THE NATION'S GOSPEL
Volume 2

Dedication

To my children Anna, James and Rebekah

THE NATION'S GOSPEL

Spreading the Christian Faith in Britain since the Reformation

Volume 2

REVOLUTION TO REVIVAL
1791 – 1900

Jeremy A. Thomas

Wilberforce Publications
London

First published in Great Britain in 2020 by
Wilberforce Publications Limited
70 Wimpole Street, London W1G 8AX

Wilberforce Publications Limited is a wholly owned subsidiary of Christian Concern

ISBN 978-1-9995842-1-4

Printed in Great Britain by Imprint Digital, Exeter

The Nation's Gospel
Spreading the Christian Faith in Britain since the Reformation

The Nation's Gospel is a unique four volume work, which takes the reader on a journey to explore how the Christian faith has been spread in Britain since the Reformation. This is living history, telling the stories of the Christian faith of past generations and its outworking in society, which has much to teach us today.

The volumes are as follows:
Volume 1: Reformation to Revolution (1516-1791)
Volume 2: Revolution to Revival (1791-1900)
Volume 3: Revival to Reports (1900-1945)
Volume 4: Reports to Renewal? (1945-2016)

Commendations
Set out below are a number of commendations received in respect of the first and second volumes and the later volumes, to be published in the future.

Volume 1: Reformation to Revolution (1516-1791)

What food for the soul there is here! Obviously written by a theologian, a historian and a Christian, it shows us the magnificent history of evangelism in the Christian church. Its great strength is that it doesn't leave us there, it inspires and motivates us to ensure that evangelism should be central to the church's ministry in our own day, it reminds us that faithful Christians throughout the history of the church have paid the price for their witness, the implied call is on us to do the same.

Rev. Tim Hanson
Vicar of Christ Church, Wharton
Trustee of the North West Gospel Partnership

This is a splendid and unique achievement in providing a panoramic history of gospel work and growth in Britain from the Reformation onwards. It contains a wealth of detail in a comparatively short space, but is exceptionally well-documented to encourage further study and research. Surveying historical, political and sociological perspectives from his strong biblical theological base, the author discerns and illuminates trends and movements which we still see being worked out today and points out significant lessons for our contemporary context. This is church history alive and makes compelling reading, because this book beats with the same gospel heart as those faithful servants of Christ down the centuries, whose labours it records and celebrates. I warmly commend it.

Rev. David Jackman

Past President of the Proclamation Trust, London

Jeremy Thomas's treatment of the English Reformation is not another account of its main events – for that you should look elsewhere. But for those familiar with the outline of the events this book offers an accessible, detailed, and rich account of what was done to advance the cause of Christ's kingdom in sixteenth-century England. Thomas draws on a wide range of primary and secondary material to describe official policy from the centre and local, even individual, action on the ground. It is a humbling and inspiring account of our predecessors' energetic and sacrificial attempts to spread the good news of the gospel.

Rev. Dr Garry J. Williams

Director, The John Owen Centre for Theological Study at London Seminary
Visiting Professor of Historical Theology,
Westminster Theological Seminary (Philadelphia)

Serving in a church where William Wilberforce and the Clapham Sect used to worship, I am only too aware of how an understanding of the past can enlighten and aid us in the present in our desire to proclaim the good news of Jesus afresh to each generation. The Nation's Gospel is church history at its best. It lays out the past so that we can learn from it in the present. I am very grateful to Jeremy for his masterful and insightful research, and his coherent and engaging presentation of the material.

Rev. Jago Wynne

Rector of Holy Trinity Clapham

Volume 2: Revolution to Revival (1791-1900)

In a time of spiritual barrenness the psalmist (in Psalm 126) remembered the past when God had acted in an unforgettable way. That recollection encouraged him to pray for the present situation. The memory was not mere nostalgia but gave rise to prayer, joy, hope and renewed service for the Lord. The psalmist did not know if there would again be sudden revival or slow slog, but he continued as 'the sower who went forth to sow'.

Jeremy Thomas is to be thanked for another thorough, readable and exciting account of an amazing period of church history. But this is a 'warts and all' story providing not only great encouragement but lessons to learn from the compromises and mistakes that the church made. They still impact us today. Jeremy Thomas's labour of love hands rich treasures for his readers. I pray that this volume will lead us to a renewed desire to sow in tears that we might return with joy, carrying our sheaves with us.

And having set aside time to read each day a portion of the first two volumes, I can't wait for the next two.

Roger Carswell
Evangelist

Jeremy Thomas has done a great service to the 21st century Evangelical Church, by reminding them of the great things the Lord has done through the preaching of the gospel in previous generations. In this well researched book, the Open-Air Mission committee were thrilled to be reminded of how the Lord has used open air preaching in our nation to bring the gospel to the many who are outside of the Church.

This is a timely reminder to Christians today to be evangelistic, and to go out into 'the highways and byways' to urge people to come to the gospel feast. May this volume stir many in our churches to go into our town and city centres to preach the gospel to a new generation.

David Gayton
Committee Member, Open-Air Mission

In this tour de force of nineteenth century church history we see the breadth and depth of the gospel's impact and its profound influence on every corner and aspect of the nation's life. This work elevates us to the height we need to comprehend and appreciate all that the church and unique figures like Charles Spurgeon achieved and the challenging legacy they have left us to continue. But it also warns us that at the height of worldly success the seeds of dissention and decline can be sown in the human and institutional heart. May this work serve as an encouragement, challenge and warning about the power of the gospel to transform, and our need to always remain faithful under God's word.

Ross Hendry

Chief Executive, Spurgeons Children's Charity

One of the best books I have ever read on church history. Vivid, interesting, inspirational and very well researched. It's very relevant for us in Britain today. I thoroughly recommend it.

Rev. Canon Roger Simpson

The Archbishop of York's Evangelist to the North

When facing a world of confusion and uncertainty, it is important for God's people, as they look forward in faith, to look back at our Christian heritage and see the faithful hand of our sovereign Lord at work. As we see the church publicly appearing to sacrifice biblical truth on the altar of political correctness, we realise that there is nothing new under the sun. Paul reminds Timothy of that in 2 Timothy 4:3, and we also see that in the past history of the church in England. Jeremy Thomas, in this authoritative and meticulously researched account of 'The Nation's Gospel', gives us great insight into the impact of evangelisation at times when the culture of the era was one of increasing secularisation. This highly informative volume should both encourage us and yet challenge us as we look back on our heritage, and give us a real sense of urgency as we share the good news of the gospel of our Lord Jesus Christ with a world that is fast descending into spiritual anarchy and chaos.

W.E.G. (Bill) Thomas

Consultant Surgeon Emeritus and former Vice President of the Royal College of Surgeons

Former International President of the Gideons

Volume 3: Revival to Reports (1900-1945)

In his very helpful history of evangelicalism in England, Jeremy Thomas identifies important lessons that are very relevant for today – that God can cause great revivals through faithful preaching of His Word but that man can cause hindrances to the Gospel through needless divisions and unbiblical practices.

Prof. Stuart Burgess
Professor of engineering design at the University of Bristol

An extremely well-researched overview of Christian mission in the UK since the Reformation – fascinating, thorough and informative. This is just the book I wish I had been able to read at theological college to give me a better understanding of why we are where we are today. I loved it!

Rev. Stephen Wookey
Rector of St David's Church, Moreton-in-March

Volume 4: Reports to Renewal? (1945–2016)

This thoroughly researched yet engaging volume is a remarkable and timely achievement. As secularism's grip on the nation appears to become ever tighter we are in urgent need of this reminder that the decline of Christianity is not just a sociological problem. History bears witness that the reasons the Bible itself gives for both the decline and the growth of the church are true. This being a history of evangelism, the gospel is at centre stage. We see there is nothing new in the self-defeating resort to a diluted or distorted gospel to make it more palatable, but we also see that whenever the biblical gospel is recovered in its fullness, often at great cost, the church recovers and the nation prospers. This book constitutes a call to resilient and hopeful proclamation of the gospel. It is also an implicit but powerful rebuke to church leaders who succumb to compromise and managerialism. The forthcoming volumes are eagerly awaited.

Rev. Canon Charles Raven
Secretary of the GAFCON Theological Commission
Former Archbishop of Kenya's Officer for Anglican Communion Affairs

CONTENTS

CONTENTS

Part 3
RESPONDING TO THE NEW CHALLENGES
(1859-1900)

GENERAL FOREWORD

For thirty years I have sat at my desk writing talks. That practice has led me to have one shelf that I can reach without getting up. On it are books that I find indispensable, for instance Jim Packer's *Knowing God* is there, and the latest edition is Tim Keller's commentary on *Mark's Gospel*. This four volume work will also be there. I think I'll reach for it most weeks in the time I have left. Why? Well, with any book you must ask these questions:

Who is it by?
What is it about?
What's it for?

So, first, who is it by? I've known Jeremy Thomas for over 20 years and I trust his motives and this work, dear reader, is motivated by a purity of heart that I've seen in very few. Jeremy is unashamedly like a medieval chronicler, bringing to bear a Bible framework on the history of evangelism in Britain. We see things from the perspective of one who fears the Lord and one who knows the gospel must lead to the obedience that comes from faith, Romans 1:5. But unlike many medieval chroniclers, Jeremy has been trained in the exacting cauldron of an international law firm, and therefore it is in his DNA to back up his argument with evidence. You will see on every page that he gives reasons for what he says.

What I need as a preacher is history presented through the lens of one who knows that God is Holy and that Christ has warned his church that sin will cause him to remove his lampstand from us, Revelation 2:5. So who is this book by? A London trained lawyer who fears the Lord and who hauntingly knows that "when God judges a people and finds them wanting and beyond corrective discipline, he leaves them" (Ezekiel 10:18).

Secondly, what is it about? It's about the gospel going out in Britain over the last 500 years and it interprets that journey with a biblical framework. So when it comes to evangelism, what has it meant to do the right thing in the right way? To be honest, I find it staggering that so many of our church leaders today are ignorant of the lessons of history. We have to look back in order to see how to go forward. I confess that I find myself close to tears as I see strategies for evangelism, which utterly fail to look back and learn from the past.

Lastly, what's it for? Answer: it's for gospel workers, be they church elders, evangelists, vicars, teachers, laity, youth workers, pray-ers or whatever. It's for those who desire to reach the lost and lift up the nation to the Lord. My job as an evangelist is Ephesians 4:12: "to equip [God's] people for works of service" in of course the area of telling others. Well, how were these works of service in evangelism done over the last 500 years? What are we missing today? Where do we need to put our energy?

Furthermore, in biblical evangelism there is always a balance between three great emphases. They all appear in 2 Corinthians 4:1-6. First, there must be integrity, we must preach Christ, and as we preach Christ, "we have renounced secret and shameful ways; we do not use deception, nor do we distort the word of God. On the contrary, by setting forth the truth plainly we commend ourselves to everyone's conscience in the sight of God."

It is therefore thrilling to read in these pages the Scottish preacher, Robert Bruce, who accepted banishment to the wilds of Inverness rather than soften the gospel. And what happened when he got to Inverness? Well, many were converted and that is the second key emphasis, sovereignty, 2 Corinthians 4:6: "For God who said, 'Let light shine out of darkness,' made his light shine in our hearts to give us the light of the knowledge of God's glory displayed in the face of Christ."

This is of course primarily God's work as we dare to preach the truth. He does the miracle and opens the blind eyes of the listeners. So wonderfully in these pages we read of the conversion of John Cardmaker, who was outside in the rain listening to Hugh Latimer preach. Despite the rain, his blind eyes were opened, and he became a leading London Edwardian preacher and in Queen Mary's reign a celebrated martyr.

I also love the story of the conversion of John Owen, who became Vice-Chancellor of Oxford University and chaplain to Oliver Cromwell. Owen, as a young chaplain, had gone with a cousin to hear Edmund Calamy, a leading preacher of the day, at St. Mary's Church,

Aldermanbury. Calamy was unable to attend. Owen was pressed by his cousin to go to listen to another eminent preacher of the day. However, Owen was too tired to go, but a "country minister" arrived, and his preaching converted Owen. In later life Owen was unable to identify that country preacher, despite much effort.

So we preach Christ, and we pray that the Sovereign Lord would open blind eyes and we watch with awe, amazement and thanksgiving, as we see the Lord at work.

But thirdly, we need creativity and energy, 2 Corinthians 4:5: We are to be your servants for Jesus' sake. So what does it mean to be rock-solid on my doctrine and belief, but in terms of practice and methodology, to keep looking to employ methods which are most appropriate for my hearers? How can I best express my concern for the desires, inclinations and sensitivities of my hearers, with one goal in mind, "to win as many as possible" (1 Corinthians 9:19)?

I have to say that as I look back on the methodologies of the past, this work has already changed where I put my energy and time as an evangelist. If you come to All Souls during the three Sundays leading up to Christmas, you will see me preaching on the street at Oxford Circus, with a gang from the church there to speak to shoppers and handing out flyers and New Testaments to passers-by asking them back to carol services. Why are we doing this? Because we learn in these pages that open-air preaching is a litmus test of gospel vigour in the local church. Come to my home and in the morning you'll see me teaching the Bible at breakfast to my four and six-year old sons. Again, it has been this book that has persuaded me of the central importance of the Bible in the home, taught by the father, to the health of the nation. We should be eternally grateful to Jeremy Thomas for giving himself to this work. I don't know of any other such history and yet, when you think about it, this is the most important history that we can read. I pray that we'll do so, to the great benefit of ourselves, our families and the country.

The Rev. Rico Tice
All Souls Church, Langham Place, London

AUTHOR'S PREFACE

My publisher suggested that a four-volume work on religious history, by a corporate lawyer, deserved a word of explanation as to how it came to be. This preface is that explanation.

As long as I can remember, I have wanted to write a history book. However, apart perhaps from a few historians who have the opportunity and gift of lucid presentation on television, my parents and I concluded that there was insufficient money in history – and so I became a pupil barrister in the Middle Temple. During my pupillage, my interest in history was not dormant – indeed, it was beginning to flourish – although it had taken an unexpected direction. I had previously taken a Master's degree at Dalhousie Law School, in Halifax, Nova Scotia, and had come under the influence of Professor Ronald St John MacDonald. Ronald's primary interest was in public international law – the laws that govern states in their relationships with one another. He had the unique distinction of being the only non-European to be elected to the European Court of Human Rights. Ronald's interests, though, were wide[1] – and embraced a deep love of history. Under his guidance and encouragement, I began to write in various academic legal journals and festschrifts on a variety of topics related to public international law – either as his research assistant, or under my own name. The articles generally approached the relevant topic from a historical perspective and, at one point, my published works made me a leading authority on the history of international law in Asia – or that's what I like to believe; but then no one else was writing at the time on the topic!

Sometime in the late 1980s or early 1990s, Ronald discussed with me the possibility of a contribution to a work on the history of public international law that he was considering editing with his great friend, Professor Douglas Johnson, of the Victoria Law School. Ronald observed that the last major overview of the history of public international law by an author writing in English was Nussbaum's *A Concise History of the Law of Nations* – which first appeared in 1947 – and the topic

[1] See J. Batten, *Judges* (1986) pp.240-260.

was long due a revisit. I wanted to be involved – and my article on the history of international law in Asia was the starting point for my intended contribution.[2] The project never materialised, but Ronald later founded the *Journal of the History of International Law* – to which I contributed an article on law and theology in the writings of Hugo Grotius; it is with Grotius that, in many people's view, modern public international law begins.[3] I then parked the idea of writing a history of international law – as to be the project of my retirement years.

As the years passed my mind returned to the prospect of writing a history of public international law. However, although Ronald sadly died, I discovered that Professor Johnson had – for many years – been working on the very same topic. He did not live to see the fruits of his labours, but my old housemate, Professor Aldo Chircop of the Dalhousie Law School, finalised Douglas's book – and it was published under the title of *The Historical Foundations of World Order: The Tower and the Arena* (2008).[4]

Therefore, I was stuck for a topic when, in 2009, I attended the School of Evangelism Conference at the Reverend Rico Tice's invitation. That day, two Scottish ministers – on separate occasions – suggested that I write something on church history. I started to read Iain Murray's magisterial two-volume biography of Martyn Lloyd-Jones[5] and visited the Evangelical Library. While there, I happened upon Iain Murray's articles published on the centenary of the 1859 Revival.[6] These articles

[2] J.A. Thomas, "History and International Law in Asia: A Time for Review?", in *Essays in Honour of Wang Tieya* (1994) (R.St.J. MacDonald (ed.)) pp.813-857.
[3] J. Thomas, "The Intertwining of Law and Theology in the Writings of Hugo Grotius", in 1 *Journal of the History of International Law* (1999) pp.61-100.
[4] That Douglas's book was published when it was, and that it deterred me from pushing forward with the plan for a work on the history of public international law, was an act of providence. Little did I know that another major work on the same topic was in the process of being completed – and that it would be published as *The Oxford Handbook of the History of International Law* (2012) (B. Fassbender and A. Peters (eds)). The early 1990s was a good time for starting work on a general history of public international law; 15 years later, the need was filled – or about to be.
[5] I.H. Murray, *David Martyn Lloyd-Jones: The First Forty Years 1899-1939* (1982) and *D. Martyn Lloyd-Jones: The Fight of Faith 1939-1981* (1990).
[6] I.H. Murray, "A Hundred Years Ago (I.) C.H. Spurgeon and the 1859 Revival", in 14 *The Banner of Truth*, February 1959, pp.4-11 and "A Hundred Years Ago (II.) The Death of John Angell James", in 15 *The Banner of Truth*, April 1959, pp.3-11.

observed that, at the same time as the Christian revival was in full strength, Darwin published *On the Origin of Species* and John Stuart Mill published his treatise *On Liberty*. The articles presented the idea that forces pointing in very different directions might be working on the churches in Britain at that time – and they stimulated a latent interest to understand better why they had suffered such numerical decline in the last 150 years. At the end of February 2010, I started research on what was happening in the nation in 1859 – which I then thought would make the starting point of my book.

The next major milestone in the shaping of this work came from discussing my reading with the Reverend Rico Tice – who ministers at my church, All Souls, Langham Place. On one occasion, I observed that the four great evangelists of the nineteenth century – namely, Charles Haddon Spurgeon, J.C. Ryle, D.L. Moody and William Booth – each perhaps represented different strands of contemporary evangelicalism: namely, a fundamentalist form of Christianity, Anglican evangelicalism, transatlantic evangelicalism, and a more experiential theology. As a result, Rico persuaded me to do a talk on these four evangelists – which I delivered a number of times.

By now, my reading suggested to me that there was a major lacuna in the literature – relating to an overview of how the faith had been spread in Britain over the generations. There were histories of evangelistic campaigns, biographies of evangelists, and histories of evangelistic organisations – but nothing which pulled them all together over time. Indeed, the only history of evangelism in Britain I found had originally been written in German – and it also embraced the history of evangelism in Germany and the United States of America.[7]

Furthermore, although evangelists were important in spreading the faith, they were only one means of doing so, and there were wider considerations on which their effectiveness depended – principally, the extent to which the basic Christian doctrines were understood. In the past, there were catechisms, liturgy, tract distribution, Sabbath observance and family religion, Sunday schools and youth work, and religious teaching in schools – all of which are now in decline. I wanted to investigate why the tools our predecessors had used in sharing the faith had been neglected.

[7] P. Scharpff, *History of Evangelism* (1966).

I was also aware of how the message proclaimed by the churches has varied over time and in different denominations, and I was interested in how church attendance had been affected by these matters.

When I started writing, I expected to be finished in two or three years at the most. That hope was, as I was to learn, illusory – because of the number of issues to be covered and the abundance of the available literature on many topics. Furthermore, I was writing on a subject that I wanted to read about. I knew – from J.R.R. Tolkien's and C.S. Lewis's experience[8] – the risk that, when you did so, the work was likely to run to three volumes. Indeed, this soon looked likely – and the ambit of the work was mightily extended when James Crabtree, a lawyer friend and former Chairman of Church Society, suggested that I sketch out in more detail the events leading up to 1859. James's comment sent me back to the Reformation. Thus it is that this work runs to four volumes!

No work of history is ever the last word, but I have endeavoured to illuminate some of the forgotten past – in the hope that we can learn lessons for the challenging times in which we live.

Jeremy A. Thomas
London, January 2017

[8] *The Letters of J.R.R. Tolkien* (1981) (H. Carpenter (ed.)) pp.209 and 378.

GENERAL INTRODUCTION

In the year 1859, around two in five of the population of England and Wales attends a religious service on a Sunday, but attendances have probably increased – since these numbers were established at the census of 1851. Around one in five of the nation attends a Church of England service.[1] The last great national religious revival is sweeping the nation; many people – who had ceased to attend church – return, and many of those who had never attended begin to do so. In London, Charles Haddon Spurgeon, the greatest preacher of the generation, whose reputation spans the English-speaking world,[2] observes that "The times of refreshing from the presence of the Lord have at last dawned upon our land."[3] To capture the fruits of revival, on 16 August 1859, Spurgeon witnesses the laying of the foundation-stone of the Metropolitan Tabernacle. It will be "the largest and handsomest place of worship in the Metropolis",[4] with space for over 6,000 people, sitting and standing. It will be barely adequate to hold those who crowd in to hear him.

Fast forward to the new millennium, no more than 6.3 per cent of the population is in church on a Sunday.[5] Furthermore, all churchmanships are in decline.[6] By the millenium's second decade, despite growth in London, and elsewhere where immigrants congregate, overall decline continues.[7] Only the new networks of independent churches, the Pentecostals and the Orthodox denominations, show growth. Not only has the great revival of 1859 passed into obscurity, so has the idea, among the general population, that God can fill the churches again.

[1] See *Census Of Great Britain 1851. Religious Worship* (1853). For a modern review of the census see M.R. Watts, *The Dissenters* (1995) vol.2, pp.25-30 and 672-675.

[2] On 17 February 1859, the *Pittsfield Sun* lamented that "All the 'distinguished strangers', the 42nd Highlanders, Charles Dickens, Mr Spurgeon, Queen Victoria, Kossuth Montalembert and others, have concluded to remain where they are for the season. Nobody is coming to the United States."

[3] See I.H. Murray, "A Hundred Years Ago (I.) C.H. Spurgeon and the 1859 Revival", in 14 *The Banner of Truth*, February 1959, p.4.

[4] C.H. Spurgeon, *The Life of the Rev. C.H. Spurgeon* (1860). See the page entitled "The Metropolitan Tabernacle" after the contents page.

[5] P. Brierley, *Pulling out of the Nose Dive* (2006) p.12.

[6] Ibid., p.52.

[7] Ibid., pp.65-66 and P. Brierley, *UK Church Statistics Number 2: 2010 to 2020* (2014) sections 0.2 and 12.1. For a more positive view on church numbers, see *Church Growth in Britain, 1980 to the Present Day* (2012) (D. Goodhew (ed.)).

This work tells the story of how the Christian faith has been spread in the lives of the British people since the Reformation, and identifies some of the factors that progress and retard its influence. The first volume, *Reformation to Revolution* (1516-1791), begins with the endeavours of the reformers to spread the gospel, moves on to those of the Puritans and the Methodists, and closes in the early years of the French Revolution with the death of John Wesley. The second volume, *Revolution to Revival* (1791-1900), traces the revival of the fortunes of Christianity – as the French Revolution made the consequences of atheism real – through to the mid-nineteenth century revival, when the proportion of the population voluntarily attending church probably peaked.[8] The third volume, *Revival to Reports* (1900-1945), covers the period from 1900 until the end of the Second World War, a period characterised by the publication of a number of important reports into evangelism. The fourth volume, *Reports to Renewal?* (1945-2016), takes our story from the end of the Second World War – and the publication of the Church of England's report *Towards the Conversion of England,* up until 2016 – when so many doubt Christianity's relevance. Matters have greatly changed with regard to the national standing of Reformation theology since the mid-nineteenth century. In 1900, the first Bishop of Liverpool, J.C. Ryle, could still tell his clergy to "Never forget that the principles of the Protestant Reformation made this country what she is and let nothing ever tempt you to forsake them."[9] Such a charge today is unthinkable.

At the heart of our story is the history in Britain of "evangelism" or, as some prefer it, "evangelisation". The history of evangelism is a surprisingly neglected subject – given its importance to the British churches and to any understanding of the rise and fall of the Christian faith within the nation. The best study of which the author is aware seems little known – being written originally in German by Paulus Scharpff, and published in English in 1966.[10] It provides a good history of evangelism

[8] Authors subscribing to some form of secularisation theory often suggest church attendances were declining in England and Wales by the 1850s but are often misty as to when they believe church numbers peaked; see S. Bruce, *Secularization: In Defence of an Unfashionable Theory* (2011) p.9. They can also be superficial in what they treat as expressions of a Christianity that the apostles would have recognised.

[9] "Dr Ryle", in *The Manchester Guardian*, 11 June 1900.

[10] P. Scharpff, *History of Evangelism* (1966) pp.ix-xii. Some works trace evangelistic endeavours from a particular perspective for a specific time such as O. Barclay,

in Germany, Britain and the United States – these countries being chosen by Scharpff as they were influenced by pietism; the ideas of which Scharpff saw as the driving force behind modern-day evangelism.

Surprisingly, neither the term evangelism, nor evangelisation, is used in the Bible. Instead, when referring to the spread of the Christian faith, the Bible uses the verb "euaggelizo" – meaning to announce good news ("evangelise") – or the noun "euaggellion", a good message, the gospel. Repeatedly, the New Testament uses these terms in the context of telling,[11] or using words[12] to communicate the good news – and especially of preaching it – with the New Testament focus being on peripatetic preaching. Indeed, St Paul declares "Woe to me if I do not preach the gospel!",[13] and his experience is common when the gospel spreads.

Agreeing a detailed definition of evangelism has in recent times become unexpectedly contentious. As the endeavour to define evangelism is a twentieth century phenomenon, its definition will be left until that time is reached in our history. In any event, Roman Catholics prefer to use the term "evangelisation" to describe reaching out to others.[14] At this stage, it is sufficient to note that the terms "evangelism" and "evangelisation" both combine the word "evangel", the good news, with a suffix pointing to the means and processes used to spread that message. Accordingly, this work, in each of the periods it covers, will look at the message being proclaimed as the gospel by the churches – and its means of delivery.

The apostles believed that the content of the gospel message was the key to its success; St Paul wrote, the gospel "is the power of God for the salvation of everyone who believes: first for the Jew, then for the Gentile".[15] In his view, a message which purports to be the gospel, but which is different from the one he preached, "is really no gospel at all". He believed that the preacher of any such gospel deserved to be "eternally condemned", because he misled his hearers.[16] In considering

Evangelicalism in Britain 1935-1995 (1997) and there are histories of particular evangelistic campaigns such as those of Billy Graham. There are also global histories of evangelism such as R.G. Tuttle Jr, *The Story of Evangelism* (2006).

[11] For example, 1 Thessalonians 2:2.

[12] For example, 1 Thessalonians 1:5.

[13] 1 Corinthians 9:16.

[14] See Apostolic Exhortation, *Evangelii Gaudium,* 24 November 2013.

[15] Romans 1:16.

[16] Galatians 1:7-9.

the spread of the genuine gospel in any of our periods, we would be wise to consider how its first advocates foresaw its future – and the extent to which they believed adherence to their message guaranteed its success.

That some claim the title of Christian and preach a message other than that of the apostles, and that they find willing listeners, is a constant of early Christian history. St Paul rebuked the church at Corinth for listening easily enough to "a different gospel from the one you accepted".[17] He was also aware of the temptation to water down the gospel, to tamper with it, to make it more pleasing to contemporaries.[18] St Paul also condemned "false apostles", and was not the only apostle to do so. Others were equally clear that those would come who offered the churches a different message, or who would distort the Scriptures.[19] St Peter, St John, and St Jude all foretold that "false prophets",[20] "many antichrists"[21] and "godless men"[22] would slip in amongst the churches to introduce "destructive heresies". Attending a church, or even leading one, does not make a person a Christian any more than standing in a garage makes someone a motor car. It is also true that it is possible to preach the word of God not to promote God's glory, or the well-being of one's neighbour, but for personal profit,[23] or for some other personal reason.[24] At least that's what St Paul found. In subsequent chapters, one issue will be whether the churches in the period under consideration have kept to the message preached by the apostles – or whether they have proclaimed something different, with all the related consequences of so doing.

Both evangelism and evangelisation add to the "evangel" a suffix. Evangelism adds an "ism" – referring to the "procedures, actions and systems that are appropriate to...help people discover it".[25] The term "evangelisation" adds to the evangel an "isation" – pointing not just to the process, but also to the results of the evangel being spread through a nation. Thus the phrase "evangelisation" is probably wider than

[17] 2 Corinthians 11:4 and Galatians 1:6-10.

[18] 2 Corinthians 4:2, 2 Timothy 4:3, 1 Thessalonians 2:3-5 and Acts 20:30.

[19] 2 Peter 3:16.

[20] 2 Peter 2:1.

[21] 1 John 2:18-19.

[22] Jude 4.

[23] 2 Corinthians 2:17.

[24] Philippians 1:15.

[25] R. Warren, *Signs of Life* (1996) p.6.

"evangelism" – pointing to outreach on a national scale, and embracing issues of justice in the outworking of the gospel – although to be too prescriptive of the meaning of these terms, and the way that they are used by any given author, is perilous.[26] English Protestants, assuming that England is historically a Protestant country, most often refer to "evangelism" – while Roman Catholics use "evangelisation" as the term to describe the spread of their respective messages. Nevertheless, it is telling that when the Church of England has wanted to convert the nation, it may speak of "evangelisation" or "re-evangelisation"[27] just as willingly as of evangelism. Perhaps the most ambitious evangelistic endeavour ever, that of the Protestant Student Volunteer Movement at the end of the nineteenth and the beginning of the twentieth century, had as its watchword "the evangelisation of the world in this generation".[28] Today, Roman Catholics still prefer to use the term "evangelisation" – and the associations of that word do not deter its use by Protestants.[29]

Our story will embrace other aspects of the life of the British churches, beyond their message, however glorious, and the means whereby it is communicated.[30] It will touch upon the way that great evangelistic zeal in any age seems to coincide with positive social, economic and political changes in the nation's life. When the gospel was proclaimed by the apostles, they expected it to produce fruit. Thus, St Paul expected the converts in the city of Colossae to "live a life worthy of the Lord... bearing fruit in every good work".[31] Jesus had already told his followers that their light should "shine before men, that they may see your good

[26] See B. Hoare and L. Griffiths, "A Decade of Evangelism – or Evangelisation", in 19(1) *Epworth Review* January (1992), pp.68-69, D.J. Bosch, *Transforming Mission* (1993) pp.409-411 and P. Knights and A. Murray, *Evangelisation in England and Wales* (2002) pp.21-22.
[27] *The Evangelistic Work of the Church* (1918) pp.18, 32 and 35.
[28] C.H. Hopkins, *John R. Mott* (1979) pp.231-233.
[29] See B. Hoare and L. Griffiths, "A Decade of Evangelism – or Evangelisation", in 19(1), *Epworth Review* January (1992), pp.68-69 and J.R.W. Stott, *Christian Mission in the Modern World* (1977) pp.38-39.
[30] On the differences between mission and evangelism see G.L. Carey, "Evangelism", in *The Oxford Companion to Christian Thought* (2000) p.221.
See also J.R.W. Stott, *Christian Mission in the Modern World* (1977) pp.14-34 and D.J. Bosch, *Transforming Mission* (1993) pp.1-2 and 409-412.
[31] Colossians 1:10.

deeds and praise your Father in heaven".[32] Indeed, some commentators suggest that Christ is presented "through a range of activities and relationships, not least as a community of people who live by the values of the kingdom of God and speak of his presence in their lives".[33] It is not necessary to decide whether right conduct, on its own, presents the gospel – but it undoubtedly reinforces any gospel call and challenges the lifestyles of others; its absence in the deliverer of a gospel call may undermine that call.

The paucity of interest in past evangelistic practices, their impact, and the theology that sustained them, points to a lacuna in the history of the British churches – and hints at an alternative to existing popular explanations for the recent decline of Christianity in Britain. Explanations for this abound; all are man-centred. They assume that there is no God, and that the decline of Christianity in Britain is not the action of the Deity – or his response, foretold by the apostles – to the wilfulness of his people, but the result of external forces acting upon the churches. Thus, the decline of Christianity is attributed to matters such as the secularisation of the culture – that is, the decline in the social significance of religion.[34] Secularisation is said to be inextricably linked with modernisation – whereby technological innovation transforms the world[35] and leads to matters such as education, politics or science being removed from the control of the religious elites. This process, it is argued, has "undermined the power, popularity and prestige of religious beliefs".[36] However, the argument is vague as to when the development of technology reached a tipping point that inevitably led to education, politics and science being removed from the control of the religious elites

[32] Matthew 5:16.

[33] R. Warren, *Signs of Life* (1996) p.5 and B. Green, *The Practice of Evangelism* (1958) p.16.

[34] See R. Wallis and S. Bruce, "Secularization: The Orthodox Model", in *Religion and Modernization* (1992) (S. Bruce (ed.)) p.11 and S. Bruce, *Secularization: In Defence of an Unfashionable Theory* (2011) p.2. For a flavour of the issues and variations within the secularisation debate generally see, *The Role of Religion in Modern Societies* (2008) (D. Pollack and D.V.A. Olson (eds)).

[35] P.L. Berger, B. Berger, and H. Kellner, *The Homeless Mind* (1974) p.15 and P.L. Berger, *Facing up to Modernity* (1979) p.101.

[36] S. Bruce, *Secularization: In Defence of an Unfashionable Theory* (2011) p.24. An earlier generation suggested that secularisation is modernisation; see G. Reid, *The Gagging of God* (1969) p.68.

– occurrences that have not been seen in many other countries of similar technological advancement. The danger of the secularisation thesis, or indeed any other man-orientated explanation for religious decline, is that it may mistake the consequence of religious decline, for its cause.

At this point, we will observe some other explanations for contemporary religious decline – to which we will refer later. Alan Gilbert links secularisation to the rise of the working class – as "the most truly 'hegemonic' class which is least influenced by Christian thought and Christian institutions".[37] A further nuance to the secularisation thesis is that secularisation takes place – at least it has done until recently – at three levels: – that of society, church organisations and the individual.[38] Today, we may add a fourth level; that of the family with the eradication of ideas such as male headship and the extension of marriage to those of the same sex.

Callum Brown puts forward a more sensational thesis for the decline of Christianity – in his insightful work, *The Death of Christian Britain.* In the 1970s, he postulated that the appearance of the "promiscuous girl", who was socially acceptable,[39] drove a wedge between the lifestyle of the Christian and secular girl. As a result, the number of young women in church fell steeply.[40] When women stopped going to church, men were less likely to go.

Hugh McLeod suggests that the decline is not due to one overriding cause, but to a variety of contributing factors. He challenges the search for a "momentous and mysterious"[41] master factor to explain the decline. He especially emphasises a long 1960s, stretching from 1958 to 1974, as a time of crisis for Christianity. He points to affluence, changes in outlook on gender and sexuality, new movements and ideas particularly associated with free speech, student protests and a rebellious youth culture, resurgence in Marxism and attacks on authority, and conflicts within the churches – including changes in their theology and practice.[42]

The secularisation thesis is also challenged by Grace Davie. In 1994, she published *Religion in Britain since 1945*: *Believing without*

[37] A.D. Gilbert, *The Making of Post-Christian Britain* (1980) p.91.

[38] See generally K. Dobbelaere, *Secularisation: An Analysis at Three Levels* (2002).

[39] C.G. Brown, *The Death of Christian Britain* (2009) p.196.

[40] Ibid., p.192.

[41] H. McLeod, *The Religious Crisis of the 1960s* (2007) p.15.

[42] Ibid., p.260. See also p.15.

Belonging. She noted that the statistics concerning "feelings, experience and the more numinous aspects of religious belief demonstrate considerable persistence in contemporary Britain".[43] Christian orthodoxy might be in an immense muddle, and church attendance might be declining, but she urged that "the concept of secularisation is getting harder and harder to sustain".[44] She graphically characterised the attitude to religion in the nation as "believing without belonging". In early 2013, Davie reaffirmed her view that it was unlikely that secular rationalism would become the overriding norm.[45]

However, in considering the reasons behind the decline of Christianity in Britain we will be wise to keep in mind the reasons that the authors of its faith give as the reasons why a church may be extinguished. For example, Moses warned Israel of the dangers of wealth leading her to forget God.[46] The apostle Peter warned of the dangers of false teachers and false doctrine destroying a church.[47] St Paul warned the church in Galatia (part of modern central Turkey) that if they continued "biting and devouring each other" they would be destroyed.[48] The apostle John foretold that the sexually immoral in churches would find themselves at war with the living God.[49] Jesus had no doubts that if the church disobeyed him, it would be trampled over.[50] The Bible teaches that God loves – but he also judges.[51] When God judges a people, and finds them wanting and beyond corrective discipline, he leaves them.[52] When a church is in decline, the reasons for its decline are rarely mysterious.

In addressing the recent decline in church membership and attendances, this work will take a longer historical perspective than most previous commentators. Many writers suggest that the decline in church attendance is something new and mysterious. A previously triumphant Christianity is portrayed, now sensationally heading for

[43] G. Davie, *Religion in Britain since 1945* (1994) p.4.
[44] Ibid., p.7.
[45] G. Davie, *The Sociology of Religion* (2013) p.142.
[46] Deuteronomy 8:10-20.
[47] 2 Peter 2:1-3.
[48] Galatians 5:15.
[49] Revelation 2:14-16.
[50] Matthew 5:13.
[51] John 3:16.
[52] Ezekiel 10:18.

an irrevocable fall. One question is whether this picture is true. Was it previously a monolithic structure able to impose its way on the nation? Was the nation a land of towns and villages, at the heart of which nestled the churches to which the citizens happily streamed, and from which Protestant sermons fanned out across the nation – until secularisation, Christianity's nemesis, emerged around the time of the Enlightenment? By going back to the Reformation, rather than the last two centuries and a little more, we can test this thesis. It will also enable us to consider over a longer period of time how changes made to the gospel message, and its means of delivery, impact its influence in any age.

To reduce this work to four volumes, its scope is limited in a number of ways. First, its focus is on England, as the country where the bulk of the British population resides; but other parts of Britain are considered, to illustrate developments of wider significance. In particular, in addition to the metropolis, there is a focus on Kidderminster – a medium-sized Midlands' town, with both rural and industrial pretensions – as a means to illustrate more widely the consequences of changes in the gospel message and evangelistic methods. Secondly, this work does not elaborate the personal characteristics, strengths, weaknesses and personal misfortunes of the leading evangelists and Christian leaders of each epoch – nor, indeed, many of the more general marks of mission that are helpful for an individual involved in evangelism to possess.[53] Thirdly, it does not explore the role of fasting – and only touches upon the role of prayer –

[53] One formulation of mission is that of the Church of England's Board for Mission and Partnership for World Mission. It sets out as the ten marks of mission:
"(1) To witness to the good news of Jesus and the Kingdom.
(2) To enable those called by God to become committed disciples of Jesus and members of his community.
(3) To renew the Church as one agent of God's concern for the world.
(4) To advance in the discernment of God in the company of others.
(5) To heal the sick, feed the hungry, clothe the naked, visit prisoners and show hospitality to strangers.
(6) To love our neighbours as ourselves and our enemies without qualification.
(7) To seek the justice and peace of the kingdom and to identify and challenge corruption of power.
(8) To suffer abuse for his sake.
(9) To be a sign of God's power to reconcile divided peoples.
(10) To enable us to be fully human after the image of Christ."
See *The Measure of Mission* (1987) p.24. See also more generally E.D.S. Woods, "The Presentation of the Gospel at Home", in *Liberal Evangelicalism: An Interpretation* (1923) pp.252-253.

in evangelism. Both deserve their own treatment.[54] Fourthly, it does not focus on the ostensible reasons why an individual might leave a church – although to some extent the reasons for coming to or leaving a church are related.[55] Fifthly, this work focuses, but certainly not exclusively so, on the evangelicals – whether in the form of the sixteenth-century reformers, the seventeenth-century Puritans and eighteenth-century Methodists, or the evangelicals of subsequent centuries – simply because they have generally been the most energetic (in seeking to add to the numbers of Christians) and innovative (in establishing institutions to do so).[56] In many ways, by their success or failure is the numerical and general health of the churches determined. However, this work is not a history of the evangelical party.

For leaders and members of the churches, an understanding of the evangelistic strategies and systems of the past, and the structures put in place to support and sustain them, may reveal lessons, and determine priorities, to draw individuals back to Christ.[57] The then Prime Minister, David Cameron, in a speech at Christ Church, Oxford, on the 400th anniversary of the King James Bible, told his audience, "We are a Christian country and we should not be afraid to say so"[58] – a remark he often repeated.[59]

This work will also be of interest to those seeking to understand our

[54] For an overview of various prayer movements relating to evangelism in the eighteenth century and early nineteenth century, see *Thoughts on the Great Duty of Prayer for the Outpouring of the Holy Spirit* (1859) pp.8-13. For the linking of prayer with revival in the Victorian period, see D. Bebbington, *Victorian Religious Revivals* (2012) p.265. Two of the most significant church-based ministries since, Spurgeon at the Metropolitan Tabernacle and David Watson at York, both attributed their respective successes to the power of prayer; see A. Dallimore, *C.H. Spurgeon* (1984) pp.48-49 and T. Saunders and H. Sansom, *David Watson, A Biography* (1992) p.307.
[55] For a recent study see P. Richter and L.J. Francis, *Gone but not Forgotten* (1998).
[56] See J.C. Ryle, "Where are we?", in 1 *The Churchman* (1879-1880) p.35, and for a recent restatement of this view see D. Erdozain, *The Problem of Pleasure: Sport, Recreation and the Crisis of Victorian Religion* (2010) p.4. David Bebbington's suggestion in *Evangelicalism in Modern Britain* (1989) of a discontinuity between the eighteenth-century evangelicals, and the reformers and Puritans is considered in J.A. Thomas, *The Nation's Gospel: Reformation to Revolution* (2017) vol.1, p.317.
[57] Martyn Lloyd-Jones expressed the same views long ago: I.H. Murray, *D. Martyn Lloyd-Jones: The Fight of Faith 1939-1981* (1990) p.369.
[58] "David Cameron says the UK is a Christian Country", http://www.bbc.co.uk/news/uk-politics-16224394, accessed 7 July 2016.
[59] See for example A. Barnett, "David Cameron Christmas Message", in *The Independent,* 24 December 2015.

own times and the collapse of moral values in both the churches and the nation. The link was acknowledged by the Prime Minister, at Oxford, when he called for a revival of traditional Christian values to counter Britain's "moral collapse". To revive those traditional Christian values, an understanding of why Christianity itself has lost its vigour –and how it can be revived – is needed. Tellingly, the Prime Minister went on to describe himself as a "committed", but only "vaguely practising", Christian – admitting he was "full of doubts" about big theological issues.

It will also provide food for thought for all those looking to find and recover what made Britain the influence that she was in the world at different times since the Reformation. There is a broad correlation between the vigour behind the spread of the gospel in Britain and her world influence, seen in terms of their respective highs during the time of Henry VIII, Elizabeth I, Oliver Cromwell and then during the second half of the eighteenth century as Methodism took root until the end of the nineteenth century. As we will see later, Lord Macaulay believed that it was Protestantism that lay behind the greatness of nineteenth century Britain while, as we have already seen, nineteenth century clergy never tired at drawing the link between the principles of the Reformation and national greatness. They would not be surprised to learn that the weakening of the doctrines of the sixteenth century reformers has coincided with the decline of the influence of the churches and Christian values within the nation and national decline on the world scene.

A work like this is built on the foundations of those who have gone before, and the footnotes reveal the author's debts to many historians and others. However, it does not seek to follow or rebut any particular interpretation of historical events. Rather, this work seeks to recast the existing materials into a study of the spread of the gospel, based upon a biblical framework. Its distinctiveness also lies in a combination of three other factors. First, it is written from the perspective of a person who believes in a God who intervenes in this world – an increasingly scarce commodity. Secondly, it is written by a lawyer who spent his career in an international law firm, with its largest office in the City of London, and who has written on a variety of legal topics – and has no need to appeal to any element of the churches for acclaim. Thirdly, in the manner of a fool rushing in, this volume aims to pull together a vast amount of material – in order to provide an overview to the reader of the key doctrinal developments, and some identification of the most important churches and personalities for the propagation of the gospel. The author identifies with the theologian Alec Vidler who, in 1940, wrote of his book *God's Judgment on Europe,* that "On page after page I have found myself making statements each of which could form the subject of a whole book, and each of which has in fact formed the subject of many books."[60]

In a book of this nature – and one written by a lawyer no less – there is the need for comment of a "boiler plate" nature. To the extent that the author has transmitted the errors of any of those who have gone before, or added to them, he asks for the reader's indulgence. The great historian of the Reformation, A.G. Dickens, noted that "even a historian with long experience and many helpful colleagues can never entirely familiarise himself with every aspect of this immense, hugely documented [topic]".[61] How much more is this statement applicable to an author seeking to embrace the scope of this work. Furthermore, like Dickens, the author hopes for the opportunity to make any necessary amendments in the future. An area requiring a particular degree of caution, and not necessarily related to the potential failings of the author, are the details of church attendances, as the original records are often either incomplete or open to interpretation – especially those before 1851.[62] However, the details provided should demonstrate the direction that church attendances are moving at the relevant time. All references to verses of the Bible, unless otherwise stated, are from the New International Version. For the sake of simplicity, academic and clergy titles have generally been avoided, unless in a context worthy of special note. Male pronouns have been used – as reflecting the theology the vast bulk of the individuals embraced by this work would have based their lives upon. Spellings, use of capitals and punctuation of quotations, have been modernised.

[60] A.R. Vidler, *God's Judgment on Europe* (1940) p.viii.

[61] A.G. Dickens, *The English Reformation* (1989) p.12.

[62] There is a debate in the literature as to which of baptisms, confirmations, church membership or attendances is the best indication of a denomination's strength in any period. For a discussion see R. Walford, *The Growth of "New London" in Suburban Middlesex (1918-1945) and the Response of the Church of England* (2007) pp.337-347.

FOREWORD TO VOLUME 2

It is said, cynically perhaps, that history teaches us that history teaches us nothing; which would be something of a pity should it turn out that Jeremy Thomas's monumental labours earn many and enthusiastic plaudits, yet few consequences of any significance. For myself, I am filled with wonder and admiration at all Mr Thomas has provided for our delight and learning – his is a very fine achievement, unique in its way. And what astounding reading lists are here! I imagine dusty book stacks, long unvisited, finally yielding up their precious information for this indomitable explorer. Thus, a great story has been told, a story that needed to be told.

The question at issue, I suppose, is how all this wealth in *The Nation's Gospel* is to be turned to good account. Here, I think, Scripture may help us. That is why I am bold to append below the words of a favourite Psalm, whose very simplicity demonstrates a seriously important pattern that runs right through our Bibles. This is the pattern of ***Remembrance*** and ***Reassurance***, with the intimate connection that exists between the two.

The claim is made that the most frequent command of all in Scripture is the call to Remember. Certainly Remembrance, with Reassurance, continues to control authentic public worship as Pulpit and Table recall the people of God to the apostolic faith of Jesus Christ and him crucified. Is it now the turn of *The Nation's Gospel* to bring to remembrance our heritage, the history of evangelistic enterprise over five centuries? And yet, in practical terms, how? Reading straight through one of these volumes, as I have done, is a remarkable experience; but it is impossible to take in and retain all the fascinating ways and byways by which gospel people have spread the light. One possible opportunity is the midweek home group or church Bible study, that invaluable aid for growth, individually and corporately, in grace and knowledge. We know the risks, monotony or inadequate leadership, causing members to wander off into conversational topics C.S. Lewis professed to have no taste for, namely politics, money, deaths and indigestion! But I ask myself whether a periodic study of 'gospel history', Bible and Thomas to hand, might not be refreshing, profitable for all, and, in a secular context, very close to reality. For example, strategies to convert a nation (vol.1, ch.3) might, one evening, dispel any complacency among us as we observe 'The epoch of personal evangelism', with old and young handing out Tyndale's New Testament from the City of London, to the universities, and on into the countryside; and this with notable success yet at risk of imprisonment, fines, public mockery, even death in the fires of the market place. That energetic person, Lady Jane Grey, sent a New Testament to her sister Katherine the night before she went to the scaffold (p.69 of vol.1), urging her to read and follow it, for if she did so she would be brought to "immortal and everlasting life". In volume 2, for instance, the quite extraordinary energy and achievements of the Victorians, particularly post 1859, take the breath away. Thankfully the word of God continues to spread and flourish in our own day; however, compared with our Victorian predecessors, we have only just begun!

And so one could go on. All in all, inspired as we must be by these records of achievement, it is words from Calvin's commentary on Micah 4:6 that alone 'explain' the survival of the cause of Christ, (often in very dark days) that Jeremy Thomas has recounted for us with such exemplary diligence.

> Although the church is at the present time hardly to be distinguished from a dead or at best sick man, there is no reason for despair, for the Lord raises up his own suddenly, as he waked the dead from the grave. This we must clearly remember, lest, when the church fails to shine forth, we conclude too quickly that the light has died utterly away. But the church in the world is so preserved that she rises suddenly from the dead. Her very preservation through the days is due to a succession of miracles. Let us cling to the remembrance that she is not without her resurrection, or rather not without her many resurrections.

In *The Nation's Gospel* we hear the wonderful story of these 'many resurrections', sufficient evidence to show that, whatever the future may hold, the message of Christ will continue to prevail.

Psalm 126: Remembrance and Reassurance

When the Lord restored the fortunes of Zion
we were like those who dreamed
Our mouths were filled with laughter,
our tongues with songs of joy.
Then it was said among the nations
'The Lord has done great things for them'
The Lord has done great things for us
And we are filled with joy.

Restore our fortunes, LORD,
like streams in the Negev.
Those who sow with tears
will reap with songs of joy.
Those who go out weeping,
carrying seed to sow,
Will return with songs of joy,
carrying sheaves with them.

The Rev. Prebendary Dick Lucas

ACKNOWLEDGEMENTS FOR VOLUME 2

In the first volume of this work, I acknowledged the contribution of a number of people who helped to shape it and the volumes to come. Accordingly, this acknowledgment recognises the endeavours of those individuals who, since January 2017, have helped bring this second volume to fruition.

The Reverend Rico Tice continues to energise and motivate me with the importance of an understanding of history for the contemporary church – when my zeal wanes under the weight of the literature to be read. Without Rico this volume would not have appeared.

Peter Parson has read this volume a number of times and his comments have assisted greatly its flow and readability. He has given lavishly of his time and experience, well beyond the call of friendship. In addition, my wife Anita has sacrificed much in order to bring this project to completion. Not only has she freed me from other matters, but she has checked the draft text's technical set-up and assisted its editing. Dr Justin Byron-Davies has again made helpful structural, technical and other points for which I am very grateful. Peter Byron-Davies's comments have also improved the text.

I'd also express my thanks to a number of additional members of the staff of the Rare Books section of the British Library for their help in making the research part of this project so enjoyable; namely, Kiana Arnott-Job, Stephen Leary, Earnest Lubwama, Jenny Modely and Patsy Russell. They are an immensely helpful team.

Finally, my thanks to John Scriven of Wilberforce Publications and to Andrea Williams, Chief Executive of Christian Concern, the holding company of my publisher. John has overseen the publication of this volume with great charm and industry, and his comments have much improved the manuscript. Andrea continues to amaze, staying with this project, while juggling so many other significant matters. She combines the commitment to the gospel with the creativity, energy and endurance that the contemporary Christian needs and which so many of our forebears manifested.

Jeremy A. Thomas
London, April 2018

INTRODUCTION TO VOLUME 2

The quiet revival (1791-1858)

Many contemporaries saw the nineteenth century as a new high-water mark of Christian influence in Great Britain. In early 1859, William Arthur, the well-known Wesleyan Methodist minister, observed that God had blessed the nation with a great revival in each of the last three centuries. He referred to the Reformation, the Puritan epoch and the Methodist revival of Whitefield and Wesley. Each successively carried forward the cause of "vital religion" in Britain to a new high-water mark. The religious stirrings in America, at the time, led Arthur to hope for

> not the conversion of a few scores in this town, or a few hundreds in that city... but a pervasive, national quickening, reaching into every parish, going into the centre of society, striking its highest and its lowest extremes, and carrying forward the cause of vital religion as far in advance of its position at this day as the revival of last century and its results have, up to this time, carried it beyond the position it then occupied.[1]

He was not to be disappointed. Later that year, the last great national spiritual revival swept the United Kingdom; around one million people were converted in that and the surrounding years. Emily Kinnaird – whose family was connected with the upper echelons of London's banking circles, the aristocracy and the nation's leading politicians – recalled, that "The questions 'Are you saved?' 'Have you been converted?' 'Do you love the Lord?' were freely used, and the answers to these were perfectly natural, because the experiences were so real; to say 'yes' was just a testimony to a great fact of experience."[2]

When I started the research for this work, I planned to begin with that great spiritual revival of 1859. God has not blessed Britain since with such a revival. Thus, the high-water mark of 1859 seemed the place to start the story of how the Christian faith had been spread in recent times in the lives of the British people and to identify some of the factors that

[1] W. Arthur, *May We Hope for a Great Revival* (1859) p.4.
[2] E. Kinnaird, *Reminiscences* (1925) p.87.

progress and retard its influence. It was, after all, a high-water mark that was maintained for a good 35 years – whatever Matthew Arnold might otherwise suggest in his poem, "Dover Beach".[3]

However, James Crabtree, a lawyer friend and a former Chairman of Church Society suggested, having read an initial draft of this work, that I sketch in more detail the events leading up to 1859. James's comment proved insightful. It both facilitated a wider and deeper study of how changes made to the gospel message and its means of delivery impact its influence; and encouraged the discernment of wider patterns in the spread of the gospel across the ages.

In studying the means to carry Christianity to the nation, from the death of John Wesley and the French Revolution to the year 1859, I was surprised by the period's spiritual riches. This period saw the foundations laid for the expansion of British Christianity – in a much quieter and less spectacular way than the great religious revivals of the past, including that of the years around 1859. The first half of the nineteenth century, with its great Christian personalities and articulation of what became known as "aggressive evangelism", witnessed the development of the most comprehensive blueprint yet for the spread of Christianity within Britain – although new technologies have, subsequently, provided additional opportunities for spreading the gospel. In this regard, one thinks of the magic lantern show well-used by Lord Shaftesbury and others in the last half of the nineteenth century, and films and radio in the twentieth century. For those wanting to understand why Christianity has the standing within the nation it has today, the study of the first half of the nineteenth century is particularly rewarding. Simply by comparing the zeal of Christians then, with their successors today, one can understand the strength of the foundations laid in the nineteenth century underpinning today's churches and yet discover a major explanation of why those same churches languish today.

This is an introduction, so it is not the place to systematically set out nineteenth century developments in the means and tools to take the gospel to the nation. Nor is it the place to explain, in full, the appearance of church parties which caused such conflict and undermined the spread of the gospel. However, it will be useful for the reader to receive some

[3] Started around 1850, or perhaps a year earlier.

preliminary guidance as to the matters of special relevance, before reaching the book's substance. The examples below illustrate how, in the first half of the nineteenth century, a great platform to spread Christianity within Britain was built. This only now is finally crumbling, by virtue of the appearance of the new parties and doctrines claiming to be Christian, and their successors, which first appeared in the first half of the nineteenth century.

The early nineteenth century was the great age of family religion and lay-driven religious organisations, especially in the field of learning. It was widely accepted that "The fear of the Lord is the beginning of knowledge".[4] Sunday schools, which had commenced in the previous century, multiplied and multiplied again. Ragged schools for the poor were established and two great societies emerged to generally promote schools across the land. They were the British and Foreign School Society (1808), which was non-denominational, and the National Society for Promoting the Education of the Poor in the Principles of the Established Church throughout England and Wales (1811) ("The National Society for Promoting the Education of the Poor"). A number of other educational movements also grew, such as the adult school movement and the mutual improvement societies. They were guided as much by the desire to teach Christianity as to provide a general education. There was also the Young Men's Christian Association, which provided educational and literary facilities. For children of the "better" classes, as they were called, governesses who taught Christianity flourished and the growth in private school education began to blossom; this drew heavily on Christian ideals.

In the years prior to 1859 the use of literature to teach the gospel was institutionalised. The Religious Tract Society, founded in 1799, evolved the techniques necessary for the mass production of reading material. Its progeny, including the Bible Society, followed behind it. These, and many other lesser publishing enterprises, supplied the materials for a host of home-visiting societies, to deliver religious materials into the hands of the people, especially in the cities. They were joined by the various 'colporteur' societies whose workers criss-crossed the land between the towns and villages, delivering religious literature to the people. Tracts

[4] Proverbs 1:7.

explaining the gospel were given out in profusion. In the cities, the great city mission societies sprouted up, like the Glasgow City Mission (1826) and the London City Mission (1835).

The first half of the nineteenth century also saw the foundations laid for the great burst of open-air lay preaching which emerged in the 1859 Revival and in the decades afterwards. The Open-Air Mission, established in 1853, almost made open-air preaching a science, "furnished with well-defined and accurate laws".[5] Even the Bishop of London preached in the open. On the steps of the Royal Exchange, clergymen preached every Sunday evening to large congregations.

In our period the widespread use of women to hold out the gospel began, especially through the work of the Bible Society and home visiting societies. In 1857 Ellen Ranyard founded the London Bible and Domestic Female Mission – to use poor lay women to reach poor lay women. Some preached, but most were involved in tract distribution or with humanitarian activities. These activities demonstrated the capacity of women for roles outside the home.

The existing churches also targeted the unconverted. To note a few of the more interesting examples, in 1797 the Baptist Home Missionary Society commenced work. The Church of England founded the Church Pastoral-Aid Society (1836) to increase the number of clergy preaching the gospel of grace. It also employed laity. In the following year the High Church Society for Promoting the Employment of Additional Curates in Populous Places was established. In 1844 Bishops Charles Blomfield and Charles Sumner established the Scripture Readers' Association – to appoint lay agents to read the Holy Scriptures to the poor, under the superintendence of the parish clergy. Blomfield, the Bishop of London (1828-1856), built over 200 new churches during his episcopacy as London rapidly grew.

There were also new denominations with a radical evangelistic zeal, first the Primitive Methodists (1811) and then, in the 1820s and 1830s, the Brethren. The latter provided many of the evangelists who led the 1859 Revival and helped bind together the diverse groups sustaining it – and who afterwards stimulated evangelistic endeavours, across the denominations.

[5] F. Cockrem, *Gawin Kirkham* (N.D.) pp.47-48.

Expectations in the 1850s as to the future influence of Christianity on the nation were high. In 1851, the first religious census in England and Wales established the facts relating to church attendance. Horace Mann, in his official report, observed that all that was needed was "the action of the rulers of the church to gather and direct", in order to overcome all spiritual opposition.[6]

Yet, if the mechanisms for taking the gospel to the nation vastly expanded, issues with the message began to emerge towards the mid-years of the century. The early years of the nineteenth century had seen evangelical doctrines spread across the Church of England. These were preached with enthusiasm from many pulpits across the denominations and in the open air by members of the Dissenting groups. The atonement, the Last Judgment, heaven and hell, becoming a "new creature", being converted, or enjoying the "new birth", were the common themes of lay evangelists, clergy and Christian literature of the time. However, from the mid-1820s, other ideas were increasingly circulated – emanating primarily from Germany and imported by Samuel Taylor Coleridge – which first challenged how the Bible was to be interpreted and, later, its key doctrines. The Broad Church began to take distinctive shape and in the 1830s the Tractarians emerged; they had distinctive but not necessarily novel ideas. They argued that through baptism and communion, rather than through the word of God, the grace which brought about the new creation was primarily conveyed. The advertisement in the first volume of the *Tracts for the Times* declared: "The sacraments, and not preaching, are the sources of divine grace."[7] Furthermore, they elevated the role of the clergy in the Church; the clergy had a special authority flowing from being the successors to the apostles. These ideas led to, first, conflict within the Church and then, conflict with the other denominations.

There were also developments in science, particularly in geology, that challenged the age of the earth, the time needed for its shaping and the universality of Noah's flood. Many evangelical leaders accommodated most of these new ideas into their interpretation of the early chapters of Genesis, by moving from what had often been a literal interpretation to one that sought to interpret the relevant text in accordance with its

[6] H. Mann, *Religious Worship in England and Wales* (1854) p.102.

[7] Cited in T. Arnold, "Introduction" to *Sermons by Thomas Arnold* (1878) (Mrs W.E. Forster (ed.)) vol.4, p.xvii.

nuances, or verses elsewhere in the Bible. Not all evangelicals agreed with such an approach, which inevitably brought division, although initially the impact of differences between evangelicals was relatively subdued. The issues became more intense across the church in the 1830s and 1840s when, spurred on by the willingness of leading evangelicals to reinterpret key passages in Genesis, more liberal elements within the churches and universities began to take similar liberties with other portions of the Bible, which geology left unchallenged.

New spiritual highs and new challenges (1859-1900)

The years around 1859 saw remarkable growth in church attendances and conversions. On 30 July 1859, a journal, *The Revival*, was launched to provide "a weekly record of events connected with the present revival of religion". A few years later, it recorded that "God raised up men for almost every class and from almost every class".[8] For the evangelicals, in the words of professor Owen Chadwick, this was their day of "national authority. The evangelicals were never triumphant. But there was an epoch when they were powerful; the epoch after 1855." Chadwick attributed this influence to their power over church and state.[9]

However, there was another side to it all. At the same time as some men were struck down by a terrible sense of sin, "whole literatures" and "whole philosophies"[10] were formulated without reference to God, to provide an alternative to the Christian way of life. Tellingly, in the 1860s, "the word *secularisation* began its metaphorical career in phrases like the *secularisation of art* or the *secularisation* of politics".[11] It acted as a unifying force behind these new literatures and philosophies – of which there were some striking developments around 1859, or thereabouts. We will look in detail at six of these new literatures and philosophies shortly. Briefly they were as follows. First – and, with the benefit of hindsight, the most important – was that within science. 1859 witnessed the publication of Darwin's *Origin of Species*, which articulated the idea of evolution and natural selection as the explanation for the development of life. It

[8] "The Revival in London", in *The Revival*, 12 April 1862 p.114. In one week *The Revival*'s circulation advanced from 8,000 to 80,000 copies, G.E. Morgan, *R.C. Morgan: His Life and Times* (1909) pp.46-47.

[9] O. Chadwick, *The Victorian Church* (1987) pt.1, p.440.

[10] F.W. Farrar, *The Witness of History to Christ* (1892) p.6.

[11] Author's italics. O. Chadwick, *The Secularization of the European Mind in the Nineteenth Century* (1975) p.229.

would be used to justify ideas challenging Christianity on other grounds. Second, in philosophy, 1859 saw the publication of John Stuart Mill's treatise *On Liberty.* It also saw Herbert Spencer revise his prospectus for the proposed series of volumes that became his *Synthetic Philosophy* – which successfully promoted the doctrine of evolution. Third, 1859 saw changes in politics, with Charles Bradlaugh becoming a new driving force among the Secularists. Furthermore, the general election of that year witnessed the beginnings of the modern Liberal Party, which would encourage conflict between Anglican and Nonconformist. Fourth, in the world of social, economic and cultural thought, 1859 saw the publication of Karl Marx's *A Contribution to the Critique of Political Economy*. It also saw the great art critic, John Ruskin, launch himself as a social and economic commentator in the intellectual tradition of Carlyle. Fifth, in literature and letters, the novelists, by the late 1850s, attained a new degree of importance – and established new means for the dissemination of views unsympathetic to Christianity. Sixth, the final challenge was to the historical accuracy and authority of the Bible.

Within certain churches and chapels the doctrines taught also changed. Liberalism took root – especially within the Church of England and among the Congregationalists, the successors to the Puritans. Broadly, theological liberals argued that if the early chapters of Genesis could be reinterpreted by virtue of new scientific ideas, why not the whole of the old orthodoxies? Indeed, liberal theological leaders had greater empathy with the creators of the new literatures and philosophies than with the upholders of orthodoxy. The spirit behind the Tractarian movement was also taking new guise, as it began to animate a group who became known as the Ritualists. They suggested that medieval ritual, with its roots in the deep past, was the solution to attracting the working class, who infrequently attended church. There was also Christian Socialism which, although primarily the creation of the liberal theologian F.D. Maurice, drew in some of those leaning towards Ritualism and some evangelicals as well. Later in the century, perhaps as a reaction to these developments, glimmerings of Pentecostalism emerged.

Not only were distinct parties forming within the denominations causing conflict within them, but the same issues caused conflicts between the denominations. Furthermore, a growing disestablishment campaign by the Nonconformists damaged relationships between them and the established churches. This made working together to teach Christianity in the schools of the nation almost impossible and created tensions further afield. It also led to the loss of control by the established churches of the ancient universities, just at the time when their Christian intellectual vigour was vitally needed. Such Christian elements that remained in the universities might tend towards a High Church perspective, especially in history. Religions from the Orient, like Buddhism and Islam, also got a positive press – and the adherents of spiritualism and the Mormons were manifest, while the newly established theosophy took further shape.

Responding to the new challenges (1859-1900)

Notwithstanding the background noise, Christians, at least from the years 1859 to the mid-1880s, maintained a broad and vigorous focus on orthodoxy and evangelism. This was the age of great preachers, of whom the Baptist C.H. Spurgeon was the greatest, but many others became household names. Aggressive evangelism manifested new levels of zeal – perhaps reaching its zenith in the work of the Salvation Army, while open-air preaching and tract distribution widely flourished. A great range of new mission organisations came into being. Some focused on the workplace; most on their locality; some were of general application; others targeted special groups such as children in a variety of ways. The latter included The Children's Special Service Mission, Christian Endeavour and the Boys' and Girls' Brigades. This work to reach the nation was fortified with the help of a number of influential American evangelists, such as D.L. Moody and Mrs Palmer; the latter was the spur for Catherine Booth to begin preaching.

Furthermore, huge effort went into reaching people with the gospel through education, whether in the form of Sunday or day-schools for most children and private schools for children of the wealthy. For adults, there was the adult school movement and the educational facilities of institutional churches. Buildings for religious purposes multiplied. Accompanying these endeavours was a great range of social help from all denominations – although the Brethren, the most evangelistically minded denomination, were less accommodating in this respect. There were many other developments which aided evangelism. As the nineteenth century drew to a close, Mary Sumner, the founder of the Mothers' Union, observed: "there never was a time when such religious enthusiasm prevailed, such zealous fighting for God and right...and still the tide of sin rolls on". She noted "the rivers of immorality, intemperance, irreligion and infidelity are streaming over our cities and villages".[12] At the same time, the view that conversion, or becoming a new creation, came through baptism was increasingly widespread. The need for personal repentance by a Christian and a turning away from sin was increasingly given up by the churches. Many taught that there was no hell. Distracted by these and other internal doctrinal challenges, orthodoxy was perceived to be slowly losing the apologetics battle (which it had won in the first half of the nineteenth century) under the onslaught of secularisation and the "whole literatures" and "whole philosophies" it had spawned. As a result, during the last stage of the nineteenth century, or slightly earlier, the Bible was less and less read and its ideas ceased to permeate the thought of the unconverted in quite the same way as in the past. Converts became fewer and Christian zeal began to dry up. The numbers in church and chapel, as a proportion of the nation, began to fall away – decline that has not really ceased since.

[12] M. Sumner, *Women's Work Among Women* (1890) p.2.

Part 1

The quiet revival
(1791-1858)

1

A BATTLE FOR SUPREMACY (1791-1809)

1.1 Deepening infidelity

The early 1790s did not seem propitious for Christianity. In revolutionary France, the centre of atheism, many were "first the victims of delusion, and afterwards the victims of destruction".[1] At home, in 1791, John Wesley, the preacher of the changed heart, died. From the perspective of renewing morality, the endeavours of his evangelistic work – and the legal endeavours of the Proclamation Society – left much to be achieved. In London in 1793 one authority suggested that one in ten females was a prostitute. This must be an exaggeration, although the author was the London magistrate of police.[2] A Spitalfields brothel specialised in the under-fourteens, as did many pimps.[3] In 1794, Thomas Paine launched his major attack on orthodoxy by publishing, in English, the first part of *The Age of Reason* – "being an investigation of true and of fabulous theology".[4] Its effect was like a bolt of electricity. It was "disseminated with inconceivable industry through every town and village of the kingdom".[5] In 1795, the second part followed. Paine declared his creed as follows: "I believe in one God, and no more; and I hope for happiness beyond this life. I believe in the equality of man; and I believe that religious duties consist in doing justice, loving mercy, and endeavouring to make our fellow creatures happy."[6] He did not believe in the historic creeds; the churches were human inventions to enslave. Jesus "was a

[1] J. Brewster, *A Secular Essay* (1802) pp.338-339.

[2] S. Tomkins, *The Clapham Sect* (2010) p.60.

[3] Ibid.

[4] T. Paine, "*The Age of Reason*", in *The Complete Writings of Thomas Paine* (1969) (P.S. Foner (ed.)) vol.1, p.463.

[5] R. Hodgson, *The Life of the Right Reverend Beilby Porteus* (1811) p.125.

[6] T. Paine, "*The Age of Reason*", in *The Complete Writings of Thomas Paine* (1995) (P.S. Foner (ed.)) vol.1, p.464.

virtuous and an amiable man", but not born of a virgin.[7] The authors of the Scriptures were dismissed as "mythologists".[8] God could only be known through his works in creation – not revelation. Paine rejected the doctrine of sin; science brought a man face-to-face with God.[9] A contemporary thought that *The Age of Reason* "was calculated to inflict a deeper wound on religion, than any that had ever appeared in this or any other country".[10]

Richard Watson, the Bishop of Llandaff – who had earlier rebutted Gibbon's onslaught against Christianity[11] with his book, *An Apology for the Bible* (1796) – is credited along with others with ultimately defeating, in his day, the arguments of *The Age of Reason*. Watson wrote, in a letter to Paine, that *The Age of Reason* was so "extraordinary a performance...not from any novelty in the objections [deist in outlook]... against revealed religion (for I find little or no novelty in them), but from the zeal with which you labour to disseminate your opinions, and from the confidence with which you esteem them true".[12] Watson charged Paine with unsettling "the faith of thousands; root[ing] from the minds of the unhappy virtuous all their comfortable assurance of a future recompense". Furthermore, he had "annihilated in the minds of the flagitious all their fears of future punishment; you will have given the reins to the domination of every passion, and have thereby contributed to the introduction of the public insecurity, and of the private unhappiness, usually and almost necessarily accompanying a state of corrupted morals".[13]

[7] Ibid., pp.466-467.
[8] Ibid., p.469.
[9] Ibid., pp.601-602. The similarity between Paine's thought and twentieth-century liberalism has often been noted, for example, see G.H. Dowkontt, *The "Deadly Parallel"* (N.D.).
[10] R. Hodgson, *The Life of the Right Reverend Beilby Porteus* (1811) p.129. On the success of *The Age of Reason* in providing converts to secularism, see S. Budd, *Varieties of Unbelief 1850-1960* (1977) pp.107-108.
[11] J.A. Thomas, *The Nation's Gospel: Reformation to Revolution* (2017) vol.1, p.367.
[12] R. Watson, "Letter I", in *An Apology for the Bible, in a Series of Letters Addressed to Thomas Paine* (1796) p.1.
[13] Ibid., p.2. Watson was not an evangelical. In 1791, he republished Fowler's, *The Design of Christianity*, which had caused so much offence to John Bunyan, see E. Fowler, "The Design of Christianity", in *A Collection of Theological Tracts* (1791) (R. Watson (ed.)) vol.6, pp.311-420. Some thought his theology Unitarian, see P. Charles, *Unitarianism Defended* (1812) p.3.

In England, scepticism was the order of the day. Scotland witnessed "the midnight of the Church of Scotland".[14] In 1796, Samuel Taylor Coleridge wrote to a friend about Charles Darwin's grandfather, Erasmus, teasing him with all the longstanding arguments against the existence of God and revealed religion. Erasmus Darwin, he recorded, had read all the works of infidels, but not one in defence of religion. Coleridge concluded that Darwin "deems that there is a certain *self-evidence* in infidelity, and becomes an atheist by intuition".[15] One writer observed that scepticism "pervaded most books of science and amusement, and he who sat down to the perusal of a treatise upon botany or geology was in danger of rising up a sceptic or an infidel...not a few of a more serious description abandoned the profession of Christianity".[16] This writer was probably referring to the first volume of Erasmus Darwin's *Zoonomia* (1794), espousing biological evolution.[17] Erasmus, was very much a polymath, achieving, according to a recent writer, "more in a wider variety of fields than anyone since".[18] However, the future Prime Minister, George Canning, and others, in *The Loves of the Triangles* (1797),[19] effectively "ridiculed" Darwin's writing style and the belief that humans evolved from lower animals[20] – but the belief lingered. In 1814, in the Unitarian *Monthly Repository*, the idea of Lord Monboddo that men were improved monkeys was mocked.[21] In 1815, Coleridge wrote to William Wordsworth about "Darwin, and all the countless believers even (strange to say) among Christians of man's having progressed from

[14] A. Haldane, *The Lives of Robert Haldane of Airthrey and of his Brother James Alexander Haldane* (1853) p.130.

[15] Author's italics. K. Raine, *The Letters of Samuel Taylor Coleridge* (1950) p.57.

[16] J.W. Morris, *Biographical Recollections of the Rev. Robert Hall* (1833) p.142.

[17] Erasmus disbelieved in revelation and, though a theist, thought "Unitarianism was a feather-bed to catch a falling Christian", see *Charles Darwin's The Life of Erasmus Darwin* (2003) (D. King-Hele (ed.)) p.63. He had "a fatal attraction to women", see A. Desmond and J. Moore, *Darwin* (1991) p.6.

[18] *Charles Darwin's The Life of Erasmus Darwin* (2003) (D. King-Hele (ed.)) p.ix.

[19] As late as 1852, *The Loves of the Triangles* was reprinted in *Poetry of the Anti-Jacobin*. Its editor observed that "public opinion never fails, sooner or later, to arrive at a just conclusion as to merits both of individuals and actions", *Poetry of the Anti-Jacobin* (1852) p.v.

[20] D. King-Hele, "Erasmus Darwin", in 10 *Interdisciplinary Science Review* (1985) p.177.

[21] "Thoughts on the Fall", in 9 *The Monthly Repository of Theology and General Literature* (1814) p.391.

an orang-utan state – so contrary to all history, to all religion, nay, to all possibility".[22]

In the metropolis, the debating rooms were open and "the most barefaced infidelity was taught, to which the lower classes were invited, often on Sunday evenings, by a variety of specious allurements".[23] The aim of the "modern sceptics", it was asserted, was "To obliterate the sense of deity, of moral sanctions, and a future world, and by these means to prepare the way for the total subversion of every institution, both social and religious, which men have been hitherto accustomed to revere".[24] Property was an "unjust possession, and marriage odious monopoly".[25] Authority fell into disrepute; "the *double-entendre*, imported from the continent", which in reality was "filthy jesting", became common.[26] "Females of tender age, decked in the slight and partial covering of Parisian dames...became accustomed to the gaze of licentiousness,"[27] and "Pictures were exhibited of the most impious, disloyal, and indecent description; and were introduced into the schools".[28] In Parliament, it was noted that the French, despairing of victory by force of arms, "had sent amongst us a number of female dancers who, by the allurements of the most indecent attitudes, and most wanton theatrical exhibitions, succeeded but too effectually in loosening and corrupting the morals of the people". By common report, the performances exceeded the "licentious theatres of Athens and Rome".[29] Cases of elopement and

[22] K. Raine, *The Letters of Samuel Taylor Coleridge* (1950) p.212. Dr Clarke suggested, in very learned fashion, that the serpent of Genesis 3 was also an ape or orang-utan, see "Extracts from New Publications", in 7 *The Monthly Repository of Theology and General Literature* (1812) pp.16-20 and "Thoughts on the Fall", in 9 *The Monthly Repository of Theology and General Literature* (1814) pp.391-393.

[23] O. Gregory, *A Brief Memoir of the Life of Robert Hall* (1833) p.103. On the various corresponding societies, see W.M. Reid, *The Rise and Dissolution of the Infidel Societies in this Metropolis* (1800) republished in *Literacy and Society* (1971) (V.E. Neuburg (ed.)).

[24] R. Hall, "Preface" to *Modern Infidelity Considered* (1800) p.v.

[25] J.W. Middelton, *An Ecclesiastical Memoir of the First Four Decades of the Reign of George the Third* (1822) p.278.

[26] Ibid., p.283.

[27] Ibid., p.281.

[28] Ibid., p.285.

[29] *The Annual Register, or a View of the History, Politics, and Literature for the Year 1798* (1800) p.230.

adultery increased and, in the latter case, "raged".[30] Mary Wollstonecraft suggested that "adultery is justifiable".[31] Lord Loughborough, the Lord Chancellor, observed, in the House of Lords, that divorces "were considered little more than matters of course".[32] A bill to render it unlawful for persons divorced for adultery to intermarry with each other failed in that House.[33] Lord Clare declared that marriage was but a civil contract – and if the contract was dissolved, the parties were free to marry again.[34] Contemporaries noted that atheism had always existed, but it was "a curiosity to be placed in a moral museum...its domestication was never anticipated".[35] All the same, the teachers of the new irreligion made warm professions of attachment to virtue and proposed "to revolutionise the morals of mankind"[36] by separating morality from religion.

Shute Barrington, the Bishop of Durham, in his 'charge' of 1797, attributed the rise of infidelity to "an almost universal lukewarmness and indifference in Christians respecting the essentials of their religion, the peculiar grounds of their faith, of their hopes and their fears, than to the ability, the arguments, or even the perseverance of the enemies of Christianity".[37] Some hoped that the war with France would moderate the desire for pleasure and amusement and advance the cause of religion. The year 1798 saw signs of this, with the "avenues to the churches filled with carriages"[38] of the great – and the simple country people onlooking and wondering what was the matter. However, the next year witnessed

[30] *Reform or Ruin!* (1823) p.15. Lord Auckland calculated that there had been four parliamentary divorces since the Reformation and 1700, but since the reign of George III there had been 198, R. Hodgson, *The Life of the Right Reverend Beilby Porteus* (1811) pp.148-149.

[31] H. More, "*Strictures on the Modern System of Female Education*" (1799) vol.1, p.48, in *Strictures on Female Education* (1995).

[32] *The Annual Register, or a View of the History, Politics, and Literature for the Year 1798* (1800) p.230.

[33] R. Hodgson, *The Life of the Right Reverend Beilby Porteus* (1811) p.148.

[34] Ibid., pp.155-157.

[35] J.W. Middelton, *An Ecclesiastical Memoir of the First Four Decades of the Reign of George the Third* (1822) p.277.

[36] R. Hall, *Modern Infidelity Considered* (1800) p.14.

[37] J.W. Middelton, *An Ecclesiastical Memoir of the First Four Decades of the Reign of George the Third* (1822) pp.335-336.

[38] *The Annual Register, or a View of the History, Politics, and Literature for the Year 1798* (1800) p.229.

the return of "the spirit of dissipation, luxury, and profusion".[39]

1.2 Orthodoxy fights back

As the sky darkened, the first glimmer of dawn appeared for orthodox Churchmen. Men like Watson, with his *An Apology for the Bible*, played their part, but it was one thing to parry the intellectual assault, it was another to change the hearts of men. In 1795, the evangelical clergyman John Newton observed:

> The times are dark; but perhaps they were darker in *England* sixty years ago, when, though we had peace and plenty, the bulk of the kingdom lay under the judgment of an unregenerate ministry, and the people were perishing for lack of knowledge. In this respect, the times are better than they were. The gospel is planted in many parts... And every year the gospel is preached in new places – ministers are still raising up – the work is still spreading.[40]

When Newton wrote, he thought that there were not less than 400 Anglican clergy who were gospel preachers, whereas, in 1740, there was not one. They, in many cases, drew the crowds.[41] Further, the existence of a powerful common enemy pushed Churchmen and Dissenters together. For example, Robert Hall, the Baptist minister, gained many plaudits from members of the Church of England for his *Modern Infidelity Considered* (1800).

1.3 The influence of Christianity on the nation is in the balance

By 1802, it remained unclear whether Christianity would triumph in the nation. Brewster, an Anglican minister, observed that "the practice of religion has undoubtedly decreased" but he went on, "still this age is proud to acknowledge a glorious assemblage of piety and virtue, breaking forth like the refreshing water in a thirsty soil".[42] By 1809, an ongoing division of views as to the prospects of Christianity within

[39] J. Brewster, *A Secular Essay* (1802) p.399.
[40] Author's italics. Cited in D.B. Hindmarsh, *John Newton* (1996) p.327.
[41] J. Bean, *Zeal Without Innovation* (1809) p.42, R. Hall, *Strictures on a Work, Intitled, "Zeal Without Innovation"* (1809) p.21 and W.H.B. Proby, *Annals of the "Low-Church" Party in England* (1888) vol.1, p.358.
[42] J. Brewster, *A Secular Essay* (1802) p.401.

the nation can be discerned. The evangelical clergyman James Bean observed declining attendances at Church of England services. No longer did the attendance of "the more considerable heads of families... with their servants as well as children", have "a good effect on families of inferior condition".[43] Bean thought a few young girls plus, perhaps, their mother, the most likely members of a congregation. Fathers wanted a little relaxation after a busy week and the young men wanted something more interesting for their unexhausted spirits. He noted that even "With a numerous attendance of ministers, the finest specimens of church music...the seats at St Paul's Cathedral are seldom half filled".[44] Bean concluded that, if the gospel was not preached, the urban middle classes would not attend church but go to the country. As he observed, "Think of the general flocking of the better conditioned men of trade into the country on a Sunday; the morning consumed in the journey, the middle of the day in conviviality, the evening in returning to their neglected homes".[45]

Furthermore, Bean noted that even if the gospel was preached and the poor cared for, the strength of the opposition meant that there was no guarantee of church growth. Converts might fall away.[46] The press was hostile to evangelicalism and a "considerable proportion" of those who drew their livelihood from literary pursuits were "open or disguised abettors of atheism".[47] Bean urged evangelical ministers to live such good lives that what the press said about them would be unrecognised by their respective flocks.[48]

Bean's views drew a sharp retort from Robert Hall, a leading Baptist minister. He thought that as the number of gospel preachers increased,[49] "profligate transgressors are reclaimed, the mere form of religion is succeeded by the power, and fruits of genuine piety appear in the holy and exemplary lives of their adherents. A visible reformation in society at large".[50] Another Nonconformist explained the lack of attendances

[43] J. Bean, *Zeal Without Innovation* (1809) p.2 and *Zeal Without Bigotry* (1809) p.10.
[44] J. Bean, *Zeal Without Innovation* (1809) p.4
[45] Ibid., pp.6-7.
[46] Ibid., pp.316-318.
[47] R. Hall, *Modern Infidelity Considered* (1800) p.15.
[48] J. Bean, *Zeal Without Innovation* (1809) pp.vii-xii and 371-372.
[49] R. Hall, *Strictures on a Work, Intitled, "Zeal Without Innovation"* (1809) p.39.
[50] Ibid., p.33.

at Church of England services simply because of "a general want of interesting pulpit labours". He added that "With the exception of a very small minority, it is notorious that the preaching of the established clergy is in direct opposition to the spirit of their own...articles and liturgy."[51]

1.4 A great spiritual battle

Hall was one of a number of Dissenting ministers who thought that a great spiritual battle for the nation's soul was going on. He exulted in "the multitude of places where the gospel is preached in its purity [The Nonconformist chapels and evangelical Anglican churches], the general disposition to attend it, the establishment of Sunday schools, the circulation, with happy effect, of innumerable tracts, the translation of the Scriptures into foreign languages, and their more extensive communication to all nations, the formation of missionary societies, the growing unanimity among Christians, and the prodigious increase of faithful ministers in the established church".[52] It was an "era of zeal".[53] However he also observed "the violent, the outrageous opposition that is made to religion by multitudes".[54] He added:

> Great Britain exhibits the singular spectacle of two parties contending, not whether Christianity shall be received or rejected, but whether it shall be allowed to retain anything spiritual; not whether the articles or homilies shall be repealed, but whether they shall be laid as the basis of public instruction. Infidelity being too much discredited by the atrocities in France to hope for public countenance, the enemies of religion, instead of attacking the outworks of Christianity, are obliged to content themselves with vilifying and misrepresenting its distinguishing doctrines. They are willing to retain the Christian religion, providing it continue inefficient; and are want to boast of their attachment to the Established Church, when it is manifest there is little in it they admire except its splendor and its emoluments.[55]

[51] *Zeal Without Bigotry* (1809) pp.10 and 25.
[52] R. Hall, *Strictures on a Work, Intitled, "Zeal Without Innovation"* (1809) p.21.
[53] D. Bogue and J. Bennett, *History of Dissenters, from the Revolution in 1688, to the Year 1808* (1812) vol.4, p.388.
[54] R. Hall, *Strictures on a Work, Intitled, "Zeal Without Innovation"* (1809) p.22.
[55] Ibid., p.26.

Other Dissenting evangelicals developed the idea of a spiritual battle for the souls of the people. Thomas Haweis, the Countess of Huntingdon's successor as the leader of her Connection, observed that against the "ungodliness, that hath come in like a flood, the Spirit of the Lord hath lifted up the standard of the everlasting gospel. A vast increase of places for worship have been erected; an host of labourers thrust forth into the harvest; multiplied schools for religious instruction".[56]

Elsewhere in a movement embracing many lands Christians came together to pray. In the words of a Religious Tract Society editor to Andrew Fuller's *The Duty of Christians to Pray for the Revival and Extent of Real Religion*, they implored "a more abundant effusion of the Holy Spirit on all the churches of Christ throughout the habitable earth, and to extend the unspeakable blessings of the gospel to all mankind". The movement embraced Holland, Germany, and the United States. In Britain missionary prayer meetings were held on the first Monday of a month and on a Saturday evening in every week not only in London, but "in most of the principal cities, towns and villages of England." The original idea behind the movement seems to have come from Scotland.

[56] T. Haweis, *A View of the Present State of Evangelical Religion* (1812) p.16.

2

THE GOSPEL TRIUMPHS

2.1 The Church of England turns towards evangelicalism and revives

At the end of the eighteenth century, the clergy of the Church of England generally lacked zeal for the spiritual, educational and moral welfare of their charges. The High Church historian, John Henry Overton, records many examples of their failings at this time and their cause, often through too close an association of the clergy with the lifestyle of the gentry.[57] Those with zeal were despised. Charles Simeon, a leading evangelical at Cambridge, later reminisced that "It was a university crime to speak to me, and was reported to parents".[58] Richard Snape, another evangelical, was represented as evil by many bishops. He had almost given up on ministry when he was ordained by Bishop Porteus, the friend of Hannah More, in 1796. In 1798, he left Nottingham because of opposition, but his endeavours laid the foundation of future Church success in that city.[59]

However, the French Revolution gave an impetus to change the mood of the Establishment. Edmund Burke, in his *Reflections on the Revolution in France* (1790), made it clear that the church establishment was essential to the stability of the state.[60] This was despite the fact that French Protestants enjoyed a more generous treatment under revolutionary governments than they had enjoyed under the monarchy. In any event, from the autumn of 1793 a systematic de-Christianisation of France set in, sweeping across Catholics and Protestants alike.[61]

As a result, the Anglican clergy reflected on the inconsistency between what they preached in the pulpit – about the jolliness of life – and

[57] J.H. Overton, *The English Church in the Nineteenth Century* (1894) pp.2-17.
[58] H.E. Hopkins, *Charles Simeon of Cambridge* (1977) p.84.
[59] See L.E. Shelford, *A Memorial of the Rev. William Cadman* (1899) pp.11-12.
[60] *Burke's Reflections on the Revolution in France* (1900) (F.G. Selby (ed.)) pp.111-113.
[61] R. Birn, "Religious Toleration and Freedom of Expression", in *The French Idea of Freedom: The Old Regime and the Declaration of Rights of 1789* (1994) (D.V. Klay (ed.)) pp.417-418.

what they read in the liturgy. Revolutionary France manifested sin and so its solution, the atonement, became acceptable.[62] Indeed, William Wilberforce thought that the liturgy provided a "faithful model of the Christian's belief, and practice, and language...preserving a living representation of the opinions and habits of better times, like some historical record which reproaches a degenerate posterity".[63] Overton thought that it also revealed to the "Church how little real hold she had upon the masses".[64] The days when it could be written that "The mass of the clergy troubled not their souls with theological difficulties, but hunted and tippled peacefully with the squirearchy", were numbered.[65]

For some, the Methodists provided a model of best practice. For example, Charles Simeon, early in his ministry, practised itinerancy and preached in a farmer's barn.[66] By 1807, a Churchman who held to spiritual regeneration by water baptism felt that the tide was "running very strongly against" him. He, and those likeminded, risked being overwhelmed; they were so "puny a race".[67]

Only towards the end of the second decade of the nineteenth century was the triumph of the gospel assured. In 1809, Bean observed that "The innocency of error was never, perhaps, a more fashionable topic of declamation...it is much in vogue to decry an attention to doctrines".[68] He thought that an "earnest piety among the ministers"[69] was needed, as "a worldly clergy is a dead weight" upon the Church. By them, he added, "her operation is impeded, and her efficiency lost".[70] In Oxford, to be an evangelical between 1810 and 1820 was almost to attach a

[62] W.J. Conybeare, *Essays Ecclesiastical and Social* (1855) pp.62-63.

[63] W. Wilberforce, *A Practical View of the Prevailing Religious System of Professed Christians, in the Higher and Middle Classes in This Country, Contrasted with Real Christianity* (1829) p.394.

[64] J.H. Overton, *The English Church in the Nineteenth Century* (1894) p.2.

[65] W.J. Conybeare, *Essays Ecclesiastical and Social* (1855) p.62. See also W.E. Gladstone, *Gleanings of Past Years* (1879) vol.7, p.219.

[66] A. Atherstone, *Evangelical Mission and Anglican Church Order: Charles Simeon Reconsidered* (2009) pp.14-19.

[67] D. Waterland, "Regeneration stated and Explained", in *The Churchman's Remembrancer* (1807) vol.1, p.v.

[68] J. Bean, *Zeal Without Innovation* (1809) p.300.

[69] Ibid., p.29.

[70] Ibid., p.30.

black letter to your name.[71] But the spiritual outlook there was changing. Oxford's primary evangelical centre was St Ebbe's. There, in William Gladstone's evocative words, under Henry Bulteel "the flame was at white heat".[72] Many were converted there in the mid-1820s who later became significant builders of the Plymouth Brethren. In London, an evangelical minister remained a "marked man", excluded from the parish churches, exiled to a friendly proprietary chapel.[73] By 1820, Gladstone suggests, the number of evangelical clergy still did not exceed five per cent, although this may be on the low side.[74]

By the end of the second decade of the nineteenth century, the evangelicals could see the spiritual trajectory of the Church. In 1818, *The Christian Observer* observed that, during the last 20 years, "those just views of Christian doctrine which characterised the wisest and best of our reformers have rapidly increased in the Church".[75] In 1820, *The Christian Observer* rejoiced that "our new systems of education, our Bible, missionary, and other charitable societies", are "so widely extending and so deeply taking root".[76] The following year, it observed the increasing numbers of clergy enlisting "under the scriptural banners of her martyrs and reformers" and the multitudes of her laity aspiring to "assist in the general extension of religious knowledge".[77] Many evangelical clergy were well-able to manage a parish with its growing parochial machinery,[78] while the wealth of the laity went to acquire rights of appointments to parishes – especially city centre parishes.[79] Furthermore, the new churches, built in the 1820s, provided new openings for able evangelical clergy. As gospel preachers entered Church pulpits, the other mechanisms for advancing the gospel increasingly made

[71] S. Minton, *The Evangelicals and "The Edinburgh"* (N.D.) p.49. See also G. Atkins, *Wilberforce and his Milieux: The Worlds of Anglican Evangelicalism, c.1780-1830* (2009) (Unpublished Ph.D. thesis, Cambridge University) p.43.

[72] W.E. Gladstone, *Gleanings of Past Years* (1879) vol.7, p.211.

[73] Ibid., p.213.

[74] Ibid., p.210.

[75] "Preface" to 16 *The Christian Observer for the Year 1817* (1818) pp.v-vi.

[76] "Preface" to 18 *The Christian Observer for the Year 1819* (1820) p.vii.

[77] "Preface" to 20 *The Christian Observer for the Year 1821* (1822) p.v.

[78] D. Wilson, *Our Protestant Faith in Danger* (1850) p.4.

[79] G. Atkins, *Wilberforce and his Milieux: The Worlds of Anglican Evangelicalism, c.1780-1830* (2009) (Unpublished Ph.D. thesis, Cambridge University) pp.61-62 and 111.

an impact – and the opposition melted away. However, Anglicanism continued to frown on open-air preaching. In 1831, the Bishop of Oxford deprived Henry Bulteel, at St Ebbe's Oxford, of his curacy for doing so. He added to his offence by preaching in "Dissenting meeting-houses".[80] Nevertheless, he remained at Oxford preaching to large open-air crowds, before founding a Strict Baptist Chapel in Oxford.[81] By the late 1820s, Simeon commented that "now my views are received with respect and even esteem by men of rank, by archbishops and bishops".[82]

Before 1830, Gladstone calculated that evangelicals made up around 12.5 per cent of the clergy.[83] In 1839, three years after Simeon's death, a Dissenting minister put the number of evangelical Church ministers at 3,000, although this may be on the high side.[84] Their ideas were increasingly influential – and talk of a union between the "Evangelical" and "Orthodox" parties appeared.[85]

2.2 Evangelicals move into high ecclesiastical office

Wilberforce tried to use his influence to get worthy evangelicals into high ecclesiastical office, but was rarely successful – even when canvassing his friend, Pitt.[86] His only real success came in 1792, with the elevation of Isaac Milner, President of Queens' College, Cambridge, to Dean of Carlisle. Although, by the second decade of the nineteenth century, "a vast body of evangelical clergy hath arisen" in the Established Church,

[80] H.B. Bulteel, *The Doctrine of the Miraculous Interference of Jesus on behalf of Believers* (1832) p.28.

[81] For a summary of Bulteel's ministry, see F.M. Turner, *John Henry Newman* (2002) pp.49-51.

[82] H.E. Hopkins, *Charles Simeon of Cambridge* (1977) p.84. For a very helpful picture of the growth of the evangelicals up to the 1820s, see G. Atkins, *Wilberforce and his Milieux: The Worlds of Anglican Evangelicalism, c.1780-1830* (2009) (Unpublished Ph.D. thesis, Cambridge University) pp.96-110.

[83] W.E. Gladstone, *Gleanings of Past Years* (1879) vol.7, p.211.

[84] See J. Walsh and S. Taylor, "Introduction: The Church and Anglicanism in the 'Long' Eighteenth Century", in *The Church of England c.1689-1833* (1993) (J. Walsh, C. Haydon and S. Taylor (eds)) p.44.

[85] See "Preface" to 61 *The Christian Observer for the Year 1861* (1861) p.iv.

[86] G. Atkins, *Wilberforce and his Milieux: The Worlds of Anglican Evangelicalism, c.1780-1830* (2009) (Unpublished Ph.D. thesis, Cambridge University) pp.96-97 and 99.

from their superiors they "received frowns, instead of favours" and "the reproach of Methodism".[87]

The first evangelical bishop[88] was Henry Ryder, at Gloucester, in 1815. This required a great struggle and the aid of Lord Harrowby, Ryder's elder brother with strong political associations. Enemies of evangelicals accused them of faction, enthusiasm, and of being disturbers of the Establishment.[89] Clergy who regarded justification by faith as a "monster" – to be marked with the "strongest reprobation" – shuddered "at the rapid growth of...*evangelical principles*, among the ministry of the Establishment". They petitioned Ryder to exclude evangelical candidates from ordination.[90] Meanwhile, evangelicals stressed their loyalty to the Church of England. In 1826, a second evangelical episcopal appointment was made – when Charles Sumner went to Llandaff. This appointment carried a whiff of scandal. It was rumoured that Charles Sumner's marriage had been entered into to protect a son of the Marquis of Conyngham from marrying the same girl. Lady Conyngham was the Prince Regent's mistress. After being introduced to the Prince Regent by Lady Conyngham, Sumner advanced rapidly.[91] In 1827, he went to the riches of the Bishopric of Winchester. He was also a second cousin of and on friendly terms with William Wilberforce. In 1828, his brother, John, became Bishop of Chester and later, Archbishop of Canterbury. However, it was impossible to get strong Calvinists into episcopal office.[92]

[87] T. Haweis, *A View of the Present State of Evangelical Religion* (1812) p.17.

[88] Ryder was on the Arminian wing, see M. Smith and S. Taylor, *Evangelicalism in the Church of England c.1790- c.1890* pp.53-85.

[89] For example, R. Warner, *A Letter to the Hon. and Right Rev. Henry Ryder D.D. Lord Bishop of Gloucester on the Admission to Holy Orders of Young Men, Holding (what are commonly called) Evangelical Principles* (1818) pp.4-5. For other criticisms of evangelicals, see R. Lloyd, *Strictures on a Recent Publication Entitled "The Church Her Own Enemy"* (1819) pp.120-126.

[90] Author's italics. R. Warner, *A Letter to the Hon. and Right Rev. Henry Ryder D.D. Lord Bishop of Gloucester on the Admission to Holy Orders of Young Men, Holding (what are commonly called) Evangelical Principles* (1818) pp.10, 18 and 36.

[91] F.K. Brown, *Fathers of the Victorians* (1961) pp.61-62.

[92] G. Atkins, *Wilberforce and his Milieux: The Worlds of Anglican Evangelicalism, c.1780-1830* (2009) (Unpublished Ph.D. thesis, Cambridge University) pp.82-110.

2.3 Methodism becomes independent and grows

Four years after John Wesley's death, Methodism separated from the Church of England. The break came when the Methodist societies started to hold services at the same time as the Established Church and to celebrate communion. Until then, Methodism operated as a para-church movement. Wesley had wanted to reform the Church of England and not set up a new denomination.[93] However, after the American War of Independence, in 1784 he was forced to appoint leaders in the United States who did not trace their authority back to England's established church. By doing so, he set himself up as an independent source of authority, pointing to the likelihood of a break between his societies and the Church of England.

Methodist enthusiasm did not die with Wesley, or with independence. There were "glorious displays of the Lord's omnipotent power, and of his willingness to save perishing sinners".[94] For example, Methodism's Sheffield circuit saw 380 souls added in the year ended August 1795.[95] In the following two years, 1,700-1,800 were added.[96] Christ was preached "as our wisdom, righteousness, sanctification and redemption" and "faith as the great duty enjoined in the gospel".[97] The eyes of a poor blind woman were miraculously opened, to the wonder of all.[98] The signs of revival continued into the first half of the nineteenth century.[99] For example, in the early 1830s, Robert Aitken, an Anglican clergymen speaking in Sheffield's Methodist chapels, witnessed, in six weeks, 3,000

[93] R.H. Martin, *Evangelicals United* (1983) pp.3-4.

[94] J. Sigston, *Memoir of the Venerable William Bramwell* (N.D.) p.97.

[95] Ibid., p.44.

[96] Ibid., p.51.

[97] Ibid., pp.46-47.

[98] Ibid., pp.63 and 99.

[99] R. Currie, *Methodism Divided* (1968) p.30. See also R. Young, *Showers of Blessing* (1844). However, even in these times of revival, the passion for souls was not universal amongst Methodists. "When Theophilus Lessey junior, came to Stourport-on-Severn, in 1811, he described his congregation as being 'very genteel, but, I fear, not a very religious or lively one. There seems to be much conformity to the world among them; I hope I shall be comfortable. They appear very friendly and affectionate.'" The next year he moved to Kidderminster as its first Methodist minister, see "Methodism in Stourport", in *The Methodist Recorder and General Christian Chronicle*, 26 April 1906, p.10.

persons pass from "death unto life".[100] Aitken himself was converted after a period of inner conviction of his sinfulness; he had heard voices asserting that he was preaching a false gospel and indicating the inadequacy of his own endeavours.[101] *The Methodist Recorder* regarded the "three years ending 1834, during which time the first visit of cholera occurred", as one of "extraordinary religious awakening".[102] In 1849, a revival at Penzance increased circuit membership of the Wesleyan Methodists "in twelve months by no less than 70 per cent".[103] In 1800 members of Methodist churches in Great Britain numbered around 96,078 people; by 1859, they numbered 495,368 people.[104] Attendances at Methodist churches always exceeded their membership numbers – but national attendances figures, as for other churches, were not taken, save for 1851, when attendances in England exceeded 1,489,000 people.[105]

Sometimes, Methodism expanded through the endeavour of a wealthy convert. For example, James Lackington, having made a fortune as a bookseller in London, in retirement built chapels at Taunton and Budleigh Salterton, as he moved around the country.[106] In 1839, Thomas Jackson, preaching to the Wesleyan Conference at their centenary, referred to "ten thousand societies of devout people, raised up by God's blessing... both at home and abroad". Jackson affirmed the great truths of Wesley Methodism: "the natural ignorance and depravity of men; their love of sin, and of flattering error; their aversion to truth and holiness; and that, therefore, they must be sought and warned, that they may repent and be saved".[107] He ended his sermon by indicating that if Wesleyan churches should ever "depart from essential truth; sink into worldliness and sloth; and, instead of promoting spiritual religion, devote their energies to the

[100] C.E. Woods, *Memoirs and Letters of Canon Hay Aitken* (1928) p.22.

[101] "Conversion of the Rev. R. Aitkin", in *The Revivalist* (1857) pp.97-99.

[102] "The District Returns", in *The Methodist Recorder, and General Christian Chronicle*, 23 May 1861, pp.57-58.

[103] D. Bebbington, *Victorian Religious Revivals* (2012) p.90.

[104] R. Currie, A. Gilbert and L. Horsley, *Churches and Churchgoers* (1977) pp.161-162. See also K.F. Inglis, *Churches and the Working Classes in Victorian England* (1964) pp.12-13.

[105] Calculation based on the figures in M.R. Watts, *The Dissenters* (1995) vol.2, p.29 and see also H. Mann, *Religious Worship in England and Wales* (1854) p.91.

[106] P. Hopkins, *The Life of James Lackington, Bookseller, 1746-1815* (2004) p.3.

[107] T. Jackson, *A Sermon Preached by Appointment before the Wesleyan Conference on Monday, August 5, 1839* (1839) p.23.

attainment of earthly objects, or objects which are directly evil" then, as the Presbyterian churches before, they would become extinct.[108] Indeed in such circumstances, Jackson suggested, Methodists would want to close down their chapels.

2.3.1 *Primitive Methodism gives Methodism a new cutting-edge*

Notwithstanding Thomas Jackson's strictures about the risks of worldliness, the Wesleyan Methodists became respectable, in places, and lost their evangelistic edge.

Hugh Bourne, a carpenter and, later, founder of the Primitive Methodists, was converted in the spring of 1799 by reading a number of books, culminating in the letters of John Fletcher "on the spiritual manifestation of the Son of God". He realised "the blessing named in John 14:21, where Christ says, 'I will love him, and will manifest myself to him;' and he manifested himself to me: and I was born again in an instant! yea, passed from death unto life".[109] On Christmas Day 1800 Bourne expounded John 14:21 to his relative – the collier Daniel Shubotham – and the need to be born again. Shubotham was converted and was soon preaching "Jesus and him crucified" in his conversations, whatever the opposition.[110] Together they set up a prayer group. Soon, "souls were saved, and God was glorified; and that most ungodly neighbourhood [the northern Staffordshire/Cheshire borderlands around Mow Cop] was greatly moralised".[111] The number of the converted kept expanding. However, the local Methodists – Bourne called them "modern Methodists" – were geographically distant and showed no interest in the revival taking place.[112] Reluctantly, Bourne began to preach – his intention emerging at the home of a nearby Methodist. However, the

[108] Ibid., p.58.

[109] J. Walford, *Memoirs of the Life and Labours of the Late Venerable Hugh Bourne* (1999) vol.1, pp.44-49.

[110] Ibid., pp.71-75.

[111] Ibid., p.79.

[112] Bourne, dismissed many of the nearby failing Methodist societies as manifesting 'modern Methodism', ruinous and without the power to convert. He suggested that modern Methodism, emphasised "building up", not making converts, although if they occurred it thought them good, and it rejected open-air preaching. Bourne thought his "converters" were better at building up, as well as converting. He thought it telling that when modern Methodists joined Primitive Methodists, conversions among the latter ceased, see ibid., pp.94-100.

numbers present were too great to preach indoors, so Bourne preached outside – and an impromptu prayer meeting followed. The first camp meeting on Mow Cop had been held; it was 12 July, 1801.[113] For his followers, extended times of prayer after a church service became standard.

The summer of 1807 saw Bourne hold another Sunday camp meeting on Mow Cop. In doing so, he was influenced by the American evangelist Lorenzo Dow's[114] ideas of camp meetings for public prayer, preaching and love feasts. Such was its success that two others were planned for two or three days, or more. At the first meeting, a number of stands were put up for preaching, prayer, exhorting and relating experiences – and a separate meeting was held for the children, at which six were converted, to add to at least six adults already converted. At different times, between 2,000-4,000 were present.[115] At the second camp meeting, considerable effort was put into obtaining a licence to avoid breaching the Conventicles Act (1664). This banned meetings over a certain number of people to worship except in accordance with practices of the Church of England – and wooden buildings were put up in order to take advantage of the protections of the Toleration Act 1690. Food and many other artefacts had to be sought. Sixty conversions were recorded.[116] Shortly thereafter, the attention of Bourne's mind was drawn to the benefits of processing, singing in a group through a town – for the purpose of influencing the public mind. Processing was soon "carried out on a large and extensive scale in the Primitive Methodist Connection".[117]

The Wesleyan Methodist Conference of ministers condemned the Mow Top camp meetings for being likely to foster indiscipline and uncontrolled initiatives among lay members. "Shouting, shaking, and rolling on the ground often accompanied the tremendous emotional release that followed upon conversion."[118] In June 1808, Bourne was put out of his local Methodist society, without being heard. In 1811, he and many who held reservations about Wesleyan Methodism formed, under

[113] Ibid., pp.89-93 and 127.
[114] See N. Scotland, *Apostles of the Spirit and Fire* (2009) pp.27-48.
[115] J. Walford, *Memoirs of the Life and Labours of the Late Venerable Hugh Bourne* (1999) vol.1, pp.130-138.
[116] Ibid., pp.137-138 and 156-163.
[117] Ibid., pp.164-165.
[118] Cited in B. Atkinson, *Land of Hope and Glory* (2003) p.158.

Bourne, the movement that became known as Primitive Methodism.[119] This appellation recalled the words used by John Wesley – to characterise the open-air endeavours of his early followers – to whose role the Primitives believed they had succeeded.[120]

Primitive Methodists believed in direct words of God, "through dreams and visions".[121] They made significant use of itinerant, including female, evangelistic preachers, who fanned out across the countryside.[122] Villages and towns were transformed as men like Johnny Oxtoby prayed for them, then knocked on doors and spoke to "any he met of Christ and the forgiveness of sins".[123] These lay evangelists suffered persecution. Often, landlords would not sell them the land to build a chapel.[124] Nicknamed "Ranters",[125] one indication of their past influence is that in the countryside, not far from Kidderminster, is the eponymous geographical feature, "Ranters Bank". In 1836, a chapel was built there. Nevertheless, their endeavours were richly rewarded; by 1851, attendances at their chapels in England numbered nearly 330,000[126] and they had built or acquired 1,500 chapels.[127] At Stanhope, in Durham, the Primitive Methodist Society increased its numbers "from 50 in September 1851 to 115, with 9 on probation six months later".[128] But they too were moving away from camp meetings and open-air evangelism

[119] Bourne provided the administrative, and William Clowes the preaching skills to establish the new movement, G. Milburn, *Primitive Methodism* (2002) pp.29-31.

[120] Ibid., p.x.

[121] H. McLeod, *Religion and the Working Class in Nineteenth-Century Britain* (1984) p.27. See also J. Walford, *Memoirs of the Life and Labours of the Late Venerable Hugh Bourne* (1999) vol.1, pp.166-167, 169-170, 182-183, 222-223, 247-248.

[122] G. Milburn, *Primitive Methodism* (2002) pp.15-16. Hugh Bourne wrote a tract to give away supporting female preaching, see J. Walford, *Memoirs of the Life and Labours of the Late Venerable Hugh Bourne* (1999) vol.1, pp.184-189, 202 and 414.

[123] F. Cook, *Fine Gold From Yorkshire* (2017) p.67. Oxtoby, himself, had been converted by travelling Methodist evangelists who passed through his village, ibid., pp.66-67.

[124] R.W. Ambler, *Ranters, Revivalists, and Reformers* (1989) pp.4 and 49-51.

[125] The name was given to them on occasion of a mission party returning home and singing in the streets of Belper, see J. Walford, *Memoirs of the Life and Labours of the Late Venerable Hugh Bourne* (1999) vol.1, pp.412-413.

[126] Calculation based on the figures in M.R. Watts, *The Dissenters* (1995) vol.2, pp.28-29. Watts gives a slightly higher figure than H. Mann, *Religious Worship in England and Wales* (1854) p.91.

[127] G. Milburn, *Primitive Methodism* (2002) p.26.

[128] D. Bebbington, *Victorian Religious Revivals* (2012) p.115.

which, for the first half of the nineteenth century, they championed and gave a cutting edge to. Although "the most thoroughly working class of major religious denominations in nineteenth-century England",[129] by the mid-century they wanted to have an educated ministry, in settled chapels – and were becoming respectable. However, before becoming so, on a winter's day in December 1849, the 15-year old C.H. Spurgeon wandered into one of their chapels – because of a snowstorm in Colchester. The snow prevented the regular preacher from attending and the sermon was taken, in Spurgeon's words, by "a shoemaker, or tailor, or something of that sort...this man was really stupid. He was obliged to stick to his text, for the simple reason that he had little else to say. The text was – 'Look unto me. And be ye saved, all the ends of the earth'". The preacher then "shouted as only a Primitive Methodist could do, 'Young man, look to Jesus Christ. Look! Look! Look! You have nothing to do but look and live!'" Spurgeon looked and found the Saviour. The Primitives had caught the greatest preacher of the nineteenth century – and one of its most influential men.[130]

2.4 Nonconformist numbers blossom

The spiritual enthusiasm and relentless itinerant preaching – at whatever personal cost to health – of many a Methodist preacher, acted as a spur to Nonconformity; what was called "Methodist fever" spread, taking many to an early death through exhaustion.[131] In 1809, the evangelical Anglican James Bean lamented: "The coventicle of a preaching mechanic overflowing; the parish church almost without a congregation".[132] In the pulpits of the Independents were "men of natural eloquence and fervid temperament...they preached with a vehemence, a solemnity, and a power which produced immense results".[133] Their preachers spoke earnestly about the "consequences of a wicked life" and that "Jesus Christ is able to save to the uttermost, all that come unto God by him": no "cold, or

[129] H. McLeod, *Religion and the Working Class in Nineteenth-Century Britain* (1984) p.26.

[130] Cited in A.A. Dallimore, *C.H. Spurgeon* (1984) pp.18-19.

[131] M.R. Watts, *The Dissenters* (1995) vol.2, pp.150-151.

[132] J. Bean, *Zeal Without Innovation* (1809) p.26 and *Zeal Without Bigotry* (1809) pp.9-11.

[133] R.W. Dale, *The Evangelical Revival* (1880) p.16.

timid"[134] sermons. They preached in the open air; "one of the most fruitful means of Nonconformist expansion". Early in the nineteenth century, the Dissenting historians Bogue and Bennett wrote: "no one denomination of Christians...can boast of so great a number of ministers who preach the gospel in purity as the English Independents".[135] They "confidently asserted" that "there is now more religion among Dissenters...than at any former period".[136] Between 1800 and 1830, Congregationalists established 500 new chapels.[137] At Carrs Lane Chapel, Birmingham, the preaching of John Angell James lifted membership from 50 in 1805, to 500 in 1833 and about 1,000 in 1855. The congregation, always more numerous in Nonconformist churches of the time than the names on the relevant church membership list, numbered 2,000, in 1833.[138] The ideals of the French Revolution helped strengthen Independency – by making the lower classes more willing to be their own judge in religion so that, if they approved the preacher and his doctrine, they felt less unwillingness to join Dissent.[139] Furthermore, Methodists were still not numerous and, after one of their wandering preachers had passed through an area, those awakened often had no more obvious refuge than a chapel of one of the other Dissenting denominations.[140] At the Old Meeting House in Kidderminster, from 1820 onwards, there was, apart from the odd interregnum, constant growth. Its historian wrote that "the desert rejoiced and blossomed as the rose".[141]

The Baptists also grew rapidly. The Particular Baptist minister Andrew Fuller, in 1810, found his Monday and Friday night meetings at Kettering "much thronged – the discourses in the latter have been much addressed to persons under some concern about their salvation".[142]

[134] J. Bean, *Zeal Without Innovation* (1809) p.37. See also D. Bogue and J. Bennett, *History of Dissenters, from the Revolution in 1688, to the Year 1808* (1812) vol.4, pp.312-314.

[135] D. Bogue and J. Bennett, *History of Dissenters, from the Revolution in 1688, to the Year 1808* (1812) vol.4, p.330.

[136] Ibid., p.395.

[137] R. Carwardine, *Transatlantic Revivalism* (2006) p.61.

[138] C.A. Haig, *John Angell James* (1961) p.21.

[139] D. Bogue and J. Bennett, *History of Dissenters, from the Revolution in 1688, to the Year 1808* (1812) vol.4, pp.204-205.

[140] Ibid., pp.314-315.

[141] G. Hunsworth, *Baxter's Nonconformist Descendants* (1874) p.56.

[142] A.G. Fuller, *The Complete Works of the Rev. Andrew Fuller* (1856) p.lxxviii.

The New Connection of General Baptists increased the number of their churches from 60[143] or so, at the turn of the nineteenth century, to 220, in 1840.[144] Between 1800 and 1860, Nonconformist members, including the Methodists, multiplied around five and a half fold, notwithstanding often fierce Anglican opposition.[145] The spiritual vitality behind this growth is highlighted when it is considered that, over the same period, Great Britain's population just over doubled – to 23.1 million.

2.5 The Brethren appear to provide an additional evangelistic cutting-edge

In the 1820s, the work of the Church of Ireland clergyman John Nelson Darby and others laid the foundations of the Brethren.[146] Darby was one of a number who were converted or became effective itinerant evangelists, moving from a High Church position in the Irish revival of the 1820s.[147] They left the Established Church because they considered it "little more than another generation of hypocritical and complaisant Pharisees and Sadducees".[148] In 1831, the first Brethren congregation in England was established at Plymouth and quickly grew, drawing a number of clergy who seceded from the Church of England.[149] The census of 1851 identifies 132 Brethren places of worship in England and Wales, although recent research suggests that this considerably underestimated their number.[150] Early Brethren members were often from the "genteel" classes, although after 1859 the movement developed a more populist ethos.[151] It had grown through a mixture of secession from most denominations and vigorous evangelism. At Hereford, John

[143] D. Bogue and J. Bennett, *History of Dissenters, from the Revolution in 1688, to the Year 1808* (1812) vol.4, p.332.
[144] R. Hayden, *English Baptist History and Heritage* (2005) pp.55-58.
[145] For Nonconformist numbers, see R. Currie, A. Gilbert and L. Horsley, *Churches and Churchgoers* (1977) p.25 and for the privations and opposition their preachers suffered, see M.R. Watts, *The Dissenters* (1995) vol.2, pp.150-156.
[146] See generally W.B. Neatby, *A History of the Plymouth Brethren* (2001) pp.15-70 and T. Grass, *Gathering to His Name* (2012) pp.9-62.
[147] Ibid., pp.12-29.
[148] F.M. Turner, *John Henry Newman* (2002) p.52.
[149] T. Grass, *Gathering to His Name* (2012) pp.34-38.
[150] H. Mann, *Religious Worship in England and Wales* (1854) p.42 and T. Grass, *Gathering to His Name* (2012) pp.115-116.
[151] Ibid., pp.86-87 and 118.

Venn (of the distinguished evangelical family) lost the most zealous of his congregation to them. They fanned out in energetic evangelism to the neighbouring towns and villages. This energy and commitment made them influential, fulfilling "a long-existing pattern of renewal and self-transformation within evangelical religion".[152]

The appellation 'Brethren' indicated that being a Christian was more important than any doctrinal slant. Creeds were eschewed as divisive. They regarded as Christians all those who held the basic tenets of salvation. They also affirmed the role of the Holy Spirit as the "all sufficient guide" to God's people. Gifts from the Spirit, especially those of teachers and evangelists, were emphasised – and those possessing these gifts were freed to exercise them outside the Brethren Assembly. There were no ordained clergymen.[153] It was upon "the Spirit's gifting rather than upon human ordination" that ministry rested.[154] Ironically, given the emphasis on their 'Brotherhood', in 1848, the Brethren split into Open and Exclusivist Brethren.

Darby and the Brethren, starting at various conferences,[155] are intimately connected with the development of dispensational theology – which divided history into various "dispensations". It included the idea that Jesus would return before a time of terror on earth (the "Tribulation"), to take away the faithful (the "Rapture"). After the Tribulation, Christ and his church would return to earth and reign for a thousand years (the "millennium") – before the resurrection of the wicked and the final judgment. The underpinning theology was complicated.[156]

In the 1830s, certain Brethren ideas entered – in simplified form – the evangelical mainstream, when the Church luminary Edward Bickersteth became a "millennial".[157] Until then, the orthodox view was that the gradual conversion of the world could be expected. Bickersteth made

[152] F.M. Turner, *John Henry Newman* (2002) p.52.

[153] For a picture of the Brethren in the early 1850s, see H. Mann, *Religious Worship in England and Wales* (1854) pp.41-42.

[154] T. Grass, *Gathering to His Name* (2012) p.18. Darby believed that the supernatural gifts of the apostolic age, such as speaking in tongues had ceased, see ibid., p.91.

[155] Ibid., pp.25-29 and 35-36.

[156] See ibid., pp.101-107 and generally T.P. Weber, *Living in the Shadow of the Second Coming* (1987).

[157] For a short background to millennialism, see F.M. Turner, *John Henry Newman* (2002) pp.39-40.

widely popular the view that the second coming of Christ preceded a reign by him of a thousand years. He took from Scripture that the "first resurrection is literal, and that Christ will establish a glorious kingdom of righteousness on earth at his final return, before the resurrection of the wicked and their final judgment".[158] Bickersteth thought that the time was short until the return of Jesus. This gave new motives for diligence in, and energy to, evangelistic efforts. There was the prospect of a speedy recompense from the Lord on the day of his appearing. By the late 1840s, probably at least half of the evangelicals favoured premillennialism.[159] Turnbull, a recent biographer of Lord Shaftesbury, attributes his energy for social reform to his moderate premillennialism.[160] Shaftesbury and Bickersteth were great friends. Martyn Lloyd-Jones attributed the lack of interest in scholarship by evangelicals later in the nineteenth century to the belief that the imminent arrival of the millennium made it superfluous.[161] Others suggest that premillennialism shifted "the centre of gravity of the gospel message from the word of the cross to the hope of the crown".[162]

As part of the final denouement, millennialists expected the mass conversion of the Jews – and their restoration to Palestine. The London Society for Promoting Christianity Amongst the Jews became a very well-funded organisation.[163] One observer of the Established Church, in an aggressive overstatement – but which points to the growing preoccupation in some quarters with the millennium – argued that the London Society had become so preoccupied with the Jews that it acted as "propaganda for converting Christians to Judaism".[164]

[158] T.R. Birks, *A. Memoir of the Rev Edward Bickersteth* (1853) vol.2, p.44.
[159] See G. Carter, *Anglican Evangelicals* (2001) p.155.
[160] R. Turnbull, *Anglican and Evangelical* (2007) pp.154-156. Turnbull suggests that the Rapture disinclined those holding the position of Darby to be involved in social reform, as they looked forward to a future dispensation. If true, they did not lack evangelistic zeal, see ibid., p.154.
[161] See T.A. Noble, *Tyndale House and Fellowship* (2006) pp.34-35.
[162] J. Macleod, *Scottish Theology* (1974) p.278.
[163] D.M. Lewis, *Lighten their Darkness* (1986) pp.206-207.
[164] W.J. Conybeare, *Essays Ecclesiastical and Social* (1855) pp.83 and 94.

2.6 Roman Catholic numbers mushroom

During much of our period, the negative perception of Roman Catholics declined. The change perhaps began in 1791. Then, moved in part by their sufferings in France from forces perceived to be committed to atheism, the Roman Catholic Relief Act allowed them, subject to taking certain oaths, to worship in their own churches.[165] Later, as they fought effectively against Napoleon, it became difficult to consider them disloyal. Furthermore, with the defeat of Napoleonic France and the continuing eclipse of Catholic Spain, the threat from the Catholic powers was insignificant.[166]

In England, Roman Catholic numbers at the beginning of our period were comparatively small.[167] However, they were numerous in Ireland, and in parts of recently acquired Canada. It was mass Irish immigration which stimulated their numerical growth in Britain – growth that was even steeper than that among the Nonconformists. In 1860, their British members totalled 1,179,000 – up from 129,000 in 1800.[168] Their numbers increasingly included a number of the nobility and landed gentry – but they less actively spread their religion than Nonconformists.[169]

2.7 Not every denomination thrives, or thrives for the right reasons

The gospel did not triumph among all denominations. The Presbyterians, "leaning to the Arian heresy...dwindled away".[170] John Brewster observed that where "disbelief and disloyalty met together…The numbers soon diminished". Some Dissenters doubted the authority of Scripture, especially St Paul's epistles, "under the sanction of reason and science, falsely so called".[171] Some joined Dissent to express their desire to demolish the Establishment – and not to advance religion.[172]

165 R. Burn, *Ecclesiastical Law* (1797) vol.3, p.233.

166 L. Colley, *Britons: Forging the Nation 1707-1837* (2009) pp.327-341.

167 F. Plowden, *The Case Stated* (N.D.) p.17.

168 The relevant calculation assumes that a Catholic member was someone who had undergone a "Catholic marriage", see R. Currie, A. Gilbert and L. Horsley, *Churches and Churchgoers* (1977) pp.25 and 27-28.

169 "To the Editor of The Christian Observer", in 13 *The Christian Observer for the Year 1814* (1815) p.768.

170 T. Haweis, *A View of the Present State of Evangelical Religion* (1812) p.22.

171 J. Brewster, *A Secular Essay* (1802) pp.349-350.

172 Ibid., pp.344 and 348-350.

2.8 In Wales, revival

The language barrier spared Wales the assault of what was regarded as 'infidel' literature. South Wales had enjoyed the fruits of the Methodist revival. In 1791 in North Wales, a great revival broke out. The "seeds of knowledge" planted by Thomas Charles and all those involved in the Welsh schools and Sunday schools had sprouted.[173] At Pwllheli, "thousands attended". At Bala, there flowed "a very great, powerful, and glorious outpouring of the Spirit". In Caernarvonshire and Anglesey, the congregations were "very numerous". As Charles wrote, "It is an easy work to preach the gospel of the Kingdom at this time."[174] For example, the Baptists – who in 1776 had launched a missionary movement to evangelise North Wales, with mixed results[175] – enjoyed a time of startling growth. Christmas Evans, their leading evangelistic preacher, in one near three-year period, saw 600 persons added to his churches in Anglesey.[176] In September 1813, Thomas Charles wrote to a friend that: "There have been added to the church in the two chapels of Clyngog, 138; in Llanllyvni, 90; in Penygraig and Tymawr, above 100; and many in other societies in the county. The Sunday schools abound with scholars."[177]

By then, the Calvinistic successors of Howell Harris and Daniel Rowlands – Thomas Charles was a convert of Rowlands – had separated from the Established Church. They had existed as private societies within it but, in 1811, they commenced administrating the sacraments and assumed the appearance of a separate connection. As the Calvinistic Methodist Church, the movement grew rapidly. An American visitor concluded that: "The Welsh are a very religious people. There is perhaps no other Christian people in the world, who manifest so much religious susceptibility, or who can be brought so much under its power."[178] In 1851, the Calvinistic Methodist Church had 828 chapels – and at their Sunday services nearly 80,000 attended in the morning, nearly 60,000

[173] M. Bruen, *History of Revivals of Religion in the British Isles* (1836) p.121. See also J.A. Thomas, *The Nation's Gospel* vol.1 (2017), pp.356-357 and 359-360.

[174] M. Bruen, *History of Revivals of Religion in the British Isles* (1836) pp.122-124.

[175] E.E. Rees, *Christmas Evans* (N.D.) pp.55-58.

[176] Ibid., pp.104-105. The Welsh at this time also benefited from other great preachers, including John Elias, a Calvinistic Methodist and Williams of Wren, the Independent.

[177] E. Morgan, *The Life and Labours of the Rev. T. Charles* (1865) p.369.

[178] Cited in R. Carwardine, *Transatlantic Revivalism* (2006) p.85.

in the afternoon and over 125,000 in the evening.[179] The secession of the Calvinistic Methodists helped the evangelicals remaining in the Church in Wales to focus on the gospel, without the need to act so as to keep the two bodies together. Most of their parishioners may have left but, slowly, the evangelicals that remained rebuilt their flocks, especially in Carmarthenshire and Cardiganshire – and bred the necessary supply of ordinands for a wider work in Wales.[180]

2.9 In Scotland, spiritual advance

In Scotland, the gospel "tide had begun to flow about 1790".[181] Many ministers were encouraged by the news from Wales.[182] In 1796, Charles Simeon visited Edinburgh and "awakened several" people, scattering tracts "along the roads and in the streets".[183] He then rode into the Highlands for a pleasure tour, mingled with ministry, accompanied by James Haldane. Around this time, Sunday schools were set up, at first to teach the poor and their parents the principles of religion in the great cities. Unlike England, there was no need to teach the people to read, as most could already do so.[184] Evangelical ministers rode out on tours to the hinterlands, handing out tracts and establishing Sunday schools. A week's tour in 1797 by John Campbell saw the formation, three months later, of 60 Sabbath-evening schools.[185] Campbell's counsellor and encourager was the Countess of Leven. His helper was James Haldane and, with the north of Scotland lying in the hands of 'careless and immoral' ministers,[186] James Haldane again soon rode out on similar ventures with others. Preaching was then added to the range of tasks undertaken on these tours. Over the next nine years, Haldane, a layman and former East India sea captain, preached in "almost every town or populous village in Scotland" – and in the northern islands of Orkney

[179] H. Mann, *Religious Worship in England and Wales* (1854) p.38.
[180] R.L. Brown, *The Welsh Evangelicals* (1986) pp.35-69.
[181] J. Macleod, *Scottish Theology* (1974) p.266.
[182] See R. Philip, *The Life, Times, and Missionary Enterprises, of the Rev. John Campbell* (1841) pp.146-152.
[183] Ibid., p.118.
[184] Ibid., p.122.
[185] Ibid., p.130.
[186] A. Haldane, *The Lives of Robert Haldane of Airthrey and of his Brother James Alexander Haldane* (1853) p.152.

and of Shetland.[187] The congregations were substantial; at Kirkwall, in the Orkneys, congregations of 3,000 and 4,000 regularly gathered.[188] Haldane thought that every Christian was bound, "wherever he has the opportunity, to warn sinners to flee from the wrath to come, and to point out Jesus as the way, the truth and the life".[189] His biographer refers to his first tour of the North as awakening "multitudes" to God. This also gave an impulse to the Established Church and to seceder churches.[190] At the end of 1797, The Society for Propagating the Gospel at Home was founded; its labours "were greatly blessed".[191] Shortly thereafter, Robert Haldane, a wealthy land owner and brother of James, opened the Edinburgh Tabernacle, the first of a series of large tabernacles in Scotland's major cities, modelled on George Whitefield's idea of stations for continuous preaching. Its opening saw Rowland Hill arrive from London to preach to crowds from seven in the morning.[192] James Haldane was its first minister. Robert also established a seminary to "qualify pious young men" to go "out literally to the highways and hedges to preach the gospel".[193] By 1805, they had trained 200 lay preachers.[194] The work of the Haldane brothers furthered Congregationalism in Scotland and, later, the Baptist cause when the brothers moved to that perspective.[195]

Generally, the Church of Scotland did not appreciate these developments. Supported by other churches, it moved to quash 'vagrant teaching' and Sunday schools – for allegedly teaching irreligion and anarchy.[196] By the second decade of the nineteenth century, observers thought that a quarter, or a fifth, of the population attended churches

[187] Ibid., p.153.
[188] Ibid., p.173.
[189] Ibid., p.155.
[190] Ibid., p.190.
[191] Ibid., p.193.
[192] R. Philip, *The Life, Times, and Missionary Enterprises, of the Rev. John Campbell* (1841) pp.165 and 280-282.
[193] A. Haldane, *The Lives of Robert Haldane of Airthrey and of his Brother James Alexander Haldane* (1853) pp.247-248.
[194] A.L. Drummond and J. Bulloch, *The Scottish Church 1688-1843* (1973) p.153.
[195] In 1985, the Baptists observed that their strength in Scotland resided in the areas where the Haldane brothers had been active, P. Brierley and F. Macdonald, *Prospects for Scotland* (1985) p.45.
[196] A. Haldane, *The Lives of Robert Haldane of Airthrey and of his Brother James Alexander Haldane* (1853) pp.256-262.

that had seceded from the Church of Scotland.[197] However, within the confines of the Church of Scotland, a number of men of "ability and standing in the ministry" were converted.[198] In the form of the Clapham Sect "they received powerful support from the south".[199] These new converts included Thomas Chalmers, one of the great, if not the greatest, nineteenth century Scotsmen, and a convert inspired by William Wilberforce's *A Practical View of Religion.*[200]

The basic structures for advancing religion in Scotland were sound, although in the fast-growing cities, like Glasgow, they were stretched and, in the remoter parts of the country, were less substantial.[201] Ministers had a duty to visit parishioners at home and to give religious and moral instruction – and to inform themselves of the material needs of the poor. Along with other parish leaders, they were also responsible for the collection and distribution of the parish poor-relief fund. Chalmers thought that this was of great benefit to Scotland, as it had the capacity to unite parishes in benevolence. In England, poor laws encouraged the poor "to think more of their rights than their responsibilities" and required the state to coerce the rich to give charity.[202] Furthermore, Scotland's schools, for which ministers were responsible, gave it a great advantage over other parts of Britain when it came to advancing the gospel. Chalmers rejoiced in the endeavours of the Society in Scotland for Propagating Christian Knowledge, whose Highland schools had helped create "the most intelligent and virtuous peasantry in Europe".[203] However, he was anxious that the Society did not make "industry and cultivation" the centre of their schools' work, but "to preach Christ to sinners, and

[197] H.M. Wellwood, *Account of the Life and Writings of John Erskine, D.D.* (1818) p.445 and J. Kirton, *A History of the Church of Scotland 1660-1679* (1992) p.v.
[198] J. Macleod, *Scottish Theology* (1974) pp.256-257.
[199] S.J. Brown, *Thomas Chalmers and the Godly Commonwealth in Scotland* (1982) p.48.
[200] J. Wolffe, "William Wilberforce's *Practical View* (1797) and its Reception", in *Revival and Resurgence in Christian History* (2008) (K. Cooper and J. Gregory (eds)) pp.180-181 and S.J Brown, *Thomas Chalmers and the Godly Commonwealth in Scotland* (1982) pp.55-56.
[201] Ibid., pp.70 and 94-99.
[202] Ibid., pp.67-68. See also D. Englander, *Poverty and Poor Law Reform: From Chadwick to Booth, 1834-1914* (2013) pp.47-48 which questions with regard to the poor law the extent of the differences between Scotland and England.
[203] T. Chalmers, *The Utility of Missions Ascertained by Expeience* (1817) p.16.

to rear human souls to a beauteous and never-fading immortality".[204] In addition, by making the "social virtues…part of religion" Chalmers thought that Scotsmen were exalted far above anything the "poet or moralist" could do for them.[205] Many Moderate clergyman had "regarded their parish as little more than a sinecure while they pursued eminence in other, academic, endeavours".[206] As evangelical clergymen moved into the parishes, a new vitality spread through the parish system – and its benefits in spreading religious knowledge began to be seen.

2.10 A great revival takes hold

By the mid-1820s, a great spiritual revival was on its way across Britain, but one unaccompanied by sensational manifestations. For Daniel Wilson, the events of previous years spoke for themselves. He wrote:

> What can mark the progress of a revival of religion, if the increased exertions of Christians in disseminating the Holy Scriptures, in planting missions, in calling back the houses of Israel and Judah to their Messiah, in scattering profusely prayer-books and homilies, and religious tracts and treatises in every quarter, in translating for foreign nations and barbarian tribes the records of our faith, do not prove it!...such a period of light and exertion has not appeared, taking it altogether, since the days of the apostles.[207]

Two letters written by the Anglican minister John Scott over a period of just over 20 years illustrate the change in spiritual atmosphere. Writing in 1812, after 13 years in Hull, he thought that his ministry had not been "attended with any peculiar degree of usefulness". Writing in the summer of 1833, he indicated that the numbers attending his church had doubled in the last ten years.[208] In Wilson's view, the spread of real

[204] Ibid., p.21.
[205] Ibid., p.20.
[206] S.J. Brown, *Thomas Chalmers and the Godly Commonwealth in Scotland* (1982) p.71.
[207] D. Wilson, "Introductory Essay" to W. Wilberforce, *A Practical View of the Prevailing Religious System of Professed Christians, in the Higher and Middle Classes in This Country, Contrasted with Real Christianity* (1829) p.lii.
[208] D. Wilson, *Recollections of the Late Rev. John Scott, M.A. of Hull* (1834) pp.10 and 20-21.

Christianity without persecution was a "certain criterion of a revival of mercy to a nation". It marked "a Divine favour to the government and country which affords such protection".[209] Nevertheless, he observed "a mass of hatred, of bitter determined hatred, against evangelical truth and holiness, lurking in our country".[210] As Maurice Quinlan observes: "By 1830 Protestantism was probably a greater force in the lives of the English people than it had ever before been."[211]

But many Christians, recognising that others were making "vigorous efforts" to lead the "lower grades of society" to "embrace the dogmas of infidelity",[212] urged their fellows to seek further revival. For example, in 1832, *The Revivalist* was founded, devoted to revival and the extension of evangelical religion. And the times did get even better. In that year, *The Revivalist* noted the "rapid spread of real piety in our established Church", as evangelicals began "the faithful preaching of the gospel" in pulpits formerly occupied by "worldly priests".[213] In 1848, the Dean of Westminster referred his congregation in Westminster Abbey to the "high religious, and moral, and political exaltation, which we may venture to affirm is without example in the past or present history of nations".[214] Furthermore, the cause of "civil and religious prosperity" was "daily and annually advancing". He attributed this to "God's blessing".

In 1856, *The Christian Observer* proclaimed that "the last ten years have witnessed a great increase in the number and influence of the decidedly evangelical clergy". The same author thought it exceedingly doubtful whether there were ever so many at any previous period in the whole history of the Church of England, or whether such noble opportunities were ever presented for the faithful preaching of the gospel...But nowhere has this change been more remarkable than in London...many of the largest and most important parishes have been placed under the parochial care of a better and abler evangelical clergy.

[209] D. Wilson, "Introductory Essay" to W. Wilberforce, *A Practical View of the Prevailing Religious System of Professed Christians, in the Higher and Middle Classes in This Country, Contrasted with Real Christianity* (1829) p.lv.
[210] Ibid., p.lvii.
[211] M.J. Quinlan, *Victorian Prelude* (1941) p.257.
[212] *The Revivalist* (1832) p.2.
[213] "Increase of Religion in the Established Church", in *The Revivalist* (1832) pp.57-58.
[214] W. Buckland, *A Sermon Preached in Westminster Abbey, on Easter Sunday Evening, April 23, 1848* (1848) p.5.

There were at least 40 such parishes containing an aggregate population of a little less than half a million people. St Paul's Cathedral experienced change – becoming "a radiating point for evangelical truth through the City". Furthermore, the Crown was exercising its powers of patronage in favour of "some of the most decidedly evangelical clergymen of the day".[215]

As evangelicals were placed in the pulpits of the nation's churches, observers noted "an increased facility of collecting congregations". In 1856 a writer in *The Christian Observer* noted that churches thinly attended ten years ago were now full. Even working men seemed more willing to attend than formerly.[216] All the same, not all attending were converted. Indeed, "sudden and marked conversions", it observed, were fewer than in Whitefield's day, but many more well-filled churches existed than ten years previously – where incumbents had "the joy of beholding a large number of precious souls to be numbered in many instances by tens, and in some by hundreds. And such translations from death to life, they are privileged to trace to the blessing of God on their own ministry."[217]

However, even in the heyday of spiritual growth in the second quarter of the nineteenth century, denominations did not necessarily grow constantly. John Angell James, in a letter to an American friend written in September 1847, observed that "The Wesleyan body had a decrease last year of five thousand. Neither we nor the Baptists are doing much, and the evangelical clergy of the Church of England as little. The excitement of the age is bearing down religion. Men's minds are wholly engrossed by the things that are seen and temporal."[218] All the same, in

[215] "On the Progress of True Religion Amongst our Home Population", in 56 *The Christian Observer for the Year 1856* (1856) pp.145-147.

[216] How willingly working men attended church was a topic of discussion. One observer believed that in no district of the masses did church attendance reach 20 per cent – and rarely 10 per cent. The more pessimistic thought attendance levels in the country were six per cent of labourers and, in London, two per cent, see ibid., p.151.

[217] Ibid., p.150. See also "Are Genuine Conversions to God as Frequent and as Decisive as they were Seventy Years Ago?", in 57 *The Christian Observer for the Year 1857* (1857) pp.73-78.

[218] R.W. Dale, *The Life and Letters of J.A. James* (1861) pp.542-543. The period of stagnation began around 1845. Peter Rylands blamed the problem on "Puseyite leaven" spreading from the Established Church to the Dissenters – and various other weaknesses within the Dissenters, especially the quality of the ministers and the use

1848, Gawin Kirkham, aged 16, and later a noted open-air evangelist, was converted by the simple rite of confirmation.[219]

In Scotland

> The decade from 1820 to 1830...witnessed a phenomenal growth of evangelical influence...Vast crowds flocked to hear fashionable evangelical preachers. There was an increase in family worship, and a marked decrease in swearing and drunkenness among the upper and middle classes. Strict religious observances became a sign of respectability. Bible study and prayer groups proliferated...The best and the brightest young men crowded into the divinity halls.[220]

Then, in 1839, a revival at Kilsyth was "more or less felt all over Scotland", as William Chalmers Burns and others preached across the nation. In particular, James Morison enjoyed "so wonderful an itineracy".[221] Robert Murray M'Cheyne wrote of the early 1840s that "I am sure there never was a time when the Spirit of God was more present in Scotland".[222] In 1860, Islay, the brother of W.C. Burns, suggested that through the Kilsyth revival "the idea of revival as the great necessity of the church...took strong possession of the minds of Christian men, and has never since lost its hold".[223]

2.11 American evangelists add fuel to the fire

In the first third of the nineteenth century, the revivals that shook America were "more frequent and copious than those experienced by

of creeds, see P. Rylands, *The Pulpit and the People* (1847) pp.6-11, 69 and 71-118. George Dawson put the problems primarily down to the priesthood within the Church of England and differences between the churches and their creeds, see G. Dawson, *The Demands of the Age Upon the Church* (1847).

[219] F. Cockrem, *Gawin Kirkham* (N.D.) pp.12-13.

[220] S.J. Brown, *Thomas Chalmers and the Godly Commonwealth in Scotland* (1982) p.211.

[221] F. Ferguson, *A History of the Evangelical Union* (1876) p.12. For the Kilsyth revival and its immediate impact, see I. Burns, *The Pastor of Kilsyth* (1860) pp.123-168 and I.H. Murray, *A Scottish Christian Heritage* (2006) pp.105-109. See also H. Bonar, *The Life of John Milne* (2010) pp.40-67 and D.J. McLean, "William Chalmers Burns", in *In Writing*, Autumn/Winter 2018 pp.4-17.

[222] A.A. Bonar, *The Life of Robert Murray M'Cheyne* (1960) p.153. See also I.H. Murray, *A Scottish Christian Heritage* (2006) p.78.

[223] I. Burns, *The Pastor of Kilsyth* (1860) p.167.

any other region of the earth". The European religious world read the reports avidly.[224] In England, a "considerable excitement throughout the country at large resulted".[225] They introduced to Great Britain many new ideas and practices to encourage conversion. For example, as we have seen, Lorenzo Dow's ideas and visits to England in 1806 and 1818 profoundly influenced the Primitive Methodists. He had earlier preached across Ireland, often in the open air.[226] In men of respectability, the revivals were commonly associated with vulgarity, emotionalism and disruption. Lorenzo Dow, the best known American revivalist of the time, for example, was not a sophisticated individual.

From the late 1820s, a number of urbane American preachers and participants in revival arrived on Britain's shores – and subsequently preached or wrote about their experiences.[227] For example, in August 1828 William Patton gave an account of the revival in America to nearly 2,000 hearers at Carrs Lane Chapel, in Birmingham. The next evening, Angell James repeated the substance of the address at the chapel's prayer gathering – at which two or three times the usual number attended.[228] Angell James believed that Providence would employ North America "as its chief instrument in the conversion of the world".[229] In the chapels of the metropolis, Calvin Colton preached on the same topic – and then wrote the *History and Character of American Revivals of Religion* (1832). A revival was there defined as "*the multiplied power of religion over a community of minds, when the Spirit of God awakens Christians to special faith and effort and brings sinners to repentance.*"[230] He thought that the history of American revivals indicated that there were two types of revival. The first type was where the instruments of revival were not

[224] M. Bruen, *History of Revivals of Religion in the British Isles* (1836) p.258.

[225] R.W. Dale, *The Life and Letters of John Angell James* (1861) pp.247, 250, 253 and 257.

[226] R. Carwardine, *Transatlantic Revivalism* (2006) pp.103-107 and N. Scotland, *Apostles of the Spirit and Fire* (2009) pp.27-48.

[227] R. Carwardine, *Transatlantic Revivalism* (2006) pp.66-68.

[228] R.W. Dale, *The Life and Letters of John Angell James* (1861) p.246.

[229] Untitled comment to *The Works of John Angell James* (1861) (T.S. James (ed.)) vol.9 p.ii.

[230] Author's italics. C. Colton, *History and Character of American Revivals of Religion* (1832) pp.1-2.

apparent;[231] and the second was where God manifestly worked "to meet his own engagements, to fulfil his promises – to work when his people work".[232] Colton suggested that to wait on God's sovereignty for the first type of revival "is not the submission of piety, but an expression of the sloth and recklessness of unbelief".[233]

The merits of transatlantic revivalism became a subject of debate.[234] The respected American preacher Lyman Beecher wrote in the pages of *The Christian Observer* that among his many fears related to revival was that "it will unavoidably array a large portion of the unrenewed part of the community against revivals and religion, and produce infidels, scoffers, Unitarians, and Universalists on every side – increasing the resistance seven-fold to evangelical doctrine".[235] *The Christian Observer* itself suggested that these revivals "blended good and evil" – and it could not but "rejoice with trembling".[236] Secular writers, like Mrs Trollope, in her *Domestic Manners of the Americans* (1832), paid particular tribute to the power in America of revivalist preachers over women, particularly the pretty young women that packed their churches. A deputation of the newly established Congregational Union was sent to America – and published two volumes of findings.[237]

The first wave of these visitors from America to Britain acted more as publicists of revival than its preachers.[238] They were less impressed with the steady growth of Christianity in Great Britain – and thought something better was possible.[239] From the late 1830s, American preachers associated with revival and ready to preach its doctrines landed on England's shores.[240] The most successful of them was the Methodist James Caughey – a substantial personality. He arrived at Liverpool in

[231] Ibid., p.2.
[232] Ibid., p.7.
[233] Ibid., p.6.
[234] M. Bruen, *History of Revivals of Religion in the British Isles* (1836) pp.258-265.
[235] "American Revivals", in 28 *The Christian Observer for the Year 1828* (1829) p.541.
[236] "Religious Revivals in America", in 29 *The Christian Observer for the Year 1829* (1830) pp.186-187.
[237] See A. Reed and J. Matheson, *A Narrative of the Visit to the American Churches by the Deputation from the Congregational Union of England and Wales* (1835).
[238] R. Carwardine, *Transatlantic Revivalism* (2006) pp.66-68.
[239] Ibid., pp.62-63.
[240] Ibid., pp.73-77.

July 1841[241] and remained in Great Britain until 1847. Although he later returned, his first visit was his most effective.

Caughey ran protracted revivalist campaigns, mainly in the great northern Methodist centres, such as the Brunswick Chapel in Leeds. Detailed records were kept of his converts, drawn from all classes except perhaps the very lowest[242] – and through his preaching an estimated 20,000 souls were saved. He powerfully influenced the future General Booth, of the Salvation Army.[243] It was not easy for him. While conducting a mission at York, "Letters of criticism and super-criticism, anonymous and otherwise, came to him almost daily."[244] Furthermore, the leaders of the Wesleyan Methodist Conference, increasingly concerned with maintaining the established order, were no admirers of him. Towards the end of his first visit, they banned him from the denomination's chapels.[245] They later wrote to the American Methodist General Conference, asking it to ensure that Caughey did not return to set foot on "Queen Victoria's soil".[246] However, he returned to England in 1857, focusing on Methodist chapels apart from those of the Wesleyans. In Sheffield, his campaign of July 1857 to January 1858, based on a chapel of each of the United Methodists, New Connection Methodists and Primitive Methodists, resulted in 3,756 people "who obtained the blessing of purity as well as those who bore public testimony of the power of God to forgive sins".[247] The campaign then continued – with equal success in other Sheffield chapels – until the end of August 1858. At a meeting to mark the end of Caughey's labours in Sheffield, a report indicated 5,364 converts. At the report's presentation, a prayer was made that "this revival may be but as the drops before the glorious shower of

[241] For an excellent summary of Caughey's impact in Britain during his first visit, see ibid., pp.102-133.

[242] Ibid., p.193.

[243] N. Scotland, *Apostles of the Spirit and Fire* (2009) pp.91-115 and J. Kent, *Holding the Fort* (1978) pp.311-13. Wherever Caughey preached, on his first visit, the Wesleyan Methodists enjoyed a marked growth in membership – with decline being interrupted and limited growth accelerated, R. Carwardine, *Transatlantic Revivalism* (2006) pp.111-115.

[244] J. Caughey, *Glimpses of Life in Soul Saving* (1868) p.18.

[245] R. Currie, *Methodism Divided* (1968) p.70.

[246] Rev. James Caughey, *The Revivalist* (1860) p.141.

[247] "The Amazing Work of God at Sheffield", in *The Revivalist* (1858) p.33.

gospel blessing that shall sweep England from one end to the other".[248]

The most famous American evangelist of the mid-years of the nineteenth century was Charles Grandison Finney. Finney's great work was his *Lectures on Revivals of Religion*, published in the United Kingdom in 1837.[249] The bedrock of his thinking was that "A revival always includes conviction of sin on the part of the church…Backslidden Christians will be brought to repentance. A revival is nothing else than a new beginning of obedience to God."[250] Finney's book sparked revival in Wales between 1839 and 1843, popularly known as "Finney's Revival".[251] In Scotland, James Morison, a young probationer minister, read it avidly as he headed north to preach. He continued to do so on arrival and under his preaching revival took hold.[252] Catherine Mumford, another great admirer of *Lectures on Revivals*, commended it to her future husband, the young William Booth.[253] One publisher in England alone sold 80,000 copies of it.[254]

Controversially, the first point of Finney's *Lectures* was that "*Religion is the work of man*. It is something for man to do. It consists in obeying God",[255] although he acknowledged that it was God's Spirit that led man to obey. He urged that "the Almighty had so ordained that particular methods would infallibly bring" revival[256] – and rejected the older view that a revival was a sovereign work of God.[257] Conversions were to be encouraged by careful planning and "excitements". This planning included protracted meetings for anxious enquirers "and the adoption of certain techniques – such as the isolated anxious seat for the troubled sinner in search of salvation".[258] This seat was to be in full view of the

[248] "Farewell Soiree to the Rev. James Caughey", in *The Revivalist* (1858) pp.145-160.
[249] See generally N. Scotland, *Apostles of the Spirit and Fire* (2009) pp.67-89 and 218 and R. Carwardine, *Transatlantic Revivalism* (2006) pp.134-135.
[250] C.G. Finney, *Revivals of Religion* (1913) p.7.
[251] K. J. Hardman, *Charles Grandison Finney* (1990) p.399. See also R. Carwardine, *Transatlantic Revivalism* (2006) pp.85 and 89-94.
[252] W. Adamson, *The Life of the Rev. James Morison* (1898) pp.55-56 and R. Carwardine, *Transatlantic Revivalism* (2006) pp.94-101.
[253] H. Begbie, *Life of William Booth* (1920) vol.1, p.175-176.
[254] N. Scotland, *Apostles of the Spirit and Fire* (2009) p.77.
[255] Author's italics. C.G. Finney, *Revivals of Religion* (1913) p.1.
[256] D. Bebbington, *Victorian Religious Revivals* (2012) p.12.
[257] M. Bruen, *History of Revivals of Religion in the British Isles* (1836) p.3.
[258] D.W. Bebbington, *Evangelicalism in Modern Britain* (1989) p.116.

congregation, who prayed for the penitent. Finney also subtly changed the meaning of the 'new birth' – away from the need for a new creation, into the exercise of natural powers and faculties in the way that they ought to be exercised.[259] Further, although he insisted that sinners deserved eternal death, he did not subscribe to penal substitution, seeing the atonement rather as a moral example.[260]

Finney toured England from late 1849 to the spring of 1851, preaching at Whitefield's Moorfields Tabernacle – to great success. "The young men of the Tabernacle...laboured...to excite the attention of the careless, and to bring them to hear the word of life".[261] Houses were visited and copies of Finney's addresses left; posters were put up and were also carried on the shoulders of men through the streets. Each weekday, at least two-thirds of his hearers were strangers;[262] thousands were converted, many paid restitution for past misdeeds totalling thousands of pounds, but not all his supporters were entirely convinced by his work.[263] However, the needs of the time were many – and anyone who seemed likely to "infuse a little more life, provided it be not the life of a lunatic or a maniac", was welcome.[264]

2.12 A new concern for morality

Coinciding with the revival of religion was a concern for decorum, manners and morality. In 1829, Francis Place, the political reformer and sceptic during the last 30 years, wrote that the people had become "wiser, better, more frugal, more honest, more respectable, more virtuous than they ever were before".[265] Drunkenness among all classes reduced, and there was "a remarkable decrease in swearing". Gambling also fell from favour – the state lottery being discontinued in 1826 – and there

[259] K.J. Hardman, *Charles Grandison Finney* (1990) p.391.

[260] For a discussion, see ibid., pp.385-388.

[261] Ibid., p.413.

[262] R. Carwardine, *Transatlantic Revivalism* (2006) p.145.

[263] R.W. Dale, *The Life and Letters of J.A. James* (1861) p.546.

[264] Ibid. There were doubts about whether Finnney's converts continued, see J.E. Johnson, "Charles G. Finney and a Theology of Revivalism", in 38 *Church History* (1969) pp. 338-358 at 348.

[265] Cited in M.J. Quinlan, *Victorian Prelude* (1941) p.173. See also "State of the Nation", in 6 *The Westminster Review* (1826) p.264.

was little demand for pornography.[266] Maurice Quinlan graphically observed that the "brutish masses of the eighteenth century were being transformed into the more decent, law abiding common people of the Victorian era".[267]

Evangelicals were unsurprised by this development. *The Christian Observer* expected their clergy to preach "the fruits of faith, as well as the root from which they spring; then no man is an Evangelical Preacher who is not a Moral Preacher". The morality taught was that flowing from the cross, not the morals of Seneca and Epictetus.[268] Converts were exhorted to immediately give up besetting sins, and to avoid being entangled in them again.[269] In Sunday schools, evangelicals ran "the great preventive of moral deterioration in our land".[270]

Writers like the Baptist Andrew Fuller spelt out in detail the differences in the efficacy of Calvinistic and Trinitarian to Socinian and Unitarian theology, in promoting true morality. The Calvinistic system taught that rebellion against God "is opposition to the general good". It destroys the "well-being of the universe, by excluding God, and righteousness, and peace, from the whole system...it is...an infinite evil, and deserving of endless punishment – and that, in whatever instance God exercises forgiveness, it is not without respect to that public expression of his displeasure against it, which was uttered in the death of his Son".[271]

Fuller also argued that "equally necessary to promote repentance is *the equity and goodness of the divine law*".[272] The Socinians thought sin no more than something worthy of "pity, but not of blame". It was in every sense natural, except where contracted by education or example. God only punished it because it tended to harm the sinner.[273] The Socinians called those who opposed them "bigots" and, like Joseph Priestley,

[266] M.J. Quinlan, *Victorian Prelude* (1941) pp.253-280.

[267] Ibid., p.178.

[268] "The Society for Promoting Christian Knowledge", in 33 *The Christian Observer for the Year 1833* (1833) p.495.

[269] W. Haslam, *From Death into Life* (1897) p.257.

[270] A. Reed and J. Matheson, *A Narrative of the Visit to the American Churches by the Deputation from the Congregational Union of England and Wales* (Jackson and Walford (1835)) vol.1, p.389.

[271] A. Fuller, *The Calvinistic and Socinian Systems Examined and Compared as to their Moral Tendency* (1815) p.23.

[272] Author's italics. Ibid., p.25.

[273] Ibid., p.24.

called for religion to be accommodated "to the notions of infidels, and then they would condescend to receive it".[274] The Calvinists thought that the Unitarians, like Hume, Bolingbroke, Voltaire and other unbelievers, were united in relying upon "the sufficiency of human reason".[275]

At Cambridge in the early 1830s interest revived in the academic and theoretical underpinnings of morality outside Calvinism. Preachers might teach a vigorous biblical morality, but many would not listen to them because of their underlying theology, so a number of devout members of Cambridge University sought to strengthen the nation's morality, primarily by going back to the standard works on morality of the more distant past. Paley's *Moral Philosophy* (1785) came under condemnation for its utilitarianism.[276] William Whewell thought its currency was due to its adoption by Cambridge University and that it "had a very large share in producing the confusion and vacillation of thought respecting the grounds of morals so generally prevalent in England, even among persons of cultivated minds".[277] At Trinity College Cambridge, Bishop Butler's longstanding works on this topic, with their emphasis on conscience, became the subject of examination. Nevertheless, Adam Sedgwick was not convinced that going back to the past was the solution to the development of the nation's future morality. He thought that "there is no English work on morals at once unexceptionable in its principles, and cast in such a form as to meet the wants of the University".[278] Whewell, though, was undeterred. He republished *Butler's Three Sermons on Human Nature* (1848) and then *Butler's Six Sermons on Moral Subjects* (1849). However, there were others, outside the churches, working to change the basis of morality.[279] The dissatisfaction of many Church leaders with the contemporary works on the basis of morality perhaps provided the opportunity for those like John Stuart Mill to advance their own ideas – which took morality in a very different direction.

[274] Ibid., p.256.
[275] Ibid., pp.256-257.
[276] A. Sedgwick, "A Discourse on the Studies of the University", in *History of British Educational Thought (British University Education)* (2000) pp.48-57.
[277] W. Whewell, "Preface" to *On the Foundations of Morals* (1837) pp.vi-vii.
[278] A. Sedgwick, 'Preface" to "A Discourse on the Studies of the University", in *History of British Educational Thought (British University Education)* (2000) pp.vi-vii. See also W. Whewell, "Preface" to *On the Foundations of Morals* (1837) p.v.
[279] See L.J. Snyder, *Reforming Philosophy* (2006) pp.8 and 204-215.

2.13 Liberty, equality and fraternity are reinterpreted

The ideals of the French Revolution (liberty, equality and fraternity) which had led to such bloodshed and which, at the beginning of our period, spurred British Christianity to new found zeal had, by its end, been given new meaning. In August 1858, Thomas Holmes, writing of the progress of the "Great Sheffield Revival" under James Caughey, observed that Christians had "shouted our victory at no palace gates, but at the trembling gates of hell".[280] He went on to say that "the weeping convert" had found his true liberty from sin; his spiritual bondage was over. He could "testify to the equality of the salvation to all, the vilest and the proudest". Together, Christians of different backgrounds had "worked and prayed in glorious brotherhood of duty",[281] to win the unconverted.

2.14 No persecution

In 1829, Daniel Wilson noted that one of the characteristics of the time was a lack of persecution. He observed that "the sincere servants of God are allowed to preach, and write, and labour, and extend themselves peaceably far and wide, 'none making them afraid'. This marks a Divine favour to the government and country which affords such protection." He contrasted the meekness, tolerance, benevolence and charity of "revived Christianity" with other religions. He wrote: "Popery has ever persecuted. Mohammedanism persecutes. Proud, declining, nominal Protestantism is inclined to persecute. Infidelity and philosophy, after all their boasts, persecute."[282]

[280] "Progress of the Great Sheffield Revival, under the Rev. James Caughey", in *The Revivalist* (1858) p.130.
[281] Ibid., pp.129-130.
[282] D. Wilson, "Introductory Essay" to W. Wilberforce, *A Practical View of the Prevailing Religious System of Professed Christians, in the Higher and Middle Classes in This Country, Contrasted with Real Christianity* (1829) p.lv.

3

SOME EVANGELICAL LEADERS

3.1 Charles Simeon becomes the leader of the Church of England's evangelical clergy

The most influential clergyman of the early nineteenth century was Charles Simeon, at Holy Trinity Cambridge. He came from a well-off family. He was thrown into a state of terror after entering Cambridge as a student and being informed that he was required to take, in three weeks, the Lord's supper. He felt utterly unworthy to do so. He read Allestree's *The Whole Duty of Man* (1658), but found relief from his spiritual distress by reading Bishop Wilson's book on the sacrament. There, he read of the need to transfer his guilt to another – namely, Jesus Christ.[283] Simeon would, according to Lord Macaulay, wield influence greater than any primate.[284] His life overlapped with that of the other great evangelical William Wilberforce – both being born in 1759. Simeon died in 1836, three years after Wilberforce. Their work in church and state was complementary and on occasion, as with the foundation of the Church Missionary Society, in partnership.[285]

Simeon embodied orthodoxy and evangelicalism. He believed in conversion and justification by faith and, from early in his ministerial career, his preaching filled a church which had not been full for a century.[286] But he also felt more strongly than most evangelicals "the claims of corporate and of national religious life".[287] He loved the Church of England and its liturgy. Of the Prayer Book, he commented: "no

[283] H.C.G. Moule, *Charles Simeon* (1948) pp.24-26.

[284] G.O. Trevelyan, *Life and Letters of Lord Macaulay* (1876) vol.1, p.74.

[285] See A. Pollard, "The Evangelical Revival, The Triumphant Phrase (1790-1830)", in 107 *Churchman* (1993) p.254.

[286] H.C.G. Moule, *Charles Simeon* (1948) p.35.

[287] Ibid., p.168. See also, for a slightly different slant A. Atherstone, *Evangelical Mission and Anglican Church Order: Charles Simeon Reconsidered* (2009).

other human work is so free from faults as it is"[288] – and the Anglican evangelicalism of the period was firmly based on the Prayer Book – thus making it part of the Establishment.[289] He avoided the dispute between the Calvinists and Arminians. He believed that the Bible taught both doctrines and therefore reasoned that the important thing was to teach both.[290] He was also a great trainer of men for the Church of England's ministry. It has been written that perhaps it "never had a more loving and devoted son and servant than Simeon".[291]

However, on arrival at Holy Trinity in 1782, his parishioners did not want to accept his gospel. They locked the church's box pews and, sometimes, the church to keep him out. Opposition of this type continued for nearly a decade.[292] Church windows were broken by stones.[293] The university and its undergraduates could also be hostile.

Simeon persevered in his doctrine and preaching, while many other clergymen also laboured to show that the doctrine of justification by faith and other evangelical doctrines were those of the Thirty-nine Articles and Homilies.[294] By the 1820s, he recalled with joy the change in terms of religion that had come over Cambridge University. He recalled, "The sun and moon are scarcely more different from each other than Cambridge is from what it was when I was first minister of Trinity Church; and the same change has taken place in the whole land".[295] In 1856, 20 years after his death, evangelical students at Cambridge were still known as "Sims"[296] – and the soubriquet lingered on into the 1860s. Simeon protected his heritage by establishing The Simeon Trust – to purchase rights to appoint parish ministers; so ensuring evangelical succession. An independently wealthy man, his money funded the trust.

Simeon also made a lasting contribution as a founder of the Church

[288] H.C.G. Moule, *Charles Simeon* (1948) p.85.
[289] See generally G. Atkins, *Wilberforce and his Milieux: The Worlds of Anglican Evangelicalism, c.1780-1830* (2009) (Unpublished Ph.D. thesis, Cambridge University)
[290] See H.C.G. Moule, *Charles Simeon* (1948) pp.77-81.
[291] Ibid., p.85.
[292] Ibid., p.45.
[293] Ibid., pp.53-60.
[294] For example, J. Overton, *The True Churchman Ascertained* (1801).
[295] H.C.G. Moule, *Charles Simeon* (1948) p.151.
[296] O. Chadwick, *The Victorian Church* (1987) pt.1, p.447. H.C.G. Moule, *Charles Simeon* (1948) p.60.

Missionary Society, a major instrument of missionary advance later in the century. By the 1850s, it had 2,000 ministers and teachers.[297] However, at the beginning of the century, the British were not geared up to be missionaries. Its first two missionaries, for lack of suitable British talent, were German. However, for Simeon, it was not all triumph. In the late 1820s, Charles Darwin's college rooms were within earshot of his Holy Trinity Church, but the Sims failed to convert him.[298] It is also worth noting that even in the long sunset of his life, Simeon and Christianity were not beyond challenge. In 1829 the Rev. Robert Taylor and Richard Carlile arrived in Cambridge. Taylor had been Simeon's curate – but had given up on Christ. Taylor and Carlile wanted to create a sensation – and sent a circular, stylising themselves as the "Infidel missionaries", to the leading figures of the University, including Simeon. In it, they invited a "discussion on the merits of the Christian religion...that such a person as Jesus Christ alleged to have been of Nazareth, never existed; and that the Christian religion had no such origin as has been pretended; neither is it in any way beneficial to mankind; but that it is nothing more than an emanation from the ancient pagan religion".[299] The challenge came to nothing.

3.2 William Wilberforce becomes the leader of the evangelical laity

The most famous British evangelical of the time, possibly of any time, was William Wilberforce.

3.2.1 *Wilberforce's conversion*

Wilberforce's conversion began on the way home from Nice, when he read a relative's copy of Doddridge's *The Rise and Progress of Religion in the Soul* (1745). Wilberforce discovered that the religion of

[297] W.J. Conybeare, *Essays Ecclesiastical and Social* (1855) p.66.

[298] A. Desmond and J. Moore, *Darwin* (1991) p.57.

[299] Ibid., pp.71-73. Taylor had already issued a challenge to all ministers, through his Christian Evidence Society, that they demonstrate the error in his propositions that the New Testament documents were not written by the persons they were purported to be written by, that they did not appear in the times they referred to, that the persons of which they treated never existed, and the events they describe never happened, see R. Taylor, *Syntagma* (1828) p.ii. He was answered, see J.P. Smith, *An Answer to a Printed Paper Entitled "Manifesto of the Christian Evidence Society" to which is annexed a Rejoinder* (1830).

Doddridge was the religion of the New Testament. True religion was not just taking part in ceremonies, but a way of life. After a time of struggle, lasting from January to November 1785, Wilberforce wrote to his friends to announce his conversion.[300] After it, "whatever was his work", Wilberforce reserved "an unbroken morning hour for religion, and an inviolate Sabbath".[301]

Doddridge's book, which so influenced Wilberforce, was more than an explanation of how to become a Christian – it provided a framework for religious observation and a philosophy for life. William Hague, the former Conservative politician, states that no other "volume [outside the Bible] would be more influential in determining [Wilberforce's] conduct".[302] Doddridge believed in judgment, heaven and hell – and forgiveness for those who repented and believed in Christ for eternal life. For Doddridge, an awareness of God led to conduct "which we have reason to believe will be pleasing to him".[303] But, apart from the essentials, Doddridge was not unduly strict in his theology – affirming "that the Scriptures allowed, and indeed, recommended, a latitude of expression, and he resolutely refused to subscribe to any man-made confession of faith, or to be a party to any attempt to impose creeds on others".[304] Wilberforce's adoption of Christianity showed to the world that it was possible to be a man of affairs and a Christian.

3.2.2 *A book to convert the upper and emerging middle classes*

Wilberforce's first publication, *A Practical View of the Prevailing Religious System of Professed Christians in the Higher and Middle Classes in This Country, Contrasted with Real Christianity* (1797), sought to convert to Christianity the upper and emerging middle classes. The latter, in the words of Sir Leslie Stephen, were growing "up as an independent society which is already beginning to be the most important

[300] See S. Tomkins, *William Wilberforce* (2007) pp.43-48 and J.C. Colquhoun, *William Wilberforce: His Friends and Times* (1867) pp.69-72.
[301] Ibid., p.289.
[302] W. Hague, *William Wilberforce* (2007) p.73.
[303] P. Doddridge, *The Rise and Progress of Religion in the Soul* (1825) p.2.
[304] See K. Hylson-Smith, *The Churches in England from Elizabeth 1 to Elizabeth 11* (1997) (vol.2: 1689-1833) p.103.

social stratum and the chief factor in political and social development".[305] Among their number, and reflecting Wilberforce's thinking with regard to Christianity, was James William Freshfield from whom the modern international law firm takes its name.[306] The growth of commerce and the professions needed to support it were seen by later evangelicals as divinely ordained for the spread of the gospel by providing the funding that its spread needed and by its bringing people together. In turn, the principles of the gospel sustained the further spread of commerce in a virtuous circle.[307] Furthermore, members of the 'better' classes, as they were known, were to be the role models for families, servants and others; if they were won, the nation would be reached. In adopting this strategy, Wilberforce widened and deepened the work of his friend Hannah More; they were to be more successful than they could ever have hoped or imagined.

Christianity, at the end of the eighteenth and beginning of the nineteenth centuries, was unpopular among Wilberforce's audience. He warned that "the time is fast approaching, when Christianity will be almost as openly disavowed in the language, as in fact it is already supposed to have disappeared from the conduct of men; when infidelity will be held to be the necessary appendage of a man of fashion, and to believe will be deemed the indication of a feeble mind and a contracted understanding".[308] In writing, he "risked everything dear to a public man, and a politician as such – consideration, weight, ambition, reputation. He exposed himself to all the misapprehension and hostility which attach to so noble an avowal of the humiliating doctrines of vital Christianity in a corrupt age".[309]

[305] L. Stephen, *English Literature and Society in the Eighteenth Century* (1904) p.193. See also M.J. Quinlan, *Victorian Prelude* (1941) pp.59 and 105.

[306] J. Slinn, *A History of Freshfields* (1984) pp.58-63.

[307] F.M. Turner, *John Henry Newman* (2002) pp.56-64.

[308] W. Wilberforce, *A Practical View of the Prevailing Religious System of Professed Christians, in the Higher and Middle Classes in This Country, Contrasted with Real Christianity* (1829) pp.367-368.

[309] D. Wilson, "Introductory Essay" to W. Wilberforce, *A Practical View of the Prevailing Religious System of Professed Christians, in the Higher and Middle Classes in This Country, Contrasted with Real Christianity* (1829) p.xii.

Christianity opens the door to the life to come

Wilberforce wrote that Christianity was of "infinite importance" because everyone would, quoting Romans 14:10, "stand before God's judgment seat".[310] This was the theology of Doddridge and the New Testament. Wilberforce was concerned not with the sceptic or the militant atheist, but with the many who had a "scanty and erroneous" understanding of "real Christianity".[311] Wilberforce's views on heaven and hell became so well known that his very presence, without saying anything, might convict the unconverted that they were heading for hell.[312]

In promoting Christianity, he was unconcerned about a charge of imposing his own views on people. He argued that he would "have a cold heart, or a most confined notion of benevolence", if he saw someone he esteemed and loved, labouring under a fatal error and withheld his "endeavours to set them right".[313] For Wilberforce, understanding the "evil of sin" was the foundation of the need for religion. Sin was endemic in man, manifesting man's rebellious nature against God's sovereignty. The just prospect of the return of the Lord,[314] to punish sin, led to "the great business of life" being "to secure our admission into heaven".[315] This life was merely the preparation for the next. Failure to regard it as such, he believed, would be a cause of lament in the life to come.

A reviewer of Wilberforce's book *A Practical View* wrote that: "It came upon the whole world of statesmen, and literati, and divines, quite by surprise" and, by reason of the standing of the author, "An electric shock could not be felt more vividly and instantaneously".[316] It sold 7,500 copies in six months and remained in print until the end

[310] W. Wilberforce, *A Practical View of the Prevailing Religious System of Professed Christians, in the Higher and Middle Classes in This Country, Contrasted with Real Christianity* (1829) p.91.

[311] Ibid.

[312] F. Cook, *Fine Gold From Yorkshire* (2017) pp.97-98.

[313] W. Wilberforce, *A Practical View of the Prevailing Religious System of Professed Christians, in the Higher and Middle Classes in This Country, Contrasted with Real Christianity* (1829) p.90.

[314] Ibid., p.306.

[315] Ibid., p.309.

[316] D. Wilson, "Introductory Essay" to W. Wilberforce, *A Practical View of the Prevailing Religious System of Professed Christians, in the Higher and Middle Classes in This Country, Contrasted with Real Christianity* (1829) pp.xvii-xviii.

of the next century.[317] It was an ambitious work, representing "the entire scheme of Christianity, in its main doctrines, precepts, spirit, tendency and character".[318] In doing so, it was the trumpet that "gathered together the dispersed professors of evangelical principles", leading to the construction of "a bridge between Establishment and Dissent".[319] Its impact on the younger clergy was particularly powerful[320] – and it corrected those who "preach evangelical doctrines without a due exhibition of their practical effects".[321] Wilberforce, by linking his name with evangelical theology and clergy, raised the tone of religion and morals in the upper quarters of society. Its argument awakened "a serious concern about their salvation in the breasts of many individuals" and converted some key figures.[322] The politician and philosopher Edmund Burke spent his last two days on earth reading it – and was thankful. By the 1820s there was "no inconsiderable number of individuals amongst the nobility and gentry" who dedicated their "time, and wealth, and influence, to the honour of God", although from that quarter there remained plenty opposed to Christianity.[323]

Christianity elevates a nation

Wilberforce saw Christianity as the means to elevate the nation's moral, economic and international standing. He affirmed that "it has graciously pleased the Supreme Being so to arrange the constitution of things, as to render the prevalence of true religion and of pure morality conducive

[317] For a brief overview of the publishing history of *A Practical View,* see J. Wolffe, "William Wilberforce's *Practical View* (1797) and its Reception", in *Revival and Resurgence in Christian History* (2008) (K. Cooper and J. Gregory (eds)) pp.178-179.

[318] D. Wilson, "Introductory Essay" to W. Wilberforce, *A Practical View of the Prevailing Religious System of Professed Christians, in the Higher and Middle Classes in This Country, Contrasted with Real Christianity* (1829) p.xiv.

[319] J. Grant, *A Summary of the History of the English Church* (1825) vol.4, p.29.

[320] D. Wilson, "Introductory Essay" to W. Wilberforce, *A Practical View of the Prevailing Religious System of Professed Christians, in the Higher and Middle Classes in This Country, Contrasted with Real Christianity* (1829) p.xxxix.

[321] Ibid., p.xlii.

[322] J.W. Middelton, *An Ecclesiastical Memoir of the First Four Decades of the Reign of George the Third* (1822) pp.300-301 and D. Wilson, "Introductory Essay" to W. Wilberforce, *A Practical View of the Prevailing Religious System of Professed Christians, in the Higher and Middle Classes in This Country, Contrasted with Real Christianity* (1829) p.xxxi.

[323] Ibid., p.l.

to the well-being of states, and the preservation of civil order".[324] By "true religion", Wilberforce meant Christianity. Events in France where atheism was flourishing, confirmed his thesis. Wilson, 30 years later, in his introductory essay to *A Practical View*, suggested that "as a noble appeal to a degenerate age – as a work which forms an era in the history of the times", parallels could only be found in Augustine and the Reformation.[325]

Wilberforce had no doubts that God was active in the world. The fate of the nation rested in his hands. Christianity, he observed, promoted "the temporal welfare of political communities" and so was a "question of great political importance".[326] Without religion, he argued, "a community could not long subsist. The cement of society being no more, the state would soon be dissolved into individuality". He also observed that moral degeneracy would follow as religion decayed, citing the authority of St Paul and the passage from Romans 1 in which St Paul stated that when a people left God, he gave them up to their desires, including homosexual practice.[327] Furthermore, he was not afraid to take his stand on Scripture in public debates and to force his opponents to think along similar lines. For example in 1807, as the abolition of the slave trade drew near, he wrote in *A Letter on the Abolition of the Slave Trade; Addressed to the Freeholders and other Inhabitants of Yorkshire* "That the Almighty Creator of the universe governs the world which he has made; that the sufferings of nations are to be regarded as the punishment of national crimes; and their decline and fall, as the execution of his sentence; are truths which I trust are still generally believed among us. Indeed to deny them, would be directly to contradict the express and repeated

[324] W. Wilberforce, *A Practical View of the Prevailing Religious System of Professed Christians, in the Higher and Middle Classes in This Country, Contrasted with Real Christianity* (1829) p.401.

[325] See D. Wilson, "Introductory Essay" to W. Wilberforce, *A Practical View of the Prevailing Religious System of Professed Christians, in the Higher and Middle Classes in This Country, Contrasted with Real Christianity* (1829) p.xli.

[326] W. Wilberforce, *A Practical View of the Prevailing Religious System of Professed Christians, in the Higher and Middle Classes in This Country, Contrasted with Real Christianity* (1829) pp.359-360.

[327] Ibid., p.395. That "degeneracy in religion was followed by a degeneracy in morals" was perceived to be "a law of God's government", see *The Life of James McCosh* (1896) (W.M. Sloane (ed.)) p.17.

declarations of the Holy Scriptures".[328]

Wilberforce reflected that: "a good national education, by training up the people in the principles of true religion, would do more even towards our political benefit than any other measure whatever".[329] Such education needed to be more than teaching Christian morality, as Christianity's particular doctrines and a living Christian faith were the keys to its success – it being generally uncontested that wherever Christianity has prevailed, it "has raised the general standard of morals to a height before unknown".[330] However, if the doctrines of the gospel were left untaught, although Christianity's "effects might, and probably would, remain for a while without any great apparent alteration… her spirit might languish, or even her authority decline".[331] He observed that the reason why the Church had been so ineffective in the eighteenth century was that, since the end of the seventeenth century, "the divines of the Established Church" had inculcated "the moral and practical precepts of Christianity...without justly laying the grand foundation of a sinner's acceptance with God, or pointing out how the practical precepts of Christianity grow out of her peculiar doctrines, and are inseparably connected with them".[332] In 1804, after the Society for Promoting Christian Knowledge failed to provide the necessary Bibles, he co-founded The British and Foreign Bible Society, with the aim of spreading the Christian religion to the working class.[333]

Wilberforce's life manifests how the particular doctrines of Christianity relied upon an active faith to motivate action. Today he is best remembered for his leadership of the abolition of the slave trade, his involvement in children's education and the campaign to abolish vice, but he was also involved in a very wide range of the philanthropic activities of his busy age. Furthermore, there were things he would not

[328] W. Wilberforce, *A Letter on the Abolition of the Slave Trade; Addressed to the Freeholders and other Inhabitants of Yorkshire* (1807) p.4.

[329] Cited in I. Bradley, *The Call to Seriousness* (1976) p.115.

[330] W. Wilberforce, *A Practical View of the Prevailing Religious System of Professed Christians, in the Higher and Middle Classes in This Country, Contrasted with Real Christianity* (1829) p.361.

[331] Ibid., p.362.

[332] Ibid., p.372.

[333] For a summary of the background to the foundation of the Bible Society, see M.J. Quinlan, *Victorian Prelude* (1941) pp.126-128.

do, such as attend the theatre – because of its connection with drinking, prostitution, and for portraying a suspect morality.[334] Born rich, he expended his treasure on good causes – the poor, and an improvident son.[335] Accordingly, in order to have a home, his last days were spent travelling between the homes of his children.

Wilberforce's campaign against vice was motivated by the belief that the disease afflicting "Britain in the late eighteenth and early nineteenth centuries was essentially moral rather than economic or political".[336] Only Christianity could effectively promote morality. Robert Hall, in his *Modern Infidelity Considered*, wrote of Christianity that

> the immaculate holiness of this revelation is precisely that which renders it disgusting to men who are determined at all events to retain their vices. Our Saviour furnishes the solution; *they love darkness rather than light, because their deeds are evil; neither will they come to the true light lest their deeds be reproved.*[337]

A few years later, Hall wrote that "the excellent work of Mr Wilberforce...is not more conspicuous for the orthodoxy of its tenets, than for the purity and energy of its moral instruction".[338]

The work of Wilberforce's Proclamation Society was not originally well-favoured by the public. Its most active period was over by the end of 1792, although it continued until 1808 – when it merged into the Society for the Suppression of Vice.[339] The latter had been established in 1802, with a wider membership drawn especially from the urban professional and commercial classes, rather than Establishment figures.[340] It also drew its membership from a wide range of theological perspectives.[341] It was

[334] W. Wilberforce, *A Practical View of the Prevailing Religious System of Professed Christians, in the Higher and Middle Classes in This Country, Contrasted with Real Christianity* (1829) pp.317-319. For a summary of other objections to the theatre, see I. Bradley, *The Call to Seriousness* (1976) p.102.

[335] Wilberforce, "regularly gave away a quarter of his income", see D. Owen, *English Philanthropy 1660-1960* (1965) p.93.

[336] I. Bradley, *The Call to Seriousness* (1976) p.115.

[337] Author's italics. R. Hall, "Preface" to *Modern Infidelity Considered* (1800) p.vi.

[338] R. Hall, *Strictures on a Work, Intitled, "Zeal Without Innovation"* (1809) p.33.

[339] A. Hunt, *Governing Morals* (1999) pp.65-68.

[340] Ibid., p.70.

[341] M.J. Quinlan, *Victorian Prelude* (1941) pp.202-203.

more willing to intervene "where it detected a lack of resolve from the authorities" in enforcing the relevant law.[342] By 1819, there had been a "striking change in the general opinion respecting" such work. *The Christian Observer* noted that the Society had stayed in some measure "the pestilence of blasphemous and infidel publications".[343] In 1820, shortly after his accession, George IV reissued his father's Proclamation for the Encouragement of Piety and Virtue. It was to be read in criminal courts before a charge was laid – and in the churches and chapels at least four times a quarter after divine service.[344] Although there were reservations about the enthusiasm with which the Proclamation was read,[345] the work of the Society for the Suppression of Vice continued until the 1880s, when it was absorbed into other social movements. Its influence and emphasis fluctuated over the years, but it had a "notable achievement…in securing the passage of Lord Campbell's Obscene Publications Act in 1857".[346] Furthermore, in three years around 1870, the Society destroyed 140,213 obscene pictures, 21,772 books and five tons of letterpress.[347] Wilberforce had made 'goodness fashionable'.

J.C. Ryle, writing in 1868 and looking back over the previous 100 years, thought "that our own times are the best times that England has ever seen". One hundred years before, "duelling, adultery, fornication, gambling, swearing, Sabbath-breaking and drunkenness were hardly regarded as vices at all". The change to the general standard of morality was attributed to the beginning of Wilberforce's work.[348] Slavery had

[342] A. Hunt, *Governing Morals* (1999) p.69.

[343] "Preface" to 19 *The Christian Observer for the Year 1820* (1821) p.vi. See also M. J. Quinlan, *Victorian Prelude* (1941) pp.215-222.

[344] See R. Carlile, "Radical Reform Begun at Carlton House, By the Order of the King", in 2 *The Republican* (1820) p.234. Those of a Republican perspective hoped that "the example as well as the precept will issue from the right quarter, for there are a certain race of beings, who…are ready to catch at a royal and fashionable vice in preference to a royal virtue", ibid., p.236. Carlile, was the subject of a series of prosecutions at this time by the Vice Society, see A. Hunt, *Governing Morals* (1999) p.71.

[345] R. Carlile, "Radical Reform Begun at Carlton House, By the Order of the King", in 2 *The Republican* (1820) p.235.

[346] A. Hunt, *Governing Morals* (1999) p.71.

[347] S. Tomkins, *William Wilberforce* (2007) p.223. For detail on the campaign against vice see I. Bradley, *The Call to Seriousness* (1976) pp.94-118. Pornography, in the sense used today, existed significantly since sometime in the middle of the eighteenth century, see J. Weeks, *Sex, Politics and Society* (1989) p.20.

[348] J.C. Ryle, *Christian Leaders of the Eighteenth Century* (1997) pp.18-19.

been abolished from the Empire, vice suppressed, education advanced, the Bible put into the hands of the working classes, and the 'better' classes converted. All this coincided with the United Kingdom, a little island, becoming the only world power – possessing the world's most advanced economy and ruling the largest empire the world had ever seen. Overseas, Wilberforce's endeavours to spread Christianity had been vigorous – including, as we have seen, co-founding the Church Missionary Society. He made godliness and church-going socially respectable. However, as Simeon found, there were those who escaped his gospel net, such as his close associate the Unitarian William Smith MP. The philosopher Jeremy Bentham, whose work influenced John Stuart Mill, was another.[349] Mill's ideas, as we will see, had a very damaging effect on Christianity.

3.2.3 *Wilberforce and the Clapham Sect*

Wilberforce was helped and strengthened in his work by members of the so-called "Clapham Sect". They were a group of wealthy and educated laymen, no more than half of whom lived for a time around the then village of Clapham, just outside London. To call them a sect, is a further misnomer;[350] they were committed to the advocacy of Christianity within the Established Church and within the nation, the elimination of vice and the extension of philanthropy.[351] After Wilberforce, their most important member was probably Henry Thornton, an MP, influential economist and banker. Thornton was much impressed and influenced by Wilberforce's piety and was taken to hear Wilberforce's favourite preachers.[352] On marriage, he reduced his philanthropy to only two-thirds

[349] J. Pollock, *Wilberforce* (2007) p.183.

[350] For an interesting account of the derivation of the "Clapham Sect", see S. Tomkins, *The Clapham Sect* (2010) pp.11-12.

[351] For a sense of the individual good works of the evangelicals, see F. Brown, *Fathers of the Victorians* (1961) pp.235-237, 242, 256, 279 and 281. Evangelicals also implemented humanitarian reform of the law. Within 20 years of the death of Wilberforce, it was written of the Evangelical party that: "The reform of prison discipline was effected by their efforts, the criminal law was robbed of its bloodthirsty severity by their aid. To their benevolent agitation it is owing that Hindu widows are no longer burnt alive, and that the natives of the most distant and barbarous colonies know they will not appeal in vain to English sympathy against English oppression", W.J. Conybeare, *Essays Ecclesiastical and Social* (1855) p.65.

[352] J.C. Colquhoun, *William Wilberforce: His Friends and Times* (1867) p.289.

of his income, rather than by giving away the six-sevenths previously.[353] Other Claphamites included the MP James Stephen – the legal mind behind the Slave Trade Act of 1807, which abolished the slave trade in the British Empire; Zachary Macaulay, Governor of Sierra Leone and a member of the Royal Society; Charles Grant, Chairman of the British East India Company; and Lord Teignmouth, a Governor-General of India. Professional theological input to the Clapham Sect was first provided by Henry Venn. His son, John Venn, succeeded him when John became rector of Holy Trinity, Clapham. On the edge of the Clapham Sect were men of increasing influence with links to the evangelical Dissenters. Their ranks included James William Freshfield whose children would be baptised into the Church of England.[354]

The members of the Clapham Sect manifested the collective power of able and determined Christians, under God, to change the nation. They, with their meetings, institutions, reports and petitions, perfected and even invented the machinery for forming popular opinion and bringing it to bear on ministers.[355] They knew the importance of Parliament in securing moral change. For Wilberforce, it was the "moral mint of the nation in which moral and political principles receive their stamp and currency".[356] Furthermore, if God was to use their endeavours, Christianity had to direct the lives of the members of the Clapham Sect. Accordingly, *The Christian Observer*, at the beginning of 1820, suggested its readers ask themselves:

> What am I doing to alleviate distress, to impart knowledge, to conciliate affection, in my own immediate circle, that, as far as in me lies, I may be instrumental in stemming the anti-moral and anti-social torrent? Am I diligently promoting that pure and undefiled religion which is the best cement of states, as well as the only guarantee for the temporal or eternal happiness of individuals? Am I setting a religious example in my own person? Am I exerting myself for the Christian discipline and instruction of my family; for the religious education of the poor; for the extension of the gospel;

[353] D. Owen, *English Philanthropy 1660-1960* (1965) p.93.
[354] J. Slinn, *A History of Freshfields* (1984) pp.58-63.
[355] G.O. Trevelyan, *Life and Letters of Lord Macaulay* (1876) vol.1, p.75.
[356] Cited in I. Bradley, *The Call to Seriousness* (1976) p.165.

for the salvation of all mankind.[357]

It was not only Wilberforce who expected to "stand before God's judgment seat."[358]

3.2.4 *Not everyone likes Wilberforce's theology*

After the publication of *A Practical View*, Daniel Wilson wrote that "Men were surprised at what Christianity was described to be: they were offended at the picture given of spiritual religion: they were dismayed at the representation of the distance to which modern Christianity had receded from its ancient limits".[359] Liberals, High Churchmen and Unitarians all impugned it with varying degrees of severity.[360] For them, the trouble was that the author, not being an ecclesiastic, could not be written-off as a dogmatist. Nor could he be charged with being ignorant, or lacking talent, or benevolence. The High Churchman, Charles Daubeny, responded to *A Practical View* with his weighty *A Guide to the Church* (1798). Daubeny disagreed with Wilberforce on the latter's strictures on the Church – and suggested that there were conditions of a moral order that were necessary before a person could receive salvation.[361] The Unitarians fiercely condemned Wilberforce and his book.[362] For example, Thomas Belsham was outraged that Wilberforce "hardly allows the name of Christian to those who call in question his unproved dogmas concerning what he styles… 'the corruption of human nature', the atonement of the Saviour, and 'the sanctifying influence of the Holy Spirit'". He added: in an "enlightened age, confident assertions no longer pass for self-evident truths".[363] There were other responses –

[357] "Preface" to 19 *The Christian Observer for the Year 1820* (1821) pp.vi-vii.

[358] *Memoir of the Life and Correspondence of John Lord Teignmouth* (1843) vol.2, p.390.

[359] D. Wilson, "Introductory Essay" to W. Wilberforce, *A Practical View of the Prevailing Religious System of Professed Christians, in the Higher and Middle Classes in This Country, Contrasted with Real Christianity* (1829) p.xix.

[360] J.W. Middelton, *An Ecclesiastical Memoir of the First Four Decades of the Reign of George the Third* (1822) pp.297-304.

[361] C. Daubeny, *A Guide to the Church* (1830) vol.1, pp.lxx and 228.

[362] J. Wolffe, "William Wilberforce's *Practical View* (1797) and its Reception", in *Revival and Resurgence in Christian History* (2008) (K. Cooper and J. Gregory (eds)) pp.181-182.

[363] T. Belsham, *A Review of Mr Wilberforce's Treatise Entitled a Practical View of the Prevailing Religious System of Professed Christians* (1798) p.2.

and they were met by a flurry of replies by supporters of Wilberforce's position. Wilberforce himself made no response. John Wolffe notes that the attacks on *A Practical View* "implicitly recognised it as an important contribution to religious discourse".[364] Wolffe adds that "It stimulated the High Church arguments of Daubeny, recognised as important antecedents of the Oxford Movement, encouraged statements of liberal and rational Christianity", and encouraged those who struggled with evangelicalism's key tenets to grapple with it.[365] Meanwhile, it found widespread acceptance.

3.3 Hannah More is the leading literary female

Hannah More's literary gifts continued to influence the nation. In 1795, she launched a series of tracts known as the *Cheap Repository Tracts* – many of which she wrote. Each tract was a short, entertaining, tale or ballad intended to "advance the cause of moral rather than political revolution by teaching the lower and middle orders of society their duties rather than their rights".[366] More dismissed "rights" as "metaphysical jargon".[367] The tracts were an alternative to the "vicious" anti-authoritarian tracts circulated by pedlars among the poor, like those of Tom Paine. Nevertheless, More's tracts appealed to all ranks and were produced in record breaking numbers – two million in 1795 alone. New tracts continued appearing into 1798, although the main series ended in 1797. After the Napoleonic Wars she, at the request of the Government, returned to tract writing, with *Stories for the Middle Ranks of Society and Tales for the Common People*. Reprints of her tracts were numerous and continued into the 1840s, stimulating others to similar endeavours.

More also wrote on female education. Her two volumes concerning *Strictures on the Modern System of Female Education* (1799) went through seven editions in their year of publication. Her thesis was that women of the higher class had influence and that "The general state of

[364] J. Wolffe, "William Wilberforce's *Practical View* (1797) and its Reception", in *Revival and Resurgence in Christian History* (2008) (K. Cooper and J. Gregory (eds)) p.183.

[365] Ibid., p.184.

[366] *Tales for the Common People* (2002) p.x. See also M.J. Quinlan, *Victorian Prelude* (1941) pp.83-90.

[367] Cited in J. Wordsworth, "Introduction" to *Strictures on Female Education* (1995), first page.

civilised society depends...on the prevailing sentiments and habits of women, and on the nature and degree of the estimation in which they are held".[368] They could either use their "boasted power over mankind to no higher purpose than the gratification of vanity or the indulgence of pleasure", or they could exert "their power, to raise the depressed tone of public morals, and to awaken the drowsy spirit of religious principle".[369]

Hannah More had high expectations of a lady's religious intellectual endeavours. After "a proper course of preparation", a lady should "swallow and digest such strong meat as Watt's or Duncan's little book of logic, some parts of Mr Locke's *Essay on the Human Understanding*, and Bishop Butler's *Analogy*".[370] One admirer described *Strictures on Female Education* as sending forth bolts "which shattered the towers and arsenals of fashionable abuses and follies".[371] On the same topic, was *Hints Towards Forming the Character of a Young Princess* (1805). More's writings helped shape the late nineteenth century commitment to teaching Christianity in the home.[372] In family religion it was not enough to infuse the minds of children with religious knowledge. Children needed to be taught the proper use of time. She urged parents to keep their children from "small talk, idle reading, and a quiet and dull frittering away of time" – for which, in today's world, perhaps means YouTube, computer games and television. The use of an expression like "children will be children", to justify failing to discipline a child, was well known to Hannah More. She accepted no such excuse. In her view, the "love of ease" prevented parental action.[373]

More's novel, *Coelebs in Search of a Wife* (1809), was instrumental in making visiting the poor – to bring them spiritual and human relief and seeking to improve their housing – "a fashion and a rage" among

[368] H. More, *"Strictures on the Modern System of Female Education"* (1799) vol.1, p.2, in *Strictures on Female Education* (1995).

[369] Ibid., pp.3-4.

[370] Ibid., p.179.

[371] W. Roberts, *Memoirs of The Life and Correspondence of Mrs Hannah More* (1834) vol.3, p.65.

[372] For her thoughts concerning the teaching of boys, see H. More, *Moral Sketches of Prevailing Opinions and Manners Foreign and Domestic* (1821) (8th ed.) pp.81-113.

[373] H. More, *"Strictures on the Modern System of Female Education"* (1799) vol.1, pp.120-125, in *Strictures on Female Education* (1995).

evangelical ladies[374] and then, generally, among ladies. Its heroine regularly devoted two evenings a week to making the rounds among the village poor – and it went through eight editions within two months. Helping the poor was not new, but now such help was systemised. In 1811 the first ladies' auxiliary of the Bible Society appeared and in 1812 the Ladies' Royal Benevolent Society.[375] These societies led to critical comments from those who did not think it fit for women to associate in large assemblies, form committees, or collect subscriptions.[376]

In later years, More returned to more general themes, such as *Practical Piety* (1811) and *Christian Morals* (1813). The latter had at least six editions in the year of its publication. In 1815, Jane Porter wrote to her that "your former literary fame was a bright forerunner to your promulgation of the gospel. It made it fashionable to read your works; and by that word, they passed into all hands, and gradually infused their contents into all hearts." Porter dated "the regeneration of the people of this country" to the works of More and the Sunday schools of Robert Raikes. The poor being in "profligate ignorance – the rich in presumptuous apostasy." [377] In 1819, More wrote *Moral Sketches of Prevailing Opinions and Manners Foreign and Domestic*. In 1821, it reached its eighth edition. In this she demonstrated a sound understanding of the new religious situation – and what would undermine it. Although she saw "every kind of religious improvement",[378] she also detected errors in some of those who professed Christianity. She felt the need to give a few friendly hints – that "Holy Scripture was given to be

[374] *Correspondence of William Edward Channing, D.D. and Lucy Aikin* (1874) (A.L. Le Breton (ed.)) pp.396-397. Overton wrote that it was so "delightful a thing" for "'the religious world' to whom all light literature was strictly tabooed, to find a writer with whom it was not only an allowable, but even a creditable thing, to be entertained. The greatest credit is due to Hannah More, as the first among the evangelicals who dared to enlist the novel and the drama on the side of virtue and religion", see J.H. Overton, *The English Church in the Nineteenth Century* (1894) p.174. Her drama that Overton referred to was *Sacred Dramas* (1782). It was intended to be read, but not acted out.

[375] For an excellent account of More and the beginnings of ladies' visiting societies, see M.J. Quinlan, *Victorian Prelude* (1941) pp.148-149.

[376] R.H. Martin, "Women and the Bible Society", in *Sowing the Word* (2004) (S. Batalden, K. Cann and J. Dean (eds)) p.49.

[377] W. Roberts, *Memoirs of the Life and Correspondence of Hannah More* (1834) vol.3, p.432.

[378] H. More, "Preface to the First Edition", in *Moral Sketches of Prevailing Opinions and Manners Foreign and Domestic* (1821) (8th ed.) p.xix.

searched...not...to be criticised".[379] And she went on, "The more we cavil, the less we shall obey."

In 1814, at the height of her fame, the poet Coleridge wrote to a friend that Hannah More "is indisputably the *first* literary female, I ever met with – in part, no doubt, because she is a Christian".[380] More, even at the end of her life, made no great claims for either herself or her sex. She was quite happy to shine as a star of the "*second* magnitude".[381]

3.4 Lord Shaftesbury takes on Wilberforce's humanitarian mantle

Inheriting Wilberforce's humanitarian impulse was the seventh Earl of Shaftesbury. Shaftesbury was active in Parliament from the 1830s onwards.[382] He drove forward measures prohibiting the employment of young children in the mills and limiting the working hours of older ones. Boys under ten were banned from the mines, as were women and girls.[383] He ensured that the laws regulating chimney sweeps were effective and properly enforced and that children were banned from the dangerous work of brick-making. In many ways, he is the father of modern health and safety legislation at work. He also did much for the care of lunatics, the poor and orphans – and was an example to others, such as Thomas Barnardo.

Shaftesbury had a very different theological perspective to that of his famous ancestor, the third Earl, whom we noted in our first volume.[384] The seventh Earl revered the Bible. Unlike his ancestor, he had no doubts about eternal punishment. Nevertheless, Shaftesbury's influence over the evangelicals was always limited; he acted as their figurehead. As they grew in number, different interest groups appeared among them – and the easy unity that the Clapham Sect and other Christians enjoyed in the first quarter of the century dissipated. In 1856, he wrote: "This [the leadership of the Evangelical party] is a position too perilous, too uncertain, and too useless for anyone to accept. No one can be an

[379] Ibid., pp.174-175.

[380] Author's italics. See *Collected Letters of Samuel Taylor Coleridge* (2000) (E.L. Griggs (ed.)) vol.3, pp.499-500.

[381] Author's italics. H. More, *Moral Sketches of Prevailing Opinions and Manners Foreign and Domestic* (1821) (8th ed.) p.167.

[382] See R. Turnbull, *Anglican and Evangelical* (2007) pp.149-152.

[383] His work with the weak and vulnerable also embraced the reform of the lunacy laws.

[384] J.A. Thomas, *The Nation's Gospel: Reformation to Revolution* (2017) vol.1, pp.264-265 and 305.

effective leader unless those who follow him are prepared to repose confidence in his judgment and guidance, not during smooth and easy times alone, but in times of doubt and perplexity. No one in these days has such a sentiment. All confidence has ceased; and people from a variety of causes take up their opinions, and let them fall, entirely in reference to themselves or their particular sections."[385]

3.5 An evangelical Archbishop of Canterbury is appointed

In 1848, John Sumner was appointed the first evangelical Archbishop of Canterbury. This was a surprise, as the Whig Prime Minister, Lord John Russell, liked to appoint bishops noted for their Whig leanings and lack of theological conviction. Lord Shaftesbury regularly proffered advice to Russell on the right man for a bishopric, but he found that his views favouring evangelicals were no more welcome than Wilberforce's to William Pitt. For example, Shaftesbury wrote on 2 November 1849, "Dear Russell, It is quite manifest that you hold my opinions, ecclesiastical and religious, in supreme contempt...Nevertheless you have always been so kind and good-humoured in allowing me to state what I think."[386] John Sumner wrote a book on evidences for Christianity which Charles Darwin read at school. It is said that Darwin found nothing "objectionable" in it, but it failed to convert him.[387]

3.6 The Baptists discover a great preacher

In December 1853, a young man left his boyhood in East Anglia behind when he was invited to preach at New Park Street Chapel, in Southwark, London. It needed a minister. It had been a great Baptist church, but at

[385] Cited in W.R. Ward, "Church and Society in the First Half of the Nineteenth Century", in *A History of the Methodist Church in Great Britain* (R.E. Davies, A.R. George and E.G. Rupp (eds)) (1978) vol.2, p.87.

[386] Cited in O. Chadwick, *The Victorian Church* (1987) pt.1, p.235. The appointment of bishops could be a burden to a Prime Minister. Lord Melbourne once affirmed "I positively believe they die to vex me", see L.E. Elliott-Binns, *The Evangelical Movement in the English Church* (1928) p.52.

[387] Sumner reduced unbelief to a dilemma - "either Jesus did not exist, or he actually lived, but was not the Son of God, hence an imposter". Non-existence was "evidently absurd," therefore sceptics must hold Jesus "deceived himself". This, the Gospels suggested, was unlikely – see for more detail A. Desmond and J. Moore, *Darwin* (1991) p.49.

that time it was said that "the greatness of its traditions" were "equalled only by the emptiness of its pews".[388] Charles Haddon Spurgeon was elected to its pastorate, aged 19. Very soon the news spread of "a pulpit phenomenon in a back street of Southwark";[389] and the chapel was full, including the standing room. His biographer, Holden Pike, describes him as preaching "the gospel with a freedom and a fulness which had not been out rivalled since the eighteenth-century revival preachers".[390] At the end of a year's ministry, the deacons resolved to build a bigger chapel.

The new chapel was the Metropolitan Tabernacle. Spurgeon had no doubt about what God would do. The new chapel was a statement, the largest church or chapel in London. Built to sit 4,200, with another 2,000 standing, its opening saw 7,000 crammed in. When the foundation-stone was laid, he was 25. Spurgeon was its pastor for the rest of his life. And it remained full for the rest of his life. Spurgeon, though, was much more than a preacher. Like John Wesley, he knew the power of print – and when he died he had more books and sermons in circulation than anyone before him.[391] In pre-civil war America, they burnt his books when he denounced slavery. Like Wesley, he also knew how to build an organisation. His orphanages alone were a major symbol of Victorian philanthropy. He reached all classes of people and was not deterred from his tasks. In his first year of ministry in London, aged 20, as a cholera epidemic raged across London, he was to be found attending the bedside of dying victims.[392] Shaftesbury confessed that, in moments of despondency, only Spurgeon and one other could meet his spiritual needs.[393] Spurgeon was heavily influenced by his reading of the Puritans.

[388] E.J. Poole-Connor, *Evangelicalism in England* (1951) p.224. It sat 1,200. At the time Spurgeon preached, the congregation was greatly reduced. Estimates vary for his first sermon. Some go as high as 200. Some as low as 80.

[389] G.H. Pike, "*The Life and Work of Charles Haddon Spurgeon*", vol.1, p.124, in G.H. Pike, *The Life and Work of Charles Haddon Spurgeon* (The Banner of Truth Trust (1991)) vol.1.

[390] Ibid., p.125.

[391] L.A. Drummond, "Charles Haddon Spurgeon", in *Baptist Theologians* (1990) (T. George and D.S. Dockery (eds)) p.267.

[392] C.H. Spurgeon, *Autobiography* (1973) vol.1, pp.272-274.

[393] C. Binfield, *George Williams and the Y.M.C.A.* (1973) p.208.

3.7 The Scots discover a great evangelical

Thomas Chalmers, it has been suggested, made a mark on the life of his country in the nineteenth century that no other Scotsman can compare with.[394] After ordination, he was a Moderate until converted, as we have seen, by reading Wilberforce's *A Practical View of Religion*. His conversion immediately created a stir. His biographer, Stewart Brown, refers us to the comment of Janet Coutts, a young clergymen's widow who lived nearby him. She observed in a letter to a friend that "we had a new miracle of Divine grace, in a Mr Chalmers of Kilmany, a great philosopher, but once an enemy avowedly to the peculiar doctrines of the gospel. For a year back the Lord has been teaching him by the rod…and now he comes forward to preach the faith which once he destroyed, and I trust we glorify God in him."[395] Crowds quickly gathered in Kilmany to see the "new miracle" while, after his move to Glasgow, his preaching drew huge crowds to the important pulpit of the Tron.[396] Stewart Brown suggests that between 1815 and 1817, as a preacher, he attained an "eminence perhaps unsurpassed in the history of the Scottish pulpit".[397] James McCosh, later President of Princeton University, came to study under him at Edinburgh and regarded him as the "greatest" man he ever met and as the deliverer of the nation from the "moderatism" (faithless Christianity) of the eighteenth century.[398]

However, in reaching the nation he was much more than just a preacher. He took parish visiting seriously, teaching the Bible and the Longer and Shorter Catechisms, encouraging family religion and looking for moral reform in his parishioners. He also organised his laity[399] and his students[400] to carry out house visitation programmes. He also used his own influence and "donated substantial sums" "to

[394] A.L. Drummond and J. Bulloch, *The Scottish Church 1688-1843* (1973) p.161. For a recent profile of Chalmers, see I.H. Murray, *A Scottish Christian Heritage* (2006) pp.73-121 and see also S.J. Brown, *Thomas Chalmers and the Godly Commonwealth in Scotland* (1982).

[395] Ibid., p.50.

[396] As an evangelical Chalmer's appointment to the influential pulpit of the Tron had been contentious, see ibid., pp.91-93.

[397] Ibid., p.106. See also *The Life of James McCosh* (1896) (W.M. Sloane (ed.)) p.40.

[398] Ibid., pp.40-41.

[399] S.J. Brown, *Thomas Chalmers and the Godly Commonwealth in Scotland* (1982) pp.75-78 and 138-139.

[400] *The Life of James McCosh* (1896) (W.M. Sloane (ed.)) p.42.

secure medical assistance, food, and clothing for the poor, in response to needs which he discovered during his visitations".[401] Furthermore, like Wilberforce in England "he was concerned to win the upper social orders",[402] encouraged their benevolence – by expecting them to curtail luxurious consumption[403] – and vigorously promoted the Bible Society.[404] He was capable of dealing with intellectual problems to the faith and was sufficiently practical to develop plans and ideas to take the faith to the unconverted. He did not shirk tackling the problems others passed by, including meeting the material needs of the poor. His thinking undergirded many of the themes in the remainder of this Part.[405]

[401] S.J. Brown, *Thomas Chalmers and the Godly Commonwealth in Scotland* (1982) pp.76-77.
[402] Ibid., p.59.
[403] Ibid., p.67.
[404] Ibid., pp.65-70 and 139.
[405] See also A.L. Drummond and J. Bulloch, *The Scottish Church 1688-1843* (1973) pp.160-179.

4

THE TOOLS TO CHANGE A NATION

4.1 An attitude of service

The Christians of the day were anxious to use their time on earth wisely. The editor of *The Christian Observer* trembled as he looked at its pages and considered that he would have to give an account for what was written.[406] Time was to be used in the service of God, not frittered away on amusement. Novel reading was out, although some allowed exceptions,[407] and listening to music was debatable. In April 1822, a writer to *The Christian Observer* asked the nuanced question of whether it was lawful to attend a concert of music: 1) at Hanover Square or the Argyle Rooms; 2) including sacred music, at a theatre; and 3) comprising secular music in a church for charitable purposes.[408] The letters to the editor, in response, emphasised the importance of avoiding a spirit of "musical dissipation"; for some, going to the theatre for musical purposes, or mixing church with entertainment, was out.[409] Christians freed from the distraction of amusement focused on serving the Lord. The Religious Tract Society noted that "A spirit of active benevolence is one of the distinguishing features of Christianity." It added, "the Christian, enlightened from above to view the state of the man as an immortal being, is most concerned for the salvation of his soul, and his eternal blessedness".[410] Just after the Crimean War, a number of newly converted

[406] "Preface" to 20 *The Christian Observer for the Year 1821* (1822) p.iii.
[407] W. Roberts, *Memoirs of The Life and Correspondence of Mrs Hannah More* (1834) vol.3, pp.77-78.
[408] "To the Editor of the Christian Observer", in 20 *The Christian Observer for the Year 1821* (1822) p.227.
[409] See "Miscellaneous", in 20 *The Christian Observer for the Year 1821* (1822) pp.347-352.
[410] Religious Tract Society, *An Address to Christians on the Distribution of Religious Tracts* (No.1) (N.D.) p.1.

men – with experience of that war – were challenged by others to begin their evangelistic careers by visiting the sick and dying and reading aloud to them.[411] Lord Radstock and Sir Arthur Blackwood would be among the leading evangelists of our next period. In the summer of 1858, it was observed that "Every denomination of evangelical Christians is at work in some department or other. Now on the moral waste and now in the vineyard; here reclaiming, there reviving; each in his own way, and all rejoicing in the results".[412]

4.2 Co-operation

Across the denominations evangelicals increasingly attended each other's services and worked together on a variety of issues, including the relief of human suffering.[413] It led to "much mutual pleasure".[414] Such an approach was not new. For example, George Whitefield had modelled the benefits of interdenominational endeavours to reach the nation for Christ by those who through the new birth enjoyed a unity in Christ. In 1795 the establishment of the interdenominational London Missionary Society, to spread the gospel overseas, challenged the churches to overcome their differences, and to go out to the unconverted at home.[415] As a result, new ventures for home mission were established that cut across denominational boundaries. In 1844, Sir James Stephen could record, half humourously, "Ours is the age of societies. For the redress of every oppression that is done under the sun there is a public meeting."[416]

4.3 Getting the Bible out

The impetus of war against France with its state atheism, produced interdenominational support for schemes to spread Christian knowledge, such as those of the Religious Tract Society. Furthermore, in a meeting of that organisation, its Secretary Joseph Hughes had the idea of a scheme

[411] E. Trotter, *Lord Radstock* (N.D.) pp.9-10 and *Some Records of the Life of Stevenson Arthur Blackwood* K.C.B. (1898) pp.149 and 169-170.
[412] "Special Services", in *The British Evangelist*, August 1858 p.65.
[413] O. Gregory, *A Brief Memoir of the Life of Robert Hall* (1833) p.142. See generally R.H. Martin, *Evangelicals United* (1983).
[414] A.G. Fuller, *The Complete Works of the Rev. Andrew Fuller* (1856) p.lxvi.
[415] D. Bogue and J. Bennett, *History of Dissenters, from the Revolution in 1688, to the Year 1808* (1812) vol.4, p.387.
[416] "The Clapham Sect", in *The Edinburgh Review*, July 1844, p.306.

to circulate the Bible without note or comment.[417] The advocates of the work of the British and Foreign Bible Society were convinced that, if the Bible was simply read, "individuals could be changed, and social and political systems thereby transformed".[418] After 1809, auxiliary branches started "as if by magic, in every town and city from Berwick to Plymouth, and from Carlisle to Dover".[419] In Scotland the same magic was at work. Societies were soon established in Edinburgh and Glasgow and, in 1812, Thomas Chalmers instituted one in his parish of Kilmany. In April that year, of his parish's population of 780, no less than 160 were subscribers.[420] At the head of the various London auxiliary branches were "their Royal Highnesses the Dukes of York, Kent, Cumberland, Sussex and Cambridge".[421] Stories of poor families converted through Bible reading, and becoming prosperous, multiplied. Often, the wife was converted first and then the husband – as he listened to his wife read the Bible to the children.[422] Occasionally, the man was converted first. A story was told of one wife who sold her husband's Bible because it had changed him and there was no longer the opportunity for "a bit of a dance or fun". The husband required her to buy it back.[423]

The Bible Society originally enabled its subscribers to buy Bibles at a discount, which they then distributed. In 1812, it was discovered that "half the population of the labouring classes in the metropolis of the British Empire were destitute of the Holy Scriptures".[424] In that year, the Bible Society introduced house-to-house visiting whereby the poor

[417] J. Leifchild, *Life of the Rev. Joseph Hughes* (1840) p.41.

[418] L. Howsam, "Preface" to *Cheap Bibles* (1991) p.xiii.

[419] A. O'Callaghan, *The Bible Society against the Church and State* (1817) p.6. Conybeare suggests that it reduced the price of the Bible to within reach of "the poorest labourer," see W.J. Conybeare, *Essays Ecclesiastical and Social* (1855) p.66. However, whether this is quite true is unclear, see *Second Report of the London City Mission* (1836) pp.17-18.

[420] S.J. Brown, *Thomas Chalmers and the Godly Commonwealth in Scotland* (1982) p.63.

[421] G. Browne, *The History of the British and Foreign Bible Society* (1859) vol.1, p.59.

[422] See for example, C.S. Dudley, *An Analysis of the System of the Bible Society* (1821). For a more easily accessible example, see R.H. Martin, "Women and the Bible Society", in *Sowing the Word* (2004) (S. Batalden, K. Cann and J. Dean (eds)) p.43.

[423] L. Howsam, *Cheap Bibles* (1991) p.183.

[424] G. Browne, *The History of the British and Foreign Bible Society* (1859) vol.1, p.60.

could buy, at low cost, a Bible on a weekly instalment plan. The paperwork for those visiting homes was substantial, but it was found that by encouraging the poor to pay for their Bible, their self-respect and ability to help themselves was inspired.[425] Middle-class ladies mostly did the visiting.

Public controversy soon surrounded the Bible Society's work. Beilby Porteus, the Bishop of London, referred "to the sneers and cavils of its intemperate opponents".[426] High Churchmen were outraged that the Bible was circulated without the benefit of guidance from the Church. Others thought that the Bible was being sold too cheaply, and was therefore undervalued, or that the Bible Society was a plot by the Dissenters to undermine the Established Church. After the war ended in 1815, hostile critics suggested that it was only because many were "alarmed by the growth of infidelity" that they were "compelled, seduced, or cajoled to lend their names and their credit to the 'venerable association'".[427] In the 1820s, the Scottish branches broke away. The issue was over the circulation by those working with Roman Catholics of the Apocrypha[428] with the Bible. Other members of the Bible Society to leave were those who would not accept Unitarian members. The latter, in 1831, formed the Trinitarian Bible Society.[429]

Yet, by the 1830s, there was still much to do to make available the Bible to all. In 1838, the London City Mission calculated that, in London, 50,000 families remained without a page of Scripture.[430] Yet a single page of Scripture could have a remarkable effect. Ridley Herschell was a Jew "who traced his conversion largely to the reading of a page torn from a New Testament and wrapped around an article he had purchased." He later became a minister and saw many Jews converted.[431]

To make the existing Scriptures go further, the London City Mission

[425] See generally C.S. Dudley, *An Analysis of the System of the Bible Society* (1821) and J. Griscom, *A Year in Europe* (1823) vol.2, p.399.
[426] R. Hodgson, *The Life of the Right Reverend Beilby Porteus* (1811) p.213.
[427] A. O'Callaghan, *The Bible Society against the Church and State* (1817) p.5. See also M. J. Quinlan, *Victorian Prelude* (1941) pp.130-133.
[428] A book that since the Reformation had not been regarded as of divine origin, but of considerable historical interest.
[429] A.J. Brown, *The Word of God Among all the Nations* (1981) pp.7-25.
[430] *The Third Annual Report of the London City Mission* (1838) p.9.
[431] F.J. Exley *"Our Hearts Desire"* (1942) p.13.

loaned out the Bibles and Testaments they received from the Bible Society.[432] Some of those from poor backgrounds, converted by Bible reading, became agents of the Bible Society. One such woman, reaching out in the early 1850s to the notorious St Giles area to the east of Oxford Street, in London, achieved 70 Bible subscribers in her first month.[433] Her work led to the establishment of the first female missionary society, the London Bible and Domestic Female Mission. It was thought that a working-class female was more effective in reaching that class than a middle- or upper-class female, since she could testify to how the Bible had transformed her life.

In the first 50 years of its existence, the Bible Society supplied from its London base nearly ten million Bibles and portions of the Old Testament, and nearly 11 million New Testaments and portions.[434] In 1854, its jubilee year, the production of Scripture portions in London exceeded one million for the first time.[435] It was "by far the largest and most ambitious" pan-evangelical organisation,[436] and was a model for evangelistic endeavours. Its work generally gave "an important impetus for the transformation of the book trades: the development of stereotype, of machine printing and paper making, and of mechanised processes at the binding shop".[437] The Bible, which had been "a neglected book – a forgotten book – an unknown book – to a vast and melancholy extent" had been "lifted high among the nations, and sent forth on its glorious mission throughout the earth".[438] During the same period, the United Kingdom was preeminent among the nations.

4.4 Reviving preaching

At the beginning of the nineteenth century, the cadre of evangelical clergymen flowing through the universities began to reach the Church. A Baptist observed that "perhaps no denomination of Christians ever

[432] *Second Report of the London City Mission* (1836) pp.17-18 and *The Third Annual Report of the London City Mission* (1838) pp.9-11.
[433] L.N.R., *The Missing Link* (1859) p.31.
[434] G. Browne, *The History of the British and Foreign Bible Society* (1859) vol.2, p.544.
[435] Ibid.
[436] R.H. Martin, *Evangelicals United* (1983) pp.91-95.
[437] L. Howsam, "Preface" to *Cheap Bibles* (1991) p.xiv.
[438] G. Browne, *The History of the British and Foreign Bible Society* (1859) vol.2, p.485.

produced so many excellent preachers".[439] Gladstone, in his review of the evangelical movement, concluded that its "reintroduction of Christ our Lord to be the woof and warp of preaching", was its "great gift… to the 'teaching Church'". By 1879, he thought the gift pervaded the "whole mass".[440] There were also passionate Anglican clergy, like Robert Aitken, who preached in the late 1830s, night after night, in his own London chapels. Each "night the anxious might be numbered by scores, and on Sundays by hundreds".[441] In the 1850s, after he had moved to the Cornish mining area of Pendeen, he preached every day – and three times on a Sunday.[442] The Church of England at the time did not run special services – missions, as they were subsequently called – with the idea of awakening souls. Conversion through the Church, if it happened, came through the normal round of services.[443] Some preachers, such as J.C. Ryle (who had a very good first-class honours degree from Christ Church, Oxford), adopted a simple style to meet the needs of their labouring hearers.

In some ways, evangelical clergy in developing their preaching were responding to developments within Nonconformity. An amalgamation of Methodist and Dissenting preaching styles had already taken place. The Dissenting historians David Bogue and James Bennett observed that "The Dissenter had adopted the more natural address and easy conversation style of the Methodist; and the Methodist has taken to the more regular divisions and orderly method of the Dissenter".[444]

The end of our period saw the greatest preacher of the century, Charles Haddon Spurgeon, take up a pulpit in London. He had an arresting voice and was the 'metropolitan marvel' of 1856. A future Liberal cabinet minister, Augustine Birrell, recorded that when he went to hear Spurgeon,

> the only seat that could be offered him was one in the top gallery, between a woman eating an orange and a man sucking peppermints.

[439] R. Hall, *Strictures on a Work, Intitled, "Zeal Without Innovation"* (1809) p.43.
[440] W.E. Gladstone, *Gleanings of Past Years* (1879) vol.7, p.224.
[441] C.E. Woods, *Memoirs and Letters of Canon Hay Aitken* (1928) p.23.
[442] Ibid., p.63.
[443] W. Haslam, *From Death into Life* (1897) p.161.
[444] Reading of sermons among Independents went out of fashion, see D. Bogue and J. Bennett, *History of Dissenters, from the Revolution in 1688, to the Year 1808* (1812) vol.4, p.346.

> Finding the combined odours unendurable, he was about to leave; 'and then', said he, 'I heard a voice, and I forgot all else'. The magic that wrought the spell was Spurgeon giving out the first hymn.[445]

Spurgeon had earnestness. A hostile reviewer commented that his speech

> was not very eloquent...it did not display great genius...It did display great earnestness. It was difficult to suppose that he who spoke did not also believe. His influence rests much on the basis of his earnestness. His hearers conclude that he is anxious to accomplish all that he says. He usually deals with truths as they merit, and as if they were what they are, dread solemnities.[446]

Yet he also "made men laugh in church. He pressed humour into the service of theology".[447]

The preaching burden carried by evangelical ministers was heavy. A Dissenting minister in a country town might preach four times a week – three times on a Sunday and once midweek.[448] His midweek sermon might repeat a Sunday sermon. In Wales, May 1838 saw Christmas Evans itinerating around that country aged 71; that month he preached 26 times.[449] Some clergy, like Spurgeon, preached ten times a week, but in doing so he ruined his health.[450]

Sermons in those days were not short. Thomas Binney, at the King's Weigh House Chapel in London, typically preached at least three times a week,[451] for 40-45 minutes on each occasion.[452] That was twice

[445] Cited in E.J. Poole-Connor, *Evangelicalism in England* (1951) pp.226-227.

[446] "Mr Spurgeon at Exeter Hall", in *The Observer,* 16 and 17 November 1856.

[447] "The Late Mr. Spurgeon", in *The Observer,* 4 February 1892. However, compare, from a similar theological perspective W.E. Smith, *Address to Evangelists* (N.D.) pp.19-20.

[448] The afternoon service was under pressure to be discontinued as a time, allegedly, unfavourable for speaking, see D. Bogue and J. Bennett, *History of Dissenters, from the Revolution in 1688, to the Year 1808* (1812) vol.4, pp.344-345.

[449] E.E. Rees, *Christmas Evans* (N.D.) pp.177-178.

[450] "Mr Spurgeon at Bristol–A Scene", in *The Observer*, 16 September 1861.

[451] W.H.B. Proby, *Annals of the "Low-Church" Party in England* (1888) vol.1, p.381.

[452] *Sermons Preached in the King's Weigh House Chapel, London. 1829-1869. By T. Binney* (1875) (H. Allon (ed.)) p.xiv.

on a Sunday and once in the week. Binney, though, was close to but not in the foremost rank of preachers. In Birmingham, a sermon by the leading Congregational preacher John Angell James might last an hour and a quarter.[453] The evangelist Charles Finney, a lawyer by early training, rarely preached for less than an hour and a half.[454] In the Church of Scotland at the turn of the nineteenth century, sermons of such length from leading preachers seem to have been common. Sometimes one preacher immediately succeeded another.[455] In the Church of England, bishops in charges to their clergy began to urge more than one sermon,[456] although Tractarian preachers tended to be brief.[457] In the 1830s, to fit more services into a Sunday (such was the demand) the leading evangelical Church of England minister Baptist Wriothesley Noel thought that a service could be cut down to an hour and a half – without trimming the sermon, it was too important for that. In 1851, it was calculated that the average service length was still one and three-quarter hours.[458]

However, the growth of gospel preaching was not without its challenges. The Religious Tract Society produced a tract addressed *To Disturbers of Public Worship*. Even in the spiritually uplifting times of the early 1850s, William Haslam observed that congregations found preaching acceptable so long as the subject was not applied "too pointedly, by telling the people, both in the pulpit and out of it, that they are now ruined and lost; and that, having been redeemed, they are responsible before God; and that, if they will not be regenerated by the Spirit, they will be damned".[459] He found himself before a special meeting

[453] A.W.W. Dale, *The Life of R.W. Dale* (1898) p.54.

[454] K.J. Hardman, *Charles Grandison Finney* (1990) p.415.

[455] A. Haldane, *The Lives of Robert Haldane of Airthrey and of his Brother James Alexander Haldane* (1853) pp.137-138.

[456] Overton comments that at the beginning of the nineteenth century, "the clergy, as a rule, were not very attentive to the rubrics; but there was one rubric which many of them religiously observed, the one which prescribes a sermon in the morning and makes no allusion to any other sermon", see J.H. Overton, *The English Church in the Nineteenth Century* (1894) p.137.

[457] D. Wilson, *Our Protestant Faith in Danger* (1850) p.18.

[458] H. Mann, *Religious Worship in England and Wales* (1854) p.91.

[459] W. Haslam, *From Death into Life* (1897) p.78. Different approaches existed to awaken the conscience. Angell James startled by "vivid representations of the Divine indignation and wrath...gathering like a thunderstorm over the future of the unsaved".

of local clergy, convened by his rural dean, to consider his "betrayal of Church principles" – but no action was taken.[460]

Other ministers found it easier to compromise. Haslam was visited by a minister who preached on ruin, redemption and regeneration with effect but, "finding that his preaching made him very unpopular, he was weak enough to change his tone, and speak smooth things". That minister, knowing he was being unfaithful – and being of private means – resigned his living.[461] Haslam identified other types of minister who also failed to advance the gospel. One minister, who allegedly had experienced conversion, refrained from its need in his preaching – and used his natural gifts to establish "a large congregation", rather than win souls.[462] There was also the evangelical minister who asked Haslam to preach, but as soon as the preaching proved effective, and disturbances arose from those who rejected his doctrine, wanted Haslam to desist.[463] There were also those who "professed to believe in salvation by *faith only;* but for all this they never urged upon their people to perform acts of faith – they only expected them to receive the doctrine...such people opposed me and my work a great deal more than even High Churchmen".[464] Haslam also had the experience of a schoolmaster and his wife going "from house-to-house, in order to set the people against me and my preaching".[465] However, shortly afterwards, they were converted. Haslam, who had been a Tractarian, was converted by his own sermon. He wryly commented that "I used to be quite a popular man: people liked me, and clergymen let me preach in their pulpits; but now that I had something to tell for the good of souls, they seemed to agree to keep me out".[466] One clergy friend, who had Haslam preach for him, had his licence withdrawn for doing so by no less a personage than Samuel Wilberforce, the Bishop of Oxford, after revival came to the parish.[467]

Finney asserted the "righteous claims and awful majesty of the Divine Law", R.W. Dale, *The Life and Letters of J.A. James* (1861) pp.613-614.

[460] W. Haslam, *From Death into Life* (1897) p.135.

[461] Ibid., p.77.

[462] Ibid., pp.146-147.

[463] Ibid., pp.161-172.

[464] Author's italics. Ibid., p.190.

[465] Ibid., pp.81-83.

[466] Ibid., p.192.

[467] Ibid., p.250.

4.5 Special meetings for conversion

In England, most conversions from preaching had come through the regular round of church and chapel sermons. They were not necessarily publicly declared or urged, except as part of a rite, such as baptism, confirmation or membership. For example, one of the converts of Thomas Binny's early preaching was the radical William Hone, who made the impromptu decision to attend the Weigh House Chapel on New Year's Day, 1832. Binney wished to make sure Hone was converted – so Hone was not admitted as a member of the Weigh House until 30 December 1834, when 13 of his family members also joined.[468]

However, in America, revivalists used "four-day meetings" to promote conversions. As a justification for such longer meetings, Charles Finney pointed to the fact that in Scotland times of communion had often not been held regularly but had been held in periodic celebrations from a Thursday until after the Sabbath and, in other churches, religious festivals often involved protracted meetings.[469]

In "April 1834, a young Baptist minister of Boston, Lincolnshire, arranged a week's revival meetings in imitation of the American practice, 'being the first of the kind ever held in this country.' Within a year, five similar 'four-day meetings' had been held in the same area and by 1836 their use had spread into Baptist and Congregational circles further afield."[470] Most of such days were devoted to meetings, building towards the evening meeting. Tract distribution and street preaching might supplement the day's events. Sometimes, two local churches combined their efforts. It was found that those converted were usually from the Sunday school, unconverted church members or the lapsed, from whatever denomination.[471] As the new techniques spread, the numbers attending Baptist and Congregational churches increased but later, in the 1840s, doubt spread over their effectiveness as "converts" drifted away.[472] All the same, the idea of special meetings or services to

[468] T. Larsen, *Crisis of Doubt* (2006) pp.47-49.

[469] C.G. Finney, *Revivals of Religion* (1913) p.297. See also J.A. Thomas, *The Nation's Gospel: Reformation to Revolution* (2017) vol.1, pp.170-171.

[470] R. Carwardine, *Transatlantic Revivalism* (2006) p.73.

[471] Ibid., pp.77-83.

[472] Ibid., pp.83-84. A Congregational Union deputation expressed doubts about them, because they downplayed the role of normal services in conversion, see A. Reed and J. Matheson, *A Narrative of the Visit to the American Churches by the Deputation from the Congregational Union of England and Wales* (Jackson and Walford (1835)) vol.2, pp.33-34.

reach the lost was widespread. In the 1850s, William Booth "achieved remarkable results as a[n]...evangelist in Guernsey, the West Country, the Midlands and the North, employing special services modelled on James Caughey's methods".[473] His work, like Caughey's before him, was unappreciated by his Methodist denomination. In Liverpool, the mid-1850s saw the lay evangelists John Hambleton, Reginald Radcliffe and others take a hall on each Sabbath, with the intention of running services from 10 am to 9.30 pm, without intermission. Each service was to last only half an hour. They sparked a revival in Liverpool.[474]

4.6 The inquiry meeting

American revivalism found benefit in having a separate meeting after the gospel had been preached, to which those affected by the sermon could be directed for help and counselling. The meeting took a variety of forms. Sometimes, it began with an appeal to come to the communion rail,[475] or to sit at a bench within the church, called the "anxious bench", so as to make a public expression of conversion. The British were cautious in adopting such ideas, although in 1829 John Angell James established his own weekly anxious inquiry meeting. Those with a troubled conscience could go to it for counselling. Immediately, it met with "considerable success".[476]

In the mid-1830s,[477] a Congregational Union deputation went to America to investigate thoroughly these matters, and to report back their findings. They found inquiry meetings unscriptural, encouraging precipitate action and conclusions. However, in 1840 Andrew Reed, one of the deputation to America, led some revival meetings at the Wycliffe Chapel; afterwards he saw inquirers personally and in private.[478] In 1850 Charles Finney, after preaching to large audiences at Whitefield's Tabernacle, asked his host for an inquiry room for an after-service meeting, to which he could invite the seeking unconverted.

[473] R. Carwardine, *Transatlantic Revivalism* (2006) pp.184-185.
[474] G. Green, *Reginald Radcliffe: The Liverpool Solicitor* (2009) p.9.
[475] R. Carwardine, *Transatlantic Revivalism* (2006) pp.120, 183-184 and 190.
[476] R.W. Dale, *The Life and Letters of John Angell James* (1861) p.254.
[477] A. Reed and J. Matheson, *A Narrative of the Visit to the American Churches by the Deputation from the Congregational Union of England and Wales* (Jackson and Walford (1835)) vol.2, pp.34-43.
[478] R. Carwardine, *Transatlantic Revivalism* (2006) p.77.

His surprised host offered him an infant school room capable of holding 30 to 40 individuals. Finney indicated that this was not large enough. Ultimately, a nearby room was settled upon that held 1,500 people. After the service, to his host's "great astonishment", the room was "perfectly crowded with people".[479]

In the 1850s, the holding of after-meetings – and the drawing of the penitent to the communion rail – spread among revivalists. For example, in 1852 William Booth, in the afternoon of his first Sunday as a Methodist minister at Spalding in Lincolnshire, found one young woman weeping in the prayer, or after-meeting. He urged her to "come to the communion rails at night. She did so, and the Lord saved her". In the evening 14 others "came to the communion rail; many, if not all, finding the Saviour". The next Sunday he was on his knees, talking to someone under conviction of their sin.[480] Danger existed for anyone induced to go to the communion rail, who was not really ready to repent. The redoubtable Catherine Mumford, in a letter of March 1853 to William Booth, warned him against the injudicious use of the communion rail and reminded him of the cautionary example of her brother. He had been induced to attend the communion rail and, although he professed to find peace, his profession lacked foundation. Soon afterwards, "his conduct was far *worse* than it *had ever been* before...his heart was closed against conviction by the vain idea that he was converted".[481]

William Haslam also made use of a public after-meeting, held away from wherever the relevant church service had been held, such as the vestry, or a schoolroom or church hall, or even the rectory. He suggests that, as late as 1858-1859, it was unusual to have an after-meeting in church.[482] Such an approach, it was argued, allowed greater liberty to individuals to express themselves in prayer, praise or singing.[483]

[479] K.J. Hardman, *Charles Grandison Finney* (1990) pp.412-413 and 417. Finney, while at the Moorfields Tabernacle, to avoid late meetings and over excitement, occasionally deferred the after-meeting to the next day. On one occasion, he invited weeping penitents to the chapel's front seats, R. Carwardine, *Transatlantic Revivalism* (2006) p.144.

[480] H. Begbie, *Life of William Booth* (1920) vol.1, pp.155-156.

[481] Author's italics. Ibid., p.176.

[482] W. Haslam, *From Death into Life* (1897) p.291.

[483] For Finney's views on the anxious bench, and anxious meetings, see C.G. Finney, *Revivals of Religion* (1913) pp.296 and 302-305.

4.7 The power of prayer

The American revivalists emphasised the power of prayer as a precursor to effective evangelistic work. It is outside the scope of this book to take a detailed look at the role of prayer in evangelism but, in the mid-nineteenth century, so effective was prayer in evangelism that it became an important means of directly bringing about conversions. Accordingly, a brief foray into certain effects of prayer is appropriate. In Warwickshire, a poor woman who had just enjoyed "the blessing of entire sanctification...thought that if cottage-prayer meetings were held about the village, God would hear, and souls would be saved. She... prayed in cottages wherever permission was given...The work spread till the whole neighbourhood was shaken, and numbers were savingly brought to God." In a Wiltshire village, the six or seven members of a small society "prayed in the chapel, till conviction seized the ungodly by their fire-sides, and falling from their seats, they screamed aloud for mercy. Their ungodly relatives would run off to the chapel for someone to come and point them to Jesus."[484] It was, though, in Northern Ireland that the most momentous testimony to the power of prayer in evangelism is found. At the end of 1857, James McQuilkin and three friends met at the Old Schoolhouse, Kells, to pray for their friends. In the following months, many of those they prayed for were converted. From the parish of Connor, each convert demonstrated "the soul's unutterable happiness in Christ, and its misery alienated from him, that he became at once a burning advocate to all around".[485] The foundations of a great revival, that would open our next period, were being laid.

4.8 A plethora of books

As the schools and Sunday schools taught more people to read, literature became an increasingly significant part of their lives. Many people spent, as an evangelical observer recalled, "an evening, sitting along the edges of the pavement, with penny periodicals in their hands, the character of which is of every varied shade of good and evil".[486] Accordingly, it was

[484] G. Warner, "Prayer and Revivals", in *The Revivalist* (1857) p.33.

[485] "Rev. W. Arthur on the Irish Revival", in *The Revivalist* (1860) p.97.

[486] L.N.R., *The Missing Link* (1859) p.32. A survey of London, in 1812, found that around 60 per cent of the population could read, see G. Browne, *The History of the British and Foreign Bible Society* (1859) vol.1, p.57. It is unclear whether the survey included young children as among those who could not read.

important to provide an alternative to the "poison far and wide" that was spread by the "advocates of infidelity".[487] The number of religious books, as a proportion of all books published, grew – the 1850s being "the high point of religious publishing".[488] The Religious Tract Society thought that preaching was "God's first way of making the gospel known" but, in a land where revelation was known, writing was "God's chief way of making himself known to the human race from age to age, and of presenting truth to the minds of men from day to day".[489] For example, as we have seen, a work by John Fletcher was used by God to convert Hugh Bourne, the founder of Primitive Methodism. Christian literature – to convert and to change the nation's thinking and ways – came in a variety of forms and from many sources. We will now look at some of the most influential and famous works. Before doing so, it is worth observing that Hugh Bourne's simple handwritten statement of his own conversion and experience led to the conversion of his relative, Daniel Shubotham, another key figure in the early days of Primitive Methodism.[490]

4.8.1 *Tracts circulated in vast numbers*

Circulation of the *Cheap Repository Tracts* had been aided by the establishment of the Cheap Repository Association, of which Henry Thornton was secretary and Wilberforce a subscriber. It founded branch societies to distribute its tracts. Members circulated them in their families, in their schools and among their dependents; they encouraged bookshops and stall holders at fairs to stock them; gave retailers and hawkers a few free copies and encouraged them to sell more; and copies were sent to hospitals, workhouses and prisons.[491] In Scotland, the Edinburgh Tract Society[492] was founded, although it is to Charles Simeon that the first

[487] M.J. Quinlan, *Victorian Prelude* (1941) p.122.
[488] P. Scott, "The Business of Belief: The Emergence of 'Religious' Publishing", in *Sanctity and Secularity: The Church and the World* (1973) (D. Baker (ed.)) pp.214 and 224.
[489] Religious Tract Society, *An Address to Christians on the Distribution of Religious Tracts* (No.1) (N.D.) p.3.
[490] J. Walford, *Memoirs of the Life and Labours of the Late Venerable Hugh Bourne* (1999) vol.1, pp.65-74.
[491] M.J. Quinlan, *Victorian Prelude* (1941) p.85 and A. Stott, *Hannah More* (2003) pp.168-190.
[492] For its background, see R. Philip, *The Life, Times, and Missionary Enterprises, of the Rev. John Campbell* (1841) pp.120-121.

public distribution of tracts in Scotland is credited, in 1796.[493]

In 1799, the interdenominational Religious Tract Society was established.[494] Its aim – to circulate the theology of the sixteenth century reformers, in contemporary language – was not new,[495] but its founders wanted to do so "on a larger scale than before attempted".[496] Unlike the ballads and stories of the *Cheap Repository Tracts,* the Religious Tract Society regarded it as important that "the incidents narrated in its tracts shall, as far as possible, be real occurrences" and not works of imagination.[497] It became "one of the chief sources of literature for nineteenth-century readers".[498]

Its first tract was, appropriately, *An Address to Christians on the Distribution of Religious Tracts.* It stated that many pious people found "it extremely difficult to speak for God, and for the salvation of their fellow-creatures". For some, the difficulty could not be overcome – but the giving of a tract made the task easy.[499] It added that it was "difficult to say in what other way there is a probability of so much good being done with so small a sum".[500] To Christians who were already doing much, the Religious Tract Society urged them to add tract distribution to the means they employed.[501] Many did so. The Reverend Samuel Kilpin, when on a business or pleasure trip, dispensed about 100 tracts every five miles. Another individual purchased no fewer than 741,000 tracts and handbills for distribution.[502] In his fifties, the future evangelist, Brownlow North, began his evangelistic endeavours by distributing

[493] A. Haldane, *The Lives of Robert Haldane of Airthrey and of his Brother James Alexander Haldane* (1853) pp.145 and 273.

[494] After the death of Benjamin Forfitt, the founder of the Society for Promoting Religious Knowledge among the Poor, in 1794, it became a book club for subscribers – so ceasing to make gratuitous grants of literature, see *Prize Essay on the Occasion of the Society for Promoting Religious Knowledge among the Poor Established the 8th of August, 1750 Completing its First Centenary* (1850) pp.99-102.

[495] S.G. Green, *The Story of the Religious Tract Society* (1899) pp.10 and 29.

[496] J. Leifchild, *Life of the Rev. Joseph Hughes* (1840) p.39.

[497] S.G. Green, *The Story of the Religious Tract Society* (1899) p.10.

[498] M.J. Quinlan, *Victorian Prelude* (1941) p.124.

[499] Religious Tract Society, *An Address to Christians on the Distribution of Religious Tracts* (No.1) (N.D.) p.3.

[500] Ibid., p.4.

[501] Ibid., p.13.

[502] M.J. Quinlan, *Victorian Prelude* (1941) pp.124-125.

tracts,[503] as did, in his early teens, C.H. Spurgeon.[504]

Tracts were written to cover every relevant topic. They embraced the biography of well-known Christians like John Bunyan – and gave guidance on important topics in titles such as the following (all published in 1799): *To a Youth on the Importance of Purity* or *To a Youth at School* or, more poignantly, an address *To the Unfortunate Female*. There were also theological works such as *The Way to Heaven*, again published in 1799. They were designed to be "pure truth...flowing from the sacred fountain of the New Testament" and to give "some account of the way of a sinner's salvation". Each was to be clearly written – the truth presented in a striking and entertaining fashion – and to be full of ideas. A tract could be re-read so it covered more ground than a sermon.[505] During its first year, the Religious Tract Society put into circulation 200,000 tracts.[506] By the end of its fourth year, the number of tracts sold reached 1.4 million.[507] Auxiliary societies were founded in larger towns such as Darlington, Liverpool and Manchester. By 1815, there were 124 such auxiliary societies.[508] The circulation of 6,000 copies of Wilberforce's *A Practical View* yielded one or two celebrity converts.[509]

In the 1820s, the Religious Tract Society focused on tracts for children. A range of children's characters – with names such as Sally Meanwell, Fanny Thoughtless, Dick Wildgoose and Tom Steady – were introduced in *Short Stories for Children Under Ten Years of Age*. In 1824, it established a monthly magazine for children, *The Child's Companion*. It sold 339,000 copies in its first year.[510] These and other publications "revolutionised the Sunday reading of the young".[511] In 1829, publications issued by the society numbered 10,113,463.[512] Legh Richmond's [513] *The Dairyman's Daughter* (1810) was the most

[503] "Mr. Brownlow North", in *The Revivalist* (1859) p.177.
[504] A.A. Dallimore, *C.H. Spurgeon* (1984) pp.23-24 and 27.
[505] Religious Tract Society, *An Address to Christians on the Distribution of Religious Tracts* (No.1) (N.D.) pp.11-12.
[506] S.G. Green, *The Story of the Religious Tract Society* (1899) p.7.
[507] Ibid., p.8.
[508] Ibid p.19.
[509] See R.H. Martin, *Evangelicals United* (1983) p.157.
[510] S.G. Green, *The Story of the Religious Tract Society* (1899) p.33.
[511] Ibid., p.47.
[512] Ibid., p.28.
[513] S.A. Allibone, *A Critical Dictionary of English Literature and British and American Authors* (1965) vol.2, p.1802.

popular of these – alone selling, by 1849, four million copies – and it was of serious length. Many testified they owed their conversion to it. Legh Richmond was converted as a young curate by Wilberforce's *A Practical View.*[514] High Church ministers, like William Haslam in his early ministry, also handed out tracts, because parishioners liked and read them. He did not know how to respond when they converted readers.[515] But the work of the Religious Tract Society in holding to evangelical ideas, or even holding its members together, was not always easy.[516] In 1825 Roman Catholics sought to change its undergirding theology, but 1,200 supporters turned up to the relevant meeting – at six in the morning – and the challenge passed.[517]

In the 1830s, newly established visiting societies used tracts to introduce their visits and as a means of "silently working good, by the evangelical truths which they place before the reader during the interval which elapses between one call and the next".[518] A number of these tracts rebutted what was perceived as the dangerous socialism of Robert Owen.[519] In 1838, the London City Mission recorded that its agents had given out 229,809 tracts in the previous year and noted many converts from them.[520] In the 1840s, the Religious Tract Society started to address secular subjects, such as science, from an evangelical perspective.[521] Improvements in scientific research and telescopes were extending new conceptions of "the power and glory of the eternal mind".[522] By 1849, the Religious Tract Society had circulated 500 million tracts – their publication being "the first exercise ever undertaken in England which involved the mass production and distribution of reading matter."[523]

[514] "William Wilberforce esq", in 34 *The Christian Observer for the Year 1834* (1834) pp.62-63.

[515] W. Haslam, *From Death into Life* (1897) pp.48-52.

[516] See generally R.H. Martin, *Evangelicals United* (1983) pp.161-168.

[517] S.G. Green, *The Story of the Religious Tract Society* (1899) p.29.

[518] *Second Report of the London City Mission* (1836) p.18.

[519] For example, *Talk about Socialism* (N.D.), E. Birch, *Remarks on Socialism* (N.D.) and J. Mather, *Socialism Exposed* (N.D.).

[520] *The Third Annual Report of the London City Mission* (1838) pp.12-13.

[521] W.J. Astore, *Observing God* (2001) p.140.

[522] J. Kitto, *Daily Bible Illustrations (Evening Series)* (1867) vol.1, p.124.

[523] I. Bradley, *The Call to Seriousness* (1976) p.42. See also R.H. Martin, *Evangelicals United* (1983) pp.148-168.

By the mid-1850s, it was also giving "large grants of periodicals" for distribution by the new street preaching organisations like the Open-Air Mission.[524] The Religious Tract Society was only the largest of many tract producers. For example, the Weekly Tract Society published tracts in leaflet form for Emily Gosse, the wife of the distinguished zoologist Philip. She produced 41 in total, and 35 in the last 18 months of her life ending on 9 February 1857. At least half a million copies were printed.[525] By the summer of 1858, the general demand for tracts was said to be doubling every month.[526] In Scotland too, tracts were being written by men like Horatius Bonar and distributed locally by his helpers, men and women alike.[527]

4.8.2 *Punchy and direct evangelistic books*

Punchy evangelistic books were republished and passed-on to make the reader directly focus on the issue of salvation. A copy of Doddridge's *Religion in the Soul*, owned by the author, is an edition of 1825. It was given as a gift on 29 October 1855. The inscription is addressed to Mr Thomas Beaman "from his friend of Ravenscroft." By 1849, the Religious Tract Society edition numbered more than 81,000 copies[528] and in the late 1870s it was still being reprinted.

The Anxious Enquirer after Salvation (1834) was a new book, by John Angell James. It was based on his experience of dealing week-by-week with those whose souls were "*already* greatly troubled by the conviction of their guilt and peril".[529] Its first heading was "You are an immortal creature...born for eternity".[530] The explanatory text under this heading went on, "eternity, vast eternity...is before you...You may die any moment, and you are as near to heaven or hell as you are to death." Its pages were proof of the "religious teaching" by which "vast multitudes

[524] *The Open-Air Mission Third Annual Report* (1856) p.6.
[525] E. Gosse, *The Life of Philip Henry Gosse* (1890) p.260.
[526] "Special Services", in *The British Evangelist*, August 1858 p.67.
[527] I.H. Murray, *A Scottish Christian Heritage* (2006) pp.171-172.
[528] By then there were those who argued that Doddridge's book was better as a tool to holiness than a challenge to the unconverted, see R. Philip, *The Life, Times, and Missionary Enterprises, of the Rev. John Campbell* (1841) pp.33-35.
[529] Author's italics. R.W. Dale, *The Life and Letters of J.A. James* (1861) p.289.
[530] J.A. James, *The Anxious Enquirer after Salvation* (1834) p.1.

of persons ... were practically guided".[531] It went through six editions in its first year – and was translated into many languages. In 1835, it was reissued by the Religious Tract Society and by 1849 it had circulated 350,000 copies.[532] The Religious Tract Society found Doddridge's and Angell James's works of "more use in guiding young and earnest souls to Christ than any others".[533] R.W. Dale, who succeeded Angell James at Carrs Lane, testified that "it was my trusted guide through anguish and fear to a quiet trust in Christ".[534] Other books used for similar purpose included Wilberforce's *A Practical View*, aimed at the influential, and Legh Richmond's *The Dairyman's Daughter*, for the popular end of the market. Older works, such as Scougal's *The Life of God in the Soul of Man* (1677), continued to find a readership, being reprinted in 1850 by the Society for Promoting Christian Knowledge. In Scotland, Horatius Bonar published *God's Way of Peace: A Book for the Anxious* (1861). By 1889, it had sold 285,000 copies.[535]

Some evangelistic works explored new avenues of argument and may have paved the way in the years to come for more liberal developments. For instance, in 1852 Thomas Binney delivered a lecture advocating the Christian life – which he then expanded into a popular book with the telling title, *Is it Possible to Make the Best of Both Worlds?* Binney's attempt to show how Christian virtues enhanced life in this world, led others to suggest that self-sacrifice was being rejected and that defective Christian foundations were being laid.[536] He had already suggested that the "special mission" of Congregationalism was to the middle classes, a view espoused by important younger men like R.W. Dale.[537] Some see Binney as a founder of a "New Evangelicalism" that took shape in the mid-decades of the nineteenth century, authorising in religious terms "the inescapable attractions of secular living which Nonconformists experienced under the increasing prosperity of the mid-Victorian years;

[531] R.W. Dale, *The Life and Letters of J.A. James* (1861) p.288.

[532] S.G. Green, *The Story of the Religious Tract Society* (1899) p.51.

[533] Ibid., p.50.

[534] R.W. Dale, *The Life and Letters of J.A. James* (1861) pp.16, 288 and 301.

[535] I.H. Murray, *A Scottish Christian Heritage* (2006) pp.173-174.

[536] *This World & the Next: The Impossibility of Making the Best of Both* (1856) and W. Clarkson, *This World, or the Next?* (1856).

[537] M.D. Johnson, *The Dissolution of Dissent, 1850-1918* (1987) p.34 and A.W.W. Dale, *The Life of R.W. Dale* (1898) p.613.

and at the same time ... insisting on religious action and participation for religious purposes to prevent Nonconformists from lapsing into a self-satisfied complacency".[538]

4.8.3 *Books to shape the nation's moral conduct*

Evangelicals believed that for God to bless the nation, moral conduct needed changing and, with an increasingly literate public, good books were the means to communicate the necessary principles, while reading them left the public less time to absorb more pernicious literature. For the working classes, the *Cheap Repository Tracts* and other tracts performed this task. For the educated, Henry Venn's weighty *The Complete Duty of Man* (1763) was regularly reprinted. In 1794, it was supplemented by Thomas Gisborne's two-volume *An Enquiry into the Duties of Men in the Higher and Middle Classes of Society in Great Britain.* By 1811, this reached its sixth edition. In 1797, Gisborne added a volume for the ladies. 1847 witnessed publication of its 14th edition. Hannah More, as we have seen, had already produced her works on moral conduct. The last of the major evangelical manuals on conduct was William Roberts's *The Portraiture of a Christian Gentleman* (1829), dedicated to Hannah More. These major manuals on conduct were supplemented by innumerable lesser works on improvement and the Christian life. During the first quarter of the nineteenth century, they together achieved "a revolution in manners",[539] remodelling, along biblical lines, the code of conduct of the upper classes. Ian Bradley, in considering the impact of these authors on the upper classes, refers to the following illuminating example. Gentlemen had always settled disputes by duels, but Christians thought this contrary to the principles of humility and forgiveness. In 1844, the Articles of War were changed to declare it "suitable to the character of honourable men to apologise and offer redress for wrong or insult committed, and equally so for the party aggrieved to accept frankly and cordially, explanation and apologies for the same". A few years later, the last duel in England was fought.[540] The standards of some professions were also remodelled by the influence of Christians and their ideals. This was nowhere truer than the civil service. A byword

[538] M.D. Johnson, *The Dissolution of Dissent, 1850-1918* (1987) p.6.
[539] M.J. Quinlan, *Victorian Prelude* (1941) pp.3 and 119.
[540] Cited in I. Bradley, *The Call to Seriousness* (1976) pp.152-153.

for corruption in the eighteenth century, it began to be characterised by new standards of personal conduct based upon "integrity, impartiality and unflinching application to duty".[541]

Supplementing the serious and detailed guides on right living were inspirational stories of godly lives. Biographies of missionaries were popular. Perhaps most popular of all was Catherine Marsh's *Memoirs of Captain Hedley Vicars*, which sold 78,000 copies in 1856.[542] Hedley Vicars, a soldier who lost his life in the Crimean War, was an example of a "true disciple". The book, which demonstrated the power of human example to influence the conduct of others, helped to make the army a popular profession for Christians in late nineteenth century Britain.[543]

4.8.4 *Books to shape the nation's understanding of providence*

Joseph Milner was Wilberforce's old school teacher, who was converted through a student of the Countess of Huntingdon's Trevecca college.[544] In 1794, he published the first volume of a multi-volume work to which his brother, Isaac, would add after Joseph's death. In *The History of the Church of Christ*, he promised "an ecclesiastical history on a new plan".[545] "Genuine piety", he wrote, "is the only thing, which I intend to celebrate".[546] His subjects were "real, not merely nominal Christians; who believed the doctrines of the gospel, loved them because of their divine excellency, and suffered gladly the loss of all things that they might win Christ and be found in him".[547] His history was not about which church men belonged to, or rites and ceremonies, or forms of church government, or even religious controversies, unless they impacted the "essence of Christ's religion".[548] Milner's view was that histories that displayed ecclesiastical wickedness and internal dissension fed enmity against the gospel. He wanted "an account of the progress of

[541] Ibid., pp.159-163.

[542] P. Scott, "The Business of Belief: The Emergence of 'Religious' Publishing", in *Sanctity and Secularity: The Church and the World* (1973) (D. Baker (ed.)) p.215.

[543] Christian pacifists were alarmed by the success of the book, see *Soldiership and Christianity Being a Review of the Memoirs of the Late Captain Hedley Vicars* (1856). During the first half of the nineteenth century there had been an increasing Christian witness in the army, I. Dobbie, *Sovereign Service* (2013) pp.14-15.

[544] F. Cook, *Selina Countess of Huntingdon* (2001) p.338.

[545] J. Milner, "Introduction" to *The History of the Church of Christ* (1834) vol.1, p.iii.

[546] Ibid., vol.1, p.iv.

[547] Ibid., p.iii.

[548] Ibid., p.iv.

godliness itself".[549] Historians, he argued, by emphasising wickedness in the church, encouraged deists and sceptics to represent [Muslims] and pagans as more virtuous than Christians.[550]

Milner's work was a success – it shaped attitudes towards church history for almost three decades – it being almost "sacrilege" to criticise it.[551] It breathed and infused "a spirit of seriousness, piety, devotedness, deadness to the world, benevolence, and activity in doing good".[552] It was observed to bring "to a serious sense of religion those who were heretofore lost in the vain pursuits of the world".[553] Such was its theological clarity, that it was "instrumental in converting half a dozen members of Parliament".[554] It instructed, established and edified sincere Christians.[555] It was one of the most influential works in the early life of Cardinal Newman – and influenced his later historical writings.[556] Such was the interest in it that in 1826 John Scott published the first of three volumes which continued Milner's story – taking it from the Diet of Augsburg in 1530 to the death of Calvin in 1564.

In the early 1830s *The History of the Church of Christ* came under violent attack. The initial cause of this was Samuel Maitland's reaction to a statement in Bickersteth's popular work, *The Christian Student,* that described Milner's work as "eminently pious and useful, having much of the mind of the Spirit. The best history of the real church and ably continued".[557] Maitland assailed the section on the medieval Albigensians and Waldensians but seemed to target the destruction of its wider standing. Maitland described the design of *The History of the Church*

[549] Ibid.

[550] Ibid., p.v.

[551] J.G. Dowling, *A Letter to the Rev. S.R. Maitland on the Opinions of the Paulicians* (1835) p.4.

[552] J. Scott, "Preface" to *The History of the Church of Christ* (1826) vol.1, p.iii. and see also J. Scott, *A Vindication of the Rev. Joseph Milner, M.A. and the History of the Church of Christ* (1834) p.45.

[553] Ibid., p.44.

[554] J.D. Walsh, "Joseph Milner's Evangelical Church History", in 10 *The Journal of Ecclesiastical History* (1959) p.185 and J. Scott, *A Vindication of the Rev. Joseph Milner, M.A. and the History of the Church of Christ* (1834) pp.44-45.

[555] J. Scott, "Preface" to *The History of the Church of Christ* (1826) vol.1, p.iii.

[556] S. Thomas, *Newman and Heresy* (1991) pp.9 and 46-49.

[557] E. Bickersteth, *The Christian Student* (1832) p.542.

of Christ as "noble", but "the execution was feeble and defective".[558] In April 1834 James Rose, an early leader of the Oxford Movement, used a divinity lecture at the newly founded University of Durham to suggest that Joseph Milner was "a man of feeble powers and limited views".[559] The Dean, the Chapter and members of the University were present. An exchange of letters followed between Maitland and Rose – about the failings of Joseph Milner and his history.[560] John Scott made a defence of Milner to Rose[561] and John King to Maitland.[562] Maitland returned the compliment in a very lengthy pamphlet and the public exchange lengthened.[563] Nevertheless, in 1839, Henry Stebbing published the first volume of a further continuation of Milner's work, again from the Diet of Augsburg (1530) but ending this time in the eighteenth century. To extend the circulation of *The History of the Church of Christ*, in 1847 Thomas Grantham produced a revised version correcting translations of quotations, verifying the references and removing other errors. Bickersteth's view of Milner's work remained unchanged by the controversy he unexpectedly initiated.[564] However, the dominance of the view that in history "Christ, his gospel and human nature are the same in all ages" had been fractured, along with the emphasis in church history on "true Christianity." Later, historians would be more interested in showing how Christianity had adapted to its times from age to age,

[558] S.R. Maitland, *Facts and Documents Illustrative of the History, Doctrine and Rites of the Ancient Albigenses and Waldenses* (1832) p.46.

[559] J. Scott, *A Vindication of the Rev. Joseph Milner, M.A. and the History of the Church of Christ* (1834) p.9.

[560] The first of which was S.R. Maitland, *A Letter to the Rev. Hugh James Rose, B.D. with strictures on Milner's Church History* (1834) and a second letter followed in 1835.

[561] J. Scott, *A Vindication of the Rev. Joseph Milner, M.A. and the History of the Church of Christ* (1834).

[562] J. King, *Maitland not Authorized to Censure Milner* (1835).

[563] For example, S.R. Maitland, *A Letter to the Rev. John King, M.A. Incumbent of Christ's Church Hull; Occasioned by His Pamphlet Entitled "Maitland not Authorized to Censure Milner* (1835), S.R. Maitland, *Remarks on that Part of the Rev. J. King's Pamphlet Entitled "Maitland not Authorized to Censure Milner" which Relates to the Waldenses, including a Reply to the Rev. R.G. Faber's supplement, Entitled "Reinerius and Maitland"* (1836) and J. King, *Examination of Milner's History of the Fourth Century and of Certain Strictures on that History, Contained in the Second Letter of the Rev. S.R. Maitland to the Rev. H.J. Rose* (1836).

[564] E. Bickersteth, *The Christian Student* (1844) (4th ed.) p.509.

"rather than directly to confute error or to establish truth".[565]

4.8.5 *The apologetics battle is won*

In 1794 William Paley's *View of the Evidences of Christianity* was published. In 1800, the leading Baptist minister Robert Hall thought that Paley's work was "probably, without exception, the most clear and satisfactory statement of the historical proofs of the Christian religion, ever exhibited in any age or country".[566] Hall wanted to contend for the faith against modern infidelity and, believing that the proofs for the being of God had already been adequately dealt with by others, he focused his attack on "the total incompatibility of sceptical principles with the existence of a society".[567] In his view, if scepticism got a grip, morality would become "a fluctuating expedient, varying with the tastes of individuals, and changing with the scenes of life."[568] In 1822, Cambridge University made an examination in Paley's *Evidences of Christianity* a "fixed subject" for its students.

In the 1820s Thomas Chalmers, the Scottish clergyman, affirmed the importance of apologetics because of "their ascendant influence over the general mind of society.[569] Chalmers commended the clergy of his day for ably discharging their apologetic task. Without such success, he believed that "The fostering hand of the legislature would soon have been withheld from all our Christian institutions."[570] Revealing the different directions in which the thought life of the nation might have gone, in 1814 a landowner in County Durham, and no evangelical, had on his bookshelves (to be read by his teenage sons) "Paley's *Theology*, *Evidences of Christianity*, and *Moral Philosophy*", along with "Darwin's *Zoonomia,* and in metaphysics the works of Locke and Hartley".[571] However, by December 1835 Chalmers wrote that "Those days have

[565] J.D. Walsh, "Joseph Milner's Evangelical Church History", in 10 *The Journal of Ecclesiastical History* (1959) p.185.

[566] R. Hall, *Modern Infidelity Considered* (1800) p.ix. The perceived strength of Paley's *Evidences of Christianity* lay in its historical work, see T. Chalmers, *A Course of Thirteen Lectures Delivered in the University of Edinburgh* (N.D.) p.3.

[567] R. Hall, *Modern Infidelity Considered* (1800) p.x.

[568] Ibid., p.21.

[569] T. Chalmers, *The Christian and Civic Economy of Large Towns* (1821) vol.1, p.306.

[570] Ibid., pp.306-307.

[571] H. Taylor, *Autobiography of Henry Taylor* (1885) vol.1, p.30.

gone by of triumphant anticipation to the enemies of the cross, when the wit of Voltaire, and the eloquence of Rousseau, and the sophistry of Hume, entered into menacing combination on the side of infidelity. These have been withstood – and on the arena, too, of literary and intellectual debate – where many a feat of championship has been performed in repelling those successive attacks, which under the semblance of philosophy have been made upon the Faith."[572]

4.8.6 *Catechisms are well taught*

Teaching the catechism was central to religious life in the first half of the nineteenth century. At the beginning of the century in Wales, Thomas Charles[573] found that it was difficult to preach to uncatechised people. They simply did not understand what was said. Charles enjoyed great success by combining preaching and catechising. In Scotland, as the preachers pushed into the wilds, they were often preceded by school teachers and catechists, often supported by the Society for the Propagation of Christian Knowledge[574] and the endeavours of the Haldane brothers that we have already noted. The leading Congregationalist R.W. Dale recalled that in his childhood (in the 1830s and early 1840s) parents and schools with a church connection taught children the catechism. He noted that "the nature of the atonement of Christ was explained in a few lines, and the doctrines of original sin, of election, of effectual calling, of the perseverance of the saints, were defined and demonstrated".[575] He added that, "The minds of men being made up, and made up in their youth and early manhood, the large measure of truth which was contained in the theology which they had learnt in their catechisms, and which they heard from the pulpit, had its fair influence on their moral and spiritual life."[576] High Churchmen attached similar significance to catechising, although the aim of the work was "to fill children with a love and knowledge of the Church's worship and sacraments".[577] They

[572] T. Chalmers, "Natural Theology", in *Select Works of Thomas Chalmers* (1857) vol.5, p.150.
[573] E. Morgan, *The Life and Labours of the Rev. T. Charles* (1865) pp.275-276 and 357.
[574] I.H. Murray, *A Scottish Christian Heritage* (2006) p.149.
[575] R.W. Dale, *The Evangelical Revival* (1880) p.263.
[576] Ibid., p.265.
[577] P. Davie, *Raising up a Faithful People* (1997) p.50.

also gave special attention to baptismal regeneration.[578]

4.8.7 *Juvenile religious literature makes an impact*

The foundation of the era of juvenile religious literature is credited to John Campbell, in Scotland. He was also one of the founding fathers of the genre in England. Many future ministers received their "first serious impressions about religion" from one of his works. He "always had his pockets full of little books for distribution wherever he met with children".[579]

4.8.8 *Colporteurs are introduced*

Colporteurs had long been known on the continent, being individuals who travelled the country selling religious literature. They generally needed some funding, as the profits from book sales rarely covered their full costs. In 1793 the Scottish Colportage Society was founded. In the mid-nineteenth century the Bible Society, finding it increasingly difficult to get the 'better' classes out to collect one penny subscriptions for its Bibles, tried colportage.[580] The first purpose of its Jubilee Fund of 1854 was to raise funds to establish "an extensive and efficient system of colportage, throughout Great Britain".[581] For the Bible Society, the era of its dependency on the voluntary service of middle-class ladies to distribute its works was ending and the era of paid agents beginning.[582]

The Bible Society found that the employment of poor women – converted through Bible-reading to reach other poor women – had unique advantages. Marian, the Bible Society's first such worker, "in the most unlikely quarters", in 20 weeks effected the sale of 250 pieces of Christian literature, 130 Bibles and 120 Testaments.[583] Marian, after making contact with her women, invited them back for tea and

[578] S. Mumm, *All Saints Sisters of the Poor* (2001) p.49.

[579] R. Philip, *The Life, Times, and Missionary Enterprises, of the Rev. John Campbell* (1841) pp.184-192.

[580] W. Canton, *A History of the British and Foreign Bible Society* (1904) vol.2, pp.163-164 and L. Howsam, "The Bible Society and the Book Trade", in *Sowing the Word* (2004) (S. Batalden, K. Cann and J. Dean (eds)) p.34.

[581] W. Canton, *A History of the British and Foreign Bible Society* (1904) vol.2, p.445.

[582] L. Howsam, *Cheap Bibles* (1991) pp.185, 186 and 200.

[583] L.N.R., *The Missing Link* (1859) p.42.

a "little talk…on their ways, and how to mend them".[584] She showed that the reserve and pride of the denizens of the poor areas of the cities could be overcome. A female agency – made up of those from a poor background, to reach the poor – was seen as the missing link.[585] Once a female colporteur was in place, she saw needs that, with a little help, could be met. Saucepans on loan were circulated around the tenements surrounding a courtyard, together with recipes for a nourishing soup. Loans, to provide cheap bedding for those who had never enjoyed a refreshing sleep and clothing, were also supplied. The Bible Society provided the Bibles, while local subscribers paid for the Biblewomen and the materials for their domestic mission. Once the poor had been taught to save for a Bible, they could learn to save for items of comfort.[586] The danger was always that the social work pushed out the focus on Bible distribution.[587]

4.9 Family religion spreads

Family religion spread the religious principles that made a Christian "holy and happy";[588] its influence expressed "the abiding mercy of God with us".[589] It was the mother of the itinerant evangelist John Hambleton who "had sown the seeds of truth" in his mind, and whose prayers for his conversion God later answered, although she did not live to see the change in his life.[590] However, the itinerant evangelist Richard Weaver's Anglican mother saw her prayers answered, although "she would have to weep and pray for long and weary years". She also saw other sons converted, including George who became a Primitive Methodist preacher.[591] In the 1840s, the evangelist Robert Aitken sent his son Hay,

[584] Ibid., pp.33-41.
[585] Ibid., pp.32, 39-42 and 54-67.
[586] Ibid., pp.68-69.
[587] Ibid., p.49.
[588] J. Bean, *Family Worship; A Course of Morning and Evening Prayers for every Day in the Month to which is Prefixed a Discourse on Family Religion* (1796) p.iv.
[589] D. Wilson, "Introductory Essay" to W. Wilberforce, *A Practical View of the Prevailing Religious System of Professed Christians, in the Higher and Middle Classes in This Country, Contrasted with Real Christianity* (1829) p.lvi.
[590] J. Hambleton, *Buds, Blossoms, and Fruits of the Revival* (N.D.) pp.12-13. See also E.H.B., *The Converted Actor* (N.D.) pp.4-5.
[591] J. Paterson, *Richard Weaver's Life Story* (2012) pp.33-34, 39, 40-41, 43, 45 and 47-48.

later also a successful evangelist, to his room, on discovering that Hay was unconscious of being converted. He was commanded to stay there until he was assured of his conversion. A "long and dreary" incarceration arose, until the child could declare that "his load of childish sins was removed".[592] Robert Aitken, as a clergyman with responsibilities of hospitality, also took in many who needed help, or who were looking for guidance, sometimes for months, thereby exposing them to his religious practice. In families that were ignorant of the need for conversion, parents might teach their children and servants "the ordinances" of the Church. This was true of Hugh Bourne's mother, Ellen, so that when he was converted he knew the "principles of godly sincerity, self-denial and the temperate use of God's good creatures; and…to abhor the sin of *drunkenness*."[593]

William Wilberforce and the other members of the Clapham Sect firmly believed in family devotions, as did Hugh Bourne, the much less establishment-minded Primitive Methodist.[594] Wilberforce wrote to one of his sons, "O my dearest boy, let me earnestly conjure you not to be seduced into neglecting, curtailing, or hurrying over your morning prayers. Of all things, guard against neglecting God in the closet. There is nothing more fatal to the life and power of religion – nothing which makes God more certainly withdraw his grace."[595] Henry Thornton's family prayers, published after his death in 1834, went through 31 editions in 20 years. Such prayer times were no unfocused, childish or mumbling affairs. Thornton's *Family Prayers* would not have disgraced the Prayer Book. In 1829 William Roberts set out the first task of a Christian gentleman as that of leading family prayers. He wrote that, in the past, the "silly dread of profane ridicule" might have discouraged many from "instituting daily recognition of man's dependence upon the author of his being". But now, "by God's peculiar blessing", the nation had arrived at a "period in its religious advancement, when family

[592] C.E. Woods, *Memoirs and Letters of Canon Hay Aitken* (1928) p.73.

[593] Author's italics. J. Walford, *Memoirs of the Life and Labours of the Late Venerable Hugh Bourne* (1999) vol.1, p.17. Soon after Hugh's conversion Ellen discovered the more excellent way, not by works of righteousness but according to God's mercy through regeneration. She then became a great source of counsel to two of her sons in the spread of Primitive Methodism, see ibid., p.18.

[594] Ibid., pp.180-181.

[595] J.S. Harford, *Recollections of William Wilberforce, Esq*. (1865) p.6.

worship at the beginning and end of each day is quite of course among all professing Christians".[596]

Family worship reached out beyond biological members. At his home near Birmingham, Francis Chavasse, later the second Bishop of Liverpool, recorded in the 1850s how, on some mornings, when the rector appeared, the children, maids and outdoor servants filed in to take their places, while the rector read from the Bible and all knelt for prayer. "So every Sunday the whole household, servants included, repaired to Warmley Church, two miles away, the weaker members traveling in the large family barouche."[597] Thomas Langton was converted at the thrice-daily family prayers of the Methodist Thomas Seymour of Green Hammerton, within ten days of beginning work for Seymour around 1857. Langton later became an important Methodist evangelist to Yorkshire.[598]

The strength of family worship is illustrated by the rapidity with which successful books on the subject went through new editions and by how widely they were circulated. For example, in 1796 James Bean published *Family Worship; A Course of Morning and Evening Prayers for every Day in the Month to which is Prefixed a Discourse on Family Religion.* A copy of the 10th London edition of the *Discourse on Family Religion* was published in the United States of America – as a tract – capable of being bought in the hundreds and given away. In the early 1850s, a number of family religious magazines started to provide edifying reading for the unoccupied portion of the Sabbath.[599] For those wanting some Bible study in their family time, specifically designed works, like J.C. Ryle's commentaries on the Gospels, were published – today, considered respectable general commentaries. The historian G.M. Trevelyan cited with approval the thoughts of an earlier writer: "Evangelicalism was the religion of the home; and in the revival of family worship it won the most signal and most gracious of its triumphs".[600] One Lord Lieutenant of a Midland shire observed in 1850 that when he was growing up, there had only been two families in the county who

[596] W. Roberts, *The Portraiture of a Christian Gentleman* (1829) p.9. By 'professing Christians', Roberts probably meant those of the upper and middle classes, being the classes in which Christianity made most headway.

[597] J.B. Lancelot, *Francis James Chavasse* (1929) p.6.

[598] I.C. Watson, *The Life Story of Thomas Langton of Malton* (1896) p.23.

[599] J.L. Altholz, *The Religious Press in Britain, 1760-1900* (1989) p.48.

[600] Cited in G.M. Trevelyan, *English Social History* (1978) p.503.

had family prayers – whereas now there were only two who did not.[601] As the Tractarian movement took a grip it emulated evangelicalism's commitment to family religion.[602]

4.10 Sabbath obedience advances[603]

In the eighteenth century, although there were legal restrictions on Sabbath activities, it was, among the "most decorous persons...a day of pleasure". It was a day for concerts and parties.[604] Sabbath observance among Nonconformists was better. In 1809 James Bean demonstrated the failure of Anglicans to use the Sabbath for religion and the formation of religious character, by setting forth a page of a diary of a gentleman – for Sunday, 9 June. Going to church was central, and the sermon was recorded as "excellent" but, Bean noted, only two of 24 hours had a religious focus; there was nothing for the formation of religious character, the balance of the time being spent on entertainment and social intercourse. Bean argued that such conduct was "calculated so to take the mind off from what was presented to it at church, as to render attendance on public worship a practice of little effect to the individual, though his example in that act is of great service to the community".[605] In London Bishop Beilby Porteus, in the early years of the nineteenth century, battled with those who wanted to introduce paid-for entertainment on the Sabbath and to take the servants away from their rest.[606] In 1809, the Society for Promoting the Observance of the Sabbath was established. By then, the Society for the Suppression of Vice was active in bringing prosecutions against those who breached the Sunday trading laws. In 1807, of its 678 prosecutions, 623 were for Sabbath violation.[607] By the 1840s, mission organisations urged employers to ensure that no secular

[601] I. Bradley, *The Call to Seriousness* (1976) p.38. There was an ongoing need for clergymen to exhort their hearers to the merits of family prayers, as business was always likely to prevent them, see J.A. James, "What is the Spiritual State of our Churches?", in *The Works of John Angell James* (1861) (T.S. James (ed.)) vol.9, pp.414-420.

[602] S. Mumm, *All Saints Sisters of the Poor* (2001) p.46.

[603] See D.M. Lewis, *Lighten their Darkness* (1986) pp.232-242.

[604] W.H.B. Proby, *Annals of the "Low-Church" Party in England* (1888) vol.1, p.100.

[605] J. Bean, *Zeal Without Innovation* (1809) pp.7-8.

[606] R. Hodgson, *The Life of the Right Reverend Beilby Porteus* (1811) pp.138-142 and 188-199.

[607] A. Hunt, *Governing Morals* (1999) p.73.

activities interfered with divine worship for servants – and, if the duties of a large family made it impracticable for both servant and mother to attend a service at the same time, it was the servant who went, as the mother was closer to her children and "her concern for the everlasting welfare of her domestics, will prompt her to make the sacrifice with all cheerfulness".[608]

As our period ended, J.C. Ryle noted the change in the use of the Sabbath when he wrote that it is "the best safeguard of our country's religion".[609] It was a means of grace, something to give thanks for, as Henry Thornton's *Family Prayers* repeatedly reveals. It was a day to attend public worship, to provide Christian teaching, to meet the needs of the soul and to perform acts of mercy. To achieve these purposes, proper planning had to go into how the day was used. William Wilberforce spent an hour and a half in the afternoon reading – often, Baxter's *Practical Works*[610] – and, if things went wrong in the proper use of the Sabbath, he lamented, "for want of a plan lost the value of this day sadly".[611] Evangelicals regarded Sunday newspapers as "pernicious", coming "forth from their presses, like thieves from their obscure haunts, to rob their readers of the only day which can be rescued for religious reflection and prayer".[612] The Sabbath was also not for train excursions, steamboat jaunts, exhibitions, sight-seeing, parties or other forms of amusement.[613] In the 1830s, agents of the London City Mission sought to get shop-keepers to shut on a Sabbath – and succeeded.[614] Public sports on the Sabbath went into decline. The Sabbath symbolised God's blessing on the nation. Revolutionary France had given it up, so God gave up Revolutionary France.[615] Ryle added, "Experience shows that there is the closest connection between Sabbath sanctification and healthy

[608] "Our Servants", in *The Female Mission Record,* March 1845 p.28.

[609] J.C. Ryle, *Expository Thoughts on the Gospels: Luke* (1983) pt.1, p.163.

[610] J.S. Harford, *Recollections of William Wilberforce, Esq.* (1865) p.7.

[611] W. Hague, *William Wilberforce* (2007) p.209.

[612] B.W. Noel, *The State of the Metropolis Considered* (1835) (3rd ed.) p.14 and D. Wilson, "Introductory Essay" to W. Wilberforce, *A Practical View of the Prevailing Religious System of Professed Christians, in the Higher and Middle Classes in This Country, Contrasted with Real Christianity* (1829) pp.lix-lx.

[613] J.C. Ryle, *Expository Thoughts on the Gospels: Mark* (1985) p.46.

[614] *Second Report of the London City Mission* (1836) p.16.

[615] I. Bradley, *The Call to Seriousness* (1976) p.103.

Christianity".[616] It was also a form of national witness to the nations "affording to our Continental neighbours the noble example of a nation fearing God, by making his law paramount to every consideration".[617] The Unitarians remained opposed to encouraging Sabbath observance.[618]

Huge effort went into strengthening the legal protection of the Sabbath; it became a political battleground. In 1831, the pan-evangelical Lord's Day Observance Society was founded. In 1834, the Prime Minister, Sir Robert Peel, discontinued Sunday Cabinet Councils to please the evangelicals.[619] In 1850, the Sunday post was abolished. The victory was short-lived. Parliament demanded, and got, its re-instatement. Encouraged by this success, the forces of anti-Sabbatarianism attempted to open on the Sabbath some major icons of British culture – namely, the Crystal Palace, the British Museum and the National Gallery. The driving force behind anti-Sabbatarianism was big business, especially the railway owners. They gradually habituated the public "to the sight of the crowded excursion-train emptying itself of its reckless Sabbath-breakers", until more powerful backers joined them.[620] Nevertheless, the demand to open the national cultural icons on a Sabbath was beaten off. Thus encouraged, it was the turn of the Sabbatarians to try to advance their cause. First, there was a parliamentary act to curtail the Sunday opening hours of drinking places. Then, in 1855, a bill was introduced into Parliament to generally limit Sunday trading. It was backed by an alliance of evangelicals and workers. Neither wanted a "large and respectable body of men who, in order to gain their daily bread, were required to sacrifice their Sunday happiness".[621] The bill was withdrawn after riots in Hyde Park. After a little more than a year, the new limits on drinking hours were also repealed.

However, the tug-of-war over the Sabbath continued. In March 1856,

[616] J.C. Ryle, *Expository Thoughts on the Gospels: Luke* (1983) pt.2, p.123.

[617] E.J. Speck, *Church Pastoral-Aid Society* (1881) p.85.

[618] M.R. Watts, *The Dissenters* (2015) vol.3, pp.155-157.

[619] S. Minton, *The Evangelicals and "The Edinburgh"* (N.D.) p.41.

[620] "On the Progress of True Religion Amongst our Home Population", in 56 *The Christian Observer for the Year 1856* (1856) p.151. Using Sunday transport, even to work in a Sunday school, remained taboo amongst evangelicals at the century's end, see P.M. St. John, *R. Hudson Pope* (1967) p.23.

[621] "On the Progress of True Religion Amongst our Home Population", in 56 T*he Christian Observer for the Year 1856* (1856) p.151.

the author of an article on the advance of religion in the land thought that the "powerful progress" of Sunday trading was the leading danger of the day, exceeding the threat of popery, Tractarianism and rationalism.[622] In the spring of 1856, military bands started playing in the parks of London. On a Sunday, in early May 1856, it was estimated that 147,352 people listened to them in Kensington Gardens and Regent's Park.[623] Many were horrified. The Prime Minister, Lord Palmerston, at the express request of Archbishop Sumner, ordered the discontinuance of the military bands. Nevertheless, on a Sunday in early June, a band – organised by the society established for securing the performance of Sunday music in the parks – played at Regent's Park.[624] Evangelical control of the Sabbath was always slippery.

The spiritual expectations of the Sabbath and the desire to resist pleasure could be excessive. John Ruskin's mother, on a Sunday, turned over the pictures on the wall – lest the bright colours distract the children from the "contemplation of man's sinful state".[625] If this story is true, undue Sabbath rigour may have helped turn Ruskin, later in life, from Christianity. Edmund Gosse, the writer, is perhaps another son of an evangelical who turned from the faith, possibly by an "excessive passivity" on the Sabbath.[626]

4.11 A more pious and fairly remunerated clergy

The evangelical leader Daniel Wilson regarded the piety and simplicity of the clergy as "the seed-plot of divine grace among our population". In 1826, he referred to the "streams of living water" flowing from the doctrine and life of the clergy, "for the refreshment and salvation of the people".[627] He also detected a "very observable progress in the activity and piety of the dignitaries of the Church which unites them more closely

[622] Ibid., p.150.

[623] "The Bands in the Parks", in *The Times*, 8 May 1856. Another source suggested that a quarter of a million persons listened to the bands on a Sunday, "The Sunday Band Question", in *The Times*, 21 May 1856.

[624] "The Sunday Bands", in *The Times*, 2 June 1856.

[625] I. Bradley, *The Call to Seriousness* (1976) p.183.

[626] E. Gosse, *Father and Son* (1907) pp.273-275 and 277-278.

[627] D. Wilson, "Introductory Essay" to W. Wilberforce, *A Practical View of the Prevailing Religious System of Professed Christians, in the Higher and Middle Classes in This Country, Contrasted with Real Christianity* (1829) p.li.

with charitable institutions, opens their affections to their pious clergy, leads to the better distribution of patronage, and augments the strictness of the previous examination of candidates for holy orders".[628]

Huge disparities in clergy incomes existed. For example, the vicarage of Stanhope, in County Durham, carried a princely income of £18,000 per annum. The Bishop of Durham trumped this with, in 1831, a magnificent £22,000 per annum.[629] Furthermore, some clergy held multiple offices – while others took the income, but were not-resident in a parish. Illustrative of this, "Great Henry of Exeter...sought on going to his Bishopric to retain the Rectory of Stanhope and his stall at Durham" worth another £5,000.[630] At the other end of things, John Scott wrote his continuation of Milner's *The History of the Church of Christ*, because writing was his preferred alternative to taking pupils, to meet the needs of a large family living in Hull. He was also an evening lecturer at another church, which paid considerably more than his parish stipend.[631] In the early years of the nineteenth century, with Dissent growing, the government gave regular grants to augment the stipends of poor clergy. However, in 1835, the government required the Church to put its own house in order. An Ecclesiastical Commission was set up to redistribute incomes. Over the ensuing decades, this was achieved and non-residency declined. Legislation limiting pluralities (holding more than one church office) was shortly afterwards put in place.

Nevertheless, redistributing income did not guarantee godliness. In 1850 the evangelist Robert Aitken was exercised by the "godless state of the clergy". Of a church dignitary like Samuel Wilberforce, he thought that he had "light" but was "altogether in the world...He is literally the idol or pet of worldlings...and he seems to enjoy the position."[632] Others had real concerns about redistributing Church endowments. Thomas Chalmers, while noting the indolence of many of the Church of England's dignitaries, observed that in the past, when error appeared, it sent forth "an armed champion...in full equipment from some high and lettered

[628] Ibid.

[629] See R. Turnbull, *Anglican and Evangelical* (2007) p.146.

[630] A.R. Buckland, "Islington and the Appeal to History", in 41 *Churchman* (1927) p.97. This author puts the value of Stanhope at £5,000.

[631] D. Wilson, *Recollections of the Late Rev. John Scott, M.A. of Hull* (1834) pp.8-9.

[632] C.E. Woods, *Memoirs and Letters of Canon Hay Aitken* (1928) p.37.

retreat of that noble hierarchy".[633]

4.12 Binding together and teaching through hymn singing and music
Methodism popularised hymn-singing. The hymns of the Wesleys were prominent and also those of Isaac Watts. The Religious Tract Society kept in circulation the latter's *Divine Songs for Children*.[634] The Religious Tract Society was also a great distributor of the *Cottage Hymn Book*, which was a little book of hymns "selected for private reading and meditation, as well as for public or family worship".[635]

Advocates of music noted its "tendency to draw men together and to bind them together, and to form a sort of moral harmony out of discordant elements, by making the pleasure of each consist in contributing to the pleasure of others". It was also "a great means of diffusing religious feeling".[636]

Good singing and music drew people to church, even if the preaching deadened.[637] Singing that was sufficiently loud might draw in unconverted passers-by. For example, in the late 1790s John Wheeler, passing a Baptist chapel in Northampton, was drawn in by the singing and was converted. Soon, he was preaching in neighbouring villages – one of his converts was to be a future President of the Baptist Union. Two of Wheeler's brothers were also subsequently converted – one of their converts allegedly brought the great Charles Haddon Spurgeon to London to preach for the first time.[638]

However, congregational hymn singing was not to the taste of all. In the late eighteenth century, the Anglican Portman Chapel appears to have sung only Psalms and, in the first quarter of the nineteenth century, this was also true of most churches in the high tradition – as well as those of other traditions.[639] James Bean, the evangelical clergyman, criticised parishes using a hymn book – as giving to that church "an appearance

[633] E.B. Ramsey, *T. Chalmers* (N.D.) p.29.
[634] Religious Tract Society, *Divine and Moral Songs* (No.5) (N.D.) p.3.
[635] "Introduction" to *Cottage Hymn Book with an Appendix Containing Hymns Particularly Selected for Seamen* (N.D.).
[636] H. Raikes, "Preface" to *The Claims of Missions Upon the Young Men of England* (1846) pp.xxxv-xxxvi.
[637] W. Haslam, *From Death into Life* (1897) pp.20-33.
[638] H.W. Robinson *The Life and Faith of the Baptists* (1946) pp.110-111.
[639] O. Chadwick, *The Victorian Church* (1987) pt.1, p.67.

of singularity" and manifesting deviance from the established order and encouraging self-will. It nourished "an affection for change and novelty". The "beauty of uniformity" was being risked.[640] Nevertheless, it was the evangelicals who made hymns part of Church worship. John Overton concluded that hymns became "one of the auxiliary causes of the life and vigour of evangelicalism".[641] In the 1840s congregational hymn singing became popular across the Church of England,[642] but the Bishop of London was not beyond attempting to limit it, "however beautiful".[643] In the 1880s, a High Church member still dismissed the *Olney Hymns* as "almost entirely occupied with descriptions of subjective feelings and emotions".[644] Elements of Congregationalism resisted singing, even the Psalms. However, Thomas Binney helped popularise singing among them, arguing that from early times congregational singing had existed among God's people but, like other spiritual benefits, the Catholic priesthood had stolen it from the people.[645] In Scotland, Horatius Bonar, who became Scotland's "greatest hymn writer",[646] wrote his first hymns for singing by children in his mission district in Leith. However, Iain Murray tells us that the hymns in the first hymn book to carry his name were "primarily intended for reading rather than singing. Bonar did nothing to introduce hymns into the regular services of his church".[647]

Music in a church service could be a cause of conflict, as the Wesleyans at Leeds discovered in 1827, when their leadership required that they accept an organ.[648] It was also found that music on its own, even with professional singers, did not necessarily fill even St Paul's Cathedral but, in the right circumstances, it could be very powerful.[649]

[640] J. Bean, *Zeal Without Innovation* (1809) pp.309-311. See also *Thoughts on the Singing of Unauthorised Hymns in Public Worship* (1835).
[641] J.H. Overton, *The English Church in the Nineteenth Century* (1894) p.133.
[642] J. Walvin, *Leisure and Society, 1830-1950* (1978) p.98. See also "Hymns and Hymn Singing", in 74 *The Christian Observer for the Year 1874* (1874) p.107.
[643] D.A. Beaufort, *The Customs of the Church* (1843) p.23.
[644] W.H.B. Proby, *Annals of the "Low-Church" Party in England* (1888) vol.1, p.262.
[645] See T. Binney, "Preface" to *Congregational Church Music* (1853) pp.5-6.
[646] I.H. Murray, *A Scottish Christian Heritage* (2006) p.159.
[647] Ibid., pp.175-176 but also see 185.
[648] Organs generally seem to have helped fill a church, see J.H. Overton, *The English Church in the Nineteenth Century* (1894) p.136.
[649] Ibid., pp.134-137.

4.13 Special efforts to reach the working classes and needy

Those associated with the Clapham Sect saw their duty to the poor as a "personal service, enjoined by the highest authority; and cannot be commuted".[650] In 1796, the Society for Bettering the Condition and Increasing the Comforts of the Poor was founded and Wilberforce, Lord Teignmouth and other members of the Clapham Sect were among the early members of its General Committee. It was a forerunner of many such societies. It produced a host of practical reports into ways of improving the lot of the poor, with good effect.[651] The poor were entitled, its members believed, to the: (1) prevention of vice and contagion; (2) promotion of virtue and industry; and (3) general diffusion of moral and religious education.[652] With regard to the latter, it was noted that the "superior advantages" of teaching about "another state of existence hereafter" and of "the fallen state of man, and the appointed means of salvation through the atonement of a redeemer", had "been felt and proved wherever the experiment had been tried".[653]

The task of reaching the poor with the gospel expanded as the population of Great Britain and Ireland grew by 11 million between 1801 and 1851. The poor crowded into the cities. London, approaching a million people in 1801, by 1851 had over 2,360,000 people. Many lost contact with the churches, as they moved from country to city, if they ever had any contact; the concern of the churches to reach them and their descendants deepened.[654] If missionaries were taking the Bible in many languages and dialects to India and elsewhere in Asia, what about the unconverted on the doorstep?[655]

In 1832, the editor of *The Revivalist's* first address suggested that "not one-half of the population of the kingdom regularly, or even

[650] *The Society for Bettering the Condition and Increasing the Comforts of the Poor* (1805) vol.1, pp.4-5.

[651] See D. Owen, *English Philanthropy 1660-1960* (1965) pp.105-108.

[652] *The Society for Bettering the Condition and Increasing the Comforts of the Poor* (1805) vol.4, p.4.

[653] Ibid., p.33.

[654] For a brief survey of the religious indifference of the working classes at the beginning of the nineteenth century, see K.F. Inglis, *Churches and the Working Classes in Victorian England* (1964) pp.1-5.

[655] *The Third Annual Report of the London City Mission* (1838) pp.16-17.

frequently, attend on the worship of God".[656] In 1835, Baptist Noel, a leading Anglican evangelical and the younger brother of the Earl of Gainsborough, made a "back of the envelope" calculation as to the proportion of the population attending Anglican and orthodox Nonconformist churches in London (excluding the City). He found that on any given Sunday, on the best possible case, no more than 31.4 per cent and 13.4 per cent of London's population attended respectively Anglican and orthodox Nonconformist churches. The proportion of London's population who were regular orthodox worshippers was nearly 39 per cent (but some regular worshippers did not attend for reasons such as illness). Just over 35 per cent of the population of London entirely neglected any form of worship (whether orthodox or otherwise) and another 20 per cent attended orthodox worship irregularly.[657] He urged, in a well-known pamphlet, action to save these lost souls and to remedy the "demoralisation" that want of instruction led to[658] – such as Sabbath breaking, excessive spirit drinking, begging, gambling, abandoned females, theft, fraud and disreputable employments.[659]

Baptist Noel's call to reach the unconverted with the gospel enjoyed widespread appeal; the sufferings of the poor gave credibility to the radical Owenites – and others – and left the poor open to their programmes. The Church needed to be seen to do something. The radicals taught that the monarchy was tyranny, the establishment irreligious, that shareholders should forgo dividends and landholders forgo rents, while the labourer was afforded a comfortable maintenance.[660] The most popular radical periodicals tended to come out on a Saturday or Sunday and it was on a Sunday that radical leaders, such as Robert Owen, held their lectures, often at the same time as church services.[661] Accordingly, the Establishment was sympathetic to alternative Sabbath occupations for the masses and many new Christian initiatives were launched. Evangelicals generally led them and, at length, the Evangelical party became "great enough to give the tone to society at large; and the practice

[656] *The Revivalist* (1832) p.1.
[657] B.W. Noel, *The State of the Metropolis Considered* (1835) (3rd ed.) p.10.
[658] Ibid., p.12.
[659] Ibid., p.24.
[660] Ibid., p.65.
[661] Ibid., p.67.

of...superintending the poor" became so general that one observer knew of "no one circumstance by which the manners, studies and occupations of Englishwomen have been so extensively modified, or so strikingly contradistinguished from those of a former generation".[662] To these new initiatives we will now turn.

4.13.1 *Building new churches*

There was little hope of winning the urban working classes for Christ if the churches lacked room for them. In the cities, and especially London, existing church buildings could not cope with the population explosion although in some urban and rural areas churches were far from full.[663] The Bishop of London noted that "From St Martin-in-the-Fields to Marylebone church inclusive, a space containing 200,000 souls, there are only five parish churches" – and St Marylebone's church was very small.[664] He called upon Parliament to remedy the need. In 1809, James Bean thought that in places of increased population "not a tenth part of the inhabitants" could "obtain seats in the parish church".[665] The Church of England attributed the growth of Nonconformity to an insufficiency of episcopal churches and chapels.[666]

The victorious conclusion of the Napoleonic Wars led Parliament to answer the Bishop of London's call, by giving the Church of England, in 1818, one million pounds towards the building of new churches – as an expression of national thanksgiving to the Almighty – and a Church Building Society was set up. The resulting churches were known as "Waterloo Churches". For example, in the parish of St Marylebone, in the early 1820s, four churches were built – including what would be the influential church of All Souls Langham Place. In 1824, a further £500,000 was provided by Parliament and in Scotland it provided "a

[662] *Correspondence of William Edward Channing, D.D. and Lucy Aikin* (1874) (A.L. Le Breton (ed.)) p.397.

[663] H. Mann, *Religious Worship in England and Wales* (1854) p.88.

[664] Namely "St Martin's, St Anne's Soho, St James's, St George's Hanover Sq and the very small church of Marylebone". There were also some chapels, J. Bean, *Zeal Without Innovation* (1809) p.35.

[665] Ibid., p.34. See also J.H. Overton, *The English Church in the Nineteenth Century* (1894) pp.145-146.

[666] For an Anglican view on how Dissent exploited its weakness in the country, see *Church of England Pastoral Aid Society* (N.D.) pp.10-12.

grant of £50,000 for building churches in the Highlands and Islands".[667] Thereafter, public money dwindled away, as the Dissenters gained a voice in Parliament. They did not want state funding for the opposition.[668]

The need for more churches remained. Baptist Noel, in a celebrated public letter to the Bishop of London, published in 1835 as *The State of the Metropolis Considered*, drew attention to the need for more church accommodation, in the hope that "some persons may be induced by it to offer their help".[669] In doing so, there were difficulties – since the law stopped the inhabitants of a parish building "a new church unless it can be shown that two-thirds of the parish are without church-room".[670] Nevertheless, private liberality did step in. Between 1831 and 1851, the Church of England embarked on a massive church building programme[671] and restructured its parishes to make them manageable. For example, in the 1840s and 1850s, All Souls reduced its district to endow the equally influential All Saints, Margaret Street, and St Andrew's, Wells Street.[672] The Nonconformists also built new chapels. In the seven years ending 1845 the Congregationalists alone built 68 chapels in London.[673] However, all this was not enough to meet London's growing needs for churches. Even if Nonconformist chapels were included, there was not space in church and chapel for more than one half of London's population to attend, even if planned building projects were fulfilled.[674] The editor of the London City Mission, in his pamphlet *A Letter to the*

[667] S.J. Brown, *Thomas Chalmers and the Godly Commonwealth in Scotland* (1982) pp.212-213.

[668] In Scotland, the Seceders took a similar position when the Church of Scotland looked for government assistance to build churches, see A.L. Drummond and J. Bulloch, *The Scottish Church 1688-1843* (1973) pp.231-233.

[669] B.W. Noel, *The State of the Metropolis Considered* (1835) (3rd ed.) p.3.

[670] Ibid., p.37.

[671] See J.H. Overton, *The English Church in the Nineteenth Century* (1894) pp.150-153.

[672] It was no different in Scotland. Thomas Chalmers, soon after arriving at the Tron, in Glasgow divided his parish – having petitioned the Town Council to raise the number of parishes from 10 to 30, see A.L. Drummond and J. Bulloch, *The Scottish Church 1688-1843* (1973) pp.172, 184-186 and 230-231. However, the Church of Scotland's church extension campaign led it into conflict with the state, which ultimately paved the way for the disruption of 1843, see S.J. Brown, *Thomas Chalmers and the Godly Commonwealth in Scotland* (1982) pp.235-379.

[673] P. Rylands, *The Pulpit and the People* (1847) p.86.

[674] *A Letter to the Clergy, Ministers, and Protestant Christians of Great Britain on the Deplorable (Spiritual) Condition of the Metropolis* (1841) pp.5-6.

Clergy, Ministers, and Protestant Christians of Great Britain on the Deplorable (Spiritual) Condition of the Metropolis (1841), publicly blasted the clergy of all denominations for allowing this state of affairs.

In the growing provincial towns, the same need emerged for new churches. By way of example, in Kidderminster in 1824 St George's was built on one side of the town and in 1843 St John's followed on the opposite side. There were still also parts of the land where the gospel had never penetrated and where Christian morality was only dimly perceived. For example, in 1844 the Church of England built at Far Forest, about eight miles from Kidderminster, a missionary church to reach its "lawless" smallholders and agricultural labourers. Many of its people lived in a common-law relationship and ministers offered a joint of meat to those who married. In Cornwall in the 1850s Robert Aitken built a church, vicarage and schools among the miners. His predecessor had been chased away.[675] The Anglicans alone built 1,400 churches between 1825 and 1849.[676] Blomfield, the Bishop of London, was responsible for more than 200.[677] The Congregationalists, in addition to their London chapels, built 60 in large towns in the seven years ending 1845 while in that period in rural districts with a similar increase in population they built 276 new chapels. Some authors suggested that the "jealousy of town ministers" kept new Congregational churches out of large towns.[678]

4.13.2 *Running additional services*

An alternative way to meet population growth was to multiply the number of Sunday services. For example, Lord Teignmouth, the first president of the Bible Society, living in Portman Square in London, worked to establish evening services in nearby churches. Simeon's Holy Trinity, Cambridge had already done so at the end of the previous century.[679] All Souls, Langham Place introduced evening prayer in 1827 and thereby doubled its weekly services. Baptist Noel in the 1830s thought that a

[675] C.E. Woods, *Memoirs and Letters of Canon Hay Aitken* (1928) p.55.

[676] P. Brierley, *UK Church Statistics 2005-2015* (2011) section 14.4, p.7.

[677] R. Walford, *The Growth of "New London", in Suburban Middlesex (1918-1945) and the Response of the Church of England* (2007) pp.91-93.

[678] P. Rylands, *The Pulpit and the People* (1847) p.86.

[679] *Sketch of the Life of the Late Right Honourable Lord Teignmouth* (1834) p.21. See also J.H. Overton, *The English Church in the Nineteenth Century* (1894) pp.141-142.

service could be cut down to an hour and a half. This meant that up to six services could be fitted into a day, if "the prayers were shortened by the removal of repetitions".[680] The Nonconformists found the afternoon the most convenient time for a service aimed at "mothers of families, to the labouring classes, and to the poor".[681] A further idea, from the 1850s, was to run the increasingly common weekday services[682] sufficiently late in the evening so that the working class could attend.[683] In 1856, All Souls, Langham Place started a Thursday evening service.[684] At St James, Clerkenwell, the evening service began at 7.30 pm and was known as the one for the working classes. It was "crowded", such a congregation being not "an everyday occurrence". The Rector Robert Maguire called it "my choicest congregation".[685] In the 1850s communion services were added to the repertoire of evening services, with both Tractarian and evangelical support; it was found that the practice drew "many to that blessed ordinance who could never come before."[686]

4.13.3 *Removing pew rents and box pews*

Pew rents helped pay for the new church buildings and their staff.[687] As a matter of law, one-third of seats in the Established Church had to be free, but those sitting in them, by doing so, identified themselves as poor.[688] Not until 1850 was the first new London church in the modern

[680] B.W. Noel, *The State of the Metropolis Considered* (1835) (3rd ed.) p.32.

[681] D. Bogue and J. Bennett, *History of Dissenters, from the Revolution in 1688, to the Year 1808* (1812) vol.4, p.345.

[682] Overton attributed the introduction of these to evangelical clergy like Legh Richmond, see J.H. Overton, *The English Church in the Nineteenth Century* (1894) pp.143-144.

[683] H. Mann, *Religious Worship in England and Wales* (1854) p.85.

[684] F. Prins, *All Souls Langham Place London* (1980) p.4.

[685] R. Maguire, *Pastoral Letter Addressed to the Congregation of St James's, Clerkenwell* (1859) p.9.

[686] G.R. Balleine, *A History of the Evangelical Party in the Church of England* (1951) pp.191-193. For an example of the operation and uptake of communion services in a specific parish, see R. Maguire, *Pastoral Letter Addressed to the Congregation of St James's, Clerkenwell* (1859) p.11.

[687] See also B.W. Noel, *The State of the Metropolis Considered* (1835) (3rd ed.) pp.32-40.

[688] Ibid., p.39. Most paid for a seat to hear Spurgeon, the greatest preacher of the day. In his early days, preaching at the Surrey Music Hall, a ticket could be purchased until a quarter of an hour before the service. At that time admission became free leading

era opened without recourse to pew rents.[689] In 1851 53 per cent of pews in English churches were subject to pew rents.[690]

However, by the 1850s, having built the new churches, box pews were thought to be an insuperable barrier to filling them. Edward Miall thought they created an "unhappy moral impression".[691] In 1853 Lord Shaftesbury also called for the abolition of all high, or "square", pews if not the substitution of all pews by open sittings[692] – and in many evangelical parishes they were dispensed with.[693] The High Church also wanted rid of box pews. However, a clergyman who did so without making himself the most unpopular man in the parish possessed, as one observer noted, "a rare union of tact and courage".[694] The Anglicans noted that the Prayer Book rubric provided for an offertory, which seemed an alternative way of securing the necessary funding.[695] The Dissenters

to an "immense rush" for seats. Boxes were put out for people leaving, to contribute, but there was no formal collection. Spurgeon did not approve of begging, see "Mr Spurgeon's Second Discourse at the Surrey Garden's", in *The Observer*, 1 Dec 1856. Once his Metropolitan Tabernacle was built, regular attenders purchased a seat on a three-monthly basis and were admitted by ticket. The poor – and irregular attenders – remained outside until five minutes before the service when they were allowed in. Again, there was a great rush – and again, there was no regular collection, but collection boxes were left near the entrance of the Tabernacle for one of Spurgeon's projects; see A.A. Dallimore, *C.H. Spurgeon* (1984) p.98. In 1890, when Arthur Porritt visited the Metropolitan Tabernacle, the collection boxes remained, A. Porritt, *The Best I Remember* (1922) p.1. Spurgeon thought that those buying a ticket to attend were more likely to value the experience, see G.H. Pike, "*The Life and Work of Charles Haddon Spurgeon*", vol.3, p.175, in G.H. Pike, *The Life and Work of Charles Haddon Spurgeon* (The Banner of Truth Trust (1991)) vol.1. When he preached at the service of National Repentance for the Indian Mutiny, the 24,000 who heard him paid the normal charge of a shilling to get into the Crystal Palace. There was also a collection, see C.H. Spurgeon, *Autobiography* (1973) vol.1, p.354.

[689] K.F. Inglis, *Churches and the Working Classes in Victorian England* (1964) p.50. Overton attributes the first absolutely free church to be built in the country to Archdeacon Daubeny's Christ Church, in Bath, consecrated in 1798, see J.H. Overton, *The English Church in the Nineteenth Century* (1894) p.157.

[690] D.A. Reid, Playing and Praying in *Cambridge Urban History of Britain (1840-1950)* (2000) (M. Daunton (ed.)) vol.3, p.793. See also H. Mann, *Religious Worship in England and Wales* (1854) p.viii.

[691] E. Miall, *The British Churches in Relation to the British People* (1850) p.283.

[692] *Practical Hints on Lord Shaftesbury's advice to the Clergy* (1853) p.4.

[693] I. Bradley, *The Call to Seriousness* (1976) p.64.

[694] W.J. Conybeare, *Essays Ecclesiastical and Social* (1855) pp.112-113.

[695] H. Mann, *Religious Worship in England and Wales* (1854) p.94.

were less concerned about pew rents.[696]

4.13.4 *Familiarising the working classes with church buildings*

By the 1850s, some thought that the church building itself deterred the working class from attending church. Many of the new churches and services were never full, for instance, those in Bethnal Green. To Bishop Blomfield's surprise, a means had to be found to get the poor to attend the new churches. A proposed solution to this difficulty was to use church buildings for a purpose to which the working class would come, so that they became familiar to them.[697]

4.13.5 *Opening churches for the destitute poor*

It was found that the very poorest were much more likely to attend churches that they regarded as exclusively their own, so churches known as ragged churches were established.[698] In 1853, the Ragged Church and Chapel Union was founded with Lord Shaftesbury as patron. Ragged churches were to act as preaching stations, proclaiming the gospel but avoiding taking baptisms or giving communion. Those who wanted to grow in their faith advanced by attending regular places of worship. By 1857 there were 35 ragged churches, with an aggregate attendance of 2,500.[699] Some ragged churches started in a shed, but there were conversions – and those converted moved on to the regular churches.[700] In its annual report that year, the Ragged Church and Chapel Union noted that "its principles and aims are being increasingly recognised and acted upon by all sections and by men of every grade and position of the church of Christ in this highly favoured land".[701] Ragged churches worked closely with the ragged schools – schools for the children of the very poorest city dwellers, since the parents of ragged school children were often too dirty to attend ordinary churches. It was found that parents were interested in what interested their children.[702]

[696] Ibid., but see E. Miall, *The British Churches in Relation to the British People* (1850) p.283.
[697] Ibid.
[698] H. Mann, *Religious Worship in England and Wales* (1854) p.94.
[699] *The Fourth Annual Report of the Ragged Church & Chapel Union* (1857) p.7.
[700] Ibid., pp.8-9.
[701] Ibid., p.5.
[702] T. Chalmers, *The Christian and Civic Economy of Large Towns* (1821) vol.1, p.344.

4.13.6 *Running services in buildings other than churches*

The use of public halls and private rooms as places to teach Christianity was another solution to the unwillingness of the working classes to attend church.[703] In 1838 the London City Mission held no less than 5,475 missionary services, mainly in the rooms of the poor.[704] In 1855, to forward the London City Mission's work, Lord Shaftesbury piloted through Parliament the Religious Worship Bill, repealing restrictions on where religious worship could take place when large numbers were involved.[705] In the late 1850s agents of the Open-Air Mission went into the common lodging houses of London to hold services; in 1856, they held 1,168 such services.[706] In less industrial parts, cottage meetings were started. In June 1856, at a cottage reading taken at Elmer's End, near Beckenham, Miss Marsh told the story of the woman at the well in John 4 – and the "religious emotions" of the future evangelist and first Secretary to the Post Office, Sir Arthur Blackwood, were deeply stirred.[707] William Haslam used cottage meetings as part of his strategy to convert the citizens of the Cornish town of Hayle in 1857-1858.[708]

4.13.7 *Using the laity to reach the working classes*

The masses in the cities were too numerous for ministers, with their increased preaching duties, to reach; lay house visitation offered the solution.[709] Methodists had shown what lay workers could achieve in house visitation and evangelical leaders noted the important part visitation played in the American revivals.[710] Furthermore, The Bible Society and its associations were well-versed in the opportunities arising from house visitation because, although the Bible Society's constitution provided that Bibles should be circulated without note or comment, its

[703] H. Mann, *Religious Worship in England and Wales* (1854) p.85.

[704] *The Third Annual Report of the London City Mission* (1838) p.12.

[705] "Religious Worship Bill", in *Hansard,* 23 July 1855.

[706] *The Open-Air Mission Fourth Annual Report* (1857) p.7.

[707] *Some Records of the Life of Stevenson Arthur Blackwood* K.C.B. (1898) p.133.

[708] W. Haslam, *From Death into Life* (1897) p.289.

[709] D. Bogue and J. Bennett, *History of Dissenters, from the Revolution in 1688, to the Year 1808* (1812) vol.4, p.351.

[710] D.M. Lewis, *Lighten their Darkness* (1986) p.34. See also A. Reed and J. Matheson, *A Narrative of the Visit to the American Churches by the Deputation from the Congregational Union of England and Wales* (Jackson and Walford (1835)) vol.1, pp. 58-60 and 378-379 and vol.2, p.14.

members often got into discussion with those visited.[711]

Thomas Chalmers provided the popular rationale and blueprint for house visitation in a series of quarterly publications beginning in 1819. So successful were they that they became the foundation upon which the publisher William Collins built "the House of Collins into one of Britain's great publishing concerns".[712] They were later drawn together into his three-volume work, *The Christian and Civic Economy of Large Towns*, a volume being published in each of the years 1821, 1823 and 1826. Each volume contained over 350 pages and much of it was based upon Chalmers's experience in, and understanding of, his home city of Glasgow. On his arrival at the Tron, Chalmers had set about revitalising its parish machinery in order to reach its multitudes of poor through house visitation by its members, schools for parish children and poor relief – at the expense of ministering to many of the middle- and upper-class congregation that it drew from across the city.[713]

Chalmers's thesis in *The Christian and Civic Economy of Large Towns* was that the benevolence of the period was being rendered abortive because the endeavours of political scientists to improve society did not include Christianity – and Christian philanthropists did not admit the validity of political science into their thinking.[714] Chalmers aimed to unite the endeavours of these two groups in order to better society. In addition, he wanted to rectify a deadly mischief of "a large class of religionists" who held a "distaste towards all kind of external machinery for the furtherance of any Christian enterprise".[715] He acknowledged the "Spirit of God, as the agent of every prosperous revolution in the Christianity of our land", but noted that when "living water flowed more abundantly than it has ever done since", the apostles provided "it with ducts of conveyance".[716] Chalmers was positive about building new churches, but did not believe they would draw the heathen to Christ.

[711] R.H. Martin, "Women and the Bible Society", in *Sowing the Word* (2004) (S. Batalden, K. Caan and J. Dean (eds)) pp.43-44.

[712] S.J. Brown, *Thomas Chalmers and the Godly Commonwealth in Scotland* (1982) p.146.

[713] Ibid., pp.99-105.

[714] T. Chalmers, *The Christian and Civic Economy of Large Towns* (1821) vol.1, pp.1 and 3.

[715] Ibid., p.18.

[716] Ibid., p.20.

The new churches might be filled, but primarily by a transfer of sitters from elsewhere.[717] His thesis was that there was a need for "an external apparatus for the transmission of Christianity",[718] a "numerous and well-appointed agency".[719]

Chalmers thought that the churches drew those who had a predisposition to religious influences, but the great majority were unwilling to respond. What was needed was an "aggressive" movement to draw the lost into Christianity. Just as in the parable of the wedding feast Jesus told messengers to "Go out quickly into the streets and alleys of the town and bring in the poor, the crippled, the blind and the lame",[720] then messengers were to go "to the roads and country lanes", so that the churches may be full. In fulfilment of this mandate, Chalmers suggested dividing the great city parishes into small manageable districts for which one or more individuals could organise systematic house visitation. The emphasis was on doing the work; city-wide management was to be avoided, as leading to superficiality. Chalmers was "most thoroughly persuaded, that the less we are linked and hampered with one another, the more effective will be all our operations".[721]

House visitation raised the issue of whether visitors should meet the temporal needs of the poor, as well as their spiritual ones. Chalmers thought that the two roles should be kept separate.[722] That way, the visitor could identify the true character of the person visited – and the latter be kept from the risk of "hypocrisy of heart",[723] pretending to religious interest for worldly advantage. However, this issue would be an ongoing concern.

[717] T. Chalmers, *The Christian and Civic Economy of Large Towns* (1823) vol.2, p.3.
[718] T. Chalmers, *The Christian and Civic Economy of Large Towns* (1821) vol.1, p.20.
[719] Ibid., p.26.
[720] See Luke 14:15-24; see also Matthew 22:8-9. The evangelist George Smith also took Christianity to the waters by pioneering ships as chapels in port, see R. Kverndal, *George Charles Smith of Penzance* (2012).
[721] T. Chalmers, *The Christian and Civic Economy of Large Towns* (1821) vol.1, p.75.
[722] Ibid., pp.249-304.
[723] Ibid., p.255. Chalmers has been credited as "one of the founders of case work in social welfare administration" for "his emphasis upon systematic visitations and visitation of relief recipients". He has also been credited as a herald of the "social gospel', because of his interest in reaching the working classes, see S.J. Brown, *Thomas Chalmers and the Godly Commonwealth in Scotland* (1982) pp.377 and 378.

Visiting societies mushroom in number

In 1826 one of the first visiting societies arose in the parish of St Giles, in London's West End. Often, a paid agent oversaw the work and identified needs, while the visitors were volunteers. The volunteers were energetic. Surviving records suggest that, on average, each volunteer looked after 17 families and paid 18 visits a year to each. That is about a visit to each family every three weeks. In 1828 a number of evangelical visiting societies came together to form a General Society for Promoting District Visiting. Its design was to "promote a general and systematic visitation of the poor, with a view of improving their temporal and spiritual condition". By the early 1830s, 19 such societies were operating.[724] For Anglican clergy, the use of the laity could be controversial, especially where their work cut across parochial boundaries. In the Diocese of London, the Metropolitan Visiting and Relief Association was established to "channel relief to the most necessitous poor through district visiting societies". In the 1840s and 1850s, it worked with 70 or 80 district societies.[725]

Individual churches and chapels responded to these new visiting societies with their own, and also societies to promote the benefit of the poor.[726] In 1826, Daniel Wilson attributed the spread of piety to the different societies, both within and outside the Church, and to their "competition, and rival exertions, and the division of labour, and mutual emulation for the dissemination of the faith under the protection of a mild and beneficient government".[727] For example, John Scott, at his parish in Hull in 1830, established a district visiting society. He then had 200 visitors and upwards of 20,000 under visitation. He visited every family first.[728] In the 1830s, that Congregational flagship, the King's Weigh House Church, established its domestic mission. It had

[724] "General Society for Promoting District Visiting", in *Supplement to the Religious Intelligence in The Christian Observer for the Year 1831* (1832), towards the end of the volume.

[725] D. Owen, *English Philanthropy 1660-1960* (1965) pp.141-143.

[726] W.J. Conybeare, *Essays Ecclesiastical and Social* (1855) p.69. See also M.J. Quinlan, *Victorian Prelude* (1941) pp.133-138.

[727] D. Wilson, "Introductory Essay" to W. Wilberforce, *A Practical View of the Prevailing Religious System of Professed Christians, in the Higher and Middle Classes in This Country, Contrasted with Real Christianity* (1829) p.lii.

[728] D. Wilson. *Recollections of the Late Rev. John Scott, M.A. of Hull* (1834) p.8.

a Christian instructional society for visiting families and distributing tracts, a Sunday school, a Bible class for young men and a mission station east of the Tower. Visitors provided material help through the Cheap Clothing Society.[729] Many of the visitors were women.[730] By 1850, virtually every parish church, even an Anglican proprietary chapel,[731] and many Nonconformist chapels, had a visiting society.

Home missions flourish

In 1826, David Nasmith brought together eight evangelical denominations to found the Glasgow City Mission, to reach the poor of that city. Nasmith's ability as a unifier and organiser of gospel work was manifest. He had already demonstrated enthusiasm for tract distribution, Sunday school work and adult evening education. Now, he sent out preachers to people's homes. In 1828, he established Dublin's City Mission and,

[729] E. Kaye, *The History of the King's Weigh House Church* (1968) p.93. For the staggering range of regular religious and philanthropic activities carried out by the Congregational Carrs Lane Chapel, Birmingham, in 1859, see J.A. James, "What is the Spiritual State of our Churches?", in *The Works of John Angell James* (1861) (T.S. James (ed.)) vol.9, pp.368-370. The activities included making substantial contributions to or establishing organisations to support: the local Congregational theological college; the London Misssionary Society; the Colonial Missionary Society; orphan mission schools in the East Indies; a Dorcas society for the poor of Birmingham; a maternal society; a female benevolent society for visting the sick poor; a religious tract society employing 90 distributors and funding the purchase of tracts; a village preachers' society; the local county association of wandering evangelists; two town missionaries; a young men's brotherly society for general and religious improvement with 2,000 volumes; night schools for young men and women; and the education of 2,000 children through Sunday and day-schools. Angell James suggested that this was "but an average of Congregational exertion and liberality in this general day of activity", see ibid., p.369. While Angell James was at Carrs Lane, the old chapel building was considerably improved and extended, seven small chapels were built in the town and two separate Independent chapels established. A third was established in partnership with another congregation and work was nearly complete on a fourth. It had bought the land for a further two chapels in the suburbs of Birmingham, see ibid. For details on how a clothing society might work, see "Miscellaneous", in 16 *The Christian Observer for the Year 1817* (1818) pp.17-20.

[730] For an excellent survey of the background to the early visiting societies see D.M. Lewis, *Lighten their Darkness* (1986) pp.34-45. See also D. Owen, *English Philanthropy 1660-1960* (1965) pp.140-143. For an example of their benefits in a rural mining parish, see C.E. Woods, *Memoirs and Letters of Canon Hay Aitken* (1928) pp.64-65.

[731] L.E. Shelford, *A Memorial of the Rev. William Cadman* (1899) p.24.

in 1835, the London City Mission.[732] Baptist Noel chaired its first meeting. The MP Thomas Buxton, who led the final charge in the House of Commons to abolish slavery in the Empire when Wilberforce was too frail to do so, was its first treasurer.[733] It regarded itself as fulfilling the Lord's command to "go out quickly into the streets and lanes of the city and bring in hither the poor".[734] By the time of its second report, 50 missionaries had "already been sent forth to give the invitation". Some of the poor had believed the message and had already gone to their new family above. Others remained "to tell what great things the Lord has done for their souls". The Mission wanted another 300 to 400 agents – that "all the poor in this metropolis may be invited".[735] An agent was trained in Hebrew – to reach Jewish people – and another spoke the "all-important truths of the gospel" in the Gaelic language of the Irish.[736] Local associations of laity were also formed which managed the work of the Mission's agents in their area. In the early to mid-1840s, the reports of the North West Marylebone Association showed signs of growing spiritual success.[737]

The Nonconformist desire for disestablishment initially limited Church involvement with the London City Mission, notwithstanding that its lay agents did not initially preach in the streets.[738] Indeed, the Bishop of London forbad his clergy's involvement, although he later

[732] Nasmith was to found a vast number of town and city missions and other societies to take forth the gospel both in the United Kingdom and the United States, see generally The Religious Tract Society, *David Nasmith* (N.D.).

[733] For the background to the formation of the London City Mission see I. Howat and J. Nicholls, *Streets Paved with Gold* (2003) pp.21-29.

[734] *Second Report of the London City Mission* (1836) p.4, being a paraphrase of Luke 14:23. Its agents also visited the manufacturers, workhouses and hospitals looking for the poor, sick, aged and infirm, see *Second Report of the London City Mission* (1836) p.18.

[735] Ibid., p.4. The agents of the London City Mission were paid so that it would not compete with the visiting societies for voluntary visitors, see ibid., p.5.

[736] Ibid., p.15.

[737] Compare *The First Annual Report of the North-West Mary-le-bone Association in Connection with the London City Mission* (1842) and *Report of the North-West Marylebone Association in Connection with the London City Mission* 1843 & 1844 (1844).

[738] G.H. Pike, *Beneath the Blue Sky* (1888) p.150.

relented.[739] Instead, in 1844 Bishops Charles Blomfield and Charles Sumner patronised what became the Church of England Scripture Readers' Association to work within their respective dioceses. Its work expanded and formed a model for other organisations, the Army Scripture Readers' Society already existed. The founding of the Church of England Scripture Readers' Association manifested "the close alliance that obtains between the political interest and religious character of a country"[740] – that Chalmers articulated. This alliance embraced the desire to bring under "Christian and humanised principle" the mass of a city's population – lest it might lift "its brawny vigour" against the authorities of the land. It was accepted that "*the grand means of converting sinners to God is the application of the word of life to the individual heart and conscience*".[741]

The Scripture Readers' Association appointed lay agents to read the Bible to the poor, under the superintendence of the parish clergy. Its agents were educated in the Scriptures and apologetics, as "the false reasoning of Shaftesbury [the eighteenth century philosopher and not the nineteenth century Christian philanthropist] and Bolingbroke" continued "to supply the superficial caviller, although overthrown again and again".[742] William Conybeare observed that its agents were "drawn from the same class of society as those to whom they are sent"[743] – and thereby got closer to the "modes of feeling, thinking, and speaking" of those they sought to reach. They were not to preach, but to engage in the reading of the Bible and the Prayer Book, the answering of objections to the word of God and in religious conversation – although some went on to careers as noted evangelists.[744] They were also not to distribute money freely, but to point the poor to where temporal relief could be

[739] J. Garwood, *The Importance of City and Town Missions preserving the Strictly Catholic Character* (1858) pp.4-5.
[740] See "Introductory Address", in 1 *The Scripture Readers' Journal* (1853-6) p.2.
[741] Author's italics. Ibid.
[742] "The Scripture Reader", in 1 *The Scripture Readers' Journal* (1853-6) p.6. On Shaftesbury and Bolingbroke, see J.A. Thomas, *The Nation's Gospel: Reformation to Revolution* (2017) vol.1, pp.264-265 and 366-367.
[743] W.J. Conybeare, *Essays Ecclesiastical and Social* (1855) p.68. This may have been a liberal attempt at disparagement, see for the background of early Scripture Readers, "Our Scripture Readers", in 2 *The Scripture Readers' Journal* (1856-60) pp.1-3.
[744] F. Cockrem, *Gawin Kirkham* (N.D.) pp.40-44.

found.[745] In 1847 the Rector of St Martin's Birmingham found the Scripture reader so useful that he invited contributions for three more. The existing reader made up to 50 visits a week, plus 20 visits to the sick, and did not mince about raising eternal issues.[746] The Rector of All Souls Langham Place, Charles Baring, thought "that in a large metropolitan parish it is impossible to carry on the work of regular visitation of the poor without the agency of lay Scripture readers".[747] All Souls appointed its third Scripture reader between April 1853 and May 1854.[748] A Scripture reader working in the East End of London between 1847-1853 visited nearly 13,000 homes, baptised 1,989 infants (many belonging to Baptist parents) and 54 adults, induced 1,048 children and 157 adults to attend school, 182 persons to attend church and 250 to be confirmed. He also visited 160 people during an illness that led to their respective deaths – and distributed 110 Bibles and 73 Prayer Books.[749] The persistence of a Scripture reader might lead to a death-bed conversion, where the clergy had failed.[750] Indeed, the Scripture reader became a link connecting the metropolitan clergy and the poor.[751] However, it was possible for spiritual teaching to drop from the Scripture reader's routine – to be replaced by "relieving temporal distress".[752]

The number of full-time evangelistic workers with the London City Mission rose rapidly, but did not reach the numbers originally desired. By the early 1850s, it employed 300 and the Scripture readers numbered 323 agents.[753] By this time, the benefits of denominations working together had been seen. The Church had the money, while the

[745] "The Scripture Reader", in 1 *The Scripture Readers' Journal* (1853-6) p.8.

[746] See J.C. Miller, *Earnest and Anxious Words to the Parishioners of St Martin's Birmingham* (1847).

[747] "Our Scripture Readers", in 1 *The Scripture Readers' Journal* (1853-6) p.345.

[748] See the "Ninth and Tenth Reports of the Church of England Scripture Readers' Association", in 1 *The Scripture Readers' Journal* (1853-6) pp.55 and 183 respectively.

[749] "Tenth Report of the Church of England Scripture Readers' Association", in 1 *The Scripture Readers' Journal* (1853-6) p.180. Only in the mid-1850s were Scripture Readers allowed to distribute tracts, approved by the Archbishop of Canterbury and the Bishops of London and Winchester, "Twelfth Report of the Church of England Scripture Readers' Association", in 1 *The Scripture Readers' Journal* (1853-6) p.386.

[750] "The Scripture Reader", in 1 *The Scripture Readers' Journal* (1853-6) p.10.

[751] "Introductory Address", in 1 *The Scripture Readers' Journal* (1853-6) pp.3-4 and "Progress of Lay Agency", in 1 *The Scripture Readers' Journal* (1853-6) p.118.

[752] W. Haslam, *"Yet Not I"* (N.D.) p.14.

[753] H. Mann, *Religious Worship in England and Wales* (1854) p.99.

character of Dissenters made them more suited to missionary work. Further, by working together, they more easily convinced the poor that they were concerned with their spiritual health – and not just filling the relevant denominational building. By the late 1850s, more London City Missionaries were superintended by Anglicans than the clergy of Dissenters.[754]

Both the London City Mission and Scripture Readers' Association employed only male agents. However, most of the poor at home were women – and their husbands did not take kindly to them receiving spiritual guidance from men, or from the ladies that visited them through other organisations. Therefore in 1857 Ellen H. Ranyard drew together the various female Bible agencies under the auspices of the Bible Society and founded the London Bible and Domestic Female Mission. Ranyard believed that the best way to reach and help poor women was through other women – Biblewomen – drawn from the same background, who could "devote themselves to the task of relieving suffering and distributing Bibles within their local area".[755] Together, these and the smaller mission operations reflected a vast increase in evangelistic resources. In 1851, there were only 1,274 clergy and ministers in London (including Roman Catholic).[756]

The benefit of clergy and laity working together was demonstrated at St Mary's Whitechapel. By 1851, William Champneys,[757] with the aid of the London City Mission and the Scripture Readers' Association, drew a congregation of 1,157 adults in the morning, over 437 adults to afternoon meetings and 1,463 adults at night.[758] Good numbers of Sunday scholars also attended each service. Furthermore, Champneys ran a school with two Sunday services – 580 children and 149 adults attending. Champneys found that an evening communion service attracted many working-class members, who would not otherwise attend.[759] The same results from

[754] J. Garwood, *The Importance of City and Town Missions preserving the Strictly Catholic Character* (1858) pp.14-15.

[755] S. Lane, "Forgotten Labours: Women's Bible Work and the BFBS", in *Sowing the Word* (2004) (S. Batalden, K. Cann and J. Dean (eds)) p.61.

[756] D.M. Lewis, *Lighten their Darkness* (1986) p.120.

[757] Previously Chamneys had been rector of St Ebbe's Oxford, being appointed in 1832 – the year after Bulteel had his licence withdrawn.

[758] Ibid., pp.128-149.

[759] E.H. Bickersteth, *Charge* (1886) p.25.

laity and clergy working together were seen in Edinburgh and Glasgow. In the summer of 1859, it was observed that "30,000 people, who were utterly neglectful of public worship in 1851, have been brought under the means of grace through the efforts of lay agency and denominational churches".[760] All the same, such success with the working class required unrelenting hard work and perseverance.[761]

4.13.8 *More clergy for the cities*

The Church recognised that population growth left many people without Christian pastoral care and subject to the ministrations of Dissenters and, even worse, the radicals. Methodist[762] and Baptist[763] ministers already systematically visited homes, although visiting styles varied. The Baptist minister Robert Hall was said to take 30 cups of tea in an afternoon – visiting four families and drinking seven or eight cups at each. Accordingly, more clergy were needed and in 1836 evangelicals in the Church of England established the Church Pastoral-Aid Society ("CPAS").[764] Lord Shaftesbury was its president and presided over its annual general meeting. Clergy were to preach the gospel of "grace in season and out of season, teaching from house to house, and labouring as one having souls for his hire".[765] In addition, the CPAS decided to employ laymen. They took services but could only preach from a homily, or deliver "a sermon from some *approved* source"; they were to be "teachers of the young, and visitors and advisers of the aged and poor".[766] The decision by the CPAS to appoint laymen led William Gladstone and others of the High Church party, who saw the priesthood "as a precious gift from God and a means of grace for his people",[767] to separate.[768] In

[760] See "Home Evangelisation", in *The British Evangelist*, July 1859 p.242.

[761] For an excellent survey of the effects of door-to-door visitation at this time, see D.M. Lewis, *Lighten their Darkness* (1986) pp.128-149.

[762] J. Sigston, *Memoir of the Venerable William Bramwell* (N.D.) p.48.

[763] O. Gregory, *A Brief Memoir of the Life of Robert Hall* (1833) pp.63 and 67-68.

[764] For an account of the background to the formation of the CPAS, see E.A. Knox, "Centenary of the Church Pastoral-Aid Society", in *Church and People*, October, 1936 p.86 and E.J. Speck, *Church Pastoral-Aid Society* (1881).

[765] *Church of England Pastoral Aid Society* (N.D.) p.5.

[766] Author's italics. Ibid.

[767] "Who are the ACS?", www.additionalcurates.co.uk/whoaretheacs.php, accessed 3 November 2016.

[768] An alternative explanation for the establishment of the Additional Curates Society

1837 the Society for Promoting the Employment of Additional Curates in Populous Places was established, primarily through the energy of Joshua Watson.[769] Among its "warmest supporters"[770] were the leaders of the Oxford Movement. The first collection for its work was taken at the forerunner of All Saints, Margaret Street.[771]

By the 1850s, the CPAS supported 300 clergymen for outreach purposes and over 100 lay assistants.[772] Lord Shaftesbury thought that the reason that the revolution of 1848 – which broke out in France and had major repercussions elsewhere – passed almost unheeded in England, was partly due to the work of the CPAS. Its agents had gone "among the people from house to house, distributing the word of God".[773] He made a similar point about the work of the London City Mission – as did Baptist Noel, although the latter was keen to make it clear that its object was to offer salvation, not to make the miserable content.[774] By 1851, the Society for Promoting the Employment of Additional Curates in Populous Places supported 323 curates,[775] although its fund-raising capacity never matched that of the CPAS.

is that the CPAS wanted to ensure that its funds were used to support only those who would preach the gospel – and wanted to weed out Tractarians and "idle or ball frequenting curates", see E.J. Speck, *Church Pastoral-Aid Society* (1881) pp.30-33. The Additional Curates Society was happy to support whoever the bishops ordained. The bishops generally preferred to support the Additional Curates Society, although the two Sumners and some other bishops were members of the CPAS, see O. Chadwick, *The Victorian Church* (1987) pt.1, p.450.

769 Watson, a layman, was a remarkable supporter of High Church causes, including the National Society for Promoting the Education of the Poor, see C. Kelway, *Centenary of the Additional Curates Society 1837-1937* (1937) pp.5-8.

770 Ibid., p.8.

771 Ibid.

772 W.J. Conybeare, *Essays Ecclesiastical and Social* (1855) p.68 and H. Mann, *Religious Worship in England and Wales* (1854) p.99.

773 "A Striking Testimony to the Influence of the C.P.-A.S. by Lord Shaftesbury in 1858", in *Church and People,* July 1940 pp.41-42. See also W. Buckland, *A Sermon Preached in Westminster Abbey, on Easter Sunday Evening, April 23, 1848* (1848) p.5.

774 I. Howat and J. Nicholls, *Streets Paved with Gold* (2003) pp.34 and 137-138.

775 H. Mann, *Religious Worship in England and Wales* (1854) p.98.

4.13.9 *Open-air and itinerant preaching expands*

At the beginning of our period, Methodists led the way in open-air and itinerant preaching. The Independents followed, reviving their county associations, many of which employed one, two or even three itinerant preachers.[776] Bogue and Bennett urged that if unassociated evangelical ministers and congregations started an association, "success will far exceed their expectations".[777] After an itinerant preacher had passed through a village – often preaching outside – meetings for prayer, preaching and reading might start in private rooms or homes. A few years later, these meetings might lead to the building of a small chapel. In 1797, the Baptists gave an impetus to their outdoor preaching by establishing The Baptist Society in London, for the Encouragement and Support of Itinerant and Village Preaching (from 1821 the Baptist Home Missionary Society).[778] However, the Church of England remained unenthusiastic. In 1797, even the stone pulpit specially built into the quadrangle of Magdalen College Oxford for preaching to listeners outside had for a long time been out of use.[779]

By 1835, the Baptist Home Mission Society had 100 missionaries – preaching, running Sunday schools and distributing Bibles and tracts in the villages. The following year, it tended to shift its resources to the towns and cities.[780] For example, the Baptist minister George Charles Smith, after cutting his teeth on open-air preaching in the south-west, turned to London and enjoyed success in numerous parts after overcoming initial "ridicule, contempt and opposition".[781] At Smithfield, he had as many as "five hundred persons standing, with fixed and devout

[776] For a list of the extensive number of Calvinistic organisations active in itinerant evangelism between 1780-1830, see D.W. Lovegrove, *Established Church, Sectarian People* (1988) pp.182-184.

[777] D. Bogue and J. Bennett, *History of Dissenters, from the Revolution in 1688, to the Year 1808* (1812) vol.4, p.364. See also D.W. Lovegrove, *Established Church, Sectarian People* (1988) pp.14-15.

[778] J. Ivimey, *A History of the English Baptists* (1830) vol.4, pp.68-72. Slightly earlier, in 1795, the Baptist Missionary Society appropriated part of its funds for home mission work, to respond to the charge of domestic neglect. Deryck Lovegrove informs us that this "represented the first attempt to organise the work on a national and denominational basis", D.W. Lovegrove, *Established Church, Sectarian People* (1988) p.25.

[779] "Mr Urban, Guildford, Dec.12", in 67 *The Gentleman's Magazine* (1797) p.377.

[780] R. Cawardine, "The Evangelist System", in 28 *The Baptist Quarterly* (1980) p.209.

[781] G.C. Smith, *Preaching in the Open Air* (N.D.) p.34.

attention, to the close of the service".[782] He was a committed propagandist of open-air preaching and a great founder of institutions – including the Christian Instruction Society, a model for other more enduring city-wide evangelistic organisations. In Scotland, the Countess of Leven was behind an effective lay scheme for itinerant preachers.[783]

In 1835, spurred on by the example of George Smith, Baptist Noel suggested open-air preaching to the Bishop of London and backed his call by reference to the practice of Jesus, the apostles and others.[784] However, bishops were traditionally unwilling to sanction open-air preaching. But times changed. In Cornwall in 1852 William Haslam preached on Perran beach and then elsewhere – when the vicar of his old church refused him permission to preach. Haslam, a little time before, had been converted while preaching in his own pulpit and felt the need to return to his old flock to give them the gospel message. Hundreds came to listen and the 50 people who cried out for mercy led him to repeat the experiment.[785] Haslam had been very much a Tractarian until his conversion, so his open-air preaching career could not have been foretold.

Others noted in London the "remarkable readiness" for "crowds who frequent the thoroughfare and the poorer localities of London to listen to plainspoken addresses delivered in the open-air". In June 1853, to take advantage of this, the interdenominational Open-Air Mission was founded – to present the gospel in the open-air to those who would not attend church. It intended to deliver regular services at "specified places and fixed hours", through carefully selected lay agents, without the use of "clerical costume". Initially, 60 sites[786] were chosen as places where services would be held. In any given week, 40 of them were used by the Open-Air Mission's nine agents for services. Congregations at

[782] B.W. Noel, *The State of the Metropolis Considered* (1835) (3rd ed.) p.49.

[783] R. Philip, *The Life, Times, and Missionary Enterprises, of the Rev. John Campbell* (1841) p.139.

[784] B.W. Noel, *The State of the Metropolis Considered* (1835) (3rd ed.) pp.43-58. George Dawson with Unitarian leanings, attributed the success of Jesus with the "common people" to his work as a street preacher, see G. Dawson, *The Demands of the Age Upon the Church* (1847) p.25.

[785] W. Haslam, *From Death into Life* (1897) pp.118-127.

[786] Although the work was very successful, the Open-Air Mission was unafraid to quickly reduce its stations to 50, see *Second Annual Report of the Open-Air Mission* (1855) p.4.

its first year's services generally numbered between 50 to 200 hearers and over 1,000 services were held.[787] It was observed that "Eloquence is not needed, but earnestness". What was required from the preacher was "rather 'speaking' than 'preaching'...a plain familiar address, not a lengthy harangue".[788]

In its *Second Annual Report*, the Open-Air Mission observed that "the work of the Mission has not only caused thousands to hear who would not otherwise have heard the word, but has called forth other agencies, as well as the efforts of individuals, for the revival of the practice of open-air preaching as a recognised mode of proclaiming Scripture truth".[789] For example, in 1854 the London City Mission removed the prohibition on its agents preaching in the streets. As a result, in 1854 it held 1,306 open-air meetings. The Country Towns Mission also turned to open-air preaching.[790] The *Second Annual Report of the Open-Air Mission* recorded that 30 clergymen of the Church of England and the ministers of 9 Congregational chapels were also preaching out of doors in London and that "this number will soon double".[791] The Islington Church Home Mission was a Church of England organisation – embracing both clergy and laity – set up at the time and dedicated, among other matters, to promoting open-air evangelism. Many ministers also preached in the open-air with the Christian Instruction Society.[792]

In 1855, members of the Open-Air Mission observed that "people are ready to attend, and willing to listen."[793] Only the papists were "violent".[794] In every locality its members could judge "the season of the year, the day of the week, and the hour of the day most proper...for preaching the gospel out of doors".[795] John MacGregor, the Mission's first Secretary, and also a barrister and the son of a general, challenged preachers by means of a tract to join them in preaching outside. He urged:

[787] *First Report of the Open-Air Mission* (1854) pp.3-5.

[788] Ibid., p.7.

[789] *Second Annual Report of the Open-Air Mission* (1855) p.3.

[790] *The Open-Air Mission Third Annual Report* (1857) p.9.

[791] *Second Annual Report of the Open-Air Mission* (1855) p.5.

[792] R. Roy, "'*Go out Quickly', 'into the Streets and Lanes of the City*'" (1855) p.3 and *Second Annual Report of the Open-Air Mission* (1855) pp.5-6.

[793] R. Roy, "'*Go out Quickly', 'into the Streets and Lanes of the City*'" (1855) p.1.

[794] Ibid., p.4.

[795] Ibid., p.1.

"Is this a time to wait till [the people] come to our empty churches? You stand and call from the pulpit, but where are they sitting all the while?"[796] MacGregor explained that the Mission was moving from the idea of drawing together a worshipping congregation in the streets. Instead, it aimed to attract a listening crowd. It perceived that there was no need to sing hymns; prayer was only to be briefly employed to solemnise the proceedings. MacGregor suggested that the way to start was "In a crowded alley or thoroughfare, converse with some idle men, or careless children, or gossiping loungers. Read the word, and begin 'open-air *speaking*'. Don't call it 'preaching'".[797] He found that though the atonement was under attack in church and intellectual circles, in the streets "no instance has been observed where the doctrine of the atonement by Christ has been openly questioned. Its mercy and justice seem to satisfy the longings of mankind." It was the doctrine "of the Fall and sinfulness of man, when plainly stated", that "excited more than any other doctrine the rancour of the wicked".[798]

The commitment to open-air preaching was not limited to London, but swiftly spread across the land.[799] It was helped by publicity from Horace Mann's official report on *Religious Worship in England and Wales* (1854). Mann regarded the time as one of "terrible emergency" because of the masses who never attended church.[800] He also observed that the Mormons were out and about and making headway across the land.[801] To Mann, open-air preaching by Christians offered a solution to both problems.[802] John MacGregor also used the sight of Mormons on

[796] Ibid. It had been first published in the *Record* in March 1855, over 17,000 being quickly produced, and a cheaper edition was also published, see *Second Annual Report of the Open-Air Mission* (1855) p.6.

[797] Author's italics. R. Roy, "'*Go out Quickly', 'into the Streets and Lanes of the City*'" (1855) p.3.

[798] Ibid., p.2.

[799] For John Hambleton's success in the open air at Liverpool at this time, see J. Hambleton, *Buds, Blossoms, and Fruits of the Revival* (N.D.) pp.10–14. See also G. Green, *Reginald Radcliffe: The Liverpool Solicitor* (2009) p.10.

[800] H. Mann, *Religious Worship in England and Wales* (1854) p.97.

[801] On the state of Mormonism in England and Wales, in the early 1850s, see ibid., p.52. See also *The Open-Air Mission Third Annual Report* (1856) p.7. The vigour of the Mormons caused the London City Mission considerable distress, see D.M. Lewis, *Lighten their Darkness* (1986) pp.224-225.

[802] H. Mann, *Religious Worship in England and Wales* (1854) pp.96-98.

a Sunday afternoon – exhorting and giving out tracts – as a reason for Christians doing likewise.[803] An institutional response to these issues was required from the Church of England and the evangelical Sumner brothers, as Archbishop of Canterbury and Bishop of Winchester, gave their assent.[804] In London in 1856 William Duncan Long, incumbent of St Paul's Long Lane Bermondsey, preached in the neighbouring streets – dark with poverty and crime – and, in doing so, trained up his Scripture reader, Gawin Kirkham, later a very effective open-air preacher. All the same, the clergy generally saw open-air preaching as a role for the laity. They, other than evangelical clergy, were too busy. Therefore, many were shocked when in 1857 Archibald Tait, the Bishop of London (and future Archbishop of Canterbury) and a Broad Churchman, preached in the open-air. Others followed suit, often with great result. For instance, in the late 1850s, Robert Maguire, the rector of St James, Clerkenwell, preached at Clerkenwell Green in the summer months after the Sunday evening service. Attendances began with a couple of hundred and "gradually augmented to over 2,000". On a Monday evening, Maguire preached on different streets to congregations averaging 700, while a curate preached at the east-end of the parish.[805] In his work, he was supported by members of the Open-Air Mission, handing out publicity bills.[806]

In 1858, under the "authority of the Bishop of London, and the patronage of the Lord Mayor of London", clergymen preached at the Royal Exchange every Sunday evening to large congregations. The Lord Mayor attended to encourage these "devoted men".[807] Thus, it was said of John MacGregor, the Open-Air Mission's founder, that he found open-air preaching "practised feebly, fitfully, and, too often, unwisely, and left it furnished with well-defined and accurate laws; he found it largely the object of the Church's averted gaze and left it, when at length his sacred trust and testimony were fulfilled, the recognised and the indispensable adjunct of its ministry among the multitude".[808]

[803] R. Roy, "'*Go out Quickly', 'into the Streets and Lanes of the City*'" (1855) p.2.
[804] *Second Annual Report of the Open-Air Mission* (1855) p.5.
[805] R. Maguire, *Pastoral Letter Addressed to the Congregation of St James's, Clerkenwell* (1859) p.8.
[806] *The Open-Air Mission Fourth Annual Report* (1857) p.13.
[807] "Special Services", in *The British Evangelist*, August 1858 p.65.
[808] F. Cockrem, *Gawin Kirkham* (N.D.) pp.47-48.

The members of the Open-Air Mission went wherever crowds assembled, such as race courses, fairs and places of execution. They travelled to county districts only on a Monday to Saturday and, if in town, walked to their mission engagements so that they kept no-one from attending church.[809] They preached, handed-out tracts and engaged in conversation with anyone who would listen. At the Epsom Derby, "All the sellers of sham jewellery were conversed with privately" and an array of other moral issues were tackled.[810] When Gawin Kirkham, Secretary of the Open-Air Mission, went north to the hard pressed cotton workers of Preston, he took funds he had collected to meet their needs – as well as intending "to tell of the Bread that would not perish".[811] The response to their work was unpredictable. There were opponents, "in order: the Romanist, the Mormonite, the Communist, Sceptic, infidel, Secularist, and the (self-styled) Teetotaller" (moralist).[812] They found that the best way of dealing with persecutions, was to carry on; it soon died away, once it was realised that it was of no avail.[813] John MacGregor recorded being hit by those who threw "mud, cabbage stalks, stones and oyster shells...Still many heard and thanked us".[814] At the races, one member was imprisoned, but the populace demanded, and got, his release.[815] At another racecourse, "Hardly one in fifty would take the tracts."[816] Nevertheless, there could be great openness. On Good Friday 1857,

[809] Ibid., p.131.

[810] Ibid., pp.52-54.

[811] Ibid., p.55.

[812] *"Street Sceptics"*, in the Theological Tracts binding of the British Library, July 1857 p.1. See also G.H. Pike, *Beneath the Blue Sky* (1888) pp.285-286.

[813] Ibid., p.158.

[814] A.J. Greenbank, *'This is the Lord's Doing': The Open-Air Mission 1853-2003* (2003) p.8. Others suffered sticks, whips, flour that made them as white as a miller and the odd stone that drew blood, see F. Cochrem, *Gawin Kirkham* (N.D.) p.93. At Liverpool John Hambleton had the experience of someone trying to set his open Bible alight and "had many narrow experiences from the fury of angry mobs", see E.H.B., *The Converted Actor* (N.D.) pp.58 and 61-62.

[815] *Street Sceptics,* in the Theological Tracts binding of the British Library, July 1857 p.4. Others, like the leading lay evangelists Reginald Radcliffe and Richard Weaver, spent a night in the cells when their listeners at Chester race track did not like their message, see J. Radcliffe, *Recollections of Reginald Radcliffe* (N.D.) p.23. Radcliffe's experience and those with him had been no better when they preached and distributed literature at Liverpool's races, see G. Green, *Reginald Radcliffe: The Liverpool Solicitor* (2009) pp.10-11.

[816] F. Cockrem, *Gawin Kirkham* (N.D.) p.92.

members of the Open-Air Mission outside Crystal Palace gave away 8,000 tracts and papers. Not 20 people refused them and hundreds gave thanks.[817]

However, as the commitment to open-air preaching spread to denominations previously resistant to it, those denominations whose growth is linked to it began to reject it. William Booth left the Methodists because he wanted the career of an itinerant evangelist and they would not sanction it. They closed the door of their chapels to him. Another Methodist minister who had learnt the art of preaching in the open-air was Thomas Champness. He would lay the foundations of Cliff College, and, by doing so, kept alive the Methodist tradition of vigorous evangelistic preaching among the laity.[818] The Congregationalists also became less enamoured of itinerant preaching, as they sought "respectability" towards the end of our period.

4.13.10 *Fighting the 'demon' drink and sexual immorality*

The London City Mission appealed for funds because "the gin palaces are multiplying around us, [and] licentiousness abounds?"[819] Baptist Noel, perhaps the leading preacher of his era, thought drink robbed a man of his "furniture, his children of their food...inspiring him with ferocious malice against the unhappy mother who complains of his unnatural selfishness". It also destroyed health, created despondency, delirium and insanity and was a sure road to destitution. It led a man "to avoid all the means of grace".[820] Men fought "with men, and women with women, till the clothes are torn from their backs".[821] In the 1830s a number of temperance associations started, although many ridiculed those involved.[822] In 1847 the Band of Hope was founded to teach

[817] *Street Sceptics*, in the Theological Tracts binding of the British Library, July 1857 p.4. The Crystal Palace seems to have been a prime place for tract distribution and for engaging passers-by in conversation. For the experience of the London City Mission, see I. Howat and J. Nicholls, *Streets Paved with Gold* (2003) pp.122-123.

[818] J.I. Brice, *The Crowd for Christ* (1934) p.19.

[819] *Second Report of the London City Mission* (1836) p.4. Intemperance and sexual immorality were just as much an issue in rural Scotand, see *The Life of James McCosh* (1896) (W.M. Sloane (ed.)) pp.17-19.

[820] B.W. Noel, *The State of the Metropolis Considered* (1835) (3rd ed.) p.16.

[821] Ibid., p.18.

[822] Ibid., p.28.

temperance to children. It was an immediate success. Nevertheless, in 1856, a survey found that on one Sabbath nearly two-thirds of the men, women and children, of a town of 15,000, visited its 61 beer-shops or public houses.[823] A year before, in the notorious St Giles area of London, a London City Missioner "ascertained that two-thirds of the poverty, misery, crime, and disease" observed were "produced by the vice of intemperance".[824]

Many specialist evangelical missions were established to help those cast off by society as adulterers, or as the victims of seducers – and to reclaim prostitutes. For example, the London Female Mission, established in 1836 – another David Nasmith foundation – sought to restore the fallen and to "guard the *innocent* from those dangers to which the young female is eminently exposed in the vicinity of London".[825] Young girls of few means coming to the city were especially vulnerable and homes were established for them. Charity sermons were preached to raise funds for the new organisation – and in them no mercy was given to males who "regard females of a certain class in no other light than as the instruments of gratifying their basest desires".[826] The preachers thundered against those for whom "Seduction has become a trade, conducted with regularity, and with business tact".[827] The congregations were not allowed to wallow in their own self-righteousness, but were reminded "What is the case of the women taken in adultery, but a general personification of your own? Caught in the very act and career of sin – in friendship with the world, which is adultery against God – arraigned for judgment and condemnation – rescued from death and hell by the imposition of Christ."[828] By December 1845 the London Female Mission had helped 1,661 females "amid many difficulties and much discouragement, in the face of much slander, opposition and jealousies".[829] It was also

823 "On the Progress of True Religion Amongst our Home Population", in 56 *The Christian Observer for the Year 1856* (1856) p.152.

824 L.N.R., *The Missing Link* (1859) p.5.

825 Author's italics. P. Hall, *The Woman Taken in Adultery* (1837) pp.6-7.

826 E.N. Kirk, *A Sermon Preached at Islington Chapel on Behalf of The London Female Mission* (1837) p.5.

827 Ibid.

828 P. Hall, *The Woman Taken in Adultery* (1837) p.8.

829 "Operations of the London Female Record", in *The Female Mission Record*, December 1845 p.134.

advising the readership of its monthly journal on how to treat servants with "fairness and honour".[830]

The mission organisations and evangelists targeted members of the working and agricultural labouring classes who lived together outside marriage.[831] The Scripture reader working in the East End of London, whose work we have already met, between 1847 and 1853 persuaded 20 persons 'living in sin' to get married.[832] In 1855, the Annual Report of the London City Mission stated that its agents had persuaded no less than 479 persons living together to marry – this being 26 more than the year before.[833] Other Christian organisations, such as the Lock Asylum for the Reception of Penitent Female Patients, sought to provide accommodation, training and religious help to those cured of venereal disease, but who otherwise would be forced on to the streets. The results of this work were often disappointing, but "a very small number" were brought to "true repentance and a Christian life".[834]

4.13.11 *Working men's education develops*

In the 1820s, mechanics institutes, teaching technical subjects to the artisans and working classes, spread across the land. Thomas Chalmers and other clergy encouraged them – not so much for their religious teaching, but because they provided an "affinity to the upper classes of life in mental cultivation...an aspiration after greater things".[835] In 1852, an attempt was made to give greater religious input to working men's education, with the launch of the Working Men's Educational Union. Among its Vice-Presidents was Thomas Hankey, the Governor of the Bank of England.

The object of the Working Men's Educational Union was the "elevation of the working classes, as it regards their physical, intellectual, moral and religious condition".[836] It believed that men trained in these

[830] "Our Servants", in *The Female Mission Record,* March 1845 p.30.

[831] I.C. Watson, *The Life Story of Thomas Langton of Malton* (1896) p.29.

[832] "Tenth Report of the Church of England Scripture Readers' Association", in 1 *The Scripture Readers' Journal* (1853-6) p.180.

[833] D.M. Lewis, *Lighten their Darkness* (1986) p.129.

[834] D.I. Williams, *The London Lock* (N.D.) pp.57-58.

[835] T. Chalmers, *The Christian and Civic Economy of Large Towns* (1826) vol.3, pp.383-384.

[836] *The First Annual Report of the Working Men's Union* (1853) p.1.

areas, even "men of the roughest exterior and of brutalised habits are susceptible of polish and capable of transformation".[837] To this end, it organised lectures "imbued with a sound Christian spirit",[838] to act as a stepping stone to an introduction to the faith. For instance, early lectures were on Nineveh and Assyria, the solar system and human physiology in relation to health.[839]

Its first year's work was a great success – one estimate of attendances at the lectures put them at nearly a quarter of a million people.[840] By the fourth year of its operation, estimated attendances at its lectures numbered 2,105,925.[841] Portions of the secular press were alarmed and regularly attacked the lectures. By 1860, the Society could deliver lectures on 500 topics, which came with "cloth wall" sheets to hang up on walls, by way of illustration.[842] Evangelicals were also the driving force behind the establishment of many lending libraries.[843] The Working Men's Educational Union had the conviction that, once the working classes had developed a taste for literary employments, "libraries will follow".[844] Sometimes the borrower, instead of asking for a novel like *Uncle Tom's Cabin,* asked at the last minute for a Bible, with remarkable results. Such was the Christian origin of the first of Ellen Ranyard's women's workers.[845]

[837] Ibid., p.40.

[838] "Court of Queen's Bench, Westminster, Nov. 22", in *The Times,* 23 November 1855.

[839] *The First Annual Report of the Working Men's Union* (1853) p.25. Some lecture topics were political – such as, "Ought we to ask for the ballot?" and another, "The voluntary principle, or an establishment – which?" These turned out to be expensive for the Working Men's Educational Union – as, by delivering them, it lost exemption from the poor-rates, see "Court of Queen's Bench, Westminster, Nov. 22", in *The Times*, 23 November 1855.

[840] *The First Annual Report of the Working Men's Union* (1853) p.24.

[841] *The Fourth Annual Report of the Working Men's Union* (1856) p.14.

[842] See generally D.M. Lewis, *Lighten their Darkness* (1986) pp.225-229. The use of illustrations and diagrams to illustrate lectures was, from the beginning, fundamental to the work of the Working Men's Educational Union – in order to make the lectures "Popular, entertaining and instructive", see *The First Annual Report of the Working Men's Union* (1853) p.9. Unexpectedly, they led to lectures for the deaf and dumb, see ibid., p.34.

[843] W.J. Conybeare, *Essays Ecclesiastical and Social* (1855) p.69.

[844] *The First Annual Report of the Working Men's Union* (1853) p.35.

[845] E. Platt, *The Story of the Ranyard Mission 1857-1937* (1937) p.15.

4.13.12 *The adult school movement emerges*

The adult school movement catered for both men and women. In embryonic form, it consisted of isolated adult Sunday schools for "Bible reading and instruction in the secular arts of writing and arithmetic".[846] In 1845, a work was begun by Joseph Sturge in Birmingham which sparked the adult school movement under the leadership of William White. White received strong assistance from the Quakers who, after a period of "comparative isolation", were returning to "this troublesome world".[847] Elements of them were reported to hold to evangelical doctrines.[848] Individual agents of the mission societies might also teach reading to those they visited so that, after they left, the Scriptures could be read.[849]

4.13.13 *A model town*

In 1853, Titus Salt's model town, Saltaire,[850] was opened. It embodied "on a splendid scale those plans for the religious, social, physical and intellectual improvement of the people".[851] Salt's milling business had previously been in nearby Bradford, but it was overcrowded, smoky and polluted. He had the belief that showing Christian sympathy for the needy would lead to their religious and moral improvement.

Salt was a Congregationalist. However, his model town, as well as having a splendid Congregational church, had Wesleyan and Primitive Methodist chapels, together with a room for the Swedenborgians (an unorthodox religious group, originating in Sweden). Nearby, there were Anglican and Roman Catholic places of worship.[852]

4.14 Fighting the failings of society and developing capitalism

As we have seen, William Wilberforce thought that Christian social principles laid the basis for a flourishing economy – and laboured to bring them about. The nation's sins threatened the judgment of God and national decline. Wilberforce, though, was not alone in his social

[846] See generally J.W. Rowntree and H.B. Binns, *A History of the Adult School Movement* (1985) pp.10-14.
[847] Ibid., p.14.
[848] B.W. Noel, *The State of the Metropolis Considered* (1835) (3rd ed.) p.5.
[849] *Second Report of the London City Mission* (1836) p.16.
[850] Today it is a UNESCO World Heritage Site.
[851] *Balgarnie's Salt* (2003) (Barlo and D. Shaw (eds)) p.87.
[852] Ibid., p.112.

concern. In 1807, a group of Christians associated with the Moorfields Tabernacle established the Aged Pilgrim's Society to provide pensions for elderly Christians who had "spent a laborious life in honest poverty".[853] The pages of *The Christian Observer* testify to its concern to eradicate sin in human working conditions, such as the use of climbing boys to sweep chimneys.[854]

North of the border, Thomas Chalmers worked first in his rural parish of Kilmany, and then in Glasgow, to remove pauperism. He sought to do so through encouraging self-help, education and community kindness – with some degree of success.[855] His book, *The Christian and Civic Economy of Large Towns*, includes an extensive analysis of the needs of the poor and the remedies that might be employed to ameliorate their position, including the establishment of a poor peoples' savings bank. It set out the means "to organise the entire British nation into a godly commonwealth of stable Christian communities".[856] He also wrote *The Application of Christianity to the Commercial and Ordinary Affairs of Life* (1820), which quickly went through many editions. In this he observed that "the spirit of enterprise… beyond the moderation of the New Testament…is sure, at length, to visit every country, where it operates with the recoil of all those calamities, which, in the shape of beggared capitalists, and unemployed operatives, and dreary intervals of bankruptcy and alarm, are observed to follow a season of overdone speculation".[857] Chalmers' social ideals had important similarities with those of Robert Owen, although Owen placed less emphasis on private property, while Chalmers placed more emphasis on communal benevolence.[858]

By the mid-1840s evangelical leaders, such as Baptist Noel, were justifiably proud of the "very distinguished place among the nations of

[853] B.H. Edwards, *When Evangelicals Care* (2017) p.27.

[854] "To the Editor of the Christian Observer", in 16 *The Christian Observer for the Year 1817* (1818) p.89.

[855] S.J. Brown, *Thomas Chalmers and the Godly Commonwealth in Scotland* (1982) pp.142-144.

[856] Ibid., p.144.

[857] T. Chalmers, *The Application of Christianity to the Commercial and Ordinary Affairs of Life* (1820) pp.v-vi.

[858] S.J. Brown, *Thomas Chalmers and the Godly Commonwealth in Scotland* (1982) pp.148-151.

the earth" that their country now held. Yet he was increasingly concerned by "a phenomenon some-what mysterious and exceedingly painful – an ever-increasing capital, together with a deepening pauperism".[859] Speaking to an audience of young men in London, he noted that the agricultural class was "exceedingly ill paid, ill lodged, and ill fed". In the cotton industry, workers were poorly paid and its factories relied too much on child labour. In the mines, "women and children laboured in subterranean darkness", but they either laboured below ground or starved. Hardware manufacture manifested the same addiction to child labour and poor pay. In the shops, young men suffered from working late hours, severely damaging their minds, morals and health. The sufferings of young women, hurried to a "premature grave" by trying to earn a living from needlework, were recorded. To these evils, he added those who find no employment on any terms.[860] Baptist Noel suggested how his audience could gain influence to eradicate such evils. Lord Shaftesbury actively sought to do so. Such work was part of the task to which God called Christians – nevertheless, he would have agreed with Thomas Chalmers when he said "I should count the salvation of a single soul of more value than the deliverance of a whole empire from pauperism".[861]

4.15 Reaching the Jews

The Jewish race always had a special claim on the gospel. St Paul had written of the gospel that "it is the power of God that brings salvation to everyone who believes: first to the Jew then to the Gentile".[862] In 1808, the first British society dedicated to taking the gospel to the Jews was established by the Hebrew Joseph Samuel C.F. Frey. Founded as an interdenominational society with the name of the London Society for Promoting Christianity Amongst the Jews, it soon became an exclusively Anglican body operating under the name of the Church Missions to Jews.[863] Under the scholarly Alexander McCaul it became "one of the

[859] B.W. Noel, "On the Means of Acquiring Influence", in *The Claims of Missions Upon the Young Men of England* (1846) p.125.

[860] Ibid., pp.125-127.

[861] S.J. Brown, *Thomas Chalmers and the Godly Commonwealth in Scotland* (1982) p.138.

[862] Romans 1:16.

[863] F.J. Exley "*Our Hearts Desire*" (1942) pp.12-13.

foremost of our Church institutions".[864] In London, "great numbers of Jews were attracted, especially at the seasons of the great festivals, by his preaching".[865] For poor inquirers the Jewish Operative Converts' Institution was founded.[866]

In Scotland, there was a deeper concern for the conversion of the Jews, which led to the establishment, in 1838, of the Church of Scotland's Committee for the Conversion of the Jews. Scotland's interest in the topic stimulated England's. In 1842 the interdenominational British Society for the Propagation of the Gospel Among the Jews was founded. The original focus of the Society's work was "London and the larger towns of the United Kingdom".[867] Most of the missionaries were Hebrew Christians; many were converts of the Society.[868]

4.16 Reaching the young for Christ

In the first half of the nineteenth century, it was religion that was the driver of education at all levels. At a great public school like St Paul's, Captain R.N. Sanderson ended his 1852 Commemoration Address, in praise of Dean Colet, by reflecting that "education is not merely practical instruction, nor the acquisition of useful or elegant accomplishments... but, religious and moral training of the soul of man, for its progress through the essentials of this world to its eternity in the next".[869] A year earlier, the government's report into education concluded that "Popular education may be said to be almost entirely the creation of the present century".[870] It was "religious zeal to which this great advance was almost wholly due".[871] Some "philosophers", with their "most brilliant and popular treatises on education", decried this.[872] They thought the mind should be kept free of "Prepositions". However, those like Hannah More thought such individuals simply endeavoured "to destroy Christianity"

[864] J.B. McCaul, *A Memorial Sketch of the Rev. Alexander McCaul* (1863) p.9.
[865] Ibid., p.12.
[866] Ibid., p.9.
[867] Ibid., p.23.
[868] Ibid., pp.26 and 29.
[869] R.N. Sanderson, *Commemoration Address in Praise of Dean Colet* (1852) p.15.
[870] H. Mann, *Education in Great Britain* (1854) p.11.
[871] Ibid., p.13.
[872] H. More, *"Strictures on the Modern System of Female Education"* (1799) vol.1, p.223, in *Strictures on Female Education* (1995).

by discouraging the religious education of youth,[873] and got on with the work embracing all classes. Chalmers made the point that one reason why so many did not attend church in cities like Glasgow, in comparison with the country parishes, was that the provision for religious instruction in the cities had not kept pace with their population growth.[874] In his Glasgow parish, he vigorously set about remedying this deficiency.[875]

In Southwark, William Cadman's work in reaching his parish through schools became a model.[876] In 1852 he took on St George's Church Borough and a congregation on the first Sunday of 25. His parish numbered 30,000. He began its spiritual renewal by dividing it into districts and establishing a ragged or national school in each district. Each day, the schoolchildren committed to memory a text of Scripture; church visitors were then able to visit the homes where these texts were carried and increased attendance of parents at religious services followed.

4.16.1 *Reaching and educating the poor through Sunday schools*

From the early 1800s, across the nation, Sunday school work developed. For example, at Worcester in 1800 the Dissenters' Sunday school started at 9 am and finished at 5 pm. Between lessons, the children joined the morning and afternoon services. To attend, a scholar required a recommendation from a member of the Evangelistic Society and five shillings annually – often paid by a member of that society. A contemporary attributed the rescue of the nation from revolution to "a singular act of divine providence" in raising up Sunday schools, whether

[873] Ibid., p.224.

[874] Chalmers identified the schools of Scotland as an example of an apparatus for the transmission of Christianity. They were instituted when the "religious spirit" ran high and when the gospel was abandoned, the schools kept alive "an intelligence, and an enlargement, and a reflective sobriety," see T. Chalmers, *The Christian and Civic Economy of Large Towns* (1821) vol.1, p.22. When the spirit reappeared, the schools provided, in Chalmers's view, a "more effectual door of access for it through the families of that land which has the apparatus, than of that land which has it not," see ibid., p.23. For details of the work to extend schooling in Scotland in the first half of the nineteenth century, see A.L. Drummond and J. Bulloch, *The Scottish Church 1688-1843* (1973) pp.186-189.

[875] S.J. Brown, *Thomas Chalmers and the Godly Commonwealth in Scotland* (1982) pp.135-137.

[876] W. Cadman, "Pastoral Visitation", in *Homiletical and Pastoral Lectures* (1879) pp.311-331 and L.E. Shelford, *A Memorial of the Rev. William Cadman* (1899) pp.33-52.

Methodist, Church of England or of whatever denomination.[877] However, the work could be misunderstood and teachers in the schools could be unfairly vilified. For instance, during the war with France, the Worcester Dissenters' Sunday school was accused of being a seminary of "sedition and atheism".[878] Teaching poor children to read and write was considered by some to be misconceived and likely to lead them to read Tom Paine and develop ideas above their station. Some High Churchmen attacked Sunday schools run by Church evangelicals as places for promoting Methodism or Nonconformity.[879]

A major landmark in Sunday school work was the establishment in 1803 of the Sunday School Union at Rowland Hill's Surrey Chapel. This sought to stimulate and encourage the religious education of youth, to improve methods of instruction and to promote the opening of new schools. Now, the Sunday school movement took on the colouring of a voluntary evangelical movement. It was a sign "of the kingdom of Christ making sensible advances".[880] In North Wales, Thomas Charles recorded that through the day schools and Sunday schools and preaching, "the spread of divine knowledge is become universal".[881] The role of Sunday schools was to prepare the minds of the young "to admit and feel the power of the truth". It was observed that for those whose minds had been so prepared, when the truth was "applied with unwonted force to the conscience, it is usually with the happiest results".[882] Sunday schools were to become "nurseries" in which "our revivals begin".[883] For example, the revival at Worcester in 1858 began in its Sunday school.[884]

For their Sunday school teaching in "cellars pestilent with fever", even those who loathed Calvinists thought them the "salt of this world".[885]

[877] J. Brewster, *A Secular Essay* (1802) p.130. See also P.B. Cliff, *The Rise and Development of the Sunday School Movement in England 1780-1980* (1986) p.74.
[878] G. Osborn, *A Sermon Preached in Angel Street Meeting House, Worcester for the Benefit of Sunday Schools* (1801) p.7.
[879] M.J. Quinlan, *Victorian Prelude* (1941) pp.162-163.
[880] R. Hall, *Strictures on a Work, Intitled, "Zeal Without Innovation"* (1809) p.21.
[881] M. Bruen, *History of Revivals of Religion in the British Isles* (1836) p.118.
[882] A. Reed and J. Matheson, *A Narrative of the Visit to the American Churches by the Deputation from the Congregational Union of England and Wales* (Jackson and Walford (1835)) vol.2, p.10.
[883] R. Carwardine, *Transatlantic Revivalism* (2006) p.160.
[884] T. Whitehouse, "One Hundred and Sixteen Conversions at Worcester", in *The Revivalist* (1858) p.121.
[885] W.J. Conybeare, *Essays Ecclesiastical and Social* (1855) p.99.

By the second decade of the nineteenth century, so effective were these schools that some observers suggested that if rich parents did not instruct their children they would "see them out-stripped in the noblest of all kinds of knowledge by the children of the poor".[886] Massive operations evolved. For instance, in February 1845 the Surrey Chapel looked after a group of schools and missions in Southwark numbering 4,441 children and 546 teachers.[887] Nationally, by 1851 there were 2.4 million Sunday scholars, with 1.8 million attending each week – out of a population under 10 of 4,440,000. Sunday school teachers numbered 250,000.[888] Many a young man was converted through teaching Sunday school – and many more who taught found it kept them from temptation and strengthened them in holiness.[889] All the same, "there were constant complaints that no more than 10 or 20 per cent of Sunday scholars ever became church members".[890] However some, like James Flanagan, partly through memorising Bible verses in Sunday school, such as John 3:16, and later reading the Bible given to him there, were, in later life, converted.[891] In our next period, Flanagan became a well-known Primitive Methodist, whose successful evangelistic ministry extended into the First World War.

4.16.2 *Mutual improvement societies*

From the 1840s, once children became too old for Sunday schools, the chapels sought the interest of young people through mutual improvement societies.[892] These brought together their members for the discussion and reading of literary matters, backed up with an appropriate library, or "classes in writing, grammar, geography, algebra, geometry and

[886] D. Bogue and J. Bennett, *History of Dissenters, from the Revolution in 1688, to the Year 1808* (1812) vol.4, p.352.

[887] C. Binfield, *George Williams and the Y.M.C.A.* (1973) p.102.

[888] H. Mann, *Religious Worship in England and Wales* (1854) p.100. Some recent estimates put the figure higher at 2.941 million children by 1850, see P. Brierley, *UK Church Statistics 2005-2015* (2011) section 14.4, p.7.

[889] B.W. Noel, "On the Means of Acquiring Influence", in *The Claims of Missions Upon the Young Men of England* (1846) pp.139-140.

[890] M.R. Watts, *The Dissenters* (2015) vol.3, p.174.

[891] R.W. Russell, *The Life of James Flanagan* (1920) pp.5 and 18. Flanagan made great use of John 3:16, in his own evangelistic ministry, referring to it in many conversions, see generally J. Flanagan, *The Romance of Evangelism* (1902).

[892] M.R. Watts, *The Dissenters* (2015) vol.3, pp.174-175.

book keeping".[893] For Wesleyan Methodists, attendance at it might be an acceptable alternative to the class meeting.[894]

4.16.3 ***Reaching and educating the inner-city poor through ragged schools***

As we have seen before, the ragged school movement focussed on the exceptionally poor of the inner cities. The first such schools emerged through the charitable impulse of individuals working independently across the nation. However, it was the London City Mission that first coined the term. In 1835, it started its first ragged school. Ragged schools taught reading and writing, with the Bible as the text. Over time, history and geography could be added for the more adept. Standards were not necessarily high but, because of the background of the children, the work often led into providing help with their accommodation, food,[895] holidays and work. Often, a Sunday school added to its work a ragged school and they might share the same teaching staff and buildings. George Williams, the founder of the Young Men's Christian Association ("YMCA"), for example, helped with both.[896]

In 1844, the ragged school movement gained profile and political clout with the foundation of the Ragged School Union. This was mainly an evangelical organisation, chaired by Lord Shaftesbury. The potential scope of the work was huge, but it did not daunt those involved. By 1857, the movement's objective (which was never reached) was stated as providing "a free education, combined with moral and religious instruction"[897] to the estimated 2,861,848 children between the age of 3 and 15 who did not receive any instruction whatsoever.[898] Contemporaries believed that the ignorance of these children was not simply a lack of head knowledge, or reasoning skills, but a "practical ignorance of man's immortal nature and destiny, an ignorance which degrades below the

[893] Ibid., p.175.

[894] Ibid., p.146.

[895] Their provision of food was the example that led to the establishment of school dinners by the Education (Provision of Meals) Act of 1906: for the background, see K. Heasman, *Evangelicals in Action* (1962) p.76.

[896] C. Binfield, *George Williams and the Y.M.C.A.* (1973) pp.101-102.

[897] M. Carpenter, *The Claims of Ragged Schools to Pecuniary Educational Aid* (1859) p.iv. All groups with a Christian background were involved, including, in some areas, the Unitarians: K. Heasman, *Evangelicals in Action* (1962) p.72.

[898] There were an estimated 4,908,690 children in all in this category.

brute creation".[899] There was also a strongly practical justification for ragged schools. Without them, it was feared many children would end up as street children, or in reform institutions, or in prison. One writer calculated that the cost of running a ragged school was one-third or one-quarter of the cost to the state of leaving the children to a life of crime.[900] In London by 1857-1858 the ragged school movement had 102 day schools and 121 evening schools, with 13,979 day scholars and 7,538 evening scholars.[901]

4.16.4 *Reaching and educating the slightly better off*

Charity schools continued. For example, the Kensington School for charity children instructed 22 boys and 11 girls in the Christian religion. They were given bed and board, and completely clothed once a year. The boys were also taught to read, write and to do accounts; the girls to read, write, sew and knit. When they had time free from their lessons, the boys were taught a useful manufacture and the girls domestic skills.[902]

The educational prospects of those children whose parents could afford a small fee and a uniform, were enhanced by the founding, in 1808, of the non-denominational Royal British or Lancasterian System for the Education of the Poor. In 1811, its Anglican counterpart followed – The National Society for Promoting the Education of the Poor. In 1814, the former changed its name to the British and Foreign School Society.[903] These societies aimed at the systematic provision of education across England and Wales – the National Society for Promoting the Education of the Poor wanting to build a Church school in every parish.[904] Some people, such as a future President of the Royal Society, thought that giving education to the poor "would be prejudicial to their morals

[899] M. Carpenter, *The Claims of Ragged Schools to Pecuniary Educational Aid* (1859) p.iv-v.

[900] T. Gutherie, *Seed-Time & Harvest of Ragged Schools* (1860) p.167.

[901] M. Carpenter, *The Claims of Ragged Schools to Pecuniary Educational Aid* (1859) p.11.

[902] *An Hymn to be Sung by the Charity Children of Kensington, at their Parish Church, on Sunday, December 15, 1793* in the British Library. For the background, in an earlier period, to the formation of charity schools, see J.A. Thomas, *The Nation's Gospel: Reformation to Revolution* (2017) vol.1, pp.283-285.

[903] See "History of the BFSS", www.bfss.org.uk/about-us/history-of-the-bfss/, accessed 28 April 2017.

[904] H.J. Burgess and P.A. Welsby, *A Short History of the National Society* (1961) p.5.

and happiness: it would teach them to despise their lot in life".[905] The driver for its foundation was the High Church party. It made teaching the national religion the foundation of national education. The "first and chief thing" to be taught to the poor was "the excellent liturgy and catechism provided by our Church".[906] It fiercely opposed teaching non-denominational religion, as its "natural consequence must be to alienate the minds of the people" from the Established Church.[907] Many clergy were deeply involved in the foundation, running and teaching within their parish school.[908] Evangelicals established two colleges to educate and train teachers in the evangelical religion of the Church of England.[909]

These new societies set standards and influenced others operating in the same field. For example, in 1829 the master's mandate at the King's Weigh House Church school was to "instruct the boys in the principles of the Christian religion and teach them the Assembly's Catechism, reading, writing and arithmetic upon the system of the British and Foreign School Society".[910] To meet the numbers needing teaching, the new educational societies adopted the monitor system. The learning environment in the schools of the Societies could be strict, because of the need to educate so many, but the poet Samuel Taylor Coleridge emphasised the need to lead in education by love and imagination.[911]

By 1833 the Church of England ran between 6,000 and 7,000 day-schools, containing half a million pupils – and half of these schools were in union with the National Society for Promoting the Education of the Poor. That year, the work grew as the government gave out grants. To encourage them to give more, Baptist Noel suggested that every £100 spent on moral and religious education saved the country £1,000 in the contemporary equivalent of social security payments, increased police

905 Ibid., p.2.
906 Ibid., p.4.
907 *First Annual Report of the National Society* (1812) p.5. For the High Church onslaught against nonsectarian religion, see M.J. Quinlan, *Victorian Prelude* (1941) pp.167-171.
908 G. Huelin, "Innovation: The National Society 1811-1934", in *Faith in the Future* (1986) p.20.
909 "Evangelical Teachers for Elementary Schools", in *The Record*, 16 January 1919, p.59.
910 E. Kaye, *The History of the King's Weigh House Church* (1968) p.87.
911 See T. Copley, *Black Tom* (2002) pp.118-119.

costs, and in prison-related expenses.[912] By 1846, the Church educated one million day-children in some 17,000 schools and was establishing a number of teacher training colleges.[913] In comparison, by 1850 the British and Foreign School Society had some 200,000 children, the Wesleyan schools 38,000 children, Roman Catholic schools 34,000 children and Congregational schools 6,000 children.[914] However, church work in education was becoming a battleground between those who wanted to secularise education and those who wanted to maintain its religious basis.[915] For example, at St George's Chapel, Kidderminster, the assistant minister preached against those who sought to remove Christian principles from education and who thought that "man needs only intellectual culture to shew him the path of duty and happiness".[916] There were also objections from the Dissenters – who did not want their children taught the Church Catechism and liturgy at their expense via government grants. There were also differences in the National Society for Promoting the Education of the Poor between evangelicals and High Churchmen – which led two or three hundred evangelicals, including Lord Shaftesbury, to leave. In 1853 they set up an alternative to it – the Church Education Society.[917] It soon attracted the support of a number of bishops,[918] but in the long term it did not flourish – and evangelical influence in the National Society for Promoting the Education of the Poor declined.[919]

[912] B.W. Noel, *The State of the Metropolis Considered* (1835) (3rd ed.) p.29.
[913] See W.E. Beck, "The History of the Cheltenham Training College", in *Church and People,* September, 1949 p.132.
[914] H.J. Burgess and P.A. Welsby, *A Short History of the National Society* (1961) p.34. See also H.J. Burgess, *Enterprise in Education* (1958) pp.42-43.
[915] For an excellent summary of the issues, see H.J. Burgess and P.A. Welsby, *A Short History of the National Society* (1961) pp.10-17 and 23-30.
[916] J.A. Baxter, *A Sermon Preached in St George's Chapel, Kidderminster* (1838) p.22.
[917] It was established because it was "imperative that members of the Church of England, who hold in their plain meaning her evangelical articles and formularies should unite to form a society, which shall have for its object: To promote national education on Protestant and Church of England principles, and to diffuse sound opinions on the subject", see Church of England Education Society, *Report of the Committee Adopted at the First Annual Meeting* (1854) p.5.
[918] Church of England Education Society, *Report of the Committee Adopted at the Fifth Annual Meeting* (1858) p.3.
[919] H.J. Burgess, *Enterprise in Education* (1958) pp.142-143.

4.16.5 *Expanding the private schools for the upper and middle classes*
In 1807 Mill Hill was established by Independents to provide the best of private school education without exposure to the traditions of the Church of England.[920] Other schools for Congregationalists followed, such as Caterham (1811), Silcoates (1820) and Taunton (1847).

The members of the Clapham Sect were generally against sending their children to public school[921] but, towards the end of our period, many public schools were established for the burgeoning middle classes. Between 1841 and 1881, a new one opened every year. All parties of the Established Church established them, their most energetic founder being the Anglo-Catholic Nathaniel Woodward, whose work started with Lancing College and continues today through the Woodward Schools.[922]

The new schools were influenced by the educational programme of Thomas Arnold, headmaster of Rugby from 1828. "He sought to produce Christians, gentlemen, and scholars – and in that order",[923] but his views on what made a Christian were moulded by German biblical criticism. Much of Arnold's preaching was along catechetical lines,[924] although from his time at Oxford he had doubts about the clauses on hell in the Athanasian Creed and certain matters related to the Trinity.[925] However, he preached that "Christ died for a proper sacrifice for sin".[926] He willingly referred in his sermons in Rugby Chapel to the need for an individual to be "born again" and to be "reconciled to God", if he was to be converted. Conversion was proved by "a manifest disposition to avoid sin, there we may be sure that Christ's Spirit has worked".[927] John Keble had counselled Arnold, when he had his doubts at Oxford about certain tenets of orthodoxy, to "pursue a good diet, practical piety, family, and parish life as the source of genuine cure for significant

[920] *Congregational Year Book* (1860) p.270.
[921] For example, see "The Late Lord Macaulay", in *The Record*, 2 January 1860, p.3.
[922] See generally K. Harris, *Evangelicals and Education* (2004).
[923] Commission on Religious Education in Schools, *The Fourth R* (1970) p.5.
[924] See H.O. Old, *The Reading and Preaching of the Scriptures in the Worship of the Christian Church* (2007) vol.6, pp.350-353.
[925] F.M. Turner, *John Henry Newman* (2002) pp.72-73.
[926] T. Arnold, *Sermons by Thomas Arnold* (1878) (Mrs W.E. Forster (ed.)) vol.4, p.184. For a recent appraisal of Arnold's theology, see T. Copley, *Black Tom* (2002) pp.183-251.
[927] T. Arnold, *Sermons by Thomas Arnold* (1878) (Mrs W.E. Forster (ed.)) vol.6, pp.154-155.

religious questioning".[928] Townsend Powell, the curate of Stretton-upon-Dunsmore in Warwickshire, observed that, while Arnold's sermons "appear to breathe the purest spirit of the gospel", in truth they undermine "the very foundations of the Christian faith".[929] Townsend Powell's strictures extended to Arnold's suggestion that people were "born Christians", that if a person persuades himself "that he loves God really, and desires to please him, he has no longer any need to regard the written law of God", that the creeds, sacraments and Church discipline could be dispensed with. Townsend Powell added: "Not that it is possible for a moment to entertain the thought that Dr Arnold is an infidel at heart".[930] After Arnold's death, a debate arose as to whether he died trusting in Christ for his salvation.[931] Nevertheless, he left an influential heritage. As biblical criticism took a grip in the last third of the nineteenth century, three Archbishops of Canterbury, Archibald Tait, Edward Benson and Frederick Temple were either his successors as headmaster of Rugby, or taught there.

4.16.6 *The role of governess*

For the education of the children of wealthy parents, there were governesses and tutors, many of whom saw as their role the conversion of their charges. Christian newspapers carried advertisements along the following lines: "To Godly parents. A lady of practical piety, opposed to Tractarianism, wishes to meet a Godly family desiring to bring up their children in the way they should go."[932] Lord Shaftesbury was a child of the nobility, converted by a governess. His parents were uninterested in Christianity.

Towards the end of our period the role of a governess would be pointed in a slightly different direction when the liberal clergyman F.D. Maurice founded Queen's College – a pioneering work in women's education, aimed at training governesses. This became the first institution in the world to award academic qualifications to women. Among Maurice's

[928] F.M. Turner, *John Henry Newman* (2002) p.73.
[929] H.T. Powell, *Liberalism Unveiled* (1830) p.4.
[930] Ibid., p.29.
[931] See S. Minton, *The Evangelicals and "The Edinburgh"* (N.D.) pp.8-9 and W.H.B. Proby, *Annals of the "Low-Church" Party in England* (1888) vol.1, p.389.
[932] W.J. Conybeare, *Essays Ecclesiastical and Social* (1855) p.96.

early students were "Dorothea Beale, the long-time principal of Cheltenham Ladies' College and Frances Mary Buss, founder and first headmistress of North London Collegiate School for Girls".[933]

4.16.7 *Higher education is reformed and expanded*

At the end of the eighteenth century, the religious exercises at Oxford were described as "hasty and irreverent".[934] It was not until the first decade of the nineteenth century that exams – and the "general struggle of personal competition" – were introduced.[935] At Cambridge things were better and, with Charles Simeon at Holy Trinity Church, a centre for the spread of evangelical influence over the youthful existed.[936] By 1826 Daniel Wilson noted "the increased diligence and piety of our students at the universities". The higher standard of preaching, morality and strictness of the divinity exams were all commended.[937] He looked forward with the words, "One generation of pious and devoted candidates for ordination, is the blossom of the next age."[938] In Scotland, at the University of St Andrews, historically a Moderate centre, Thomas Chalmers' arrival to the chair of Moral Philosophy led, within two years, to the comment that "our college seems at present to present an aspect of something similar to that of the University of Oxford in the days of Hervey and Wesley".[939] But elsewhere there were new challenges to the dominance of the Established Church in higher education.

By the late eighteenth century, the challenge of the Dissenting academies was extinguished – but in 1828 a new academic institution was opened in Bloomsbury, London, mainly by free thinkers, including the Utilitarians Jeremy Bentham and James Mill, although the evangelical

933 G.J. Worth, *Macmillian's Magazine, 1859-1907* (2003) p.76.

934 Cited in H.C. Barnard, *A Short History of English Education* (1947) p.29.

935 F.C. Conybeare, *Letters and Exercises of the Elizabethan Schoolmaster John Conybeare* (1905) p.138.

936 Simeon's influence at Cambridge was enhanced by the presence of a number of distinguished evangelicals with university appointments, see J.H. Overton, *The English Church in the Nineteenth Century* (1894) pp.62-66.

937 D. Wilson, "Introductory Essay" to W. Wilberforce, *A Practical View of the Prevailing Religious System of Professed Christians, in the Higher and Middle Classes in This Country, Contrasted with Real Christianity* (1829) pp.l-li.

938 Ibid., p.li.

939 S.J. Brown, *Thomas Chalmers and the Godly Commonwealth in Scotland* (1982) p.168.

Zachary Macaulay was also involved. Thomas Chalmers was offered the chair of Moral Philosophy.[940] It became University College, London. There were no religious tests for entry. Its curriculum was modern and practical. It aimed at the newly emerging middle classes. In London, there was an aggregate of such persons "the like to which exists in no other spot on the surface of the earth".[941] As a counterweight, in 1831 the Church of England opened King's College on the Strand. At the meeting calling for its establishment, a resolution was passed affirming that "while the various branches of literature and science are made the subjects of instruction, it shall be an essential part of the system to imbue the minds of youth with a knowledge of the doctrines and duties of Christianity as inculcated by the United Church of England and Ireland."[942] In 1836 London University was founded – to award degrees to students of a growing number of constituent colleges. Among its alumni were men like the Congregationalists James Brown, R.W. Dale and Newman Hall, and John Clifford of the Baptists – all of whom would take their respective denominations in later years in a liberal direction. In 1832, the Bishop of Durham, Van Mildert, founded the University of Durham, aimed at educating the clergy of the North too poor for the older universities.

4.16.8 *The Young Men's Christian Association is founded*

Another means of reaching the young was through the YMCA, founded in 1844. This grew out of a prayer meeting. Its leading spirit was the draper George Williams, who had been heavily influenced by Finney's *Lectures on Revivals*.[943] Its object was to arouse "converted men in the different drapery establishments in the metropolis to a sense of their obligation and responsibility as Christians in diffusing religious knowledge to those around them".[944] The medium to fulfil this objective included the prayer meeting but the work was combined with social concerns, such as literary lectures and opportunities for physical training. Members of the YMCA were often energetic in their evangelism. For example, in

[940] Ibid., pp.177 and 183.

[941] "State of the Nation", in 6 The *Westminster Review* (1826) p.270.

[942] Cited in H.C. Barnard, *A Short History of English Education* (1947) p.101.

[943] K.J. Hardman, *Charles Grandison Finney* (1990) p.379.

[944] C. Binfield, *George Williams and the Y.M.C.A.* (1973) p.120.

1851, for the Great Exhibition, young men distributed 350,000 tracts concerning eternity in Hyde Park. In the late 1850s YMCA members were "gradually pressing forward" in open-air preaching.[945]

4.17 Women at the spiritual cutting edge

At the beginning of the nineteenth century, Christian observers feared that English women were being led astray by the sexual freedom of the French Revolution. This was a "melancholy prospect for the nation at large", because it was an old observation that, as female "religious conduct and purity of manners increase or diminish, those of men will do the same".[946] By the early 1820s, the general esteem of women had risen through the literary and other endeavours of Hannah More and others[947] – as they responded positively to the encouragement to refrain from luxury and to help differentiate the nation from the French. Ladies of the 'better' classes were known for their practical benevolence, personal generosity and evangelical activity. In 1821 it was thought that at least 10,000 ladies were involved in the work of the Bible associations. They made up most of the auxiliaries collecting subscriptions for Bibles in the towns and villages.[948] Some traditional Churchmen disapproved of these developments. Richard Lloyd wrote, "the *evangelical* piety of the present times...generates a low, vulgar spirit of equality, without a due sense of subordination."[949] In 1841 Lucy Aiken thought that the concern of evangelicals for the poor "had given rise among the ladies to much spiritual pride and self-inflation; much of an imperious, pragmatical meddling habit".[950] Shortly some ladies, inclined towards Tractarianism, would begin to form themselves into distinctive Anglican religious communities to pursue a life of active good works. However,

[945] *The Open-Air Mission Fourth Annual Report* (1857) p.4.

[946] *A Serious Address to the Public, Upon the Present Times: but More Particularly to the Religious Part of it (*1803) p.39.

[947] C.S. Dudley, *An Analysis of the System of the Bible Society* (1821) p.345.

[948] Ibid., p.501 and L. Howsam, "Preface" to *Cheap Bibles* (1991) p.xiv.

[949] Author's italics. R. Lloyd, *Strictures on a Recent Publication Entitled "The Church Her Own Enemy"* (1819) p.120.

[950] *Correspondence of William Edward Channing, D.D. and Lucy Aikin* (1874) (A.L. Le Breton (ed.)) p.398.

they were generally frowned upon as being a manifestation of Roman Catholic practices.[951]

In George Eliot's *Scenes of Clerical Life* (1858), ladies "cut out garments for the poor, distributed tracts, quoted Scripture, and defined the true gospel...teaching at the Sunday school, visiting the poor, and striving after a standard of purity and goodness"[952] – and such a list undervalues them. They also played a central role in house-to-house visitation, made up most of the teachers in ragged schools and, in some of the smaller Methodist groupings, at times made up to 20 per cent of the preachers.[953] Lord Shaftesbury thought Mrs Ranyard of the London Bible and Domestic Female Mission, possessed "directing and controlling administrative powers, such as few statesmen have possessed".[954] Women were also some of the "gifted ones" in the Catholic Apostolic Church. In America, spiritual revival often saw women praying in assemblies[955] and then preaching. In July 1840 Zilpha Elaw arrived from America at London Docks to preach. She was a person of colour[956] and, for a decade, found an active preaching ministry – especially with the Primitive Methodists, but also the Wesleyans. She found Britain less receptive soil than America for the gospel. However, she wrote "I am more justified in saying that my God hath made my ministry a blessing to hundreds of persons; and many who were living in sin and darkness before they saw my coloured face, have risen up to praise the Lord, for having seen my coloured face."[957] Anecdotal evidence suggests that by

[951] S. Mumm, *All Saints Sisters of the Poor* (2001) pp.xi-xiii.

[952] G. Eliot, *Scenes of Clerical Life* (Oxford University Press (1988)) p.228.

[953] M.R. Watts, *The Dissenters* (1995) vol.2, pp.149-150. For one striking example, see J. Paterson, *Richard Weaver's Life Story* (2012) pp.59-60.

[954] E. Hodder, *The Life and Work of the Seventh Earl of Shaftesbury, K.G.* (1887) p.711.

[955] Women praying in mixed assemblies was not seen positively by some members of *The Christian Observer*, see "American revivals", in 28 *The Christian Observer for the Year 1828* (1829) p.480.

[956] Evangelists of ethnic minorities, although unusual in the nineteenth century and thereafter, were not novel in Britain, see D. Killingray, "Black Evangelicals in, Darkest Britain 1770s-1930s", in *British Evangelical Identities Past and Present* (2008) vol.1, pp.128-142. The sight of one preaching at Milnthorpe Market Cross on 6th September 1855 manifested to the mind of the future open air evangelist Gawin Kirkham that "Legitimate attraction…formed an element of effective preaching in the open-air" and the potential of the medium, F. Cockrem, *Gawin Kirkham* (N.D.) p.38.

[957] Cited in N. Scotland, *Apostles of the Spirit and Fire* (2009) p.64. On Elaw, see generally ibid., pp.49-65.

the 1850s two-thirds of the members of the churches were women.[958]

We only have space to mention a few other women of note. We have looked at Hannah More who, through her schools and educational endeavours, encouraged the working classes towards godliness, encouraged ladies to house visitation, provided guidance on family life and appealed to the religious instincts of the nobility. More or her characters modelled the female roles described by George Eliot (see above). If the spread of evangelical religion among the upper classes was primarily through wives and daughters, their first mentor was Hannah More.[959] Later, to provide regular instruction for ladies, Charlotte Elizabeth established *The Christian Lady's Magazine* (1834).[960] This "included theological essays, reviews of serious books and regular articles on politics". She "believed that 'It is the peculiar work of Christianity, wherever it is established, to elevate women from the debased position in which they are elsewhere placed'."[961] Another woman of note is the Quaker Elizabeth Fry, who was involved in prison and other humanitarian reforms. In Fry's work, advancing biblical understanding played an integral part.

Florence Nightingale brought about the possibility of a dedicated female order forming part of the clergy. Nightingale was an Anglican, with a Unitarian background[962] and somewhat unorthodox religious views. In 1850 she visited the Lutheran religious community at Kaiserswerth-am-Rhein in Germany. There, she observed deaconesses working for the sick and the deprived. She published her findings anonymously in *The Institution of Kaiserswerth on the Rhine, for the Practical Training of Deaconesses, etc.* (1851). The work of the Kaiserswerth deaconesses inspired the evangelical William Pennefather to found the Mildmay deaconesses – the forerunners of modern deaconesses (in our next period). On the Tractarian side, the Anglican sisterhoods were also developing their provision of nursing skills.[963]

Two other Christian organisations dedicated to working with women

958 R.W. Dale, *The Life and Letters of J.A. James* (1861) p.545.

959 I. Bradley, *The Call to Seriousness* (1976) p.40.

960 See J.L. Altholz, *The Religious Press in Britain, 1760-1900* (1989) p.47.

961 J. Wolffe, *The Expansion of Evangelicalism* (2006) p.134.

962 She was a granddaughter of William Wilberforce's friend William Smith.

963 S. Mumm, *All Saints Sisters of the Poor* (2001) p.xv.

also put down roots; they would later merge into the Young Women's Christian Association ("YWCA"). In 1855 Lady Kinnaird, with two or three friends, opened a Christian home in London for nurses en-route to, or from, Florence Nightingale's Crimean wartime hospitals. The home was for provincial girls who could pay only moderate fees. It was at first called a Society for the Christian and Domestic Improvement of Young Women and was later joined by others.[964] In the same year, Miss Emma Roberts of Barnet started a group to pray for young women. Miss Roberts soon had a "world-wide object"[965] for her group, which included social concerns. It became known as the Young Women's Christian Association.

The Crimean War made Florence Nightingale a national figure for her nursing work and opened up opportunities for women to play a greater role in society. By following Florence Nightingale to war, "some young women made the really stupendous step of asserting their independence".[966] Furthermore, the service of women in "the Crimean War brought into enduring prominence" their part "in the nation's life, and [their] right to share in its efforts and rewards".[967]

4.18 Evangelicals in the Church of England develop a voice[968]

In 1802 certain members of the Clapham Sect launched a monthly periodical, *The Christian Observer*. Its prospectus noted that "dramatic compositions, novels, tales, newspapers, magazines and reviews" disseminated "doctrines subversive of all morality". It intended to combat these developments by stripping "scepticism and imposture of their artful disguise" and by promoting "the increase of sound theological knowledge".[969] The founders of *The Christian Observer* were loyal

[964] Young Women's Christian Association, *Our Eighty Years* (1935) p.14.
[965] Ibid., p.1.
[966] Ibid., p.8.
[967] Ibid., p.1.
[968] For an excellent introduction to the parties, literature and organisation of the Church of England in the nineteenth century, see K. Harris, *Evangelicals and Education* (2004) pp.11-63.
[969] See page 1 of the Prospectus bound into 1 *The Christian Observer for the Year 1802* (1802). See generally J.N. Pratt, *The Thought of the Evangelical Leaders* (1978) pp.92-94. In response to the flood of infidelity the numbers of the religious press increased fourfold between 1790 and 1825, see J.L. Altholz, *The Religious Press in Britain, 1760-1900* (1989) p.10.

to the Church and intended to defend its doctrines, but to treat other Christian denominations with charity. The individual pieces, including book reviews of a wide range of works touching upon religion, were thoughtful, well-written, often learned and lengthy. By 1813 it met a growing demand and approval.[970] In 1822, *The Christian Observer* noted, with "peculiar satisfaction...the diffusion among the ministers and members of the National Church of sound scriptural principles and personal piety, combined with candour, moderation, intelligence, and good taste, and animated by ardent zeal and unwearied philanthropy".[971] It wished these improvements to be universal. By its 30th anniversary, its editor rejoiced that its pages had been instrumental in "The great increase of pure religion in our own church during the last quarter of a century."[972] By 1834, it was "one of the oldest periodical works extant" – and no episcopal publication was still in circulation that had existed when it began.[973] In Scotland, and partly modelled on it, Scottish evangelicals founded in 1810 *The Edinburgh Christian Instructor*.

To spread Christian learning to all parts of the nation, many other literary and often innovative works appeared, both Anglican and Nonconformist.[974] Josef Altholz, the historian of the religious press, calculated that around 3,000 religious periodicals were published between 1824 and 1900.[975] They included learned quarterly and monthly publications, penny-a-month periodicals such as *The Friendly Visitor* (1819) and the early children's magazine *The Children's Friend* (1824), both edited by the strong Calvinist clergyman Carus Wilson, together with Saturday magazines "and a multitude of other small weekly publications".[976]

Nevertheless, as far as evangelical Anglicans were concerned, the baneful consequences of reading the daily newspapers remained. So, in 1828, *The Record* was established to provide an alternative to them. Its prospectus noted that newspapers were "one of the most dangerous,

[970] "Preface" to 13 *The Christian Observer for the Year 1814* (1815) p.iii.
[971] "Preface" to 20 *The Christian Observer for the Year 1821* (1822) pp.v-vi.
[972] "Preface" to 32 *The Christian Observer for the Year 1832* (1832) p.iii.
[973] "Preface" to 34 *The Christian Observer for the Year 1834* (1834) p.iii.
[974] For an overview of the religious publications of the time, see J.L. Altholz, *The Religious Press in Britain, 1760-1900* (1989).
[975] Ibid., p.2.
[976] "Preface" to 34 *The Christian Observer for the Year 1834* (1834) p.iii.

though perhaps least suspected, publications that can gain admittance into a family". The influence of the newspapers, and especially *The Times*, was acknowledged by all. Robert Owen, writing from a very different perspective, thought their editors were "now the great instructors of the human race".[977] Edward Miall, a Nonconformist, observed that "nothing has exerted more power, in this country, to crush all the holier virtues out of our churches than our newspaper press, metropolitan and provincial". He added that *The Times* manifested an "utter want of virtuous principle" and that all newspapers followed it in this, although their influence was less.[978]

The Record aimed to "furnish a journal of passing events, which shall offer nothing offensive to the eye of decency, or derogatory to the sacred claims of morality and religion."[979] Its first editor explained that he expected to frequently "insist that the good alone are qualified to be free; that liberty to the bad is only a licence to injury, oppression, contention, and every evil work...that, if there is ever to be perfect freedom, there must be perfect virtue".[980] Published on a Tuesday and Friday (later three times a week) and adopting a broadsheet newspaper format, *The Record* included commodity and government bond prices. By 1838, it had "the largest circulation by far of the religious prints".[981] Of its influence in the 1840s onwards, a theological liberal later wrote that "it needed some courage for a clergyman, at least one not belonging to the High Church party, to do what his conscience bade him, if *The Record* said one thing and his conscience another".[982] *The Church of England Newspaper* is its descendant.

Meanwhile, it was recognised that evangelicals in the Church of England needed to meet regularly. The obvious place was London, but they were weak there. In the first third of the century, Gladstone did not believe that they held a single parish west of Temple Bar. Such strength as they had in London lay in the proprietary chapels to which the wealthy held the power of appointment. From the late 1820s evangelical

[977] R. Owen, *The Life of Robert Owen* (1857) vol.1, p.iii.
[978] E. Miall, *The British Churches in Relation to the British People* (1850) pp.302-303.
[979] "Prospectus of '*The Record*'", in *The Record*, 1 January 1828, p.1.
[980] "*The Record*", in *The Record*, 1 January 1828, p.4.
[981] Cited in D.M. Lewis, *Lighten their Darkness* (1986) p.17.
[982] *The Life of Frederick Denison Maurice* (1884) (F. Maurice (ed.)) vol.2, p.371.

Anglicans wanting the truths of the gospel went to hear Baptist Noel at St John's Chapel Bedford Row, Holborn. However, in the north they held St Mary's Islington. Gladstone regarded this as an accident.[983] In 1827 its vicar, Daniel Wilson, established the evangelical Islington Clerical Conference.[984] By 1833 its attendance numbered 50 but in 1863 those attending numbered about 300.[985] It was the largest and most influential of a number of conferences for evangelical clergy. Its strength, or weakness, at any time revealed much about the standing of evangelicalism until the Islington Clerical Conferences ceased in the early 1980s.

4.19 The Nonconformists do the same

The Nonconformists were also committed to new organisations and the religious press. In 1818, *The Congregational Magazine* was founded, which helped to "instil a denominational consciousness" and in the early 1830s the Congregational Union was established "To promote evangelical religion, in connection with the Congregational denomination."[986] Some periodicals were more literary, like *The Eclectic Review* (1805) and the later *The British Quarterly Review* (1845). The former reviewed, monthly, the most noteworthy books, while the latter gave "ample coverage to religious subjects but [devoted] most of the space to literature, science, and especially politics".[987] Other publications were populist, such as *The Christian's Penny Magazine* (1846), with its circulation of over 100,000, or acted as mouthpieces for the leading religious figures of the day.[988]

The most strident Nonconformist publication was *The Nonconformist*, first published on 14 April 1841. Its chief aim was to show that "a national establishment of religion is essentially vicious in its constitution", in order to encourage the severing of the union of Church and state. Edward Miall, its founder, thought that "At present we have government

[983] W.E. Gladstone, *Gleanings of Past Years* (1879) vol.7, p.213. See W.H.B. Proby, *Annals of the "Low-Church" Party in England* (1888) vol.1, pp.343-344.

[984] For the background to the first meeting of the Islington Clerical conference, see D. Bebbington, "The Islington Conference", in *Evangelicalism and the Church of England in the Twentieth Century* (2014) (A. Atherstone and J. Maiden (eds)) pp.49-51.

[985] "Islington Clerical Meeting", in *The Record,* 19 January 1863, p.4.

[986] A. Peel. *A Brief History of English Congregationalism* (1953) pp.71-74.

[987] J.L. Altholz, *The Religious Press in Britain, 1760-1900* (1989) pp.59-60.

[988] See generally ibid., pp.57-65.

in excess. Every limb of the nation is pinioned by acts of Parliament. Nothing is left to spontaneous growth."[989] However, by speaking "of nothing but free trade, the franchise, and the individual's political rights ... instead of making radicalism Christian, it [*The Nonconformist*] ended by secularising Christianity".[990] Miall later wanted to establish "a daily newspaper upon the broad principles of Christianity"[991] and encouraged Christians to use the provincial press and other methods of swaying the minds of others for gospel purposes.[992]

4.20 Exeter Hall is built and provides a physical focus for evangelicalism

From 1831, for 50 years, Exeter Hall in London served as the headquarters of the evangelical movement and "the centre of evangelical England".[993] In the words of *The Revivalist*, it was a "splendid building". It thought that "Few objects can be contemplated more grand and imposing than the view presented from the platform when the hall is crowded."[994] A picture of Exeter Hall adorned the frontpiece of the first volume of *The Revivalist*. Forgotten today, it stood where the Strand Palace Hotel now stands on the Strand, in the centre of London. There, in May, the Nonconformists and the great missionary societies held their meetings. Inside, were three halls – the largest held 3,000[995] – and office space. The numbers attending an annual meeting of a great missionary society would be well into four figures. Christians streamed in to the capital for the May missionary season. Such meetings facilitated the building of relationships and understanding between Nonconformist and Church evangelicals – and Exeter Hall also provided a meeting place where evangelicals planned and held evangelistic campaigns. As someone who was no evangelical observed: in May at Exeter Hall, "The Church and

[989] "Address to the Reader", in *The Nonconformist*, 14 April 1841 p.1.

[990] Cited in J.L. Altholz, *The Religious Press in Britain, 1760-1900* (1989) p.61.

[991] E. Miall, *The British Churches in Relation to the British People* (1850) p.305.

[992] Ibid., p.306.

[993] C. Binfield, *George Williams and the Y.M.C.A.* (1973) p.95. See generally I. Bradley, *The Call to Seriousness* (1976) pp.140-141.

[994] *The Revivalist* (1832) p.280.

[995] Some suggest more, see D.M. Lewis, *Lighten their Darkness* (1986) p.91. Others suggest a slightly different configuration for Exeter Hall, but it was clearly capacious, I. Bradley, *The Call to Seriousness* (1976) p.140.

Conventicle meet together, the platform and the pulpit kiss each other."[996] No evangelical speaker of note visited London without the anticipation of being asked to speak there. For those who disliked evangelicals, "Exeter Hall Christianity" was a term of contempt.

4.21 Theological education expands

A burgeoning population required more ordinands. A solution for Church of England evangelicals was to emulate the work of the Elland Society. In 1795, the Bristol Clerical Education Society was founded, and flourished, helping more than 100 ordinands over the next 30 or so years.[997] In 1816, the London Clergy Education Society was founded. In the hands of Charles Simeon, it supported the band of preachers flowing out of Cambridge and across the nation.

Another solution to the lack of ordinands was to establish new Church of England theological colleges. Between 1816 and 1857, nine were established, including the theological department in King's College, London.[998] Most of them were High Church/Tractarian foundations, offering ordination for those without an Oxbridge background – especially for areas of the country where Oxbridge men were less willing to go. They sought to instil in their students a new conception of the priestly role.[999] There was also Cuddesdon College, founded by Samuel Wilberforce in 1854 in the Catholic tradition for university graduates. He wanted the younger clergy to adopt "a clerical tone" and "religious habits". In November 1854, it had eight students.[1000] *The Christian Observer* was troubled by the appearance of these new colleges with their theological perspectives different to its own – and suggested an evangelical equivalent, but nothing was done in this direction for many years. It was also anxious about the theology being taught in the universities. It discerned "their secret want of confidence in the doctrines which they would undertake to preach". Men were, as a result, being

[996] Cited in C. Binfield, *George Williams and the Y.M.C.A.* (1973) p.95.

[997] G. Atkins, *Wilberforce and his Milieux: The Worlds of Anglican Evangelicalism, c.1780-1830* (2009) (Unpublished Ph.D. thesis, Cambridge University) p.36.

[998] *Handbook of the Theological Colleges of the Church of England and the Episcopal Church in Scotland 1884-5* (1885).

[999] See generally "Theological Colleges", in *The Modern Churchman* (1911-1912) vol.1, p.441.

[1000] J.O. Johnston, *Life and Letters of Henry Parry Liddon* (1904) p.34.

discouraged from the ministry, or were being poorly trained for it.[1001]

At the beginning of our period, Congregationalists also renewed their commitment to theological education, for ministry candidates who showed clear evidence of conversion. Their academies were centred on "theological studies", rather than "classical or philosophical learning".[1002] It was observed that in them "the study of the Scriptures, either in their original tongues, or in the form of systematic theology, the knowledge of the best divines or ecclesiastical historians, the art of preaching or of spending time in the study to the greatest advantage, form the incessant objects of laborious attention".[1003] The same observers noted in 1812 that it was to the "new turn" in the affairs of their academies that "much of the prosperity which the churches have of late enjoyed" should be attributed.[1004]

Between 1803 and 1850, the number of Congregational theological colleges increased from three to eight,[1005] including colleges in London and Birmingham's Spring Hill College.[1006] There was also Cheshunt College, which was Calvinistic in its articles of foundation and left its students free to choose the denomination within which to pursue ministry. But, towards the end of our period, the leading Congregationalist minister in Birmingham, John Angell James, became concerned lest his denomination's colleges produced learned, but not "earnest preachers and judicious pastors".[1007] At Kidderminster, another Congregationalist minister lamented how seldom the theological colleges were lifted before the throne of grace in prayer – and the risk that "it be presumed that they are safe without God's guidance".[1008]

[1001] "The New Year", in 57 *The Christian Observer for the Year 1857* (1857) p.4.

[1002] D. Bogue and J. Bennett, *History of Dissenters, from the Revolution in 1688, to the Year 1808* (1812) vol.4, p.301.

[1003] Ibid., p.307.

[1004] Ibid., p.305.

[1005] H. Mann, *Religious Worship in England and Wales* (1854) p.20.

[1006] E. Kaye, *Mansfield College, Oxford* (1996) pp.6-24.

[1007] J.A. James, "What is the Spiritual State of our Churches?", in *The Works of John Angell James* (1861) (T.S. James (ed.)) vol.9, p.367. See also P. Rylands, *The Pulpit and the People* (1847) pp.72-73. Ironically in choosing R.W. Dale as his successor, Angell James chose someone who would be known for impressiveness in public speaking, but one by virtue of his difference in doctrine would lead the Congregationalists in a different direction.

[1008] W. Wright, *The Church Bereaved* (1857) p.17.

The Baptists were equally busy creating an educated pastorate. Between 1804 and 1843, they established five of their six theological colleges that existed at the end of our period.[1009] The Baptist C.H. Spurgeon also founded his Pastors' College. In its original conception, it "aimed at making preachers rather than scholars", as did other institutions.[1010]

In 1834, the Wesleyan Methodists established the Wesleyan Theological Institution. Here, the response of members to a more learned ministry was mixed. A number were so appalled at this innovation that they left to found the Wesleyan Methodist Association. The Welsh Calvinistic Methodists established theological colleges in less controversial circumstances – at Bala in 1837 and Trevecca in 1842.

4.22 The power of art

Woodcut art had been used by the sixteenth-century reformers – perhaps most effectively by John Foxe, in his record of the Protestant martyrs, *Acts and Monuments* – but British Protestants thereafter generally ignored art as a means of communicating their message. However, early in the nineteenth century, David Wilkie "started a fashion for genre paintings of religious history that gave support to the Protestant faith."[1011] From the 1840s onwards, interest in the use of religious art intensified as both Protestants, like John Ruskin, and Roman Catholics, such as the future Archbishop Wiseman, reflected on how it could be used to communicate the true meaning of the Bible and the merits of their respective faiths.[1012] William Michael Rossetti observed, "The learning of the age may be a benefit to its art, or a misfortune; but it is a fact, and cannot be ignored."[1013] Holman Hunt, the most Protestant of the Pre-Raphaelite painters,[1014] ironically seems to have been both led

[1009] H. Mann, *Religious Worship in England and Wales* (1854) p.22.

[1010] M. Hopkins, *Nonconformity's Romantic Generation* (2004) p.156. See generally C.H. Spurgeon, *An All-Round-Ministry* (1960) pp.viii-xix and M.R. Watts, *The Dissenters* (2015) vol.3, pp.202-203.

[1011] T. Buser, *Religious Art in the Nineteenth Century in Europe and America* (2002) vol.1, pp.79-80.

[1012] M. Giebelhausen, *Painting the Bible* (2006) pp.1-20.

[1013] Cited in ibid., p.1.

[1014] For a brief background to the Pre-Raphaelite Brotherhood, see G.P. Landow, "William Holman Hunt's 'Shadow of Death'", in 55 *Bulletin of the John Rylands University Library of Manchester* (1972) p.200.

towards religious conversion, and had his eyes opened to typological symbolism as a means of painting, by reading the second volume of Ruskin's *Modern Painters* (1846). This was given to him by a fellow student who wanted to convert Hunt to Roman Catholicism and who was "under the mistaken impression that its author belonged to this faith".[1015] Around this time, Hunt began work on *The Light of the World* (finished 1853) in which he depicted Revelation 3:20, with Jesus standing at the door and asking to be let in. The painting reflected his own personal experience, as he read the Bible and searched for the truth.[1016] William Bell Scott, the Scottish painter, in referring to it, said "For the first time in this country a picture became a subject of conversation and general interest from one end of the island to the other, and indeed continued so for many years."[1017] In later life, Hunt wrote "when the critics as usual assailed it violently, I have been comforted by hearing of persons in sickness who knew not the painter's name, and troubled themselves not at all about the manner of its production, or the artistic question, speaking of the picture as one that had haunted them and given them hope – the hope that makes death have no terrors".[1018]

It was, though, the Roman Catholics who were to make most use of religious art in their buildings. Pointing to the future use of religious art by Roman Catholics, Wiseman observed that "religious art had always been 'essentially *for the people*'; works were 'to be hung over some altar, or to adorn the walls of a cloister, or perhaps a public hall'".[1019]

4.23 The High Church is re-energised

The growing influence of the Evangelical party stimulated the High Church to action, especially that part of it known as the Hackney Phalanx.[1020] In many areas, they became as activist as the evangelicals, and adopted a similar morality. The Church's existing organisations for distributing its ideas – such as the Society for Promoting Christian Knowledge and the Society for the Propagation of the Gospel – were

[1015] G.P. Landow, *William Holman Hunt and Typological Symbolism* (1979) pp.6-7.
[1016] W.B. Scott, *Autobiographical Notes* (1892) vol.1, pp.312-313.
[1017] Ibid., p.310.
[1018] Ibid., p.313.
[1019] Author's italics. M. Giebelhausen, *Painting the Bible* (2006) p.6.
[1020] For the Hackney Phalanx, see C. Podmore, *Aspects of Anglican Identity* (2005) pp.9-16 and M.J. Quinlan, *Victorian Prelude* (1941) pp.118 and 132-133.

reinvigorated. The National Society for Promoting the Education of the Poor was established and, in 1818, the Church Building Society. Quinlan states that "the body of orthodox members became more zealous, certainly – and more genuinely religious, perhaps – than at any time since the seventeenth century".[1021]

4.24 Dreams and visions

Dreams and visions could not be planned for and were not a common means of conversion. However, Brownlow North, a great nephew of Lord North, the Prime Minister of an earlier age, experienced, while playing cards in his Scottish shooting lodge, "a kind of sensation as if he were going to drop down dead". He immediately retired to his bedroom, feeling the need for mercy and that he was a few minutes from hell. He knelt, and prayed, while the maid lit the fire. He rose a changed man and became, in our next period, a very important gentleman evangelist.[1022] Another important evangelist of our next period was W.P. Lockhart. In 1855 while walking alone by the Menai Straits, his biographer records that, "the words 'It is finished' were flashed into his mind with as much force and distinctness as though he heard them spoken from heaven: from that moment the great fact of Christ's death for sinners became the central thought of his life."[1023] At Liverpool in 1855 the evangelist John Hambleton's sister Hannah had a dream in which "she saw running waters of revival flowing through the streets of Livepool."[1024] Duly encouraged, Hambleton and others who were considering hiring a hall for evangelistic services throughout each Sabbath, did so. By eleven o'clock on the first day of their services, "God's power began to take hold of sinners: by twelve, it was expedient to remove anxious mourners, groaning under conviction of sin".[1025] The revival that broke out that day in Liverpool was still continuing in 1865.[1026] William Haslam also records – referring to Joel 2:28-29, that "your old men shall dream dreams, your young men shall see visions" – that dreams and visions led to a number

[1021] Ibid., p.118.
[1022] "Mr. Brownlow North", in *The Revivalist* (1859) p.177.
[1023] M.J. Lockhart, *W.P Lockhart* (1895) p.7.
[1024] G. Green, *Reginald Radcliffe: The Liverpool Solicitor* (2009) p.9. See also J. Hambleton, *Buds, Blossoms, and Fruits of the Revival* (N.D.) pp.15-16.
[1025] Ibid., pp.16-17.
[1026] Ibid., p.17.

of conversions, or the spiritual advance of the church, as a "spiritual atmosphere", towards the end of our period, took hold in Cornwall.[1027]

[1027] W. Haslam, *From Death into Life* (1897) pp.88-106, 111-117, 129, 186-187, 284, 286-289 and 304-307.

5

CALVINISM IS THE THEOLOGICAL DRIVER OF THE TIMES

5.1 Overview

It was Calvinism that energised much of orthodoxy in Britain in the first half of the nineteenth century, but it was "moderate and quietly taken for granted".[1028] It was also never dominant, often misunderstood and, in many places unpopular.[1029] Porteus, the bishop most open to working with Methodists, heartily rejected it,[1030] and lay evangelical leaders of the Church of England, such as William Wilberforce and Hannah More, did not "entertain any tenet *peculiar* to Calvinism".[1031] More did not affirm Arminianism either, lest she be taken for a Methodist. Her "zealous attachment was to the *church* and practical Christianity".[1032] They and their friends wanted to see conversions, but were nervous over a disproportionate statement of the doctrines of election and predestination, lest they generate a dispute similar to that which wrought havoc between

[1028] R. Hall, *Strictures on a Work, Intitled, "Zeal Without Innovation"* (1809) p.35, I.H. Murray, "A Hundred Years Ago (II.) The Death of John Angell James", in 15 *Banner of Truth*, April 1959, p.9, R.H. Martin, *Evangelicals United* (1983) pp.16-20, R. Tudur Jones, *Congregationalism in England 1662-1962* (1962) pp.259-261 and B. Hilton, *The Age of Atonement* (1991) p.9.

[1029] J. Bean, *Zeal Without Innovation* (1809) pp.47-75 and G. Atkins, *Wilberforce and his Milieux: The Worlds of Anglican Evangelicalism, c.1780-1830* (2009) (Unpublished Ph.D. thesis, Cambridge University) pp.82-110.

[1030] R. Hodgson, *The Life of the Right Reverend Beilby Porteus* (1811) pp.265-276.

[1031] Author's italics. W. Roberts, *Memoirs of the Life and Correspondence of Hannah More* (1834) vol.3, p.129. See also J. Pollock, *Wilberforce* (2007) pp.200-201.

[1032] Author's italics. W. Roberts, *Memoirs of the Life and Correspondence of Hannah More* (1834) vol.3, p.130.

the followers of Whitefield and Wesley.[1033] In Scotland, Thomas Chalmers had an unease with certain aspects of Calvinism – perhaps giving the role of education and of moral change a greater significance in conversion than Calvinists thought right – and was censured for this.[1034]

Their successors also emphasised the practical, aiming for conversions, without getting into Calvinism. They wanted the clergy to be "less solicitous about their own reputation as preachers and more anxious to win souls, even at the risk of giving some offence".[1035] They urged more "stirring appeals to the conscience and solemn warnings".[1036] Robert Aitken, the leading Church evangelist, "conceived a strong antipathy to the Calvinistic teaching of the church in which he had been brought up".[1037] The influence of the Evangelical party was such that leaders of the other Church parties started to accept many of their statements of truth and phraseology. In the words of *The Christian Observer*, a "marvellous unity"[1038] developed between them all, although the Church evangelicals were always aware of doctrinal pressure points which might lead others to break from them. *The Christian Observer* thought the other non-evangelical groupings delivered a "dry, historical belief",[1039] rather than a living faith.

In Scotland, the first two decades of the nineteenth century saw the same process of evangelical growth and then assimilation, as differences between the members of the Moderate and Evangelical parties gradually

[1033] For a criticism of Calvinism from the perspective of a correspondent of *The Christian Observer,* see "To the Editor of the Christian Observer", in 13 *The Christian Observer for the Year 1814* (1815) pp.620-630 and 764-768. See also "To the Editor of the Christian Observer", in 17 *The Christian Observer for the Year 1818* (1819) pp.12-13. Zachary Macaulay tended to Arminianism, "The Late Lord Macaulay", in *The Record*, 2 January 1860, p.3. Lord Teignmouth thought the less the study of writings on Calvinism the better, *Memoir of the Life and Correspondence of John Lord Teignmouth* (1843) vol.2, p.511 and was against "invidious party names", *Sketch of the Life of the Late Right Honourable Lord Teignmouth* (1834) pp.10 and 14-15.

[1034] S.J. Brown, *Thomas Chalmers and the Godly Commonwealth in Scotland* (1982) pp.76-77, 113-115, 182 and 377, but see also 145.

[1035] "The Perils of the Church in the Present Day", in *59 The Christian Observer for the Year 1859* (1859) p.221.

[1036] Ibid., p.220.

[1037] C.E. Woods, *Memoirs and Letters of Canon Hay Aitken* (1928) pp.18 and 33.

[1038] "The Perils of the Church in the Present Day", in 59 *The Christian Observer for the Year 1859* (1859) p.219.

[1039] Ibid.

disappeared, until they became barely apparent. In Scotland, though, this was perhaps because, in both parties, Calvinism grew in influence. Iain Murray notes the publication of Thomas M'Crie's *Life of Knox* (1811) as playing a "significant part" in this.[1040]

[1040] I.H. Murray, *A Scottish Christian Heritage* (2006) p.161. See also S.J. Brown, *Thomas Chalmers and the Godly Commonwealth in Scotland* (1982) p.211.

6

YET INFIDELITY LINGERS AND UNEXPECTED DEVELOPMENTS

6.1 Introduction

As revival grew in strength, keen-eyed observers noted that the sky was not cloudless. The clouds of infidelity and deism thickened in the skies, while ominous clouds drifted in which might yet bring the perfect storm, once fully gathered.[1041] For one thing, there were always members of the radical fringe. For example, Richard Carlile, who we earlier saw riding in to challenge Simeon in Cambridge, had already founded *The Republican* in 1819. He closed the work of its first volume with a piece that included the resolution that "whilst religion is made the engine of the state to forge fresh fetters, and whilst the established priesthood…are the supple tools of every existing authority; I for one shall live and die its foe".[1042] There would be other radicals, like Robert Owen, of much more illustrious standing in society, who would also want rid of Christianity. To him, we will come shortly. But the initial significant challenger to Christianity came from the more traditional foe of Unitarianism. Later, the challenge to Christianity came through developments in its ritual and through liberalism. Those considered to be evangelicals could also unleash surprises. The rise of Christian morality was also not beyond challenge.

[1041] See for instance the two volumes of *The Deist or Moral Philosopher* (1819).

[1042] R. Carlile, 1 *The Republican* (1819) p.xi. In later life, Carlile seems to have been influenced more positively by the Christianity of the age – although he never became an orthodox believer, see T. Larsen, *Crisis of Doubt* (2006) pp.261-263.

6.2 Unitarianism becomes legal and is energised

In 1791 Joseph Priestley fled from Birmingham to Hackney, because the mob had been aroused by his support for the French Revolution and his Unitarian religious principles. That same year, the Unitarian Book Society was founded to establish a common bond between Unitarians and to circulate their ideas through books. From then onwards, Unitarianism began to move from an intellectual movement within mainly Presbyterianism to draw in a wider group of participants. The Unitarian Book Society never drew a large number of members, but its existence encouraged the formation of similar societies elsewhere – and its rules articulated clear theological principles, such as "there is one man Christ Jesus, who was commissioned by God to instruct men in their duty, and to reveal the doctrine of a future life". Moral conduct, it was argued, depended on the extent to which these principles were received into the mind.[1043] However, the Unitarians did not believe in the divinity of Jesus. Neither did they believe in hell and eternal punishment; rather, they believed in annihilation of the soul at death.[1044]

In 1804, William Vidler founded a Unitarian Evangelical Society. In 1806, he was among the founders of a Unitarian Fund, to fund missionaries of Unitarian principles among the poor.[1045] At the time, Unitarianism was very much for the educated who rejected orthodoxy. That year, *The Monthly Repository of Theology and General Literature* was launched as "the only periodical publication which is open to free and impartial theological inquiry and discussion". Its editor noted "The rapid increase of the friends of rational religion",[1046] but correspondents

[1043] R.W. Davis, *Dissent in Politics 1780-1830* (1971) p.196. See also T. Belsham, *Memoirs of the Late Reverend Lindsey, M.A.* (1873) pp.196-200. By 1806, the Unitarian Book Society had distributed £3,000 in books, see "Unitarian Book Society", in 1 *The Monthly Repository of Theology and General Literature* (1806) p.220.

[1044] M.R. Watts, *The Dissenters* (1995) vol.2, pp.83-87. They attracted "surprisingly few [converts] from the Church of England", see ibid., p.87.

[1045] R.W. Davis, *Dissent in Politics 1780-1830* (1971) p.197. The Christian Tract Society was also established to provide cheap tracts for the poor which inculcated "moral conduct on Christian principles". They were to avoid doctrinal issues, save where some tenet is "brought forward for reprobation on account of its obvious tendency to sap the foundation of Christian morality," see T. Rees, "On the Christian Tract Society", in 7 *The Monthly Repository of Theology and General Literature* (1812) pp.124-125.

[1046] "Preface" to 1 *The Monthly Repository of Theology and General Literature* (1806) p.vi.

thought Unitarianism still lacked Calvinism's vigour. Michael Watts observes, "the liberal gospel preached by the Unitarians could never have either the compelling power or the motivating force of the evangelical gospel which taught that acceptance or rejection issued in either eternal joy or everlasting misery".[1047] Furthermore, within Unitarian ranks, a key source of contention was the use of the laity to spread its tenets.[1048]

Nevertheless, Unitarian missionaries went out and they made an impact, proving to be attractive to Dissenters becoming liberal on the topic of hell.[1049] For example, in late 1811 William Vidler preached in Reading after local people asked the Unitarian Fund to send someone there. His preaching led to the establishment, after a few weeks, of a morning congregation of 100 to 130 persons with 400 in the evening, although that congregation soon halved.[1050] In Scotland, the missionary tour by Mr Wright of 1812 lasted 80 days and he preached 68 times. In Glasgow especially, he found Unitarianism "firmly established" and drew "large and deeply attentive audiences" of up to 700 or 800 people. Wright believed the cause of Unitarianism was "advancing in the West of Scotland" and that Scotland generally "was favourable soil for the spread of Unitarianism".[1051] In Wales, an entire Baptist church turned Unitarian, save for a few refugees,[1052] although converts to Unitarianism might later revert to orthodoxy.[1053]

The ability to advance Unitarianism was limited by law. The clause in the Toleration Act 1690, which exempted persons denying the Trinity from the benefit of that Act's provisions, remained. Unitarians existed by "connivence".[1054] For example, in an earlier period, Theophilus Lindsey commenced his preaching at the Essex Street chapel by virtue of the skill

[1047] M.R. Watts, *The Dissenters* (1995) vol.2, p.96.

[1048] "Want of Zeal in Unitarians", in 1 *The Monthly Repository of Theology and General Literature* (1806) pp.641-644.

[1049] M.R. Watts, *The Dissenters* (1995) vol.2, pp.83-87.

[1050] "Intelligence", in 7 *The Monthly Repository of Theology and General Literature* (1812) p.772.

[1051] Ibid., pp.51, 55 and 123.

[1052] "Unitarianism in Wales", in 7 *The Monthly Repository of Theology and General Literature* (1812) p.23.

[1053] "Intelligence", in 7 *The Monthly Repository of Theology and General Literature* (1812) pp.722-727.

[1054] "Unitarian Society", in 9 *The Monthly Repository of Theology and General Literature* (1814) p.252.

of his legal adviser and the support of many Establishment figures.[1055] In 1811, the opportunity to repeal the provisions that left non-trinitarian belief open to prosecution arose as a reaction to Lord Sidmouth's Bill to further regulate the registration of Dissenting Ministers under the Toleration Acts. Lord Sidmouth's Bill came at a time of national emergency and it was thought that men might be avoiding their duty to fight in the Napoleonic Wars by registering as Dissenting ministers. The Dissenters of all denominations, including the Unitarians, were outraged and united, with the support of Wilberforce and his friends, to defeat the Bill.[1056]

The new unity of the Dissenters and Church evangelicals led to moves in the direction of greater religious liberty. In 1812 the Conventicle Act and the Five Mile Act – which had limited preaching and assembling by Dissenters, but which had for long not been enforced – were repealed. The Unitarian MP William Smith – a close associate of William Wilberforce – and Wilberforce himself, supported the repeal. In 1813, 'Mr William Smith's Bill' was passed to finally remove the legal consequences of denying the Trinity. Smith and the Unitarians then turned to campaign for the repeal of the Test and Corporation Acts, which required those holding public office to be practising members of the Church of England.[1057] Of that time, Richard Davis writes: "Unitarianism was already growing into a separate and very aggressive sect", in "response to the aggressiveness of evangelical trinitarians". Of the latter, Davis adds, "having, in a sense, brought Christ back into religion, they were not about to see him turned out again."[1058] Wilberforce, Macaulay and others close to them all tried, without success, to convert Smith to the trinitarian position.[1059] In 1819 the Association for Protecting the Civil Rights of Unitarians was founded with 48 congregations, although some prominent ones, such as that at Essex Street, London, remained outside.[1060] Some Unitarian congregations now consisted "almost entirely of poor people" and the

[1055] T. Belsham, *Memoirs of the Late Reverend Lindsey, M.A.* (1873) pp.68-70.
[1056] See generally R.W. Davis, *Dissent in Politics 1780-1830* (1971) pp.148-169.
[1057] "Unitarian Society", in 9 *The Monthly Repository of Theology and General Literature* (1814) pp.252-253.
[1058] R.W. Davis, *Dissent in Politics 1780-1830* (1971) p.195.
[1059] Ibid., pp.108-109.
[1060] Ibid., p.209. See also "Intelligence", in 14 *The Monthly Repository of Theology and General Literature* (1819) pp.48-55.

conversion of some Methodists to Methodist Unitarians raised Unitarian hopes of making further inroads into the working classes.[1061] The 1819 report of the Unitarian Fund noted that a number of Independent Calvinistic ministers were now preaching Unitarianism in important centres, including that of Reading.[1062]

6.3 The Owenites

In 1829 a London newspaper carried an advertisement that every Sunday at 11 am at No.2 Leicester Place, Leicester Square, Robert Owen would set out the principles upon which to "found an entire new state of society, in which truth will be substituted for religion, beneficial realities for injurious mysteries and ceremonies; knowledge for ignorance; riches for poverty, universal charity, kind feelings, and union for discord, evil passions, unkind feelings, and uncharitableness".[1063] It all sounded utopian, the prouncements of a radical but, in 1829, Robert Owen was a captain of industry with an international reputation.

Owen, in his childhood, had contact with some Methodist women who tried to convert him while living in Newtown in mid-Wales. However, he was more attracted to the theology of the Anglican Lawrence Sterne, of whom Henry Venn had been dismissive.[1064] By the age of ten, he felt strongly that "there must be something wrong with all religions".[1065] Owen married the evangelical daughter of the evangelical David Dale,[1066] the owner of New Lanark's cotton mills "and one of the most extraordinary men in the commercial world of Scotland".[1067]At around the same time as his marriage, Owen and his associates acquired the New Lanark mills on "singularly generous terms".[1068] Dale's regime at New Lanark combined financial success with the promotion of the education of its workforce and general benevolence towards them. It

[1061] "Report of the Committee of the Unitarian Fund", appended to 14 *The Monthly Repository of Theology and General Literature* (1819) pp.2-4.
[1062] Ibid., p.8.
[1063] R.E. Davies, *The Life of Robert Owen* (1907) p.41.
[1064] J.A. Thomas, *The Nation's Gospel: Reformation to Revolution* (2017) vol.1, p.364.
[1065] R. Owen, *The Life of Robert Owen* (1857) vol.1, pp.4 and 16.
[1066] For Owen's courtship, see R.D. Owen, *Threading my Way* (1967) pp.51-56. It took two years for David Dale to be won to the marriage but he was.
[1067] R. Owen, *The Life of Robert Owen* (1857) vol.1, p.45.
[1068] R. Davis and F. O'Hagan, *Robert Owen* (2010) p.37.

was also technologically innovative, using Arkwright's new water-frame machines.[1069] Owen vigorously built on these solid foundations so that New Lanark became "famous throughout Great Britain".[1070] Achieving great commercial success, with Jeremy Bentham for a time as a partner,[1071] Owen attracted the attention of the nation. Or, as one critic put it, for a time he "deluded the visitors of New Lanark by the exhibition of the practical fruits of Christian culture, as if they were the result of his own wild and ungodly theories".[1072]

Owen built upon his father-in-law's education programmes although, unlike his father-in-law, his educational programmes were increasingly devoid of religious content.[1073] At New Lanark, he started to educate children at the age of one, or as soon as they could walk, creating – in his own words – "the first institution for the formation of the infant and child character".[1074] He was also a powerful financial backer of Lancaster and Bell, who established the monitor system – whereby a teacher taught a number of others, who then taught the rest. His views on education were adopted by the Kingdom of Prussia.[1075] New Lanark also became well-known for its model conditions of employment – and Owen became a champion of factory and social reform, teaching that all working men had a right to a comfortable existence. So successful an expression of the merits of industrialisation was Owen's New Lanark, that a future Czar of Russia,[1076] and many other foreign dignitaries, visited it and spread the message of its merits across Europe.

Owen's father-in-law, David Dale, was a Calvinist and unafraid to make a stand for the gospel. He left the Church of Scotland over powers of patronage given to secular authorities. He helped found and became the pastor of his Old Scotch Independents church and also became "the pastor of upwards of forty churches or congregations, dissenters from

[1069] Ibid., pp.28-32. See also R.D. Owen, *Threading my Way* (1967) pp.27-36.

[1070] J. Griscom, *A Year in Europe* (1823) vol.2, p.375.

[1071] Allegedly Bentham's only successful pecuniary speculation, R. Owen, *The Life of Robert Owen* (1857) vol.1, pp.95-96 and 129.

[1072] A. Haldane, *The Lives of Robert Haldane of Airthrey and of his Brother James Alexander Haldane* (1853) pp.159-160.

[1073] R. Davis and F. O'Hagan, *Robert Owen* (2010) pp.55-56.

[1074] R. Owen, *The Life of Robert Owen* (1857) vol.1, p.134.

[1075] Ibid.

[1076] Grand Duke Nicholas, later Nicholas I of Russia, see ibid., pp.145-146.

the Church of Scotland".[1077] Dale and Owen's sisters-in-law sought to convert Owen, but to no avail. His wife prayed for his conversion.[1078] She gave their children the religious education in which she was brought up, teaching them that there was no salvation from hell, except by the vicarious atonement of Christ's death and sufferings.[1079] She ensured that the Bible was read at home each day – and a copy provided for those staying overnight.[1080] However, Owen thought belief was "an involuntary act of the mind, and for which no one could be justly or rationally praised or blamed, rewarded or punished".[1081] It was all a matter of the circumstances of birth. Those born and educated in China followed Confucius; in Turkey, they followed Mohammed; and in Rome, they were papists. His experience taught him that "human nature is radically good"[1082] and that men are what they are "by nature, education, and circumstances; and consequently, that persons are not justly the objects of praise or blame for any of their moral qualities; that there can be no such thing as sin, nor any desert of praise".[1083] Owen did not interfere in his wife's spiritual education of his children. However, when his eldest son, Robert Dale Owen, just before he reached his teenage years, sought to convert his father, the father sufficiently unsettled his son's theological understanding so that, shortly after, the son turned to universalism (the belief that salvation is given to all – whatever they believed). His mother, on discovering this change in her son, spent the night in tears.[1084]

Owen's first well-known work was *A New View of Society*. This comprised four essays devoted to the well-being of his country. The first essay, published in 1813, promoted the power of education to shape character and improve society and urged its extension to all. The first edition of this essay was dedicated to William Wilberforce. Later essays encouraged full employment – by advocating that the unemployed build

[1077] Ibid., p.71. David Dale's wife initially followed him but left his church after turning Baptist. She died before her daughter Caroline Dale met Owen.
[1078] R.D. Owen, *Threading my Way* (1967) p.79.
[1079] Ibid., p.76.
[1080] J. Griscom, *A Year in Europe* (1823) vol.2, pp.382-383.
[1081] R. Owen, *The Life of Robert Owen* (1857) vol.1, pp.71-72 and 101.
[1082] Ibid., p.131.
[1083] B.W. Noel, *The State of the Metropolis Considered* (1835) (3rd ed.) p.59.
[1084] R.D. Owen, *Threading my Way* (1967) pp.82-88.

public infrastructure projects, such as roads.[1085] His essays, combined with his pecuniary and social success at New Lanark, won him "golden opinions" among "men of rank and talent" and he was equally popular with the masses.[1086]

In 1817, Owen's antagonism to religion was made public.[1087] On 14 August, he held a widely publicised public meeting at the City of London Tavern. This considered a plan to meet the needs of all by relieving the country from its present distress, by remoralising the lower orders, reducing the rate levied in the parishes to help the poor and gradually abolishing pauperism.[1088] The meeting, amid tumult, was adjourned for a week and during this time the public mind became "highly excited" by Owen's plan. Unknown to all but himself, although his religious principles were an increasing cause of suspicion, Owen was determined to give the death blow to all religions and to replace them with "the reign of charity".[1089] As his speech reached its crescendo, he dramatically paused before declaring that the ability of implementing his plan was held back by error, "combined with the fundamental notions of every religion that has hitherto been taught to men". By them, man had been made "the most inconsistent, and the most miserable being in existence". It was religion that brought "disunion, division and separation".[1090] Forty years later, he wrote that the consequences of those proceedings "have been fermenting to this day, and are continuing to ferment, throughout society".[1091] He had "discovered that the great obstacle to all substantial and lasting progress and improvement among men, was the religions

[1085] Owen's mind was fertile. For a full introduction to his thought and influence, see G. Claeys, "Introduction" to *Selected Works of Robert Owen* (1993) (G. Claeys (ed.)) vol.1, pp.xv-lxii.

[1086] R.D. Owen, *Threading my Way* (1967) pp.191-192.

[1087] His eldest son thought his father a deist and, during the active portion of his life, a Secularist – in omitting from "his system, as a motive to human conduct, all reference to another life; believing that men can be made to see so clearly how much it is for their interest to be temperate and industrious, just and kind, that, in virtue of such insight and without other prompting, they will act uprightly through life", see ibid., pp.192-194.

[1088] "A Public Meeting is to be Held at the City of London Tavern", in *The Times*, 30 July 1817.

[1089] R. Owen, *The Life of Robert Owen* (1857) vol.1, pp.160-161.

[1090] Ibid., p.161 and R. Owen, *The Life of Robert Owen* (1858) vol.1A, p.115.

[1091] R. Owen, *The Life of Robert Owen* (1857) vol.1, pp.154 and 163.

of the nations".[1092] Owen's public career ultimately "led to virtual separation" from his wife. After their honeymoon, she disappears from his autobiography.[1093]

In the 1820s and 1830s, Owen's star was impacted by the failure of various ventures, particularly in the United States, to establish a community manifesting the benefits of his new society. In some members of these communities, sloth and an unwillingness to submit to authority appeared. As a result, his personal finances were badly damaged, but he intrepidly continued to propagate his ideas. On 1 May 1835, Owen established a "communitarian organisation, the Association of All Classes and of All Nations", later known as the Rational Society. The name 'socialism' was given to its meetings and to the new movement;[1094] by the 1840s, its members were styled 'socialists'. Attendees at its lectures included the young Friedrich Engels. Through public meetings, public lectures, public discussions and cheap publications, Owen aimed to change public opinion to bring about his new moral order. He also sought – through activities, such as presiding over a marriage and the singing of social hymns exalting "the virtues of community and sociability" – to supplant "the social function of organised religion".[1095] *The Westminster Review* of 1839 reflected that Owen's antipathy to commercial competition was apparently "the actual creed of a great portion of the working classes".[1096]

Owen's new moral world required the end of the "Priesthood and its various institutions".[1097] The latter included the existing law of marriage, which he alleged the priests had devised. It was immoral, he suggested, for men and women to "live day and night together for their lives after nature has caused their love for each other to cease".[1098] He

[1092] Ibid., p.158.

[1093] R.W. Leopold, *Robert Dale Owen* (1940) p.5. She died in 1831.

[1094] R.E. Davies, *The Life of Robert Owen* (1907) pp.43-44.

[1095] See G. Claeys, "Introduction" to *Selected Works of Robert Owen* (1993) (G. Claeys (ed.)) vol.1, p.xliii.

[1096] Cited in ibid., p.xlii.

[1097] R. Owen, *The Catechism of the New Moral World* (N.D.) p.9.

[1098] R. Owen, "Lectures on the Marriages of the Priesthood of the Old Immoral World", in *Selected Works of Robert Owen* (1993) (G. Claeys (ed.)) vol.2, p.315. He suffered early disappointment when a lucrative promise of a partnership with the owner of a mill enterprise was withdrawn when the owner's daughter was due to be married and

also foreshadowed later developments in the twentieth century, with his view that "The pure and genuine chastity of nature is to have connection only with affection."[1099] He introduced "social missionaries" to spread his new ideas and to expound upon "popular topics like phrenology, mesmerism and the conquests of science."[1100] Many were ex-ministers, and one was George Holyoake, later a major advocate of secularism. To aid their work and to teach his new moral world, Owen published a catechism.[1101] Strangely, for a man so opposed to religion, he adopted traditional Calvinistic language to express his over-arching view of man's needs, but he gave the words new meaning. He aimed to create a new society by "regenerating" the human mind, that it should be "born again". The millennium was to be introduced by accepting that a man's character was formed for him and that society, by its practical measures, could "make all future generations, without any exception, good, wise, and happy".[1102]

6.4 Miraculous happenings within evangelicalism

Edward Irving was Thomas Chalmers's assistant before becoming the minister at the Church of Scotland's Caledonian Church in Hatton Garden, London. In the early 1820s, he was a metropolitan sensation.[1103] Attendances rose from 50 to 1,500 in three months. Royalty, politicians and unbelievers all eagerly attended. Samuel Taylor Coleridge held that Irving "possesses more of the spirit and purpose of the reformers... he has more of the head and heart, the life, the unction, and the genial power of Martin Luther, than any now alive".[1104] Irving's preaching took on an apocalyptic overtone. Prophetic foretellings told of the battle

the mill owner's future son-in-law demanded that the family business be kept solely in the family, R. Owen, *The Life of Robert Owen* (1857) vol.1, pp.39-42, and see also p.7 for another experience of Owen relating to marriage in his early years.

[1099] R. Owen, "Lectures on the Marriages of the Priesthood of the Old Immoral World", in *Selected Works of Robert Owen* (1993) (G. Claeys (ed.)) vol.2, p.293.

[1100] G. Claeys, "Introduction" to *Selected Works of Robert Owen* (1993) (G. Claeys (ed.)) vol.1, p.xliii.

[1101] R. Owen, *The Catechism of the New Moral World* (N.D.).

[1102] R. Owen, *The Life of Robert Owen* (1857) vol.1, p.iv.

[1103] Shortly after his conversion, in 1812, the evangelist Charles Finney also spoke in tongues – but he did not know what to make of it, see D.P. Williams, *The Prophetical Ministry* (1931) p.98.

[1104] Cited in C. Hill, *The Wilberforce Connection* (2004) p.195.

of Armageddon occurring in 1846. Irving spoke as if infallible. In the early 1830s, the gift of tongues – whereby church members spoke in unknown languages – was restored to his church.[1105] A group of six "gifted ones" appeared, including four women. Specified parts of the service were allowed for prophecy, or for members to speak in tongues. Irving explained these activities as the work of the Holy Spirit. He also began to believe that if prayer did not heal the sick, it was through a lack of faith. Most evangelicals were unconvinced of the divine origin of these manifestations.[1106] In 1833, the Church of Scotland dismissed Irving for teaching error relating to Christ's human nature.[1107] He died the following year, but the ritualistic Catholic Apostolic Church arose out of his work, prospered and spread across the world. By 1856, it was said "No Christian community in England of equal size can boast of so many families of rank or wealth".[1108]

Some evangelicals were influenced by Irving's experiences. Perhaps most importantly for the future, Henry Bulteel was "fully convinced... of the reality of the manifestations of the Holy Ghost in Mr Irving's Church"[1109] – and Bulteel was said to have miraculously healed several chronically-ill women.[1110] He argued, in *The Doctrine of the Miraculous Interference of Jesus on behalf of Believers* (1832), that the interposition of the hand of Jesus to heal was likely and "certain, where ever the person

[1105] For the appearance in Scotland at this time of the tongues phenomena, see A.L. Drummond and J. Bulloch, *The Scottish Church 1688-1843* (1973) pp.198-199. John Darby was unconvinced that the manifestations of the Spirit were authentic, see T. Grass, *Gathering to His Name* (2012) p.31.

[1106] W.H.B. Proby, *Annals of the "Low-Church" Party in England* (1888) vol.1, pp.337-338.

[1107] Pentecostals in the twentieth century thought Irving was "of most noble character, holy and faithful in his unwearied labour, and has never been surpassed in zeal". However, his followers exercised the gift of tongues in a "disorderly" way, and thereby "brought reproach on the work of God," see D.P. Williams, *The Prophetical Ministry* (1931) p.97.

[1108] J.B. Marsden, *History of Christian Churches and Sects* (1856) vol.11, p.67.

[1109] H.B. Bulteel, *The Doctrine of the Miraculous Interference of Jesus on behalf of Believers* (1832) p.30. One of the friends of the future Emma Darwin spoke in tongues, E. Healey, *Emma Darwin* (2001) p.132.

[1110] Ibid., pp.30-33. See also R.W. Dale, *The Life and Letters of John Angell James* (1861) p.263.

desiring it has faith to rely on Jesus for it".[1111] It was argued that the age of the miraculous had not ended with the apostles. Gladstone, it is said, turned from evangelicalism to a High Church Christianity while at St Ebbe's, Oxford, perhaps in reaction to this kind of evangelicalism.[1112] Certainly, some thought that "Newmanism", to which we shall turn shortly, "would never be the success it is if it hadn't been for that flood of Irvingism".[1113] The increasingly liberal Baden Powell, the Savilan Professor of Geometry at Oxford, in his critique of miracles, later used the "miraculous" speaking of tongues as an example of something to be "ascribed to natural causes, as yet perhaps little understood".[1114]

6.5 Old challengers take new shape

In 1817, while *The Christian Observer* noted the spread of the "doctrine which characterised the wisest and best of our reformers", it also noted the growth of "two evils; very opposite".[1115] On the one side, was liberalism, to which we will come shortly. On the other side, popery which created a fog within Protestantism. It linked "the baptismal rite with spiritual regeneration", rejected "a sinner's justification only by faith in the merits of a crucified Saviour" – and was unwilling to circulate the Bible without a note on its interpretation. In 1831, Henry Bulteel, in Oxford, was noting how the "formalists" were dropping the words of Christ from their vocabulary, such as "holiness", "taking up the cross", "born again", "born of the spirit" and "new creature". He thought they were ashamed of them and recounted the consequences for them personally that would follow.[1116]

[1111] H.B. Bulteel, *The Doctrine of the Miraculous Interference of Jesus on behalf of Believers* (1832) p.7.
[1112] See L.S.H. Wright, *Samuel Taylor Coleridge and the Anglican Church* (2010) p.244. Gladstone accepted the validity of baptismal regeneration, see M.R. Watts, *The Dissenters* (1995) vol.2, p.578. Bulteel, subsequently rejected Irvingism, becoming a Strict Baptist before joining the Plymouth Brethren, see F.M. Turner, *John Henry Newman* (2002) pp.50-51.
[1113] Cited in G. Carter, *Anglican Evangelicals* (2001) p.194.
[1114] B. Powell, "On the Study of the Evidences of Christianity", in *Essays and Reviews: The 1860 Text and its Reading* (2000) (V. Shea and W. Whitla (eds)) p.241.
[1115] "Preface" to 16 *The Christian Observer for the Year 1817* (1818) p.vi.
[1116] H.B. Bulteel, *A Sermon on 1 Corinthians II. 12* (1831) p.40.

6.5.1 *The Oxford Movement arises*

In 1833, the "formalists", as Bulteel would have called them, took shape in the distinctive form of the Oxford Movement – its members being known as Tractarians.[1117] The immediate cause of their movement was voting reform in the national electoral system. First, in 1828, the civil disabilities on Nonconformists were removed by the repeal of the Test and Corporation Acts and then, in 1829, the Catholic Emancipation Act removed the restrictions on Roman Catholics. These developments, together with the extension of the parliamentary franchise by the Reform Act of 1832, opened up many offices to Catholics and Nonconformists[1118] and changed the electorate. The Oxford Movement was to be the most significant Christian movement to spring from such reforms. Its founders, being High Churchmen, were concerned that a Parliament elected by, and composed of, non-Churchmen, might use its power to dictate to the Established Church in ways contrary to its formularies. There was a good basis for this, as "with its growing efficiency, there was, oddly enough, a growing odium against it, and that for just those very faults which it was doing its best to amend".[1119] Within Parliament, the call for the disestablishment of the Church of England, without compensation, could be heard.[1120]

Matters came to a head when Parliament suppressed ten Anglican bishoprics in Ireland, and increased state funding to a Catholic theological college in Ireland. Many were concerned, including the evangelicals. As we have seen, especially in the 1820s, evangelicals had made inroads into Roman Catholicism in Ireland;[1121] and the translation of the Bible into the vernacular Irish in 1827 provided the further means to secure the

[1117] Frank Turner notes that it was "one of the supreme ironies of English religious history that a radical high church movement rather than the evangelical movement came to be called the Tractarian Movement and its activists the Tractites", see F.M. Turner, *John Henry Newman* (2002) p.60.

[1118] For a helpful summary of the background to the repeal of the Test and Corporation Acts and the rise of the Tractarian movement, see C. Podmore, *Aspects of Anglican Identity* (2005) pp.16-23.

[1119] J.H. Overton, *The English Church in the Nineteenth Century* (1894) p.10.

[1120] Ibid., p.12.

[1121] W.J. Conybeare, *Essays Ecclesiastical and Social* (1855) p.98. John Darby refers to Roman Catholics becoming, in 1827, Protestants at the rate of 700 or 800 a week, see T. Grass, *Gathering to His Name* (2012) p.16.

reformation of the Irish Church.[1122] One commentator, reflecting on the Irish situation, observed that "In every direction there are evident signs of revival", as what was called a "New Reformation" broke out.[1123] The abolition of the bishoprics, and state funding of a Catholic theological college, seemed a betrayal of these successes. Furthermore, if the state had the power to abolish bishoprics, it could remove from, or foist upon, the Church other matters – or interfere with it in other ways.

John Keble, a fellow of Oriel College, Oxford, preached in July 1833 on national apostasy, at St Mary's Church, Oxford. He raised the prospect that a Christian nation which, in her legislation and policy, reflected the fundamental rules of Christ's church, nevertheless might go on to throw off all restraint and forsake and trample the church. The target of this sermon and the work of the Tractarians, John Henry Newman subsequently alleged, was liberalism. However, Frank Turner, in his work *John Henry Newman* (2002), regards Newman's view as a rewriting of history. In Turner's cogent analysis, the Tractarian Movement of the 1830s and 1840s targeted not liberal theology but was "the most extensive, vigorous theological and intellectual assault of the century on evangelical Protestantism".[1124]

Certainly, in the 1830s, it was the growing strength of the generally evangelical Dissenters that appeared to pose the greatest threat to the privileges of the Church. But one should not entirely dismiss the threat of theological liberalism to the Church, since the Unitarians bulked up Dissenting numbers. Furthermore, within the Established Church, evangelicals were arising who were much more critical of it than members of the Clapham Sect. Only two years before Keble's apostasy sermon Henry Bulteel, also preaching before the University of Oxford at St Mary's Church, assailed the way that the Church's bishops and ministers were appointed. Many of them, he asserted, were "to be generally found in the front rank of Baal worshippers in his temples". He added "that the heads and resident fellows of colleges" in Oxford had

[1122] C. Cator, *The Work of an Evangelist* (1833) p.22.

[1123] M. Bruen, *History of Revivals of Religion in the British Isles* (1836) p.164. See also T. Grass, *Gathering to His Name* (2012) pp.14-15.

[1124] F.M. Turner, *John Henry Newman* (2002) p.7. For the shift of Newman from 'conversion' and his evangelical roots to being a founder of Tractarianism, see ibid., pp.111-126.

"no small share" in these "corruptions".[1125] The sermon was published and regularly reprinted – and also a pamphlet in which Bulteel accused the Bishop of Oxford, Bagot, of being "an officer of the Church of antichrist".[1126] The influence of William Wilberforce was passing – symbolising, in his self, the unity of Church and state; he died within two weeks of Keble's sermon.

Newman later argued that "Reformation principles were powerless to rescue"[1127] the Church from her foes. However, as Frank Turner argues, the Tractarians wanted "a Second Reformation, first by resisting the political influence of evangelical Dissent on the Established Church, then by purging the Establishment of Protestant innovations, especially recent evangelical ones, and finally by recovering Catholic faith and practice".[1128] In bringing about the Second Reformation, Newman knew he needed to undermine the principles of the first. The Broad Churchman Julius Charles Hare observed that "the battle of the Reformation is renewed, now that the reformers are attacked with unscrupulous ignorance and virulence, now that the principles which animated them are impugned and denied".[1129] The Tractarians argued that it was through baptism and communion that grace was primarily conveyed. The advertisement in the first volume of the *Tracts for the Times* declared: "The sacraments, and not preaching, are the sources of divine grace."[1130] Newman and his colleagues also affirmed the authority flowing from apostolic succession. They argued that bishops had inherited divine authority in matters of the church, faith and morals from the apostles. This authority, no state could challenge.[1131] Yet, strangely, the doctrine of apostolic authority and sacramental grace was employed chiefly against the growing number of evangelicals, both Dissenters and Church.[1132]

The Tractarians, as yet, had no desire to emphasise ritual. But the emphasis on apostolic succession pointed towards Rome. By 1841, in

[1125] H.B. Bulteel, *A Sermon on 1 Corinthians II. 12* (1831) p.46.
[1126] F.M. Turner, *John Henry Newman* (2002) p.50.
[1127] J.H. Newman, *Apologia Pro Vita Sua and Six Sermons* (2008) p.158.
[1128] F.M. Turner, *John Henry Newman* (2002) p.2.
[1129] J.C. Hare, "Preface" to *The Mission of the Comforter, with Notes* (1850) p.x.
[1130] Cited in T. Arnold, "Introduction" to *Sermons by Thomas Arnold* (1878) (Mrs W.E. Forster (ed.)) vol.4, p.xvii.
[1131] F.M. Turner, *John Henry Newman* (2002) pp.168-180.
[1132] Ibid., pp.180-193.

the notorious *Tract 90*, Newman declared that the Thirty-nine Articles were no difficulty to a Roman Catholic. It was "possible to sign the articles in one sense and to interpret them in another".[1133] A year earlier, the possibility of a post-death conversion experience was sanctioned by the courts. Prayer for the dead might be more efficacious than the evangelism of the living.[1134] By the mid-1840s, Puseyism, named after Edward Bouverie Pusey – a Tractarian leader and Regius Professor of Hebrew at Oxford University[1135] – was "rampant", especially among the younger clergy.[1136] There were signs that it was "creeping about among the upper classes".[1137] It was also making an appeal to art lovers, through the work of a number of the Pre-Raphaelite brotherhood,[1138] although Holman Hunt – who was influenced by Ruskin in the latter's Christian epoch – was more Protestant.[1139] A reaction set in and there was talk of Tractarianism being a bar to preferment.[1140] However, in 1854, W.K. Hamilton went to Salisbury as the first Tractarian bishop. Among the Dissenters, its spirit existed "without its name".[1141] Evangelicals feared that the young men trained in the universities for ministry were being tainted there by the errors of an "active and popular" Romanising party.[1142] Thus, for example, Henry Liddon's evangelical mother was concerned about him going to Oxford, but his father overcame such concerns.[1143] At Oxford, Henry Liddon came "into the closest intimacy" with the Tractarian leaders there and, in due time, became one of their successors.[1144]

[1133] A.W.W. Dale, *The Life of R.W. Dale* (1898) p.169.
[1134] W.H B. Proby, *Annals of the "Low-Church" Party in England* (1888) vol.1, pp.446-447.
[1135] Pusey was also a cousin of Lord Shaftesbury.
[1136] R.W. Dale, *The Life and Letters of J.A. James* (1861) p.535.
[1137] Ibid., p.537.
[1138] T. Buser, *Religious Art in the Nineteenth Century in Europe and America* (2002) vol.1, pp.87-114. See also L. Errington, *Social and Religious Themes in English Art 1840-1860* (1984).
[1139] T. Buser, *Religious Art in the Nineteenth Century in Europe and America* (2002) vol.1, pp.92-93 and 106-114 and also M. Giebelhausen, *Painting the Bible* (2006) pp.16-17.
[1140] R.W. Dale, *The Life and Letters of J.A. James* (1861) p.537.
[1141] P. Rylands, *The Pulpit and the People* (1847) p.69.
[1142] D. Wilson, *Our Protestant Faith in Danger* (1850) p.16.
[1143] J.O. Johnston, *Life and Letters of Henry Parry Liddon* (1904) p.8.
[1144] Ibid., p.14.

Contemporaries thought that either the Tractarians wanted to change evangelicalism, or to establish a rival and antagonistic religion.[1145] The preface to *The Christian Observer* for 1833 thought that Tractarians were scattering "throughout the land publications which, for bigotry, popery and intolerance, surpass the writings even of Laud and Sacheverell".[1146] Tractarians thought that evangelicalism was deficient for not containing within it any principle of spiritual progress.[1147] A future Prime Minister, William Gladstone, saw the Tractarians – by putting Christianity at the heart of the nation – as the successors to the previous century's Evangelical Revival.[1148] Not everyone agreed with Gladstone although, with evangelical parents, he understood evangelicalism.[1149] The idea of spiritual progress in doctrine would later prove damaging to all forms of Christianity. However, this is to move ahead of ourselves. By 1856, although there were decided Tractarians and large Tractarian congregations in Brighton and Pimlico, *The Christian Observer* rejoiced that they had "failed to gain the slightest hold on the feelings or judgment of the British people".[1150] Indeed, at Perranzabuloe in Cornwall, William Haslam, one Sunday morning in the early to mid-1840s, found that reading an abridged Newman sermon in the pulpit led to his musicians, choir and others walking out.[1151] Haslam himself was later converted by his own sermon and saw at least the conversion of one Tractarian clergyman who had moved from what his mother had taught him.[1152]

However, for the Establishment, its Protestantism seems to have been partly a reaction to French imperialism. After the Napoleonic Wars, with Roman Catholic states no longer a military threat, resistance to Roman Catholic doctrines not only declined, but the doctrines themselves crept back. Among many leading Tractarian and High Church historians, two

1145 W.H.B. Proby, *Annals of the "Low-Church" Party in England* (1888) vol.1, p.396.
1146 "Preface" to 33 *The Christian Observer for the Year 1833* (1833) p.iii.
1147 W.H.B. Proby, *Annals of the "Low-Church" Party in England* (1888) vol.1, p.362.
1148 W.E. Gladstone, *Gleanings of Past Years* (1879) vol.7, pp.209 and 223. See also J.H. Rigg, *The Present Position of Christianity and the Christian Faith in this Country* (1878) p.7.
1149 R.W. Dale, *The Evangelical Revival* (1880) p.4.
1150 "On the Progress of True Religion Amongst our Home Population", in *The Christian Observer for the Year 1856* (1856) p.149.
1151 W. Haslam, *From Death into Life* (1897) pp.31-32.
1152 Ibid., pp.193-200. See also F. Pigou, *The Acts of the Holy Ghost* (1908) pp.38-39.

attitudes to the Reformation began to appear: either the extent to which the Reformation broke with the past was minimised, or its doctrines were virulently assailed. By doing so, the 'big idea' – that national greatness hinged upon obedience to the doctrines of the Reformation – began to be undermined. In its place, the idea was propagated that the medieval period was the time of national greatness.[1153]

6.5.2 *Roman Catholicism makes a comeback*

The Roman Catholic Relief Act of 1791 and Catholic Emancipation Act of 1829, by removing the restrictions on the civil liberties of Roman Catholics, facilitated their return in significant numbers to prominence in Great Britain. They began to influence the nation in certain areas, such as architecture, through the work of the architect Augustus Pugin and his Gothic Revival style. His commitment to stained glass windows helped "to create in the church an otherworldly cosmos".[1154]

In England Roman Catholicism gained recruits of standing from the Tractarians, including two of William Wilberforce's sons, Robert and Henry, both former Anglican clergy, and John Henry Newman.[1155] These and other leading seceders "drew scores, nay hundreds, in their train".[1156] Newman gave Roman Catholicism intellectual weight and, in 1845, he published *An Essay on the Development of Christian Doctrine*. In this he argued that Protestant criticism of Roman doctrinal innovation since early Christian times was unjustified, as the developments were a natural growth of what had gone before. In launching this defence of Roman Catholicism, he paved a highway for others wanting doctrinal innovation. Roman Catholicism also benefited from the 400,000 Irish immigrating to England between 1841 and 1851. Missioners of the London City Mission ascertained that one in every seven families they visited was Irish Roman Catholic.[1157]

[1153] J. Kirby, *Historians and the Church of England: Religion and Historical Scholarship, 1870-1920* (2016) pp.165-188.

[1154] T. Buser, *Religious Art in the Nineteenth Century in Europe and America* (2002) vol.1, p.116.

[1155] A third son of William Wilberforce also became a Roman Catholic, see S. Baring-Gould, *The Church Revival* (1914) p.335.

[1156] Ibid.

[1157] L.N.R., *The Missing Link* (1859) p.7.

The Roman Catholics also introduced itinerant missionaries and missions, often using personnel from abroad.[1158] For instance, Luigi Gentili from Rome enjoyed great success in evangelising the Leicestershire villages of Shepshed, Belton and Osgathorpe from June 1840. By the following May, he had over 500 converts from them.[1159] His work of preaching in the open, house visiting and talking to people in the country lanes was continued by his wealthy Oxford convert, William Lockhart. In 1843, Lockhart, at Loughborough, became the first member of the Oxford Movement to be received into the Roman Catholic church.[1160] Later, Lockhart would travel the United Kingdom as a missionary, winning converts.[1161]

In 1850, the pope thought that in England, "every day the obstacles are falling off which stood in the way of the extension of the Catholic religion".[1162] Accordingly, he reintroduced Roman Catholic bishoprics to England, together with the Archbishopric of Westminster. This, it is said, roused Protestant feeling as it had not been roused since the Glorious Revolution of 1688.[1163] However, the advent of the Crimean War, the alliance with Catholic France and the use of Catholic Irish soldiers in the British Army, made it difficult to maintain political anti-Catholicism.[1164]

[1158] K.F. Inglis, *Churches and the Working Classes in Victorian England* (1964) pp.17-18.

[1159] N. Schofield, *William Lockhart* (2011) p.49.

[1160] Ibid., pp.32-35.

[1161] Ibid., p.50.

[1162] *The Apostolic Letter of Pope Pius IX for the Re-Establishment of the Roman Catholic Episcopacy in England* (N.D.) p.5.

[1163] R.W. Dale, *The Life and Letters of J.A. James* (1861) p.545 and "On the Progress of True Religion Amongst our Home Population", in 56 *The Christian Observer for the Year 1856* (1856) p.149.

[1164] See D.M. Lewis, *Lighten their Darkness* (1986) pp.200-202. The impact of the Crimean War on Britain as a Protestant state needs consideration. In it, she sought to prop-up Muslim Turkey, with the help of Catholic France, against Orthodox Russia. At the Peace Treaty of Paris (1856) Turkey became the first non-Christian state to be admitted to the "Family of Nations" – and to enjoy the protection of the international legal system. In doing so, the parties were accepting that "no essential difference exists within the Family of Nations between Christian and non-Christian States", see L. Oppenheim, *International Law* (1912) vol.1, pp.154-155. As a result, the issue of religion in international law and politics tended to fall away, making it more acceptable for the religious ideas of other nations to circulate in Britain. The test of whether a state could join the Family of Nations shifted from its religion, to its level of civilisation, see ibid., p.155. See also W.E. Hall, *International Law* (1880) pp.34-35.

All the same, Roman Catholicism found it hard to keep its new recruits actively living the faith.[1165] For example, William Haslam, the Tractarian turned revivalist, had six friends who joined Rome in the winter of 1856. However, none were enthused long-term by the experience, either becoming miserable or abandoning their faith.[1166] On 30 March 1851, only 252,500 Roman Catholics attended mass in England and Wales.[1167]

In Scotland, the 1790s saw an increased flow of Roman Catholics from Ireland. Their priests followed them into the burgeoning cities and schools were started. They formed distinct communities and, by 1831, one calculation put their numbers as 15 per cent of Glasgow's population.[1168]

6.5.3 *Liberalism*

On the liberal horizon and darkening the sky was the view that "The only evidence required to entitle a man to regard himself as a member of the [redeemed community], is the persuasion that he belongs to it; and this persuasion is made the substitute for that 'faith which worketh by love' and holy obedience".[1169] The Baptist minister, Andrew Fuller, explained how someone could come to hold such a view as follows:

> Longing for ease to his troubled spirit, he is in the most imminent danger of taking up his rest in anything that will afford him a present relief; and if in such a state of mind he receive an impression that God has forgiven and accepted him, or read a book or heard a sermon favourable to such a mode of obtaining comfort, he will very probably imbibe it, and become inebriated with the delicious draft. And now he thinks he has discovered the light of life, and feels to have lost his burden.[1170]

Fuller, before his conversion, had undergone such a time.[1171]

[1165] See G. Best, *Mid-Victorian Britain* (1979) p.200.

[1166] W. Haslam, *From Death into Life* (1897) p.274.

[1167] H. Mann, *Religious Worship in England and Wales* (1854) p.45.

[1168] A.L. Drummond and J. Bulloch, *The Scottish Church 1688-1843* (1973) pp.137-141 and 146.

[1169] "Preface" to 16 *The Christian Observer for the Year 1817* (1818) p.vii.

[1170] Cited in E.D. Burns, "Andrew Fuller's Heavenly-Minded Piety: The Blessedness of Rest and Rewards for the Dead in Christ", in 128 *Churchman* (2014) p.151.

[1171] A.G. Fuller, *The Complete Works of the Rev. Andrew Fuller* (1856) pp.xvi-xvii.

Developments in Germany

In Germany, a few years before Fuller started preaching, Friedrich Schleiermacher, the son of a Prussian Army chaplain brought up among the Moravian Brethren, concluded that he could not accept the divinity of Christ, penal substitution or hell – and doubted the authenticity of the documents upon which Christianity rested. At the time, orthodoxy was being challenged in German literature. Further, in 1784, shortly after his death, the deist Gotthold Emphraim Lessing's *New Hypothesis Concerning the Evangelists Regarded as Purely Human Historians* had been published. It opened up new issues with regard to how the four Gospels had been written and their historicity.[1172] In 1791, after a time of study at the rationalist University of Halle, Schleiermacher wrote to his father, from whom his theological views had led to estrangement, to claim that his heart was now "properly cultivated" – even if the erudition of his intellect contradicted this. Schleiermacher believed he had returned to the Moravian faith, but only of a higher order.[1173] His new faith appreciated the Moravian community in which he had been nurtured, but rejected doctrinal formulas as "simply the result of reflection upon religious feeling". Historic creeds and teaching had to be tested against the contemporary needs of the religious community that produced them.[1174] It was religious feeling that was key – and one of his ideas was "that music is a more basic medium of religious expression than the spoken word".[1175]

Schleiermacher, in his *On Religion: Speeches to its Cultured Despisers* (1799), addressed "modern men and women whose education has interested them in just about everything except religion". Their "rich and many-sided" lives meant that they no longer needed the eternal.[1176] Schleiermacher did not point to the thunderings of hell, but to Christianity's "inspiration of science, of art, of morality and of everything else", as the reason for cultural despisers of religion to turn to it. It provided "a sense of the infinite" – and it was religion, not Christianity that was the subject of the bulk of the material making up

[1172] See generally, H. Chadwick, *Lessing's Theological Writings* (1956).
[1173] B.A. Gerrish, *A Prince of the Church* (1984) pp.10-13. See also R. Crouter, *Friedrich Schleiermacher On Religion* (1988) p.5.
[1174] B.A. Gerrish, *A Prince of the Church* (1984) pp.13 and 24-25.
[1175] Ibid., p.15.
[1176] R. Crouter, *Friedrich Schleiermacher On Religion* (1988) p.77.

this work. For Schleiermacher, "the original intuition of Christianity" was "an unsatisfied longing that is directed towards a great object and of whose infinity you are conscious". In the Son, this "feeling was wholly dominant"[1177] and Christians were "People who made the same intuition the basis of their religion".[1178] Thus, the Son was a mediator, but not the only mediator between God and man; and neither had the writing of Scripture closed with the end of the apostolic age.[1179] Contemporaries could not understand "how a man who adheres to such a system could be an honest teacher of Christianity".[1180] To meet criticisms, Schleiermacher made various amendments to later editions of *On Religion*, but this merely led to what modern scholars call the "conceptual incoherence" of the later editions.[1181] Around the time that it was published, Schleiermacher fell in love with the wife of a clergyman. However, she rejected his blandishments and stayed with her husband.[1182] It is commonly said that *On Religion* "inaugurated the modern period in religious thought".[1183]

Developments in England

The liberalism of which John Henry Newman was possibly nervous came from Germany – via Samuel Taylor Coleridge[1184] and his principal disciples: Connop Thirlwall, Bishop of St David's for 34 years, Archdeacon Julius Hare and Thomas Arnold of Rugby.[1185] Coleridge went through a period of what looks like conviction of sin in his early 20s, which has led some to suggest that he went through an "evangelical conversion".[1186] Nevertheless, his letters that point to

[1177] Ibid., p.217.
[1178] Ibid., p.220.
[1179] Ibid., pp.219-220.
[1180] A.C. Dole, *Schleiermacher on Religion and the Natural Order* (2010) p.4.
[1181] Ibid., p.5.
[1182] For a brief overview of Schleiermacher's attitude to women, see K. Clements, *Friedrich Schleiermacher* (1987) pp.21-22.
[1183] B.A. Gerrish, *A Prince of the Church* (1984) p.4.
[1184] Ironically a later liberal thought that "Coleridge's far-reaching vision did...discern the best part of the speculative truths which [the Tractarians]...exaggerated and perverted", J.C. Hare, "Preface" to *The Mission of the Comforter, with Notes* (1850) p.xiv.
[1185] See generally V.F. Storr, *Freedom and Tradition* (1940) pp.44-69.
[1186] P. Edwards, *The Statesman's Science* (2004) p.230.

conviction of sin lack any firm conviction in the atonement of Christ as the means of peace with God.[1187] Certainly, by the end of 1797, he had made up his mind to become a Unitarian minister[1188] and, on Christmas Day of that year, he received a letter offering him a Unitarian chapel in Shrewsbury. However, in the same post, he received a second – and entirely unexpected – letter from Josiah and Thomas Wedgewood, containing a draft payable to bearer of £100 to decline this engagement. This, he finally accepted – when the Wedgewood's offer was increased to an annuity of £150.[1189] With an "active zeal for Unitarian Christianity", he was now free of money concerns. After standing in for Dr Toulmin, the Unitarian minister at Taunton,[1190] he headed for Germany in the autumn of 1798. Here, on his first visit, he collected the materials for a biography of the eighteenth-century dramatist Gotthold Lessing. In later life, Coleridge came to accept the Trinity, although there were doubts about the orthodoxy of his formulation of it,[1191] and he favoured a national church. However, it was a church without doctrinal content and one whose role was to act as a "civilising force" to improve culture. He "has been seen as a founder of the Broad Church movement" that emerged later in the nineteenth century.[1192] In 1859, one reviewer of the theology of Coleridge noted that it is "remarkable how readily almost all the various phases of modern heresy may be traced to Coleridge as their author".[1193] That reviewer hoped that at the very close of his life, Coleridge had "died a true believer in the atonement of Christ".[1194]

Coleridge's most important idea was to rest the authority of the Bible not on its ultimate divine author, but on its spiritual nature. Coleridge wrote that, in the Bible, he "found words for my inmost thoughts, songs

[1187] *Collected Letters of Samuel Taylor Coleridge* (1966) (E.L. Griggs (ed.)) vol.1, pp.63-68. Penal atonement "continued to trouble him throughout his life", see J.W. Barbeau, *Coleridge, the Bible, and Religion* (2008) p.21.

[1188] *Collected Letters of Samuel Taylor Coleridge* (1966) (E.L. Griggs (ed.)) vol.1, p.362.

[1189] Ibid., pp.361-385.

[1190] Ibid., p.407.

[1191] "The Theology of Coleridge", in 59 *The Christian Observer for the Year 1859* (1859) p.636.

[1192] P. Edwards, *The Statesman's Science* (2004) pp.180-183.

[1193] "The Theology of Coleridge", in 59 *The Christian Observer for the Year 1859* (1859) p.634.

[1194] Ibid., p.638.

for my joy, utterances for my hidden griefs, and pleadings for my shame and feebleness? In short whatever *finds* me, bears witness for itself that it has proceeded from a Holy Spirit."[1195] This statement suggested that the only portions of the Bible with authority were those that chimed with the spirit of the reader. Man was to be central in thoughts about God. As Coleridge added, the Bible might be "a continual source and support of true belief...but what the right interpretation is – or whether the very words now extant are corrupt or genuine – must be determined by the industry and understanding of fallible, and alas! more or less prejudiced theologians".[1196]

Coleridge did not publish his views. They were too controversial for the times. He did not believe in the doctrine of the Fall and the atonement.[1197] All the same, the work in which they were set out, *Confessions of an Inquiring Spirit*, was circulated privately among those of sympathetic view. In 1825, a first draft was with the printer. However, it was not until 1840, six years after his death, that his nephew published it.[1198] As the years rolled by, Coleridge's ideas gained currency; further, the portions of the Bible that chimed with the spirit of liberal leaders diminished. At the heart of his theology was the desire to separate "two distinct conceptions – revelation by the Eternal Word, and actuation of the Holy Spirit".[1199] Julius Hare, one of Coleridge's pupils, believed that Coleridge had spiritualised "not only our philosophy, but our theology, to raise them both above the empiricism into which they had long been dwindling, and to set them free from the technical trammels

[1195] Author's italics. S.T. Coleridge, *Confessions of an Inquiring Spirit* (1886) p.15. In some ways, Coleridge's approach to interpreting the Bible was quite medieval in looking for deeper meanings in the text. "He aimed to penetrate the surface level of a text to discover, or experience, some truth to which he could respond and, in responding, assent to its authority," see G. Neville, *Coleridge and Liberal Religious Thought* (2010) p.5. Tellingly, Neville goes on, "When this was applied to the way of reading the Bible, it provided an escape route for those who were distressed by rigid doctrines claiming authority from its literal interpretation."

[1196] S.T. Coleridge, *Confessions of an Inquiring Spirit* (1886) pp.44-46.

[1197] "The Theology of Coleridge", in 59 *The Christian Observer for the Year 1859* (1859) p.637.

[1198] See A.J. Harding, *Coleridge and the Inspired Word* (1985) pp.95-99 and J.W. Barbeau, *Coleridge, the Bible, and Religion* (2008) pp.4-6. On the immediate response to the publication of the *Confessions of an Inquiring Spirit,* see ibid., pp.161-169.

[1199] S.T. Coleridge, *Confessions of an Inquiring Spirit* (1886) p.73.

of logical systems".[1200] "Primary truths" were now established "on irrefragable grounds, philological, historical, and philosophical, as well as theological".[1201]

Later, theological liberals developed more direct attacks on those who upheld the authority of the Bible – and along what became well-travelled lines. Conybeare, in a well-known essay in *The Edinburgh Review*, argued that evangelicals believed that "every casual allusion in Scripture to a fact in history, geology, or astronomy, however unconnected with religion, must be literally and infallibly accurate". No suggestion was made that evangelicals believed that the Bible might use at times popular, or figurative, language. He also suggested that evangelicals regarded each part of the Bible as possessing equal weight. However much the charges were rebutted,[1202] by dint of repetition the mud began to stick.

Conybeare's essay also illustrates some less theological arguments by which the liberals in future generations sought to weaken the confidence of evangelicals in the Bible. He argued that they were too involved in practical and parochial work to sufficiently engage competently with literature and theological learning.[1203] He characterised the Evangelical party as being "intolerant". There was also abuse. Evangelicals, he alleged, possessed "feeble minds", "low understandings" and "bad education".[1204] In heaping up his abuse, Conybeare followed the path of earlier liberals such as Sydney Smith who indicated that, through evangelicals, "piety had come to be associated in men's minds with intellectual weakness".[1205] Sydney Smith's liberality did not extend to those who disagreed with him; in this, many later liberal divines would follow him.[1206]

Conybeare's essay blamed evangelicalism for "driving half-educated

[1200] J.C. Hare, "Preface" to *The Mission of the Comforter, with Notes* (1850) p.xiii.
[1201] Ibid., p.viii.
[1202] For example, S. Minton, *The Evangelicals and "The Edinburgh"* (N.D.).
[1203] W.J. Conybeare, *Essays Ecclesiastical and Social* (1855) pp.70 and 74.
[1204] Conybeare's strictures were aimed at what he called the "Recordite" section of the Evangelical party, that is, the readers of *The Record*. Minton argued that the distinction drawn was "purely imaginary", S. Minton, *The Evangelicals and "The Edinburgh"* (N.D.) p.3.
[1205] J.H. Overton, *The English Church in the Nineteenth Century* (1894) p.121. See also "Jowett and the Broad Church", in 16 *The Westminster Review* (1859) pp.42-45 and W.E. Gladstone, *Gleanings of Past Years* (1879) vol.7, p.210.
[1206] J.H. Overton, *The English Church in the Nineteenth Century* (1894) p.112.

men into atheism" and of promulgating views "repulsive to the multitude". This was untrue; as Conybeare elsewhere acknowledged, evangelicalism's members included "the most *popular* preachers".[1207] However, at a time when the growth of Christianity led to the widespread belief that everyone ought to be a Christian – and they were not – it sounded a convincing explanation. Few theological liberals remembered, or could accept, the summons of Jesus: "Enter through the narrow gate. For wide is the gate and broad is the road that leads to destruction, and many enter through it. But small is the gate and narrow the road that leads to life, and only a few find it."[1208]

Another who struggled with the fact that so many failed to accept the gospel, was F.D. Maurice, who had been influenced by Coleridge. Maurice suggested that: "Baptism declares that those who will are taken out of that inconsistent condition to which they are prone, and are taken into a reasonable condition, in which they may live so long as they remember the covenant of God."[1209] Maurice, though, sought to distinguish his views on baptism from the Roman Catholic one. He argued that the purpose of baptism was to make a person a member of the "holy communion of saints", rather than bestowing "certain individual blessings".[1210] For Maurice, who was a universalist, "The truth is that every man is in Christ; the condemnation of every man is, that he will not own the truth; he will not *act* as if this were *true,* he will not believe that which is the truth."[1211] Maurice was criticised in *The Christian Observer* for attempting "to introduce the so-called religious views of Schleiermacher and his school into our English theology, adopting for that object the phraseology of our sound English divines and religious writers, but using it in another sense." It called this "*misuse of words*" a "new and subtle form of error".[1212]

By the mid-1850s, *The Christian Observer* was anxious about the rise among the clergy of the Rationalistic School, which subjected the

1207 Author's italics. S. Minton, *The Evangelicals and "The Edinburgh"* (N.D.) p.4.
1208 Matthew 7:13-14.
1209 F.D. Maurice, *The Kingdom of Christ* (1958) (A.R. Vidler (ed.)) vol.2, p.18.
1210 Ibid., p.286.
1211 Author's italics. *The Life of Frederick Denison Maurice* (1884) (F. Maurice (ed.)) vol.1, p.155.
1212 Author's italics. "Past and Present Aspect of German Theology", in 58 *The Christian Observer for the Year 1858* (1858) p.145.

Bible and Christian doctrine to interrogation. It thought the coming generation of clergy "much less hopeful than that passing from the field of labour."[1213] The rationalists seemed determined to pull down the "whole fabric of evangelical faith". However, it found it "almost impossible to suppose a really anxious enquirer resting there for the salvation of his soul". It added, "It may, perhaps, attract to its ranks a certain class of men who have never felt conviction of sin, and yet believe in the necessity of religion; and this class is numerous."[1214] William Wright, at the Union Street Chapel, in Kidderminster, expressed a similar view. In Wright's sermon of 16 March 1857, he noted: "Our times, moreover are remarkable for what (for want of a better name) we denominate as rationalistic Christianity; a phase of mental belief in which Christ is dishonoured, and the distinctive doctrine of his atonement is systematically ignored. Then there is open and avowed infidelity, to which this rationalistic system tends; running absolutely wild and rampant."[1215]

Troubles in Scotland

In Scotland, as popular piety grew, so did Calvinism, especially in the Highlands. John Macdonald, the 'Apostle of the North', preached in the open-air to thousands.[1216] However, Calvinism's growing strength stirred a reaction, especially manifested in the rejection of the idea that Christ died only for the elect. Although many evangelicals had always been uncertain about the latter point, they did believe that, until Christ's death was accepted by an individual, that individual lay under God's wrath. Some of those now rejecting limited atonement went on to suggest that, since God loved man, everything would be fine whatever one's response to him – and that penal substitution could be rejected without consequence. In the 1830s, a flurry of ministerial deprivations resulted

[1213] "On the Progress of True Religion Amongst our Home Population", in 56 *The Christian Observer for the Year 1856* (1856) p.147.
[1214] Ibid., p.150.
[1215] W. Wright, *The Church Bereaved* (1857) pp.18-19.
[1216] R. MacLeod, "John MacDonald", in the *Dictionary of Scottish Church History and Theology* (1993) (N.M. de S. Cameron (ed.)) pp.510-511 and. I.H. Murray, *A Scottish Christian Heritage* (2006) pp.125-156.

– including that, as we have seen, of Edward Irving.[1217]

6.6 Christian socialism appears

In 1850, 'Christian socialism' emerged in a series of tracts carrying that name addressed to "common Englishmen and Englishwomen".[1218] They were written by the Anglican minister F.D. Maurice. Maurice was concerned that the Christians were unsocial, and the socialists unChristian.[1219] He believed that "Christianity is the only foundation of socialism, and that a true socialism is the necessary result of a sound Christianity."[1220]

Maurice, to many, was a most attractive theologian. He emphasised the Fatherhood of God; the brotherhood of man; and that God is love.[1221] In his view, baptism was the "seal of God's children", the ground of "a real brotherhood" among men.[1222] He censured evangelicalism for not reaching out to the working classes as brothers and equals, explaining that this was the reason why the working classes had not been reached. He redefined the call to "repent and believe". "Repentance meant turning to a Father, and...believing meant trusting in him to set them right".[1223] In doing so, Maurice turned the focus from repenting of sin, and looking towards the atonement, to a focus on the minister and the act of baptism.

Maurice also emphasised co-operation, rather than competition, between men and emphasised education as the antidote to human problems. He was light on sin. The initial Christian socialist thrust of Maurice – and of his chief colleagues, Charles Kingsley and John Malcolm Ludlow – waned, along with socialism, around the end of 1854.

[1217] A.L. Drummond and J. Bulloch, *The Scottish Church 1688-1843* (1973) pp.194-219 and J. Macleod, *Scottish Theology* (1974) pp.257-259.

[1218] F.D. Maurice, "Dialogue between Somebody (a person of respectability) and Nobody (the writer)", in *Tracts on Christian Socialism No. I* (N.D.) p.11.

[1219] *The Life of Frederick Denison Maurice* (1884) (F. Maurice (ed.)) vol.2, p.35.

[1220] F.D. Maurice, "Dialogue between Somebody (a person of respectability) and Nobody (the writer)", in *Tracts on Christian Socialism No. I* (N.D.) p.1.

[1221] For a sense of the warmth felt towards Maurice, see C.E Raven, *Christian Socialism 1848-54* (1920) pp.75-93 and F. Higham, *Frederick Denison Maurice* (1947).

[1222] F.D. Maurice, "What Christian Socialism has to do with the Question which is now Agitating the Church", in *Tracts on Christian Socialism No. III* (N.D.) p.7. See also *The Life of Frederick Denison Maurice* (1884) (F. Maurice (ed.)) vol.2, p.242.

[1223] F.D. Maurice, "What Christian Socialism has to do with the Question which is now Agitating the Church", in *Tracts on Christian Socialism No. III* (N.D.) p.7.

It returned, with renewed vigour, during the last quarter of the nineteenth century. In the meantime, in 1854 Maurice and his friends established the Working Men's College to foster adult education. It gave many of the great sceptics of this and our next period a platform to lecture, including George Holyoake, Thomas Huxley, John Stuart Mill and John Ruskin.

6.7 The progenitor of the civic gospel establishes himself

George Dawson articulated the civic gospel at Birmingham. He gave up being a Baptist minister to establish his own church and stood "nearer to the Unitarians than any other church".[1224] Dawson became "hostile to the evangelical faith". He was also no enthusiast for the Evangelical Alliance founded by his neighbour John Angell James. In the sermon preached on the opening of his Church of the Saviour, in 1847, he contrasted "The unity which the Evangelical Alliance asks for...that of men bound by an iron ring of authoritative stereotyped opinion" with 'The unity we seek...that of free vitality, the unity of the Spirit, of independent men, brought together and kept together, not by a retrospective bond of sectarian opinion, but by oneness of spirit; and the prospective bond of common aim and purpose."[1225] This sounded appealing. However, he ignored the possibility that one would expect that the unity of the Spirit, for the spiritually mature, would lead to the same theological ideas. Though for his followers his "fervent utterings" attracted "numerous intelligent hearers", who "he bound together in one golden chain of unity and strength".[1226]

Dawson rejected Wilberforce's idea that Christianity's peculiar doctrines were the key to its power[1227] and he vigorously rejected creeds. In his view, "the only bond of union needful for a Christian Church is

[1224] A.W.W. Dale, *The Life of R.W. Dale* (1898) p.51. Dawson could be critical of the Unitarians, but they regarded his religious teachings as "harmonising with that form of liberal Christianity, which Unitarian Christians have laboured to diffuse", see J. Tamplin, *A Discourse Preached in the Baptist Chapel, King's Norton, on Sunday Evening, December 10, 1876 on Occasion of the Lamented Death of George Dawson* (1876) p.14.

[1225] G. Dawson, *The Demands of the Age Upon the Church* (1847) p.19.

[1226] J. Tamplin, *A Discourse Preached in the Baptist Chapel, King's Norton, on Sunday Evening, December 10, 1876 on Occasion of the Lamented Death of George Dawson* (1876) p.10.

[1227] See for the princples upon which Dawson's chapel was established, W. Wright, *The Life of George Dawson* (1905) pp.54-55.

a common recognition of Christ as their leader up to God, and...such a free love and search for spiritual truth, as would naturally grow out of an utter abandonment of all orthodoxies".[1228] For Dawson, politics and literature assumed the importance of religion in other men's thinking; his enthusiasm was for improvement in this life and not eternal bliss. "He dwelt upon the duty and the dignity of municipal work; he insisted that a man in becoming a Christian did not cease to be a citizen, and that his Christianity, if it was real, must reveal itself in a higher and nobler ideal of citizenship."[1229] In his own words, "political work is part of the service Christian men owe to Christ".[1230]

6.8 New religions

The first half of the nineteenth century saw a number of new religious groupings make an impact on the British religious scene.

6.8.1 *The Mormons arrive*

The Mormons started in America in the 1820s,[1231] but were soon active in Britain. It has been calculated that between 1837 and 1851, 17,000 emigrated from England to join their brethren in Salt Lake City. In 1851, their numbers in England and Wales were calculated at 30,000 – they had succeeded mainly with the working classes.[1232] In 1853, the number of Mormon converts sailing from England to the United States numbered 2,609.[1233] Their zeal across the nation was a cause of comment.[1234] In 1840, a mission to rural Herefordshire yielded 1,000 converts, including "virtually the entire membership of a local Wesleyan schism".[1235] Contemporaries also believed that their success illustrated the weakness

[1228] J. Tamplin, *A Discourse Preached in the Baptist Chapel, King's Norton, on Sunday Evening, December 10, 1876 on Occasion of the Lamented Death of George Dawson* (1876) p.8.

[1229] A.W.W. Dale, *The Life of R.W. Dale* (1898) p.52.

[1230] Cited in M. D. Johnson, *The Dissolution of Dissent, 1850-1918* (1987) p.41.

[1231] For an overview of the Mormon story, see H. Brogan, *The Pelican History of the United States of America* (1986) pp.238-251.

[1232] H. Mann, *Religious Worship in England and Wales* (1854) pp.50 and 52.

[1233] W.J. Conybeare, *Essays Ecclesiastical and Social* (1855) p.327.

[1234] For example, ibid., pp.280-376 and R.W. Dale, *The Life and Letters of J.A. James* (1861) p.545.

[1235] T. Grass, *Gathering to His Name* (2012) p.52.

of the Established Church.[1236] Their successful spiritual aggression was held out as worthy of emulation by orthodox evangelists. For example, Mitt Romney, the 2012 Republican candidate for the Presidency of the United States, had ancestors (Miles and Elizabeth Romney) who were converted to Mormonism at Preston in 1837.[1237] They left for the United States in 1840. Miles returned to England, as a Mormon missioner, in 1858.

6.8.2 *Spiritualism arrives*

In the late 1840s, Margarita and Catherine Fox in America allegedly experienced contact with the dead. Their disciples and other mediums shortly afterwards arrived in the United Kingdom, to create "no little stir".[1238] In the metropolis of 1853, "Table-turning" reached the proportions of an "epidemic" among the classes with leisure to indulge it, before a letter from Professor Faraday challenged it.[1239] Nevertheless, Mrs Hayden, a spiritualist who set up at No 22, Queen Anne St, Cavendish Square, in London impressed Robert Owen. At the end of his life he become a spiritualist, accepting the existence of God and some form of "Creating Power of the Universe".[1240] Mrs Hayden claimed to have put him in touch with the spirits of President Jefferson, Benjamin Franklin, the father of Queen Victoria and others.[1241] These manifestations informed Owen that they were made to change "the present false, disunited, and miserable state of human existence for a true, united and happy state, to arise from universal education".[1242] Owen concluded that Jesus Christ was the first coming of the truth, being "*an inspired medium from his birth, to teach the world the necessity for it to acquire* universal love and charity".[1243] The second coming of the truth

[1236] W.J. Conybeare, *Essays Ecclesiastical and Social* (1855) pp.v-vi, and 376.

[1237] C. Hebblethwaite, "Mitt Romney's Roots in Northern England", www.bbc.co.uk/news/magazine-18422949, accessed 15 December 2016.

[1238] D. Wilson, *Satanic Agency not Connected with Table Turning* (1853) p.4.

[1239] "Spirits and Spirit-Rapping", in 13 *The Westminster Review* (1858) p.30.

[1240] R. Owen, *The Life of Robert Owen* (1857) vol.1, p.iv.

[1241] R. Owen, *Manifesto of Robert Owen to all Governments and Peoples* (1853) pp.1-2.

[1242] Ibid., p.2.

[1243] Author's italics. R. Owen, *The Future of the Human Race* (1854) front cover and p.29.

had now arrived, "to instruct mankind *how to have* universal charity and love"[1244] – and he and his disciples were the people to do this. Owen's conversion to spiritualism intrigued his son, Robert Dale Owen – for a time a member of the United States House of Representatives. In his later years, Robert Dale Owen was "perhaps America's ablest advocate of spiritualism".[1245] In 1860, after he published in England his work on American spiritualism, *Footfalls on the Boundary of Another World*, Holyoake and other freethinkers declared that the heroism of the line of Robert Owen was extinct.[1246]

6.9 New poor-laws remove religion from state social help

The philanthropy of the period did not meet every need of the poor and the state began to extend further the involvement of the secular law to them. In England and Wales, 1834 saw a new poor-law which brought "a new rigour in the treatment of the poor".[1247] It eliminated the outdoor distribution of parish-based relief and introduced the confinement of paupers within regimented workhouses, where conditions were made sufficiently harsh to discourage application for admittance to them. There were also to be secular poor-law districts, with poor-law guardians elected by local ratepayers.[1248] Thomas Chalmers battled against the extension of the English system of poor-law relief to Scotland. He believed it discouraged community-based benevolence, which combined greater self-reliance of the poor with discreet generosity of the rich[1249] but, in 1845, the traditional system of Scottish parish poor relief was replaced with secular poor-law districts and workhouses.[1250]

[1244] Author's italics. Ibid., p.29.
[1245] R.W. Leopold, *Robert Dale Owen* (1940) p.viii.
[1246] Ibid., pp.336-337.
[1247] S.G. and E.O.A. Checkland, "Introduction" to *The Poor Law Report of 1834* (1974) p.9. For an introduction to the old poor law, see J.D. Marshall, *The Old Poor Law 1795-1834* (1985) and for an introduction to the application of the poor-law post 1834, see D. Englander, *Poverty and Poor Law Reform: From Chadwick to Booth, 1834-1914* (2013).
[1248] S.J. Brown, *Thomas Chalmers and the Godly Commonwealth in Scotland* (1982) pp.204-205.
[1249] Ibid., pp.78-84.
[1250] Ibid., pp.205, 290-295 and 366.

6.10 Conclusion

As the 1820s ended, Church evangelicals like Daniel Wilson were only too aware of the ongoing "attempts of infidelity on the one hand, and popery on the other, to undermine the foundations of religion and evangelical doctrine". However, they remained thankful that, "in a considerable number of our countrymen", the desire to follow the sentiments of the fifteenth and sixteenth centuries reformers remained.[1251] *The Christian Observer* thought that if "infidelity and licentiousness" were on the increase, so "true religion" was "greatly on the increase also".[1252]

However, the very success of the evangelicals brought them further danger. They had made "fashionable" a term like "justification by faith" so that it was often repeated, while those reciting the term were "very ignorant both of faith and justification".[1253] Many a young man was entering the ministry in search of preferment, or because of the respectability of the Church, or to gain a seat in the House of Lords, or because it offered a good living. Many were charged with being unconverted. Only time showed what they would do as they climbed the Church hierarchy. They performed only "a mock exercise of the shepherd's office."[1254] To them, the ideas of what made a Christian – such as water baptism, or by doing as much good as possible and leaving God to forgive the misdeeds – would appeal and influence many.[1255] Indeed, because of the pervasiveness of the evangelical challenge, those who resisted the evangelicals were forced to develop and harden their own thinking, so that more distinct parties emerged.[1256]

In 1830, the editor of *The Christian Remembrancer* thought that the tide was no longer running against those who regarded the Church of England as the "ark" of pure religion and baptism as the key to salvation. He argued that those baptised had been regenerated, even if inward grace

[1251] J.W. Middelton, "Preface" to *Memoirs of the Reformers, British and Foreign* (1829) vol.1, p.v.

[1252] "Preface" to 32 *The Christian Observer for the Year* 1832 (1832) p.iv.

[1253] H.B. Bulteel, *A Sermon on 1 Corinthians II. 12* (1831) p.15.

[1254] In addition, the clergy were charged with being "habitual gamblers, drunkards, misers, gluttons, fornicators, adulterers, or even worse", see ibid., pp.44-46.

[1255] *A Marvel of Grace, the Late William Taylor* (1895) pp.14-15 and 29-30.

[1256] G. Atkins, "'True Churchmen?' Anglican Evangelicals and History, c1770-1850", in 115 *Theology* (2012) pp.339-349.

"had been rejected and overborne" by and in them. He was anxious to make public the difference in the principles avowed by his publication and that of *The Christian Observer*.[1257] *The Christian Remembrancer* was convinced that it, and not *The Christian Observer*, was the true propounder of the principles of the Established Church. Soon, this new clericalism, through the Oxford Movement, burst forth as a distinctive group seeking to sweep all before it.

By the 1850s, members of the Oxford Movement were discussing whether the Evangelical party should be turned out of the Church of England. Samuel Wilberforce, William Wilberforce's son, desired to keep them – to be comprehensive.[1258] An evangelist, although friendly to the Oxford Movement, discovered that it robbed his preaching "both of its popularity and power".[1259] Yet, by 1857, matters seemed to be changing once again. The editor of *The Christian Observer*, in his preface for 1857, wrote of the publication's original purpose: "to recall the attention of the Church to the teaching of the reformers,"[1260] that "the victory, as to many points, is won, and there is really nothing to fight for."[1261] Yet that periodical was nevertheless troubled about the spiritual state of the nation. It looked back on the work of the Spirit in the nation – both at the beginning of the century and at its mid-point – and concluded that spiritual life was now broader, but lacked the depth of the past.[1262] "The gay, the dissipated, the worldly minded"[1263] attended church and happily listened to the call of the cross, but it seemed not to move them. It was concerned that too many of the converted had become worldly, leading lives no different from worldlings, so why should the unconverted want to change? It noted that "music has too often proved the connecting link between the Church and the world."[1264] A new work of the Holy Spirit, it believed, was the need of the times.

[1257] "Review of New Publications", in *The Christian Remembrancer* (1830) vol.12, pp.534-535.

[1258] J.O. Johnston, *Life and Letters of Henry Parry Liddon* (1904) pp.27-28.

[1259] C.E. Woods, *Memoirs and Letters of Canon Hay Aitken* (1928) p.48.

[1260] "Preface" to 57 *The Christian Observer for the Year 1857* (1857) p.iii.

[1261] Ibid., p.iv.

[1262] "Are Genuine Conversions to God as Frequent and as Decisive as they were Seventy Years Ago?", in 57 *The Christian Observer for the Year 1857* (1857) p.74.

[1263] Ibid., p.75.

[1264] Ibid., p.76.

The following year, in his preface, the editor to *The Christian Observer* thought that "Tractarianism has dwindled, popery has not increased, but Broad Churchism, comprehending in the term the various degrees of Broad, Broader, and Broadest – in other words of Latitudinarianism, scepticism, and rank infidelity – has entrenched itself."[1265]

[1265] "Preface" to 58 *The Christian Observer for the Year 1858* (1858) p.iv.

7

RESPONSES TO RELIGIOUS REVIVAL

7.1 Religion becomes important in politics

By the end of the 1830s, the Prime Minister, Lord Melbourne, always unenthusiastic in religious matters, remarked how religious everyone was becoming.[1266] Lord Melbourne's remark was stimulated by the increasing importance of Christianity to the political world. The removal, in 1828, of civil disabilities on Nonconformists and, in 1829, on Roman Catholics – and the reform of the franchise, in 1832 – opened up many offices to Catholics and Nonconformists[1267] and changed the electorate. After these changes many of the new voters still had religious grievances that could be remedied by political action. The five principal Nonconformist and Catholic grievances related to the privileged position of the Church of England, namely: 1) the duty, via the local rates, to contribute to the repair of the parish church; 2) access to the Universities of Oxford and Cambridge being limited to those who subscribed to the Thirty-nine Articles; 3) that births could only be registered in the baptismal registers of parish churches; 4) that a marriage, save for Jews and Quakers, must take place in the parish church; and 5) that, for most people, the only option was burial in the parish church – often with a Church rite of which the deceased disapproved. The religious revival was also impacting relations between, across and within the denominations.

[1266] See O. Chadwick, *The Victorian Church* (1987) pt.1, p.325.

[1267] For a helpful summary of the background to the repeal of the Test and Corporation Acts and the rise of the Tractarian movement, see C. Podmore, *Aspects of Anglican Identity* (2005) pp.16-23.

7.2 Agitation for disestablishment begins

In the 1830s, the Nonconformists vigorously articulated the case for separating the Church of England from the state. Thomas Binney, minister at the King's Weigh House Church and a major religious figure, declared "that the Established Church is a great national evil... it destroys more souls than it saves".[1268] The Nonconformists expected support from evangelicals in the Church of England for their campaign of disestablishment and were signally disappointed.[1269] Instead, *The Record* newspaper saw an unholy conspiracy. It believed that, for many, "the overthrow of the Establishment is only a present step to an ulterior object, viz., the overthrow of Christianity altogether". Infidelity was far from dead[1270] and would "gladly take the assistance of the orthodox Dissenters as far as they will go, in destroying those with whom, on all that is vital and essential, they agree – and then turn upon, and rend them". It added, "Paganism has persecuted; popery has persecuted. Can infidelity not persecute?"[1271] Notwithstanding these strictures, in 1844, The British Anti-State Church Association was formed to campaign for disestablishment. Many of the great Nonconformists, such as C.H. Spurgeon, were supporters.[1272] In 1850, Daniel Wilson expressed concern about the intentions of the liberal politicians. Many seemed to be no friend of distinctive gospel principles. Wilson thought they wanted to give free scope to all religions and to sever literature and science from Christianity. The radicals suggested that the general laws of science supported atheism – pointing to fate, rather than their very existence and consistency demanding a divine author.[1273] Wilson sensed a conspiracy against the gospel where religious and political parties would "unite in harmony and peace; and truth is to be merged in a spirit of enlarged charity".[1274]

[1268] R.H. Martin, *Evangelicals United* (1983) p.197.

[1269] D. Wilson, *Our Protestant Faith in Danger* (1850) p.4.

[1270] For example, see G.S. Faber, *The Fruits of Infidelity Contrasted with the Fruits of Infidelity* (1831) and E. Bather, *Hold Fast that Which is Good* (1831). The British Library's copy of the letter has appended to it an extensive list of books and tracts for the counteraction of infidel and blasphemous publications.

[1271] Cited in D.M. Lewis, *Lighten their Darkness* (1986) p.18.

[1272] The Wesleyan Methodists though, with their roots in the Church of England, were always less supportive of disestablishment.

[1273] G.J. Holyoake, *The Logic of Death* (1902) p.9.

[1274] D. Wilson, *Our Protestant Faith in Danger* (1850) p.20.

7.3 Anti-Catholic reaction

Voting reform led many Protestants to be concerned about the growth of Roman Catholic influence. On 11 July 1835, the Protestant Association was formed – to express the peculiar dangers of the times. Its work was predicated upon the following resolutions:

> That the influence of true religion over a people forms the best security for their individual rights, and the surest basis of national prosperity.
>
> That the British constitution acknowledges in its principle and laws the sovereignty of Almighty God, and the supreme authority of his holy word, and has provided for the Scriptural instruction of the people by its religious Establishments.
>
> That in opposition to this principle of the constitution, doctrines have of late been propagated, that religion is unconnected with the duties of legislation – that in the eye of the state all religions are alike – and that support should equally be given or denied to all.

Earlier, Protestant associations had furthered particular initiatives, but the Protestant Association was the first in a line of organisations pledged to maintain the Protestant nature of Church and state. Giving force to such organisations was the view that when England turned Protestant, she held about tenth place among the nations but, by the 1830s, she was "far above the mightiest of the empires". This, it was believed, was due "to that special favour and protection of God, which is never withheld from any nation which publicly honours him".[1275] Many local Protestant institutes sprang up for a similar purpose. T.R. Birks, in a lecture to the one at Islington, thought that it was its Protestant faith that enabled England to stand "calm and erect" during the anarchy that shook the other European nations during 1848. His thesis was that "Protestant Christianity…is the true foundation of our national peace and greatness… Faith in relics and crucifixes, in steam-engines and railways can never save us, but only faith in Christ."[1276] However, absent a political threat from a Roman Catholic power to focus the mind, this viewpoint became less persuasive than formerly to those without strong Protestant beliefs.

[1275] See D.M. Lewis, *Lighten their Darkness* (1986) p.22.

[1276] T.R. Birks, *Protestant Truth the Basis of National Prosperity* (1848) pp.1-2.

As the Royal Navy ruled the waves and British industry was the world leader, it was the time to try alternative theological perspectives – and for those espousing a range of Christian beliefs to fall out with one another.

7.4 Evangelicals unite while some follow the civic gospel

In 1846, evangelicals of all denominations, and from many different countries, formed the Evangelical Alliance. The idea of a pan-Evangelical organisation, an early form of ecumenicalism, is attributed to John Angell James. In its original conception, some wanted it to fight popery and the Plymouth Brethren. The latter were perceived as deviant – for rejecting the ordained ministry – but opposition to them soon fell away.[1277]

As plans for the Alliance ripened, its object was clarified – as reuniting Christians and cultivating union of belief and purpose between them. Those involved confessed their guilt for past divisions between Church and chapel and agreed on the need to counteract "infidelity" and "Romanism".[1278] Nevertheless, the birth of the Evangelical Alliance was not easy. A split over slavery occurred and American slave owners were barred. At home, many Anglicans were wary of an organisation that included disestablishment Nonconformists. Some evangelicals refused to join because they thought the problem was not in agreeing general principles, but in their application.[1279] All the same, by 1859, the Evangelical Alliance had 6,000 members.[1280]

At a parochial level, in August 1856, William Pennefather held "a Conference of the Lord's people" in Barnet "to promote personal holiness, brotherly love, and increased interest in the work of the Lord".[1281] The annual Barnet and, as it became, Mildmay Conference in

[1277] See generally I. Randall and D. Hilborn, *One Body in Christ: The History and Significance of the Evangelical Alliance* (2000) p.30.

[1278] E. Bickersteth, *A Brief Practical View of the Evangelical Alliance* (1846) p.24.

[1279] R. Whately, *Thoughts on the Proposed Evangelical Alliance; in a Letter to a Clergyman* (1846) p.16.

[1280] I. Randall and D. Hilborn, *One Body in Christ: The History and Significance of the Evangelical Alliance* (2000) p.68. Non-evangelicals considered that members of the Evangelical Alliance might transfer their loyalty to it – so that it became "virtually, a new, self-constituted church", see R. Whately, *Thoughts on the Proposed Evangelical Alliance; in* a *Letter to a Clergyman* (1846) p.14.

[1281] R. Braithwaite, *The Life and Letters of Rev. William Pennefather, BA* (N.D.) p.305.

Islington later wielded considerable influence, as its numbers reached 3,000.[1282]

In Scotland, Thomas Chalmers, who had been actively involved in organising Scottish participation in the Evangelical Alliance, started an interdenominational campaign, whereby all Protestant denominations would come together to plant "community-building" societies in different areas, with an emphasis on reaching the working class, although the plan did not last for more than a couple of years.[1283]

Some evangelicals though were pulling away from their heritage and into new paths, such as the civic gospel. For example R.W. Dale, after starting theological college in 1847, preferred listening to George Dawson, rather than to John Angell James – to whom he succeeded at the latter's pre-eminent pulpit. As Dale rose to the forefront of Congregationalism, Dawson's thought influenced him, although he always regretted that Dawson lacked "more of the old evangelical doctrine".[1284] The prominent politician Joseph Chamberlain was a member of Dawson's church – and Dale, Chamberlain and John Bright (a Quaker) in our next period, provided a concrete expression of the civic gospel, as the municipal services of Birmingham were transformed.

7.5 Differences in the chapels

By the end of our period, the doctrine of the Congregational church stood upon a knife-edge. It was historically Calvinistic so[1285] in 1852 William Booth turned down a free place to train as a Congregational minister because it meant studying Calvinism.[1286] However, its doctrinal slippage had already been revealed in 1846 with the publication of Edward White's *Life in Christ*. From his pulpit at Eignbrook Chapel in Hereford, White challenged the immortality of the soul, suggesting that immortality was the "peculiar privilege" of the converted. The unregenerate would, after judgment, be punished for their misdeeds and then they would die. This was a challenge to the contemporary theology expressed in works

[1282] *Some Records of the Life of Stevenson Arthur Blackwood* K.C.B. (1898) p.316.

[1283] S.J Brown, *Thomas Chalmers and the Godly Commonwealth in Scotland* (1982) pp.364-366.

[1284] A.W.W. Dale, *The Life of R.W. Dale* (1898) p.53. On Dawson and his influence over Dale see generally M.R. Watts, *The Dissenters* (2015) vol.3, pp.231-233.

[1285] H. Mann, *Religious Worship in England and Wales* (1854) p.19.

[1286] H. Begbie, *Life of William Booth* (1920) vol.1, pp.140-142.

like John Angell James's massively successful, *The Anxious Enquirer after Salvation*. In his later years, James was apprehensive about the orthodoxy of the younger ministers.[1287]

The next widespread controversy occurred in 1856, when Samuel Davidson published the Old Testament volume of the tenth edition of a standard text book – Horne's *Introduction to the Sacred Scriptures*. Davidson was a professor at the Lancaster Independent College and, for his previously published works, held an honorary Doctorate of Theology from the University of Halle. Horne had written the previous editions of this work, but Davidson thought an entire rewrite was necessary in the light of scholarly developments in countries such as Germany.[1288] Davidson abandoned Mosaic authorship of the Pentateuch and limited biblical inspiration to religion and morals. Nevertheless, he believed that he maintained "the completeness and sufficiency of Holy Scripture as an unerring rule of faith and practice, man's original depravity, regeneration by the Holy Spirit, justification by faith, the atonement made by the divine Redeemer for the sins of the world, and the application of it in redemption".[1289] Davidson's work was slated by *The Record* and Dr Horne disassociated himself from it.[1290] In 1857, a motion against Davidson, in his college's governing body, for alleged liberalism was carried, but by only 18 votes to 16. Davidson resigned and afterwards his "critical opinions rapidly advanced in the direction of pure rationalism".[1291] New appointments at Lancaster Independent College to enhance conservative scholarship did not succeed. "Imperceptibly the teaching of the lecture-rooms came into practical accord with the volume which had deprived the college of its greatest scholar."[1292] Elsewhere, within Congregationalism, men like Thomas Binney, although not apparently repudiating evangelical doctrines, began to repudiate "the

[1287] R.W. Dale, *The Life and Letters of J.A. James* (1861) p.617.

[1288] For an account of the issues from the perspective of the Davidson camp, see *The Autobiography and Diary of Samuel Davidson* (1899) (A.J. Davidson (ed.)) pp.35-70.

[1289] Ibid., p.44.

[1290] See S. Davidson, *Facts, Statements, and Explanations Connected with the Publication of the Second Volume of the Tenth Edition of Horne's Introduction to the Study of the Holy Scriptures, Entitled "The Text of the Old Testament Considered," etc.* (1857) pp.4-8.

[1291] *The Autobiography and Diary of Samuel Davidson* (1899) (A.J. Davidson (ed.)) p.67.

[1292] Ibid., p.69.

formulas and phrases" in which they were generally stated.[1293]

Nineteenth-century Methodism was more resistant to theological liberalism than any other major denomination, but it was more likely to split than any other.[1294] The issues over which it split were generally not doctrinal, but related to who controlled it and/or a lack of enthusiasm for evangelism. The Methodist New Connection appeared at the end of the eighteenth century. It arose because of a concern that Methodism's governing conference was giving too much power to ministers. In 1811, the more important and numerically strong Primitive Methodists separated off, as the evangelistic zeal of the Wesleyan Methodists languished.

The Bible Christians began in 1815. Although not a formal breakaway from the Methodists, they were started by William O'Bryan, a Wesleyan preacher in Cornwall. He adopted Methodist forms and by 1852 Bible Christians possessed 293 chapels, being the smallest Methodist community. In 1834 the Wesleyan Methodist Association split off from the old Wesleyan Connection. The crisis came over the establishment of the Wesleyan Theological Institution. In 1849, a very substantial group broke away over the power of the Wesleyan Conference and of its President, Jabez Bunting. They became known as the Reformers.[1295] There were other, smaller, Methodist breakaways. All had at least one material thing in common – a few wealthy supporters to sustain them.[1296] In 1857, the Wesleyan Methodist Association and the Reformers came together to create the United Methodist Church. Towards the end of our period, some Methodist groups found it difficult to keep up their numbers.

7.6 Contention emerges within the Church of England

The editor of *The Christian Observer for the Year 1822* suggested in his preface that seldom had a year gone by "less marked by acrimonious

[1293] A.W.W. Dale, *The Life of R.W. Dale* (1898) p.50.

[1294] For the divisions within Methodism, see generally R. Currie, *Methodism Divided* (1968) pp.54-82. There were other Methodist groups apart from the main ones mentioned here.

[1295] For details of the respective strengths of the various communities making up the Methodists in the early 1850s, see H. Mann, *Religious Worship in England and Wales* (1854) pp.27-39.

[1296] R. Currie, *Methodism Divided* (1968) p.82.

religious controversies among good men". He was also looking forward to the children "of sainted sires" stepping forward to fulfil "the duties to which they were so anxiously trained".[1297] However, Alexander Haldane, effectively editor of *The Record*, looking back in 1853, claimed that by the 1820s a younger generation of evangelicals was concerned that

> a wide-spread spirit of worldly wisdom and sinful compromise had come over a considerable portion of the Evangelical party in the Church. There is no doubt that the great anti-slavery struggle had induced an amalgamation between its leaders and Socinians [Unitarians], Romanists, and worldly men. We have heard of a distinguished prelate who was arguing with Mr Wilberforce, Mr Macaulay, and others, on the danger of the combination, who thus concluded his prophetic warning, 'It may not injure you, but what will be the influence on your sons?'[1298]

By the mid-twentieth century, a writer, looking back, observed that "there is an impressive roll of Victorian notables who were evangelicals in their youth, through parental influence or early teaching or both," but who did not continue. The list included

> Charlotte, Emily and Anne Brontë, Henry Thomas Buckle, Mark Pattison, Samuel and Robert Isaac Wilberforce,[1299] Sir James Stephen and Sir George Stephen, Lord Glenelg, Sir Gilbert Scott, Samuel Butler, Benjamin Jowett, Elizabeth Barrett, George Eliot, Kingsley, De Quincey, Ruskin, Macaulay, Peel, Gladstone, Pusey, Manning, and Newman. Of these men nine were sons of the evangelical high command.[1300]

For those who turned Roman Catholic, some attributed it to their attendance at Oxford, rather than the more evangelical Cambridge which, in the case of the Wilberforce sons, was their father's alma mater.[1301]

[1297] "Preface" to 22 *The Christian Observer for the Year 1822* (1823) p.iv.

[1298] See D.M. Lewis, *Lighten their Darkness* (1986) p.16.

[1299] Another brother, Henry Wilberforce, joined the Roman Catholic faith.

[1300] F.K. Brown, *Fathers of the Victorians* (1961) p.6. Not all the children of leading nineteenth-century evangelicals walked away from the faith of their fathers, I. Bradley, *The Call to Seriousness* (1976) p.194.

[1301] W.E. Gladstone, *Gleanings of Past Years* (1879) vol.7, p.231. However, Wilberforce's oldest son William – and the most profligate – went to Cambridge.

As the doctrinal perspective of the Church of England widened, disturbances arose. The creeds and the Thirty-nine Articles were attacked as the work of men.[1302] The issues were most sensitive where great minds and positions were involved. Appointments of those suspected of unorthodoxy (whether liberal or Catholic) to senior professorships at Oxford[1303] and to bishoprics[1304] caused a storm of protest. Oxford University condemned the books of those heading to Rome, while claiming allegiance to the Church of England.[1305] Pusey, after a sermon containing high sacramental language, was suspended from preaching for two years. In 1848, Baptist Noel, who had written against baptismal regeneration, left the Church of England and joined the Baptists.[1306] Furthermore, congregations which could get no relief from their bishop with regard to their parish's movement towards Tractarianism might move towards separation, often with the help of a clergyman supplied by the Countess of Huntingdon's Connexion.[1307] Daniel Wilson, another evangelical leader, thought the Church of England was in crisis and risked resuming "her ancient position as a vassal of the See of Rome".[1308] In 1851 the Nonconformist John Angell James, writing to a friend, observed that "the Church of England is shaken to its centre."[1309]

On the theologically liberal wing of the Anglican church, men like Frederick W. Robertson, at Trinity Chapel Brighton, revised their theology of the atonement and limited the authority of the Scriptures.[1310] Robertson wrote in a "pure, clear, and agreeable style; presenting what

[1302] S. Thomas, *Newman and Heresy* (1991) pp.71-79.

[1303] For example, Hampden to the Regius Professorship of Divinity.

[1304] Hampden to Hereford.

[1305] W.G. Ward and *The Ideal of a Christian Church* (1844).

[1306] During the first half of the nineteenth century, it has been calculated that around two percent of evangelical clergy left for the Nonconformist ministry, see *G. Carter, Anglican Evangelicals* (2001) p.55. The reasons for secession are usefully summarised in ibid., pp.31-57.

[1307] J. Fenwick, *The Free Church of England* (2004) pp.42-53.

[1308] D. Wilson, *Our Protestant Faith in Danger* (1850) p.2.

[1309] R.W. Dale, *The Life and Letters of J.A. James* (1861) p.545.

[1310] The atonement was "nothing more than an essentially common incident" and the Scriptures were to be interpreted through "the light of the life of Christ". The latter, although sounding pious, was what the apostles thought they did, yet Robertson "*Shut out the light of the other Scriptures*" outside the Gospels. Author's italics. See "A Broad Church Preacher", in *The Family Treasury of Sunday Reading* (1866) p.145.

the author considered the truth in an original and suggestive way".[1311] This threw up a debate over whether it was right to criticise novel views presented in such a "fascinating" way and which made the critics sound harsh.[1312] The fate of those who died without faith became a real issue. For example, in 1849, Sir James Stephen, the son of James Stephen of the Clapham Sect, expressed in print his doubt whether the punishment of those outside Christ was eternal. He thought that such a view threw a "portentous cloud" over whether God is love. Such a view was not novel. George Taylor, a land owner in County Durham, wrote to his son in similar terms in 1814,[1313] but then the momentum of that time was in favour of eternal punishment. Sir James Stephen's view showed the theological pendulum swinging back. Sir James added that the doctrine of eternal punishment was also "the most effective of all the causes which are at present inducing amongst us that virtual abandonment of Christianity."[1314] He assured his readers that

> the doctrine of the eternity of the future retribution forms no necessary substratum of any other Christian doctrine. If it could be completely disproved, its disappearance from the Christian system would not dissolve, nor apparently impair, the strength of any other part of that mighty fabric.[1315]

As history would show, if there was no form of future judgment and retribution, then doctrinal disputes and issues over whether any form of conduct was sinful became meaningless – simply a matter of interpretation or opinion. Jesus had made the point that the Father had "entrusted all judgment to the Son, that all may honour the Son just as they honour the Father".[1316] As the significance of the Day of Judgment lost significance, so did reverence within the nation for Jesus Christ.

Perhaps the most famous incident relating to the emerging new theology occurred when F.D. Maurice was dismissed from his theological chair at King's College, London, for his work *Theological Essays* (1853).

[1311] Ibid., p.141.
[1312] For a summary of the debate, see ibid., p.142.
[1313] H. Taylor, *Autobiography of Henry Taylor* (1885) vol.1, pp.39-40.
[1314] Sir James Stephen, *Essays in Ecclesiastical Biography* (1853) vol.2, p.504.
[1315] Ibid., pp.498-499.
[1316] John 5:22b-23.

To the common man, he was known as the parson who did not believe in hell, or any system of eternal rewards and benefits. The worst God did to a man was to leave him alone.[1317] One reason for his rejection of hell was that it "scared many into unbelief".[1318] Maurice, in our next period, gained huge stature as a theologian.[1319] He was unwilling to recognise that a man needed to be regenerated, or born again, before he could be freed from sin for service. He believed education could ensure that God's love penetrated human hearts and that men would therefore love God and each other.[1320] "If sin were minimised into something that did not require supernatural treatment" then, as Dominic Erdozain notes, "the Christian 'cure' would be redundant and the Christian religion would be on borrowed time".[1321] Maurice had lodged within the pale of the Church of England "a new faith", dissonant with the one he had pledged to maintain.[1322]

There were also court proceedings, often involving Bishop Phillpotts of Exeter as he, in his long episcopacy of 1830 to 1869, moved his diocese in a Tractarian direction.[1323] However, the case for which he is best remembered occurred in 1850, when he was successfully taken to court by Gorham, an evangelical. Phillpotts had refused to institute Gorham into his parish because Gorham rejected unconditional regeneration at baptism.[1324] In another legal case, the Anglo-Catholic George Denison was taken to court for suggesting "the inward reality of the sacrament

[1317] Maurice adopted as Christian a view previously seen as atheistic, see R.N. Watson, *The Rest is Silence* (1994).

[1318] G. Rowell, *Hell and the Victorians* (1974) p.81.

[1319] Of nineteenth-century churchmen "we shall reckon him as incomparably the greatest, alike in life, in vision and in achievement", see C.E Raven, *Christian Socialism 1848-54* (1920) p.75.

[1320] Maurice was often accused of a form of universalism and of eschewing individual sin: E. Norman, *The Victorian Christian Socialists* (2002) pp.26 and 102. See also B.M.G. Reardon, *Religious thought in the Victorian Age* (1995) pp.118-158 for a sense of the difficulty of categorising Maurice's theology.

[1321] D. Erdozain, "The Secularisation of Sin in the Nineteenth Century", 62 *Journal of Ecclesiastical History* (2011) p.59.

[1322] See H. Burgess, *Maurice's Essays* (1854) p.2.

[1323] J. Fenwick, *The Free Church of England* (2004) pp.42-46.

[1324] See D. Phillips, "Goreham and the Penzance Commission", in 128 *Churchman* (2014) pp.199-217. Phillpotts was more successful in removing William Haslam from his diocese, after he moved away from baptismal regeneration, see W. Haslam, *From Death into Life* (1897) pp.225-233.

was received by all, wicked as well as faithful". In 1858, he escaped on a technicality. Overall, the litigation was a mixed triumph for the Evangelical party. The Gorham action was a vital success but it may have led them to be over-zealous later in resort to litigation.

7.7 Conflict between Church and chapel and the voluntary principle

Underpinning the evangelistic energies of the Dissenters was the acceptance of the voluntary principle – the principle that religious groupings should be left free of state aid to reach the unconverted. After the Dissenters obtained the right to vote, they increasingly agitated with militancy and focus for its application to all forms of government action. Compulsory religion was said to bolster the Established Church – and did not inspire faith in those attending services out of duty. The Congregationalist Edward Miall thought that the existence of the Church Establishments was "fatally potent in retarding the spiritual reign of Christ in the British realms".[1325]

In Scotland, by the end of 1833, voluntary associations existed in dozens of Scottish towns and villages. As we have seen, the British Anti-State Church Association was formed in 1844. In 1853, it was renamed the Society for the Liberation of Religion from State-Patronage and Control. Thereafter, it became known as The Liberation Society, its meetings often being held at the largest church of the day, Spurgeon's Metropolitan Tabernacle.

The result of the application of the voluntary principle was that the state became unwilling to aid the building programmes of the Established Churches, as the nation's population rapidly expanded – and in Scotland the Established Church lost its long-standing administration of support for the poor, after a considerable battle.[1326] The state's involvement in education – and any help that it provided to the schools of the established churches – became increasingly contentious.

At a time when Dissent had tremendous vigour, the voluntary principle had an appeal – but it undermined the role of Christianity, as mediated through the Established Churches of Britain and in government policy. It also meant that Christianity was more likely to focus on the upper

[1325] E. Miall, *The British Churches in Relation to the British People* (1850) p.299.
[1326] S.J. Brown, *Thomas Chalmers and the Godly Commonwealth in Scotland* (1982) pp.289, 290-295, 350 and 366.

and middle classes, as they had the funds necessary to support churches lacking endowments. For this reason, in Scotland, Thomas Chalmers, as a Church of Scotland minister, fought for long against the voluntary principle as its application was likely to leave members of the growing working classes without access to the churches, since they could not afford the pew rents.[1327] Upper- and middle-class Dissenters much preferred paying pew rents – they could afford to pay them – to the alternative of paying taxes used for the benefit of Established Churches.

7.8 Ritualism engenders conflict between Church and chapel

The growth of Ritualism deepened the rift between Church and chapel and encouraged spats between them. For instance, in 1856, there was delivered at Kidderminster's Congregational church "twelve controversial lectures on 'The Right and Duty of Dissent', as a result of the High Churchism which prevailed in the town, and which assumed to itself the right to 'Rebuke Dissenters with sharpness'."[1328]

7.9 Disruption in Scotland

In Scotland, 1839 saw a peculiarly combustible mixture of spiritual revival and court involvement in the affairs of its established church. The Court of Session decided that the new churches recently established by the Church of Scotland could not be parish churches, but effectively only chapels-of-ease – without territorial boundaries and with no right to keep church-door collections for the relief of the poor and church extension.[1329] Further judgments of the Court of Session, unfavourable to the Church of Scotland, followed.

In the Seceder Church (from the Church of Scotland), 1839 saw its probationer James Morison sent to the far north to preach the gospel to "rude agricultural people".[1330] During this time, his own doubt of whether he was among God's elect was resolved by the conclusion that Christ died for all, including himself.[1331] Soon, influenced by Finney's *Lectures*

[1327] Ibid., pp.246-247.

[1328] G. Hunsworth, *Baxter's Nonconformist Descendants* (1874) pp.67-68.

[1329] S.J. Brown, *Thomas Chalmers and the Godly Commonwealth in Scotland* (1982) pp.234 and 276-277.

[1330] F. Ferguson, *A History of the Evangelical Union* (1876) p.6.

[1331] Ibid., pp.9-10.

on Revivals of Religion, he was issuing "loud calls to repentance – and forcible warnings in view of eternity"; and a church built to hold 600 was crammed full – with 1,000 listeners.[1332]

Morison's views on universal atonement were not generally accepted by his denomination. So, in 1843, after three years of proceedings against him and a few other fellow ministers, they left to establish the Evangelical Union of Scotland. During this struggle, their theology broadened from moderate Calvinism – whereby Christ died for all, but God's irresistible grace chose some – to a position whereby God's grace could be resisted; and question marks about Morison's view on original sin emerged.[1333] The Evangelical Union soon started to draw numbers from the Congregationalists.

A few days after the basis of the Evangelical Union was drafted, well over a third of the clergy of the Established and Presbyterian Church of Scotland left it – to form the Free Church of Scotland.[1334] During the afternoon of 18 May 1843, Thomas Chalmers dramatically led the departees out of the Church of Scotland's General Assembly hall, in procession – "solemnly through the New Town of Edinburgh".[1335] The background to this disruption concerned the right of the gentry – and others holding the power of appointment of ministers – to impose their appointees on the Established Church, notwithstanding local opposition. The Court of Session again was involved and decided against the Church of Scotland. The House of Lords upheld its decision.[1336] The dispute broadened – and the serious issues over the church's independence of the state arose. The General Assembly of the Church of Scotland was evangelical. By the time separation came, the dispute had been going on for a decade.[1337]

The Free Church of Scotland, led by Dr. Thomas Chalmers, enjoyed

[1332] Ibid., p.13.
[1333] W. Adamson, *The Life of the Rev. James Morison* (1898) pp.127-128, 131-132 and 292.
[1334] S.J. Brown, *Thomas Chalmers and the Godly Commonwealth in Scotland* (1982) p.335.
[1335] Ibid., p.334.
[1336] W. Adamson, *The Life of the Rev. James Morison* (1898) pp.299-300 and 329.
[1337] See generally A.L. Drummond and J. Bulloch, *The Scottish Church 1688-1843* (1973) pp.220-265 and S.J Brown, *Thomas Chalmers and the Godly Commonwealth in Scotland* (1982) pp.225-228 and 296-379.

great energy. It quickly built hundreds of churches and schools, as evangelists like John Milne were sent out[1338] – and the Free Church of Scotland spread out. Its members gave freely to its work, but the ministers previously in the Church of Scotland, who lost their stipends and manses, suffered real hardship. Contemporaries knew "no parallel to it". The ministers "had sacrificed personal interest for their principles".[1339] Iain Murray suggests that it was their willingness to accept hardship that made the message that they preached real to their listeners.[1340] However, not all the evangelicals left the Established Church – especially in the cities, they remained to declare the "message of evangelical orthodoxy".[1341]

[1338] H. Bonar, *The Life of John Milne* (2010) pp.97-112.
[1339] S.J. Brown, *Thomas Chalmers and the Godly Commonwealth in Scotland* (1982) p.334.
[1340] I.H. Murray, *A Scottish Christian Heritage* (2006) pp.111-113.
[1341] J. Macleod, *Scottish Theology* (1974) p.266.

8

DOUBTS ABOUT GOD

8.1 Introduction

As Christianity became increasingly influential in the nation, opposition forces began to consolidate and to express themselves in well-used arguments – dressed in the fashion of the age. As Christianity was advocated by its adherents, those who were uncertain about its truth, or who simply did not want it, found these arguments – in their new garb – attractive.

8.2 Is God good?

Eve, in the Garden of Eden, doubted the goodness of God's command not to eat from the tree of the knowledge of good and evil. After all, the fruit "was good for food, and pleasing to the eye, and also desirable for gaining wisdom".[1342] The same doubt echoed down the ages. In our period, the growth of the population, and the masses of urban poor, sharply raised again the issue of whether God was good. God might command (in Genesis) man to be fruitful and multiply, but was he good if the fulfilment of this command led to mass human deprivation? In 1798, the question arose most vigorously in the context of *An Essay on the Principle of Population, as it Affects the Future Improvement of Society*, by Thomas Malthus. Agricultural production was increasing – with the new rotation and breeding techniques introduced by Arthur Young (another convert of Wilberforce's *A Practical View*[1343]) – but some questioned whether agricultural production could keep pace with population increase. If not, starvation and famine would result. In his

[1342] Genesis 3:6.

[1343] J.S. Harford, *Recollections of William Wilberforce, Esq.* (1865) p.9 and J. Wolffe, "William Wilberforce's *Practical View* (1797) and its Reception", in *Revival and Resurgence in Christian History* (2008) (K. Cooper and J. Gregory (eds)) pp.183-184.

essay, Malthus fully developed this thesis. His starting point was that the inability of food supplies to keep up with population growth was a cause that "impeded the progress of mankind towards happiness".[1344]

In the decade before he published his essay, Malthus was a curate, while leading "a contemplative life of reading and discussion with his father".[1345] The principle that he laboured to establish was that it was part of the creation order that there is a "constant tendency in all animated life to increase beyond the nourishment prepared for it".[1346] This challenged the goodness of God and the harmony in the natural order and its beneficence. The challenge did not go unmet. In 1802, Paley published his *Natural Theology*. Some did not believe that Malthus believed in the "existence of God as the Supreme Governor of the world."[1347] His "pretended *principle of population* is nothing else but a mere name which these speculative philosophers have invented, for the purpose of deceiving the rest of mankind".[1348]

Natural theology sought to trace the evidence of the being and attributes of God in the works of creation and providence. The undergirding theme was that of the Psalmist: "The heavens declare the glory of God; the skies proclaim the work of his hands."[1349] Thus "science was presented as a subject which demonstrated divine design in nature" and natural theology was "needed as part of a proper clerical education".[1350] Furthermore, science and Christianity were intertwined; the latter creating the pre-suppositions for the success of the former. As David Livingstone observed of the work of Thomas Chalmers in this area: "He urged that science in both its theoretical structure and its vocational rationale should be grounded in natural theology's argument from design."[1351]

1344 T. Malthus, *An Essay on the Principle of Population, as it Affects the Future Improvement of Society* (1807) vol.1, p.1.
1345 F.W. Elwell, *A Commentary on Malthus' 1798 Essay on Population as Social Theory* (2001) p.1.
1346 T. Malthus, Ibid., p.2.
1347 J. Leslie, *A Summons of Wakening* (1807) p.84.
1348 Author's italics. Ibid., p.83.
1349 Psalm 19:1.
1350 N.A. Rupke, *The Great Chain of History* (1983) p.25. See also J.H. Brooke, *Science and Religion* (1991) pp.192-225.
1351 D.N. Livingstone, *Darwin's Forgotten Defenders: The Encounter Between Evangelical Theology and Evolutionary Thought* (1987) p.9.

Paley's *Natural Theology* was perceived by contemporaries as the latest contribution to well-defended ground, bringing together many ideas from the past[1352] and it "initiated the heyday of natural theology".[1353] John Sumner – casting around for a topic to confirm God's goodness and existence, in order to put in a submission for a prize from a bequest provided by a Scottish gentleman – found it difficult to find a "vacant spot in a district so fully occupied" by authors, of whom Paley was the latest. Sumner decided "to rest my principal evidence of the existence of the Creator upon the credibility of the Mosaic records of the creation".[1354] Sumner identified three options to explain the origins of the universe. Either, as the ancient Greeks had posited, it had existed from eternity, or it was formed by a fortuitous combination of pre-existing materials or, as the Bible taught in Genesis 1:1, it was moulded by an intelligent deity.[1355] This last view gained wide circulation. For example, John Kitto – a popular mid-nineteenth century writer – in his *Daily Bible Illustrations* (1849) for the morning, adopted Sumner's approach and commented that: "To them who had deemed it natural to believe that the world was self-created, and had no intelligent author, it is a great and astounding revelation – it lets in a flood of light upon the mind, to know, that 'in the beginning God created the heaven and the earth.'"[1356]

Sumner added a second volume to his work concerning the moral attributes of the Creator. This included examination of the consistency of the principle of population with the wisdom and goodness of the Deity. Referring to the latter principle, Sumner concluded that it fills "the world with competitors for support, enforces labour and encourages industry, by the advantages it gives to the industrious and laborious at the expense of the indolent and extravagant. The ultimate effect of it is, to foster those arts and improvements which most dignify the character and refine the mind of man."[1357] Sumner's entry won £400 – and was published as *A Treatise on the Records of Creation* (1816). In 1833, *The Records of Creation* was into its fifth edition.

1352 For the background to, and an assessment of Paley's work, see A.E. McGrath, *Dawkins' God* (2015) pp.98-107.
1353 Ibid., p.234.
1354 J.B. Sumner, *A Treatise on the Records of Creation* (1816) vol.1, p.ix.
1355 Ibid., p.5.
1356 J. Kitto, *Daily Bible Illustrations (Morning Series)* (1866) vol.1, p.2.
1357 J.B. Sumner, *A Treatise on the Records of Creation* (1816) vol.2, p.172.

In 1818, Thomas Gisborne published *The Testimony of Natural Theology to Christianity*. Gisborne's aim was to show that natural theology was a valuable aid to demonstrating the plan of salvation through a redeemer.[1358] Paley's work, although pointing to the element of design in nature, did not adequately deal with the "state of ruinous disorder" on earth – such that "it cannot be supposed to have originally proceeded thus from the forming hand of the Creator".[1359] The expansion of the domain of natural theology – and the desire to use every argument to present the case of Christianity demonstrated by Sumner's *Records* and Gisborne's *Natural Theology* – moved Noah's flood into the field of natural theology and brought, as we shall see shortly, the latter acutely into contact with the latest musings of the geologists.[1360] Indeed, in the first half of the nineteenth century, geology became "a branch of natural theology"[1361] as men like William Whewell "sought a kind of 'logic' that could 'embrace everything' – that is, a philosophy that would apply to all areas of thought".[1362]

The early 1830s were perhaps the high point of natural theology. Adam Sedgwick, preaching in the Chapel of Trinity College, Cambridge, on the day of Commemoration 1832, suggested that "The religion of nature and the religion of the Bible are…in beautiful accordance."[1363] He thought that "It is in vain that we attempt to shut out the belief in an intelligent Creator by referring all phenomena to a connected succession of material causes, not one of which is fully comprehended."[1364] 1833 saw the first of the eight volumes of the *Bridgewater Treatises* published to illustrate "the Power, Wisdom and Goodness of God as manifested in the Creation."[1365] The authorship of these volumes was prized and the

1358 T. Gisborne *The Testimony of Natural Theology to Christianity* (1818) p.8.

1359 Ibid., p.7.

1360 "*The Testimony of Natural Theology to Christianity*", in 17 *The Christian Observer for the Year 1818* (1819) pp.544-545. See also N.A. Rupke, *The Great Chain of History* (1983) pp.235-240.

1361 Ibid., p.267.

1362 L.J. Snyder, *Reforming Philosophy* (2006) p.25.

1363 A. Sedgwick, "A Discourse on the Studies of the University", in *History of British Educational Thought (British University Education)* (2000) p.16.

1364 Ibid., p.19.

1365 On the Bridgewater Treatises generally, see J.M. Robson, "The Fiat and Finger of God: The Bridgewater Treatises", in *Victorian Faith in Crisis* (1990) (R.J. Helmstadter and B. Lightman (eds)) pp.71-125.

authors distinguished; they included Thomas Chalmers. Each volume was funded to the tune of £1,000, by a bequest of the Earl of Bridgewater. For the remainder of our period, "theologies of nature remained popular and persuasive in shaping devotional practices". A number of authors were committed to explaining science to the nation from a Christian perspective.[1366] In 1848, William Buckland thought that the study of philosophy was greatly changed since the end of the previous century, when it was "too justly suspected to be allied to infidelity; the study of second causes halted short of arriving at the first".[1367] He thought "modern professors…in every fresh discovery" found "a further and another revelation of the infinite wisdom and power, and goodness of the Creator".

However, by the late 1830s, some writers, especially those of a Tractarian bent, reacted to the dominance of natural theology – holding that it "weakened man's reliance on the Scriptures as the only source of religious instruction". One of their number, William Irons, "firmly concluded that natural theology was untenable on philosophical, political, and theological grounds"[1368] – to the delight of the radicals.[1369] Furthermore, there were those like Lord Brougham, a lawyer who, in his *A Discourse of Natural Theology*, took natural theology into dangerous territory. He sought to extend its scope so that it embraced the discovery of God's will and intention for his creatures[1370] – thereby suggesting that man could work out these matters for himself and rendering revelation unnecessary, if not improbable. For this, he was condemned.[1371] Traditionally, natural theology was used only to establish certain characteristics of God and, in apologetic terms, to "remove arguments against God",[1372] rather than to set out his purposes.

[1366] W.J. Astore, *Observing God* (2001) p.239.

[1367] W. Buckland, *A Sermon Preached in Westminster Abbey, on Easter Sunday Evening, April 23, 1848* (1848) pp.9-10.

[1368] P. Corsi, *Science and Religion* (1988) p.180.

[1369] "The Religious Weakness of Protestantism", in 13 *The Westminster Review* (1858) p.152.

[1370] H. L. Brougham, *A Discourse of Natural Theology* (1835) pp.10 and 98-137.

[1371] "Lord Brougham on Natural Theology", in 12 Fraser's Magazine (1835) p.385.

[1372] D.N. Livingstone, *Darwin's Forgotten Defenders: The Encounter Between Evangelical Theology and Evolutionary Thought* (1987) p.8.

Overall, in looking at the creation, perhaps not enough consideration was being given to the impact of the Fall on the glories of God's creation. The future Cardinal Newman, in a lecture given in 1852, suggested that natural theology "has been taken out of its place, has been put too prominently forward, and thereby has almost been used as an instrument against Christianity".[1373] Elsewhere, Darwin and Alfred Russel Wallace (Darwin's co-proponent of the theory of evolution by random natural selection) pondered the work of Malthus and, in our next period, used the struggle for existence as a reason to doubt the goodness of the God revealed in the Scriptures.[1374] Meanwhile, a medical doctor George Drysdale had published in 1854 what ultimately became known as *The Elements of Social Science; or, Physical, Sexual, and Natural Religion.* This accepted the Malthusian doctrine that population growth led to poverty and starvation, but rejected his suggestions of abstinence or late marriage. Rather, Drysdale suggested that "Chastity or sexual abstinence causes more real disease and misery in one year, I believe, in this country, than sexual excesses in a century."[1375] He affirmed that "Nine out of ten cases of hysteria are owing to sexual abstinence."[1376] Drysdale believed that Malthus may have seen the "law of population" but not "its awful nature; for he did not see the evil of one of his three necessary checks, namely, sexual abstinence".[1377] This was an especial evil "in the years immediately after puberty, as then the imagination on sexual subjects is most vivid and powerful".[1378] As his nephew C.V. Drysdale later wrote, there was a "fundemental disharmony of nature – the antagonism between the satisfaction of food and sex hunger to which the greater part of human misery was due".[1379] Drysdale's solution to the problem of population growth was various forms of what later became know as contraception.[1380] He also regarded marriage as leading "to the most

[1373] A.E. McGrath, *Dawkins' God* (2015) pp.103-104.
[1374] F.W. Elwell, *A Commentary on Malthus' 1798 Essay on Population as Social Theory* (2001) pp.57-64.
[1375] By a graduate of medicine [G.R. Drysdale], *The Elements of Social Science; or, Physical, Sexual, and Natural Religion* (1861) p.186.
[1376] Ibid., p.498.
[1377] Ibid., p.345.
[1378] Ibid., p.82.
[1379] Cited in R. Ledbetter, *A History of the Malthusian League 1877-1927* (1976) p.9.
[1380] Summarised in ibid., pp.15-16.

fearful evils" because of its "irrevocable nature…and the impossibility of procuring divorce".[1381] Marriage he added, "delivers women bound into the hands of man".[1382] *The Elements of Social Science* was a popular book with 90,000 copies being sold by 1905.[1383]

8.3 Is God nature?

In our period, the success of the learned in demonstrating the goodness of God perhaps opened the way for the confusion of the Deity with nature. In the 1850s, the Romantic Movement led aspiring ministers away from orthodoxy and into the worship of a different god, namely nature. Wordsworth's poems were seen as the prime example of this. One fictional character was made to say – by an author expelled from the Congregational ministry – that Wordsworth's God "is not the God of the church, but the God of the hills, the abstraction Nature, and to this my reverence was transferred".[1384] This new view of God was seen to have affected the hymns of the time – when a Congregational minister published *The Rivulet: A Contribution to Sacred Song* (1855). The hymns therein were described as "a constant 'stream of Nature worship', threatening to swallow up the reader 'in the dread abyss of an impersonal pantheism'".[1385] God was not transcendent over the creation, but immanent within it.

8.4 Are the geologists right?

Past generations of Christian apologists had drawn together the stories from many ethnic groupings to show how embedded in their cultures were stories supporting the Mosaic account of the creation, the early life of man on earth and the destruction by a universal flood of all humanity, bar Noah and those who sought safety in the Ark.[1386] However, it was as late as the 1650s that Archbishop Ussher first suggested that the earth was created in 4004 BC. His stature in the church, and the clarity of this

[1381] By a Medical Doctor [G.R. Drysdale], *The Elements of Social Science; or, Physical, Sexual, and Natural Religion* (1861) p.355.

[1382] Ibid., p.356.

[1383] R. Ledbetter, *A History of the Malthusian League 1877-1927* (1976), p.19.

[1384] M.R. Watts, *The Dissenters* (2015) vol.3, p.4.

[1385] Ibid., p.8.

[1386] For example, H. Grotius, *The Truth of the Christian Religion* (1829) (Le Clerc (ed.)) pp.22-65.

pronouncement, meant that his calculation was often cited, but never gained universal endorsement in the churches.[1387] Towards the end of the eighteenth century and beginning of the nineteenth century, geologists began to focus on the ground under their feet – rather than the written records of the past, biblical or otherwise – to put forward a number of new theories as to the age of the earth and the impact or existence of a universal flood. Many were deists, or atheists.[1388] However, it was Georges Cuvier's *Theory of the Earth*, first published in English in 1813, that generated the most significant response from the advocates of natural theology.[1389]

Cuvier considered "That if there is any circumstance thoroughly established by geology, it is that the crust of our globe has been subjected to a great and sudden revolution, the epoch of which cannot be dated back much further than five or six thousand years ago."[1390] He acknowledged that there may have been a succession of earlier wholesale extinctions and creations – the last, comparatively recently, being the product of Noah's flood, of which there were many lingering traditions in the histories of many cultures, thus establishing the 'Catastrophist' theory. For Cuvier, linking Noah's flood with various sedimentary layers was

[1387] From the time of the Church Fathers a cause of dispute was whether and to what extent the early chapters of Genesis were intended to be taken literary or as allegory, see generally F. Watson, "Genesis Before Darwin", in *Reading Genesis after Darwin* (2009) (S.C. Barton and D. Wilkinson (eds)) pp.23-37; A. Louth, "The Six Days of Creation According to the Greek Fathers", in *Reading Genesis after Darwin* (2009) (S.C. Barton and D. Wilkinson (eds)) pp.39-55; and D. Wilkinson, "Reading Genesis 1-3 in the Light of Modern Science", in *Reading Genesis after Darwin* (2009) (S.C. Barton and D. Wilkinson (eds)) pp.129-130. For an analysis of early approaches to the interpretation of Genesis 1, as far as it pertains to geology and observations relating to the age of the earth, see M.B. Roberts, "Genesis Chapter 1 and Geological Time from Hugo Grotius and Marin Mersenne to William Conybeare and Thomas Chalmers (1620-1825)", in *Myth and Geology* (2007) (L. Piccardi and W.B. Masse (eds)) pp.39-49; J.P. Lewis, "The Days of Creation: An Historical Survey of Interpretation", in 32 *The Journal of the Evangelical Theological Society* (1989) pp.433–455; L. Lavallee, "Augustine on the Creation Days", in 32 *The Journal of the Evangelical Theological Society* (1989) pp.457-464; and T. Mortenson, *The Great Turning Point* (2004) pp.19-30 and 40-42.

[1388] Ibid., p.224.

[1389] Cuvier's daughter prayed for his conversion, although nominally he was a Protestant, see J.H. Brooke, *Science and Religion* (1991) pp.247-248.

[1390] G. Cuvier, *Theory of the Earth* (1815) p.171.

made problematic by the lack of human bones.[1391]

Cuvier's thesis drew many responses – seeking to reconcile it to the first chapter of Genesis. Robert Jameson's preface to Cuvier's work – referring to the six days of creation – suggested that "many physical considerations...render it probable that...the day, or period between morning and evening may have been indefinitely longer than it is at present".[1392] Thomas Chalmers was unconvinced of this. The following year, he suggested that the chaos referred to at the beginning of Genesis occurred during geological time. Thereafter, God reordered the world in six 24-hour periods – and the era of human existence began with its history of around 6,000 years.[1393]

Another key evangelical response to Cuvier's ideas was that of John Sumner's *A Treatise on the Records of Creation* (1816). Sumner observed that the Mosaic record offered no guidance on "the motions of the heavenly bodies, or...on the formation of the globe. The expressions of Moses are evidently accommodated to the first and familiar notions derived from the sensible appearances of the earth and the heavens."[1394] Sumner maintained that the great outlines to be drawn by the sacred historian were that God was the original Creator; that at creation the earth was in a state of chaos; and that, not exceeding 5,000 years ago, it "underwent a mighty catastrophe". He was willing to acknowledge that "the materials of the globe were in a fluid state previous to its organisation, and that the mode of its organisation was not instantaneous, but a gradual process".[1395]

However, many writers in the first half of the nineteenth century

[1391] Ibid., pp.127-132.

[1392] Ibid., p.vi.

[1393] T. Chalmers, "Remarks on Cuvier's Theory of the Earth", in *Select Works of Thomas Chalmers* (1857) vol.5, pp.629-632. Thomas Chalmers had first made this suggestion when delivering some chemistry lectures at St Andrews in the winter of 1803-1804, see M.B. Roberts, "Genesis Chapter 1 and Geological Time from Hugo Grotius and Marin Mersenne to William Conybeare and Thomas Chalmers (1620-1825)", in *Myth and Geology* (2007) (L. Piccardi and W.B. Masse (eds)) p.46. For other Scottish evangelicals who subscribed to an old earth, see D.N. Livingstone, *Darwin's Forgotten Defenders: The Encounter Between Evangelical Theology and Evolutionary Thought* (1987) pp.9-16.

[1394] J.B. Sumner, *A Treatise on the Records of Creation* (1816) vol.1, pp.270-271.

[1395] Ibid., p.272.

remained committed to a young earth.[1396] For example, the leading evangelical Thomas Gisborne was unconvinced that the present world had been created out of the remnants of an earlier world. In *The Testimony of Natural Theology to Christianity* (1818), he suggested that the convulsions evident in the earth's rock layers demanded a moral explanation – and that explanation was that "a moral change calling for such an event had taken place in that portion of the inhabitants of the earth, which was endued with moral agency and responsibility".[1397] The evidence of the piling up of masses of sea remains on mountain tops gave credibility to this theory. Gisborne's support for a creation of short duration was criticised in *The Quarterly Review*, but not his view as to the reality of Noah's flood. The anonymous author of this piece, citing an earlier author, did not believe that the flood had left geologic evidence behind.[1398]

In 1819, William Buckland, in his inaugural lecture as reader of geology at Oxford, announced that "we may henceforth consider geology as exalted to the rank of the sciences, the teaching of which forms part of our established system of education."[1399] He continued that geology held "the keys of one of the kingdoms of nature" and its science would compel "the primeval mountains of the globe to unfold the hidden records of their origin".[1400] Buckland was a Catastrophist and regarded Cuvier as "the very centre of continental philosophy".[1401] Buckland was sure that, before man appeared, the earth had gone through the "most terrible catastrophes" and cited Sumner, "a divine whose rational and sober piety no person will venture to dispute".[1402] Buckland suggested that the opening words of Genesis "in the beginning" described an immense period; that the six "days" of creation were periods of indeterminate length, and not 24 hours.[1403] By 1860, this was widely accepted by those seeking to uphold the Bible's authority – but a Broad Churchman might

[1396] T. Mortenson, *The Great Turning Point* (2004) pp.43-47.

[1397] T. Gisborne, *The Testimony of Natural Theology to Christianity* (1818) pp.64-65.

[1398] See "The Testimony of Natural Theology to Christianity", in 21 *The Quarterly Review* (1819) pp.51-52.

[1399] W. Buckland, *Vindiciae Geologiciae* (1820) p.2.

[1400] Ibid., pp.5 and 7.

[1401] Ibid., p.24.

[1402] Ibid., p.25.

[1403] Ibid., pp.31-32.

suggest that only a literal view of the relevant words was possible, in order to generally disprove the authority of the Bible.[1404]

In the published version of Buckland's inaugural lecture as reader of geology, he added by way of an appendix a summary of the proofs afforded by geology of the Mosaic deluge. A few years later, in his important work *Reliquiae Diluvianae* (1823) – following an investigation into various organic remains made on the advice of the Bishop of Durham, Shute Barrington – he "found the strongest evidence of an universal deluge". He hoped "that it will no longer be asserted, as it has been by high authorities, that geology supplies no proofs of an event in the reality of which the truth of the Mosaic records is so materially involved".[1405]

The most active opponent of the impact of Noah's flood was Buckland's pupil, Charles Lyell. Lyell, unlike most leading English geologists, was not a clergyman having trained as a lawyer. Charles Darwin considered him "thoroughly liberal in his religious beliefs or rather disbeliefs; but he was a strong theist".[1406] Lyell argued that

[1404] "Broad Church Theology", in 60 *The Christian Observer for the Year* 1860 (1860) p.394. Some leading evangelicals were willing to leave open the meaning of a "day" in Genesis, see R. Maguire, *The Sabbath and its Perpetual Obligation* (1859) p.4. There were some who thought that Buckland, Sumner and others gave too much away to the "speculations of geologists" (see *Scriptural Geology* (1826) vol.1, p.8.), when they suggested a number of creations. Such authors accepted that "Astronomy is a matter of science", but Scripture needed not to accommodate itself to any "familiar notions derived from the appearance of the constitution of the earth", see ibid., pp.xi and xiii. Sumner stuck to his views in the fifth edition of *A Treatise on the Records of Creation* (1833), as did Chalmers in his *Natural Theology* (1835). In 1849, Gray published his *The Earth's Antiquity,* which reconciled the earth's antiquity with the Mosaic record of the creation by seeing the six days as God's work of renovation of the earth after "the last pre-Adamite catastrophe", see J. Gray, *The Earth's Antiquity* (1851) p.146. His reconciliation was perceived to be so successful that, in 1851, a second edition was published, see ibid., p.ixx. Philip Gosse, the distinguished marine biologist, Fellow of the Royal Society and Plymouth Brethren preacher, while leaving open the exact or approximate age of the earth, also suggested that the heavens and the earth had been made in six days, as God had created the earth at a particular point in the life cycle of each plant and animal and therefore the earth appeared to have a history, see P.H. Gosse, *Omphalos* (1857) pp.339 and 372. For other Nonconformist approaches to geological developments, see M.R. Watts, *The Dissenters* (2015) vol.3, pp.10-13.

[1405] W. Buckland, *Reliquiae Diluvianae* (1824) dedication. For a review of the critical response to this work, see N.A. Rupke, *The Great Chain of History* (1983) pp.42-50.

[1406] N. Barlow, *The Autobiography of Charles Darwin* (1969) p.100.

"a regular and uninterrupted series of changes in the animate and inanimate world, may give rise to such breaks in the sequence, and such unconformability of stratified rocks, as are usually thought to imply convulsions and catastrophes."[1407] Lyell's view prevailed. By the early 1830s, Lyell was understood to deny the universality of Noah's flood, or to assert that it covered only the inhabited part of the world at the time.[1408] A number of individuals, whom Terry Mortenson characterises as "scriptural geologists", responded to Lyell[1409] in defence of a young earth. They very much affirmed geology, but took the view that it pointed to a young earth. In their view, geology "was different from other sciences, because it dealt with history and origins".[1410]

The leading Church of England geologists with status in the ancient universities were persuaded by Lyell's views on geology: these were men such as Adam Sedgwick, William Buckland, William Conybeare and William Whewell. With regard to the key issues of salvation, such as human sin and the need for the atonement to satisfy God's law, Whewell, for one, continued to preach and affirm them,[1411] as did Sedgwick[1412] and Conybeare.[1413] Buckland continued to affirm that all would appear before "the judgment-seat"[1414] and was a firm believer in a moral universe. Conybeare continued to uphold the inspiration of Scripture. He referred to inspiration being given "to secure a certain and infallible standard of *religious truth*, from which no appeal could lie, so we have no authority for extending it beyond this object". However, he was wary of the accuracy of the Bible on "some minute chronological points connected with the periods of Jewish history".[1415] Nevertheless,

[1407] C. Lyell, *Principles of Geology* (1853) p.181.
[1408] L.G. Wilson, *Charles Lyell* (1972) pp.308-313. For the problems with Lyell's view, assuming Noah's flood left an imprint in the geological strata, see N.A. Rupke, *The Great Chain of History* (1983) pp.194-199 and 217-218.
[1409] See generally T. Mortenson, *The Great Turning Point* (2004) and especially p.235.
[1410] Ibid., p.232.
[1411] W. Whewell, *On the Foundations of Morals* (1837) pp.86-87.
[1412] A. Sedgwick, "A Discourse on the Studies of the University", in *History of British Educational Thought (British University Education)* (2000) pp.79-82. See also the sermon preached at his funeral, R. Burn, *God Our Refuge* (1873) pp.9-15.
[1413] W.D. Conybeare, *An Elementary Course of Lectures, on the Criticism, Interpretation and Leading Doctrines of the Bible* (1834) pp.160-196.
[1414] W. Buckland, *Sermon on the Removal of the Cholera* (1849) p.26.
[1415] Author's italics. W.D. Conybeare, *An Elementary Course of Lectures, on the Criticism, Interpretation and Leading Doctrines of the Bible* (1834) pp.6-7.

the failure by some of the great Church minds of the day to explain in detail and define what was meant by the Bible containing "religious truth" in the context of geology, left it open – as we shortly see – for others to provide their own definition of what was "religious truth", across the whole scope of the Bible. They would be much more radical in disposing of core biblical doctrines.

Lyell left open the origin of species, a discussion of which the fossil record invited, as this made clear that species became extinct and that others replaced them. From before his marriage in 1839 and afterwards, Charles Darwin saw more of Lyell than any other man. Before setting sail to South America on the *Beagle,* at the end of 1831, he had been recommended to get and study the first volume of Lyell's *Principles of Geology* "but on no account to accept the views therein advocated".[1416] Darwin tried to get Lyell to adopt the principle of natural selection; but Lyell did not bite,[1417] although he encouraged Darwin to write *On the Origin of Species* (1859).

The interest in natural theology, especially at Cambridge University, led to a great sensation in 1844 when Robert Chambers published, anonymously, his *Vestiges of the Natural History of Creation.* This presented "a sweeping view of cosmological, planetary, and organic transmutation [the contemporary word for evolution] that extended even to people and social institutions".[1418] Chambers took the view that "The Creator has programmed the law of development into nature."[1419] The theory of evolution became a matter of general conversation, although its underpinning science and philosophy in *Vestiges* meant that it did not find general acceptance by the scientific community. Chambers constantly updated his thesis in subsequent editions until it reached its final form in 1860, the year after Darwin's *Origin of Species* was published. Up until then, as Thomas Huxley observed, one was either a Mosaist or an Evolutionist. Huxley was inclined to say "a plague on both your houses".[1420]

[1416] N. Barlow, *The Autobiography of Charles Darwin* (1969) p.101.
[1417] Ibid., p.124. See also J.H. Brooke, *Science and Religion* (1991) p.251.
[1418] J.T. Costa, *Wallace, Darwin, and the Origin of Species* (2014) p.17. On the contemporary reception of *Vestiges,* see J.A. Secord, *Victorian Sensation* (2000).
[1419] P.J. Bowler, *The Eclipse of Darwinism* (1983) p.48.
[1420] A. Ellegard, *Darwin and the General Reader* (1990) p.12.

One admirer of *Vestiges* was Baden Powell.[1421] Slightly earlier he had published *The Connection of Natural and Divine Truth* (1838). He looked at the discoveries of geology and concluded that they were at direct variance with the early chapters of Genesis and that "The only alternative is to admit that it was *not intended for an historical narrative*; and if the representation cannot have been designed for *literal history*, it only remains to regard it as...the language of *figure* and *poetry*."[1422] Baden Powell from this "maintained the essential independence of physical and revealed truth"[1423] – although both revealed the same divinity in their "order and design".[1424] Indeed, he suggested that you needed to be a scientist to rightly understand Scripture when he concluded that "The investigation of God's works is an essential introduction to the right reception of his word."[1425] Science was now being used to give shape to theology, rather than theology being used to shape thinking about science. At the time, Baden Powell was developing his relationship with the Unitarians.[1426]

In conclusion, what is clear is that in the first half of the nineteenth century – when the old earth idea received wide circulation and acceptance by many leading evangelicals, such as John Sumner and Thomas Chalmers – Christianity continued to grow. Its vitality did not only depend upon the Bible's ability to be used as a geological text book, although most Christians thought that the early chapters of Genesis offered insight into the creation of the world. For those who did not accept that the world was created in seven days, or believed that the world was older than roughly 6,000 years, a number of means of reconciling the Bible with the latest conclusions of science were established. However, no one approach gained universal acceptance.[1427] As we will see in our next period, it was only when it was widely

[1421] R. Chambers, *Vestiges of the Natural History of Creation* (1884) pp.xxx-xxxi.

[1422] Author's italics. B. Powell, *The Connection of Natural and Divine Truth* (1838) p.260.

[1423] B. Powell, *The Connection of Natural and Divine Truth* (1838) p.268.

[1424] Ibid., p.272.

[1425] Ibid., p.273.

[1426] P. Corsi, *Science and Religion* (1988) pp.203-208 and 265.

[1427] See W. Grudem, *Systematic Theology* (2005) pp.262-314 for an overview of different Christian perspectives on the age of the universe and the interpretation of the early chapters of Genesis.

suggested that science and theology were in conflict – and especially that you needed to investigate science to understand the Bible and theology – that the Bible and Christianity lost their power. However, a platform was being built for such a view – especially through the approach that Lyell was championing and which was being advocated in other fields of academic study – that everything "occurred according to the laws of nature but which pre-scientific people did not understand".[1428] This approach assumed that such laws just happened to exist by accident and, wrongly, that such a possibility had never been considered before.

8.5 Can the Bible be trusted?

Questions about the historical accuracy of the Bible were not new. For instance, Hugo Grotius, in the seventeenth century, addressed Book III of his influential *De Veritate Religionis Christianae* (1627) to objections to the authority of the Bible, including that the books of the Bible are inconsistent with one another. By the mid-nineteenth century, it had been a leading work of Christian apologetics for over two centuries. Bishop Watson said it was a "book so common that almost everybody has it, and so excellent that no person ought to be without it".[1429] Grotius defended the Bible from the charge of inconsistency on the basis that those "places which contain anything of moment, whether in doctrine or history...manifest agreement" not to be found in other writers.[1430] Grotius did not deny that there might appear to be inconsistencies in the Bible, but affirmed that had he lived in an earlier age, the information would have been available to reconcile them.[1431]

[1428] T. Mortenson, *The Great Turning Point* (2004) p.227.

[1429] R. Watson, "Letter III", in *An Apology for the Bible, in a Series of Letters Addressed to Thomas Paine* (1796) p.29. Lord Acton considered Grotius "a pivotal figure in the history of freedom", see H. Lauterpact, "The Grotian Tradition in International Law", in 23 *British Yearbook of International Law* (1946) p.53.

[1430] H. Grotius, *The Truth of the Christian Religion* (1829) (Le Clerc (ed.)) pp.138-139 being a translation of *De Veritate Religionis Christianae.*

[1431] Written originally in Dutch, it was translated, in 1628, into Latin and then, during the life of Grotius, into English, French and German. The final edition under his pen appeared in 1639. It was one of the most widely read books of the seventeenth and eighteenth centuries. By the early nineteenth century, additional translations had appeared in Greek, Persian, Swedish, Danish, Chinese and Arabic – although there are doubts over whether the Greek and Persian translations were realised, see J.P. Heering, "Hugo Grotius' *De Veritate Religionis Christianae*", in *Hugo Grotius Theologian*

However, by the 1850s if not before, doubts about the accuracy of the Bible were spreading among the religious – and beyond the Unitarians, who were always in the vanguard when it came to challenging orthodoxy.[1432] They regarded education as the evangelical equivalent of conversion.[1433] The Tubingen School, in Germany, dated the books of the Bible and their provenance to some years after the events they purported to describe. These views seemed so learned and unsettled many.

8.6 Is Christian doctrine static?

Thomas Carlyle, the historian and social critic, was perhaps the best known of those who won a reputation as a sage of the day, while ceasing to be an orthodox Christian. Carlyle's parents attended the staunchly Calvinistic Burgher Seceder Church of Ecclefechan. He admired his father and his faith, but he believed that it belonged to a lost world. All the world was moving onward: Watt's steam engine and Arkwright's water frame – which created such prosperity at New Lanark – had ushered in the factory age and mechanisation;[1434] and Carlyle would not believe religious truth stood still. Ironically, the discoveries of science, which framed his outlook on the Bible, were from the sixteenth century. They included the relationship between the earth, the sun[1435] and the stars. The differences between the Bible and reality on these matters John Calvin had long ago explained by the doctrine of accommodation.[1436]

Carlyle had a deep appreciation for religious sentiment and experience, but without the doctrine. He believed that it was possible to reject "the literal narrative of the sacred writers" while believing "in the spiritual truths of religion."[1437] However, he thought some belief was better than none. With his emphasis on heroes, stylistic mannerisms of a biblical

(1994) (H.J.M. Nellen and E. Rabbie (eds)) p.51.

[1432] M.R. Watts, *The Dissenters* (2015) vol.3, pp.10-11 and 22-27.

[1433] Ibid., p.205.

[1434] Robert Owen provides a good sense of how his contemporaries thought the world had changed so much between 1758 and 1858 in R. Owen, "Dedicated to the Faithful unto Death", in R. Owen, *The Life of Robert Owen* (1858) vol.1A, pp.3-4.

[1435] J.A. Froude, *Thomas Carlyle* (1896) vol.2, p.4.

[1436] J.A. Thomas, *The Nation's Gospel: Reformation to Revolution* (2017) vol.1, pp.131-134.

[1437] J.A. Froude, *Thomas Carlyle* (1896) vol.2, pp.3-4.

hue,[1438] biblical sexual morality[1439] and willingness to make biblical admonitions the centre piece of his thought,[1440] Carlyle wrote in a way that looked sufficiently Christian to make his work acceptable and the rejection of doctrinal Christianity intellectually fashionable. His writings sounded biblical, but they were not. He was one of those who flocked to hear Edward Irving preach.

However, one never quite knew what Carlyle believed.[1441] He was no follower of Thomas Huxley and the idea that humanity was descended from monkeys.[1442] He willingly invoked the divine, dedicating his *Early Kings of Norway* (1875) to "dear aethereal Ruskin, whom God preserve". But Carlyle had long before given up on biblical Christianity.

Carlyle's influence was huge. One leading clergyman thought that, of those living on Britain's shores, it was Carlyle who most encouraged the younger clergy to be dissatisfied with established doctrine or commonly received phraseology.[1443] Frederick W. Robertson attributed to Carlyle the primary influence in his shift to a Broad Church position.[1444] George Eliot famously wrote of him; "It is an idle question to ask whether his books will be read a century hence; if they were all burnt as the grandest of Suttees on his funeral pile, it would only be like cutting down an

1438 For example, he used the "voice and techniques of the sage or Old Testament prophet as a means of moral suasion. *Past and Present* employs the four-part pattern in which the prophet 1) calls his or her audience's attention to their grievous condition; 2) points out that they have fallen into this state because they have neglected God's law; 3) promises worse misery if they fail to return to God; and 4) offers visions of bliss if the listeners return to God", see T. Carlyle, *Past and Present* (2005) pp.xix-xx.

1439 He could only achieve "tolerant civility" with George Eliot, who was in a relationship with George Lewes, a married man, and one of Carlyle's literary friends, see G.S. Haight, "The Carlyles and the Leweses", in *Carlyle and his Contemporaries* (1976) (J. Clubbe (ed.)) p.196. The wife of Lewes, Agnes Jervis, was in a relationship with the married Thornton Hunt, a co-editor with Lewes on *The Leader* magazine. Carlyle thought Lewes justified in departing such a marriage, but could never overlook the impediment to his union with Eliot, ibid., pp.189-202.

1440 Work was a key imperative to Carlyle. When he wanted to add weight and urgency to the notion, he gave it expression through the words of Jesus, "Work while it is called today, for the night cometh wherein no man can work", T. Carlyle, *Sartor Resartus* (1987) p.149.

1441 See generally J.A. Froude, *Thomas Carlyle* (1896) vol.2, pp.1-23

1442 *Life and Letters of Thomas Henry Huxley* (1900) (L. Huxley (ed.)) vol.1, pp.275-276.

1443 R.W. Dale, *The Life and Letters of J.A. James* (1861) p.545.

1444 "A Broad Church Preacher", in *The Family Treasury of Sunday Reading* (1866) pp.141-146.

oak after its acorns have sown a forest. For there is hardly a superior or active mind of this generation that has not been modified by Carlyle's writings; there has hardly been an English book written for the last ten or twelve years that would not have been different if Carlyle had not lived."[1445] And Carlyle was no Eliot admirer.

Carlyle's religious influence extended to both the theological liberal and the Anglo-Catholic. The former liked him since he was against the religion of the past governing that of the day. He thought a new belief was needed and the theological liberal thought that he could meet that need. Carlyle also established the "literary genre of the autobiography or autobiographical novel", as the means that future theological liberals would use to express their "crisis of faith".[1446] Coleridge, on the opening page of his *Confessions of an Inquiring Spirit*, credited Carlyle as his stimulus. Carlyle's influence over the Anglo-Catholics arose from his social and economic work and his idea of progress. Carlyle attacked the capitalist system, based on the emerging industrial cities. It was a system based on "the cash nexus". He compared it unfavourably with the medieval world of the monasteries and the social relations that they engendered. Thus, Carlyle made popular certain aspects of Roman Catholicism. After 1859, this yearning for the medieval past appeared in the church ritual of the Tractarians. Carlyle's thinking also lay behind the university settlement movement of our next period. To many, that movement seemed like a latter-day form of the Franciscans living among the people.[1447]

8.7 Ridding morality of God

In England, during the latter half of the second decade of the nineteenth century, *The Christian Observer* observed that the moral law was being given up and it intended to watch and to "arrest"[1448] this threat. In this,

[1445] *Essays of George Eliot* (1963) (T. Pinney (ed.)) pp.213-214.

[1446] See F.M. Turner, "The Victorian Crisis of Faith and the Faith that was Lost", in *Victorian Faith in Crisis* (1990) (R.J. Helmstadter and B. Lightman (eds)) p.15.

[1447] W. Besant, "On University Settlements", in *University and Social Settlements* (1898) (W. Reason (ed.)) pp.1-10.

[1448] "Preface" to 16 *The Christian Observer for the Year 1817* (1818) p.viii. Bean had warned evangelical preachers attacking pharisaism to ensure that in doing so the way was not made for Antinomianism, J. Bean, *Zeal Without Innovation* (1809) p.331.

it enjoyed short-term success.[1449] Perhaps, as a response, its opponents unleashed new views about what constituted morality. The morality of an evangelical like William Cowper was dismissed as "altogether guided by his own conception of what was agreeable and what was disagreeable to the Deity". The editor of *The Westminster Review* suggested the "test of utility, or conduciveness to the happiness of the greatest number... is the only directive rule".[1450] This was the time when Jeremy Bentham was developing his utilitarian ideas. He did not believe that whether a religion was true or not mattered. Rather, "Utility as to affairs of this life being the sole object…any argument founded on the will of the founder of the religion, or on any other part of Scripture, cannot be in place here".[1451] Furthermore, he "consistently postulated" an "antithetical relationship between utility and religion, viewing the gain of the one as invariably the loss of the other. Religion, he would say, contributed to fear and so caused pain and suffering."[1452] For Bentham, his rejection of hell and the views of his own importance made acceptance of the need for a saviour difficult.[1453]

The notion of morality without God and the trappings of religion appealed to the Secularists, led by George Holyoake, a founder of the co-operative movement. He briefly attended the Sunday school of John Angell James at Carrs Lane, Birmingham. In 1843, Holyoake began regular publication of *The Movement* magazine – which had as its logo "Maximise morals, minimise religion". The morality that Holyoake espoused was "ethical truth". He believed that "Ethics are independent of Christianity"[1454] and he rejected what he found in the

[1449] In 1826, Daniel Wilson noted that "*the standard of holiness*, the details of Christian duty, the doctrine of morals, the obligation of the holy law, the necessity of effort, and vigilance, and prayer, and self-denial, and separation from the world are all in progress. The divorce, once too common, between doctrine and practice, is now much more rarely met with". Author's italics. See D. Wilson, "Introductory Essay" to W. Wilberforce, *A Practical View of the Prevailing Religious System of Professed Christians, in the Higher and Middle Classes in This Country, Contrasted with Real Christianity* (1829) pp.xlvii-xlviii.

[1450] "Private Correspondence of William Cowper", in 2 *The Westminster Review* (1824) pp.49-50.

[1451] J.E. Crimmins, *Secular Utilitarianism* (1990) p.278.

[1452] Ibid., pp.13-14.

[1453] Ibid., pp.10, 271 and 287.

[1454] G.J. Holyoake, "The Organisation of Free Thinkers", in 11 *The Reasoner* (1852) p.130.

Bible as incompatible with this.[1455] This principally meant the Fall of man, the atonement, the sin of unbelief in Christ and future unending punishment.[1456] He thought "*that justification by conduct* is a higher and more reliable truth than 'justification by faith in Christ'"[1457] and that "science is the providence of man."[1458] Holyoake also thought that "Nature and God were one" and that the universe had always existed and, being self-existent, always would be.[1459] He articulated these ideas in many widely-circulated pamphlets. For example, *The Logic of Death* (1850) had its 101st edition in 1902 – by which time, 100,000 had been produced – and it was not the last edition.

Holyoake, in 1851, coined the expression "Secularism", having been advised by his friend and funder of his publications and university studies, the City lawyer W.H. Ashurst, to call himself a "secularist".[1460] Its adoption was a "symbolic break with the older labels of atheism and infidelity",[1461] which suffered from connotations of moral depravity and negativism.[1462] In the mid-1850s, the first Secular societies were founded which, in "structure, outlook, organisation and philosophy resembled nothing so much as a loose structure of independent chapels".[1463] Yet, in doctrine, secularism was very different to religious orthodoxy. A contemporary described Secularism's "principal tenet being that, as the fact of a future life is (in their view) at all events susceptible of *some* degree of doubt, while the fact and necessities of a present life are matters of direct sensation, it is therefore prudent to attend exclusively to the concerns of that existence which is certain and immediate – not wasting energies required for present duties by a preparation for remote, and

[1455] G.J. Holyoake, *The Origin and Nature of Secularism* (1896) p.52.

[1456] G.J. Holyoake, *The Logic of Death* (1902) pp.5-6.

[1457] Author's italics. G.J. Holyoake, *Secularism, the Practical Philosophy of the People* (1854) p.5.

[1458] Ibid., pp.5-6.

[1459] G.J. Holyoake, *The Logic of Death* (1902) pp.10 and 12.

[1460] O. Chadwick, *The Secularization of the European Mind in the Nineteenth Century* (1975) pp.90-91 and 271. See also E. Royle, *Victorian Infidels: The Origins of the British Secularist Movement* 1791-1866 (1974) pp.91, 93, 97, 154-155, 221 and 307.

[1461] Ibid., p.3.

[1462] G.J. Holyoake, *Secularism, the Practical Philosophy of the People (*1854) p.5.

[1463] O. Chadwick, *The Secularization of the European Mind in the Nineteenth Century* (1975) p.91.

merely possible contingencies".[1464] This view offered a strong contrast to that affirmed by contemporary Christian writers, like John Angell James. In his view, "Unconcern about the soul, indifference to salvation is a most irrational as well as most guilty state of mind. The wildest enthusiasm about these matters is less surprising and unreasonable than absolute carelessness."[1465]

Secularism was built on four rights: 1) the right to think for one's self; 2) the right to differ; 3) the right to assert differences of opinion; and 4) the right to debate all vital opinion.[1466] Its aims included the conversion of "churches and chapels into temples of instruction for the people. To solicit priests to become teachers of useful knowledge. Emancipation of the Sunday from superstitious restrictions, that it may be devoted to art, culture, public exercises, and pure recreations. Establishment of an effective school system, free from the dogmatism of creeds."[1467]

Auguste Comte, who died in 1857, was another who wanted to establish society on new moral foundations, but without reference to God. However, in doing so, he "pictured himself as the founder of a new religion – the Religion of Humanity."[1468] It had all the trappings of a church, including worship services, hymns and a religious calendar with 84 festivals and 9 sacraments,[1469] but no God. The topic for a Sunday sermon could be the philosopher René Descartes. It was not a success, although Brazilians with a military background liked it; their church, the "Positivist Church of Brazil", continues. Comte's ideas attracted John Stuart Mill. Comte himself turned to daily prayer on the death of his beloved Clotilde de Vaux; at the end of his life he made *The Imitation of Christ* by Thomas à Kempis his daily reading.[1470]

[1464] Author's italics. H. Mann, *Religious Worship in England and Wales* (1854) p.93.
[1465] J.A. James, *The Anxious Enquirer after Salvation* (1834) p.1.
[1466] G.J. Holyoake, *Secularism, the Practical Philosophy of the People* (1854) p.4.
[1467] Ibid., p.12.
[1468] J.E. Crimmins, *Secular Utilitarianism* (1990) p.286.
[1469] J. Waddington, *Congregational History, 1850-1880* (1880) vol.5, pp.519-521. For the development of Comte's idea's, see O. Chadwick, *The Secularization of the European Mind in the Nineteenth Century* (1975) pp.229-239 and 255-257.
[1470] Ibid., pp.239 and 257.

8.8 Ridding literature of Christian influences

At the beginning of the nineteenth century, the works of the imagination, mainly novels, became a universal "mania"[1471] and the mania gripped the religious public.[1472] We will now look at how this universal mania influenced the outlook of the general population in certain areas, especially how it influenced the nation's understanding of Christianity and what living a Christian life looked like.

8.8.1 *Creating alternative worlds*

In 1799 John Newton wrote to Hannah More to express his desire to proscribe all novels "without mercy and without exception".[1473] However, in the pages of *The Christian Observer,* a vigorous debate arose over novel-reading for Christians. Some people thought that novels, unless having a Christian purpose, were a distraction from the serious things of life, a "private dissipation"[1474] and "the most fruitful source both of individual and national vice". For this observer, it was the "feeding of the imagination in which the great danger of novels consists". Novels divested all the dull moments of life from their portrayal of common life – and thereby discouraged the reader from "taking their proper part in the more tame and familiar incidents of common life".[1475] They also resulted in a "fictitious acquaintance" with the world and "erroneous notions of happiness".[1476] Others argued that modern literature provided

[1471] "To the Editor of the Christian Observer", in 14 *The Christian Observer for the Year 1815* (1816) pp.512-513.

[1472] "To the Editor of the Christian Observer", in 16 *The Christian Observer for the Year 1817* (1818) pp.298-299.

[1473] Hannah More was unwilling to agree, W. Roberts, *Memoirs of the Life and Correspondence of Mrs Hannah More* (1834) vol.3, pp.77-78. Newton's friend William Cowper was more sympathetic to his view, see "Progress of Error", in *The Works of William Cowper* (1835) (T.S. Grimshawe (ed.)) vol.6, p.39.

[1474] "To the Editor of the Christian Observer", in 14 *The Christian Observer for the Year 1815* (1816) p.513.

[1475] W. Roberts, *Memoirs of the Life and Correspondence of Mrs Hannah More* (1834) vol.3, p.79.

[1476] "To the Editor of the Christian Observer", in 14 *The Christian Observer for the Year 1815* (1816) pp.513-515 and see also for this line of argument "To the Editor of the Christian Observer", in 16 *The Christian Observer for the Year 1817* (1818) pp.298-301.

few good role models for the young and that the recent growth of novel reading was a sign of a secularised world.[1477] It was impossible to be unaffected by novels[1478] and, it was foretold, "Wait till another generation rises, formed by the novel readers of the day, and the standard of morals will then be perceived to decidedly have fallen."[1479] The argument that novel reading was acceptable – because a book "blends the good, the passable, and the positively bad together" – was dismissed as "a vague sort of argument".[1480] There were few books "wholly unexceptionable in their nature".[1481]

However, not all contributors to *The Christian Observer* were against novel reading. The future Lord Macaulay, in an anonymous article, led the charge in their favour. His father Zachary, no novel reader, was its editor at the time. The younger Macaulay and others thought fiction could be subservient to religion and morality.[1482] It was a case of choosing between the good and the bad. Others thought novel reading brought relief to the weary mind[1483] and that only an excessive love of works of imagination was to be condemned, as with excessive love of anything. The debate ended with a general acceptance of novel reading, but Lord Macaulay was in a distinct minority in seeing good in Fielding and Smollett. The general conclusion of Christians on them was "universal proscription".[1484] The comment of Lord Macaulay's biographer on

[1477] "To the Editor of the Christian Observer", in 16 *The Christian Observer for the Year 1817* (1818) pp.371 and 374.

[1478] William Lockhart, the first member of the Oxford Movement to be received into the Roman Catholic church, in 1886, "argued that 'perhaps most of those who have become Catholic during the last fifty years can trace the attractions of Divine Grace, through the Providence of God, in the pure literature which came into their hands in their early youth'", such literature meaning especially the novels of Sir Walter Scott, see N. Schofield, *William Lockhart* (2011) p.10.

[1479] "To the Editor of the Christian Observer", in 14 *The Christian Observer for the Year 1815* (1816) p.515.

[1480] "Review of Plumptre's Original Dramas, and Letter", in 19 *The Christian Observer for the Year 1820* (1821) p.125.

[1481] Ibid.

[1482] "To the Editor of the Christian Observer", in 15 *The Christian Observer for the Year 1816* (1817) pp.784-787. See also "To the Editor of the Christian Observer", in 16 *The Christian Observer for the Year 1817* (1818) pp.230-231.

[1483] Ibid., p.227.

[1484] Ibid., pp.230, 299 and 372 and "Review of Plumptre's Original Dramas, and Letter", in 19 *The Christian Observer for the Year 1820* (1821) p.125.

Zachary's approach to his children's penchant for novel reading was that he was "too indulgent to insist on having his own way in any but essential matters; he lived to see himself the head of a family in which novels were more read and better remembered than in any household of the United Kingdom".[1485]

The influence of the novelists grew as their works achieved greater circulation after publication of books in serial form commenced. The first such work was Dickens's *The Pickwick Papers* in 1836-1837. "Hereafter", as A.N. Wilson notes, "many of the great novels by Dickens, Thackeray, Trollope, George Eliot and others would be published serially in one of the many periodicals of the day".[1486] None of these writers was a friend to biblical Christianity. All struggled with Christian doctrine and some with Christian morality. For example, George Eliot did not follow the prohibition on sex outside marriage, giving rise to Carlyle's dislike of her. It was she who translated, from German, the influential *The Life of Jesus* (1835), by David Friedrich Strauss, who had been influenced by the works of Schleiermacher. Strauss's book popularised the idea that the Gospels were myth, expressing religious truth, but the miraculous needed stripping away.[1487] The justification for such an approach was the apparent inconsistencies in the records relating to the miracles of Jesus, which others had previously noted and sought to explain.[1488] In adopting this approach, the miracles of Jesus were attributed to causes such as "excitement"[1489] or even natural causes.[1490] In treating the Scriptures as religious truth, revealing what he called "a deeper religious life",[1491] Strauss very broadly took the same approach to Scripture that men like the geologist Conybeare applied to the early chapters of Genesis, although his conclusions as to what was religious truth were very different. Julius Hare described them as the latest form

[1485] G.O. Trevelyan, *The Life and Letters of Lord Macaulay* (1876) vol.1, p.60.
[1486] A.N. Wilson, *The Victorians* (2002) p.19.
[1487] See O. Chadwick, *The Victorian Church* (1987) pt.1, pp.530-533.
[1488] J.H. Brooke, *Science and Religion* (1991) pp.265-267.
[1489] *Strauss' Life of Jesus* (J.L. M'Ilraith (trans.)) p.170.
[1490] Ibid., pp.173-174. Strauss did not believe in a bodily resurrection of Jesus. The resurrection was real in the minds of the apostles because of the excitement of persecution or, in St Paul's case, because of witnessing the calmness of the persecuted, see ibid., pp.234-235, or in St Peter's case aided by a "visionary disposition", see ibid., p.243.
[1491] Ibid., p.258.

of Socinianism and that Strauss "has rolled out of the chaos of pantheism into the blank abyss of atheism".[1492] George Eliot also translated, after Frederich Engels failed to do so, Ludwig Feuerbach's *The Essence of Christianity* (1841), which suggested that religion existed only in man's mind.[1493] Feuerbach's ideas powerfully influenced Karl Marx and the materialist view of history.

The clergy were a target of the novelists. Hannah More noted that "jacobinical writers", at the beginning of the French Revolution, alienated "the people from the church, by undermining their respect for its ministers".[1494] Professor Owen Chadwick, in his magisterial work *The Victorian Church*, illustrates how systematically, starting with Anthony Trollope's mother, the "Trollopes held up evangelical clergymen to reprobation".[1495] By the time Frances Trollope had completed her novels Professor Chadwick suggests that all evangelical Christianity was seen "as canting, snivelling, sanctimonious hypocrisy".[1496] Christians saw what some novelists were doing. One wrote that they confirmed "the native infidelity of the human heart in the rising generation", and that even the ministers did not believe the Bible.[1497]

However, some novelists concerned about their reputation handled barbs aimed at Christianity with care. For instance, Dickens, in a preface to later editions of *The Pickwick Papers*, explained that his satire was aimed at the "cant of religion", "the pretence of piety" and an "audacious" adhesion to the letter of the law, rather than "religion", "piety" and the "great truths of Scripture" respectively. All the same, as he acknowledged, "well intentioned" readers of the original edition had

1492 J.C. Hare, "Preface" to *The Mission of the Comforter, with Notes* (1850) p.viii.

1493 S.K. Padover, *Karl Marx* (1978) p.135.

1494 W. Roberts, *Memoirs of the Life and Correspondence of Hannah More* (1834) vol.3, p.130.

1495 O. Chadwick, *The Victorian Church* (1987) pt.1, pp.446-447.

1496 Ibid., p.447. Charlotte Brontë did something similar to deeply Calvinistic clergy, although perhaps more targeted to an individual, in her portrayal of Mr Brocklehurst in *Jane Eyre* (1847), see R. Barnard and L. Barnard, "Wilson, Rev William Carus (1791-1859)", in *A Brontë Encyclopedia* (2007) pp.377-378. Her treatment in the same work of St John Rivers, who is committed to Calvinistic teaching, although not wholly condemnatory, leaves the impression that Calvinists lack compassion and joy, see N. Cervetti, *Scenes of Reading* (1998) pp.65-66.

1497 J. Ivimey, "Preface" to *The Life of Mr William Kiffin* (1833) pp.vi-vii.

not always spotted that the author made the distinction.[1498] In his later work *Bleak House* (serialised 1852-1853), he was more circumspect in linking unattractive characters to religion. Instead, his general assault is directed against philanthropists, a body closely linked with the evangelicals. For example, Mrs Jellyby, who devoted "herself entirely to the public", to the neglect of her children, has as her latest concern Africa, rather than religion. She is also a tract distributor, although the subject matter of the tracts remains undisclosed.[1499]

Nevertheless, strongly Christian writers also enjoyed great popularity.[1500] Catherine Marsh's *Memoirs of Captain Hedley Vicars* outsold Dickens's *Bleak House* in the year of their respective publications by more than two to one.[1501] Catherine Marsh was a remarkably effective personal evangelist and on friendly terms with many of the leading figures of the period.[1502]

8.8.2 *Reshaping heaven and hell*

By 1790, when William Blake began work on his *Marriage of Heaven and Hell*, he was already "obsessed" with Milton".[1503] In this work, he both recast traditional conceptions of heaven and hell – and many other key issues of orthodox belief – and raised questions about Milton's orthodoxy, especially regarding his attitude to the devil.[1504] Blake's hell seemed to have advantages over heaven with its energy, while heaven seemed rather a passive place. William Michael Rossetti, an admirer of Blake's genius, observed that in Blake's Prophetic Books there are "many passages which show the author to have been possessed by

[1498] C. Dickens, *The Posthumous Papers of the Pickwick Club* (Chapman & Hall (1911)) pp.10-11.

[1499] C. Dickens, *Bleak House* (Bradbury and Evans (1858)) pp.21 and 60.

[1500] See generally E. Jay, *The Religion of the Heart* (1979).

[1501] P. Scott, "The Business of Belief: The Emergence of 'Religious' Publishing", in *Sanctity and Secularity: The Church and the World* (1973) (D. Baker (ed.)) p.215.

[1502] L.E. O'Rorke, *The Life and Friendships of Catherine Marsh* (1917). W.H. Dawson, a young adjutant, was converted through reading the *Memoirs of Captain Hedley Vicars*. Puzzled as to why 1 John 1:7 was so significant to Hedley Vicars, he prayed for the same experience. Awakening the next day he found that "he had passed from death unto life", I. Dobbie, *Sovereign Service* (2013) pp.67-68.

[1503] E. Larrissy, *William Blake* (1985) p.116.

[1504] See ibid., p.117. Daniel Defoe had, in *The Political History of the Devil* (1726) pp.63-77, already suggested that Milton had made mistakes with regard to the devil and hell in *Paradise Lost,* including being too positive about them. He wrote, "In a word, Mr *Milton* has indeed made a fine poem *but the devil of a history*". Author's italics. Ibid., p.71. See also P.K. Alkon, *Defoe and Fictional Time* (1979) pp.44-45.

ideas which he could not regulate or control...he asserted that he wrote under immediate dictation, and without the exercise of any option of his own".[1505] In his work on Milton, and in other work, Blake joined a number who were reviving religious art in Britain around the turn of the nineteenth century.[1506]

Anne Brontë also articulated unorthodox ideas about hell in *The Tenant of Wildfell Hall* (1848), as "among other vital concerns" she dealt with "the salvation of a man's soul".[1507] Arthur Huntingdon, the novel's villain, lies dying as he discusses with his wife Helen matters drawn from the Bible relating to the life to come, including the story of Lazarus and the rich man.[1508] However Helen, who has suffered greatly at Huntingdon's hands, could not "endure to think that that poor trembling soul was hurried away to everlasting torment?" After his death, Helen took comfort "not only from a vague dependence on the possibility that penitence and pardon might have reached him at the last, but from the blessed confidence that, through whatever purging fires the erring spirit may be doomed to pass – whatever fate awaits it, still, it is not lost, and God, who hates nothing that he has made *will* bless it in the end!"[1509] The scene of Huntingdon's death has been described as a "pioneering commitment to the doctrine of universal salvation".[1510] *The Tenant* "was an immediate and sensational success", outselling all contemporary Brontë novels, save *Jane Eyre*.[1511]

8.8.3 *Milton's genius as a support for orthodoxy is further undermined*

Around 1800, Blake lived in a cottage on William Hayley's estate, acting as his amanuensis and producing, among other works, the illustrations for Hayley's biography of his friend, William Cowper (a firm evangelical who died in 1800) – *The Life, and Posthumous Writings, of William*

[1505] M. Bishop, *Blake's Hayley* (1951) p.280.
[1506] T. Buser, *Religious Art in the Nineteenth Century in Europe and America* (2002) vol.1, p.79.
[1507] W. Gërin, "Introduction" to Anne Brontë, *The Tenant of Wildfell Hall* (Penguin (1979)) p.7.
[1508] Anne Brontë, *The Tenant of Wildfell Hall* (Penguin (1979)) p.446. Luke 16:19-31.
[1509] Author's italics. Anne Brontë, *The Tenant of Wildfell Hall* (Penguin (1979)) p.452. See also W. Gërin, *Anne Brontë* (1976) pp.xii and 361.
[1510] B. Prentis, *The Brontë Sisters and George Eliot* (1988) p.161.
[1511] W. Gërin, *Anne Brontë* (1976) p.260.

Cowper (1803-1804).[1512] This biography was a tremendous success and encouraged a great demand for Cowper's poetry, which aimed at teaching the gospel.[1513] However, Blake while in Hayley's employment began work on his epic poem *Milton*, in which he was again to explore new and very different theological ideas in the company of his hero. In doing so, Blake advanced the cause of literature as a central focus of life as "Milton leaves heaven and returns to earth to do battle with forces opposed to art and the human spirit".[1514] Hayley probably did not know where Blake's thinking was taking him, while they lived near each other.[1515] Blake's development of "a surrogate for religious orthodoxy"[1516] gained wide currency when Alexander Gilchrist's *Life of Blake* was published in 1863. Thomas Carlyle was Gilchrist's next door neighbour and encourager; the epic quality of Blake's work – and its biblical resonance – without being orthodox, struck a deep chord with him.

Meanwhile, in 1823, further claims about Milton's orthodoxy were raised when an unpublished manuscript, *De Doctrina Christiana*, was discovered, which had on it Milton's name. The work was interpreted at the time as advocating Arian doctrines.[1517] Whether it actually does so, or was written by Milton, or has any value in interpreting *Paradise Lost*,[1518] is now a cause of contention – but the existence of *De Doctrina*

[1512] G.M. Ella, *William Cowper* (1993) p.587.

[1513] Ibid., pp.586-588 and 591-592. On Cowper's evangelicalism, see J.A. Thomas, *The Nation's Gospel: Reformation to Revolution* (2017) vol.1, pp.351-353.

[1514] R.N. Essick and J. Viscomi, "Introduction" to W. Blake, "Milton a Poem", in *Blake's Illuminated Books* (1993) (R.N. Essick and J. Viscomi (eds)) vol.5, p.9. George Eliot, in her novels, was another who entered into dialogue with Milton and his works, and by doing so, advanced literature as an independent measure of life, see A.K. Nardo, *George Eliot's Dialogue with John Milton* (2003).

[1515] M. Bishop, *Blake's Hayley* (1951) pp.281-282.

[1516] E. Larrissy, *Blake and Modern Literature* (2006) p.34.

[1517] See C.A. Patrides, *Milton and the Christian Tradition* (1979) pp.15-16.

[1518] C.A. Patrides reaffirms that *Paradise Lost* was perceived by Milton and his contemporaries as a distinctly Christian Protestant poem, see C.A. Patrides, *Milton and the Christian Tradition* (1979) p.5. See also G. Campbell, Thomas N. Corns, *John Mliton* (2008) pp.337-338. Patrides also suggests that *De Doctrina Christiana* was "an abortive venture into theology", cited in M. Lieb, *Theological Milton* (2006) p.16. Others question whether Milton was the author of *De Doctrina Christiana,* see W.B. Hunter, *Visitation Unimplor'd* (1998) and Michael Lieb, questions whether the views expounded of Jesus in *De Doctrina Christiana* are Arian, see M. Lieb, *Theological Milton* (2006) pp.261-278. One recent study of the authorship of *De Doctrina Christiana* concludes: "But since it was abandoned while still a work-in-progress,

Christiana continues to detract from an unequivocal use of Milton's genius to defend orthodoxy. A little earlier, Percy Bysshe Shelley suggested that Milton's genius was demonstrated by his portrayal that "Milton's devil as a moral being is...far superior to his God".[1519] Shelley especially objected to the biblical idea that "God considers punishment inevitable if Adam eats the apple"[1520] but then he also objected to the family and "the institution of marriage and the fanatical convention of chastity".[1521] A belief in hell was also becoming a practical matter. In the 1850s, not to believe in hell could lead to the loss of a case by a defendant, because his oath was invalid. The Secularists campaigned for a change in this law.[1522]

8.9 Civilisation determines a nation's religion

In 1857 Henry Thomas Buckle published the first volume of his unfinished *History of Civilisation in England.* It advanced the premise that "human societies were governed by universal laws"[1523] which could be identified by applying deductive and inductive reasoning. Such an approach undermined the role of Christianity in holding together the state and its need to depend on God's providence for its success.

According to Buckle, it was a nation's civilisation that determined its religion. Its "intellectual culture" needed to change before it was able to accept new religious doctrines,[1524] rather than the new birth, or the Lord opening the eyes of the blind. He explained the rise of Protestantism in Europe on the basis that "In the sixteenth century…credulity and ignorance, though still considerable, were rapidly diminishing, and it was found necessary to organise a religion suited to their altered circumstances".[1525] In his view: "According to the natural order, the most

probably half a decade before the completion of *Paradise Lost*, its value as a guide to the interpretation of the epic is limited", see G. Campbell, Thomas N. Corns, J.K. Hale and F.J. Tweedie, *Milton and the Manuscript of De Doctrina Christiana* (2007) p.161.

[1519] W. Empson, *Milton's God* (1978) pp.9-35.

[1520] See ibid., pp.19-21.

[1521] G. Gordon, *Shelley and the Oppressors of Mankind* (N.D.) p.5.

[1522] E. Royle, *Victorian Infidels: The Origins of the British Secularist Movement* 1791-1866 (1974) pp.268-272.

[1523] J. Kirby, *Historians and the Church of England: Religion and Historical Scholarship, 1870-1920* (2016) p.189.

[1524] H.T. Buckle, *History of Civilisation* (1873) vol.1, p.261.

[1525] Ibid.

civilised countries should all be Protestants, and the most uncivilised ones Catholics."[1526] With such a view, it is unsurprising that the High Church Anglican historians – who were the Church historians of our next period – rejected Buckle's view that a nation's intellectual activity determined its religion. However, in doing so, as we shall soon see, they like Buckle rejected the view that it was the obedience of the nation to God's laws that determined its prosperity.[1527]

8.10 God does not prefer Protestants

The leading nations[1528] of the time were Protestant, but the radicals sought to show that it was not Protestantism that was the cause of Britain's success, stability and prosperity. Rather, *The Westminster Review* attributed Britain's success to its freedom and science. It thought that orthodoxy was always "on the side of resistance" to freedom. It believed that it was the private liberty that accompanied Protestantism, what it called its "negative" side, "not to the positive side of Protestantism, that we must ascribe our mental energy and intelligence". It added an observation that "The more Protestantism has been developed into its own characteristic prosperity, the more atheistic is the aspect of public affairs." Moses would have understood this. In Deuteronomy 8:10-20 he warned that prosperity led to pride and forgetfulness of God.

Thomas Carlyle was also, with subtlety, shifting the perceived basis of the nation's success away from its Protestant establishment. He agreed that it was not wealth, or material development or pleasure that made a nation strong, but he did not agree that it was Protestantism's "peculiar doctrines" that made a nation strong. Rather, in his view, the fate of nations rested "as had been said in the Bible, and among all serious peoples, on the moral virtues, courage, veracity, purity, justice and good sense".[1529] In other words, he helped shift the emphasis away from the "peculiar doctrines" to what William Wilberforce would have said were the results of those doctrines.

[1526] Ibid., p.262.

[1527] J. Kirby, *Historians and the Church of England: Religion and Historical Scholarship, 1870-1920* (2016) pp.189-215.

[1528] "The Religious Weakness of Protestantism", in 13 *The Westminster Review* (1858) p.137.

[1529] J.A. Froude, *Thomas Carlyle* (1896) vol.2, p.18.

9

THE RELIGIOUS STATE OF THE NATION PRIOR TO 1859

9.1 A nation dependent on God

At the beginning of the nineteenth century, Christians thought divine judgment fell on France for its atheism and infidelity and that England was not above God's sanctions. An Anglican clergyman, writing in 1817, noted that "England...was alarmed by the judgments, of which, without feeling them, she was a close spectatress, and panted for an opportunity to take the lead in restoring erring man to his allegiance to his heavenly sovereign".[1530] In 1826, Daniel Wilson, in his introductory essay to Wilberforce's *A Practical View*, urged that

> Legislators must act fully as Christians. The public mind expects this... England must rise to her high destiny. If she remain stationary... she will decline and perish...be deeply persuaded that every national sin fatally contributes to the dissolution of our power; whilst every act of reformation and piety goes to arrest the deadly gangrene.[1531]

Christians understood that religion made for the "social happiness of man", not the civil institutions of the nation. The latter could not be transferred between nations and necessarily have the same impact. Experience showed that "a form of government, securing peace and happiness in one country, may be followed by anarchy and misery in another".[1532]

[1530] A. O'Callaghan, *The Bible Society against the Church and State* (1817) p.4. See for example *Reform or Ruin!* (1798).

[1531] D. Wilson, "Introductory Essay" to W. Wilberforce, *A Practical View of the Prevailing Religious System of Professed Christians, in the Higher and Middle Classes in This Country, Contrasted with Real Christianity* (1829) pp.lxxi-lxxii.

[1532] A. Sedgwick, "A Discourse on the Studies of the University", in *History of British Educational Thought (British University Education)* (2000) p.73.

By the 1850s, Britain could be said to have pressed on to "the noble career which Providence" had opened before her.[1533] Wilson thought that "at no period since the Reformation has the faithful preaching of the distinctive doctrines of the gospel been so extensive in the Church of England as during the last thirty years".[1534] When things went wrong, the nation searched her soul and, if necessary, repented. After the Indian Mutiny of 1857, Queen Victoria proclaimed a day of National Humiliation. At a service of repentance, the young Baptist preacher, C.H. Spurgeon, preached to an audience of 24,000, the largest congregation of his spectacular career. On that day, the railway traffic ceased, the shops were closed and the streets quiet. It was like a Sunday. The churches were filled with attentive listeners. *The Record* noted: "The preachers seem to have used their opportunities well, and instead of discussing general principles, to have dealt with the special import of the chastisement which had fallen upon the nation."[1535] In the previous quarter of a century there had been similar days of National Humiliation for the Irish famine, two epidemics of cholera and the Crimean War.

9.2 No lack of zeal, but the perils of respectability

There was no shortage of Christian "zeal, activity, liberality"[1536] in looking after the poor and reaching out to them with the gospel. A man who would not lend a hand to help the evangelisation of his county was viewed with suspicion.[1537] In 1859, John Angell James looked back over half a century of Christian ministry and thought that, in comparison with the little that was going on when his ministry began, it was hard to believe that it was the same church or planet. He wrote that nothing like it "had been known in the Christian church since the days of the apostles".[1538] "In the public mind the word 'philanthropist' became all but

[1533] D. Wilson, "Introductory Essay" to W. Wilberforce, *A Practical View of the Prevailing Religious System of Professed Christians, in the Higher and Middle Classes in This Country, Contrasted with Real Christianity* (1829) p.lxxii.

[1534] D. Wilson, *Our Protestant Faith in Danger* (1850) p.4.

[1535] See "The Day of Humiliation in '57", in *The Record*, 5 January 1900, p.9.

[1536] J.A. James, "What is the Spiritual State of our Churches?", in *The Works of John Angell James* (1861) (T.S. James (ed.)) vol.9, p.370.

[1537] Ibid.

[1538] Ibid., pp.367 and 372. See also E. Miall, *The British Churches in Relation to the British People* (1850) p.87. A comparison of the nineteenth century with the "days of the apostles" was a well-used superlative for religious developments of the time.

synonymous with 'evangelical'".[1539] And in the building of new churches, religion "stimulated a degree of personal giving unparalleled since the Reformation".[1540] Yet, possibly there was a growing unwillingness among middle-class evangelicals to give offence by articulating in public the Fall of man, the atonement, free grace in Jesus Christ and the final judgment. They had become "respectable". There may well be more than a grain of truth in the view of one critic that "Their domestic action was no longer that of the prophet preaching in God's name against palpable iniquity, but that of the patronising philanthropist anxious to do so much good to the poor as can be done without too great offence to the wealthy and comfortable."[1541]

9.3 An increasingly moral nation

Even where evangelistic endeavours failed to convert, the presence of the gospel and Christian teaching still had effect. A report of the CPAS commented that populations "Christian little more than in name...rude in manners, uneducated, and subjected to no moral restraint or discipline, have been, in a most striking manner, advanced in civilisation, decency of behaviour, general intelligence, and religious knowledge". *The Christian Observer* thought that though such change fell "short of actual conversion, it is clearly of the utmost value in its bearing on the general tone of society".[1542] However, there were still problems on the moral landscape, namely: excessive alcohol consumption and, increasingly, unmarried couples lived together. Prostitution grew in London and spread to the country towns. *The Christian Observer* noted: "There is increased intensity given to almost every phase of society. The bright parts are brightening and the dark shades are darkening."[1543]

[1539] D. Owen, *English Philanthropy 1660-1960* (1965) p.93. See generally S. Flew, *Philanthropy and the Funding of the Church of England 1856-1914* (2015) which also draws out giving by members of the High Church.
[1540] P.T. Marsh, *The Victorian Church in Decline* (1969) p.4.
[1541] "Jowett and the Broad Church", in 16 *The Westminster Review* (1859) pp.43-44.
[1542] "On the Progress of True Religion Amongst our Home Population", in 56 *The Christian Observer for the Year 1856* (1856) p.148.
[1543] Ibid., p.153.

9.4 Parliament seeks to follow the law of God

By custom, the law of the Church was the law of England. The emergence of democracy[1544] raised the issue whether the law of England could diverge from Scripture, especially over moral precepts. The existing law of divorce was unsatisfactory because, although divorce was forbidden, if one were wealthy or influential enough, a divorce could be obtained by an Act of Parliament. The Owenites used this as a sign of the unfairness of the existing laws related to marriage. Furthermore, a novelist like Charles Dickens, in *Hard Times* (1854), painted with great pathos the horror of being in a marriage which could only be escaped at vast expense, the wife having changed from a pretty young lass to "a creature so foul to look on", while another, with so neat a figure, waited patiently.[1545]

In 1857, jurisdiction over marriages was moved to the civil courts and divorce and remarriage permitted on the grounds of adultery. Much of the preceding debate in Parliament hung on the meaning of the biblical texts. Gladstone wrote what has been described as a "vast" article on the topic.[1546] Over 600,000 petitioned Queen Victoria against the Act.[1547] The bishops could not agree, but supported the changes in sufficient numbers for it to be claimed that Scripture supported divorce in the limited circumstances proposed. Divorce and remarriage in Church were allowed for adultery, although a wife had to prove a man's adultery was incestuous, bigamous, or accompanied by rape, sodomy, bestiality, cruelty or desertion. The number of divorces swiftly rose. For the future, the tricky element was whether a clergyman, whose conscience did not permit him to remarry someone, could be compelled to do so. The conclusion was no; but he had to surrender his church for such purpose if there was another clergyman in the diocese who would marry the couple.

9.5 Convocation is restored to give the Church a collective voice

In 1854, for the first time in over 100 years, Convocation, the Church's deliberating body, met – with authority to meet regularly, debate a little,

[1544] For a stimulating consideration of how conversionary Protestants encouraged democracy across the nations, see R.D. Woodbury, "The Missionary Roots of Modern Democracy", in 106 *American Political Science Review* (2012) pp.244-274.
[1545] C. Dickens, *Hard Times* (Penguin Classics (2003)) pp.69-78 and see also 321.
[1546] O. Chadwick, *The Victorian Church* (1987) pt.1, p.482.
[1547] E. Abbott, *A History of Marriage* (2010) p.199.

and to appoint committees to report and advise the Established Church. *The Times* suggested that Lord Derby's government encouraged this development because elections were pending and the assistance of the High Church party was not to be despised.[1548] The Evangelical party and theological liberals were against reviving the powers of Convocation. It was a clergy body and likely to be dominated by High Churchmen. High Churchmen were strong in the Church, but not in the country, and with the country being against popery evangelicals wanted lay involvement. Furthermore, Archbishop Sumner thought Convocation would become a forum to express partisanship. Considerable political and ecclesiastic wrangling followed until the right to meet was granted. In the years that followed, the authority of Convocation grew and it did not split the Church of England.[1549] However, the laity were not involved.

9.6 The first national church survey

In 1850 *The Record* commented about the mid-eighteenth century, comparing it with the current times, that "all was dead – now all is life."[1550] It added that "in the incomprehensible providence of the Almighty he has permitted the spirit of evil to work also, and the children of the wicked one likewise stand up on their feet an exceeding great army". The following year, the opportunity arose to examine the factors underlying these sentiments, when the first national census of England and Wales was taken.

9.6.1 *The 1851 census in England and Wales*

The 1851 census suggested that, out of a population of nearly 18 million people in England and Wales, 7,261,000 people attended a religious service on census Sunday – which happened to be Mothering Sunday that year.[1551] This meant that in England 39.13 per cent of the population

[1548] "Among the Questions", in *The Times*, 8 February 1853.

[1549] See O. Chadwick, The *Victorian Church* (1987) pt.1, pp.309-324.

[1550] "London", in *The Record*, 3 January 1850, p.4.

[1551] On census Sunday, 4,647,482 attended church in the morning, 3,184,135 in the afternoon, and 3,064,449 in the evening. The census did not provide the means of identifying how many people attended two or more services. Horace Mann assumed that half of those attending in the afternoon were not present in the morning – and one-third of those attending in the evening were not at either previous service. If these assumptions were correct, 7,261,000 people attended at least one service on census Sunday, see *Census of Great Britain 1851. Religious Worship* (1853) p.clii. The census

willingly attended a Sunday service, while the figure in Wales was 57.34 per cent – giving a combined figure for the two nations of just over 40 per cent of the population,[1552] a proportion probably as high as it ever was before, or after. For a specific example, in Kidderminster, out of a population of nearly 18,462 people on census Sunday, 5,027 attended morning, 801 attended afternoon and 4,066 attended evening worship.[1553] These numbers included 311 Unitarians and 300 Roman Catholics at morning, 157 Unitarians at evening and 150 Roman Catholics at afternoon services.

The 1851 census showed that Wilberforce's pitch to the upper and middle classes had borne a rich harvest. The upper classes now ranked "regular church-attendance as among the recognised proprieties of life." The middle classes had augmented their attendances at religious services, for "which, for several centuries, they have so eminently been distinguished".[1554]

numbers also included other worshipping communities – Jews, Mormons etc., although such numbers were small. M.R. Watts, *The Dissenters* (1995) vol.2, pp.25-30 and 672-675 provides a recent review of the double-counting issue and an alternative approach.

From early days, the accuracy of the 1851 census was challenged. For example, see *The Truth about Church Extension: An Exposure of Certain Fallacies and Misstatements contained in the Census Reports on Religious Worship and Education* (1857), but its general thrust is now accepted, see O. Chadwick, *The Victorian Church* (1987) pt.1, p.368-369; W.S.F. Pickering, "The 1851 Religious Census – A Useless Experiment?", in 18 *British Journal of Sociology* (1967) pp.385-387; and M.R. Watts, *The Dissenters* (1995) vol.2, pp.25-26.

Pickering suggests that the maximum figure for attendance at a religious service of those over ten on census Sunday was not more than 54 per cent, see W.S.F. Pickering, "The 1851 Religious Census – A Useless Experiment?", in 18 *British Journal of Sociology* (1967) p.393. However, this figure assumes that no children under ten were included in Mann's figures for attendances and this was not the case. In 1851, there were as many as 4,440,446 children in England and Wales.

The treatment of Sunday school-age children is a weakness in the 1851 census figures. Mann included in his figures those attending religious services and those attending Sunday schools which met at the same time as religious services – but he excluded returns of services attended only by Sunday scholars, because the "services partook more of the nature of school duties than of formal public worship," see *Census of Great Britain 1851. Religious Worship* (1853) p.clxxi. The total number of children attending Sunday school on a Sunday was 1.8 million, see ibid., p.clvii, although, of course, the attendance of many of these were included in the census figures.

1552 M.R. Watts, *The Dissenters* (1995) vol.2, pp.28 and 674. See also D. Ollerton, *Mission in a Welsh Context* (2015) (Unpublished Ph.D. thesis, University of Chester) pp.62-63.

1553 *Census of Great Britain 1851. Religious Worship* (1853) p.cclx.

1554 Ibid., p.clviii.

But the census suggested that 5,288,000[1555] of those who could do so neglected religious ordinances of their own free choice – although the missing on any given Sunday were inevitably not always the same. Horace Mann, the author of the official report on the census, observed that the prevalence of infidelity had been exaggerated – in the sense of implying some degree of antagonistic intellectual effort and decision. There was, though, plenty of spiritual indifference. Robert Aitken, the evangelist, was in turmoil "that so few responded to the call" in comparison with the needs of the time.[1556] Attendances in London were particularly weak. At Shoreditch, Marylebone and Hampstead, the proportion of their respective populations in church were respectively 15.3 per cent, 27.9 per cent and 48.9 per cent.[1557] The paucity of artisans in the congregations of churches in the cities and large towns was noted. Horace Mann wrote that they filled the day-schools of church and chapel and the Sunday schools. There they received "the elements of a religious education; but, no sooner do they mingle in the active world of labour than, subjected to the constant action of opposing influences, they soon become as utter strangers to religious ordinances as the people of a heathen country".[1558] Mann added that the masses of the working population, skilled or otherwise, had become "*unconscious Secularists*".[1559] This "sect" had "originated recently", and the labouring classes, "engrossed by the demands, the trials, or the pleasures of the passing hour, and ignorant or careless of a future", had, without thinking, adopted its creed.[1560] The report recommended that the means to fill the churches was "a great addition to the number of efficient, earnest, religious *teachers*, clerical or lay, by whose persuasions the reluctant population might be won".[1561]

[1555] Ibid. Interestingly, one informed estimate, made just before the census, was that the non-churchgoing portion of the nation numbered six million – not far from, but slightly higher than, the census, see *Prize Essay on the Occasion of the Society for Promoting Religious Knowledge Among the Poor Established the 8th of August, 1750 Completing its First Centenary* (1850) p.116.

[1556] C.E. Woods, *Memoirs and Letters of Canon Hay Aitken* (1928) pp.32 and 35.

[1557] M.R. Watts, *The Dissenters* (1995) vol.2, pp.682-683.

[1558] *Census of Great Britain 1851. Religious Worship* (1853) p.clviii.

[1559] Author's italics. Ibid. For a discussion of the appropriateness of this term, see O. Chadwick, *The Secularization of the European Mind in the Nineteenth Century* (1975) pp.90-91 and 100.

[1560] *Census of Great Britain 1851. Religious Worship* (1853) p.clviii.

[1561] Author's italics. Ibid., p.clxvii.

For all denominations, the census was revealing about their respective public standing. That not half the population attended church on a Sunday was a major concern to the Established Church.[1562] Further, of those attending services, only just over half were Anglican; and of the entire population, only 21 per cent attended an Anglican service on census Sunday. The Nonconformists drew 17.58 per cent of the population and the Roman Catholics 1.7 per cent.[1563] An additional cause of Anglican anxiety was that the growth rate of Dissent exceeded its own.[1564] Given that the majority of the people no longer attended the Established Church, The Society for the Liberation of Religion from State Patronage and Control urged that "the Establishment ought to be altered or modified".[1565]

The Methodist communities were now the second biggest religious grouping. In England, over 8.9 per cent of the population attended one of their services on census Sunday.[1566] The Wesleyan Connection alone numbered 924,000 worshippers.[1567] In Wales, over 22.4 per cent of the population attended a Methodist service on census Sunday.[1568] The Calvinistic Methodists alone had nearly 16 per cent of the Welsh population in their chapels on census Sunday.[1569] The extensive use of the laity by Methodists made them the most effective denomination in reaching the working classes. They possessed, perhaps, as many as 20,000 preachers and class leaders outside the ministerial order.[1570]

[1562] *"What Can I Do?" A Question for Church-goers About Half-empty Churches* (1854).

[1563] Watts, in his analysis of the 1851 Census, suggests that the difference between the aggregate attendance at Church of England and Nonconformist services was closer than Mann suggested. Watts puts attendances at their respective services as 19.68 per cent and 18.62 per cent of the population, see M.R. Watts, *The Dissenters* (1995) vol.2, p.674.

[1564] *The Truth about Church Extension: An Exposure of Certain Fallacies and Misstatements Contained in the Census Reports on Religious Worship and Education* (1857).

[1565] *The Ecclesiastical Census of 1851, and its Results* (1854).

[1566] Calculation based on the figures in M.R. Watts, *The Dissenters* (1995) vol.2, pp.28-29. Watts gives a slightly higher figure than H. Mann, *Religious Worship in England and Wales* (1854) p.91.

[1567] See above Note 1566.

[1568] See above Note 1566.

[1569] See above Note 1566.

[1570] *Census of Great Britain 1851. Religious Worship* (1853) p.clxv.

In England and Wales, the Independents were the next biggest Christian grouping; 4.4 per cent of the population attended their services on census Sunday.[1571] However, there were concerns, especially in the larger Independent churches, that the ministers were exercising too much control over the "spiritual teaching" and that members were no longer being encouraged to exercise their gifts and abilities.[1572]

The Baptist family of chapels made up 3.3 per cent of the population of England and Wales worshipping on census Sunday.[1573] The Particular Baptists made up the overwhelming majority of the Baptists. The census confirmed the Quaker numerical decline. Many had emigrated, but they recognised that their decline was also attributable to the "feebler endeavours now than formerly to gain proselytes".[1574]

9.6.2 *The 1851 census in Scotland*

In Scotland, a separately published census revealed higher levels of church attendance but that, relatively, the Established Church was weaker. The census showed "the attendants of the Church of Scotland at 19.9 per cent of the population, of the Free Church at 19.2 per cent, of the United Presbyterians at 11.7 per cent and of others at 10.1 per cent – or just over 60 per cent in all. However, the statistics rested on a greater degree of mere estimate than in England."[1575]

[1571] Calculation based on the figures in M.R. Watts, *The Dissenters* (1995) vol.2, pp.28-29. Watts gives a slightly lower figure than H. Mann, *Religious Worship in England and Wales* (1854) p.91.

[1572] *Census of Great Britain 1851. Religious Worship* (1853) p.clxv.

[1573] Calculation based on the figures in M.R. Watts, *The Dissenters* (1995) vol.2, pp.28-29. Watts gives a slightly lower figure than H. Mann, *Religious Worship in England and Wales* (1854) p.91.

[1574] *Census of Great Britain 1851. Religious Worship* (1853) p.lxvii.

[1575] O. Chadwick, *The Victorian Church* (1987) pt.1, p.369. See also C.G. Brown, *Religion and Society in Scotland since 1707* (1997) pp.42-46.

9.7 A remarkable capacity for spiritual growth appears in the late 1850s

By the end of the 1850s a clergyman observed of religious revivals that "Of this age they have been the glory."[1576] Some churches and chapels witnessed remarkable spiritual and numerical growth, none being more influential than the Baptist, New Park Street Chapel, Southwark. A building capable of holding 1,200 people, its former glories seemed to be past when, in 1854, the young Charles Haddon Spurgeon arrived, aged 19, to preach. Twelve months later, it was full. In February 1855, the congregation moved temporarily, while a new building was built. Exeter Hall, holding 3,000, was found not to be big enough. By October 1856, congregations numbering over 10,000 regularly assembled to hear him, with many not able to get in.[1577] Spurgeon did much more than attract the committed. As he said of 1857, "In one year it was my happiness personally to see not less than a thousand who had been converted."[1578] In Spurgeon, the chapels discovered the greatest preacher of what would be the great age of preachers.

Elsewhere, in the Cornish district of Pendeen, Robert Aitken found his voice "quite gone" as he prayed with penitents, day and night.[1579] Aitken, in 1851, was visited by William Haslam, a High Church minister with a Cornish parish. Convinced that Haslam was not converted, he told him to shut his church and not to preach until he was converted. Haslam refused to listen, but (as described earlier) his own sermon converted him the next time he preached.[1580] Thus began what Haslam later described as "the beginning of a great revival work in my parish" of Baldhu. It continued into 1854.[1581] When Robert Aitken arrived to preach, 1,500 packed into a church designed for 600.[1582] As the revival at Baldhu ebbed, Haslam was summoned to a parish in Staffordshire by the Bishop of Lichfield after Aitken had stopped a night there and left a "gloom hanging" over its souls. "A scene which, for noise and confusion, was quite Cornish"

[1576] A. Barnes, "Every Christian Should be a Revivalist", in *The Revivalist* (1859) p.81.
[1577] "Frightful Calamity at the Royal Surrey Gardens, Lambeth", in *The Observer*, 27 October 1856.
[1578] C.H. Spurgeon, *Autobiography* (1973) vol.1, p.452.
[1579] C.E. Woods, *Memoirs and Letters of Canon Hay Aitken* (1928) p.68.
[1580] W. Haslam, *From Death into Life* (1897) pp.55-64.
[1581] Ibid., pp.65 and 201.
[1582] Ibid., p.70.

soon followed. When, a week later, Haslam left for the railway station, he was accompanied by at least 200 people.

But it was not only the preaching and teaching of the leading evangelistic clergy of the day that witnessed results. In the spring of 1857, a series of special religious services was launched at Exeter Hall, with the opening service conducted by the Bishop of Carlisle. Three thousand attended from all classes, especially the elusive working class. The preaching was "delivered with dignity and power...the presiding hand and goodness of God" was felt. A few weeks later, when the services ended, 5,000 were attending and many more could not get in.[1583] In 1858, Glasgow's "largest edifice" could not contain "the multitudes who flocked to hear" the gentleman-evangelist Brownlow North. They were people drawn "from the highest to the lowest". Many were awakened.[1584] In little Kepwick, at around the same time, a revival broke out, prompted by the teaching of a tailor, Thomas Langton, and it lasted 12 years. Seventy of its 200 inhabitants joined the local Methodist society. "There was not a single house in the place which did not contain one or more members [Methodists] the public-house included."[1585] And not all were converted by the preaching. Some were overwhelmed by the need to make peace with God and knelt to pray.

9.8 Disquieting signs

But for evangelicals there were also disquieting signs. In 1850, Daniel Wilson attributed the failure to respond adequately to the Tractarian movement to a decline in personal piety. He thought that although preachers taught the same principles as Newton, Venn and Milner, they lacked their "holy unction and deep spirituality of mind".[1586] They were, perhaps, distracted by the many public works that sprang up and the demands of running the machinery of their large and growing parishes. The churches had grown quickly. In 1855 J.C. Ryle thought that two-thirds of all professing Christians were unsound in their beliefs.[1587] The

[1583] E. Hodder, *The Life and Work of the Seventh Earl of Shaftesbury, K.G.* (1887) p.542.
[1584] "The Scotch Revivalist", in *The Revivalist* (1858) p.125.
[1585] I.C. Watson, *The Life Story of Thomas Langton of Malton* (1896) pp.27-29.
[1586] D. Wilson, *Our Protestant Faith in Danger* (1850) p.6. See also W.H.B. Proby, *Annals of the "Low-Church" Party in England* (1888) vol.1, pp.356-357.
[1587] J.C. Ryle, *What Time is it?* (1855) p.74. See also D.M. Lewis, *Lighten their Darkness* (1986) pp.124-125.

Broad Churchman W.J. Conybeare thought that the evangelicals had lost their first love: "their creed has now become an hereditary system, which must often be adopted more from habit than conviction".[1588] He also detected among the upper classes – over the previous 10 to 15 years – a new scepticism. He thought this had been caused by dissensions within the churches.[1589] There was also the need to establish the authority of the Bible on more concrete grounds than that its pages contained religious truth. Such an approach had led to the very different conclusions of Strauss and Conybeare on the reality of the divinity and resurrection of Christ.

As the century wore on, the Nonconformists became more respectable, especially those involved with denominational central institutions.[1590] Perhaps the Congregationalists were in greatest peril. In 1851, John Angell James, their leading minister, wrote in a letter to a friend:

> I do not think I ever preached with less saving results since I was a minister; and this is the case with most others. It is a general complaint. We have no diminution of Christian activity and associated activity; but individual piety is undevout and feeble.[1591] A spirit of worldliness characterises the church...But there is a still more serious ground of apprehension in the minds of some of us, and that is for the orthodoxy of some of our young ministers. It is obvious to everyone that a spirit of scepticism is coming over our land...from Germany and France, and all the great verities of religious truth are to be tried over again.[1592]

The Record, from an Anglican perspective, had already observed the same trend. In 1850, it observed that "the rising power of infidelity" was rivalling Tractarianism as the principal threat to biblical Christianity – and its challenge was mainly directed at "the integrity of the word

1588 W.J. Conybeare, *Essays Ecclesiastical and Social* (1855) p.70.
1589 Ibid., p.163.
1590 K.F. Inglis, *Churches and the Working Classes in Victorian England* (1964) pp.13-16.
1591 See also W.H.B. Proby, *Annals of the "Low-Church" Party in England* (1888) vol.1, pp.356 and 358.
1592 R.W. Dale, *The Life and Letters of J.A. James* (1861) p.545.

of God."[1593] A few years later, *The Christian Observer* noted that "the extravagances of Tractarians have issued in infidelity. In the effort to escape credulity, men have sunk into scepticism."[1594]

These concerns were not transient. In an article published in 1859, during the last year of his life, John Angell James expanded on the problems he saw in the church. There might be great generosity, but he identified worldliness, a love of comfort and a lack of love as characteristic. People might go to church on a Sunday, but all religious feeling lapsed on a Monday.[1595] Another issue was a willingness to regard talent, genius and eloquence in a preacher as the test of his merit and to tolerate vice if "decked by the Muses".[1596] People were not coming to church for the great business of working out their salvation with fear and trembling, but to have "their taste gratified, and their understanding regaled".[1597] They were "contented with the mere elements of truth, its most rudimental principles...They are easily led away by the plausible objections of the abettors of error."[1598] Listening to preaching was not enough to lead to an understanding of the deep things of God – there had to be private Bible study.[1599] He also thought that "The battle of the Reformation may yet have to be fought over again."[1600] In 1851, he had thought scepticism a greater danger than popery. These strictures might be affirmed as the counsel of a wise pastor who, over a long life, had seen it all – or dismissed as the grumblings of an old man. Only time would tell.

[1593] "London", in *The Record*, 3 January 1850, p.4.

[1594] "Preface" to 56 *The Christian Observer for the Year 1856* (1856) p.v.

[1595] J.A. James, "What is the Spiritual State of our Churches?", in *The Works of John Angell James* (1861) (T.S. James (ed.)) vol.9, p.407. See also E. Miall, *The British Churches in Relation to the British People* (1850) p.95.

[1596] See also J.A. James, "What is the Spiritual State of our Churches?", in *The Works of John Angell James* (1861) (T.S. James (ed.)) vol.9, p.402.

[1597] Ibid., p.405.

[1598] Ibid., p.429.

[1599] Others thought private Bible study might be more talked about than done. For example, see W.H.B. Proby, *Annals of the "Low-Church" Party in England* (1888) vol.1, p.253.

[1600] J.A. James, "What is the Spiritual State of our Churches?", in *The Works of John Angell James* (1861) (T.S. James (ed.)) vol.9, p.433. Evangelicals in the Church of England agreed, see D. Wilson, *Our Protestant Faith in Danger* (1850).

10

SUMMARY OF PART 1

10.1 A great change in the nation

As 1858 drew to a close, the religious situation had vastly changed from the time just before the French Revolution – when "scepticism was one of the privileges of high life. Religion was reckoned a *vulgar* prejudice, much beneath the dignity of a gentleman, and utterly incompatible with the pretensions of wit."[1601] At the end of 1858, compliance with Christian morality was the hallmark of respectability. Its grip on society was sufficiently strong that John Stuart Mill thought it a moral tyrant. Voluntary church-going probably reached an all-time high and the number of services and church buildings multiplied. In an official Government report, the further advancement of Christianity was advocated as a means of advancing the prosperity of the state. This report, addressed to Viscount Palmerston, concluded that the "influence exerted by religious principle – controlling conscience, rather than refining taste – is seldom felt without conferring, in addition to its higher blessings, those fixed views and habits which can scarcely fail to render individuals prosperous and states secure...Christian men become, almost inevitably, temperate, industrious, and provident, as part of their religious duty; and Christian citizens acquire respect for human laws from having learnt to reverence those which are divine. The history of men and states shows nothing more conspicuously than this – that in proportion as a pure and practical religion is acknowledged and pursued are individuals materially prosperous and nations orderly and free. It is thus that religion 'has the promise of the life that now is, as well as of that which is to come.'"[1602]

Under God, the possibility of spiritual change in the nation had

[1601] Author's italics. "Religious Prosecutions", in 2 *The Westminster Review* (1824) p.11.
[1602] *Census of Great Britain 1851. Religious Worship* (1853) p.clxviii.

arisen with Whitefield and Wesley and their colleagues. In establishing Methodism, they created a spiritual force that sat half-way between Dissent and the Established Church, arousing both to fresh endeavour. As the Wesleyan Methodists became respectable, the Primitive Methodists arose to fly the flag for Wesley's methodological and theological insights. It was the French Revolution – and its manifestation of the consequences of atheism – that provided the opportunity for Simeon and others to make a vigorous Christianity acceptable in the Church of England, while Wilberforce, More and other members of the Clapham Sect made Christianity fashionable and moved it into the nation's culture and legal system. Shaftesbury and others continued their work. The evangelical leaders gave a new impetus to the methodologies of teaching Christianity that had energised it in the past – preaching, catechising, family spiritual life and a God-centred use of the Sabbath. Due attention was given to Christian apologetics. The training and funding of the clergy were improved, new churches built and the number of services increased.

Hymn-singing gained prominence as a means of teaching doctrine and uniting the faithful; and new enterprises were launched to meet the challenges of the times. The first wave of these enterprises, established at the beginning of the nineteenth century, focused on writing and distributing tracts and Bibles. The second wave, from the 1820s onwards, used the laity to visit and win the nation's poor with the same weapons and, increasingly, through open-air preaching, in which ministers might join. Even the Anglican leadership, always hostile to lay leadership, sanctioned the use of the laity to reach the masses for Christ. It was, in the words of Daniel Wilson, "an era of peculiar grace".[1603] Indeed, such were the times, that women, having proved themselves, were employed in numbers and in distinct societies to hold out the gospel. Buttressing and forming part of the work of the visiting societies was an array of philanthropic work. Further, a very large number of Christians taught in the Sunday, ragged and other schools. A crusade against alcohol abuse was launched. As a result, the churches had constant contact with the different social groupings of the nation; and new clergy and cross-denominational organisations were established to push evangelistic and

[1603] D. Wilson, "Introductory Essay" to *A Practical View of the Prevailing Religious System of Professed Christians, in the Higher and Middle Classes in This Country, Contrasted with Real Christianity* (1829) p.lvi.

philanthropic work forward and to promote the sharing of ideas and best practice.

10.2 Still a time of 'religious emergency'

Religious leaders, at the end of our period, had high expectations for the conversion of the nation. Yet it was a time of "emergency", because the population had tripled since John Wesley's day and the churches seemed "inefficient" in reaching them all.[1604] Lord Shaftesbury thought that the higher classes had been reached for Christ together with some of the very "lowest and poorest" of the working classes but, in his words, "there is a large intermediate class, comprising persons of intelligence, artisans of comparative affluence", outside the church.[1605] Others thought that, despite all the efforts, no more than one in fifty of the working classes attended church.[1606] Edward Miall suggested that the gospel had been subtly changed, so that admiration of God was second to "delight in our own destiny".[1607]

There were other signs that Christianity was far from secure. Even in those halcyon days, an earnest Christian could still receive contempt and be laughed at for their religion.[1608] A Christianity that was only fashionable because of the quality and energy of its leaders might be skin deep. Many who attended church did not understand doctrine. Also, a Christianity that gained its standing from the public influence of its leaders would weaken as they passed away. At Kidderminster in 1857 – in reference to the death of one leading evangelical minister – William Wright in his sermon took as his text "Your fathers, where are they? And the prophets do they live forever?"[1609] As the Clapham Sect generation passed away, the grip of Christianity on the upper classes weakened. Their children often did not hold to their father's theology. Further, Christian unity was breaking. In politics, the differences between denominations were emphasised, rather than glossed over. Ritualism grew within the Church of England and the latter found discipline

[1604] E. Miall, "Preface to the First Edition", in *The British Churches in Relation to the British People* (1850) p.v.

[1605] *Practical Hints on Lord Shaftesbury's Advice to the Clergy* (1853) p.3.

[1606] "How Wears the Missing Link?", in *God's Message in Low London* (N.D.) p.9.

[1607] E. Miall, *The British Churches in Relation to the British People* (1850) p.93.

[1608] J.C. Ryle, *Expository Thoughts on the Gospels: Luke* (1983) pt.1, pp.155-156.

[1609] W. Wright, *The Church Bereaved* (1857) pp.5 and 10.

difficult to impose. In 1850, Daniel Wilson envisaged the day when the Romanising party would exclude the Evangelical party from the Anglican Church.[1610] Methodism was prone to splits.

Furthermore, as Christianity became more assertive, it sparked a revolt from the unbelieving who, in more languid times, might have remained passive. The most popular "intellects of the age [were] employed in systematically or habitually holding up all really serious religion to contempt and scorn, as so much cant and hypocrisy, swindle, or foolishness".[1611] A group of exceptionally talented writers formed who did not like Christianity. Church and chapel were a target of their wit. They also marketed the attractions of "entertainment", in opposition to "seriousness". In geology, new theories of the history of the world gained traction, elements of which raised issues about the interpretation of the early chapters of the book of Genesis which were not decisively answered. Outside the country, especially in Germany, ideas antagonistic to faith grew. Those who were intellectually curious, but to whom orthodoxy lacked appeal, looked to import such ideas. The missionaries of a new fast-growing sect, the Mormons, arrived. In the Church of England and the universities, especially at Oxford, theological controversy arose. At Cambridge, from 1851, to combat these developments, the duration of the examination that every degree student sat – on Paley's *Evidences of Christianity* – was tripled.[1612]

There were also signs that the Established Church was insecure. Ironically, as it became more effective, it became the object of greater challenge. Attacked by Dissenters, both evangelical and Unitarian, and subject to public criticism from its more extreme members, distinct parties began to form within its ranks. As the parties developed, so did their ideas. These, in turn, brought greater dissension to the Church, both in its relationship to its own members and with outsiders. Some of the new ideas and practices within the Church of England also began to seep into the Dissenters and bring the potential for conflict there. The Church of Scotland had also suffered the 'Disruption' of 1843. Yet,

[1610] D. Wilson, *Our Protestant Faith in Danger* (1850) p.21.

[1611] J. Kitto, *Daily Bible Illustrations (Evening Series)* (1867) vol.4, p.278.

[1612] R. Potts, "The Editor's Preface" to W. Paley, *A View of the Evidences of Christianity, in Three Parts* (1850) (R. Potts (ed.)) p.xiii.

during our period, the Evangelical Alliance was formed to bring together evangelicals across the nation.

The impact of these varied forces could be perceived in very different ways. In government quarters – looking at the numbers attending the churches and advances in church machinery, buildings and resources and not at their doctrine – there was great confidence and the anticipation of further advance. The religious census of 1851 had established the facts relating to church attendance – and the "precise requirements of the times". Horace Mann observed that all that was needed was "the action of the rulers of the Church to gather and direct"[1613] their forces – and the "spiritual emergency" would be over. However, from his Congregational pulpit in Kidderminster, William Wright saw it differently. He thought that the time was "a peculiar juncture in the history of the church, and of the moral world at large; presenting features of the most ominous and portentous nature". He continued: "The corruptions of the church appear as fresh and rife as ever; priestly domination is practised on every hand; rampant infidelity sneers and triumphs at these results; and, as a necessary consequence, vice and immorality, blasphemy and impiety, widely prevail." It was only "a band of men whose hearts God has touched" that stood in the way of utter spiritual collapse.[1614] There were also men like the Reverend J.H. Wilson, the editor of *The British Evangelist*, launched in the summer of 1858. In his year-end summary, he looked back on a year of progress, but observed "we have only received the first drops of the coming shower". With appropriate prayer and consecration, he looked forward to the Lord opening the windows of heaven and pouring out "such a blessing that there will not be room to receive it".[1615] Whether such hope was justified, we will now explore.

[1613] H. Mann, *Religious Worship in England and Wales* (1854) p.102.
[1614] W. Wright, *The Church Bereaved* (1857) pp.9-10.
[1615] "To our Readers", in *The British Evangelist* (1858) p.iv.

Part 2

New spiritual highs and new challenges (1859-1900)

11

THE ZENITH OF EVANGELICAL INFLUENCE: THE YEARS EITHER SIDE OF 1859

11.1 A strong base

With the benefit of hindsight, during the years either side of 1859 Christianity reached its zenith of influence over the nation's culture. *The Christian Observer* noted: "The man of fashion is not ashamed to acknowledge that he reads his Bible, that he takes his place in religious meetings, and that he attends the ministry of his favourite preacher".[1] For evangelicals, this epoch was, in the words of Owen Chadwick, their day of "national authority. The evangelicals were never triumphant. But there was an epoch when they were powerful."[2] There were many reasons for this, including the growth in church-going, the conversion of the upper classes, the penetration of the nation's moral standards by Christianity and the grip of Christianity on philanthropy and education. However, this did not mean that they were entirely free from suffering abuse, if not persecution. John Kitto, in his *Daily Bible Illustrations*, refers to the "godly" experiencing "alienation of relatives and friends…the forfeiture of many social advantages…the quiet neglect, the cold shrug, the contemptuous sneer, the derisive laugh, the unworthy depreciation".[3] Furthermore, the appearance of theological liberalism and Tractarianism demonstrated that, even within the Church, evangelicals were not unchallenged; but, all the same, the prevalence of sin, the Fall and the atonement were widely accepted.[4] The evangelicals were also numerous.

[1] "The Perils of the Church in the Present Day", in 59 *The Christian Observer for the Year 1859* (1859) p.217.

[2] O. Chadwick, *The Victorian Church* (1987) pt.1, p.440. See also E. Russell, *That Man of Granite with the Heart of a Child* (2008) p.155.

[3] J. Kitto, *Daily Bible Illustrations (Evening Series)* (1867) vol.4, p.278. This was written originally in 1854.

[4] "The Perils of the Church in the Present Day", in 59 *The Christian Observer for the*

The *Christian Observer* suggested that "while the evangelical clergy are still numerically inferior to the rest, yet the majority of the people who attend Church at all are found in their congregations".[5] A more recent suggestion puts the number of evangelicals at between two and three million people.[6] Furthermore, as at St James Clerkenwell, it was found that "the desire of the people to hear the word preached is not declining; but the more they hear, the more is their spiritual appetite whetted for further supplies of spiritual food".[7] As to the number of evangelical clergymen, one estimate puts them at a third of the total of 18,300 clergy in 1853.[8] However, this estimate may be too high, conflicting with later perceptions that we will consider in our next Part.[9]

11.2 Lord Shaftesbury has the Prime Minister's ear

For Church of England evangelicals, the state of affairs looked providentially rosy. Lord Shaftesbury, fortuitously, became the stepson of the Prime Minister, Lord Palmerston. The days when Lord Shaftesbury's views on the appointments of bishops were snubbed by the Prime Minister of the day were over. Lord Palmerston turned to Shaftesbury for advice when choosing bishops.[10] Prince Albert was also sympathetic to Shaftesbury's religious views.[11] Nevertheless, there were limits to the recommendations that Shaftesbury could successfully make. Shaftesbury never persuaded Palmerston to elevate the most vigorous evangelicals, unless they were already well-known. But the bulk of the appointments to the House of Bishops, in Palmerston's two administrations, were evangelical in outlook – a cause of "thankfulness and hope" to *The Christian Observer*.[12] At that time, the Broad Church

Year 1859 (1859) p.219 and B. Hilton, *The Age of Atonement* (1991) pp.26-27.

[5] "'A Rope of Sand'", in 58 *The Christian Observer for the Year* 1858 (1858) p.9.

[6] I. Bradley, *The Call to Seriousness* (1976) p.52.

[7] R. Maguire, *Pastoral Letter Addressed to the Congregation of St James's, Clerkenwell* (1859) p.7.

[8] W.J. Conybeare, *Essays Ecclesiastical and Social* (1855) p.158. See also D.M. Lewis, *Lighten their Darkness* (1986) p.5.

[9] O. Chadwick, *The Victorian Church* (1987) pt.1, p.446.

[10] N. Scotland, *'Good and Proper Men': Lord Palmerston and the Bench of Bishops* (2000) pp.30-36 and G. Battiscombe, *Shaftesbury* (1974) pp.263-264.

[11] G.H. Pike, *Albert, The Prince Consort* (1888) pp.213-214.

[12] "The New Year", in 57 *The Christian Observer for the Year 1857* (1857) p.4.

did not get much of a look in.[13]

11.3 Some gifted preachers make their mark

The last half of the nineteenth century, as the later Prime Minister Lloyd George said, was an age of great preachers – and Spurgeon "was the greatest" of them all.[14] In 1859 he was 25 and, on 16 August, the foundation stone of his new church, the Metropolitan Tabernacle, was laid. It was designed as "the largest and handsomest place of worship in the Metropolis", with space, sitting and standing, for over 6,000 people. Once complete, the Metropolitan Tabernacle remained full for the rest of his life. The impact of Spurgeon on the church cannot be overestimated. Hearing Spurgeon preach inspired D.L. Moody, the great transatlantic evangelist, to fresh endeavours. In 1875, Moody was one of *Vanity Fair's* "Men of the Day".[15] In the 1880s, the greater growth of the Baptists – in comparison with other major denominations – was attributed to the Spurgeon phenomenon.[16] Another preacher making his mark on the church was William Booth. In 1859 Booth was 30. He had gone the year before (with the Methodist New Connection) to Gateshead, where his predecessor had "turned infidel". The chapel was in a poor state when he arrived. He soon had it full, with 2,000 people crowded in. The local iron workers dubbed it the "Converting Shop".[17] In the 1870s and 1880s some thought that the Salvation Army was the fastest growing Christian movement since the apostles.[18] Booth modelled his preaching on Spurgeon.[19]

11.4 The nation has lots of money

By the 1850s, the Industrial Revolution made Britain "by far the richest country in the world"[20] and by a huge margin. Competition from a re-

[13] Four out of six and eight out of thirteen in the second administration.
[14] L.A. Drummond, *Spurgeon: Prince of Preachers* (1992) p.277.
[15] J. Pollock, *Moody Without Sankey* (1983) p.xiv. Spurgeon himself, William Booth and also many other clergy made *Vanity Fair's* "Men of the Day".
[16] O. Chadwick, *The Victorian Church* (1987) pt.2, p.228.
[17] H. Begbie, *Life of William Booth* (1920) vol.1, pp.311-312.
[18] W. Booth, *All About the Salvation Army* (1885) p.7.
[19] *East End Observer*, 6 April 1867 cited in St J. Ervine, *God's Soldier: General William Booth* (1934) p.293.
[20] G. Best, *Mid-Victorian Britain* (1979) p.21.

energised France, a re-united Germany and an industrialised United States, was yet to be. The guiding hand behind these developments was seen by many to be Protestantism – even by those outside the evangelical fold. For example, Lord Macaulay, in his *History of England* (1848), compared "The loveliest and most fertile provinces of Europe" which, under Roman Catholic rule, had become

> sunk in poverty, in political servitude, and in intellectual torpor, while Protestant countries, once proverbial for sterility and barbarism, have been turned by skill and industry into gardens, and can boast of a long line of heroes and statesmen, philosophers and poets.[21]

He then compared and contrasted different parts of Britain and Europe to give a factual basis to his point. Part of this new wealth flowed into the hands of those deeply committed to reaching the nation for Christ, whether at home or abroad,[22] and they used it to fund a growing range of evangelistic and philanthropic initiatives. Kathleen Heasman, a writer on evangelical social work, records, "The number of [voluntary[23]] charities in London increased by a quarter in the decade from 1850 to 1860 and their income by 35 per cent. Though this rate of increase was not maintained in the following decades, it did not fall far short".[24] Heasman adds that "as many as three-quarters of the total number of voluntary charitable organisations in the second half of the nineteenth century can be regarded as evangelical in character and control".[25]

11.5 Great Britain reaches out to the nations

The nation's resources also flowed into missionary work outside Great Britain. By 1860 five vessels belonging to missionary societies sailed the Pacific. Contemporaries recognised that attitudes had changed to missionary work. One author wrote, our "grandfathers or great grandfathers, though good people, were content to live for themselves...

[21] *Macaulay's History of England* (1957) vol.1, p.36.

[22] W.J. Conybeare, *Essays Ecclesiastical and Social* (1855) pp.156-157.

[23] Charities were divided up into two types, endowed and voluntary. The former being funded by often long-standing legacies or bequests, while the latter were funded by regular contributions, see K. Heasman, *Evangelicals in Action* (1962) p.7.

[24] Ibid., p.8.

[25] Ibid., p.14.

With exceptions hardly worth mentioning, the churches of Christ did nothing for the conversion of the heathen, either abroad or at home".[26] The Swiss historian Jean Henri Merle d'Aubigné thought that the Anglo-Saxon race was "called more than any other to circulate the oracles of God throughout the world".[27] As Simon Green comments, "The Victorians believed that they were perhaps the first successfully to disseminate, that is to systemise and to popularise, a truly Christian understanding of God and his works in the world".[28]

11.6 Reinforcements from North America arrive

In a different direction, significant reinforcements for the conversion of Britain flowed in from the United States. These men and women appealed to all classes, bar the vagrants.[29]

James Caughey was already in England having returned in 1857 for his second visit. In July 1859 he left for the United States, after a time of "extraordinary usefulness" – such that his listeners had "the most earnest desires for his return to England".[30] He arrived back at Liverpool on 28 July 1860, soon labouring "with his usual success".[31] By January 1859, Charles Finney, off the back of a great revival in America, was also active in England. His time in Bolton was his best success, with 2,000 inquirers and 1,200 converts.[32] His wife also took a "significant part in the proceedings" of this mission.[33]

New evangelists to Britain's shores were Walter and Phoebe Palmer. They started a four-year tour of the country in 1859.[34] They had

[26] T. Gutherie, *Seed-Time & Harvest of Ragged Schools* (1860) pp.116-117.
[27] J.H. Merle d'Aubigné, *The Reformation in England* (1985) vol.1, p.143.
[28] S.J.D. Green, *The Passing of Protestant England* (2011) p.11.
[29] R. Carwardine, *Transatlantic Revivalism* (2006) pp.193-194.
[30] "Rev. James Caughey at Louth", in *The Revivalist* (1859) pp.140-143.
[31] "Rev. J. Caughey at Liverpool", in *The Revivalist* (1860) p.152. See also R. Carwardine, *Transatlantic Revivalism* (2006) pp.175-176.
[32] K.J. Hardman, *Charles Grandison Finney* (1990) p.439 and R. Carwardine, *Transatlantic Revivalism* (2006) pp.176-179. Books on revival by Americans were also in circulation in England, such as J.W. Alexander, *Revival Lessons* (1859) and S.I. Prime, *The Power of Prayer* (1859).
[33] N. Scotland, *Apostles of the Spirit and Fire* (2009) p.79 and K.J. Hardman, *Charles Grandison Finney* (1990) pp.437-438.
[34] In Britain the Palmer's travels, incidents and evangelistic labours are detailed in Dr and Mrs Palmer, *Four Years in the Old World* (1865).

previously enjoyed success as 'holiness advocates' in New York City; their "success in Britain matched or exceeded anything they had known in North America".[35] Phoebe Palmer was already "extensively known"[36] in Britain for her numerous publications, especially the delicately written book, *The Way of Holiness* (1843) – on its way to best-seller status. Its theme was that there was "but *one* way to heaven, and that, 'The way of holiness'".[37] In this book she combined theology with moving personal experiences of men and women finding Christ. Its success opened the way for Mrs Palmer's public speaking, mainly on Wesleyan circuits. A woman speaking in public was highly unusual, but she never spoke without her husband and did not take the platform. Rather, if moved by the Holy Spirit, she walked to the communion rail and simply talked to the people "with all the gracefulness of an intelligent and well-educated lady".[38] One estimate puts the converts of Dr and Mrs Palmer's visit to England and Wales at over 18,500.[39] Separation from the world was required: alcohol and jewellery were out.[40] The preaching in Gateshead by Mrs Palmer in 1859 was instrumental in leading Catherine Booth, the wife of General Booth (the future founder of the Salvation Army), to preach.

11.7 A great revival sweeps in from North America

Meanwhile, in the spring of 1859 the widespread spiritual awakening, which began in Canada and moved to the United States[41] and which brought Charles Finney hurrying to these shores, swept Northern Ireland. People knew something supernatural was happening as conversions

[35] H.E. Raser, *Phoebe Palmer* (1987) p.68.

[36] R. Wheatley, *The Life and Letters of Mrs Phoebe Palmer* (1984) p.349.

[37] Author's italics. P. Palmer "The Way of Holiness", in *The Devotional Writings of Phoebe Palmer* (1985) (D.W. Dayton (ed.)) p.7.

[38] See P.J. Walker, *Pulling the Devil's Kingdom Down* (2001) p.23. She might speak for about half-an-hour, see "Newcastle", in *The Revival*, 17 September 1859, p.63.

[39] N. Scotland, *Apostles of the Spirit and Fire* (2009) pp.124-127 and 137-138. See also R. Carwardine, *Transatlantic Revivalism* (2006) pp.182-185 and Dr and Mrs Palmer, *Four Years in the Old World* (1865).

[40] N. Scotland, *Apostles of the Spirit and Fire* (2009) pp.130-132.

[41] On the American revival of 1857-1858, see R. Carwardine, *Transatlantic Revivalism* (2006) pp.159-169. Contemporary writers also refer to Sweden, India, "and some parts of Germany, Africa and the islands of the seas", as having also been subject to "those mighty outpourings of the Spirit", see W. Cooke, *The Revival of Religion* (N.D.) p.1.

in the years before had been few.[42] Now, "Day by day the papers... endeavoured to furnish a record of [the Revival's] progress".[43] From London newspaper correspondents and others went to Northern Ireland to investigate. It was news "throughout the British Empire", as the Broad Church *Macmillan's Magazine* acknowledged.[44] Visitors discovered men and women, in numbers, convicted of their sin and crying for God's mercy (and not necessarily in church).[45] Conviction might be accompanied by sobbing, groaning, or even something akin to apoplectic or cataleptic fits, or even hysteria. Some fell as if "dead under a very quiet sermon".[46] Church attendance and the number of services multiplied, as did the number of prayer gatherings and their attendees. The moral conduct of many changed radically. Contemporaries noted that, where the revival took hold, cases of drunkenness ceased,[47] the profane swearer sang the praises of God, the Sabbath desecrator devoted the "sacred hours of the day of rest to public and private worship…the Magdalenes, the depraved, the abandoned, forsaking their course of shame" and called "upon benevolent Christians to come and help them to turn their backs upon their former sinful practices".[48]

The revival then spread to other parts of the United Kingdom. *The Christian Observer* declared: "We require a larger outpouring of the Holy Ghost...We want the heavenly gale from above".[49] Many sensed the presence of God and were converted. In 1859 and the years shortly afterwards more than a million people were added to the Christian

[42] W. Arthur, *May We Hope for a Great Revival?* (1859) pp.9 and 13.

[43] "The Religious Revival Movement", in *The Irish Times and Daily Advertiser*, 19 August 1859.

[44] J.L. Davies, "The Revivals of 1859", in 1 *Macmillan's Magazine* (1860) p.363.

[45] "The Revival Movement in Belfast", in *The Irish Times and Daily Advertiser*, 9 August 1859 and "The Physical Phenomena of the Revival", in *The Irish Times and Daily Advertiser*, 10 September 1859.

[46] "The Chamberlain of London on the Irish Revivals", in *The Observer*, 2 October 1859.

[47] For example, "The Revival in Clones", in *The Irish Times and Daily Advertiser*, 21 September 1859 and "The Effects of the Revival in Ballymena", in *The Irish Times and Daily Advertiser*, 21 November 1859.

[48] "The Religious Revival Movement", in *The Irish Times and Daily Advertiser*, 19 August 1859 and also "A Eye Witness on the Irish Revivals", in *The Observer*, 16 October 1859.

[49] "The Perils of the Church in the Present Day", in 59 *The Christian Observer for the Year 1859* (1859) p.220.

churches.[50] 1859 saw many books and tracts published[51] on the topic of revival and, on 30 July 1859, a journal, *The Revival*, was launched to provide "a weekly record of events connected with the present revival of religion".[52] Some call this movement of God's Spirit "the Second Great Awakening". It was the last national religious revival. The numbers converted led to comparisons with the day of Pentecost. Even *The Westminster Review* which rejected the Christian faith could not deny the 1859 Revival. It sought to explain it away as due to the ignorance, excessive religious excitement and the insanity of certain members of the poor and uneducated classes, to which it primarily appealed.[53]

The origins in the United Kingdom of the 1859 Revival can be traced back to 1856 and a certain Mrs Colville in Ballymena, Northern Ireland. She was an English lady doing missionary work, visiting people and telling the dying of the power of God. Her work led to the conversion of James McQuilkin who one day overheard her conversation. His conversion led to the conversion of three friends who prayed for the salvation of many. At first, their prayers seemed to receive no response. Then, as a contemporary put it, "a large number of persons were converted so suddenly as to draw all eyes to the work".[54] Interest was stimulated because, from fairly early on, the revival was accompanied by "bodily prostrations" – as strong men staggered and fell "down under the wounds of their conscience".[55] Ultimately, over 100,000 in Ulster came to a knowledge of God. Ulster's vigorous commitment to Protestantism is traced back to the revival of 1859.[56] A contemporary noted that visitors

[50] J.E. Orr, *The Second Evangelical Awakening in Britain* (1949) pp.5 and 207.

[51] For example, J.G. Small, *Restoration and Revival* (1859); *Shall there be a Revival of Religion?* (1859); W. Arthur, *May We Hope for a Great Revival?* (1859); and *The Great Revival* (1859).

[52] In 1870, it changed its name to *The Christian*, to reflect its broadening scope. From its 1 May 1862 edition, as the revival took root in London, it dropped the words "weekly" and "present" from its stated purpose of recording "a weekly record of events connected with the present revival of religion".

[53] "Christian Revivals", in 17 *The Westminster Review* (1860) pp.167-218.

[54] "The Chamberlain of London on the Irish Revivals", in *The Observer*, 2 October 1859.

[55] W. Gibson, *The Year of Grace* (1860) pp.32-33 and "The Revival in Portadown", in *The Revivalist* (1860) p.31. These prostrations and other pathological affectations were a cause of concern, see ibid., pp.326-369.

[56] Ian Paisley was converted in a Baptist chapel established at the time of the 1859 revival, and wrote a book on it, see I.R.K. Paisley, *The "Fifty Nine" Revival* (1958).

came from Continental Europe, Asia or America to admire the "spiritual change" wrought within Ireland's "northern province".[57]

From Ulster, the revival reached Scotland. It was described as "the most stupendous movement" that Scotland had seen in over 300 years. A

> host of zealous enthusiastic converts carried the message of divine love and practical sympathy, not only into the dark abodes of human woe, in the slums of our great cities; but also to the dark places of the earth, which were full of the habitations of cruelty, and, as a consequence, many of those moral wastes are now blooming.[58]

Even at Scotland's northerly town Thurso, 4,000 assembled in the open to hear the preaching of Hay Macdowall Grant.[59] Along the fishing villages of the North-east coast of Scotland, James Turner passed "like a flame of fire".[60] At Portgordon, "famed for drunkenness...many were smitten down under the mighty power of God. Those who were nearest the door were carried out, others had to lie till they got power to rise... Country people came down to scoff...but painful convictions seized upon many of those also".[61] Aberdeen, where a number of leading lay evangelists had assembled, saw an increasing number of conversions from the autumn of 1858.[62] It is estimated that in the years around 1859 "at least 300,000 converts were won in Scotland".[63]

In Wales, the years around 1859 witnessed the conversion of over 100,000.[64] To illustrate the numbers, *The Observer* reported that, in six months Aberdare's Independents gained 1,000 to 1,200 new members

[57] W. Gibson, *The Year of Grace* (1860) p.372.
[58] *Reminiscences of the Revival of '59 and the Sixties* (1910) pp.xi-xii.
[59] For a contemporary analysis of one revival making up the 1859 revival in Scotland, see D. Bebbington, *Victorian Religious Revivals* (2012) pp.159-191.
[60] R. Radcliffe, "Introductory Note" to E. McHardie, *James Turner; or, How to Reach the Masses* (1875).
[61] E. McHardie, *James Turner; or, How to Reach the Masses* (1875) p.25. Near contemporaries, even of sympathetic persuasion, had reservations about prostration, see V.J. Charlesworth, "The Apostle of the Scottish Fishermen", in *The Sword and the Trowel* (1875) pp.529-533.
[62] J. Radcliffe, *Recollections of Reginald Radcliffe* (1896) pp.36-74.
[63] J.E. Orr, *The Second Evangelical Awakening in Britain* (1949) pp.5 and 207. See also C.E. Woods, *Memoirs and Letters of Canon Hay Aitken* (1928) pp.81-86.
[64] J.E. Orr, *The Second Evangelical Awakening in Britain* (1949) pp.5 and 207.

and 4,000 went to a mountainside to pray.[65] The town of Denbigh, between 27 November and 5 December 1859, saw 200 join its Dissenting congregations.[66] Many converts came under conviction from a sermon heard long before.[67] The fame of the Welsh as great singers is traced back to their joy in God at this time.[68] The annual report of the Church of England Scripture Readers' Association recorded with regard to conversions outside the metropolis, that "a large effusion of the Holy Spirit has been vouchsafed to the Church".[69]

The revival reached London, after Baptist Noel and some other ministers visited Ulster and witnessed its progress.[70] *The Times* knew something special was going on. Its editorial commented: "there are local revivals going on always in the Methodist districts in this country; it is only when the spiritual inoculation is on a particularly large scale that it attracts notice, as it does now".[71] Nevertheless, in England the momentum was slower and spilled out beyond 1859-1860.[72] *The Revival* observed, in its edition of 20 August 1859, that the Revival had reached England's borders "but, with a few happy exceptions, can scarcely be said to have penetrated into England".[73] But by the end of the year, it

[65] "Religious Revivals in Wales", in *The Observer,* 18 and 19 September 1859.

[66] "The Revival in Wales", in *The Revivalist* (1860) p.30.

[67] E. Evans, *Two Welsh Revivalists* (1985) p.27.

[68] *The Religious Revival in Wales* (2004). The tonic sol-fa system was by coincidence introduced in that year.

[69] "Sixteenth Report of the Church of England Scripture Readers' Association", in 2 *The Scripture Readers' Journal* (1856-60) p.407.

[70] "Lecture – Religion in London", in *The Irish Times and Daily Advertiser*, 21 August 1860. For detail of the revival in London, see J. Radcliffe, *Recollections of Reginald Radcliffe* (N.D.) pp.98-136.

[71] "The Irish Religious Revivals", in *The Times*, 17 September 1859. For the growth rates in membership of the various Methodist denominations, see R. Currie, *Methodism Divided* (1968) p.95. These generally enjoyed substantial growth in the periods 1857-1859 and 1860-1862 – after periods of, in many cases, decline.

[72] It has been suggested that, in England, the marked spiritual uplift in the nation began in certain places well before 1859. For example, in Liverpool in 1855 onwards (as we saw in our first period) John Hambleton and Reginald Radcliffe were seeing a remarkable number of conversions and the summer of 1857 witnessed conversions accompanied by physical manifestations at Tipton, Staffordshire. See "Princes' End, Tipton, Staffordshire", in *The Revival*, 17 December 1859, p.165 and generally M.R. Watts, *The Dissenters* (1995) vol.2, pp.656-662.

[73] "The Revival in its Relation to the Churches in England", in *The Revival*, 20 August 1859, p.25 and also "Testimonies to the Reality of the Revival", in *The Revival*, 24 September 1859, p.69 and *The Great Revival?* (1859) pp.7 and 12.

observed that "the revival of religion is spreading throughout the length and breadth of the land".[74] The navvy and future evangelist William Smith was converted at this time while meditating, at Finchley Road Station, on "God's love to a guilty world".[75] In April 1862 *The Revival* believed that on reflection, in London, 1859-1860 was the "praying winter"; 1860-1861 a time of transition; and 1861-1862 the "ingathering winter".[76] William Cooke, a Methodist, thought that "the church is both strengthening her bulwarks and extending her empire".[77] Emily Kinnaird – whose family was connected with the upper echelons of London's banking circles, the aristocracy and the nation's leading politicians – recalled of this time that "The questions 'Are you saved?' 'Have you been converted?' 'Do you love the Lord?' were freely used, and the answers to these were perfectly natural, because the experiences were so real; to say 'yes' was just a testimony to a great fact of experience."[78]

In July 1862, the Secularist leader, John Gordon, was converted after his mother took him to listen to the preaching of the Congregationalist John Conder at the Belgrave Chapel. The text that Sunday morning was the words of Jesus – "He that hath seen me hath seen the Father."[79] *The Revival* recorded that:

> God raised up men for almost every class and from almost every class...there were those high in life, some from the noble and rich... some newly converted ministers...There were also converted stage-players, infidels, blasphemers, thieves, drunkards, pickpockets, and roughs preaching the word. There was an acrobat and a conjuror besides miners, colliers, pugilists; and not a few converted Roman

[74] "East End", in *The Revival,* 31 December 1859, p.178.

[75] *A Marvel of Grace, the Late William Taylor* (1895) p.26. Reaching the navvies may have been a special concern of the evangelicals of the time. Certainly, the Pre-Raphaelite painter Ford Madox Brown, in his well-known painting, *Work* – in which he seeks to encapsulate all aspects of mid-Victorian life – includes a woman who is distributing tracts, although the relevant navvy has a "sneering face", see T. Barringer, *Men at Work* (2005) pp.50-51 and 63-66.

[76] "The Revival in London", in *The Revival*, 12 April 1862, p.115.

[77] W. Cooke, *The Revival of Religion* (N.D.) p.1.

[78] E. Kinnaird, *Reminiscences* (1925) p.87.

[79] T. Larsen, *Crisis of Doubt* (2006) pp.120-121. Joseph Barker was another leading Secularist who turned to Christianity at this time, see ibid., pp.160-172, as was John Bebbington who did the same, see ibid., pp.189 and 191-196.

Catholics came to the help of the Lord.[80]

The work in London was "slow and without much demonstration or excitement".[81] This stimulated activity in the provinces which in turn animated London's workers.[82] For example, at Bewdley, near Kidderminster Mr Alexander, a London working man, ignited a revival. Before his visit the town's vestry and cottage prayer meetings were already pervaded by a "hallowed influence". At the Baptist chapel the twice daily services were crowded and the anxious enquirers numbered 31. Between services house-to-house visiting took place and occasionally a few people paraded in the streets singing hymns, such as "There is a Fountain Filled with Blood", a favourite of the 1859 Revival.[83] Returning a few weeks later, in hay-shed and home, he found prayers for salvation; entire families were moved, the fathers in tears. Mr Alexander wrote that "Scores of souls in Bewdley" had "the blood sprinkled upon them, and the Spirit to answer with the blood to assure them they are born of God".[84] The revival "touched even the great public schools", such as Eton.[85] At Silcoates Hall, 40 boys out of 50 professed faith in one day and night, including the young W.T. Stead,[86] a pioneer of modern investigative journalism. Indeed, among the young conversions were most likely, especially those who had some Christian understanding by virtue of having attended Sunday school and among females.[87] Contemporaries thought the revival was over by June 1864, when an "awful deadness" descended,[88] although there were aftershocks.[89] Yet, in the summer of 1866, Spurgeon thought "there never was a time when people were more

[80] "The Revival in London", in *The Revival*, 12 April 1862, p.114. At this time fewer prayer meetings took place – but it was not a concern, as other Christian activities included so much prayer, see "Thanksgiving and Prayer", in *The Revival,* 3 July 1862, p.249.

[81] "The Revival in London", in *The Revival*, 12 April 1862, p.113.

[82] Ibid., p.115.

[83] "Bewdley", in *The Revival*, 8 March 1862, pp.77-78.

[84] "Bewdley", in *The Revival*, 19 April 1862, p.126.

[85] E.M. Wood, *The Polytechnic and its Founder Quintin Hogg* (1932) pp.31-32. See also "Religious Revivals", in *59 The Christian Observer for the Year 1859* (1859) p.726.

[86] W.T. Stead, "The Revival in the West", in *The Revival of 1905* (1905) pp.5-6.

[87] R. Carwardine, *Transatlantic Revivalism* (2006) p.193.

[88] "Has God's Work Stopped?", in *The Revival*, 2 June 1864 p.342. See also R. Carwardine, *Transatlantic Revivalism* (2006) p.197.

[89] See W. Haslam, *"Yet Not I"* (N.D.) pp.300-301.

willing to listen to the gospel of Christ than now".[90] He thought that the problem was that Christians had just ceased to expect conversions; he sought to stir them to action.[91]

The impact of the revival in England was weaker in denominations with more theologically liberal elements, like the Congregational Union.[92] The New Connexion of General Baptists saw a membership increase in its best revival year, 1861-1862, of only 3.3 per cent.[93] However, its numbers had been static for the decade 1846 to 1856 and increased by just over ten per cent between 1856 and 1865.[94] *The Methodist Recorder*, in the opening paragraph of its first issue, stated that "The Wesleyan Methodist body is increasing daily."[95]

There were other views of the revival. The secular press was hostile.[96] Hints were dropped "that there is room for the interference of magistracy and police, to protect the sober-minded community from the contagion of a fanaticism, which the world dreads as much as it hates".[97] Horatius Bonar responded by arguing that every religious movement had its human side, and that to condemn religious work for its disturbances was like banning commerce because its merchants contained so many "frauds and knaveries".[98]

Others thought the numbers were not so great and pointed with justification to some play-acting among those enjoying visions.[99] Some thought that to judge a moral change in "six or seven weeks of a new career is too short a probation".[100] And, as in the time of Jesus, some

[90] C.H. Spurgeon, "Fields White for Harvest", in *Metropolitan Tabernacle Pulpit* (1867) vol.12, p.460.
[91] Ibid., pp.457-468.
[92] See *Congregational Year Book* (1860) p.303.
[93] M.R. Watts, *The Dissenters* (1995) vol. 2, p.657.
[94] R. Currie, A. Gilbert and L. Horsley, *Churches and Churchgoers* (1977) pp.148-149. See denominational growth charts in R. Carwardine, *Transatlantic Revivalism* (2006) pp.194-195.
[95] "To our Readers", in *The Methodist Recorder, and General Christian Chronicle,* 4 April 1861, p.1. See also "The District Returns", in *The Methodist Recorder, and General Christian Chronicle,* 23 May 1861, pp.57-58.
[96] H. Bonar, "Modern Hostility to Revivals", in *The Revivalist* (1860) p.49.
[97] Ibid.
[98] Ibid., pp.50-51.
[99] "The Irish 'Revival'", in *The Daily Scotsman*, 22 September 1859 and "Revival Movement and Irish Insanity", in *The Observer*, 18 September 1859.
[100] "The Irish Religious 'Revivals'", *Manchester Guardian*, 17 September 1859. See also "Christian Revivals", in 17 *The Westminster Review* (1860) pp.198-213.

thought excessive commitment to him likely to lead to madness.[101] There were also mockers. For example, when a group of Christians travelling by train to Armagh for a great revival meeting sang hymns in their carriage, the passengers in a neighbouring carriage, in the words of an accompanying newspaper correspondent, responded with "a burlesque hymn, the words of which will not bear type".[102]

However, 60 years after the 1859 Revival, the Church of England turned to its events to consider what a true revival might look like – after its own botched endeavour during the First World War. It noted the lasting practical and social effects. Even "Mill owners and managers, magistrates and policemen, men sceptical as to the cause, indifferent to the movement, or hostile to it, have all concurred in bearing witness to the change on the face of society; to the almost entire disappearance of certain vices, to the sobriety and honesty that characterise all classes".[103]

11.8 But...

The 1859 Revival, unlike the Great Awakening of Whitefield and Wesley in the mid-eighteenth century, did not raise up a new generation of ministers and theologians equipped to meet the serious intellectual challenges that lay ahead or, except in Northern Ireland, have a deep influence. Except, perhaps, in London, the 1859 Revival was mainly a spontaneous turning to God, led by the laity. It was the "Layman's Revival" and left behind a Christian vigour among the lower classes (but not exclusively so).[104] In Ireland, *The Record* noted, the emphasis was on prayer – "Prayer was everywhere the grand element of the people's being – the special object of their assembling! They met only to pray; they lived only to pray!"[105] London emulated the emphasis on prayer as

[101] J.S. Bushnan, *Religious Revivals in Relation to Nervous and Mental Diseases* (1860).
[102] "The Irish 'Revival'", in *The Daily Scotsman*, 22 September 1859.
[103] Cited in the Report of the Archbishops' Third Committee of Inquiry, *Evangelistic Work of the Church* (1918) pp.51-52.
[104] Critics of the 1859-1860 awakening dismissed it as "nothing else than a religious ferment among the ignorant rabble". Later in the century, the critics dismissed Moody and Sankey for failing to reach "the lowest strata of society". They said their work was nothing other than "a fever of pious sensationalism among the more religiously inclined sort of people", J. Macpherson, *Revival and Revival Work* (N.D.) p.293.
[105] "The 'British Standard' on Revivals and Mr Reginald Radcliffe's Preaching", in *The Record*, 4 June 1860, p.3. See also J. Radcliffe, "Preface" to *Recollections of Reginald Radcliffe* (1896) p.iv.

the secret behind revival. *The Revival* of 31 December 1859, listed for its London readers over 20 daily special prayer meetings for revival and over 45 additional weekly ones. Outside London, *The Record* counted 90 prayer meetings for revival in England.[106]

Lay preaching expanded: the motto being "every man a missionary". For example, W.P. Lockhart – aged 24 and later to be a merchant – preached for the first time on 15 January 1860 and, by the end of that year, he had spoken 76 times, addressing thousands and seen many converted.[107] "There were services for police and cabmen, for lamplighters, postmen, sweeps, dustmen, and scavengers, boatmen and bargemen."[108] The American evangelists preached night after night. For instance, James Caughey preached at the Baille Street Chapel, in Rochdale, from 2 December 1860 to April 1861 and 1,800 names were entered in the chapel's Revival Register. Around 20 per cent were aged 14 or under.[109] At Liverpool, the visit of Richard Weaver manifested the need for a city hall to hold 3,000-4,000.[110]

The learned and certain elements of the evangelical press did not approve of the preaching style of the new leading lay evangelists. *The Record* circulated the criticism of Reginald Radcliffe (a solicitor) that appeared first in *The British Standard* – a Nonconformist publication. This noted Radcliffe's zeal, and that he had been a blessing to some, but it thought that he had "been pushed forward by mistaken and indiscreet friends into a false position".[111]

Further, the time of service in Britain for Radcliffe and the other two members making up the key triumvirate of "gentleman evangelists"[112] – namely, Brownlow North[113] and Hay Macdowall Grant (the Laird of

[106] "London", in *The Record*, 31 December 1860, p.2. For some examples of prayer meetings inside and outside London, see *Some Records of the Life of Stevenson Arthur Blackwood* K.C.B. (1898) (H.S. Blackwood (ed.)) pp.203-204.
[107] M.J. Lockhart, *W.P. Lockhart* (1895) p.61.
[108] "The Revival in London", in *The Revival*, 12 April 1862, p.114.
[109] J. Kent, *Holding the Fort* (1978) pp.77-87.
[110] "Liverpool", in *The Revival*, 5 February 1863, p.69.
[111] "The 'British Standard' on Revivals and Mr Reginald Radcliffe's Preaching", in *The Record*, 4 June 1860, p.3.
[112] See generally E.J. Poole-Connor, *Evangelical Unity* (1941) pp.69-100.
[113] I. Murray, "A Hundred Years Ago (III.) The Ministry of Brownlow North", in 16 *Banner of Truth*, August 1959, p.1.

Arndilly)[114] – was limited. Brownlow North was not converted until November 1854,[115] having been "a terrible reprobate".[116] Hay Macdowall Grant did not start preaching until 1856 and then almost by accident and under pressure.[117] In 1859, he and Brownlow North were already in, or close to, their 50s. Grant died, after a long illness, in March 1870; Brownlow North at the end of 1875. Reginald Radcliffe was only 34 in 1859, but his health was never good.[118] In 1862, after a vigorous preaching campaign in Geneva, he returned to England for rest. His wife Jane's biography, *Recollections of Reginald Radcliffe* (1896) suggests that it was not until 1870 that he resumed major preaching duties and then in Paris. That biography, for the rest of Radcliffe's life, focuses upon his work overseas, although he was much involved in England with the Moody mission of 1874 and the establishment of Strangers' Rests, for the spiritual and general care of seamen and foreigners. He also, somehow, kept up his practice as a solicitor.

After the 1859 Revival the time left for some of its other leading, but less wealthy, lay evangelists was short – or marred by illness, or simply less spectacular in terms of conversions. James Turner, who set the North-east coast of Scotland alight with his preaching, died in early February 1863, aged 44. For more than a year before his death, he was ill and did not preach – worn out by his earlier spiritual labours long into the night. Richard Weaver, the "converted collier", lived until 1896 – but his last 25 years were marked by illness and the "pain and travail of sadness and sorrow".[119] In his later years, "he counted himself happy if he could work for 12 or 13 weeks out of 52".[120] Nevertheless, at the end of 1881, his preaching in Glasgow still filled its three largest

[114] On the work of Hay Macdowall Grant in 1859, see M.M. Gordon, *Hay Macdowall Grant* (1879) pp.64-73. The life of an evangelist of those days was not without its troubles. Louisa, wife of Hay Macdowall Grant, converted to Roman Catholicism because of doubts over the proprietary of lay-preaching. He was forced to issue a denial that he too had converted, after a newspaper announcement to that effect, ibid., p.79.

[115] "Mr. Brownlow North", in *The Revivalist* (1859) p.177.

[116] "The Scotch Revivalist", in *The Revivalist* (1858) p.125.

[117] See C.E. Woods, *Memoirs and Letters of Canon Hay Aitken* (1928) pp.76-81.

[118] G. Green, *Reginald Radcliffe: The Liverpool Solicitor* (2009) p.31.

[119] J. Paterson, *Richard Weaver's Life Story* (2012) p.247.

[120] Ibid., p.196. His success was attributed to his "marvellous sympathy" for the working man, see ibid., p.193.

halls, over five weeks.[121] It was not until Sunday 5 December 1895 that he started his last mission – one of two weeks – using such texts as "The great day of his wrath" and "My Spirit shall not always strive with man".[122] Easily assessable information about the later life of John Hambleton, who worked closely with Reginald Radcliffe in the revival years around 1859, is limited. His autobiography, *Buds, Blossoms, and Fruits of the Revival*, is full of wonderful tales of conversions, but finishes in 1865, although it was written around 1870. He seems to have continued his itinerant preaching, before spending the last ten years of his life undertaking similar work in Australia.[123]

The 1859 Revival lacked the support of a distinctive and united group of devoted Christians of the standing, wealth, literary talents and energy of William Wilberforce and the Clapham Sect, although Lord Shaftesbury was supportive and attempts were made to reach the upper classes by lay preachers known to them, with some degree of success.[124] As "the chief Revival movement of the century, among the masses",[125] the 1859 Revival did not draw the attention of the scholarly, nor has it done since. Of Brownlow North's preaching, it was noted that it "makes no attempt at exegetical preaching...he has but one doctrine to expound". It was "the fervour of his earnestness" in which his spiritual power lay.[126] Further, of its converts, those most remembered did not contribute directly to the Church. An apologist of the 1859 Revival lists its outstanding converts as "Tom Barnardo, founder of Barnardo's homes; James Chalmers, the pioneer missionary to New Guinea; Hugh Price Hughes, the Methodist stalwart; and Evan Hopkins, the founder of the Keswick Convention."[127] Of these, only Hugh Price Hughes played a central role in his denomination. Perhaps the most important evangelist converted through the 1859 Revival and its aftermath was Henry Moorhouse, converted through Richard Weaver. Moorhouse had

[121] Ibid., pp.188-189.
[122] Ibid., p.237.
[123] G. Green, *John Hambleton* (2009) p.29. Among Hambleton's converts was the young Thomas Barnardo, G.E. Morgan, *R.C. Morgan: His Life and Times* (1909) p.146.
[124] *Some Records of the Life of Stevenson Arthur Blackwood* K.C.B. (1898) (H.S. Blackwood (ed.)) pp.215-219 and 222.
[125] J. Macpherson, *Henry Moorhouse* (N.D.) p.v.
[126] "The Scotch Revivalist", in *The Revivalist* (1858) p.124.
[127] J.E. Orr, *The Second Evangelical Awakening in Britain* (1949) p.5.

an effective ministry among the masses and influenced D.L. Moody, but he died in 1880 aged 40. Moorhouse would be one of a number of lay Brethren evangelists who were workers during, or converted by, the 1859 Revival and who, in the years ahead, would be effective evangelists working across and bringing together the evangelical elements of the denominations.[128]

There was some ministerial input to the 1859 Revival. In Dublin, the theological wing of the Guinness brewing family emerged in the form of the powerful preaching of Henry Grattan Guinness. In London, Baptist Noel preached with a "new earnestness and greater success than he had ever before obtained".[129] In Wales, Dafydd Morgan saw many conversions until the end of 1860.[130] In London, from late 1859 many of the leading preachers of the age joined in using its theatres to reach the working classes. In Barnet, William Pennefather opened, in December 1860, a portable "iron room" for reaching the working classes[131] – and "Hundreds were melted to tears under the simple message of the gospel, brought home by the divine Spirit...A feeling of awe seemed for a time to pervade the town, and the public-houses were, comparatively speaking, empty."[132] In April 1862, two and a half years after London's theatres had been opened as preaching venues, they remained "filled with attentive, and often riveted listeners, week after week".[133]

Nevertheless, the 1859 Revival had a less lasting influence than otherwise it might have had – because in the main it took place outside the churches. As men speculated whether the Holy Spirit, having visited America, would visit these shores, William Arthur, a Methodist, wrote that some good men "shrink from the idea of a revival, lest it should be attended with extravagance".[134] As the revival unfolded, with a few exceptions, Anglican sources sounded ongoing cautions about the

[128] T. Grass, *Gathering to His Name* (2012) pp.140-144. James McQuilkin, with whom the 1859 Revival began, later became a member of the Brethren, ibid., p.143.
[129] "Lecture - Religion in London", in *The Irish Times and Daily Advertiser*, 21 August 1860.
[130] E. Evans, *Two Welsh Revivalists* (1985) p.49.
[131] R. Braithwaite, *The Life and Letters of Rev. William Pennefather* (N.D.) pp.339-342.
[132] Ibid., pp.344-345.
[133] "The Revival in London", in *The Revival*, 12 April 1862, p.115.
[134] W. Arthur, *May We Hope for a Great Revival?* (1859) p.2.

dangers of revival, and the risk of "indiscreet zeal"[135] and of hysteria.[136] The Nonconformist ministry, also with a few notable exceptions, was unsympathetic. They tried to dampen down 'mere enthusiasm'. Lay preaching was perceived as dangerous, likely to bring religion into contempt.[137] Handley Moule, later the Bishop of Durham, writing with the benefit of hindsight, thought that the 1859 Revival had possessed the power, if "utilised thoughtfully for the glory of God", to "have put another face on English Christianity ever since, in the way of spiritual power and ecclesiastical peace and cohesion".[138]

However, the 1859 Revival did provide the momentum to oppose the growing scepticism in the nation's thought life and the growing divisions within the churches. In Wales, "a new generation of preachers, missionaries and leaders emerged".[139] A book, published in 1910, to commemorate the Revival's jubilee in Scotland, recorded:

> all the mission movements – home and foreign – philanthropic schemes, and measures for the alleviation of human suffering, have been mainly manned and maintained during the last fifty years by the converts of the Revival of '59 and the sixties, and those who sympathised with it. There are men and women still living, many of them of birth, rank, and intellectual ability to say nothing of the host of home ministers, foreign missionaries, and evangelists, and others – who were converted, or received a never-to-be-forgotten quickening and impetus to their spiritual life, during that time.[140]

[135] When the evangelist Reginald Radcliffe made use of "an uneducated youth" – converted at a prayer meeting – to address a meeting on his conversion and spiritual experience, Radcliffe was publicly condemned for fostering "spiritual pride" and fixing "the whole work of revival" with a character of "ranting fanaticism", see "The 'British Standard' on Revivals and Mr Reginald Radcliffe's Preaching", in *The Record*, 4 June 1860, p.3. This seems very unfair given that Jesus had told the demon possessed man, after his healing, to "Go home to your family and tell them how much the Lord has done for you, and how he has had mercy on you," see Mark 5:19.

[136] T. Macneece, *Words of Caution and Counsel* (1859).

[137] J. Macpherson, *Henry Moorhouse* (N.D.) pp.vii-viii. See generally J. Kent, *Holding the Fort* (1978) pp.100-128.

[138] H.C.G. Moule, *The Evangelical School in the Church of England* (1901) p.59.

[139] E. Evans, *Two Welsh Revivalists* (1985) p.26.

[140] *Reminiscences of the Revival of '59 and the Sixties* (1910) p.xii.

It was the energy of this cadre of people that enabled the churches to meet the challenges that lay ahead. As they passed away, the ability of the churches to meet those challenges waned. Elsewhere, where the spirit of 1859 did not pass, the nation grew cold to Christianity. To those challenges, we now turn.

12

CRITICS OUTSIDE THE CHURCH

12.1 1859 – The year of the sceptic

If 1859 witnessed remarkable spiritual activity, its growth drew a "corresponding reaction" from the "carnal mind".[141] In Barnet, "The remarkable revival season had been succeeded by a burst of opposition and persecution such as is not often seen in a quiet English parish. Hymns were parodied in the street, prayer meetings travestied, and such open mockery and scoffing exhibited", that a visitor to the parsonage remarked that "I have seen much opposition to God's truth, but I never met with such bitter enmity as I have heard expressed between this house and the railway station."[142]

But something much more significant was at work than vituperation. Different shades of churchmanship could see the challenges ahead. At the end of 1859, *The British Evangelist* noted that although 'infidelity' was "beaten from every ground, and driven from one position to another", it was now arising in "new power and entrenching itself in new positions... vile poisonous publications" were "issuing from the press by millions".[143] The editor to *The Christian Observer* noted in his preface, for the year 1860, that:

> Intellectual restlessness, impatience of all established forms of thought and long accepted creeds, is the strongly marked feature of the age. Substantially, it is the old battle with the ancient foe; but the assailants have adopted new methods, and fight with weapons hitherto untried. The revolution which is going forward in our naval

[141] J.H. Rigg, *The Present Position of Christianity and the Christian Faith in this Country* (1878) pp.3 and 16. See generally F.M. Turner, "The Victorian Crisis of Faith and the Faith that was Lost", in *Victorian Faith in Crisis* (1990) (R.J. Helmstadter and B. Lightman (eds)) pp.9-38.
[142] R. Braithwaite, *The Life and Letters of Rev. William Pennefather* (N.D.) pp.349-350.
[143] "The Evangelisation of our Home Population", in *The British Evangelist*, December 1859 p.442.

and military warfare has its counterpart in the warfare of morals and theology.[144]

The Record, in 1863, thought: "Never before did infidelity assume so daring a front, and present itself in such treacherous guise."[145] The 1859 Revival mainly affected the working classes. The response struck at the movement's weakness – its lack of intellectual leadership. *The Record* added that the attacks were not from some "esoteric philosophy", or from the base elements of society, but from those who "sit in high places, and aspire, perhaps, to lift their 'mitred fronts in courts and parliaments'".[146] In his Hulsean lectures of 1870, F.W. Farrar looked to history and how the church had survived the "stormiest waves of past assault" to provide an "undaunted confidence...amid the decuman billows of modern scepticism".[147] Later, Farrar, as Archdeacon of Westminster, observed that it was no "longer against this or that treatise that we must defend the most vital principles of Christian doctrine. It is against whole literatures; it is against whole philosophies; it is against the vague doubts of eminent thinkers; it is against innumerable sneers, the repeated assumptions, the ever-varying criticisms of a powerful and intellectual press."[148]

The possibility of a spiritual challenge, at a time of revival, did not surprise the earnest. Indeed, on the eve of the 1859 Revival, men speculated that any major revival would be succeeded by "anti-Christian times".[149] William Arthur noted that each of the revivals in the three previous centuries had produced a new denomination. The sixteenth century had witnessed the establishment of the Church of England; the seventeenth century the Dissenters; and the eighteenth century the Methodists. He hoped that any new revival would not produce a further denomination, but that it would draw the existing denominations together.[150] His hopes as to the result of revival would, in some way, be realised – as the evangelicals drew together. In the London of late 1861-

[144] "Preface" to 60 *The Christian Observer for the Year* 1860 (1860) p.iii.
[145] "London", in *The Record,* 2 January 1863, p.2.
[146] Ibid.
[147] F.W. Farrar, *The Witness of History to Christ* (1892) p.5.
[148] Ibid., p.6.
[149] "Responsibility in Regard to the Present Revival", in *The Revival,* 7 January 1860, p.1.
[150] W. Arthur, *May We Hope for a Great Revival?* (1859) p.8.

1862, *The Revival* commented: "Brethren of different communities felt compelled to draw together, labourers in the different spheres and fields of operation seemed forced into a union of love, a union of which Christ was the real though the invisible centre and magnet. This union was as easy, God having wrought in the work, as it was difficult or impossible heretofore."[151] No major new denomination came out of the 1859 Revival, although one might see the appearance of the Salvation Army as an aftershock. Later, perhaps as an imitation of what evangelicals achieved in the 1860s – as we will see in the next Part of this volume – the broad ecumenical movement took root.

The evangelical reversal that followed the 1859 Revival was not a new denomination, but something more dangerous; it was the crystallisation of a "quasi-religious movement away from religion".[152] Infidelity, atheism and materialism became rivals to religion; that man had a soul was denied.[153] Farrar thought the key assault was launched at the "Divinity of Christ". However, the supernatural and most of the doctrinal elements of Christianity were targeted, leaving only a weakened morality. Religion itself was not generally denied, as without it, society "might otherwise disintegrate into materialism, amoralism and selfish individualism".[154] Rather, the purpose of many leaders of thought was to change and soften religion, especially its doctrinal component, in such a way as to make it irrelevant and powerless. There ceased to be a God to be obeyed; rather, to claim the name of Christian, and to submit to a few rites, was thought to give access to eternity. Wilberforce's view that "the moral and practical precepts of Christianity...grow out of her peculiar doctrines and are inseparably connected with them" became forgotten, or unacceptable. A new deism was taking grip, but without reference to its earlier form of expression.

The Bible warned about seeking a wisdom to live by outside that of God.[155] The rejection by many of orthodox Christianity was not

[151] "The Revival in London", in *The Revival*, 12 April 1862, p.113 and "Revival Truths", in *The Revival*, 31 July 1862, p.41.

[152] G.M. Trevelyan, *English Social History* (1978) p.502.

[153] "Another Sigh for a Revival", in *The Revival*, 17 December 1859, p.161.

[154] D. Roberts, "Introduction" to George Eliot, *Middlemarch* (Wordsworth Editions Limited (2000)) p.x.

[155] Proverbs 3:5-7. In Ecclesiastes, the teacher sought to personally determine wisdom, but he did not find it. He breached many commandments in the process – see Ecclesiastes 2.

new, but what was new was the number of "whole literatures" and "whole philosophies" that were formulated, without reference to God, to justify that rejection, or to provide an alternative way of seeing life. Tellingly, in the 1860s, "the word *secularisation* began its metaphorical career in phrases like the *secularisation of art* or the *secularisation* of politics".[156] It acted as a unifying force behind these new literatures and philosophies. We will now look at six of them – and some striking developments around 1859 in each. The first – and, with the benefit of hindsight, the most important – was that, within science, 1859 witnessed the publication of Darwin's *Origin of Species*. Second, in philosophy, 1859 saw the publication of John Stuart Mill's treatise *On Liberty*. It also saw Herbert Spencer revise his prospectus for the proposed series of volumes that became his *Synthetic Philosophy*. This drove home the significance of the doctrine of evolution. Third, 1859 saw changes in the world of politics, with Charles Bradlaugh becoming a new driving force with the Secularists. Furthermore, the general election of that year witnessed the beginnings of the modern Liberal Party. Fourth, in the world of social, economic and cultural thought, 1859 saw the publication of Karl Marx's *A Contribution to the Critique of Political Economy*. It also saw great art critic John Ruskin launch himself as a social and economic commentator in the line of Carlyle. Fifth, in literature and letters, by the late 1850s the novelists had attained a new degree of importance, helping to make literature a central focus of life and establishing new means to disseminate views unsympathetic to Christianity. Sixth, the final challenge was to the historical accuracy and authority of the Bible. 1859 was also the year that Sigmund Freud moved to Vienna. There, he helped establish and develop psychology as an independent academic discipline. It, too, would present serious challenges to Christianity. In 1859 though, Freud was but three; his assault on religion we will defer to later.

[156] Author's italics. O. Chadwick, *The Secularization of the European Mind in the Nineteenth Century* (1975) p.229.

12.1.1 *Charles Darwin and science*

The work of Charles Darwin is today generally seen as epitomising a long-standing conflict between science and Christianity. But, in reality, for centuries before, there had been unity. In the past, science was a vocation or hobby and the man of science was as likely to be a clergyman as anyone else; the word 'scientist', David Knight tells us, was only coined in 1833.[157] Indeed, the great Edmund Burke had seen the role of the established church as "receiving and meliorating, and above all of preserving, the accessions of science and literature, as the order of Providence should successively produce them".[158] It was Thomas Carlyle, as we have seen, who prepared the way for the conflict between science and religion narrative by suggesting, earlier than Darwin's work, a discordance between the Bible and science.

Darwin's early career very much reflects how closely linked religion and science were at the time. Prior to departing on his great expedition on the *Beagle*, he studied at Cambridge with the intention of taking Church orders. After that expedition, he was an uncertain deist. His issue with Christianity was that he could not believe in the Bible as the revelation of God, or that Jesus was the Son of God. He had personal reasons for his conclusion. He thought it was "a damnable doctrine" that all those who do not believe will be everlastingly punished, as "this would include my father, brother and almost all my best friends".[159] He might also have mentioned both his grandfathers, including Erasmus Darwin, who had already propounded the theory of evolution.[160] All the same, his feelings might point to heaven.[161] He could be "agnostic about his agnosticism".[162] Towards the end of his life, he considered

[157] See D. Knight, *The Making of Modern Science* (2009) p.x.

[158] *Burke's Reflections on the Revolution in France* (1900) (F.G. Selby (ed.)) p.112.

[159] N. Barlow, *The Autobiography of Charles Darwin* (1969) pp.85-87.

[160] A. Desmond and J. Moore, *Darwin* (1991) pp.5-12. Darwin has been criticised for "neglecting to acknowledge the influence of his predecessors", including Erasmus, see J.T. Costa, *Wallace, Darwin, and the Origin of Species* (2014) p.253.

[161] Darwin was troubled by the thought that all human struggle would end with that "of the solar system – a dark, dead, lifeless lump careering through the depths of space". The idea of complete annihilation to him was "intolerable". His hope was that in "the distant future" man "will be a more perfect creature", see O. Lodge, "Introduction" to T. Huxley, *Lay Sermons* (1910) p.ix.

[162] A. Desmond and J. Moore, *Darwin* (1991) p.636.

himself a "theist"[163] and suggested a man can be "an ardent theist and evolutionist".[164] Emma Darwin, his wife, seems to have followed her family's Unitarianism, with concessions to the Church of England.[165] She read the Bible to her children and ensured that they were baptised and confirmed into the latter.[166] Charles Darwin's problem in relation to Christianity was that he had no real sense of sin – so he had no need for Christ.[167] Certainly, his work did much to undermine the reality of the Fall in the mind of the common man. Furthermore, if there was no Fall, there was no need of the Saviour.

Darwin did not invent evolution; the idea was already popularly known by the appellation 'transmutation'. What Darwin provided, through the principle of natural selection, was "an explanation of a mechanism by which evolutionary change could take place". He also suggested that all life was descended from a few organisms, if not a common ancestor. It was not until the sixth edition of his work that he used the word evolution – and even then, "with some hesitation".[168]

Darwin did not court controversy by publicly rejecting Christianity. He carefully placed echoes of the divine within the *Origin of Species* to make the book more acceptable to its likely readership. For example, he concludes – echoing the book of Genesis – that all "organic beings...

[163] N. Barlow, *The Autobiography of Charles Darwin* (1969) p.93. See also A.L. Moore, *Science and the Faith* (1889) p.170.

[164] A. Desmond and J. Moore, *Darwin* (1991) p.636.

[165] See E. Healey, *Emma Darwin* (2001) pp.79, 131, 158, 199 and 333. Before marriage, the future Emma Darwin wrote to Charles to ask him to read John 13 onwards, A. Desmond and J. Moore, *Darwin* (1991) p.270. Before his engagement, his father advised him to conceal his doubts from any future wife, see N. Barlow, *The Autobiography of Charles Darwin* (1969) p.95. Shortly after marriage, his wife wrote to him again in what he called "her beautiful letter", ibid., p.97. She cautioned against "casting off" what Jesus had "done for your benefit as well as for all the world". She wanted to spend eternity with Darwin and finished her letter saying that it would be most unhappy "if I thought we did not belong to each other for ever", ibid., pp.236-237. He read the "beautiful letter" many times in his life. It was not his wife's last letter on this theme, see A. Desmond and J. Moore, *Darwin* (1991) pp.506-507.

[166] R. O'Hanlon, "Charles Darwin, the Man: An Overview", in *Charles Darwin 1809-1882: A Centennial Commemorative* (1982) (R.G. Chapman and C.T. Duval (eds)) p.28.

[167] For Darwin's religious position generally, see A. Desmond and J. Moore, *Darwin* (1991) pp.622-637.

[168] D.N. Livingstone, *Darwin's Forgotten Defenders: The Encounter Between Evangelical Theology and Evolutionary Thought* (1987) p.xi.

have descended from some primordial form, into which life was first breathed".[169] Furthermore, in its final paragraph, he states: "there is a grandeur in this view of life...having been originally breathed into a few forms or into one".[170] In the second edition, Darwin added an express reference to "the Creator" as the person providing the breath of life. The book also begins with two epigraphs that affirm a creator. The second edition added a third, where the point was made even more explicit. However, Darwin's rejection of a loving Creator, and any form of orthodox Christianity, was fortified, in 1851, by the death of his favourite daughter, Annie.[171]

Christian critics observed the inadequate reference to the "Records of Creation", in the *Origin of Species*.[172] His work also shocked people because the mechanism of change that Darwin proposed was "nature red in tooth and claw", thereby assailing the beneficent image of the universe and its Creator that had been suggested by the natural theologians.[173] The natural theologians may have failed to give proper recognition to the consequences of the Fall in their accounts of a beneficent creation, but Darwin exaggerated their deficiency. Nevertheless, the prestige of natural theology – the value of which, as we have seen, was already being questioned – was severely dented. Natural selection replaced natural theology as the explanation of life. Furthermore, Darwin seemed to dismiss the idea that man had been made in God's image. The reviewer of *Origin of Species* in *The Christian Observer* thought that Darwin, "By choosing exceptional instances, abnormal developments, for the purpose of argument, and filling up from imagination every lapse or hiatus that occurs, the most preposterous opinions may be made to appear plausible – the most erroneous to wear the semblance of truth."[174]

At the time that Darwin wrote, science was making momentous strides – impacting, among other things, food production, transport,

[169] C. Darwin, "*On the Origin of Species*", in *The Annotated Origin* (2009) (J.T. Costa (ed.)) p.484.
[170] Ibid., p.490.
[171] A. Desmond and J. Moore, *Darwin* (1991) pp.375-387.
[172] "Darwin on the Origin of Species", in 60 *The Christian Observer for the Year* 1860 (1860) p.563. See also "The Atonement and its Repudiators", in 60 *The Christian Observer for the Year* 1860 (1860) p.732.
[173] J.H. Brooke, *Science and Religion* (1991) p.231.
[174] "Darwin on the Origin of Species", in 60 *The Christian Observer for the Year* 1860 (1860) p.561.

communications, industry and mining and thereby changing economic and political interests. New scientific societies were coming into being; the idea of the research university was spreading, with its Ph.D. cadres. Science had become "both public knowledge and meritocratic. A route to social mobility."[175] Accordingly, recent writers see the conflict that Darwin's views brought with Christianity as an expression of the new power of the Dissenting captains of northern industry – seeking their place in the sun, at the expense of the Anglican gentry;[176] or as part of a clash between the men of science and men of theology for intellectual dominance;[177] or as reflecting the desire of younger professional scientists to advance themselves professionally and socially against the older clerical elites.[178] David Livingstone, more generally, sees the "Darwinian episode" as centred "on the role science was to play in the future of human society";[179] and Ruth Barton writes that those seeking to advance the interests of science were challenging the clergy who had "the unique role of cultural leadership, educating the public mind, guiding public morals and legitimating the social order".[180]

A further reason for the success of Darwin's views was the popular perception of his character from those of very different theological perspectives. Philip Gosse, with a Brethren outlook – on meeting him for the first time – "was captivated";[181] and Aubrey Moore, an honorary canon of Christ Church Oxford, referred to his almost 'saintly' character:

> his intense modesty, his self-forgetfulness, his shrinking from popularity or applause, while gladly welcoming the testimony of those who were competent to judge of the truth of his work, his devotion to truth as shown by the weight he gives to unfavourable

[175] D. Knight, *The Making of Modern Science* (2009) p.ix.
[176] A. Desmond, *Huxley: The Devil's Disciple* (1994).
[177] P. White, *Thomas Huxley: Making the Man of Science* (2003) p.106.
[178] F.M. Turner, "The Late Victorian Conflict of Science and Religion as an Event in Nineteenth-century Intellectual and Cultural History", in *Science and Religion* (2010) (T. Dixon, G. Cantor, and S. Pumfrey (eds)) pp.98-99 and 106.
[179] D.N. Livingstone, *Darwin's Forgotten Defenders: The Encounter Between Evangelical Theology and Evolutionary Thought* (1987) pp.51 and 185-186.
[180] R. Barton, "'Huxley, Lubbock and Half a Dozen Others': Professionals and Gentlemen in the Formation of the X Club", in 89 *Isis* (1998) p.414.
[181] E. Gosse, *The Life of Philip Henry Gosse* (1890) p.256.

facts, his humility his simplicity his reverence.[182]

However, Darwin did not need to overly draw attention to himself or his work; others did this. As Owen Chadwick observes; "The spearhead of scientific aggression against Christianity"[183] came not from him, but from Thomas Huxley, John Tyndall, Francis Galton and William Draper; and from the work of the X Club, a private dining club made up mainly of Fellows of the Royal Society of Science.[184] It constituted a "body-guard of sound and experienced naturalists".[185] Three of its members, being Sir Joseph Dalton Hooker, William H. Spottiswoode and Thomas Huxley each succeeded the other as President of the Royal Society between the key years of 1873 to 1885.[186] They were united by a "devotion to science, pure and free, untrammelled by religious dogmas".[187] They sought to "speak with one voice" as "representatives of impartial science" – and, through use of media, patronage and craft, achieved institutional power in the societies that "stood for science as a whole".[188]

[182] A.L. Moore, *Science and the Faith* (1889) p.215.

[183] O. Chadwick, *The Victorian Church* (1987) pt.2, p.14. Darwin appreciated the importance of having Huxley on his side. He invited Huxley to stay at Downe House, prior to the publication of the *Origin of Species*. Hitherto, Huxley's views were not those of Darwin; Darwin wanted a propagandist of Huxley's ability to think and say the right things, see A. Desmond and J. Moore, *Darwin's Sacred Cause* (2009) pp.274-276.

[184] For the story from of the X Club, see R. Barton "'An Influential Set of Chaps': The X-Club and Royal Society Politics 1864-85", in 23 *The British Journal for the History of Science* (1990) pp.53-81. The one member of the X Club who was not a Fellow of the Royal Society was Herbert Spencer, but he refused to allow his name to go forward for nomination, see ibid., p.56.

[185] E. Gosse, *Father and Son* (1907) p.118.

[186] This triumvirate of Presidents of the Royal Society was succeeded, first by Sir George Stokes (1885-1890) and then Lord Kelvin (1890-1895) – both of whom were Christians who doubted various aspects of Darwinism, see D.B. Wilson, *Kelvin and Stokes* (1987) pp.84-90. Stokes had been earlier edged out of the presidency by Spottiswoode, a wealthy amateur scientist – but one supported by the X Club, see R. Barton, "'Huxley, Lubbock and Half a Dozen Others': Professionals and Gentlemen in the Formation of the X Club", in 89 *Isis* (1998) p.415. Stokes would be, by quite some way, the longest serving Royal Society Council member in the period 1840-1900, see R. Barton "'An Influential Set of Chaps': The X-Club and Royal Society Politics 1864-85", in 23 *The British Journal for the History of Science* (1990) p.59. On the politics of his appointment as President of the Royal Society, see ibid., pp.68-72 and 79-80.

[187] R. Barton, "'Huxley, Lubbock and Half a Dozen Others': Professionals and Gentlemen in the Formation of the X Club", in 89 *Isis* (1998) p.411.

[188] Ibid., p.444. For more detail on how the X Club used the media, see R. Barton,

Of these men who spearheaded Darwinism, one stands out – Thomas Huxley. Little is known of Huxley's early scepticism. His mother was devout; his father taught the future Cardinal Newman at an evangelical school before it closed. However, by the age of 15, he "had only a residue of Calvinistic 'moderate' evangelicalism left in him".[189] Like Darwin, he had a wife, Henrietta who, prior to marriage, expressed concern for his soul and prayed for him. However, in courtship, his doubts "rendered him a hindrance to her spiritual pursuits";[190] her education with the Moravians in Germany originally gave her a much more orthodox outlook than Emma Darwin. Later, as she became caught up in her husband's work, her doctrinal views became more ambiguous. She certainly rejected the idea that Christ died for sin and it has been suggested that she moved towards Unitarianism.[191] Nevertheless, she took their children to Christ Church, Lisson Grove in St Marylebone, where Llewelyn Davies – a personal friend of F.D. Maurice and a Christian Socialist – "drew intellectuals from far and wide".[192]

Huxley's dislike of Christianity went back before the publication of the *Origin of Species* and was focused on its doctrinal and supernatural elements. Yet, all the same, he believed that:

> The doctrines of predestination, of original sin, of the innate depravity of man and the evil fate of the greater part of the race, of the primacy of satan in this world...of a malevolent demiurgus subordinate to a benevolent Almighty...appear to me to be vastly nearer the truth than the 'liberal' popular illusions that babies are all born good, and that the example of a corrupt society is responsible for their failure to remain so; that it is given to everybody to reach

"Scientific Authority and Scientific Controversy in *Nature:* North Britain Against the X Club", in *Culture and Science in the Nineteenth-Century Media* (2004) (L. Henson, G. Cantor, G. Dawson, R. Noakes, S. Shuttleworth, and J.R. Topham (eds)) pp.223-235.

[189] A. Desmond, *Huxley: The Devil's Disciple* (1994) p.387.

[190] P. White, "Science at Home: The Space Between Henrietta Heathorn and Thomas Huxley", in 34 *History of Science* (1996) p.40.

[191] M.H. Cooke, *The Evolution of Nettie Huxley 1825-1914* (2008) pp.12-16, 22-23, 29-30, 36-37, 108-109, 110, 113-115, 124-125, 132-134 and also A. Desmond, *Huxley: The Devil's Disciple* (1994) pp.75-76, 86-87, 132, 285-286 and 394-395.

[192] Ibid., pp.285-286.

> the ethical ideal if he will only try.[193]

The way Huxley's mind developed is revealed in a letter to a friend, written on 30 January 1859. In it, he wrote:

> I recognise in their truths [referring to the Bible writers] that they were in the truest and highest sense scientific – I recognise in their truths the results of a long and loving if sorrowful, study of man's nature and relations...Thou shalt love thy neighbour as thyself is the law of gravitation of society.
>
> Theology and parsondom...are in my mind the natural and irreconcilable Enemies of science. Few see it but I believe we are on the eve of a new reformation and if I have a wish to live 30 y[ea]rs, it is to see the god of science on the necks of her enemies. But the new religion will not be a worship of the intellect alone.[194]

It has been said that "This letter might be read as the kind of declaration of war between science and religion for which Huxley has become famous".[195] He aimed to sever the long-standing alliance between them and to set the scientific community and the clergy against each other. Continuing the military metaphor, Huxley believed "the evolutionary theory was the strongest possible weapon which could be wielded against religious faith".[196] Ruth Barton suggests "the secularisation of society through the cultural domination of science was Huxley's chief aim".[197]

Huxley attacked the supernatural, but not the moral, element of Christianity. It is said that he taught a "rational Puritanism".[198] His wife observed that; "No husband 'manifested more of the moral

[193] *Life and Letters of Thomas Henry Huxley* (1900) (L. Huxley (ed.)) vol.2, pp.303-304. See also M.H. Cooke, *The Evolution of Nettie Huxley 1825-1914* (2008) p.115.
[194] Cited in P. White, *Thomas Huxley: Making the "Man of Science"* (2003) pp.105-106.
[195] Ibid., p.106.
[196] O. Chadwick, *The Victorian Church* (1987) pt.2, p.19.
[197] R. Barton, "Evolution: The Whitworth Gun in Huxley's War for the Liberation of Science from Theology", in *The Wider Domain of Evolutionary Thought* (1983) (D. Oldroyd and I. Langham (eds)) p.262.
[198] A. Desmond, *Huxley: Evolution's High Priest* (1997) p.xi.

presuppositions of a Puritan evangelicalism.'"[199] He was not against religious feelings; he thought they lay too deep to be eradicated.[200] Furthermore, he conflated the language of religion and science so much and used so much Pauline language that he was named the "apostle Paul of the new teaching".[201]

Darwinism did not destroy Christianity although it appealed strongly to those rationalists[202] already committed to "a self-progressing natural organic world".[203] It also acted as a unifying idea to many, but not all, critics of Christianity. It never received universal acclamation within the scientific community.[204] For example, Sedgwick was unconvinced by Darwin[205] and Darwin was "deeply hurt" by his attacks.[206] Indeed,

[199] A. Desmond, *Huxley: The Devil's Disciple* (1994) p.285. It is said he was "not really against Religion...it was against the Fetishism, the Polytheism, the Theism or Atheism and many other isms" that he was against. He coined, in 1869, the expression "agnosticism", as a more positive alternative to atheism – and not tainted with the sectarianism of religious strife; the scientist with clean hands. All the same, after Huxley, theology was not the same – because "the theology of the present had become more scientific than that of the past", O. Lodge, "Introduction" to *T. Huxley, Lay Sermons* (1910) p.xi.

[200] R. Barton, "Evolution: The Whitworth Gun in Huxley's War for the Liberation of Science from Theology", in *The Wider Domain of Evolutionary Thought* (1983) (D. Oldroyd and I. Langham (eds)) pp.263-267.

[201] A. Desmond, *Huxley: The Devil's Disciple* (1994) p.xvii and A. Desmond, *Huxley: Evolution's High Priest* (1997) p.xiii.

[202] S. Budd, *Varieties of Unbelief 1850-1960* (1977) pp.124-149.

[203] A. Desmond, *The Politics of Evolution* (1989) p.1. On the reception of Darwin's evolutionary ideas, see A. Ellegard, *Darwin and the General Reader* (1990) and D.L. Hull, *Darwin and his Critics* (1973).

[204] Many experts were, for long, against the principle of natural selection, as Darwin accepted in 1878 (see A.L. Moore, *Science and the Faith* (1889) p.165) – even if they accepted evolution, see A. Ellegard, *Darwin and the General Reader* (1990) p.47. For a rejection of the latest Darwinian account of the origins and evolution of life by a non-Christian philosopher, see T. Nagel, *Mind and Cosmos: Why the Materialist Neo-Darwinian Conception of the Universe is Almost Certainly False* (2012). For a recent summary of scientific arguments against Darwinism today by a leading Christian scientist, together with an analysis of the early chapters of Genesis, see A. McIntosh, *Genesis for Today* (2014). For a modern overview of the Darwinian view of evolution from a Christian theologian, see W. Grudem, *Systematic Theology* (2005) pp.279-287.

[205] E. Ashby and M. Anderson, "Introduction" to A. Sedgwick, *A Discourse on the Studies of the University* (1969) p.15.

[206] See J.H. Brooke, "Genesis and the Scientists", in *Reading Genesis after Darwin* (2009) (S.C. Barton and D. Wilkinson (eds)) pp.99-100.

around the turn of the century, Darwinism was itself subject to eclipse.[207] This only passed, in 1942, when Julian Huxley published his *Evolution: The Modern Synthesis*.[208] There continued to be,[209] and continues to be, Christian scientists. Some scientists maintained that, by introducing the idea of fixed laws into the development of species, Darwin strengthened the argument for the existence of God – by pointing to the evidence of a design underpinning the universe, which demanded a designer.[210] A speaker at the Church Congress of 1879 suggested that it was wonderful for a world to have been created out of diffuse matter which was inherently capable of development.[211] Consistent with this, "Huxley stated that 'the theological equivalent of the scientific conception of order is providence.'"[212] Darwin also pointed to the common origin of man, in Adam, which Christian apologists also found helpful.[213]

Nevertheless, by the time of Darwin's death in 1882, *The Record* noted that "the speculations of the school of which Mr Darwin was the founder have done more than perhaps anything else in the world to promote the cause of unbelief in this world".[214] As Sir George Stokes observed, even if evolution explained the development of species, it only operated as a "mode", not as the "cause", but it tended towards "the

[207] P.J. Bowler, *The Eclipse of Darwinism* (1983). See also D. Knight, *The Making of Modern Science* (2009) pp.276-278.

[208] This wedded Darwinian selection "with new insights from genetics, systematics and paleontology", see J.T. Costa, *Wallace, Darwin, and the Origin of Species* (2014) p.275.

[209] When the great physicist, Sir George Stokes, was asked whether his experience was that the greatest scientists were irreligious his answer was "but the reverse", see *Memoir and Scientific Correspondence of the Late Sir George Gabriel Stokes* (1907) (J. Larmor (ed.)) vol.1, p.78.

[210] For example, the Asa Gray, Fisher Professor of Natural History (Botany) at Harvard University, see A. Gray, *Darwiniana: Essays and Reviews Pertaining to Darwinism* (1876). On Gray generally, see D.N. Livingstone, *Darwin's Forgotten Defenders: The Encounter Between Evangelical Theology and Evolutionary Thought* (1987) pp.60-77 and J.R. Moore, *The Post-Darwinian Controversies* (1981) pp.269-280.

[211] "The Church Congress", in *The Times*, 10 October 1879.

[212] Cited in D.N. Livingstone, *Darwin's Forgotten Defenders: The Encounter Between Evangelical Theology and Evolutionary Thought* (1987) p.49.

[213] J. Kitto, *Daily Bible Illustrations (Morning Series)* (1866) vol.1, p.171.

[214] "Darwin and Darwinism", in *The Record*, 5 May 1882, p.167. George Bernard Shaw perceptively commented, "Darwin had the luck to please everyone who had an axe to grind", see D. Wilkinson, "Reading Genesis 1-3 in the Light of Modern Science", in *Reading Genesis after Darwin* (2009) (S.C. Barton and D. Wilkinson (eds)) p.129.

denial of a First Cause".[215] Furthermore, the mechanistic approach to life that Darwinism seemed to encourage, took out of Christianity much of the wonder in the creation that the author of Psalm 19 had known – and which had been such a characteristic of the natural theologians of the 1820s and 1830s. Darwin himself, in his later years, observed that whereas "formerly pictures gave me considerable, and music very great delight", in his later years he could not "endure to read a line of poetry". He had also "almost lost any taste for pictures or music", although, he added, "I retain some taste for fine scenery, but it does not cause me the exquisite delight which it formerly did."[216]

Accordingly, we need to balance the nineteenth century view of the times with recent research which suggests that it was the orthodox view of Scripture – and its morality with regard to "eternal punishment, hell, the atonement, and damnation for unbelievers" – that led secularists to reject Christianity, rather than science or anything else.[217] For example, Sir George Gabriel Stokes, the leading physicist, who succeeded Thomas Huxley as President of the Royal Society, was more concerned that the doctrine of hell and eternal torment led to scepticism than evolution did. Stokes abandoned belief in the former,[218] but continued to resist aspects of the latter.[219] In his view, "science never has explained, nor does there seem to be the remotest prospect that it ever will be able to explain, the origin of life".[220] Elsewhere, he wrote: "There are vast gaps between the life of a grass, that of a fish, that of a bee, that of a man. I do not think that science has succeeded, and I doubt if it will ever succeed, in filling these in."[221] He also did not believe that all living things came from a "single form"[222] and believed that man was the result of the special

[215] *Memoir and Scientific Correspondence of the Late Sir George Gabriel Stokes* (1907) (J. Larmor (ed.)) vol.1, p.90.

[216] He found "novels, which are works of the imagination, though not of a very high order…a wonderful relief and pleasure…I often bless all novelists", see N. Barlow, *The Autobiography of Charles Darwin* (1969) p.138. We will see more shortly on the novelists.

[217] See M.R. Watts, *The Dissenters* (2015) vol.3, p.46.

[218] See G.G. Stokes, *Conditional Immortality* (1897).

[219] See D.B. Wilson, *Kelvin and Stokes* (1987) pp.84-90.

[220] *Memoir and Scientific Correspondence of the Late Sir George Gabriel Stokes* (1907) (J. Larmor (ed.)) vol.1, pp.79-80.

[221] Ibid., p.82.

[222] G.G. Stokes, *Natural Theology* (1893) p.149.

creative act of God.[223] That Stokes suggested that the doctrine of hell led more to scepticism than the doctrine of evolution should not surprise us, as it was the doctrine of hell that led Darwin to reject Christianity.

The impact of Darwinism on the general approach to the interpretation of Scripture by many clergy underlay the spread of unbelief that *The Record* discerned above – just as much as its direct challenge to the Creation and Fall. It did this in a number of ways. First, it gave the justification of contemporary science to theological liberals in their interpretation of the Bible. They no more believed in doctrines such as heaven and hell, final judgment, penal substitution and the inspiration of Scripture than did members of the X Club mentioned earlier. So they happily joined common cause with the Darwinians, as a non-literalistic approach to the early chapters of Genesis provided a rationale to dispose of any other doctrine they disliked. Indeed, members of the X Club reached out to support theological liberals in the 1860s when the latter challenged orthodoxy.[224]

Secondly, it introduced division between those who were orthodox in their belief on heaven and hell, final judgment etc. Some of this group broadly construed Genesis as compatible with Darwin's hypothesis of evolution and geological discoveries. They took the approach that the early chapters of Genesis were "accommodated" to man's understanding at the time they were written – otherwise contemporaries would have thought them nonsense – but nevertheless manifesting timeless truths.[225] They did not think that such an approach impacted the correct construction of the rest of the Bible. Their general approach was broadly to take the Bible literally, unless the text or other matters suggested otherwise. Within this perspective, there were a range of views as to what within the early chapters of Genesis was literally true. The key issues were that God created the heavens and the earth and the historicity of the Fall, without which penal substitution did not make sense. Other members of orthodoxy robustly dismissed atheistic evolution, and the

[223] Ibid., pp.151-152.

[224] R. Barton, "'Huxley, Lubbock and Half a Dozen Others': Professionals and Gentlemen in the Formation of the X Club", in 89 *Isis* (1998) p.435. See also O. Chadwick, *The Victorian Church* (1987) pt.2, p.26.

[225] See M. Tinker, "Clearing Away Conceptual Fog: Genesis, Creation and Evolution", in 121 *Churchman* (2012) p.106.

view of the formation of life, as suggesting that the "impossible will happen if you wait long enough".[226] The variety of these responses[227] to Darwinism created uncertainty as to the meaning of the first chapters of Genesis and division on the vital issues of Creation and the Fall. A house divided against itself, Jesus had said, will not stand.[228] Certainly, as a means to explain the world pithily, the evangelicals did not have in their armoury a word with the resonance "evolution", or the two words, "natural selection", whatever their merits.

In sum, as we have seen, in the first half of the nineteenth century, as the geologists worked at extending the antiquity of the earth, a number of leading British evangelicals, but not all, sought to harmonise the Bible with their work and the gospel spread. But Darwin gave added challenge, both to those who kept to a literal interpretation of the early chapters of Genesis and those who sought to harmonise the book of Genesis with the new scientific ideas. The evangelicals met Darwin's challenge with less success than in the issue of the true age of the earth.[229] Darwin had, as the scientist William Whewell regretted, made "the clear definite

[226] For a more learned statement of this view, see M.J.S. Hodge, "The History of the Earth, Life, and Man: Whewell and Palaetiological Science", in *William Whewell: A Composite Portrait* (1991) (M. Fisch and S. Schaffer (eds)) p.286.

[227] For the complexity of the responses, see D.N. Livingstone, *Darwin's Forgotten Defenders: The Encounter Between Evangelical Theology and Evolutionary Thought* (1987), a complexity that endures to this day. For a summary of present evangelical responses to the interpretation of the early chapters of Genesis see A. McIntosh, *Genesis 1-11* (2016) pp.9-11.

[228] Mark 3:25.

[229] J.H. Brooke, "Genesis and the Scientists: Dissonance Among the Harmonisers", in *Reading Genesis after Darwin* (2009) (S.C. Barton and D. Wilkinson (eds)) pp.93-109. In America, there was a much more vigorous endeavour to accept evolution, by evangelical theologians. Of Asa Gray, it was said that he "tried to show to the American people that Darwinism was probably true, and was quite consistent with Christianity; but Gray's influence was confined to scientific circles". It was the Scotsman, James McCosh, who, as President of Princeton University, convinced the intelligent public that whether "Evolution is sound or erroneous…it is not dangerous to Christianity", see *The Life of James McCosh* (1896) (W.M. Sloane (ed.)) pp.123-124. Other important evangelical supporters of evolution were B.B. Warfield and, to a lesser extent, Charles Hodge, see D.N. Livingstone, *Darwin's Forgotten Defenders: The Encounter Between Evangelical Theology and Evolutionary Thought* (1987) pp.100-131. See generally, for the development of evangelical attitudes to Darwinism, M. Wellings, *Evangelicals Embattled* (2003) pp.189-226 and D.N. Livingstone, *Darwin's Forgotten Defenders: The Encounter Between Evangelical Theology and Evolutionary Thought* (1987).

line, which used to mark the commencement of the human period of the earth's history…obscure and doubtful".[230] Darwin, towards the end of his life, commented: "Nothing is more remarkable than the spread of scepticism or rationalism during the latter half of my life".[231] Only, perhaps, a Church of England bishop – in this case Harvey Goodwin, the Bishop of Carlisle – could have preached Darwin's funeral sermon on the Sunday after his death, at Westminster Abbey, saying that it was "suitable to bury the remains of the most conspicuous man of science in this generation with the fullest expression of Christian hope".[232] By burying Darwin in Westminster Abbey, his supporters symbolically placed Darwinism at the centre of the nation. In the late 1880s, theological issues over evolution began to die down – partly through the work of the High Churchman Aubrey Lackington Moore,[233] who expounded theistic evolution. But Darwin was dead; and the time of the X Club's influence – containing his leading protagonists – was also over; most of its members being either deceased or infirm. It was in the late 1880s, as we shall see, that the growth of Christianity in the nation began to stall. This was also the time, as we will shortly see, when the doctrine of hell was being given up and in theology there was a shift from the atonement to the incarnation as the central idea.

12.1.2 *John Stuart Mill, Herbert Spencer and philosophy*

John Stuart Mill was one of the most influential British philosophers of the nineteenth century. Like Darwin, he did not repudiate Christianity in public.[234] In his posthumously published autobiography, his rejection of Christianity also fastened on the existence of hell and God's intention – being, he suggested, that "the great majority were to be consigned to horrible and everlasting torment".[235] Critics commented that it was

[230] Cited in M.J.S. Hodge, "The History of the Earth, Life, and Man: Whewell and Palaetiological Science", in *William Whewell: A Composite Portrait* (1991) (M. Fisch and S. Schaffer (eds)) p.287.
[231] N. Barlow, *The Autobiography of Charles Darwin* (1969) p.95.
[232] "The Late Mr Darwin", in *The Times,* 1 May 1882.
[233] For a summary of A.L. Moore's work, see J.R. Moore, *The Post-Darwinian Controversies* (1981) pp.259-269.
[234] J.S. Mill, *Three Essays on Religion* (1874) pp.ix and x.
[235] J.J. Cross, "Preface" to *Autobiography of John Stuart Mill* (1948) p.29.

unclear as to the extent that he had ever read the Bible.[236] From our perspective, his most pertinent work is *On Liberty*, published in 1859. Its influence was comparable with that of Karl Marx's *Critique of Political Economy*, published almost contemporaneously. However, it is said, "the influence on political thought of Mill's treatise was more immediate, and perhaps no less permanent".[237]

Mill lacked personal enthusiasm for the Christian moral values undergirding Victorian social life; he undermined their authority by elaborating a higher principle by which to judge their validity. *On Liberty* asserted "one very simple principle...that the sole end for which mankind [is] warranted, individually or collectively, in interfering with the liberty of action of any of their number, is self-protection".[238] To interfere with someone, to promote his good, whether physical or moral, was insufficient warrant. The American commentator Thomas Sowell suggests that Mill was one of those who regarded themselves as part of "an *anointed* elite, people with a mission to lead others in one way or another to better lives".[239]

Mill's aim was to free people from the moral "tyranny of the prevailing opinion" as to personal or social excellence, rather than from the legal penalties for failing to conform to them.[240] By this, he probably meant the standards propagated by the likes of Hannah More, Gisborne, Roberts and others in their books on conduct. He suggested that such standards destroyed independent thought. His approach weakened the notion that the nation's morality (and religion) was important to God and that national prosperity hinged on its fidelity to God's purposes.

Having established a new non-Christian touchstone by which to judge morality, Mill went on to release into human consciousness a number of subsidiary principles which proved equally damaging to Christianity. His first principle was the idea of human development or progress beyond

[236] "Autobiography of John Stuart Mill", in 74 *The Christian Observer for the Year 1874* (1874) p.50.

[237] I. Berlin, "John Stuart Mill and the Ends of Life", in *J.S. Mill On Liberty in Focus* (1991) (J. Gray and G.W. Smith (eds)) p.132.

[238] J.S. Mill, "*On Liberty*", in *J.S. Mill On Liberty in Focus* (1991) (J. Gray and G.W. Smith (eds)) p.30.

[239] Author's italics. T. Sowell, *Intellectuals and Society* (2009) p.76.

[240] J.S. Mill, "*On Liberty*", in *J.S. Mill On Liberty in Focus* (1991) (J. Gray and G.W. Smith (eds)) p.26.

Christianity. He referred to Christian morality as incomplete and quoted a portion of the Koran to suggest a useful addition.[241] Furthermore, he asserted non-Christians have produced "a large portion of the noblest and most valuable moral teaching".[242] And he added that the ethical doctrine of the Old Testament was "barbarous, and...intended only for a barbarous people".[243] In essence, Mill recommended what the book of Revelation condemns – adding to, or taking away from, what is written in the Scriptures.[244] Later writers developed this idea so that the Bible, or any other religious movement, was only a stage in human development. Once a purer light arose, the Bible (or the relevant religious movement) could be discarded. This left free the people of any age to develop religion according to the prevailing voice. The Tractarians used this form of argument to suggest that they were the divinely appointed successors to the Church evangelicals. Mill's second principle was to suggest that we can never be certain of anything. While he does not state this categorically, he does suggest that "Complete liberty of contradicting and disproving our opinion, is the very condition which justifies us in assuming its truth for purposes of action."[245] This leads to the position whereby no one can be sure of anything, since the events of tomorrow may change the strongest convictions. Any notion that God, by definition, might be able to speak with authority, appeared unconsidered.[246] The third principle was that Christianity lacked the power "to produce the moral regeneration of mankind". God was not up to the task. Any system capable of doing so needed "secular standards" beside Christian ethics. A too pure form of Christianity was bad. Mill wrote that the interests of "truth require a diversity of opinions".[247] God could not be trusted to get

[241] Ibid., pp.67-68. Contemporary thinking about the benefits of a multi–faith society may have its origins in Mill's thinking about the need to supplement Christianity with the thinking of other faiths.

[242] Ibid., pp.68-9.

[243] Ibid., p.66.

[244] Revelation 22:19.

[245] J.S. Mill, "*On Liberty*", in *J.S. Mill On Liberty in Focus.* (1991) (J. Gray and G.W. Smith (eds)) p.39. Many of Mill's ideas echoed the earlier thinking of Holyoake, without the open disavowal of Christianity, see G.J. Holyoake, "The Organisation of Free Thinkers", in 11 *The Reasoner* (1852) pp.129-131.

[246] For a criticism of *On Liberty* from a Christian perspective contemporary with Mill, see J. Parker, *John Stuart Mill On Liberty* (1865).

[247] J.S. Mill, "*On Liberty*", in *J.S. Mill On Liberty in Focus* (1991) (J. Gray and G.W. Smith (eds)) p.68.

it right. His fourth principle was the idea of utility. This was "the ultimate appeal on all ethical questions: but it must be utility in the largest sense, grounded on the permanent interests of man as a progressive being". Mill's language is opaque.[248] However, it was only these interests that permitted such limited intervention to liberty that he accepted. How Mill kept together his ideas on liberty and utility, or whether they can be kept together, is debated by scholars. The general view is that they cannot.[249] However, whatever the philosophical difficulties, the idea that the highest good is that people should be free, unless they harm others, to pursue their own pleasure or happiness, was a powerful one for future ages.

On Liberty was well received by certain clergymen, which suggests that popular opinion was not subject to the theological oppression, nor as destructive of independent thought, as Mill suggested.[250] In *The Spectator*, the Bishop of St David's expected any reader to be "thrilled by a sense of the ethical sublime". F.D. Maurice, also writing in *The Spectator*, thought Mill would contribute more wisdom to Parliament than "almost any other man".[251] However, many Christians remained unpersuaded of the merits of *On Liberty.* Joseph Parker, the leading Congregational preacher, noted that these critics had originally sworn to test their doctrines by the word of God. He added: "we have well-nigh lost all those broad lines of separation which in apostolic times marked off *faith* from *unbelief*...The church is dying of a spurious charity".[252]

Another philosopher working in 1859 on an important publication, was Herbert Spencer. Spencer, in the late nineteenth century, was probably better known than Mill, although his reputation has since faded. Spencer achieved a degree of notoriety with his publication *The Principles of Psychology* (1855), then labelled "Modern Atheism".[253] In 1860, he gave

[248] Ibid., p.31.

[249] J. Gray and G.W. Smith, "Introduction" to *J.S. Mill On Liberty in Focus* (1991) (J. Gray and G.W. Smith (eds)) pp.1-19.

[250] For a review of the early critics of *On Liberty*, see J.C. Rees, *John Stuart Mill's On Liberty* (1985) pp.78-105 and 84 for how they believed that there was freedom of debate in religious matters.

[251] Cited in J. Parker, *John Stuart Mill On Liberty* (1865) pp.32-35. In the general election of 1868, notwithstanding a liberal landslide, Mill lost his seat to the statio-ner-statesman W.H. Smith.

[252] Author's italics. Ibid., p.37.

[253] H. Spencer, *An Autobiography* (1904) vol.1, pp.468-472.

notice that he intended to publish a system of philosophy embracing First Principles – being The Principles of Biology, The Principles of Psychology, the Principles of Sociology and the Principles of Morality. Spencer toiled at this ambitious project until 1896, when the last volume of what became known as the *Synthetic Philosophy* was complete. The foundations of his thought rested on rejecting theism, the Fall and hell.[254] The ultimate religious idea, he argued, was "that the power which the universe manifests to us is utterly inscrutable".[255] Instead, Spencer looked to general laws to provide a systematic interpretation of life, mind and society. The big idea at the time was the law of evolution. Spencer was a member of the X Club. The publication of Spencer's *Synthetic Philosophy* led to the historian J.B. Bury commenting that it "did more than any other work...both to drive home the significance of the doctrine of evolution and to raise the doctrine of progress to the rank of a commonplace truth".[256] These doctrines became almost articles of faith, in some quarters, in the last quarter of the nineteenth century.

In Spencer's hands, both doctrines of evolution and progress assumed optimistic, even utopian, overtones. Human nature was capable of change; it was capable of attaining perfection through adaptation to the conditions of social life, rather than the new birth by the Holy Spirit. Herbert Spencer suggested: "Progress is not an accident but a necessity. What we call evil and immorality must disappear. It is certain that a man must become perfect."[257] There was no struggle with sin; evil could be eliminated by "gradual adaptation, gradual psychological change".[258] He also believed morality was progressing and that "the secularisation of morals is becoming imperative", as the existing moral injunctions lost the authority derived from their alleged sacred origins.[259] His philosophy blessed whatever was the dominant social idea of the time.[260] Christian

[254] J.R. Moore, "1859 and all that: Remaking the Story of Evolution-and-Religion", in *Charles Darwin 1809-1882: A Centennial Commemorative* (1982) (R.G. Chapman and C.T. Duval (eds)) pp.184-185.

[255] H. Spencer, 1 *First Principles,* Oct 1860, p.46.

[256] J.B. Bury, *The Idea of Progress* (1955) p.341. Darwin, though, was not an admirer of Spencer, see N. Barlow, *The Autobiography of Charles Darwin* (1969) pp.108-109.

[257] Cited in A.G. Hebert, *Liturgy and Society* (1935) p.31.

[258] J.B. Bury, *The Idea of Progress* (1955) p.340.

[259] "Darwin and Darwinism", in *The Record*, 5 May 1882, p.167.

[260] Shortly after the First World War, Dean Inge labelled the idea of progress as

commentators thought Spencer's formulation of evolution much more dangerous than that of Darwin.[261]

To the universities, the idea of the world's progress was especially attractive. It gave philosophical justification to the labours of the various academic disciplines. Christianity, in comparison, did not indulge the egos of the new non-religious elites that, as we will see, ran the universities after 1870. Christianity, at best, told them they were thinking God's thoughts after him and, at worst, that they were sinful and under judgment, whatever their academic distinction.

The notion of inevitable progress allowed scholars to indulge in prophetic foresights as to the future achievements of their respective discipline. Even the lawyers were led astray, including one as great as Lassa Francis Lawrence Oppenheim, the Whewell Professor of International Law at Cambridge. In his textbook on public international law, he predicted that, in regulating the relationships between states, "immeasurable progress is guaranteed to international law, since there are eternal moral and economic factors working in its favour". Two years after he wrote, World War One started. The book, duly updated, remains a standard legal practitioner's work.[262]

Meanwhile, Leslie Stephen had rewritten the recent history of English philosophy, in his *History of English Thought in the Eighteenth Century* (1876). The topic, since the 1860s, was already subject to a process of revision.[263] Stephen saw the work of Hume as "a turning-point" in its history.[264] He noted that "If Hume's scepticism was a potent influence at the time, it was not because similar doubts had never occurred to other thinkers, or never been expressed by them, but because the social conditions happened to be favourable to their development."[265] As we saw in an earlier volume, this did not fit with perceptions of the

"superstition", W.R. Inge, *The Idea of Progress* (1920) p.9.

[261] For example, see D.N. Livingstone, *Darwin's Forgotten Defenders: The Encounter Between Evangelical Theology and Evolutionary Thought* (1987) pp.64 and 138 and J.R. Moore, *The Post-Darwinian Controversies* (1981) pp.253-254 and 262.

[262] L. Oppenheim, *International Law* (1912) p.83.

[263] See generally O. Chadwick, *The Secularization of the European Mind in the Nineteenth Century* (1975) pp.143-160.

[264] L. Stephen, *History of English Thought in the Eighteenth Century* (1876) vol.1, p.1.

[265] Ibid., p.19.

standing of Hume's work at the end of his life.[266] It was also as though the coming of the Methodists, William Wilberforce and the Clapham Sect and the halcyon days of evangelical Christianity in the first half of the nineteenth century had never been. Stephen also resurrected deism and imbued it with new force which made it appear as the driving force of the "soul of the nation",[267] even though, by 1859, no one read the deistic writers.[268] Anyone who rejected scepticism, or even toyed with Christianity, was destroyed with verve by a few strokes of Stephen's acidic pen. For example, "Joseph Butler belonged to the exceedingly small class of men who find in abstract speculation not merely the main employment, but almost the sole enjoyment, of their lives."[269] The writings of Philip Doddridge, despite the conversion of William Wilberforce, were "a faint reflection, from the older Puritans...the fire no longer communicates much heat".[270] William Warburton "led the life of a terrier in a rat-pit, worrying all theological vermin".[271] Even Mill, lauded as "the most distinguished of Hume's recent disciples", was trashed as possessing "A pathetic desire to find some remnant of truth in the ancient dogmas."[272] This was because Mill, towards the end of his life, and in an essay published posthumously, stated that there was "a large balance of probability in favour of creation by intelligence", but he was not finally convinced.[273]

In the last quarter of the nineteenth century, how far philosophy, even that with a religious basis, had moved from orthodox Christianity, is illustrated in the work of T.H. Green's influential philosophy of idealism. It has been described "as a variant of Christianity designed to cope with

[266] J.A. Thomas, *The Nation's Gospel: Reformation to Revolution* (2017) vol.1, p.367.
[267] L. Stephen, *History of English Thought in the Eighteenth Century* (1876) vol.1, p.2.
[268] O. Chadwick, *The Secularization of the European Mind in the Nineteenth Century* (1975) p.145.
[269] L. Stephen, *History of English Thought in the Eighteenth Century* (1876) vol.1, p.278.
[270] L. Stephen, *History of English Thought in the Eighteenth Century* (1876) vol.2, p.388.
[271] L. Stephen, *History of English Thought in the Eighteenth Century* (1876) vol.1, p.345.
[272] Ibid., pp.311-312.
[273] J.S. Mill, *Three Essays on Religion* (1874) p.174.

religious difficulties".[274] In 1860, Green took up a fellowship at Balliol College Oxford. He rejected the supernatural elements of Christianity and "deprecated the attempt to reconstruct from uncertain documents the precise details" of the teaching of Jesus. He dwelt on their salient features from the Sermon on the Mount, the epistles of St Paul and John's Gospel.[275] One writer explains his thought as follows:

> For Green the essential attribute of the true Christian was not subscription to certain beliefs and dogma, but rather having a proper relationship with God. 'Faith', he wrote, 'is a personal and conscious relation of man to God, forming the principle of a new life.' Green defined this relationship in terms of conscience and duty. God, he argued, dwelt in every individual, taking the form of his higher self. It was by responding to this higher self, and leading a life of self-sacrifice, love and service to the community, that man fulfilled his divine and his human destiny.[276]

It was a religion/philosophy of works. Green's emphasis on the importance of a relationship with God made his thinking sound truly Christian. However, it was not possible to have a relationship with God if one disbelieved what he said. Furthermore, how could a person's relationship with God be authentic if the biblical signposts to the Christian life were rejected? One of his students discovered his knowledge of "Christ as a person, had been dissolved by criticism".[277]

Green paid insufficient attention to human sin. He acknowledged that sin separated man from God, but its horror is missing from his work. He believed that the benefits of the cross could be secured by "a life of charity" and through "sincerity and truth".[278] Without accepting the historical facts of the faith – and faith in the atonement – to secure pardon, Christianity became a religion of good works. Furthermore, as

[274] P. Nicholson, "Introduction" to T.H. Green, *Collected Works of Thomas Hill Green* (1997) (P. Nicholson (ed.)) vol.1, p.viii.
[275] R.L. Nettleship, "Memoir, T.H. Green", in T.H. Green, *Collected Works of Thomas Hill Green* (1997) (P. Nicholson (ed.)) vol.3, p.cii.
[276] I. Bradley, *The Call to Seriousness* (1976) p.201.
[277] R. Horton, *An Autobiography* (1917) p.43.
[278] T.H. Green, "The Witness of God", in *Collected Works of Thomas Hill Green* (1997) (P. Nicholson (ed.)) vol.3, p.248.

Wilberforce had indicated, if its peculiar doctrines were not taught, it would decay. However, the decay was not immediate and Green heavily influenced those who launched the Settlement Movement and the attempt to bring civilisation and better ways of living to the East End.[279]

12.1.3 *Politics and political thought*

The general election of 1859 witnessed the beginnings of the modern Liberal Party.[280] This did not in itself necessarily herald a political attack on Christianity, as the party drew its strength from the Nonconformists, but there was a radical element within it, hostile to traditional Christianity. However, more dangerous to Christianity was the fact that the two main political parties drew much of their strength from different Christian camps, the Tories relying upon the Church of England, and the risk that mutual conflict between the parties over religious issues would weaken the Christian fabric of the nation. Again, it is worth recalling the words of Jesus that a house divided cannot stand.

Openly opposed to Christianity was the Secularist movement, the fortunes of which revived in 1859 as Charles Bradlaugh came to prominence.[281] In 1866 Bradlaugh founded the National Secular Society and in the 1880s he became the first openly atheistic MP. Bradlaugh had no role for God – in this world, or the next. He wrote of the atheistic position: "the conception of creation is impossible. We are utterly unable to construe it in thought as possible that the complement of existence has been either increased or diminished, much less can we conceive an absolute origination of substance."[282] Secularists were also very much behind what became known as neo-Malthusian theory.[283] This accepted Malthus's ideas on population but added the solution of family limitation to the alleged dilemma that nature presented of population or poverty. In 1877 the Malthusian League was founded. The ideas of George Drysdale

[279] K.F. Inglis, *Churches and the Working Classes in Victorian England* (1964) pp.150-152, 154, 159-160.

[280] For an analysis of the elements making up the Liberal Party, see J.R. Vincent, *The Formation of the British Liberal Party 1857-1868* (1976).

[281] E. Royle, *Radicals, Secularists and Republicans: Popular Freethought in Britain, 1866-1915* (1980) p.4.

[282] C. Bradlaugh, *A Plea for Atheism* (1880) p.5.

[283] R. Ledbetter, *A History of the Malthusian League 1877-1927* (1976) pp.25-26.

were very much its underpinning philosophy, although he did not allow his name to be associated with it publicly.[284]

Secularism's "golden age" was the 1860s to the 1880s. Then, it occupied the "front of the political stage". The National Secular Society had branches throughout Britain.[285] In 1868, one Christian leader viewed it as "the sea into which all other evils converge and pour their united streams".[286] Whether national religion could survive seemed questionable. One night, in the 1883-1884 mission of the American evangelist D.L. Moody, hundreds of Secularists attended the East End hall where he was speaking, with the aim of disrupting the service. As events transpired, at least one Secularist was converted.[287] Indeed, as Timothy Larsen observes of secularism generally, in his iconoclastic work *Crisis of Doubt* (2006): "A far greater percentage of Secularist leaders became Christians than Christian ministers became sceptics."[288]

The Secularists held much in common with others campaigning against doctrinal Christianity. They were agreeable to the trappings of religion. At the end of 1860, John Gordon received the "call" to become the first full-time lecturer of a British Secularist society. He intended to build a congregation at Leeds.[289] They used songs and ceremonies – just as long as the God-talk was out. Here, to give a flavour, is the opening verse of their song, "Heaven on Earth":

> The parson may preach and the fanatic rave[290]
> Of existence eternal beyond the dark grave;
> Their heaven, they say, is far up above,

[284] Ibid., p.57.

[285] E. Royle, *Radicals, Secularists and Republicans: Popular Freethought in Britain, 1866-1915* (1980) p.x.

[286] T.R. Birks, "That the Evangelical Body have a Special Duty at this Crisis, as Faithful Representatives of our Reformed Church", in *Present Danger and Present Duty* (1868) (E. Auriol (ed.)) p.117.

[287] For a summary of that night, see J. Pollock, *Moody without Sankey* (1983) pp.211-213.

[288] T. Larsen, *Crisis of Doubt* (2006) p.vii.

[289] Ibid., pp.114-115 and 118-119. Gordon was shortly afterwards converted to orthodoxy, see ibid., pp.119-126.

[290] This line seems to echo a line from Cowper's *Progress of Error*, swap "deist" for "fanatic", see J.A. Thomas, *The Nation's Gospel: Reformation to Revolution* (2017) vol.1, p.352.

But mine is on earth, and I call it love[291]

And here is their song, entitled "Death", in its entirety:

Thy sable, vast, and shadowy form, O death,
Hovers around us in the prime of life,
Till in thy folds we sigh away our breath,
And lose all interest in this mortal strife.

We die, and pass away we know not where,
The world forgets us ere we scarce have fled;
Yet shall our actions long survive us here,
Good deeds work blessings though their author's dead.[292]

The significance of the Secularists diminished in the mid-1880s. Bradlaugh was an atheist and, in drawing many in that direction, he may have drawn them away from the Secularist party – with its more religious feel.[293] For those who wanted to retain the trappings of religion, while developing the political attack on Christianity, the socialists offered possibilities. They identified Christianity with capitalism and blamed the former for the latter's treatment of the poor. Yet, in its early days, socialism found it expedient, at times, to pose as a new religion. William Morris, the patron of the Arts and Crafts Movement, suggested that "the aim of the socialists should be the founding of a religion".[294] Morris popularised the expression the "religion of socialism" by writing the peroration to the 1885 manifesto of the Socialist League. This stated that the religion of socialism is "the only religion which the Socialist League professes".[295] Another socialist leader wrote: "A new conception of life is taking shape, to which it is affection, if not folly, to refuse the

[291] A. Holyoake and C. Watts, *The Secularist's Manual of Songs and Ceremonies* (1871) p.30.
[292] Ibid., p.29.
[293] O. Chadwick, *The Secularization of the European Mind in the Nineteenth Century* (1975) p.92.
[294] S. Yeo, "A New Life: The Religion of Socialism in Britain, 1883-1896", in 4 *History Workshop Journal* (1977) p.19.
[295] Ibid., p.6.

name of religion."[296] A separate Labour Church was founded "to develop the religion of the Labour movement, to destroy all forms of slavery, to work for true comradeship, and to fill the hearts of the people with new confidence in themselves, in each other, and in God."[297]

In the 1890s Robert Blatchford's Clarion Press took on a role equivalent to that of the Religious Tract Society, but printing a very different viewpoint, by publishing a socialist journal, tracts and novels. Blatchford wrote of *The Clarion* journal that it "had more influence on public opinion in this country than any other English journal, *The Times* included".[298] His *Merrie England* (1893), having sold 20,000 copies at a shilling, was reduced to a penny tract and, within a year, sold three-quarters of a million copies. Blatchford recalled being repeatedly offered a copy by amateur hawkers – and of being given a copy by those who thought it important but who did not know that he was the author.[299] "A year before its issue, there were not 500 socialists in Lancashire; twelve months after, there were 50,000."[300] Morality tales of a new nature then followed – such as *A Bohemian Girl* (1898), in which the singer Daisy Spanker played the heroine.

As the twentieth century dawned, reference to the religious basis of socialism declined. A number of reasons are commonly given for this. First, for socialists, alternative work interests (primarily trades unions and administrative bodies like the London County Council) made them too busy to spend time on religion. Secondly, leisure activities grew in significance. Thirdly, other bodies dedicated to party politics took the lead in implementing the interests of the working classes – that is, the Independent Labour Party and then the Labour Party.[301] Perhaps more decisive was that by the early twentieth century, as Christianity's grip on the culture weakened, there was no longer quite the need to pretend that socialism was a religion.

[296] Robert Blatchford cited in ibid.

[297] John Trevor cited in ibid., p.33. On the Labour Churches which began in Manchester in 1891 see H. McLeod, *Religion and Society in England, 1850-1914* (1996) pp.208-211. They would not prosper and few survived the First World War, see G.I.T. Machin, *Politics and the Churches in Great Britain 1869-1921* (1987) p.282.

[298] R. Blatchford, *My Eighty Years* (1931) p.197.

[299] Ibid., pp.196-197.

[300] Ibid., p.xiii.

[301] Ibid., pp.41-49.

Tom Mann's pamphlet, *A Socialist's View of Religion and the Churches* (1896), illustrates how socialism undermined Christianity. In it, Mann asks whether the churches fulfil their function of providing guidance as to conduct in this life and qualifications for the life hereafter. It was a time of poverty for the poorest classes; in his view, guidance on how to make a living was what the working man wanted. He acknowledged that the churches taught the virtues – including "honesty, sobriety, and obedience" – but "exactly how to apply them being, of course, too great a task". As to churches who taught people to "flee from the wrath to come" and find salvation in the cross, this led, in Mann's view, to "a narrow, saving, squeezing creature, taking little or no part in the vigorous life of the community, but very commonly becoming, by his isolated action, a source of weakness in any real democratic movement".[302] It took someone sure of his doctrine – and generous – to be willing to warn of the "wrath to come", if he was going to be thought of as "a narrow, saving, squeezing creature". As we will see however, those who warned of the wrath to come were not, like St Paul before them, narrow, saving, squeezing creatures – but often the ones who built the orphanages, cared for the sick and educated the poor.

Nevertheless, with 400,000 people – in London alone – in a state of semi-, or actual, starvation, Mann highlighted a burning issue. And the issue gained resonance with the Christian public, through the Scriptural references in his work (he had strong Christian contacts and associations) – especially to those in the Old Testament – relating to the rich grinding the poor. Another repeated refrain in his work is the line from the Lord's prayer, "Thy kingdom come; thy will be done, as in heaven, so upon earth." Mann did not reject the truth of the atonement so as to be dismissed as in error. Rather, he left it open and justifiably asks whether a person is accepted by God "irrespective of the life he leads".[303] He concludes that, for preachers and people, "The social salvation of the entire community is the religious duty in which...to engage."[304] The command to love your neighbour as yourself was assuming priority over that to love the Lord your God with all your heart – and again, good works were becoming central.

302 T. Mann, *A Socialist's View of Religion and the Churches* (1896) p.2.
303 Ibid., p.7.
304 Ibid., p.16.

12.1.4 *The world of social, economic and cultural thought*

1859 is a watershed year in social, economic and cultural thought. In 1859 Marx published, in German, *A Contribution to the Critique of Political Economy*. This was intended to stimulate interest in the materialist conception of history, in preparation for his later work – the massive *Capital: A Critique of Political Economy* (1867). *A Contribution* was not an immediate publishing triumph and the first translation into English did not appear until 1904. However, Marx's aim in "writing a multi-volume attack on 'bourgeois' economics was now reaching fruition".[305] Some saw "Marxist doctrine as a secular form of religion".[306]

Of more immediate impact on the standing of Christianity in the popular mind was that, in 1859, John Ruskin turned to writing social and economic criticism. In the 1840s and 1850s he was the dominant critic in the fields of art and architecture, owning the power to make or break reputations. He turned to his new sphere of influence the year after rejecting Christianity.

Ruskin's parents were evangelical, although overprotective. His early works, such as his *The Seven Lamps of Architecture* (1849), manifest an "aggressive evangelical Protestantism".[307] In it, he argued that architecture points to the moral life of the nation and that "certain right states of temper and moral feeling were the magic powers by which all good architecture has been produced".[308] However, after a long period of debate, around the age of 40, he rejected his parents' religion. In 1858, in a Waldensian chapel in Turin, he heard, as he was to write, a "little squeaking idiot" preach damnation "to an audience of seventeen old women and three louts". He left "a conclusively *un*converted man".[309] He turned, for a time, to a "religion of Humanity", centred in man.[310] This was unsurprising, as the problem troubling his mind was how could

[305] V. Barnett, *Marx* (2009) p.129.

[306] Ibid., p.1.

[307] J. Batchelor, *John Ruskin: No Wealth but Life* (2000) p.75.

[308] Cited in ibid., p.76.

[309] Author's italics. J. Ruskin, "Letter 76", in *Fors Clavigera; Letters to the Workmen and Labourers of Great Britain* (1877) vol.7, p.104.

[310] He was "contemptuous of this phrase for its association with positivism". See generally S.B. Southwell, *Religion in the Life and Thought of John Ruskin* (1956) (unpublished Ph.D. thesis, University of Texas) p.12.

religion be true when the painters he most esteemed were worldly?[311] His conclusion was to teach that "resolving to do our work well is the only sound foundation of any religion whatsoever; and that by that resolution only, and what we have done, and not by our belief, Christ will judge us, as he has plainly told us he will (though nobody believes him)".[312]

After his rejection of "Evangelical-Protestant" religion, especially during the years 1860-1867[313] he thought himself a disciple of Carlyle and turned to Carlyle for religious guidance. He had done so before. He refused to republish his earlier work as a mixture of "Protestant egotism and insolence".[314] His first attack of delirium came in 1878; he became permanently insane in 1889.[315]

In the period after 1858 elements of Christianity did not disappear from his work. Like Carlyle, he loved a rhetorical flourish with a Christian echo. But his dependence on the Bible went much deeper than that. The Bible was treated as a resource for shaping and justifying his moral vision. He selected from it those portions that explained his ideas. But the Bible had no special authority; it was just another book. When he relied upon it, he was simply pointing to "a portion, divinely appointed, of the best wisdom which human intellect, earnestly seeking for help from God, has hitherto been able to gather between birth and death".[316]

In 1906, W.T. Stead[317] wrote to the 51 MPs of the Labour Party to ask which books had been most useful to them. Of the 45 who responded, Ruskin's works were the most popular, followed by the Bible. Ruskin's economic and architectural thought also stimulated interest in the

[311] He later found the solution. The worldly painters he admired had a better grip of perspective than their religious forbears. The latter though, in other ways, he came to see, reached a higher "human achievement", J. Ruskin, "Letter 76", in *Fors Clavigera; Letters to the Workmen and Labourers of Great Britain* (1877) vol.7, p.106.

[312] Ibid., p.103.

[313] G.A. Cate, *Ruskin's Discipleship to Carlyle: A Revaluation in Carlyle and his Contemporaries* (1976) (J. Clubbe (ed.)) pp.227-256.

[314] J. Ruskin, "Letter 76", in *Fors Clavigera; Letters to the Workmen and Labourers of Great Britain* (1877) vol.7, p.105.

[315] Gertrude Himmelfarb observes that the Victorian intellectual community suffered "a larger proportion of nervous breakdowns, it would seem, than almost any other", see *Victorian Minds* (1975) p.219.

[316] J. Ruskin, *Time and Tide by Weare and Tyne* (1994) p.43.

[317] "The Labour Party and the Books that Helped to make it", in 33 *The Review of Reviews*, June 1906, pp.568-582.

medieval past, particularly the Gothic, encouraging those wanting more ritual in church services.

Equally influential – and again, wanting to take the scissors to the supernatural and doctrinal in the Bible, so that the ethical might stand out – was the educator and poet Matthew Arnold.[318] The basis of his *Culture and Anarchy*[319] was first published between 1867 to 1868 in *The Cornhill Magazine*.[320] His solution to the prospect that "In politics, in literature, in religion, things appear to be sweeping on to anarchy",[321] was to "recommend culture...a pursuit of our total perfection". The doctrine of perfectionism that Arnold affirmed was not that of John Wesley or the Bible.[322] It was more akin to a process than an end destination. It was not being transformed into the likeness of Christ. Rather, perfection was achieved "from a thorough disinterested study of human nature and human experience".[323] The study was to be of the "best which has been thought and said in the world".[324] Its attainment required a "harmonious expansion of *all* the powers which make the beauty and worth of human nature, and is not consistent with the over-development of any one power at the expense of the rest".[325] For Arnold, perfection had two elements: the "scientific passion for pure knowledge" and "the moral and social passion for doing good". The justification and motif for this second element was pious – "To make reason and the will of God prevail!"[326] But God was not to be worshipped; religion was subordinated to culture – as "the greatest and most important of the efforts by which the human race has manifested its impulse to perfect itself".[327]

Arnold was not against the Bible. It underpinned his moral and social

[318] For an assessment of Arnold's role in creating a doctrinally empty religion, see L. Trilling, *Matthew Arnold* (1982).
[319] For the background to *Culture and Anarchy* and brief critique of it, see M.R. Watts, *The Dissenters* (2015) vol.3, pp.181-182.
[320] The bulk of the pieces published in *The Cornhill Magazine* had the much less engaging title of "Anarchy and Authority".
[321] P.W. Burt, "*Culture and Anarchy*. An Essay in Political and Social Criticism", in 33 *The London Quarterly Review* (1869) p.210.
[322] For example, Matthew 5:48 and 2 Corinthians 13:9-11.
[323] M. Arnold, *Culture and Anarchy* (2009) p.36.
[324] Ibid., p.5.
[325] Author's italics, Ibid., p.36.
[326] Ibid., p.34.
[327] Ibid., p.35.

passion for doing good. He just thought it needed a fresh interpretation of his own devising. This had to be done, in his view, if the people were to accept it.[328] Arnold rejected the Bible's supernatural and doctrinal elements. As he wrote: "Remove the schemes of doctrine, Calvinistic or Arminian...and all that is most valuable in the Church of England would still remain".[329] He went to the Bible for its standard of conduct and culture was the key to its interpretation. Applying this approach, he concluded that Jesus had discovered the Bible's secret – and that secret was "sweet reasonableness".[330] It was to discover "sweet reasonableness" that one read and reread the Bible and, in his conclusion, in "sweet reasonableness" did our righteousness consist.[331] A new lens through which to read the Bible was being fashioned.

Arnold wanted to cure Christianity of the advocates of the supernatural; those whom he variously called the "Puritans" – the members of the Church of England Evangelical party and the Nonconformists.[332] Piquancy was given to Arnold's views on the latter when their journal, *The Nonconformist*, in reviewing one of his poetical works referred to his "faithless, hopeless, all but loveless poems".[333] Arnold thought that the Nonconformists were guilty of "provincialism" or, as he called them, the "hole-and-corner organisations", and the appellation stuck in the popular culture.[334] At this time, many Nonconformists started to seek greater

[328] M. Arnold, *Literature and Dogma* (Smith, Elder, & Co (1873)) pp.xii-xiii. This sold as many as 100,000 copies and was the first of Arnold's books to be translated. It appeared as *La Crise Religieuse* (1876) in France: C. Machann, *Matthew Arnold* (1998) p.111.

[329] M. Arnold, *St Paul and Protestantism* (1875) pp.4-5.

[330] Arnold's theological justification for this was that St Paul had written "By the meekness and gentleness of Christ, I appeal to you" (2 Corinthians 10:1). The correct interpretation of mildness was said to be reasonableness with sweetness M. Arnold, *St Paul and Protestantism* (1875) p.xix.

[331] M. Arnold, *Literature and Dogma* (Smith, Elder, & Co (1873)) pp.378-380.

[332] Arnold thought "there is this difference between the Evangelical party in the Church of England and the Puritans outside her – the Evangelicals have not added to the first error of holding this unsound body of opinions, the second error of separating for them", see M. Arnold, *St Paul and Protestantism* (1875) p.vi. The cure for these people – and he was quite open about this – was to bring "Puritanism more into contact with the main current of national life" and, in particular, to call it into the "liberally conceived Anglican establishment", see M. Arnold, *Culture and Anarchy* (2009) p.18.

[333] Cited in C. Machann, *Matthew Arnold* (1998) p.103.

[334] This author was brought up with it, without reading *Culture and Anarchy*.

contact with contemporary culture.[335] By the turn of the century, there were complaints to the press that the Nonconformist ministry had become so cultured that it shot over the heads of the laity and had "disregarded the central truths of the gospel in favour of 'the latest theories of the... *Fortnightly [Review]*'".[336] The collapse in Protestant church attendance since 1900 has been greatest among Nonconformists.

To sharpen his attack on Puritanism, Arnold drew a distinction between "Hebraism" and "Hellenism". Hebraism was the "philosophy of English Puritanism, strict in conscience and in obeying the law".[337] Hellenism was about the "spontaneity of consciousness", seeing things as they are and responding to them. Arnold thought that the country had received too strong a dose of Hebraism and needed a counterbalancing dose of Hellenism. Spontaneity, a love of beauty and an openness to apparently new doctrines were to be among the hallmarks of Nonconformity in the next century.

Matthew Arnold has a major place in the formation of theologically liberal Protestantism. The Bible was to be read and valued for the poetic experience it provided – but the elimination of its doctrinal element emptied it of its power to transform and guide lives. Further, as *The London Quarterly Review* complained, in Arnold's scheme "The prevailing sentiment of cultured people...becomes the sole standard of morals."[338] Here is possibly the root of modern-day ideas of political correctness, especially as far as human sexuality is concerned. Like Darwin, Arnold had no real conception of human sin. Arnold believed that the fundamental thing for the Christian was not the miracle of the atonement, but the imitation of Christ – as if sinful man could follow him without spiritual transformation.[339] He also propagated the idea that a place of neutrality exists where the Olympian observer can sit and impartially assess the merits of religious argument. Arnold called that place "disinterestedness".[340] The success of this idea is illustrated by the strength of the present-day perception that, because of their culture

[335] See generally J. Munson, *The Nonconformists* (1991) pp.67-157.
[336] Ibid., p.114.
[337] See N. Murray, *A Life of Matthew Arnold* (1996) p.246.
[338] P.W. Burt, "Art. VIII. – *Culture and Anarchy*. An Essay in Political and Social Criticism", in 33 *The London Quarterly Review* (1869) p.214.
[339] See C. Machann, *Matthew Arnold* (1998) p.105.
[340] M. Arnold, *Culture and Anarchy* (2009) p.17.

and learning, the universities and other establishment institutions, such as the BBC, are somehow neutral when it comes to religious and moral issues.[341] The same claim to the place of "disinterestedness" is made by secularism; it believes that it is above the squabbles of the religions.

Arnold's ideas today pervade the social views and mannerisms of society and church. The popular modern attitudes – such as the importance of balance[342] and sincerity – are heavily influenced by his ideas.[343] He states that "to be reared a member of an establishment is in itself a lesson of religious moderation, and a help towards culture and harmonious perfection".[344] Here also is boarding school religious education; it emasculated the impact of the earlier work of Hannah More and her associates in making obedience to biblical precepts part of the culture of the 'better' classes. The new view did not allow doctrine to be applied in any meaningful way, or for the purpose for which it was given – namely, "teaching, rebuking, correcting and training in righteousness".[345] From the 'better' classes, the same approach spread to the others. At the end of the nineteenth century, a commentator noted that the great change in the culture of the previous generation was "the diffusion of culture, or at least of a desire and need for it, among the mass of the middle and lower classes". There were a number of reasons for this which need not detain us, but it was written that "no two men have been as efficient in their work as Matthew Arnold and Ruskin".[346] Both of them offered the Bible in diluted form – sufficient to inoculate against any more vigorous interest.

[341] See I.H. Murray, *Evangelicalism Divided* (2000) p.211. Murray, suggests that because of "human depravity", the desire by evangelicals to influence the theology faculties of secular universities has met less success than might be hoped, see ibid., pp.173-214.

[342] M. Arnold, *Culture and Anarchy* (2009) p.36.

[343] Ibid., p.28.

[344] Ibid., p.12.

[345] 2 Timothy 3:16.

[346] C. Waldstein, *The Work of John Ruskin: Its Influence upon Modern Thought and Life* (1894) pp.8 and 12.

12.1.5 *The novelists*

1859 was a remarkable year for the English novel, as its grip on the reading habits of the nation expanded.[347] It also saw the first issue of two publications, which advanced the cause of novel reading and the spread of liberal theology whilst promoting ideas antagonistic to the spread of Christianity. In October 1859 the first issue of *Macmillan's Magazine* was published. It was one of the first monthly literary periodicals selling for a shilling; its pages included novels and it became the vehicle for the dissemination of the ideas of F.D. Maurice. In its pages, Maurice advocated "a truly national Church embracing a variety of theological opinion and of an ultimate unity of Christians of all persuasions based on liberty of conscience, or in their opposition to ecclesiastical dogmatism, sectarianism and authoritarianism".[348] Like Maurice, contributors to *Macmillan's Magazine* took the view that baptism made for a Christian, not the new birth.[349] *Macmillan's Magazine* has been called "the most respectable and respected magazine of 'serious' literature and comment of its time".[350] Huxley, Tyndall and other members of the X Club were all contributors.[351] It abandoned the periodical practise of not naming the authors of their respective articles.

Later, in 1859, came *The Cornhill Magazine*; its original editor was William Makepeace Thackeray, who was disenchanted with Christianity. Its first issue contained the opening part of *Framley Parsonage*[352] by Anthony Trollope, who delighted in genteel satire of contemporary Church life. It is telling that when Lord Macaulay – the son of that leading member of the Clapham Sect, Zachary – died, in December 1859, he did not die with the Bible open beside him, as his forbears might have. He died in his easy-chair, with the first issue of *The Cornhill Magazine* open at the first page of a story by Thackeray. The magazine lay open at that

[347] G.J. Worth, *Macmillan's Magazine, 1859-1907* (2003) p.1.
[348] Ibid., p.64.
[349] J.L. Davies, "The Revivals of 1859", in 3 *Macmillan's Magazine* (1860) pp.363-373.
[350] G.J. Worth, *Macmillan's Magazine, 1859-1907* (2003) p.1.
[351] R. Barton, "Scientific Authority and Scientific Controversy in *Nature:* North Britain Against the X Club", in *Culture and Science in the Nineteenth-Century Media* (2004) (L. Henson, G. Cantor, G. Dawson, R. Noakes, S. Shuttleworth, and J.R. Topham (eds)) pp.225-227 and 233.
[352] Book form 1861.

spot for some hours during his last hours of illness.[353] The picking out of this detail by his biographer – his nephew, G. Otto Trevelyan – was expressive of the change that had come over a portion of the better and literary classes in Lord Macaulay's lifetime. *The Cornhill Magazine* would go on to draw and bind together critics of Christianity.[354]

Increasing sales made the novelists ever more influential. In 1870, religious books made up the largest portion of the book market. Works of fiction were fifth. By 1886, fiction was the largest portion of the book market.[355] Anti-Christian novelists formed coteries of like-minded writers, together with the other literary critics of biblical Christianity. For instance, George Eliot, George Lewes, John Stuart Mill, Matthew Arnold and Thomas Carlyle all knew each other and would dine together.[356] Often their relationships were fortified by the common rejection of a strong Christian family heritage – this was the case with Robert Louis Stevenson, Robert Browning and Edmund Gosse.

Novel reading made entertainment acceptable for those from evangelical backgrounds. For members of the book-reading public, it absorbed time, set out new standards of acceptable behaviour and helped change the way people thought about many matters. By the "arrogance of assertion", without opportunity for reply, a character might dismiss

[353] G.O. Trevelyan, *Life and Letters of Lord Macaulay* (1876) vol.2, pp.478-479.
[354] The pages of *The Cornhill Magazine* made public Ruskin's first social and economic essays, launched the literary career of Robert Louis Stevenson and established that of Thomas Hardy. Its then editor was Leslie Stephen – later to renounce his status as a clergyman. Leslie Stephen was the grandson of James Stephen, the leading member of the Clapham Sect. His father, Sir James, had been one of the first to have doubts about the eternal nature of future punishment. His first wife's father was Thackeray. Through his second marriage, he fathered Virginia Woolf. While Leslie Stephen edited *The Cornhill Magazine*, George Henry Lewes, living with George Eliot, was involved with editorial policy. In its pages, he asserted of *The Origin of Species* – manifestly overstating the case – that "Darwin's book is in everybody's hands". We have already seen that Matthew Arnold's *Culture and Anarchy* was first circulated in *The Cornhill Magazine*. He also published in it the article that led to his *St Paul and Protestantism* (book form 1870).
[355] I.H. Murray, *The Undercover Revolution* (2009) pp.5-6. See generally P. Scott, "The Business of Belief: The Emergence of 'Religious' Publishing", in *Sanctity and Secularity: The Church and the World* (1973) (D. Baker (ed.)) pp.213-224.
[356] The depth of their relationship with one another varied. Carlyle, who held to biblical sexual morality, achieved only a "tolerant civility" with George Eliot, G.S. Haight, *The Caryles and the Leweses in Carlyle and his Contemporaries* (1976) (J. Clubbe (ed.)) p.196.

the narratives of the New Testament as "fairy tales", while supernatural events were dismissed as "out of court with men of education".[357] Furthermore, as the philosopher T.H. Green wrote in his 1862 Oxford prize essay: "The novel furnishes the standard for the measurement, and the data for the comparison" of human life. "It presents us with a series of fictitious experiences, in the light of which we read our own, and become more critically conscious of them."[358] The result was that the novelist acted as a leveller in society. Even the highest minds became "conformed insensibly to the general opinion which the new literature of the people creates".[359] Some observers thought that M.E. Braddon's popular novels *Lady Audley's Secret* (1863) and *Aurora Floyd* (1863) were "baits for suicide".[360]

Evangelical clergy were one of the first groups whose public standing many novelists sought to reduce. For example, the characters of George Eliot's *Adam Bede*, her first novel and one of the remarkable novels published in 1859, included the parson – "a very favourable specimen of the moral preachers" of the previous century and his successor, an evangelical curate. "A rough and ready" farmer describes the parson as "like a good meal o' victual; you are better for him without thinking on it; but [the evangelical curate] is like a dose o' physic; he gripes you and worrets you, and after he leaves you much the same". *The Times* reviewer of *Adam Bede* picked out the above quotation to illustrate the accuracy of the author's character sketches.[361] Evangelical ladies were another target of the novelists. In *Middlemarch* (1872) George Eliot gently mocked those who visited the rural poor and who were concerned for their housing. Dorothea was described by Eliot as "a girl so handsome and with such prospects", but she undermined her public standing by her capacity to kneel "suddenly down on a brick floor by the side of a sick labourer", praying "fervidly as if she thought herself living in the time of the apostles".[362] As to the Nonconformists, taking a swipe at them was

[357] H. Games, *The Bible and Some Current Sceptical Thought* (1890) pp.1-2.
[358] T.H. Green, "An Estimate of the Value and Influence of Works of Fiction in Modern Times", in T.H. Green, *Collected Works of Thomas Hill Green* (1997) (P. Nicholson (ed.)) vol.3, p.38.
[359] Ibid., p.45.
[360] O. Anderson, *Suicide in Victorian and Edwardian England* (1987) p.242.
[361] "Adam Bede", in *The Times*, 12 April 1859.
[362] G. Eliot, *Middlemarch* (Wordsworth Editions Limited (2000)) p.7.

"part and parcel of Victorian literature".[363] The attacks were carefully executed, the target "small, unrepresentative backwater communities outside the mainstream of Nonconformity".[364] Chapels in wealthy areas, drawing the captains of industry, were ignored. Furthermore, in a fictitious world, it was possible to idealise life without identifying its true cause. For example, *The Christian Observer* censured *Adam Bede* for suggesting that, at the end of the eighteenth century, village life without vigorous evangelical preaching was a "state of tranquil happiness and innocent enjoyment".[365] Hannah More's experience was that it was a life of "*ignorance and vice*".[366]

The target of Mrs Humphry Ward's[367] *Robert Elsmere* (1888), the "best-seller of the decade"[368] and "one of the publishing events of the century",[369] was Christian doctrine. In that novel, the hero, clergyman Robert Elsmere, gives up his living and Orders, once he concludes that "*miracles do not happen!*".[370] He came to believe that "It is not that Christianity is false, but that it is only an imperfect human reflexion of a part of truth".[371] He then goes in search of a neo-Christianity, based upon theism. It was a very successful example of the auto-biographical novel in which the hero represented the author's purely intellectual grounds for rejecting Christianity. Mrs Ward, in a subtle dig at contemporary clergy, observed of her hero that "In other men it might be right and possible that they should live on in the ministry of the Church, doing the humane and charitable work of the Church, while refusing assent to the intellectual and dogmatic framework on which the Church system rests; but for himself it would be neither right nor wrong, but simply

[363] J. Munson, *The Nonconformists* (1991) p.208.

[364] Ibid., p.212.

[365] "Recent Semi-Religious Works of Fiction", in 60 *The Christian Observer for the Year 1860* (1860) p.27.

[366] Author's italics. Ibid., p.28.

[367] A granddaughter of Thomas Arnold and niece of Matthew Arnold, see B. Lightman, "*Robert Elsmere* and the Agnostic Crises of Faith", in *Victorian Faith in Crisis* (1990) (R.J. Helmstadter and B. Lightman (eds)) pp.285-286.

[368] W.S. Peterson, *Victorian Heretic* (1976) pp.160 and 221-222.

[369] Cited in B. Lightman, "*Robert Elsmere* and the Agnostic Crises of Faith", in *Victorian Faith in Crisis* (1990) (R.J. Helmstadter and B. Lightman (eds)) p.285.

[370] Author's italics. H. Ward, *Robert Elsmere* (Smith, Elder, & Co (1888)) vol.2, p.291.

[371] Ibid., p.337.

impossible."[372] "The novel made such a deep impression on young Julian Huxley, who was Mrs Ward's nephew, that it helped to convert him to religious humanism 'but without belief in a personal God'."[373] Mrs Ward knew it was "religious propaganda".[374]

By the end of the century, as the influence of evangelicalism declined, it "ceased to command the eager attention of the secular novelist".[375] It had been dealt with. Nevertheless, the Cambridge Simeonites received a parting shot in Samuel Butler's *The Way of all Flesh* (1903). It was exceptional though. Butler had started writing it towards the beginning of the third quarter of the nineteenth century, but it was only published after his death. It portrayed the Simeonites as mainly poor scholars whose Christian zeal was animated by the expectation that it would lead to the zealots' improved social standing.[376]

The nation's moral framework was a further target for some novelists. Thomas Hardy said, "I am determined – to exhibit what I feel ought to be exhibited about life, to show that what we call immorality, irreligion, &c, are often true morality, true religion." True morality was said to include opposition to the evils of marriage and the marriage laws.[377] Certain literary figures were also developing relationships[378] – the nature of which was never clear, but which were not conducive to existing marriages. The best known of these are Dickens' relationship with Ellen Ternan – an 18 year-old actress – and John Stuart Mill's relationship with Harriet Taylor, before the death of her husband. George Eliot had three children out of wedlock, with George Lewes, a married man. At the other end of the moral scale, Ruskin's marriage with Effie Gray was dissolved for non-consummation. Catherine Booth thought that works of fiction "made young people impatient 'of parental restraint' and produced 'a premature forcing of...sexual instincts'".[379]

[372] Ibid., pp.294 and 315.
[373] W.S. Peterson, *Victorian Heretic* (1976) p.160.
[374] Cited in B. Lightman, "*Robert Elsmere* and the Agnostic Crises of Faith", in *Victorian Faith in Crisis* (1990) (R.J. Helmstadter and B. Lightman (eds)) p.306.
[375] E. Jay, *The Religion of the Heart* (1979) p.11.
[376] S. Butler, *The Way of all Flesh* (Penguin (1966)) pp.231-234.
[377] I.H. Murray, *The Undercover Revolution* (2009) p.38. Hardy would also fly the flag for suicide, see O. Anderson, *Suicide in Victorian and Edwardian England* (1987) p.69.
[378] See generally G. Himmelfarb, *Victorian Minds* (1975) pp.275-276.
[379] Cited in M.R. Watts, *The Dissenters* (2015) vol.3, p.184.

Nevertheless, a new morality was slow to emerge from the pen of the novelists. In part, this was because, in an age of vigorous Christianity, they generally adopted a high moral tone. Writing in 1868, J.C. Ryle thought that the light reading of the nation was distinctly better than that in vogue a hundred years before. He remarked (rejecting the view of the young Lord Macaulay at the beginning of the century) that the "indecency" of Fielding, Smollett, Swift and Sterne "is so glaring and gross, that few people now-a-days would like to allow their works to be seen on their drawing room table".[380] Mrs Humphry Ward might be "quite willing, even eager, to discard" Christian doctrine, but to her, "traditional ethical standards were completely sacred".[381] At her funeral, in 1920, Dean Inge of St Paul's Cathedral described her as "perhaps the greatest Englishwoman of our time".[382]

However, by the end of the century there were signs that certain novelists were increasingly willing to challenge contemporary morality. In December 1894, Thomas Hardy's novel of complex relational entanglements, *Jude the Obscure*, began to be serialised. Marriage was "trivialised through the farcical events surrounding it…all the marriages contracted in the novel involve deceit, social necessity or compulsion to religious dictates."[383] In 1895, Grant Allen published *The Woman Who Did*, a story sympathetically told of "a woman who deliberately broke the rigid conventions of the period and bore an illegitimate child as 'her very own'".[384] The following year H.G. Wells published *The Island of Dr Moreau* (1896) which expressed the collapse of Christian morality in the face of "the Darwinian revolution". That work presented "man as no more than a talking animal, that all moral systems are arbitrary and man-made, that the sanctions traditionally endorsing the social order are illusions".[385] In 1896, H.G. Wells was very positive in *The Saturday*

[380] J.C. Ryle, *Christian Leaders of the Eighteenth Century* (1997) pp.18-19.
[381] W.S. Peterson, *Victorian Heretic* (1976) p.5.
[382] Cited in ibid., p.1.
[383] G. Buzwell, "An Introduction to *Jude the Obscure*" (published 15 May 2014), https://www.bl.uk/romantics-and-victorians/articles/an-introduction-to-jude-the-obscure, accessed 16 July 2018. See generally, N. Holland, Jr., "'*Jude the Obscure*': Hardy's, Symbolic Indictment of Christianity", in 9 *Nineteenth-Century Fiction* (1954) pp.50-60.
[384] H.G. Wells, *Experiment in Autobiography* (1969) vol.2, p.548.
[385] J. Batchelor, *H.G. Wells* (1985) p.21.

Review about *Jude the Obscure*.[386] However, the reviewer in *The Pall Mall Gazette* concluded his review of the book with the words "So, Mr Hardy, don't disappoint us again. Give us quickly another and a cleaner book to take the bad taste out of our mouths."[387] The reviewer was to be disappointed. *Jude the Obscure* was to be Hardy's last completed novel.

12.1.6 *The historians*

The doubts that came from Germany about the dates of the books of the Bible and their provenance unsettled many until 1885, when J.B. Lightfoot published his *Apostolic Fathers*. This, by establishing the early dates of the writings of the apostolic fathers, pushed the dating of the books of the New Testament into the first century. All the same, works assailing the dating of the New Testament continued to sell, as anti-biblical propaganda, well into the early twentieth century.[388]

Historians also questioned the supernatural elements in the Bible. These ideas were popularised in a variety of works. Applying the assumption that God cannot do miracles, in 1863 a natural history of Jesus appeared. It was by the Frenchman, Ernest Renan. It has been called the "first effective biography" of Jesus.[389] Renan, unlike Strauss in his *Life of Jesus*, treated "Jesus as an actual person, the events of whose career were rather nuclei of legendary tradition than pure myths."[390] However, the *Life of Jesus* portrayed him, as F.D. Maurice wrote, as "a Jesus who was not the Christ, who is not the King of Men, who came from no Father in heaven, who baptised with no Spirit, who did not rise from the dead". The same critic added – pointing out the inconsistencies of Renan – "Though this Jesus claimed titles which were not his, though he practiced mean deceptions, he has been recognised as a hero both by his biographer, and by numbers who have read the biography".[391] Holman Hunt, the painter, dismissed the work as "simply

[386] G. Buzwell, "An Introduction to *Jude the Obscure*" (published 15 May 2014), https://www.bl.uk/romantics-and-victorians/articles/an-introduction-to-jude-the-obscure, accessed 16 July 2018.

[387] "*Reviews*", in *Pall Mall Gazette*, 12 November 1895, p.4.

[388] O. Chadwick, *The Victorian Church* (1987) pt.2, p.71.

[389] Ibid., p.62.

[390] W.G. Hutchison, "Introduction" to *Renan's Life of Jesus* (1897) (W.G. Hutchison (trans.)) p.xi.

[391] F.D. Maurice, *The Gospel of the Kingdom of Heaven* (1864) p.vi.

puerile nonsense".[392] However, "The quest for the historical Jesus" had begun.[393] In 1866, *Ecce Homo* was published anonymously, but it was later acknowledged to be by J.R. Seeley. It was not a biography, but an attempt to emphasise Jesus as moral teacher, rather than Saviour.[394] Later in the century, as we have seen, Mrs Humphry Ward, in her novel *Robert Elsmere*, sketched for the literary public, in a moving way, the struggles of her hero, as he abandoned his faith and became convinced that "the Gospels are like other books, full of mistakes, and credulous, like the people of the time".[395]

Such doubts about the miracles were not new. Neither the Pharisees nor the Sadducees at the time of Jesus believed in his miracles. Neither were they the result of an Enlightenment inheritance. Hugo Grotius, that doughty seventeenth century Christian apologist, was also informed by his contemporaries that miracles do not happen. However, his reply was that if Christ were God, one would expect miracles. Indeed, "the most certain proof of Divine Providence is from miracles, and the predictions we find in histories".[396] And he adds that, had it been possible to explain away the miracles, it "would have been said so at first, by those who either professed themselves enemies of Christ when he was upon earth or of his gospel".[397] Nor would the apostles have gone to the "most exquisite death" if they had disbelieved the miracles and, most of all, the resurrection.[398] However, as Professor Chadwick observes of this period, history – assuming that there was no God capable of the miraculous – "to remain history, must seek a natural explanation of prophecy in the Old Testament".[399]

392 W.B. Scott, *Autobiographical Notes of the Life of William Bell Scott* (1892) (W. Minto (ed.)) vol.1, p.314.

393 O. Chadwick, *The Victorian Church* (1987) pt.2, p.64.

394 Remarkably, reading *Ecce Homo* led R.A. Torrey, one of the great evangelists of the next century, to a public profession of faith: see R. Martin, *R.A. Torrey: Apostle of Certainty* (1976) p.35. It also acted as a stepping stone for Secularists to turn towards Christ, see T. Larsen, *Crisis of Doubt* (2006) pp.164-165.

395 H. Ward, *Robert Elsmere* (Smith, Elder, & Co (1888)) vol.2 p.333.

396 H. Grotius, *The Truth of the Christian Religion* (1829) (Le Clerc (ed.)) p.18.

397 Ibid., p.83. Jesus had said to his critics that if they would not believe in him they should "believe the works, that you may know and understand that the Father is in me, and I in the Father". The response of his critical hearers was to try and kill him (John 10:38-39). In the late nineteenth century, critics made miracles a reason for unbelief.

398 H. Grotius, *The Truth of the Christian Religion* (1829) (Le Clerc (ed.)) p.87.

399 O. Chadwick, *The Victorian Church* (1987) pt.2, p.61.

Lord Macaulay in his five volumes of *The History of England* published between 1848 and 1861 popularised amongst historians the idea of 'inevitable progress' as the dominant driver of history. This developed as the secular competitor to that of providence and the idea that God rules the nations and lifts them up as he chooses. In his analysis of religion and historical scholarship, James Kirby observes that even in the work of Christian historians in the period from 1870 to 1920, "The idea of divine providence as a regular moral governor or as intervening dramatically in human affairs (except in the most critical circumstances) receded from view."[400] He did not attribute this to Buckle and his idea of fixed laws governing societies. Instead, Kirby attributes this in part to "the anti-rationalism of the Oxford Movement".[401] "God's actions were too mysterious, too inscrutable by fallible human reason to be known and predicted in the way which had hitherto been attempted." 'Providentialism' changed into the idea of "a mysterious force which constantly drew good out of evil, straightening out the contingencies of the world and the evil acts of man into gradual progress for the better".[402] Kirby draws us to the words of High Church historians, like Mandell Creighton, Bishop of London at the end of the nineteenth century, that the possibility of progress was due to "the divine presence which, thanks to the church, had remained in the world since the incarnation".[403]

Some writers of history directly undermined Christianity by asserting a long-standing conflict between Christianity and science. This began in 1874 when J.W. Draper, a professor of New York University – and distinguished in a number of academic fields – published the *History of the Conflict between Religion and Science*, in which he provocatively stated: "the history of Science...is a narrative of the conflict of two contending powers, the expansive force of the human intellect on one side, and the compression arising from traditionary faith and human interests on the other. No one has hitherto treated the subject from this point of view."[404] Indeed, they had not.

[400] J. Kirby, *Historians and the Church of England: Religion and Historical Scholarship, 1870-1920* (2016) p.211.
[401] Ibid., p.193.
[402] Ibid., p.195.
[403] Cited in ibid., p.208.
[404] J.W. Draper, *History of the Conflict between Religion and Science* (1875) pp.vi-vii.

Draper, brought up in Britain as a Wesleyan Methodist, specifically targeted the faith of Roman Catholics, but not that of Protestants and the Orthodox. The index of Draper's book does not mention Darwin, only one page being given to the topic of evolution. Nevertheless, he wrote: "In England and America, religious persons perceive with dismay that the intellectual basis of faith has been undermined by the spirit of the age. They prepare for the approaching disaster in the best manner they can."[405] The seed of the modern popular conception – that science and theology were in inevitable conflict – had been sown. By 1901, the *History of the Conflict between Religion and Science* reached its 23rd edition. In 1923, the Secular Society published a new edition.[406]

In 1896, A.D. White, President of Cornell University, changed the target of the attack when he published his two-volume *A History of the Warfare of Science with Theology*.[407] White thought the struggle was not between science and the Catholic Church but, like Huxley, between science and dogmatic theology. White was positive about religion, as seen in the recognition of "a Power in the universe, not ourselves, which makes for righteousness". He foretold that "the love of God and of our neighbour, will steadily grow stronger and stronger, not only in the American institutions of learning but in the world at large".[408] At the time of the twentieth anniversary of the publication of *A History of the Warfare of Science with Theology*, the British, French and Germans would be mired in the killing fields of Verdun and the Somme. The Americans joined the First World War the following year.

[405] Ibid., p.328. On the role of Draper in creating the popular view of a conflict between science and religion, see O. Chadwick, *The Secularization of the European Mind in the Nineteenth Century* (1975) pp.161-165.
[406] For a brief biography of Draper relating to *History of the Conflict between Religion and Science*, see J.R. Moore, *The Post-Darwinian Controversies* (1981) pp.20-29.
[407] For a brief biography of White relating to *A History of the Warfare of Science with Theology*, see J.R. Moore, *The Post-Darwinian Controversies* (1981) pp.29-40.
[408] A.D. White, *A History of the Warfare of Science with Theology* (1896) vol.1, p.xii.

12.1.7 *Summary*

From 1859 the intellectual attacks on Christianity, which had been building from earlier in the century, reached new levels of vigour, intensity and subtlety. The attacks involved a variety of intellectual disciplines and we have only looked at a representative selection. They often overlapped and gained strength from one another. For instance, Thomas Huxley was on friendly terms with many Unitarians, often dined with Matthew Arnold, George Eliot and John Stuart Mill, gave financial support to George Holyoake, corresponded with Spencer while on honeymoon at Tenby (the latter visited him there), taught in the schools of the Christian socialists and was "Darwin's bulldog".

The principal target of these attacks was Christianity's doctrinal and supernatural elements. The leaders of contemporary thought wanted rid of any dues to their Creator, Judge and Saviour, but most were willing to accept his moral laws. Indeed, Thomas Huxley supported Bible reading in secular schools as the means to cultivate the religious feelings necessary to sustain contemporary morality.[409] Furthermore, in these attacks religious language was often used – but with new meanings.

Nevertheless, there were also softening-up attacks on the Christian moral code, in preparation for later onslaughts – as in the case of John Stuart Mill. Perhaps, only the novelists launched a general attack on Christianity, mocking its leaders, absorbing Christians in entertainment and beginning to set up alternative codes of behaviour. Once the church was no longer sure of its doctrine, these new forms of behaviour seeped into national life and the church. However, this is to move ahead of our times. In 1874, *The Christian Observer* noted that Christians had "been shocked and pained by extravagant speculations and fierce assaults upon the existence of God, and upon the revelation of his will", but this did not surprise it. It knew that "The rapid dissemination of the Bible, unparalleled in any former age, would alone serve to stimulate antagonism...Meanwhile, in the increase of morality, in thronged churches, in habits of family devotion, in philanthropic exertion – the fruits of faith in Christ" were all visible.[410]

[409] R. Barton, "Evolution: The Whitworth Gun in Huxley's War for the Liberation of Science from Theology", in *The Wider Domain of Evolutionary Thought* (1983) (D. Oldroyd and I. Langham (eds)) pp.263 and 266-267.
[410] "Preface" to 74 *The Christian Observer for the Year* 1874 (1874) p.v.

It took until the 1890s for the new ideas and new meanings given to religious language to diffuse across the land. Religion itself was left in place and religious feelings encouraged but, if Christian doctrine was disposed of, a new religion resulted. The socialist Robert Blatchford recognised this when he wrote of a "new religion" sweeping the North of England. He thought everyone was involved, but it is

> more largely the result of the labours of Darwin, Carlyle, Ruskin, Dickens, Thoreau, and Walt Whitman...This new religion...is something much higher and much greater than a wage question, an hours' question, or a franchise question, based though it be upon those things; it is something more than a mere system of scientific government, something more than an economic theory, something more even than political or industrial liberty, though it embraces all these. It is a religion of manhood and womanhood, of sweetness and of light. As John Trevor said in the *Labour Prophet*, 'It has not been to a new economic theory merely that these converts have been introduced. It has been to a new life. Their eyes shine with the gladness of a new birth'.[411]

Blatchford went on to "Contrast the new religion with the old. The old religion obeys half the command: 'Thou shalt love the Lord thy God with all thy heart, and thy neighbour as thyself.' It stops short before it comes to its neighbour. The new religion begins at its neighbour, though it does not necessarily end there."[412]

The key to passing-off the new religion for the old was to accept as the golden rule – rather than as the silver rule – the tenet that "you shall love your neighbour as yourself". The British were generally too morally sensitive to move – yet – from that axiom. However, a nation with a vigorous and united church would have better resisted the passing off of morality as religion, but the church, as we will see, was divided. Once the love of man replaced the love of God as the central doctrine of Christianity, a different Christianity emerged; ironically, one lacking in moral vigour. Only the more theologically attuned saw the significance of the difference. Confusion and lukewarmness spread. Those who have

[411] R. Blatchford, *The New Religion* (1898) p.3.
[412] Ibid., p.6.

examined the death of "moral Britain" discern its origins in the last years of the nineteenth century.[413]

[413] C. Davies, *The Strange Death of Moral Britain* (2004) p.xiii.

13

DOCTRINAL DISSENSION WITHIN THE CHURCHES

13.1 Calvinism and orthodoxy under attack

The leaders of the revival of 1859 were Calvinistic; for example, Spurgeon drew great crowds in London – and Brownlow North stirred Scotland and Ireland. Contemporary observers commented: "Calvinism... has been used in our day, and in our land by the great head of the church".[414] But orthodox doctrine, especially Calvinism, had antagonists within the churches; and in the years leading up to, and especially after, 1859, encouraged by the outside attacks on doctrine, they redoubled their efforts. In a fine example of psychological warfare, everything that the evangelicals did was wrong. For example, in 1860, one opponent argued that the Church could never again "lead a grand attack on vice, and folly, and worldliness" while a "large proportion" of her clergy were animated by evangelical principles;[415] while another took almost the opposite tack. He referred to the decay of Church evangelicals, while acknowledging their lingering influence on religious ideas and on Church life.[416] Such a valediction for them, including their Calvinistic members, was premature. Troubled times lay ahead, but also great achievements.

[414] See generally C.H. Spurgeon, *Revival Year Sermons* (1996) p.15. See also R.W. Dale, *The Evangelical Revival* (1880) p.195.

[415] "The English Evangelical Clergy", in 3 *Macmillan's Magazine* (1860) p.119.

[416] M. Pattison, "Tendencies of Religious Thought in England, 1688-1750", in *Essays and Reviews* (1860) p.257.

13.2 Weaknesses in the defences of the Established Churches

The outside attacks on orthodoxy had significant impact because many ministers were unconverted. In the first half of the nineteenth century, the standing of the Church drew into its ministerial ranks the unconverted, as the number of clergy expanded from 11,006 in 1841 to 19,043 in 1871.[417] Hugh Stowell noted that many clergy "had avowed themselves believers in the revelation of God" while being "hollow at heart and unfixed and unsettled in conviction".[418] Leslie Stephen – who was ordained in 1859 and who later renounced holy orders and became a fierce critic of Christianity – was probably one of these.[419] In 1869, J.C. Ryle, later the first Bishop of Liverpool, commenting on the passage in John's Gospel[420] where Jesus likens himself to a door to God's sheep-pen, wrote: "Thousands of ordained men in the present day know nothing whatever about Christ, except his name. They have not entered 'the door' themselves, and they are unable to show it to others... Unconverted ministers are the dry rot of the Church. When 'the blind lead the blind', both must fall into the ditch."[421]

Another problem area was that the theological training of ministers undermined, rather than energised, faith. Daniel Wilson noted, at the Islington Clerical Conference of 1863, that the "peculiarity" of the times was scepticism proceeding from within the pale of the Established Church.[422] At Oxford,[423] the more sceptical the view of Scripture, the better the Common Room received it. At Cambridge, many young men who went up intending to seek ordination were deterred from doing so "by the doubts thrown into their minds, respecting the canonical

[417] T.M. Macdonald, "How to Reach Working Men", in *Homiletical and Pastoral Lectures* (1879) p.386.

[418] "Islington Clerical Meeting", in *The Record*, 19 January 1863, p.4.

[419] Q. Bell, *Virginia Woolf* (1990) pp.8-9.

[420] John 10:1-9.

[421] J.C. Ryle, *Expository Thoughts on John* (1987) vol.2, p.197. Phoebe Palmer had a story of a curate converted by one of her helpers. The curate, having started preaching the new birth, was promptly dismissed by his rector, see Dr and Mrs Palmer, *Four Years in the Old World* (1865) pp.404-405.

[422] "Islington Clerical Meeting", in *The Record*, 19 January 1863, p.4.

[423] For the evangelicals at Oxford in this period, see J.S. Reynolds, *The Evangelicals at Oxford 1735-1871* (1975).

Scriptures".[424] At Oxford, by the mid-1870s, it was said that any university student winning an academic prize and contemplating Holy Orders was considered a "freak".[425]

Some ministers made no attempt to lead anyone anywhere. Philip Snowden, the future Labour Cabinet Minister, wrote of the Anglican church where he grew up in the 1870s, that it had

> no Sunday school...and no church choir. Mr Blaydon [the rector] used to watch from one of the windows of the vestry to see if any congregation was coming, and if no one turned up on the stroke of eleven he made his way through the back door of the church down into the woods below. If a person happened to come, the vicar would meet him at the entrance and say: 'Well now, we are not having much of a congregation this morning. Perhaps you would like a very short service?'[426]

J.C. Ryle, however, suggests that, by the late 1860s, shooting and fox hunting parsons, and those who were idle, were fewer than one hundred years before, although extant.[427]

In Scotland, the disruption of 1843 and the need for the Established Church to replenish its ministerial ranks opened up opportunities for a revived moderatism – paralleling the Broad Church movement in England – to seep in along with High Church Sacramentalism. In permitting the latter, the Church of Scotland looked to adopt the practices of the Church of England to help buttress itself against the onslaught of the Liberation Society[428] and disestablishment. All the same, in some places, the disruption energised the churches in Scotland and, in the early 1860s, a visitor from England thought it led to two ministers – where there had been one – in a parish "both teaching pretty much the same

[424] "Islington Clerical Meeting", *The Record*, 19 January 1863, p.4. The liberals claimed few of the abler university students went into the Church of England because of widespread disbelief in the Church of England's formal view of the authority of Scripture, see J.W. Colenso, "Preface" to *The Pentateuch and Book of Joshua Critically Examined* (1862) (second edition) pt.1, p.xxiii.
[425] R. Horton, *An Autobiography* (1917) p.31.
[426] P.V. Snowden, *An Autobiography* (1934) vol.1, p.31.
[427] J.C. Ryle, *Christian Leaders of the Eighteenth Century* (1997) pp.17 and 19-20.
[428] J. Macleod, *Scottish Theology* (1974) pp.298-306.

truths".[429] The same visitor "was also surprised to find so much Bible knowledge, especially among the working classes". He attributed this to seeing "in the little shop windows the children's lesson-book, with the 'A, B, C' on one page, and a short catechism on the opposite side".[430]

13.3 New doctrines to win the people for Christ

Many evangelicals looked to a traditional spiritual revival[431] to send the church out into the highways and byways and to bring the lost under the preaching of the gospel. Possibly because a traditional revival did not continue after the years around 1859 or come again, Arminianism became stronger,[432] or possibly the all-pervading assault on Calvinism made Arminianism a more appealing dwelling place.[433] Towards the end of the century, as society turned from the gospel, evangelicals sought a new weapon to break down the opposition and found it in an emphasis on doctrines related to the Holy Spirit, the power behind revival. The first signs of incipient Pentecostalism became evident.

For others, the failure to reach the masses was used to justify the development of three distinctive theological perspectives – those of the theological liberal, the Ritualist and the Christian socialist. The assumption underlying each of them was that the reason why some educated people – and many of the multiplying working class – did not attend church, was because the modern mind could not accept the orthodox view of Scripture and the morality it taught with regard to "eternal punishment, hell, the atonement, and damnation for unbelievers". To get the people back to church, each of these groups argued that long-established doctrines and practices needed updating, modifying, or dropping. Particularly to ministers, the prospect of no longer having to deal with the loudly expressed views of contemporary sceptics made this view very attractive, as did the popular theory "that the Church belongs to the nation, not the nation to the Church".[434] That the Pharisees and Romans at the time of Christ – and many others after them – had not

[429] W. Haslam, *"Yet Not I"* (N.D.) pp.152-153.
[430] Ibid., p.157.
[431] W. Arthur, *May We Hope for a Great Revival?* (1859) p.12.
[432] R.W. Dale, *The Evangelical Revival* (1880) pp.194-195.
[433] The growing numbers of Brethren among evangelicals defused tensions in this area.
[434] "Preface" to 60 *The Christian Observer for the Year 1860* (1860) p.v.

believed in the miracles, the prophecies and other Christian doctrines, did not occur to the critics or those willing to compromise biblical truth. Nor did the critics concern themselves with whether the mass of the population had ever been enthusiastic churchgoers. As had been noted by Bogue and Bennett – writing of the impact of the Arian controversy on the Dissenting congregations in the early church – "A religion from God can never be agreeable to the depraved heart of man".[435] The truth of this sentiment was now to be seen across the denominations.

The differences between the new theological parties broadly hinged on their attitudes to human learning, old and new, but all rejected Scripture alone as the guide to faith. The theological liberal looked to modern thinking and morality to refresh the people with Christian truths.[436] Robert Horton wrote: "relentless criticism on the Bible...releases the living waters which abound in the Book, waters which are often bound by the rigid and deadening traditions of interpretation".[437] The Ritualist looked to the ritual of Rome and the medieval past to draw the lost to church.[438] The Christian socialist sought Christian influence in the working classes "through a re-statement of Christian principles in terms relevant to contemporary social relations and problems".[439] He wanted to make Christianity "relevant" by building the kingdom of God on earth. Christian socialists might be Arminian, theologically liberal or Ritualist. However, these groupings were only the most vigorous groupings within the churches. Members of the old High Church party[440] remained and some, like Thomas Stuart Lyle Vogan – with his *The True Doctrine of the Eucharist* – made a widely-valued contribution.[441]

[435] D. Bogue and J. Bennett, *History of Dissenters, from the Revolution in 1688, to the Year 1808* (1810) vol.3, p.250.

[436] For an example of a bishop holding this view, see J.W. Colenso, "Preface" to *The Pentateuch and Book of Joshua Critically Examined* (1862) (second edition) pt.1, p.xxvi.

[437] R. Horton, *An Autobiography* (1917) p.95.

[438] H.W. Webb-Peploe, "The Church of England", in *Our Churches and Why We Belong to Them* (1898) pp.369-370.

[439] R. Harrison, *Before the Socialists. Studies in Labour and Politics, 1861-1881* (1965) p.15.

[440] See also J.H. Rigg, *The Present Position of Christianity and the Christian Faith in this Country* (1878) p.9.

[441] H.C.G. Moule, *The Evangelical School in the Church of England* (1901) p.52.

13.4 The growth of theological liberalism and the inability to discipline
Through "the fearless advocacy of...a mere handful of men like-minded",[442] the small Broad Church of the early nineteenth century, with uncertain beliefs, expanded in the late nineteenth century into the theologically liberal wing of the church. Perhaps, in part, this was because – as John Angell James and the American William Patton discussed – revivals risked "spurious conversions" and of welcoming to the church persons who have "mistaken the temporary excitement of natural feeling for the spirit of true piety".[443] Certainly, some applied to theology the new ideas appearing in other areas of learning. This might lead theology off in a number of different directions. Others, with a philosophical turn of mind, thought they discerned a spirit of progress at work in humanity. If other disciplines, such as science, could progress then, by analogy, so must theology.[444] For a few, the rising status of the scientific method meant that every theological doctrine had to be independently verified and, unless personally verified, it could not be accepted.[445] This was fine for a theologian with time on his hands but, for others, working out the creeds from scratch led to uncertainty.[446] Without the creeds, people lost their theological moorings and many drifted spiritually. Everything was up for discussion, but everything, the theological liberals said, was done in the pursuit of the truth – and those seeking it had nothing to worry about. In the 1860s, some evangelicals saw the attractions of the new theology which was "flattering to intellectual pride". However, they did not "apprehend any serious difficulty in coping with this new form of infidelity." It was "amazingly superficial". Nevertheless, they expected it "to spread widely for a time". What they dreaded was the "new theology" reducing Christianity "to a mere scheme of generous

[442] R. Farrar, *The Life of Frederic William Farrar* (1905) p.113.

[443] R.W. Dale, *The Life and Letters of John Angell James* (1861) p.252. See also "American Revivals", 28 *The Christian Observer for the Year 1828* (1829) pp.473-476.

[444] D.W. Bebbington, *The Dominance of Evangelicalism* (2005) p.125.

[445] See generally H. McLeod, *Religion and Society in England, 1850-1914* (1996) pp.182-193.

[446] J. Marchant, *Dr John Clifford* (1924) p.xiv and R.W. Dale, *The Evangelical Revival* (1880) pp.273-278. The attack on creeds also came from the opposite wing of the church through the Brethren: see J.C. Ryle, "The Importance of the Clear Enunciation of Dogma", in *Be Thou a Faithful Dispenser of the Word of God* (1878) p.86.

philanthropy" which could "soon be thrown aside entirely".[447]

13.4.1 *Seven Church ministers and Essays and Reviews*

The new ideas crystallised in a book written by seven Anglican clergy who attempted to illustrate the advantages of free and honest discussion of "religious and moral truth". In March 1860, *Essays and Reviews* was published. By 1869, it was into its 13th edition, with 22,500 copies of its voluminous pages in print. In comparison, by 1876, Darwin's *Origin of Species* had sold 16,000 copies.[448] *Essays and Reviews* contained seven essays, written (the note to the reader at the front of the book asserts) by seven authors in "entire independence of each other, and without concert or comparison". All the same, contemporaries noted – and recent research confirms[449] – a plan to the work. One essay introduced German higher criticism; a second advocated a new hermeneutic; others questioned the function of prophecy and the historicity of miracles; and another rejected the linear view of history in favour of cycles. There was also an essay questioning the literal meaning of Genesis and one reformulating the relationship between Church and state which advocated getting rid of the Thirty-nine Articles. As it has been observed, "taken together" they were "an affront to the Establishment doctrines of Church and state alike".[450] The book's scepticism encouraged Nonconformists to urge ending the funding of the Church out of public revenues.[451] The Wesleyan *The Methodist Recorder* dismissed it as "elaborately-woven sophistries".[452]

The vision sketched out in *Essays and Reviews* suggested that what Doddridge had thought impossible in *The Rise and Progress of Religion in the Soul* (which so influenced William Wilberforce) was about to happen. Doddridge had suggested that men delayed turning to God in the hope that God might alter the method by which he pardoned and

[447] "Preface" to 60 *The Christian Observer for the Year 1860* (1860) p.v.
[448] R.M. Young, *The Impact of Darwin on Conventional Thought, in the Victorian Crisis of Faith* (1970) p.25.
[449] "Broad Church Theology", in 60 *The Christian Observer for the Year 1860* (1860) p.376. "The Broad Church Compromise", in *Essays and Reviews: The 1860 Text and its Reading* (2000) (V. Shea and W. Whitla (eds)) p.123.
[450] Ibid.
[451] A.W.W. Dale, *The Life of R.W. Dale* (1898) p.164.
[452] "Oxford 'Essays and Reviews'", in *The Methodist Recorder, and General Christian Chronicle*, 18 April 1861 p.1.

accepted sinners. He suggested that men hoped that God would publish a new gospel, "if they will but call themselves Christians, and submit to a few external rites".[453] The learned (and liberal-leaning) Connop Thirlwall, Bishop of St David's, summarised the work as suggesting

> a National Church, without a theology, without a confession, without a creed, with no other basis of united worship than a system of universal equivocation...It proposes to attract larger congregations to our services, by extinguishing as much as possible the devotional element in them, and turning our churches into lecture-rooms, for the inculcation of ethical commonplace[s].[454]

Christianity was also to be subjective. Baden Powell concluded his essay, "On the Study of the Evidences of Christianity", with the words that "The '*reason* of the hope that is in us'…consists of such assurance as may be most satisfactory to each earnest individual inquirer's own mind."[455]

There were no new ideas in *Essays and Reviews.* The Archbishop of York commented that the arguments set out "were wont to be the weapons of the avowed adversaries of our religion".[456] Thirlwall observed: had the authors intended to revive "the speculations of Spinoza and Hume on the absolute impossibility, or incredibility of miracles", there would have been no public sensation.[457] What was new, he added, was "the character of the authors...They were ministers of a Church which aims at a definite teaching, and exacts conformity to that teaching from those whom she admits into her ministry."[458] Thirlwall also correctly foresaw two future issues. First, "The scheme...seems to exhibit an incongruity, almost amounting to direct opposition, between the means and the end. It aims at the cementing of religious unity, by

[453] P. Doddridge, *The Rise and Progress of Religion in the Soul* (1825) p.31.
[454] C. Thirlwall, "The Charge of October 1863", in *Essays and Reviews: The 1860 Text and its Reading* (2000) (V. Shea and W. Whitla (eds)) p.647.
[455] Author's italics. B. Powell, "On the Study of the Evidences of Christianity", in *Essays and Reviews: The 1860 Text and its Reading* (2000) (V. Shea and W. Whitla (eds)) p.261.
[456] "The Archbishop of York on '*Essays and Reviews*'", in *The Derby Mercury*, 17 April 1861.
[457] C. Thirlwall, "The Charge of October 1863", in *Essays and Reviews: The 1860 Text and its Reading* (2000) (V. Shea and W. Whitla (eds)) p.644.
[458] Ibid., p.643.

a process apparently tending to the most complete disintegration of all religious community." Secondly, "there is...no room for any difference of opinion in the audience".[459]

Essays and Reviews met a host of rebuttals, including two substantial works, one edited by William Wilberforce's son Samuel, the Bishop of Oxford[460] and the other edited by William Thomson, the Archbishop of York.[461] Its principal challenge to orthodoxy lay in its call for a "free handling" of the Bible because, it was stated, the Bible was not sourced from the divine but from the words of men. Such a view would have surprised the apostles Peter and Paul. However, in the years preceding the publication of *Essays and Reviews*, such a development had perhaps been prepared for, as many spoke "of poets as prophets, and of men of genius as inspired". As one preacher observed, "The tendency of such perversion of language is – and they must know it – to disparage the word of God, and to reduce it to the level of ordinary writings."[462] Furthermore, in the authors of *Essays and Reviews*, contemporaries detected "a common object and purpose"[463] – to question whether God had really taught men anything that they could not otherwise have found out. In doing so, they suggested – as Lord Brougham had, in his *A Discourse of Natural Theology* – that the creation could be examined to discern God's will for his creatures. This was just at the time that Darwin's work was encouraging men to give up on natural theology. It was not good timing – and Lord Brougham's work had not been found convincing.

Neither the Archbishop of Canterbury, the evangelical octogenarian John Sumner,[464] nor the bench of bishops, liked the book. The difficult issue was what to do about it. Some, such as Renn Dickson Hampden, the Bishop of Hereford, himself suspected of error in the 1830s, thought it "a question of Christianity or no Christianity".[465] In the end, an Episcopal Manifesto was published by the Archbishop of Canterbury in

459 Ibid., p.647.
460 S. Wilberforce, *Replies to Essays and Reviews* (1862).
461 W. Thomson, *Aids to Faith* (1862).
462 Stowell, "Inspiration", in *"Things that Accompany Salvation"* (1858) p.2.
463 G.S. Denison, *Analysis of Essays and Reviews* (1861) pp.2-3 and R.J. Cooper, *A Brief Defence of the Bible against the Attacks of Rationalistic Infidelity* (1861) p.4.
464 Died 6 September 1862.
465 "The Episcopal Manifesto", in *Essays and Reviews: The 1860 Text and its Reading* (2000) (V. Shea and W. Whitla (eds)) p.648.

The Times, to which the Archbishop of York and the bench of bishops appended agreement. Sumner stated that he could not understand how the opinions expressed in *Essays and Reviews* "can be held consistently with an honest subscription to the formularies of our Church, with many of the fundamental doctrines of which they appear to us essentially at variance".[466] The clergy were, after all, required to subscribe "willingly, and from my heart" to, amongst other things, the Thirty-nine Articles. Samuel Wilberforce thought that to put forward the views set out in *Essays and Reviews* was impossible for honest men bound by "voluntary obligations to teach the Christian revelation as the truth of God".[467] He added – in a prophetic utterance – "if such matters are admitted by us to be open...we shall leave to the next generation the fatal legacy of universal scepticism".[468]

However, censuring *Essays and Reviews* was not enough. To stop others adopting its approach, disciplinary action was required. Sumner, involved with the Gorham decision a few years earlier (which had permitted clergy to reject unconditional regeneration at baptism), had witnessed the intricacies and dangers of the legal process. He refused to issue proceedings. However, others in the Church hierarchy prosecuted two contributors to *Essays and Reviews*. The resulting case was a disaster. Although, at first instance, the two offenders were suspended for one year in February 1864, on appeal the Judicial Committee of the Privy Council cleared them. The Privy Council could only consider whether the few extracts from the book put before the court at first instance, were contrary to that which is, by law, established to be the doctrine of the Church of England. Although some of the extracts looked suspect, the essayists had elsewhere been careful to say the right thing. It was the technique of speaking both ways. It undermined orthodoxy, and yet

[466] Conveniently found in ibid., pp.649-650. See also "The School of the Essayists, and the Church of England", in 61 *The Christian Observer for the Year 1861* (1861) pp.29-38.

[467] A criticism made by others: G.S. Denison, *Analysis of Essays and Reviews* (1861) p.73.

[468] S. Wilberforce, *Replies to Essays and Reviews* (1862) p.xv. Leslie Stephen attributed his gleeful narrative of the scepticism of the eighteenth century to Pattison's essay on the "Tendencies of Religious Thought in England from 1688 to 1750", in *Essays and Reviews*, see L. Stephen, *History of English Thought in the Eighteenth Century* (1876) vol.1, p.v.

made prosecution difficult. A third essayist was also prosecuted, but the action was thrown out on procedural grounds.

Other measures were tried to distance the Church of England from the book. A protest against specified ideas in *Essays and Reviews* was circulated among the clergy and signed by approximately 8,500 of them. This, although under half of the clergy, was a high proportion for such a declaration.[469] In 1864, the Convocation of Canterbury condemned it, although less than half its members voted in the Upper House. That year a declaration was produced and circulated among the clergy maintaining, "without reserve or qualification", the inspiration and divine authority of the Bible and teaching that the punishment of the "cursed" and the life of the righteous is everlasting.[470] It obtained a greater number of signatures than the earlier protest of the clergy. Its circulation "consolidated" the relationship between Pusey and his cousin Lord Shaftesbury, from different wings of the Church, as they sought unity against the common enemy.[471]

[469] "The Protest of Clergy", in *Essays and Reviews: The 1860 Text and its Reading* (2000) (V. Shea and W. Whitla (eds)) pp.654-655. Some refused to sign – not necessarily because they accepted the contentious statements in *Essays and Reviews* but, (1) because persecution encouraged further heresy (F.D. Maurice's view concerning Jowett's article, which he deplored) or (2) to in order to preserve the "liberty of free discussion" (G.J. Wild, *A Brief Defence of the "Essays and Reviews"* (1861) p.6). The evangelical Bishop of Winchester, the brother of the Archbishop of Canterbury, observed that "I prize, in common with the memorialists, the liberty our Church has ever allowed in the fair interpretation of the Holy Scriptures" while deploring "the abuse of this latitude". He saw the memorial as a stimulant to more earnest watchfulness in the gospel of Christ and rejoiced that his diocese was "free from the taint of opinions subversive of the very foundations of our faith", see G.H. Sumner, *Life of Charles Richard Sumner* (1876) p.401.

[470] "Declaration on the Inspiration of the Word of God", in *Essays and Reviews: The 1860 Text and its Reading* (2000) (V. Shea and W. Whitla (eds)) pp.660-665 and O. Chadwick, *The Victorian Church* (1987) pt.2, p.84. Jowett, for contributing to *Essays and Reviews*, was refused, until 1865, an increment in his professional salary. Baden Powell who, in his contribution to *Essays and Reviews,* questioned the reality of miracles – and commended as "masterly", Darwin's *Origin of Species* for its exposition "of the grand principle of the self-evolving powers of nature" – died in June 1860, see B. Powell, "On the Study of the Evidences of Christianity", in *Essays and Reviews: The 1860 Text and its Reading* (2000) (V. Shea and W. Whitla (eds)) p.258. Otherwise, Baden Powell would have become "the first outspoken theological supporter of Darwin's theory" of evolution, P. Corsi, *Science and Religion* (1988) p.8.

[471] "Declaration on the Inspiration of the Word of God", in *Essays and Reviews: The 1860 Text and its Reading* (2000) (V. Shea and W. Whitla (eds)) p.661.

Years later, one of the contributors, Frederick Temple, became Archbishop of Canterbury (1896-1902). Though Temple's essay on education was itself not so controversial – and he withdrew it in 1870 – his association with theological liberalism illustrates that it was soon to be no bar to ecclesiastical preferment. In understanding theological development, it should be observed that Temple had been a pupil and, later, friend of Alexander Campbell Tait. The friendship hit a rocky patch when Tait, as Bishop of London, signed the Episcopal Manifesto that condemned *Essays and Reviews*. Temple regarded Tait's action, in signing the Manifesto, as "treachery".[472] Yet the friendship was restored. Later, Tait was a member of the Privy Council in the *Essays and Reviews* case that acquitted the defendants. He was the only clergyman in the majority, and the judgment bore his annotations. Tait was Archbishop of Canterbury when Temple, amid much opposition, was raised to the see of Exeter, on the way to becoming Archbishop of Canterbury. Temple's son, William, was Archbishop of Canterbury in the 1940s.

13.4.2 *F.D. Maurice and theological liberalism*

After F.D. Maurice vacated his chair at King's College – for denying the existence of hell – he became the rector of St Peter's Vere Street, off Oxford Street. An unsuccessful petition was launched by *The Record* to prevent his appointment. The defeat that *The Record* suffered in this matter, Maurice's son wrote later, was "so crushing that virtually from this moment it ceased to be a serious power for harm".[473]

At St Peter's Vere Street, Maurice preached, on 9th September 1860, two sermons intended to demonstrate his commitment to the Prayer Book and the Thirty-nine Articles; they were immediately published. To *The Christian Observer*'s reviewer, they failed to achieve their aim. The reviewer thought that there was "a strange obliquity in [Maurice's] mind, which hinders his perception of the true meaning of the simplest propositions when expressed in the plainest language".[474] Perhaps the

[472] "Reception and Response", in *Essays and Reviews: The 1860 Text and its Reading* (2000) (V. Shea and W. Whitla (eds)) pp.41-42.
[473] *The Life of Frederick Denison Maurice* (1884) (F. Maurice (ed.)) vol.2, p.371.
[474] "Mr Maurice's Two Sermons", in 60 *The Christian Observer for the Year 1860* (1860) p.788. Maurice's incomprehensibility was a widely held criticism, see "The Religious Weakness of Protestantism", in 13 *The Westminster Review* (1858) p.152.

greatest failing, in the reviewer's view, was Maurice's failure to tell his hearers that they are "by nature dead, dead in trespasses and sins".[475] Maurice preached that all men were children of God in some way, through the Spirit, but he gave no indication of how this was so. *The Christian Observer* thought he was a universalist, omitting the need to have a personal faith in the atonement. Its reviewer commented on his sermons that

> the system which is evolved is far too agreeable to the pride and corruption of the hearts of men, to allow us to hope that he will not have many followers and many triumphs. That he will turn many to righteousness, we cannot hope. He does not set forth Christ as the end of the law for righteousness, and his ministry will therefore be unproductive and unblessed. It is a return to the Latitudinarianism which burst in upon the Church of England just one hundred and fifty years ago. It will probably be followed in time by the same results; first Arianism, then scepticism, then an age of shameless infidelity.[476]

The same November issue of *The Christian Observer* began with an article entitled "The Atonement and its Repudiators". It thought that a belief, deemed secure for 50 years past, was now in question.

13.4.3 *Bishop Colenso and The Pentateuch and the Book of Joshua Critically Examined*

In 1862 a fresh challenge to Anglican orthodoxy arose, when Bishop John Colenso, a friend of F.D. Maurice, published the first part of *The Pentateuch and Book of Joshua Critically Examined.* He made use of Samuel Davidson's earlier work and, being a bishop, "he had access to a wider circle of readers, and his influence was all the more extensive".[477] In the twentieth century, certain bishops achieved a degree of notoriety for their beliefs, or rather lack of them; Bishop Colenso of Natal is their forerunner.

[475] "Mr Maurice's Two Sermons", in 60 *The Christian Observer for the Year 1860* (1860) p.786.
[476] Author's capitals. Ibid., p.790.
[477] *The Autobiography and Diary of Samuel Davidson* (1899) (A.J. Davidson (ed.)) p.82.

Colenso's aim was ambitious. He called for an end to teaching that the Bible is infallibly true in matters of common history and "not to look for the inspiration of the Holy One" in the pages of the "Sacred Book".[478] A modern commentator notes that "Among other startling statements", Colenso in his book "declared that little if any of the Pentateuch was written in the Mosaic age, that Moses may never have lived, that Joshua is a purely mythical figure, that the Books of Chronicles are fictitious, and that Christ's knowledge of history in speaking of Moses was not more than of any educated Jew of his day and might be faulty".[479] The evangelical T.R. Birks noted in his criticism of the volume that Colenso "quietly assumed that that general overthrow of faith in the authority and truth of Scripture, which a thousand adversaries have failed to effect, from Celsus and Porphyry to Paine and Voltaire, will at length be attained, at least in England, by this solitary home thrust from episcopal hands".[480]

Nevertheless, *The Pentateuch* was a publishing triumph. Colenso understood his market; there was already an inarticulate distrust of the authority of Scripture.[481] On 21 November 1862, after several impressions had already flowed from the presses, Colenso penned the preface to a second edition. This enabled Colenso the opportunity "to establish...still more decisively", some of his positions – the "sole object being to arrive at truth".[482]

The Pentateuch was not a great work of scholarship. Owen Chadwick, writing long after Colenso's passing, observed that "He had no sense of history, no idea how to criticise documents, no wide reading, and no profundity of mind."[483] At the time an enormous number of books, pamphlets and articles were written in response. Birks wondered how Colenso could make "a confident prophecy that in six or seven years

[478] J.W. Colenso, *The Pentateuch and Book of Joshua Critically Examined* (1862) (second edition) pt.1, p.152.

[479] K.S. Latourette, *A History of Christianity* (1975) p.1176.

[480] T.R. Birks, *The Exodus of Israel* (1863) pp.iv-v.

[481] J.W. Colenso, "Preface" to *The Pentateuch and Book of Joshua Critically Examined* (1862) (second edition) pt.1, p.xxiii.

[482] J.W. Colenso, "Preface to the Second Edition" of *The Pentateuch and Book of Joshua Critically Examined* (1862) (second edition) pt.1, p.iv.

[483] O. Chadwick, *The Victorian Church* (1987) pt.2, p.91. Some are more supportive of Colenso, see P.T. Marsh, *The Victorian Church in Decline* (1969) p.38.

faith in the Pentateuch will be dying out from the minds of educated men".[484] *The Record* circulated a piece from *The Bulwark* to the effect that Bishop Colenso was giving his flock "deadly poison" and should be removed.[485] Bishop Colenso was deposed by a synod of bishops in Cape Town. Again, the matter ended up in the Privy Council. Again, the church establishment lost. Those who had given up on orthodoxy celebrated. John Ruskin gave to the British Museum a diamond of 139 carats, for which he paid £1,000. He stipulated that it was to be called the Colenso Diamond.

This was not the end of the matter. In a pointer as to how future Lambeth Conferences might be used, at the very first in 1867 there was an attempt to publicly condemn Colenso. Indeed, the conference was called when the Canadian bishops objected to Colenso's teaching. The response was not clear and loud. No condemnation was given by the conference, but only in a private paper circulated among the bishops. Only just over half of the bishops invited attended. During the 1875 Moody mission to London, prayers were said "for careless and godless clergy".[486] Colenso penned new parts to his *The Pentateuch*, until 1878. The following year the seventh part, of 528 pages, plus a 28 page preface and a 216 page appendix, was published.

In earlier periods, when there had been doctrinal disputes within the church, as distinct from those outside, the issue had been over the right interpretation of the Bible and its proper grammatical construction. Now, the issue was the denial of the Bible's authority. If a different source of authority was proposed, a different religion was emerging.

13.4.4 *F.W. Farrar and hell*

F.W. Farrar had been a pupil of F.D. Maurice[487] and was a member of the Royal Society, having been nominated by Charles Darwin. In 1870, he delivered the Hulsean lectures – to strengthen "faith in the great truths of Christianity".[488] His initial priority was to challenge those who insisted that the impossibility of miracles "needs no demonstration".[489] In

[484] T.R. Birks, *The Exodus of Israel* (1863) p.iii.
[485] "Church Discipline and the Colenso Volume", in *The Record*, 5 January 1863, p.4.
[486] "The Revivalists", in *The Times*, 3 April 1875.
[487] R. Farrar, *The Life of Frederic William Farrar* (1905) pp.23-26 and 28.
[488] F.W. Farrar, *The Witness of History to Christ* (1892) p.vi.
[489] Ibid., p.15.

1874, as Headmaster of Marlborough College, his publisher asked him to write *The Life of Christ*. It was an uncontroversial sketch of the life of Christ – the "work of a believer",[490] he wrote – and obtained a vast circulation.[491] The miracles and the general authenticity of the Gospel narratives were all affirmed. It converted at least one Russian Jew.[492]

The next stage in Farrar's life was more controversial. In 1877, shortly after arriving as a canon of Westminster Abbey, he there undermined the relevancy of hell in a series of sermons. Since 1846, when the Congregationalist Edward White published *Life in Christ*, a large number of writers had subscribed to the conditional immortality of the soul. In 1876, White published a new version of his earlier work, which he had expanded and entirely rewritten, excepting a few pages.[493] He noted that, in the meantime, his "burden of evil theological repute had been somewhat lightened". In the same year, a sketch of the leading Congregationalist preacher Thomas Binney appeared. Its author, Henry Allon, was clear that Binney did not believe in the eternal torment of the wicked, but propounded no alternative theory.[494]

Farrar's sermons were taken down, in shorthand – against Farrar's will – and sold by thousands in unauthorised form. In 1878, they were published as *Eternal Hope*. The sermons awakened "an echo throughout the world", as Farrar poetically wrote in the "Preface to the Thirtieth Thousand copy".[495] Farrar wanted to remove "the greatest of all stumbling-blocks from the path of the faith" by, amongst other things,

[490] F.W. Farrar, *The Life of Christ* (1894) p.vii.

[491] So many were the copies sold, that his publisher voluntarily gave him a sum four times greater than that originally agreed, which was not small – but Farrar – did not think it enough and a public controversy ensued, see "Farrar and his Publishers", in *The Spectator*, 18 October 1890 p.10. For his defence, see R. Farrar, *The Life of Frederic William Farrar* (1905) p.196.

[492] Ibid., p.307.

[493] E. White, *Life in Christ* (1876) pp.vi-vii. See also R. Tudur Jones, *Congregationalism in England 1662-1962* (1962) pp.265-266. White, by 1882, was sufficiently reputable to be the Nonconformist representative at a symposium on how to reach non-churchgoers, organised by the evangelical *The Christian Monthly and Family Treasury*, see E. White, "The Non-Church Going: How Can Our Churches Reach Them?", in *The Christian Monthly and Family Treasury* (1882) pp.75-77.

[494] H. Allon, "Biographical and Critical Sketch", in T. Binney, *Sermons Preached in the King's Weigh House Chapel, London. 1829-1869* (1875) (H. Allon (ed.)) p.liv.

[495] F.W. Farrar, "Preface to the Thirtieth Thousand", in *Eternal Hope* (1892) p.vii.

restoring "the widespread, ancient reasonable" belief in an intermediate state in which the "vast majority...may still be reached by God's mercy beyond the grave".[496] He also thought that a God of love would not allow eternal punishment and that the fire of hell was metaphorical. The contemporary teaching on hell, in his view, "caused infidelity to some, temptation to others, and misery without virtue to most".[497] In penning these words, Farrar may have been thinking of Charles Darwin whose funeral sermon, for the nave service at Darwin's burial at Westminster Abbey, he preached.[498] The decisive offensive, which had been in preparation for the previous 20 years, against the church's teaching on hell had been launched.[499]

In the year that Farrar preached his famous sermons against a literal hell at Westminster Abbey, J.C. Ryle preached, at Peterborough Cathedral, against the growing idea that punishment was not eternal. The theory, he argued, was "pleasant to flesh and blood",[500] but he observed that Jesus, St John (the apostle of love) and St Paul had all taught the eternal reality of hell – as did the Prayer Book, the Catechism, the Burial service and orthodox divines down the ages. He foresaw that if "there is heaven at last, or, at any rate, no eternal punishment, even for those who live and die in sin", no young man would turn from his "riotous living".[501] The attack on the eternity of hell, Ryle argued, was also an attack on the eternity of reward. The two were impossible to separate. After Ryle later read Farrar's contribution to the debate about hell, he saw nothing new. When he published his sermon, he added a postscript

[496] See ibid., pp.xxxv and xxvi-xxviii. The idea of a second bite at the cherry – post-death repentance – was not new, see J. Smith, "The Poor Penitent", in *Essex Dove* (1629) pp.50-52 – but now it was believed by church leaders.
[497] F.W. Farrar, "Preface to the First Edition", in *Eternal Hope* (1892) p.lxi. See also E. White, *Life in Christ* (1876) p.72.
[498] See R. Farrar, *The Life of Frederic William Farrar* (1905) pp.109-110. Farrar's son enumerated the elder Mill and Sir Leslie Stephen as others who turned from Christianity, because of the doctrine of hell, ibid., p.264. Sir George Stokes the scientist and Christian also thought that the doctrine of hell made "so many men sceptics". He solved the problem by adopting the view of conditional immortality of the soul, see generally G.G. Stokes, *Conditional Immortality* (1897) p.86.
[499] On the evolving attitude to hell, see generally G. Rowell, *Hell and the Victorians* (1974) and M. Wheeler, *Heaven, Hell, and the Victorians* (1994).
[500] J.C. Ryle, *Thoughts on Immortality* (1883) p.30.
[501] Ibid.

to respond further to Farrar's arguments.[502] He also warned his readers to "Beware of manufacturing a God of your own – a God who is all mercy, but not just – a God who is all love, but not holy – a God who has a heaven for everybody, but a hell for none – a God who can allow good and bad to be side by side in time, but will make no distinction between good and bad in eternity. Such a God is an idol of your own."[503] In 1896, Ryle's sermon was being printed as a tract, entitled *Eternity!*, to be given away. It could be purchased by the dozen.[504]

Many other divines contested Farrar, including the Tractarian, Dr Pusey.[505] However, Farrar understood which way the clergy were thinking. In his preface to *Eternal Hope*, dated Christmas Eve 1877, he wrote that though his view was not that of the majority, he was "unalterably convinced" that the view he had professed would be the "deeply-treasured belief of another generation of the English clergy".[506] Indeed already, in 1876, at St Michael and St Mary Magdalen Easthampstead, Berkshire, a stained glass window of the Last Judgment was fitted in which "Figures rise from their graves to eternal life; no one seems to be condemned."[507] At the Islington Clerical Conference of 1878, J.C. Ryle referred to the "misty system" of theology emanating from extreme Broad Churchmen, and their incessant "strange and loose utterances" targeted at the inspiration of the Bible, the atonement, the sacrifice and death of Christ, the incarnation, the miracles, satan, the Holy Spirit, and future punishment. They seemed to regard "all religions as more or less true".[508] If there was no judgment, or hell, it was understandable that the attitude in London, in 1882, towards devout Christians, became: "You like religion; it gives you comfort and enjoyment, and therefore you are perfectly right in cultivating it. We

[502] Ibid., pp.52-71.
[503] Ibid., p.83.
[504] J.C. Ryle, *Eternity!* (1896).
[505] E.B. Pusey, *What is of Faith as to Everlasting Punishment?* (1879).
[506] F.W. Farrar, "Preface to the First Edition", in *Eternal Hope* (1892) p.xxx.
[507] T. Buser, *Religious Art in the Nineteenth Century in Europe and America* (2002) vol.1, p.117.
[508] J.C. Ryle, "The Importance of the Clear Enunciation of Dogma", in *Be Thou a Faithful Dispenser of the Word of God* (1878) p.80. The success of *Eternal Hope* was attributed by some to its "rhetoric" rather than its "close reasoning", see R. Farrar, *The Life of Frederic William Farrar* (1905) p.267.

can do without it, do not feel the need for it, and therefore prefer not to be troubled with the subject. You are entitled to hold your opinions, and we ours, let us be good friends, and agree to differ."[509] By 1892, Sir George Stokes, a believer in the authority of Scripture, observed that "large numbers of Christians" no longer believed in hell and eternal torment.[510] He was of the same view; while Henry Drummond observed "The revolt of the moral sense of this country against the doctrine of a physical hell, and the appeal to a Judgment Day."[511] In 1915, J.C. Ryle's son, Herbert Ryle, as Dean of Westminster Abbey, preached a series of sermons entitled *Life after Death*. He stated that the doctrine of hell in the popular consciousness belonged to another age.[512]

13.4.5 *Charles Gore and Lux Mundi*

In 1889, the publication of *Lux Mundi: A Series of Studies in the Religion of the Incarnation* led to theological liberalism fusing with Anglo-Catholicism.[513] Its publication also signified the completion of the process whereby the Church of England shifted its theological emphasis from the atonement to the incarnation.[514] *Lux Mundi* – like that other epoch-making book, *Essays and Reviews* – was a collection of essays by Anglican clergy, teachers and scholars. The authors were together at Oxford between 1875-1885. There they had "put the Catholic faith into its right relation to modern intellectual and moral problems".[515] *Lux Mundi* was the fruit of their "happy companionship".[516] Of this time, a Nonconformist student concluded "that Oxford Anglicanism is not only

[509] J.T. Davidson, "The Non-Church Going: How Can Our Churches Reach Them?", in (1882) *The Christian Monthly and Family Treasury* p.141.

[510] G.G. Stokes, *Conditional Immortality* (1897) pp.11 and 27.

[511] H. Drummond, *The New Evangelism and Other Papers* (1899) p.60.

[512] H.E. Ryle, *Life After Death* (1916) pp.8-10.

[513] B.M.G. Reardon, *Religious Thought in the Victorian Age* (1995) pp.318-337. The inevitability of a link between Anglo-Catholicism and liberal theology is highlighted by Wright, who draws out how Gladstone used the theology of Coleridge in his first theological work, see L.S.H. Wright, *Samuel Taylor Coleridge and the Anglican Church* (2010) pp.259-271.

[514] B. Hilton, *The Age of Atonement* (1991) p.5. Hilton argues that, in theology, the period 1785 to 1865 was the age of atonement – and the years thereafter, to 1889, were ones of doctrinal transition.

[515] C. Gore, "Preface" to *Lux Mundi* (1904) (C. Gore (ed.)) p.vii.

[516] Ibid.

'very genuine, very earnest, very sure of its own propagandist capacities,' but also 'essentially liberal'".[517]

The most important essay within *Lux Mundi* was Charles Gore's, on biblical inspiration. His reason for challenging the historical basis of the Old Testament was the traditional justification for changing orthodoxy – the removal of "great obstacles from the path to belief of many who certainly wish to believe".[518] The other essays, on matters such as the atonement, were generally orthodox. However, critics recognised that, if the proper approach to the Bible was lost, everything else would slip.[519] Now, not only was it lawful for Anglicans to doubt the historicity of the Old Testament, but also "*acceptable*".[520] Gore's essay in *Lux Mundi* again demonstrated that a radical line in theology was no bar to ecclesiastic preferment. He became the Bishop of Oxford and, for the first two or three decades of the twentieth century, was the leading intellectual force in the Church of England.

All the same, Anglicanism did not completely lose its ability to enforce elements of orthodoxy. Its parties could combine where a particularly public and vitriolic attack on its doctrines was made – as Professor Alfred Williams Momerie of King's College, London discovered in May 1891. He "delivered his 'oration' on 'The Corruption of the Church' at Prince's Hall, Piccadilly...before a large and distinguished audience". He declared as "nonsense" the orthodox doctrines "of original sin, the atonement, predestination and the Holy Trinity".[521] An infallible Bible was also rejected. For expressing his opinions with "scant regard for tact",[522] his chair at King's College was declared vacant.

[517] A. Peel and J.A.R. Marriott, *Robert Forman Horton* (1937) p.105.
[518] C. Gore, "The Holy Spirit and Inspiration", in *Lux Mundi* (1904) (C. Gore (ed.)) p.266.
[519] See generally M. Wellings, *Evangelicals Embattled* (2003) pp.230-235.
[520] Author's italics. O. Chadwick, *The Victorian Church* (1987) pt.2, p.97. For a criticism from a friend, see A.M. Ramsey, *From Gore to Temple* (1960) pp.7-10. There were many critical works at the time.
[521] "Dr. Momerie on the Church of England", in *The Times*, 27 May 1891.
[522] M. Wellings, *Evangelicals Embattled* (2003) p.230.

13.4.6 *Unity of theological outlook between liberal clergymen and those leading the outside assault on orthodoxy*

One of the striking unifying features between liberal clergymen and those assailing orthodox Christianity, was the affection liberal theologians had for the assailants – and the similar perspective they had on the theological issues which divided them from the orthodox, on topics like the atonement, the Day of Judgment and heaven and hell. For example, "Dean Stanley enjoyed an intimate relationship with Tyndall for many years"[523] and F.W. Farrar met with Matthew Arnold and Thomas Huxley. He enjoyed "very earnest and delightful conversations with Professor Huxley on religious subjects" and on many theological issues their outlook was the same. However, Farrar failed to convince Huxley "that Christianity is one thing, and that *current opinions about Christianity* may be quite another".[524] Ironically, Farrar's son thought his father "never fully accepted the Darwinian theory of evolution in the animal kingdom, inclining to the belief that species were immutable".[525]

13.4.7 *Liberalism within Nonconformity*[526]

Liberalism was most advanced amongst the Congregationalists. Its cause was enhanced in October 1859, when R.W. Dale took over its provincial flagship at Carrs Lane, Birmingham. Dale was no admirer of the Calvinism which his predecessor, John Angell James, had preached in building up his congregation. For Dale, James lacked originality; and for Dale, originality, not the gospel "was the pearl of great price".[527] Some already criticised Dale for "preaching deficient in gospel truth" and Dale had problems with certain clauses in the church's trust deed;[528] yet John Angell James was sufficiently impressed by Dale's intellectual ability, oratory and enthusiasm for preaching, to open the way for Dale to the Carrs Lane pulpit – and to protect him when others criticised

[523] J.R. Moore, "1859 and all that: Remaking the Story of Evolution and Religion", in *Charles Darwin 1809-1882: A Centennial Commemorative* (1982) (R.G. Chapman and C.T. Duval (eds)) p.193.

[524] Author's italics. R. Farrar, *The Life of Frederic William Farrar* (1905) p.111.

[525] Ibid., p.108.

[526] See generally M.R. Watts, *The Dissenters* (2015) vol.3, pp.28-82 and M. Wellings, *Evangelicals Embattled* (2003) pp.133-226.

[527] A.W.W. Dale, *The Life of R.W. Dale* (1898) pp.50 and 80.

[528] Ibid., pp.67 and 89.

him.[529] Shortly after the death of James, Dale published *The Life and Letters of J.A. James* (1861). In it, he savaged elements of the theology undergirding James's popular *The Anxious Enquirer after Salvation.*[530] Dale soon began to take the great congregation he had inherited in a theologically liberal direction.[531]

Further, in December 1859, the Congregationalist minister James Baldwin Brown published *The Divine Life in Man*. Brown abandoned justification through faith and penal substitution. A critic called it "the first open inroad into English evangelical Nonconformist churches of a theology fatally deficient in the truth and power of the gospel".[532] Brown had been "deeply influenced" by F.D. Maurice and, in turn, influenced other Congregationalists.[533] In 1864 Henry Allon, from the chair of the Congregational Union, maintained the divinity of Christ, the incarnation and the atonement as the means by which "the sinful are restored to God". However, he also wanted to "fully and fearlessly" recognise "the human element in the authorship of Scripture"[534] and that "the dogma of verbal inspiration has, in thousands of religious men, produced a widespread revolt".[535] Samuel Morley, a great funder of Christian causes and shortly to become a member of Parliament, retorted: "I should be wanting in fidelity to my own deep convictions if I did not feel that some slight injury had been done to God's word by what we have heard today".[536] A particular problem, to many, was the talking donkey – found in the book of Numbers.[537]

In 1875, Baldwin Brown joined Edward White and others in

[529] Ibid., pp.57-59, 75-77, 111-115 and 121-124. James first preached at Carrs Lane as a college student, and he may have been drawn to Dale as another who stood out in his student days, hoping that Dale's views were but a youthful fling. When Dale was criticised, the younger members of Carrs Lane supported him. Later, Dale offered protection – similar to that he received from Angell James – to younger clergy experimenting in theology.

[530] See A.W.W. Dale, *The Life of R.W. Dale* (1898) pp.151-155.

[531] M.R. Watts, *The Dissenters* (2015) vol.3, pp.42-45.

[532] J.H. Hinton, *Strictures on Some Passages in the Rev. J.B. Brown's "Divine Life in Man"* (1860) p.47.

[533] E. Kaye, *Mansfield College, Oxford* (1996) pp.29 and 34.

[534] J. Waddington, *Congregational History, 1850-1880* (1880) vol.5, pp.427 and 430.

[535] See also R. Tudur Jones, *Congregationalism in England 1662-1962* (1962) pp.256-257.

[536] J. Waddington, *Congregational History, 1850-1880* (1880) vol.5, p.431.

[537] Numbers 22:21-41.

coming out "strongly against both eternal punishment and conditional immortality and, though he also rejected Universalism, he did commit himself to the suggestion that there might be opportunities for spiritual development after death".[538] That year, Dale penned his introduction to Emmanuel Pétavel-Olliff's *The Struggle for Eternal Life; Or the Immortality of the Just, and the Gradual Extinction of the Wicked* – which argued for the total destruction of "impenitent and irreclaimable sinners", but reserved the possibility of a "fresh trial", or "special appeal", after death to those who had never heard or understood the good news.[539] Dale, in his introduction, thought that "The re-organisation of a single doctrine involves the re-organisation of that theological province to which it belongs." He went on to suggest that Pétavel's ideas would not enfeeble evangelical doctrine, but would make it "more intense and more vivid". He thought that, although the theory of eternal sin and suffering was the creed of the majority of both the Anglicans and the Nonconformists, preachers did not have the conviction "to preach it with adequate earnestness and energy" and private Christians could not tolerate its "vigorous and relentless" enunciation by their ministers.[540]

Nevertheless in 1880 Dale, in a sermon, referred to members of the churches departing from the "Christian tradition" and inventing a "new kind of religion". It was a "religion without God",[541] or a religion in which God had a secondary place. In his view, the church no longer had much to say about the "forgiveness of sin". In the past, men had known that God was angry with them and, when they knew his forgiveness, they were filled with joy that rose to ecstasy.[542] Now, man was the centre of religious thought.[543] Dale added: "In our very worship we are chiefly solicitous for the Epicurean indulgence of religious sentiment, and are satisfied with whatever awakens it."[544] A few years before Dale wrote, James Picton had read a paper at a major Congregational Conference

[538] M.R. Watts, *The Dissenters* (2015) vol.3, p.57.
[539] E. Pétavel *The Struggle for Eternal Life* (N.D.) pp.16-17.
[540] Ibid., p.vi.
[541] R.W. Dale, *The Evangelical Revival* (1880) p.161.
[542] Ibid., p.160.
[543] Ibid., p.169.
[544] Ibid.

suggesting that "religious communion should be based on religious feeling and not on creedal uniformity".[545] Religious feeling was an elastic concept on which to base communion. The Congregational Union saw off that suggestion, but its suggestion illustrated where things were heading.

In Congregational churches, the disposal of reliance upon historic creeds and beliefs was far advanced.[546] By the mid-1880s, "while one thing was sure, viz. salvation in Christ, other things were either unsettled or liable to much reconstruction".[547] Dale did not note any connection between the disposal of those creeds and the new devotion to religious sentiment.[548] In his view, Methodism was the church least affected by "recent changes in the moral and intellectual condition of Christendom".[549] They had been least disposed to "the reconstruction of their theological theories". Dale thought their relief "from the troubles by which we have been tried can be only temporary".

How prevalent theological liberalism became is illustrated by Spurgeon's withdrawal, in 1887, from the Baptist Union – on grounds of its laxity of faith. At the heart of what became known as the "Down-grade Controversy" was the "Saviour's all-atoning blood".[550] In his view, "Things are not now as in our early ministry. There has been a sudden growth of the toadstools of error. I never heard of universalism then, nor of its *post-mortem* salvation, nor of probation in the next state. Until very lately, I have not heard of ministers holding up the blood of Jesus to scorn."[551] Spurgeon thought that the Congregationalists were, by 1887, far gone – but he "then discovered that the error in the Baptist Church is ten times more than we knew of". When the Baptist Union failed to discipline those in error, he withdrew from it. The Baptist Union sought to entice him back by adopting a new and evangelical statement

[545] R. Tudur Jones, *Congregationalism in England 1662-1962* (1962) p.263. The emphasis on religious feeling solved many potential sources of conflict, for the holder. Thomas Huxley left religion and its "province" of feelings alone. His conflict was with theology, see R. Barton, "Evolution: The Whitworth Gun in Huxley's War for the Liberation of Science from Theology", in *The Wider Domain of Evolutionary Thought* (1983) (D. Oldroyd and I. Langham (eds)) p.263.

[546] R.W. Dale, *The Evangelical Revival* (1880) p.22.

[547] R. Horton, *An Autobiography* (1917) p.60.

[548] R.W. Dale, *The Evangelical Revival* (1880) pp.273-278.

[549] Ibid., p.22.

[550] "The Down-grade of Dissent", in *The Record*, 4 November 1887, p.1071.

[551] C.H. Spurgeon, *An All-Round Ministry* (1960) p.298.

of faith. Spurgeon was not to return. For him, there was no adequate machinery to ensure compliance. He wrote, "Fellowship with known and vital error is participation in sin."[552] In the view of those nearest and dearest to him, it probably cut short his life.[553]

In the year after the Down-grade Controversy, Robert Horton, increasingly Congregationalism's dominant figure, published his *Inspiration and the Bible.* It confirmed Spurgeon's worst fears for the denomination in which his father and grandfather had been ministers. Horton later explained his reasons for writing the book. Chief among them, in his view, were "the moral stumbling-blocks in the Old Testament". The Bible was not free from "the mistakes and limitations to which all writings, however old and venerable are liable". He aimed to "shift the authority of the Bible from [its] crumbling basis to the indisputable quality and power of the literature itself".[554] As always, the rationale for expounding this new view was that "infidelity among the people" rested on the old view of the authority of the Bible.[555] Horton was one of the first sons of Nonconformity to enter Oxford – after it was reopened to them – and, like many other Nonconformists, he was influenced by his training there at the time when Charles Gore and his associates were in full vigour. Due to the strength of the High Church party in 1870s Oxford – a party never sympathetic towards Nonconformists – the latter were pushed or drawn towards Oxford's increasingly influential liberal theologians. Horton hoped that "it might be the high privilege of Oxford to 'promulgate some new evangel which should be not the making of a sect, not the destruction of the sects, but the healing of the sects'".[556]

Scotland also drifted towards theological liberalism. Even in the Free Church of Scotland, biblical criticism undermined old certainties. Robertson Smith lost his Chair at the Free Church College at Aberdeen – but only after a long campaign against him, which began after his liberal article on the Bible was published in the *Encyclopedia Britannica.* In

552 I.M. Murray, *The Forgotten Spurgeon* (1973) p.153.
553 C.H. Spurgeon, *Autobiography: The Full Harvest 1860-1892* (1973) p.470 and M.R. Watts, *The Dissenters* (2015) vol.3, p.74.
554 R. Horton, *An Autobiography* (1917) pp.84-85.
555 Ibid., pp.84 and 90.
556 A. Peel and J.A.R. Marriott, *Robert Forman Horton* (1937) p.105.

other Scottish churches, he would probably have had fewer problems.[557]

13.5 The growth of Ritualism and the failure to discipline

Some suggested that the theological liberalism emerging in the 1860s had no spiritual substance to offer the working man. They went on to argue that the Protestant Reformation had gone too far.[558] The revivalists had not adequately reached the working man and, it was argued, their failure had impoverished the church service. In the 1860s, the Ritualists emerged in strength. They looked back to before the Reformation for inspiration, and suggested that medieval ritual, with its roots in the deep past, was the solution to attracting the working class. They were an amalgamation of the 'High and Drys' – those affirming the relationship between the Church and state and the "fast dying out"[559] Oxford Movement. This emphasised the authority of the Church flowing from apostolic succession. The Ritualists' early strength was in Samuel Wilberforce's Diocese of Oxford.[560] They sought to resist attacks on the Church by appeals to its authority (which was what those attacks disputed)[561] rather than reliance upon the word of God.

Many date the appearance of the Ritualists to 1859 and the foundation of what, shortly thereafter, became known as the English Church Union. Its primary object became the defence and maintenance of the unimpaired doctrine and discipline of the Church of England, which they believed affirmed ritual.[562] Its members protested "against the profanation of public worship, by the consorting of certain clergymen of the Church of England with Dissenting preachers in the use of theatres for public worship".[563] 1859 also saw incense first used at a Christmas midnight service of Holy Communion at St Mary Magdalene's Munster Square, London and the first usage in London of eucharistic vestments.[564] The edition of *The Record* published on the 15 February 1860 illustrates

[557] A.L. Drummond, *The Church in Late Victorian Scotland 1874-1900* (1978) pp.40-78.
[558] D. Wilson, *Our Protestant Faith in Danger* (1850) p.16.
[559] "Preface" to 60 *The Christian Observer for the Year 1860* (1860) p.iii.
[560] Ibid.
[561] A. Burroughs, *The Valley of Decision* (1916) p.170.
[562] G.B. Roberts, *The History of the English Church Union 1859-1894* (1895) p.12.
[563] Ibid., p.19.
[564] F. Penhale, *The Anglican Church Today: Catholics in Crisis* (1986) p.10.

what was going on spiritually in the different parts of the country. In one column, articles ran successively on disturbances at St George's-in-the-East, London, where its rector sought to advance Ritualism; the revival in Wales; and the effects of the Irish revival.[565] In 1863, the Anglo-Catholic *Church Times* was founded.

At the heart of Ritualism was the desire for a "Reformation in Worship". This took the form, inter alia, of increasing the use of vestments, surpliced choirs (previously limited to the cathedrals), incense, candles on the altar and the eastward position of the celebrant. There was also an emphasis on more ornate church buildings and more sophisticated music. In many ways, Christianity began to be focused on what happened in the church service on a Sunday, rather than what happened during the rest of the week. This new ritual was sometimes combined with hard work, by ritualistic parish priests, among the poor. Behind the facade, new "doctrines, strange and unheard...for 300 years" were "gradually reintroduced".[566]

In 1865, as a means of enforcing church discipline by law, the evangelical Church Association was formed. In doing so, Parliament was supportive; anything that smacked of popery engendered its antipathy.[567] Queen Victoria was also dismayed by defiant Ritualists[568] but the Prime Minister, William Ewart Gladstone, favoured them.[569] Only with his fall did the Public Worship Regulation Act of 1874[570] clarify and shorten the procedure for bringing cases concerning the propriety of worship

[565] See "St George's-in-the-East", "Revivals in Wales" and "Effects of the Irish Revival", in *The Record*, 15 February 1860, p.3.

[566] H.W. Webb-Peploe, "The Church of England", in *Our Churches and Why We Belong to Them* (1898) p.369.

[567] At the 1868 General Election, the victorious candidate in Buckingham – and President of the Evangelical Alliance – said of his opponent (who had presented a notorious Ritualist with his living): "if you [the voters] are Protestants you will not return a Ritualist", cited in G.I.T. Machin, *Politics and the Churches 1869-1921* (1987) p.6.

[568] Prince Albert was also no friend of popery, see G.H. Pike, *Albert, The Prince Consort* (1888) pp.202-228.

[569] See S. Dark, *Archbishop Davidson and the English Church* (1929) pp.2-3. Gladstone's defeat at the general election of 1874 was attributed, by some, to his having "dallied with popery", see "Preface" to 74 *The Christian Observer for the Year 1874* (1874) pp.iv-v.

[570] For the background to this act and the subsequent case law, see G.W. Graber, *Ritual Legislation in the Victorian Church of England* (1993).

to court. As a result, the ecclesiastic dress code in the time of Edward VI became a matter of national interest. Looking back to such days, it was thought that "If Hooper's views had been allowed to prevail, one half of the Ritualistic controversy of our own day would never have existed at all".[571] There were successes for the evangelicals. The Judicial Committee of the Privy Council condemned eucharistic vestments in 1871 and in 1877. However, the use of the courts to regulate worship did not raise the general esteem of the Church and it distracted the evangelicals, although Ritualism was doing that anyway.[572] Neither did it halt the flow of innovation. Ritualists, if they disagreed with a judgment of the courts, could not be suspended or deprived of their living, only imprisoned. They were content to go to prison. As many clergy who themselves would not break the law supported those who did, Ritualist martyrs were created. Despite the court judgments against their practices, their numbers grew. Some observers suggested that dealing with the law-breaking was best left to the bishops.[573] In 1886 Edward Bickersteth, the Bishop of Exeter, publicly declared that he would exercise his right to veto all prosecutions subject to the Public Worship Regulation Act – as they "aggravate the evil they are meant to suppress".[574] Indeed, during the last decade of the nineteenth century, the bishops were left to "firmly put down the more serious extravagances of the clergy". However, the "years of comparative peace" were "used by the extreme High Churchmen to advance their position on all sides",[575] until a Protestant reaction at the end of the century brought renewed conflict.

[571] J.C. Ryle, *Five English Reformers* (1890) p.49. At the time of the Reformation, there had been a dispute between the leading English reformers over the dress code for clergy. John Hooper, the Bishop of Gloucester, had advocated less elaborate vestments. However, his views had not prevailed over those of Cranmer, the Archbishop of Canterbury and Ridley, the Bishop of London.

[572] See for example J.H. Titcomb, *A Plea for Obedience: A Sermon on the Public Worship Regulation Act* (1875).

[573] J.C. Ryle, *Principles for Churchmen* (1884) p.x.

[574] E.H. Bickersteth, *Charge* (1886) p.27.

[575] A.R. Buckland, "The Protestant Revival: What Has It Done?", in 15 *Churchman* (1901) p.529. In 1884 J.C. Ryle, foretold that leaving discipline to the bishops was unlikely to be successful, see J.C. Ryle, *Principles for Churchmen* (1884) p.x.

13.5.1 *Reasons for the growth of Ritualism*

Ritualists were committed to theological reading and revived ancient learning related to the Church Fathers and the historic saints. They also knew how to win promising adherents in the universities. They were busy with the press, in the teacher training colleges[576] and in the training of nurses[577] – and lavished their time, energy and resources on all aspects of art. The evangelicals, with a few honourable exceptions, were to be too busy in their parishes to compete in most of these fields.[578]

There is some evidence that these initiatives – and especially the greater use of music, painting and architecture – appealed to the working classes already in church. However, they also appealed to the more refined taste of the 'better' classes. The number of churches using eucharistic vestments vastly increased – from 336, in 1882, to 2,158 in 1901 – and embraced a belt of often substantial churches, running across South London.[579] "Evidently the movement nourished the devotional and aesthetic instinct of the educated more than it attracted the interest of the uneducated."[580]

Some evangelicals, although deprecating the excesses of Ritualism, thought it gave a prominence to the sacraments, to the corporate idea and "to the greatness of worship" that they had lost.[581] The latter factor was particularly significant in explaining the success of Ritualism – it gave participants an experiential buzz. Bishop Ryle, a critic, wrote: "It is very annoying to see our younger members slipping away to churches where there are processions, banners, flowers, incense, and a thoroughly histrionic and gorgeous ceremonial. It is vexing to hear them say, that 'they feel so much better after these services.'"[582]

[576] D. Wilson, *Our Protestant Faith in Danger* (1850) pp.7-10 and 17.

[577] "Link after Link; or Bible Women Nurses", in *God's Message in Low London* (N.D.) pp.5, 10-11 and 63.

[578] D. Wilson, *Our Protestant Faith in Danger* (1850) pp.6-7.

[579] G.I.T. Machin, *Politics and the Churches in Great Britain 1869 to 1921* (1987) p.234. For example, St Stephen's Lewisham (1,443 attendants) and St Peter's West Norwood (1,429 attendants), see O. Chadwick *The Victorian Church* (1987) pt.2, p.317.

[580] Ibid. See also W.J. Conybeare, *Essays Ecclesiastical and Social* (1855) p.106; J.L. Lang, "The Decline in Church Attendance", in *The Christian Monthly and Family Treasury* (1882) p.13; and M. Wellings, *Evangelicals Embattled* (2003) pp.54-55.

[581] H.C.G. Moule, *The Evangelical School in the Church of England* (1901) p.31.

[582] J.C. Ryle, *Knots Untied* (1964) (G.E. Duffield (ed.)) p.17.

13.5.2 *Consequences of the spread of Ritualism*

The spread of Ritualism had profound consequences on Protestant Christianity in Britain and greatly weakened "that general dislike and aversion to popery which was once almost universal in this realm".[583] Below, we will consider some of those consequences as it affected the transmission of the gospel.

Ritualism undermines spreading the gospel

Ritualism gave renewed energy to the old idea that a person became a Christian on baptism – and thereby made spreading the knowledge of the gospel unnecessary. If an individual became a Christian on baptism, why bother to seek God further? All that was necessary for the Christian life was the (very occasional) reception of the Real Presence of Christ at communion. A vigorous commitment to spreading the knowledge of the gospel – and to teaching discipleship – was unnecessary. Spurgeon thought that the doctrine of baptismal regeneration took away the gospel's voice. In 1864, he preached that the doctrine is "increasing, fearfully increasing, until all grades of society are misled by this belief".[584] In his view, it penetrated the Dissenters, as well as the Church of England, in an idolatrous way, with its emphasis on the sacredness of places, things and men and its concern for ceremony.[585] Bishop Ryle also thought Ritualism shifted the focus of ministers from gospel communication to the accompaniments of worship on a Sunday. In his view, some evangelical ministers were being led into the same trap when they started to use "New church decorations,[586] new church music, and a semi-histrionic mode of going through church worship". He thought that these may "have a 'show of wisdom'",[587] but that they never would convert the world, although they might constitute a vain attempt to conciliate it.

Just as significantly, Ritualism undermined the idea that it was the

[583] J.C. Ryle, *Principles for Churchmen* (1884) p.xx.

[584] C.H. Spurgeon, "Baptismal Regeneration", in *Metropolitan Tabernacle Pulpit* (1865) vol.10, p.321.

[585] Ibid. See also J. Munson, *The Nonconformists* (1991) pp.129-156 and M.R. Watts, *The Dissenters* (2015) vol.3, pp.161-163.

[586] Including the use of flowers.

[587] J.C. Ryle, *Knots Untied* (1964) (G.E. Duffield (ed.)) p.16.

spread of the gospel that led a nation to be uplifted by God to pre-eminence among its peers – which idea gave energy to many evangelistic endeavours. Protestants had always seen the Reformation as "the greatest blessing God ever gave to this land".[588] However, the Ritualists vilified the Reformation and sneered at Protestantism. Neither did Ritualists believe that the spread of the Christian faith explained the nation's pre-eminence, as by doing so they fortified the Protestant cause. Instead, as we have seen, High Church historians Christianised the idea of progress. In doing so, they gave up one of the great motivators of evangelism – that the evangelists of the past had used – to demand moral change from their hearers. A national church that did not believe that it was God who lifted up the nation – according to its obedience to his will – was less likely to be a church energetic in teaching his ways to the nation and calling it to repentance.

Furthermore, Ritualism undermined the theological unity of the Church of England which assisted the gospel's spread. Across the land, services were conducted according to the Prayer Book and its Protestant theology – whatever the theological persuasion of the incumbent – although local nuances existed. Ritualism meant that instead of enjoying a theological unity to facilitate a focus on growth, the Church of England became involved in many long, expensive, time-consuming and often fruitless court proceedings against ritualistic practices. Indeed, Ritualism split the Evangelical party – between those in favour of litigation against it and the moderates.[589]

In some cases, Ritualism directly discouraged people attending certain Church of England services, or led to the withdrawal of services. For example, in the 1890s, the two archbishops supported the view of advanced Ritualists that "Evening Communion is England's greatest sin".[590] Many of these services had been started earlier in the century – to successfully draw people to church.

[588] J.C. Ryle, *Principles for Churchmen* (1884) p.xx.

[589] J.C. Whisenant, *A Fragile Unity: Anti-Ritualism and the Division of Anglican Evangelicalism in the Nineteenth Century* (2003).

[590] "Evening Communion", in *The Methodist Times*, 6 April 1893, p.211.

Ritualism lowers the wider standing of the Church of England

Ritualism damaged the reputation of the Church of England as the upholder of wisdom. It appeared intellectually backward-looking, allying itself with the "'ideas' that warred against the Renaissance of the fifteenth century, the Reformation of the sixteenth, the philosophical thinkers of the seventeenth century, the political revolutions of the eighteenth century and the general progress of the nineteenth century". As a result, it "alienated thinking men from Christianity",[591] men who were unwilling to subordinate the mind to the aesthetic and, by the late 1860s, "not a few bankers, lawyers, and doctors and members of Parliament" left the Church.[592]

Ritualism damaged the reputation of the Church of England as the upholder of concord and courtesy. Apart from the court cases, the vitriol that could be expended was unedifying. For example, the two volumes, each of 500 pages plus, of W.H.B. Proby's *Annals of the "Low-Church" Party in England* contain comments like: the Low Church party "has never been celebrated for its intellect or learning, but has produced the most striking instances of ignorance and stupidity".[593]

Ritualism could also be said to have modelled the rejection of established authority to the nation and to the wider church. One clergyman thought that if the bishops had united to take firm action in the 1830s, the movement might have been "nipped in the bud".[594] However, nothing was done. Another hostile observer of the mid-1850s thought that, by then, the Ritualistic party took "a schoolboyish pleasure in showing the annihilation of Episcopal power, and the unlimited licence of disobedience practically possessed by the clergy".[595]

Perhaps the successful defiance of episcopal authority by the Ritualists showed to the authors of *Essays and Reviews* the likelihood of their success if they did likewise – as they penned their essays. Certainly, Ritualist innovations destroyed the homogeneity of the Church's "brand" and, by challenging its boundaries, destroyed its doctrinal unity – and

[591] *Proceedings of the Fourth National Council of the Evangelical Free Churches* (1899) p.10.

[592] J.C. Ryle, *We Must Unite!* (1868) p.16.

[593] W.H.B. Proby, *Annals of the "Low-Church" Party in England* (1888) vol.1, p.5.

[594] D. Wilson, *Our Protestant Faith in Danger* (1850) p.9.

[595] W.J. Conybeare, *Essays Ecclesiastical and Social* (1855) p.127.

thereby made its penetration by theological liberalism easier. If what was Catholic and medieval was acceptable, what about that which was liberal and modern?

For Church of England evangelicals, Ritualism was a tragedy – as it led to the charge that, by assenting to the Prayer Book, but teaching the opposite on baptism, evangelical clergy emulated the practice of theological liberals on other doctrinal matters. The Church Catechism required catechists to affirm: "in my baptism; wherein I was made a member of Christ, the true child of God, and an inheritor of the kingdom of heaven". Evangelicals did not literally believe this, nor did they believe that the reformers had equated conversion with baptism. Accordingly, antagonists argued that – in failing to believe what the Prayer Book said on its face – evangelicals had "no moral right to serve in any office of ministry".[596] Further, the idea of religious truth was brought into disrepute. Spurgeon preached that: "I know of nothing more calculated to debauch the public mind than a want of straightforwardness in ministers; and when worldly men hear ministers denouncing the very things which their own Prayer Book teaches, they imagine that words have no meaning among ecclesiastics, and that vital differences in religion are merely a matter of tweedle-dee and tweedle-dum, and that it does not matter much what a man does believe so long as he is charitable towards other people."[597]

Ritualism leads to conflict with the Nonconformists[598]

The growth of Ritualism led the Church of England into conflict with the Nonconformists, intensifying their desire for disestablishment. For instance, in 1864 Spurgeon (in a sermon already mentioned) assailed the Catechism and the Prayer Book for allegedly teaching automatic

[596] W.H.B. Proby, *Annals of the "Low-Church" Party in England* (1888) vol.1, pp.v and 87.

[597] C.H. Spurgeon, "Baptismal Regeneration", in *Metropolitan Tabernacle Pulpit* (1865) vol.10, p.317.

[598] Ritualism also created tensions within Methodism – as its liturgy was based on the Prayer Book. In the same way that the Prayer Book "promoted un-Protestant" ritualism in the Church, within Methodism it "promoted un-Protestant and un-Methodistic ritualism". Inevitably issues arose over the meaning of baptism, see C. Oldstone-Moore, *Hugh Price Hughes* (1999) pp.80-81 and 87.

regeneration at baptism.[599] The drafting of the Catechism and the Prayer Book was infelicitous on the spiritual effects of baptism and, because of the way they were being used, Spurgeon felt rebuke was necessary. He made the same charge in a sermon three weeks later. He declaimed:

> I see before me now a church which tolerates evangelical truth in her communion, but at the same time lovingly embraces Puseyism… This is no time for us to talk about friendship with so corrupt a corporation. The godly in her midst are deceived if they think to mould her to a more gracious form.[600]

The duty of believers, in such a situation, he urged, was to "come out of her, and bear your witness to the truth".

In fact, a number had done so since the Tractarian challenge began and, in 1863, many of them had been brought together, with the help of and often under leaders drawn from the Countess of Huntingdon's Connexion, to create the Free Church of England.[601] It began with about 18 churches in the United Kingdom.[602] What held those remaining in the Church of England, Spurgeon added, was the cost of leaving it. A few years later, he attributed the likelihood of divine judgment on the nation

[599] C.H. Spurgeon, "Baptismal Regeneration", in *Metropolitan Tabernacle Pulpit* (1865) vol.10, pp.313-328. Over ten years later a Congregational preacher still felt the need to warn his flock of the dangers of Ritualism, see C.S. Carey, *Ritualism: A Sermon*, 25 April 1875.

[600] C.H. Spurgeon, "'Let us go Forth'", in *Metropolitan Tabernacle Pulpit* (1865) vol.10, p.370. R.W. Dale also referred to the Prayer Book's reference to baptismal regeneration, to challenge the fidelity of evangelical clergy to their church, see A.W.W. Dale, *The Life of R.W. Dale* (1898) p.171.

[601] See *A History of the Free Church of England* (1960) pp.27-38.

[602] J. Fenwick, *The Free Church of England* (2004) p.53. In 1873, for similar reasons to those leading to the Free Church of England, the Reformed Episcopal Church was established out of episcopalianism, in the United States of America. In 1877, it established a branch in England, see ibid., pp.111-117. This development led to further fragmentation in the body of believers purporting to be the true successors to the Church of England, see ibid., pp.110-127. The foundation of the Free Church of England offers practical insight into the difficulties of forming a new denomination out of an existing one – where the driving force of separation is rejection of a doctrine that has taken over the relevant denomination, without a powerful evangelistic impetus, see ibid. By 1900, the Reformed Episcopal Church had 21 congregations and, the following year, the Free Church of England had 20 congregations, ibid., pp.137-138, the number of churches having fluctuated, at fairly modest levels, over the years.

to "barefaced popery" within the Established Church.[603] Such comments drove a wedge between Church evangelicals and those outside, at a time when a common front was required against theological liberalism. Spurgeon resigned from the Evangelical Alliance over the baptismal regeneration controversy, where it caused division.

13.6 The rise of the evangelical Arminians

Most evangelicals in the late nineteenth century became Arminians, or were inclined to Arminianism, including some of the movement's greatest names. William Booth, founder of the Salvation Army, was no lover of Calvinism. In his *The Doctrines and Discipline of the Salvation Army* (1881), ten pages are devoted to refuting Calvinism's biblical basis.

13.6.1 *D.L. Moody, his friends and the gospel of God's love*

In the 1870s, the great American evangelist, D.L. Moody, with Ira David Sankey to lead the music, arrived in Britain – they would preach to packed meetings. Moody was fuzzy over the distinctions between Calvinism and Arminianism. This encouraged all to support his missions, but he was no Calvinist. He liked to say that becoming a Christian was like joining the Masons (not that he approved of them). The individual decided whether to join. The Masons decided whether to elect the candidate to membership. Furthermore, Moody, by affirming the need to make 'a decision for Christ', was criticised for suggesting that becoming a Christian was an act of the human will, rather than the decision of God. It was also found that in the urgency of a person making a decision for Christ, the essentials of biblical faith could be whittled away, one doctrine after another. This, though, was not true of Moody himself.[604]

Moody and Sankey also popularised another growing theological emphasis – one which General Booth did not share. Even those who regarded them as "two wise-hearted evangelists"[605] thought their work possessed a "certain slightness or lack of conviction of sin"[606] and of hell. Moody mentioned them in his preaching – indeed, he preached

[603] C.H. Spurgeon, "The Voice of the Cholera", in *Metropolitan Tabernacle Pulpit* (1867) vol.12, p.449.
[604] G.A. Smith, *The Life of Henry Drummond* (1899) pp.58-59.
[605] J. Macpherson, *Revival and Revival Work* (N.D.) p.311.
[606] Ibid., p.307.

against "your new doctrine...that is just doing away with Christ, with hell and even with heaven"[607] – but they lacked prominence. The success of Moody's preaching, as a reviewer in *The Times* noted "with pleasure... owed little to the 'terrors of the law'". The reviewer went on to state that the gospel Moody preaches is one of "'glad tidings'...his theme in the main is the boundless compassion of the Saviour, not the terror of hell".[608] Looking back nearly 50 years later, A.W. Robinson commented: "Mr Moody was translating into popular language, and illustrating in homely ways, much [but not all] of the teaching of Frederick Maurice... The new presentation of the gospel of the Fatherhood of God quietly melted away what remained of the hardness of Calvinism, and altered the whole temper and method of evangelistic work."[609]

Moody's example was influential. Even elements of the Brethren adopted his Arminianism and emphasis on experience.[610] Hugh Price Hughes, secretary to the Wesleyan London Mission – launched in 1876 and modelled on Moody's mission of the previous year – did not denounce individual sins. For him, sin was the failure of the comfortable middle classes to put their blessings to good account.[611] Hugh Price Hughes was the leading Methodist figure of the last third of the nineteenth century.

Contemporaries drew a distinction between the revival of 1859-60 and the Moody missions of 1873-75. The former was "ruder" and more "emotional", but "deeper". One writer observed that "Fifteen years ago we never heard inquirers or converts asking how much of the world and its gaieties they might have along with salvation".[612] One explanation suggested was that Moody provided "little dealing with conscience". This, it was thought, explained his success among the upper and middle classes, but limited his influence with the masses.[613] It was said that the

[607] D.L. Moody, *The London Discourses of D.L. Moody* (1875) p.152.

[608] "The American Revivalists", in *The Times*, 16 July 1875.

[609] A.W. Robinson, "Appendix 1" to Report of the Archbishops' Third Committee of Inquiry, *The Evangelistic Work of the Church* (1918) p.52.

[610] T. Grass, *Gathering to His Name* (2012) pp.119 and 123. The influence of Moody on the Brethren was reciprocal. It is said that it was the Brethren evangelist, Harry Moorhouse, who transformed Moody's stern preaching – so that he became the apostle of God's love, see W.R. Moody, *D.L. Moody* (1930) pp.117-120.

[611] C. Oldstone-Moore, *Hugh Price Hughes* (1999) p.71.

[612] J. Macpherson, *Revival and Revival Work* (N.D.) p.308.

[613] M.R. Watts, *The Dissenters* (2015) vol.3, p.127. Nevertheless, when he preached

minds of people of intelligence could be reached by many methods, but – perhaps somewhat arrogantly –

> if you cannot take hold on conscience with a strong, rude grasp, you will not touch the lower orders of men; you cannot so much as *talk religion* to them. The only religious thing in them is conscience... And however men may talk about love and all the sweet sentiments, we must still get the whole business of religion and of the soul well bottomed in repentance, in righteousness, in holiness; we must still come back to conscience and to God.[614]

By 1879, Pusey, the Tractarian leader, rejoiced that the "rigid Calvinistic school...is now happily all but extinct, if not altogether extinct in England",[615] although the enemies of Calvinism were always anxious to announce their demise – often prematurely.

One of Moody's most important helpers in his British mission work was Henry Drummond – a "charming personality" and "one of the most influential men of the latter part of the nineteenth century".[616] He was especially influential with the young and enjoyed the distinction of both holding the Chair in Natural Science at the Free Church College in Glasgow and of being a Fellow of the Royal Society of Edinburgh. His talents were such that Gladstone invited him to consider a seat in Parliament.[617] Drummond sided with Robertson Smith in his dispute with the latter's Free Church College;[618] Drummond's theology changed markedly over the years.[619] Drummond's life illustrates the dangers

in the East End those who met to pray were mainly working class, see J. Macpherson, *Revival and Revival Work* (N.D.) p.96.

[614] Author's italics. Ibid., p.308.

[615] E.B. Pusey, *What is of Faith as to Everlasting Punishment?* (1880) p.6. Henry Allon, the Congregationalist leader thought that it was progress for theology to be freed from "the terrible and disabling bondage of fatalistic Calvinism", H. Allon, "Biographical and Critical Sketch", in T. Binney, *Sermons Preached in the King's Weigh House Chapel, London. 1829-1869* (1875) (H. Allon (ed.)) pp.l and liv. Allon delivered the benediction and prayer at the end of the first evening of the Moody mission to London in 1875, see "The American Revivalists", in *The Times,* 10 March 1875.

[616] A.H. Walker, *Radiant Christianity* (1913) pp.14-15.

[617] M.J. Toone, *Evangelicalism in Transition* (1985) (unpublished Ph.D. thesis University of St Andrews) p.206.

[618] G.A. Smith, *The Life of Henry Drummond* (1899) pp.130-131.

[619] M.J. Toone, *Evangelicalism in Transition* (1985) (unpublished Ph.D. thesis, University of St Andrews) pp.14 and 149-219.

to orthodoxy of the effective liberal evangelist. He was a delightful personality and much influenced by contemporary ideas.

Drummond was made famous by his book *Natural Law in the Spiritual World* (1883). It sold half a million copies in 25 years, excluding foreign translations.[620] In it, he sought to demonstrate that the idea of law running through science continued into the spiritual world. This resulted in a comparison of the views of Jesus on eternal life with those of Herbert Spencer on the conditions of eternal existence for biological life. It was clever, but the grandeur of eternal life and of the God who gives it was missing. The approach showed how inverted human thinking could become. In the seventeenth century, science developed because man assumed that just as God had created spiritual laws, so his cosmos must also reflect his character and be one of order, rather than chaos. Now the order in the universe was being used to justify God's purposes; God was becoming an end thought.[621] Furthermore, Drummond enunciated "spiritual law in the exact terms of biology and physics".[622] Given the esteem for him, for a time at least, a sermon by "Every young minister and local preacher…was punctuated with scientific terms, such as 'biogenesis', 'classification', 'organic and inorganic', 'degeneration', 'semi-parasitism', and 'parasitism'." Such terms may have made the preacher look clever and contemporary, but how it helped to explain the gospel, this author has been unable to ascertain.[623] It did not convince the young H.G. Wells.[624]

Drummond also championed evolution as a means of reconciling "many things in the Bible…with our ideas of a just and good God". He found that "The moral difficulties of the Old Testament are admittedly great."[625] In his view, "Evolution has given Christianity a new Bible." It was "a nursery of growing truths."[626] George Adam Smith, Drummond's biographer, thought that Drummond had "found a basis for his faith

[620] Ibid., p.167.

[621] For more general criticisms of *Natural Law in the Spiritual World* (1883), see G.A. Smith, *The Life of Henry Drummond* (1899) pp.140-146.

[622] H. Drummond, "Preface" to *Natural Law in the Spiritual World* (1883) p.vii.

[623] A.H. Walker, *Radiant Christianity* (1913) pp.34 and 51-52.

[624] H.G. Wells, *Experiment in Autobiography* (1934) vol.1, p.162. Wells turned from Christianity over the existence of hell, see ibid., pp.163-165.

[625] G.A. Smith, *The Life of Henry Drummond* (1899) p.234.

[626] Ibid., pp.235-236.

more stable than ever the older was ever imagined to be…better vantage grounds for preaching the gospel of Christ and loftier summits."[627] Science was to be used to give a "new authority to replace the fading power of the Westminster Confession and Scripture".[628]

From 1884 for a decade he ran meetings in Edinburgh for the young, and thousands were won as his disciples.[629] He visited other universities, and his listeners spread his ideas. In a paper read to the Free Church Theological Society in Glasgow, he articulated the need for a "New Evangelism". As had so often been the case, a key basis for the proposed change was because the number of people attending church did not meet the author's high expectations. Therefore, Drummond argued, the gospel preached was "neither good nor new". The other reason articulated for change was because "There must be progress in everything, and more in theology than anything".[630] Of Reformation theology, he observed, we "cannot honestly say that it kindles or moves us". He had "respect" for it, not "enthusiasm".[631] However, in the Bible he found "boundless elasticity".[632]

The new evangelism was to be "new, intelligent and living."[633] This meant that biblical truths were not to be conveyed in 'propositional' form, nor by reason, but by the imagination.[634] In doing so, Drummond looked back to Coleridge, Maurice and Hare.[635] What the content of the new evangelism was, Drummond did not articulate in detail – but then he was against propositions. It seems to mean rejecting the practice (to the extent that it existed) of going to the leading Calvinistic writers for sermons, and in sermons for the preacher to unearth a principle of his own.[636] The new evangelism was said to be spiritual. To be against it was to be unspiritual and lazy.[637] Drummond was not against preaching

[627] Ibid., p.244.
[628] M.J. Toone, *Evangelicalism in Transition* (1985) (unpublished Ph.D. thesis, University of St Andrews) p.183.
[629] Ibid., pp.186-194.
[630] H. Drummond, *The New Evangelism and Other Papers* (1899) p.7.
[631] Ibid., pp.10-11.
[632] Ibid., p.10.
[633] Ibid., p.19.
[634] Ibid., pp.21 and 28.
[635] Ibid., pp.35-36.
[636] Ibid., pp.49-50.
[637] Ibid., p.42.

on the atonement – only conventional words were not to be used, which inevitably militated against preachers preaching on the topic; after 2,000 years, it was difficult to be wholly original.[638]

In *The Ascent of Man* (1894), Drummond returned to the topic of evolution. Critics thought that "the argument for evolution was never stated in a more fascinating manner; seldom has the gift of language been used with greater skill".[639] Drummond thought that evolutionary philosophy had gone astray, for misreading nature. It had fixed on the "struggle for life" while ignoring the "*struggle for the life of others*" – what Drummond called "altruism".[640] He argued that history demonstrated the "gradual tempering of the struggle for life. Its slow amelioration is the work of ages." A new social ordering was being created through "the reign of love which must one day, if the course of evolution holds on its way, be realised".[641] In his view, "The path of progress and the path of altruism are one. Evolution is nothing but the involution of love, the revelation of infinite spirit, the eternal life returning to itself."[642] Samuel Smith MP observed that Drummond's scheme did away with the Fall and sin, together with "the miraculous birth, resurrection, and ascension of the Lord Jesus Christ" and many other fundamental Christian doctrines. Smith was not convinced by Drummond's thesis.[643] He thought that "The Bible clearly teaches that this dispensation will end in failure, like the previous ones." He wrote 20 years before the outbreak of the First World War – and with Europe at the time "one armed camp" – adding, with much truer biblical insight than Drummond, that "it is easy to see that what men call an accident might cause the powder magazine to explode, and shatter modern civilisation to pieces".[644]

Samuel Smith was not the only evangelical to attack Drummond's evolutionary thinking. But Drummond managed to stay within the evangelical fold; neither D.L. Moody or Sankey would renounce their

[638] Ibid., pp.56-58.
[639] S. Smith, "*The Ascent of Man*": *A Review* (1894) p.3.
[640] Author's italics. G. Drummond, *The Ascent of Man* (1894) pp.16-17.
[641] Ibid., p.45.
[642] Ibid., p.46.
[643] See generally, S. Smith, "*The Ascent of Man*": *A Review* (1894).
[644] Ibid., p.12.

old helper.[645] It is said that the burden of Drummond's message was "make Christ your constant companion – salvation by friendship with Christ – love, the inspiration of life – Christ the abundant life – a fully evolved life only possible through fellowship with Christ."[646] In making these statements, Drummond was assuming that sin did not separate man from the divine; Drummond was becoming weak on sin – for him it was possibly all a matter of environment;[647] penal substitution dropped from his view.[648] Neither did he come to believe in a personal hell – and his conception of heaven was vague, if not earthly.[649] His approach, with his personal magnetism, appealed to many moving in a theologically liberal direction. It certainly looked clever and contemporary. For evangelicals heading in that direction, they could claim the endorsement of a friend of the great D.L. Moody. From his meetings in Edinburgh, beginning in 1884, thousands were won as his disciples.[650]

Drummond was not the only senior academic with influence over the young who significantly changed the gospel message. Marcus Dods, who became Principal of New College Edinburgh and who in Drummond's early days oversaw a mission station run by Drummond, was also doing so. He thought it was a "proclamation of forgiveness and restoration to God". He did not deny the atonement, but he did not think "that the acceptance of theories" of the atonement were relevant. Rather, it was "the belief of the grand fact that Christ, by his life and death, reunites sinners to God, the yielding up of your heart to him and submitting to his will, that is what entitles a man to be called a Christian".[651] What was important was to "believe on him", but an "earnest enquirer" was not told to repent.[652] The message of Jesus from the beginning of his

[645] A.H. Walker, *Radiant Christianity* (1913) pp.39-42 and 61 and M.J. Toone, *Evangelicalism in Transition* (1985) (unpublished Ph.D. thesis, University of St Andrews) pp.291-293.
[646] A.H. Walker, *Radiant Christianity* (1913) p.57. See also M.J. Toone, *Evangelicalism in Transition* (1985) (unpublished Ph.D. thesis, University of St Andrews) pp.188-190.
[647] A.H. Walker, *Radiant Christianity* (1913) p.73. See also M.J. Toone, *Evangelicalism in Transition* (1988) (unpublished Ph.D. thesis, University of St Andrews) pp.178-179, 196-198 and 200.
[648] Ibid., pp.179 and 196-197.
[649] Ibid., pp.199-200.
[650] Ibid., pp.186-194.
[651] G. Renny, *The Rev. Marcus Dods, D.D.: His Views Reviewed* (1890) p.10.
[652] Ibid., p.12.

ministry had always been "repent and believe";[653] a message that the apostles had taken up.[654] If sin had not been repented of, was there any real unity with Christ?[655] Henry Drummond acknowledged that no one had a greater influence over him than Marcus Dods, including in relationship to biblical criticism and "the application of the hypothesis of evolution to the interpretation of religion".[656]

13.6.2 *Differences within evangelical Arminianism*

The evangelical Arminians were never a united party. Some of their greatest figures were even scornful of each other's work. Booth dismissed many professed followers of Jesus Christ as being "full of humanitarian pleasant Sunday afternoon Moodyism or the like".[657] And Moody was no admirer of Booth. He worked with Church and chapel, while Booth separated from them. Arminians also made changes in practice in other areas. For instance, in the Salvation Army, female preaching[658] and leadership were in and the communion and baptism were out.[659]

13.6.3 *Developments in Scotland*

In Scotland, "the most thoroughly Calvinistic country in Europe",[660] the 1860s also saw a softening of theology attributed, in part, to James Morison and the Evangelical Union[661] and the intellectual ideas of the time. Keir Hardie, the future Labour politician, was in the late 1870s a member and lay preacher of an Evangelical Union church, before going on to join the Scottish Congregationalists until ceasing regularly to attend church in 1884.[662] Temperance was a key issue for both Hardie and the Evangelical Union. The influence of the softening of theology in the Free Church professors Drummond, Dods and Robertson Smith,

[653] Mark 1:15.
[654] Acts 2:38.
[655] 1 John 1:8-10.
[656] G.A. Smith, *The Life of Henry Drummond* (1899) p.133.
[657] H. Begbie, *Life of William Booth* (1920) vol.2, p.181.
[658] W. Booth, *The Doctrines and Discipline of the Salvation Army* (1881) section 27.
[659] Ibid., section 26.
[660] W. Adamson, *The Life of the Rev. James Morison* (1898) p.355.
[661] Ibid., pp.353-355.
[662] A Hardie biographer describes his Christianity as "highly flexible, a religion of humanity with little doctrinal content, utopian, romantic, outward-looking, democratic and egalitarian", see K.O. Morgan, *Keir Hardie* (1975) p.9.

we have already noted; they were not the only Scottish church leaders so influenced.

13.7 The beginnings of Pentecostalism

In 1856, William Arthur's *Tongues of Fire* was published. In its final paragraph, Arthur called for the "adorable Spirit" to "descend upon all the churches, renew the Pentecost in this our age, and baptise thy people generally – O, baptise them yet again with tongues of fire! Crown this nineteenth century with a revival...greater than that of the last century, greater than that of the first, greater than any 'demonstration of the Spirit' ever yet vouchsafed to men!"[663]

Around the time of the 1859 Revival, the need for the work of the Holy Spirit to bring about the new birth was being repeatedly emphasised by many of the leading evangelists. For instance, Reginald Radcliffe was castigated in the religious press for every so often in his preaching referring to "our dependence on the Holy Ghost", but then not demonstrating that fact by speaking less and praying for longer.[664] Furthermore, many conversions were attributed to a special working of the Holy Spirit in the life of the preacher and his (or her) preaching. For example, it was observed of the work of the Reverend and Mrs Haslam at Buckenham, that "The gracious Spirit of God crowned their labours with special blessing; a time of spiritual revival commenced." They were assisted by Geraldine Hooper, the most successful female preacher of the 1860s – of whom it was written that "She seemed to come under the influence of the same blessed Spirit of Revival, and to get a fresh baptism on high."[665] Phoebe Palmer, around the same time, referred to a Church of England minister listening to her as sharing in the "baptism of fire",[666] while in Manchester, where she was ministering, a number of "Independents sought and obtained the full baptism of the Spirit."[667] Methodist evangelists, with their denomination's emphasis

[663] W. Arthur, *Tongues of Fire* (1856) p.363.

[664] It was said that "The Spirit is honoured, not by the incessant repetition of his blessed name, but by a correct and scriptural exhibition of his own truth concerning Christ", see "The 'British Standard' on Revivals and Mr Reginald Radcliffe's Preaching", in *The Record,* 4 June 1860, p.3.

[665] G. Guinness, *"She Spake of Him"* (1872) p.35.

[666] P. Palmer, "Mrs Palmer's Labours", in *The Revivalist* (1859) p.186.

[667] Dr and Mrs Palmer, *Four Years in the Old World* (1866) p.697.

on seeking perfection, affirmed "the second blessing" as the source of their effectiveness,[668] or urged the seeking of a "richer baptism" for those wanting more spiritual fruit.[669] In the mid-1870s a number of those who would be involved in the foundation of the Keswick Convention emphasised the need for, or an experience of, a new or second indwelling of the Spirit.[670]

The Spirit's work was also given a renewed emphasis by Moody and Spurgeon – as they sought power to break down the increasing hardness of society to orthodox Christianity[671] – and a belief took shape that there was a special 'baptism in the Holy Spirit', which gave spiritual power to the individual. Such baptism, it was argued, often occurred post-conversion, and should be sought.[672]At a time when orthodoxy was failing to influence society in the way that it had earlier in the century, the failure to undergo such an experience was an attractive explanation for the church's weakness.[673] Moody, at the end of the nineteenth century, accepted the doctrine and encouraged R.A. Torrey, his most influential successor, to preach it.[674] Both underwent a baptism in the Holy Spirit,

[668] H.T. Smart, *The Life of Thomas Cook* (1913) p.32.

[669] W. Cooke, *The Revival of Religion* (N.D.) pp.2 and 8-9.

[670] I. Randall, "The Keswick Convention and Anglican Evangelical Tensions in the Early Twentieth Century", in *Evangelicalism and the Church of England in the Twentieth Century* (2014) (A. Atherstone and J. Maiden (eds)) pp.90-91.

[671] C.H. Spurgeon, *An All-Round Ministry* (1960) pp.315-363.

[672] Brice lists an impressive array of evangelists from this period who subscribed to "the second work of grace" – namely, Booth, Spurgeon, Murray, Hudson Taylor, Bishop Moule, Moody, Fullerton, Meyer, W.H. Tindall, Edward Davidson, Samuel Chadwick, J.D. Brash, Josiah Mee and Thomas Cook, see J.I. Brice, *The Crowd for Christ* (1934) p.58. Samuel Chadwick experienced "a mighty baptism of Pentecostal power" when "At three o'clock one Sunday morning I burnt all my sermons. I surrendered my reputation and the effort at merely clever sermons, and determined to go to the people only in the presence and power of my Redeemer. The surrender brought a mighty baptism of the Spirit's power", see ibid., p.97.

[673] Shortly after his conversion, in 1812, the evangelist Charles Finney was baptised in the Spirit, and spoke in tongues, but he did not know what to make of it, see D.P. Williams, *The Prophetical Ministry* (1931) p.98 and M. Harper, *As at the Beginning* (1965) pp.26-27. Hugh Bourne and other early leaders of the Primitive Methodists had also spoken of being "sealed by the Spirit" and enjoying full assurance as a post-conversion experience. It was accompanied by a "spirit of burning", a sense of burning love, see J. Walford, *Memoirs of the Life and Labours of the Late Venerable Hugh Bourne* (1999) vol.1, pp.115-123.

[674] R.A. Torrey, *Why God Used D.L. Moody* (1923) pp.51-59.

believing it explained their effectiveness as evangelists, compared to others. F.B. Meyer suggested that Moody's baptism in the Spirit explained why Moody affected the world. The idea of a second baptism was inherently attractive to those engaged in evangelistic work, because it shifted the focus from the word of God, which was under attack, to the work of the Spirit. The danger was that the word of God in evangelism might be given up, as people relied exclusively on the Spirit giving power to their utterances, rather than relying upon the word of God – which the Bible stated was "the sword of the Spirit".[675] For the great evangelists of the nineteenth century, this was not a danger – but for lesser mortals it might be. Furthermore, there was also the danger of separating the role of the Spirit and the word of God and fulfilling Coleridge's aim of separating, in practice, "two distinct conceptions – revelation by the Eternal Word, and actuation of the Holy Spirit".

In 1891, the Pentecostal League of Prayer was founded by Richard Harris – a prominent London barrister and later a King's Counsel – to pray for all believers to be filled with the Holy Spirit, for revival in the churches and for holiness.[676] At around the same time, others, such as Mary Boddy, the wife of the Church minister Alexander Boddy, demonstrated gifts of healing and her husband "used a service of anointing the sick and taught on the subject of healing".[677] Elsewhere, in the 1890s, Smith Wigglesworth, born in the year 1859 and later a Pentecostal pioneer, became aware of a divine healing ministry in Leeds and orientated in that direction his mission in Bradford.[678] He also received what a later generation might call[679] "words of knowledge" and practised the casting out of 'the devil' from a human body.[680] He had witnessed in Salvation Army meetings, and in those of his own, people "prostrated under the power of the Spirit".[681]

[675] Ephesians 6:17.

[676] See D. McCasland, *Oswald Chambers* (1993) pp.90-91.

[677] G. Wakefield, *The First Pentecostal Anglican* (2001) p.6.

[678] C.C. Whittaker, *Seven Pentecostal Pioneers* (1981) p.22 and S.H. Frodsham, *Smith Wigglesworth* (1974) pp.22-25 and 33-38.

[679] Ibid., pp.26-28 and 32-33.

[680] Ibid., pp.36-38. The text suggests the devil, rather than a demon.

[681] Ibid., pp.15 and 42.

13.8 Christian socialism

Christian socialism waned in the mid-1850s, but its influence re-emerged during the last quarter of the century. Christian socialists believed that the working classes were alienated from the churches because of their harsh conditions and sufferings. This, it was argued, was the result of the individualism and competition of the age; the remedy was a society based on co-operation. Their early leader, F.D. Maurice, believed in the "Fatherhood of God" and, therefore, church members had a special responsibility for the less fortunate. That this was socialism, as distinct from kindness, was not necessarily understood by contemporaries. In the hands of others, Christian socialism took on many different hues.

Stewart Headlam was Maurice's student at Cambridge and a leading light in the Guild of St Matthew (1877-1909), a Church organisation committed to promoting the holy communion, the teachings of the Prayer Book and "the study of social and political questions in light of the incarnation".[682] This revived Christian socialism, after the initial thrust by Maurice waned. Indeed, it was to be "the red hot centre of Christian socialism in England".[683] Like Maurice, Headlam rejected the doctrine of hell[684] and also the divine inspiration of the Bible.[685] He believed in the Real Presence of Christ in the eucharist – "that men could only approach God in community"[686] – and was not bound by convention.[687] It is said that his greatest act of courage was standing bail for Oscar Wilde in 1895 when the latter was tried for sodomy. Headlam hardly knew Wilde.[688]

Headlam's Guild of St Matthew appealed to radicals; it never exceeded 400 members and its most flourishing period was the years around 1884.[689] It campaigned for a land tax and other means of redistributing

682 F.G. Bettany, *Stewart Headlam: A Biography* (1926) p.80.

683 K. Leech, "Stewart Headlam, 1847-1924 and the Guild of St Matthew", in *For Christ and the People* (1968) (M.B. Reckitt (ed.)) p.63.

684 His evangelical father, in the hope of curing him of Maurice's theology, sent him to assist an evangelical minister for a year. The cure was unsuccessful. Other clergy, aiming at the same remedy, were equally unsuccessful, see ibid., pp.61-62. In adult life, he preferred Charles Bradlaugh to the likes of Moody and Sankey, ibid., p.65.

685 Ibid., p.84.

686 Ibid., p.63.

687 See generally E. Norman, *The Victorian Christian Socialists* (2002) pp.98-120.

688 Headlam's wife was a lesbian, see J.C. Cort, *Christian Socialism* (1988).

689 F.G. Bettany, *Stewart Headlam: A Biography* (1926) p.83.

wealth, free secular schools (the churches doing the religious teaching), a minimum wage, and a maximum length of the working day. The religious basis of the movement was "an endeavour to bring the 'great principle of the Oxford Movement home to those who might not otherwise have grasped it' – the eucharistic centre of Christianity, the religious basis of all their work".[690] The eucharist spoke of "brotherhood, solidarity, co-operation" as the sacrifice offered was for all.[691] Many received their "first intimation of the social gospel" through the Guild of St Matthew.[692] Headlam took action to wind it up in 1909, since other views of socialism's content began to prevail among its members and interest in religion flagged.[693]

The most important Church of England move to advance Christian socialism was the Christian Social Union ("CSU"), founded in 1889. It drew those holding a wide variety of doctrinal positions.[694] Its membership peaked at 6,000. Sixteen of the 53 men appointed as a bishop, between 1889 and 1913, were CSU members.

Its first president was Bishop Westcott, who had inclinations towards universalism,[695] but his massive scholarly abilities encouraged some conservatives to join, without undue risk to their reputation. His successor was Charles Gore, the editor of *Lux Mundi*. To illustrate Christian socialism's development, we will briefly consider one of Gore's principal contributions to the CSU – his pamphlet, *The Social Doctrine of the Sermon on the Mount* (1892). Gore was concerned to work out the details of a Christian's moral duty from the Sermon on the Mount. He emphasised the importance of character: "social improvement must always have its stronghold in the regeneration and sanctification of individual characters".[696] The point was made that the Lord in the sermon spoke to the church and not the state. The Sermon on the Mount

[690] E. Norman, *The Victorian Christian Socialists* (2002) p.106.
[691] K. Leech, "Stewart Headlam, 1847-1924 and the Guild of St Matthew", in *For Christ and the People* (1968) (M.B. Reckitt (ed)) p.71.
[692] E. Norman, *The Victorian Christian Socialists* (2002) p.120.
[693] F.G. Bettany, *Stewart Headlam: A Biography* (1926) p.92.
[694] There were also Nonconformist societies such as the Christian Socialist League, of which John Clifford was the first president, M.R. Watts, *The Dissenters* (2015) vol.3, pp.310-313.
[695] P. Blair, *What on Earth?* (1993) p.45.
[696] C. Gore, *The Social Doctrine of the Sermon on the Mount* (1892) p.7.

was said to express the "*social principle*" – being "*the principle of the sonship and brotherhood of man as based on the Fatherhood of God*".[697] This fundamental principle involved, among others, three subordinate principles – namely, the principles of justice, trust in God's Fatherhood and the principle of co-operation, not competition.

The Social Doctrine is a carefully drafted pamphlet. It uses biblical language to draw the evangelicals, but Gore is critical of the contemporary practices of both the Ritualist[698] and Evangelical parties.[699] And, as an ecclesiastical statesman, he concludes with an appeal to which all can agree: "We want…'to seek first the kingdom of God and his righteousness;' to consolidate Christian moral opinion in each district of Church life; to let it be known what Christian living means."[700] All the same, the pamphlet does not provide any detailed social programme apart from suggesting that the church should be supportive of the latest social trends. Reformers, like Tom Mann, described Gore's three subordinate principles as "mere threadbare phrases".[701] Ironically, by focusing on the 'social principle', rather than Christ and what he has done for humanity's eternal future, the pamphlet encourages a materialistic view of the universe – not the purpose of the Sermon on the Mount.

To buttress the 'social principle', Gore and the other Christian socialists called upon Christians to seek the kingdom of God, and to speed its coming. God's Kingdom was a biblical concept; it was the place where God's commands were obeyed. However, in the late nineteenth century, the doctrine gained unexpected prominence and was often given a new twist. Gore suggested that social change, and the coming kingdom of God, required a regenerated man. This was achieved through the "life-giving word of Christ alone which could impart life", but its power was limited. Obstacles needed to be removed before it could exercise influence – such as "Bad dwellings, inadequate wages, inadequate education, inability to use leisure – these are stones which lie upon the graves of men spiritually dead." Gore contended that they had to be taken

[697] Author's italics. Ibid., p.10.
[698] Gore wrote: "we are making much too much of the development of the outward exhibition of worship. We trust too much to church building and organising of 'plant'", ibid., p.16.
[699] "We try too much 'to get people to come to church'", ibid.
[700] Ibid.
[701] T. Mann, *A Socialist's view of Religion and the Churches* (1896) p.6.

away by men before the word of Christ proved effective.[702] Here was the suggestion that something else needed to be done, before evangelism took place. This thesis reappeared in later generations, but in a different guise, with other social issues to be sorted out before evangelism could take place.[703] If the thesis was adopted, evangelism must come to a halt and the church must weaken, until the relevant obstacle to evangelism was removed – unless a further obstacle to evangelism was identified and also had to be cleared away.

Elsewhere, proposals for social or political change were elevated to the status of fulfilling the kingdom of God – without the need to regenerate mankind. In practice, the approach was similar to that suggested by Gore. The church was to sort out people's housing, wages, etc, although there was no aspiration to hold out to them the word of life once these had been achieved. In a lecture to his students in 1889, C.H. Spurgeon complained: "A new theory has lately been started, which sets forth as its ideal a certain imaginary kingdom of God, unspiritual, unscriptural, and unreal. The old-fashioned way of seeking the lost sheep, one by one, is too slow: it takes too much time, and thought, and prayer, and it does not leave space enough for politics, gymnastics and sing-song. We are urged to rake in the nations wholesale into this imaginary kingdom by sanitary regulations, social arrangements, scientific accommodations, and legislative enactments. Please the people with the word 'democratic', and then amuse them into morality...our Lord's Kingdom is, after all, to be of this world; and, without conversion, or the new birth, the whole population is to melt into an earthly theocracy."[704]

Christian socialism's emphasis on this life, to the exclusion of the hereafter, points to why socialism became, in some quarters, more important than Christianity – and Christianity no more than the means to implement socialism. For example, Percy Dearmer, the secretary of the CSU from 1891 to 1912, ended a passionate exposition of Christian socialism by drawing his readers to the need to convert the heart of man, for socialism to spread. He adds, "You will only convert him by giving

[702] C. Gore, *The Social Doctrine of the Sermon on the Mount* (1892) p.7.

[703] Most recently, the successors of those taking this view have identified the need for female ministers/bishops – or the church – to affirm homosexual marriage before they can countenance evangelism.

[704] C.H. Spurgeon, *An All-Round Ministry* (1960) p.322.

him a moral ideal. Is there a better one than Christ?"[705] This leads to his point that socialism has only spread in Christian lands – with the implication that if socialists want socialism to spread, they had better make other lands Christian. Christianity had become the servant of socialism; not the means of saving mankind from the wrath to come.

Overall, Christian socialism appealed to men from all theological parties and denominations – including many "who would call themselves evangelicals". Maurice and his "brilliant exponent [Charles] Kingsley" were admirable personalities, captivating many.[706] John Clifford – President of the Baptist Union at the time of the Down-grade Controversy with Spurgeon – was also a Christian socialist and spoke at Fabian meetings.[707] Hugh Price Hughes, the leading Methodist at the end of the nineteenth century, started to elaborate social Christianity. To these men, Christian socialism seemed to offer the opportunity of enabling the working classes to find self-expression through Christianity – when traditional orthodoxy had not drawn that many. Both Clifford and Hughes developed churches and, in Hughes's case, a movement to meet the physical needs of working men, as well as their spiritual needs, while rejecting the doctrine of eternal torment.[708]

In conclusion, one commentator on the CSU wrote that it was "extraordinarily successful...in preparing the English Christianity of the early twentieth century for a new appreciation of the need for social change".[709] This commentator adds that its principal role was as an educator and propagandist, although he notes that on occasion practical action resulted.[710] In the longer term, it became "the major vehicle by which the social gospel arrived".[711] Neither it, nor any of the

[705] P. Dearmer, *Christian Socialism* (1897) p.16.

[706] H.C.G. Moule, *The Evangelical School in the Church of England* (1901) p.116.

[707] In our period, Clifford sought to prove that the "collectivist arrangement has at least four distinguishing merits, demonstrating its closer and stronger affinities with the teaching of Jesus Christ than the present method of administering the physical life of man: (1) it destroys the occasions of many of the evils of modern society; (2) it advances, elevates, and enables the struggle of life; (3) it offers the development of Christ's teaching concerning wealth and brotherhood; and (4) it fosters a higher ideal of human and social worth and well-being", see J. Clifford, "Socialism and the Teaching of Christ", in *Fabian Tract No. 78* (1897) pp.6-7.

[708] C. Oldstone-Moore, *Hugh Price Hughes* (1999) p.334.

[709] E. Norman, *The Victorian Christian Socialists* (2002) p.173.

[710] Ibid.

[711] J.C. Cort, *Christian Socialism* (1988) p.158.

other Christian socialist organisations, broke through the class barrier to make sustained communication with the urban masses. This was also true of the short-lived Labour Church Movement founded, in 1891, by the former Unitarian minister John Trevor. It sought to link the emerging Labour movement with the divine. It rejected traditional theology.[712]

13.9 Theological education

Many thought better, and more learned, ministerial training was the key to winning their vision of the future. In 1864, the Congregational Union was rocked when Henry Allon denigrated the fact that nearly half of all ministers of Independent Churches lacked an academic qualification.[713] From 1871 they had full access to the older universities but, as a result, there was the danger that, while attending them, the sons of Congregationalists drifted into Anglicanism, or away from the faith altogether.[714] To prevent this, in 1886 the Congregational Spring Hill theological college, in Birmingham, was transferred to Oxford and, with enlarged resources, renamed Mansfield College. Its task was to act as a centre to nurture Nonconformity in Oxford and to train ministers to challenge 'Anglicanism and Agnosticism'.[715] Its ambition and that of its staff knew no limit. Mansfield College's first principal, Andrew Fairbairn, was described by his biographer as having the "self-appointed task of reconstructing Christian theology".[716] Of Fairbairn's intellectual capacity there was no doubt. Lord Acton "doubted whether anyone at Oxford equalled him".[717] The danger, though, for the college, was that it would be assimilated into the mainstream of thought – a mainstream that previous generations of Nonconformists had "assiduously denounced".[718] The likelihood of such a development had already been prepared for by

[712] K.F. Inglis, *Churches and the Working Classes in Victorian England* (1964) pp.215-249.

[713] J. Waddington, *Congregational History, 1850-1880* (1880) vol.5, pp.435-440. See also M.R. Watts, *The Dissenters* (2015) vol.3, pp.191-206.

[714] E. Kaye, *Mansfield College, Oxford* (1996) pp.43-44 and 50-51.

[715] D. Inman, *The Making of Modern English Theology: God and the Academy at Oxford, 1833-1945* (2014) p.186.

[716] W.B. Selbie, *The Life of Andrew Martin Fairbairn* (1914) p.202.

[717] See R. Tudur Jones, *Congregationalism in England 1662-1962* (1962) p.266.

[718] H. Schlossberg, *Conflict and Crisis in the Religious Life of Late Victorian England* (2009) p.125 and E. Kaye, *Mansfield College, Oxford* (1996) p.90.

a considerable softening in the doctrinal content of the college's trust deed when it changed its name and location. Indeed, Mansfield College under Fairbairn raised up a generation of Liberal Evangelicals.[719] Its first students included the gifted William Selbie and Silvester Horne.[720]

Within the theological colleges and universities, theological liberalism grew and, from them, through the training of ministers, it entered the churches. The means of disseminating the new ideas expanded when Fairbairn started, in 1892, a very successful summer school for younger Free Church ministers. Three hundred attended. The impact of the theological colleges was widely known; one member of the laity suggesting that Nonconformist theological colleges sent out men whose "mission is to entertain and enlighten the sceptical *dilettante* of their congregation with polished essays on the literary curiosities of Scripture". Thus, instead of offering "Jesus Christ as the Jehovah of the Old Testament" to the millions clamouring to know God, there were only "sentimental vapourings of universal love and fatherhood".[721] The result was half-empty churches.

For the Church of England, the colleges founded in an earlier period for "raising an inferior class of clergy" proved successful. For example, in 1862, St Aiden's College, Birkenhead contributed five percent of the candidates for the entire English ministry.[722] Nevertheless, a further 16 Anglican theological colleges were founded in England between 1859 and 1900, although some closed. Many of these new colleges aimed at recruiting graduates wanting specialist clerical training. Evangelicals tended to regard them with suspicion, as entities that would fall to the High Church party.[723] In 1863, they founded the evangelical London College of Divinity (also known as St John's Hall, Highbury, later St

[719] R. Tudur Jones, *Congregationalism in England 1662-1962* (1962) pp.266-269. For further detail relating to the foundation of Mansfield College and its early influence on Nonconformity, see M.D. Johnson, *The Dissolution of Dissent, 1850-1918* (1987) pp.165-293.

[720] *The Life of Charles Silvester Horne* (1920) (W.B. Selbie (ed.)) pp.31-32.

[721] W.J.C. Ward, "Are Nonconformists Departing from the Faith?", in *The British Weekly*, 11 November 1887, p.30. See also T.A. Noble, *Tyndale House and Fellowship* (2006) pp.34-35.

[722] J.W. Colenso, "Preface" to *The Pentateuch and Book of Joshua Critically Examined* (1863) pt.2, p.xi.

[723] D. Dowland, *Nineteenth-Century Anglican Theological Training* (1997) p.69.

John's, Nottingham) for urban non-graduates. This was followed, after the ancient universities began to be secularised, by the establishment of the colleges of Wycliffe Hall in Oxford and Ridley Hall, in Cambridge. In February 1879, *The Times* carried an article stating that the former had been open a year and that the latter had just purchased an "excellent site" to educate candidates for Holy Orders from the great universities in "the principles of our reformed Protestant Church and to train them to be good ministers".[724] Their first 20 years were times of trial.[725] By 1900, Wycliffe Hall had grown to only 32 students.[726] In Wales, the foundation on Tractarian lines, in 1892, of St Michael's College, Aberdare for graduates, contributed "to the progressive catholicisation of the Welsh Church".[727]

Even the Primitive Methodists took up scholarship. In 1868, the Sunderland College was established and, in 1881, a college in Manchester followed. This soon became known as Hartley College.[728] In 1892, A.S. Peake, an influential Liberal Evangelical of the next century, became a tutor there. He later became the first Nonconformist professor of divinity when he took up the Rylands chair at Manchester University. Peake, between 1890-92, had lectured at the recently opened Mansfield College, Oxford.

The faith missions, the nature of which we will come to later, were not left out of this expansion of theological education. For instance, in 1873, Henry Grattan Guinness, part of the theological wing of the Guinness brewing family, founded Harley College, in Bromley-by-Bow, to train-up youth for home and foreign missions. Its students were not "side-tracked on to the lower level of social work and reformation".[729]

724 "Theological Halls at Oxford and Cambridge", in *The Times*, 7 February 1879 and "Theological Halls at Oxford and Cambridge", in 77 *The Christian Observer for the Year 1877* (1877) p.577. For more detail see J.B. Harford and F.C. Macdonald, *Handley Carr Glyn Moule* (1922) pp.91-98.

725 H.C.G. Moule, *The Evangelical School in the Church of England* (1901) p.107. See also J.B. Lancelot, *Francis James Chavasse* (1929) pp.103-110.

726 M. Wellings, *Evangelicals Embattled* (2003) p.92.

727 D.D. Morgan, *The Span of the Cross* (1999) p.25.

728 G. Milburn, *Primitive Methodism* (2002) pp.40-42 and 74-75.

729 C.W. Mackintosh, *Dr Harry Guinness* (1916) p.18.

13.10 Seeking agreement

In the 1870s and beyond, attempts were made through various Church conferences to identify common ground between the contending parties and to establish the truth. A comprehensive theology was wanted, although popery, even for a High Churchman like Edward Benson, the Archbishop of Canterbury, was unacceptable. Many evangelicals, but certainly not all, willingly reached out to other groupings. Bishop Ryle, in an oft quoted passage, said: "I frankly allow that many of those who disagree with the views I have expressed today are just as loyal to the Church of England as myself, and I have not the slightest wish to ostracize them, or drive them from the communion. Of course I think them mistaken and in error...But I do not want to unchurch them, so long as they honestly and 'ex animo' subscribe to the Thirty-nine Articles. Papists, Socinians, and infidels, are certainly in the wrong place in the Church of England, and I cannot tolerate them. Within these limits I can tolerate a great deal, and cultivate hope, charity and others."[730]

But there could be uncomfortable consequences for an evangelical speaker at a conference drawing those from a broad spectrum of theological positions. Ryle was labelled a "Neo-Evangelical" by certain more conservative evangelical Churchmen, for doing so. Spurgeon told him to come out from the Church of England and "to no more touch the unclean thing". However, by the end of our period, Handley Moule thought that such conferences had modified evangelical views on other systems of thought for the good and enabled them to reach out to other groupings although, in doing so, some might have become unduly tolerant.[731]

13.11 Further consequences of doctrinal variety

The first victim of growing doctrinal disunity was the circulation of the Bible. By the late 1860s, the Bible Society found it difficult to get support from Broad Churchmen, Tractarians or political dissenters.[732] Further, in seeking religious harmony, the danger arose that truth might be surrendered. In the mid-1860s Spurgeon complained in a sermon that

[730] J.C. Ryle, *Church Principles and Church Comprehensiveness* (1879) pp.40-41.
[731] H.C.G. Moule, *The Evangelical School in the Church of England* (1901) pp.72-75.
[732] L. Howsam, *Cheap Bibles* (1991) p.196.

"Modern professors have discovered a very easy way of religion...the modern theory of universal charity, let him believe that a lie is a truth and that whether it be a lie or a truth is of no consequence at all".[733]

13.11.1 *Experience is emphasised*

Given the inability to agree on doctrinal matters, some evangelical leaders emphasised "experimental and practical preaching".[734] On this, the blessing of God could be seen. The Salvation Army was especially instrumental in forwarding what worked in practice. It was criticised for its abandonment of the communion and baptism but if, as Booth claimed, it was possibly the fastest growing Christian movement since the days of the apostles,[735] who could argue? Booth affirmed:

> We are opposed to all that teaching of the Bible which is merely theoretical, speculative, and controversial, and which has no bearing on the immediate experience and walk and warfare of our soldiers... We...are doing a great work, and we cannot come down to discuss questions on which the most eminent doctors of divinity disagree.[736]

Moody was another pragmatist. He invited Christians of a variety of doctrinal positions to his supporter's platform, making doctrine appear to be of secondary importance. In 1890, in a series of lectures on why believers continued to believe in God, R.W. Dale's first answer was the argument from personal experience.[737] As his biographer recalled,

[733] C.H. Spurgeon, "'Let us go Forth'", in *Metropolitan Tabernacle Pulpit* (1865) vol.10, p.365. Ryle was of a similar view. In 1891, he commented that there was "a jelly-fish Christianity in the land; that is, a Christianity without bone or muscle or power...of which the leading principle is 'No dogma, no distinct tenets, no positive doctrine.' We have hundreds of jelly-fish clergymen, who seem not to have a single bone in their body of divinity...we have thousands of jelly-fish sermons preached every year – sermons without an edge or a point or a corner, smooth as billiard balls, awakening no sinner and edifying no saint…we have myriads of jelly-fish worshippers – respectable church-going people who have no distinct and definite views about any point in theology...They think everybody is right and nobody is wrong, everything is true and nothing is false", J.C. Ryle, *Thoughts for the Times* (1891) p.7.

[734] I. Murray, "A Hundred Years Ago (II.) The Death of John Angell James", in 15 *Banner of Truth*, April 1959, p.9.

[735] W. Booth, *All About the Salvation Army* (1885) p.7.

[736] Ibid., p.16.

[737] R.W. Dale, *The Living Christ and the Four Gospels* (1890).

his "contention was that faith in Christ is trust in a person, not belief in a book; that we believe in Christ, not because we believe the Bible to be supernaturally inspired, but that we believe in the inspiration of Scripture, because we believe in him; that the ultimate foundation of faith is personal knowledge of Christ".[738]

13.11.2 *Music and other attractions gain in prominence*

As it became difficult to agree the message, music gained prominence and started to fill its place. Spurgeon thought apostolic preaching was being abandoned for more sensational methods. He provided the following analysis of the times:

> The heaving of the masses under newly invented excitements we are too apt to identify with the power of God. This age of novelties would seem to have discovered spiritual power in brass bands and tambourines... The tendency of the time is towards bigness, parade, and show of power, as if these would surely accomplish what more regular agencies have failed to achieve.[739]

By the turn of the century, an observer wrote: "It is a fatal hour for a church when she comes to regard doctrine as more important than life".[740] And by 'life' was meant the quality of the attractions on offer by the churches, including the music.

13.11.3 *Pastoral work becomes more difficult*

An inability to provide either comfort or challenge in pastoral situations appeared. In 1844, Edward Mannering published his *Christian Consolation*. Mannering was clear that only believers could be expected to receive comfort from God – and then only if they did not "live in habitual violation of any one of the Redeemer's precepts".[741] In 1860, Charles Kingsley wrote to console Thomas Huxley on the death of his son, Noel. Kingsley refers to his "instinct" for the immortality of the

[738] A.W.W. Dale, *The Life of R.W. Dale* (1898) p.593.
[739] Cited in I.H. Murray, *The Forgotten Spurgeon* (1973) p.226.
[740] E. McCulloch, *The Open Church for the Unchurched or How to Reach the Masses* (1905) p.193.
[741] E. Mannering, *Christian Consolation* (1844) p.3.

soul. Huxley responded by indicating that he lacked the "instinct of the persistence of that existence". There was not much more to say.[742]

13.12 Some hold to the Bible and succeed

Some maintained belief in the Bible as the path to life in this age and the age to come, especially those who faced practical challenges. Lord Shaftesbury, to the end of his life, thought that "there was one, and only one, way out of every difficulty" – the spread of the message of the Bible. He considered that "Amid all the conflicts of the nations that are coming upon the earth, that book shall be our life, our light, our security, our joy, our pillar."[743] Ryle also had confidence in its power. In a congress of 1882 entitled "Can we reach the masses?" he pointed to Richard Hobson at St Nathaniel's Windsor who, 14 years before, had begun a church alone with four people in a cellar. When Ryle spoke, Hobson had 800 communicants, 1,700 Sunday scholars and 600 adults in Bible classes. He suggested that Hobson was successful because he "tries to preach Christ in the pulpit, and to visit his people in a Christ-like, sympathizing way as a pastor, at the rate of 75 families a week".[744] Ryle's preaching also drew many. In 1882, he entered Liverpool as its first bishop. Liverpool was notorious for its lapsed masses. After 18 months in the role, that "preaching prelate" witnessed wherever he went, "the church of two thousand seats, with its scanty fifty or one

[742] P. White, *Thomas Huxley: Making the Man of Science* (2003) p.116.

[743] E. Hodder, *The Life and Work of the Seventh Earl of Shaftesbury, K.G.* (1887) p.744.

[744] J.C. Ryle, *Principles for Churchmen* (1884) pp.418-420. On Hobson generally, see R. Hobson, *Richard Hobson of Liverpool* (2003). For others who enjoyed similar success, see I.D. Farley, *J.C. Ryle, First Bishop of London* (2000) p.108. Francis Chavasse, Ryle's successor as Bishop of Liverpool, while principal of Wycliffe Hall, recommended that students keep their morning for sermon preparation and their afternoon for home visiting. He thought that a clergyman should spend 12 hours a week on home visiting, during which time they should manage 25 visits in the countryside and 40 in the town, see A. Atherstone, "'The Prince of Pastoral Preachers': The Oxford Sermons of Francis Chavasse", in *British Evangelical Identities Past and Present* (2008) vol.1, pp.209-210. Some evangelicals were criticised for believing that only preaching was essential. They were perceived to prefer a comfortable study, to trudging through sleet and snow and kneeling beside a filthy bed of a dying pauper, see W.J. Conybeare, *Essays Ecclesiastical and Social* (1855) p.89 and for a response S. Minton, *The Evangelicals and "The Edinburgh"* (N.D.) pp.24-25.

hundred of a regular congregation, being unequal to receive those who would enter".[745] At Cambridge, Paley's *Evidences of Christianity*, which affirmed the miraculous, was just as much a topic of study at the end of the century as it had been at the beginning, even if there was increasing dissatisfaction with it.[746]

For many of the most enthusiastic Christians the developments and practices within their denominations were not to their taste. Some left their existing denominations to establish independent missions, and with the nation's growing prosperity independent mission halls began to proliferate. For example, Thomas Waugh believed that between 1875 and 1895 no less than 100,000 people left the ranks of Methodism for undenominational missions, including the Salvation Army. They preferred "aggressive effort" to "decorous dulness". Waugh thought that the success of the Moody mission of 1873-1875, especially gave impetus to this movement.

Interestingly, Moody had first preached in Great Britain at a gospel hall in 1867. The gospel hall in turn had been established by the publisher R.C. Morgan out of open-air preaching and cottage meetings that followed the 1859 Revival.

[745] Author's italics. J.W. Bardsley, "The Non-Church Going: How Can Our Churches Reach Them?", in *The Christian Monthly and Family Treasury* (1882) p.139.
[746] J.P. Taylor, *A Consideration of Some Recent Strictures on Paley's Evidences of Christianity* (1898).

14

THE GROWTH IN RELIGIOUS ALTERNATIVES

14.1 Overview

By the early 1850s, writers of daily Bible reading notes needed to deal with arguments that there was nothing unique in many Christian doctrines – they were common to "oriental mythology".[747] Others suggested "that there is a substratum of common truth at the bottom of all religions, whether Buddhism, Mohammedanism, or Christianity".[748] In the late 1880s, C.H. Spurgeon complained that the Muslim faith and Buddhism were being praised, to the disparagement of Christianity. He regarded it as a sign of the times. He thought "there is an unbelief abroad which creates a market for anti-Christian literature".[749] Beatrice Webb, of Fabian fame, grew up in the late Victorian period. She noted that for those who could not accept traditional Christian doctrines, "an alternative form of religious emotion" was arising "out of the opening up of the religions of the Far East".[750] Such religions rarely produced converts, but they provided alternatives to explore, distraction and a hint of mysticism. Beatrice Webb's Christianity was already unorthodox when she sensed the allure of Buddhism and Hinduism. She believed that Jesus saved the world not by his death (she could not accept the atonement), but by his word.[751] Guided by her minister that acceptance of the atonement was the way to gain knowledge of God, she only resolved to live better. But this desire, she wrote, "vanished after a series of house

[747] J. Kitto, *Daily Bible Illustrations (Evening Series)* (1867) vol.3 p.78. See generally ibid., pp.78-91.
[748] See J.C. Ryle, *Principles for Churchmen* (1884) p.xxi.
[749] C.H. Spurgeon, *An All-Round Ministry* (1960) p.286.
[750] B. Webb, *My Apprenticeship* (1979) p.83.
[751] Ibid., p.77.

parties and dances in Gloucestershire; and at the conventional age of eighteen I joined my sisters in the customary pursuits of girls of our class, riding, dancing, flirting and dressing-up".[752] In the end, her study of the Buddha and Hinduism did not convert her, but it did detach her from Christianity.[753] In many ways, Webb's response to Christianity was illustrative of her time. Disliking the claim that she was so sinful that only the death of God's Son could save her, the leisure activities of a young girl of wealthy parents led her away from God. She then tested out the religious alternatives, finding them, to human nature, more attractive than Christ, but false. Finally, she adopted the "religion of science" and sought to restore the world through her own political efforts.[754]

Beatrice Webb is perhaps typical of many, looking for a substitute to God – having rejected contemporary Christianity – and flitting from one idea, ideology or religion, to another. In this Part, there is no space to cover all the other ideas, ideologies or religions. We should though note that theosophy took shape in the late nineteenth century. Its adherents included Annie Besant, an earlier atheist leader.[755] In the late twentieth century, it influenced the New Age movement. Mormonism, as we have earlier noted, had its converts. Spiritualism continued to grow, attracting positive interest from a number of ministers interested in the supernatural;[756] and the scientist Alfred Wallace, before Darwin the first proponent of natural selection, was a spiritualist.[757] Sometimes, spiritualism was a staging post back to orthodoxy from scepticism.[758]

[752] Ibid., p.81.
[753] Ibid., p.83.
[754] Ibid., p.90.
[755] T. Larsen, *Crisis of Doubt* (2006) pp.258-259.
[756] M.R. Watts, *The Dissenters* (2015) vol.3, pp.36-41.
[757] J.T. Costa, *Wallace, Darwin, and the Origin of Species* (2014) pp.xv-xvii.
[758] T. Larsen, *Crisis of Doubt* (2006) pp.165 and 207-210.

15

CONFLICT BETWEEN THE CHURCHES

15.1 Introduction

Prior to the nineteenth century, the law buttressed the position of the Established Church in society. However, in the first half of the nineteenth century, the disabilities on Nonconformists and Roman Catholics voting and holding public office were abolished and some of the worst excesses of the existing political system were swept away. In 1867 and 1884, Reform Acts extended the franchise to around two-thirds of male voters; the electorate was no longer the landed and middle classes. However, women did not have the vote.

Giving the vote to the Nonconformists and Roman Catholics led to an upswell against the privileges of the Church of England. The Nonconformists sought redress through the Liberal Party, sharing "a common belief in the virtues of hard work, independence, self-reliance and personal probity".[759] The leading Congregationalist R.W. Dale thought its work on behalf of the Nonconformists was to remove "one incidental and subordinate grievance after another".[760]

15.2 The Church of England loses its grip on the old universities

In the first-half of the nineteenth century Thomas Chalmers, Scotsman though he was, defended the endowments of Oxford and Cambridge as the means whereby science and theology had been maintained at the highest level.[761] In the second half of the nineteenth century, it was not the Church's grip on the endowments of the ancient universities that

[759] M.R. Watts, *The Dissenters* (2015) vol.3, p.271.

[760] R.W. Dale, *The Politics of Nonconformity* (1871) p.10. Dale, later, is said to have repudiated his emphasis on politics, see *Nonconformity and Politics* (1909) pp.236-237 and G. Jackson, *Reasonable Religion* (1922) pp.39-40.

[761] "E.B. Ramsey", in *T. Chalmers* (N.D.) pp.30-31.

was lost, but the control of the universities themselves. In the 1850s, Acts of Parliament opened lower degrees at Oxford and Cambridge to members of any religion, or none. However, the government of these universities and their colleges was reserved to members of the Church of England. Then, in 1871, these restrictions were swept away by Gladstone's government,[762] as were similar ones at Durham. By these changes, the Church of England's supremacy in theological and other areas of scholarship,[763] and its ability to influence the mind of the nation, was gravely diminished. Instead, from these centres, ideas in conflict with Christianity could flow freely.

Accompanying these changes was a move away from the belief that no education can be good without religion. The aim of the university was increasingly to be the advancement of knowledge, harnessed to the social and economic welfare of the nation. The older view, though not neglecting scholarship, affirmed virtue, its promotion and an understanding of, and consent to, the doctrines of the Established Church, as the source from which they flowed. It was religion that permeated, and gave meaning to, the various disciplines. That way, God would bless the nation. In the new world of the secular university, it was the university itself that seemed "the elect instrument for social reform and the salvation of the country".[764]

As a result of these developments, it was found necessary to establish in the universities distinctive Christian groups, such as the Cambridge Inter-Collegiate Christian Union ("CICCU"), founded in 1877, and its Oxford equivalent, in 1879. These groups thrived but, at an institutional level, the ancient universities rapidly lost their religious feel. In 1878, it was said that "agnostic unbelief...has withered so much fair promise in our universities".[765] By the mid-1890s, a member of the Government noted: "A candidate for high university position is

[762] For the background to this development, E. Kaye, *Mansfield College, Oxford* (1996) pp.39-40.

[763] "Dr. A.S. Peake", in *The Times*, 20 August 1929. See also J. Kirby, *Historians and the Church of England: Religion and Historical Scholarship, 1870-1920* (2016) pp.219-221.

[764] R. Horton, *An Autobiography* (1917) p.53.

[765] J.H. Rigg, *The Present Position of Christianity and the Christian Faith in this Country* (1878) p.10.

handicapped by holy orders."[766] In 1895, evangelicals established at Oxford the Oxford Pastorate, as a response to the spread of agnosticism through the student body by "the modern young don who mixes freely with the undergraduates".[767] It was made up of two or three evangelical clergy tasked to build relationships with undergraduates and to spread evangelical influence within the university. However, as James Kirby reminds us, it is possible to exaggerate the extent of the withdrawal of the Church of England from scholarship in the late nineteenth century. In history, for example, "A large proportion of all leading historians were dedicated Anglicans, clerical or lay".[768] The problem for evangelicals, and the doctrines that stimulated church attendance, was that these scholars were, in the main, High Churchmen and were committed to undermining the impact and influence of the doctrines that gave rise to the Reformation.[769] They tended to try, as we have seen, to Christianise the secular idea of 'inevitable progress', rather than defend the idea that it was obedience to God's laws that lifted up a nation to greatness and spared it judgment. It is interesting to note that, in 1857, the editor of the *Christian Observer*, that champion of the sixteenth century reformers and their theology, observed that it was becoming more difficult to obtain contributions of the same quality as those of the past. He believed that the "evangelical body abounds" with capable men, but it was "very difficult to drag them from the cloistered cells, or those busy wheels of life, where they are mainly to be found".[770]

15.3 School education is a battleground

The involvement of Church and chapel in education was another source of conflict. The Nonconformists wanted to minimise the amount of public money received by Church schools and to ensure that their children were not taught Church principles. In 1862, the Committee of the Council on

[766] A.D. White, *A History of the Warfare of Science with Theology* (1896) vol.1, p.xi.
[767] M. Smith, "A Foundation of Influence: The Oxford Pastorate and Elite Recruitment in Early Twentieth-Century Anglicanism", in *The Rise of the Laity in Evangelical Protestantism* (2002) (D.Y. Lovegrove (ed.)) p.202.
[768] J. Kirby, *Historians and the Church of England: Religion and Historical Scholarship, 1870-1920* (2016) p.1.
[769] Ibid., pp.39-40 and 165-188. For the leading evangelical theologians, see D.W. Bebbington, *The Dominance of Evangelicalism* (2005) pp.120-121.
[770] "Preface" to 57 *The Christian Observer for the Year 1857* (1857) p.v.

Education insisted, although as yet ineffectually, that Church schools receiving a government grant must allow pupils, if their parents wished, to withdraw from any religious instruction. To those like Matthew Arnold, it was a battle which epitomised the squabbling nature of the sects.[771] The battlefield was complicated by the fact that Nonconformists split themselves into those who wanted a voluntary education system, those who wanted a state system with religious teaching, and those who wanted a state system with no religious teaching.[772]

The 1870 Education Act created the first national elementary education system.[773] Denominational schools continued with governmental grants but, where they were inadequate, state board schools were established. The right to withdraw children from religious education continued, but was rarely used.

The Education Act of 1870 was exceedingly unpopular with many Nonconformists. They thought it likely to provide more state money to Church of England schools than their own, thereby increasing the teaching of Church principles. Where public money was involved, they wanted public control. It is said that Gladstone, by rejecting Nonconformist antagonism to the Education Act of 1870, caused his disastrous defeat at the subsequent general election.[774] Disagreements between Church and chapel over education continued to influence politics well into the early twentieth century.[775] For example, Church influence over the training colleges was an ongoing cause of friction as, in many parts of the country, Nonconformists "were practically excluded from the teaching profession".[776] Such disagreements made it well-nigh impossible for Christians to unite in major mission work between Moody's last major mission in the 1880s and the beginning of the twentieth century. Only then would another American, R.A. Torrey,

[771] F.G. Walcott, *The Origins of Culture and Anarchy* (1970).

[772] See L.E. Elliott-Binns, *Religion in the Victorian Era* (1936) pp.314-316 and R. Tudur Jones, *Congregationalism in England 1662-1962* (1962) pp.273-276.

[773] The school leaving age was 10; by 1900, it had been raised to 13.

[774] R. Jenkins, *Gladstone* (1995) p.572. For the hostile spirit of Nonconformity towards the Liberals after the passage of the Education Act 1870, see R.W. Dale, *The Politics of Nonconformity* (1871).

[775] G.I.T. Machin, *Politics and the Churches in Great Britain 1869-1921* (1987) pp.225-230.

[776] A.W.W. Dale, *The Life of R.W. Dale* (1898) p.577.

who stood outside their tribal loyalties, unite them.[777]

15.4 Disestablishment

The established church, the Church of England had great privileges. As the electoral franchise was extended, especially in Ireland, it seemed increasingly difficult to justify them. In Ireland, its entrenched position seemed a symbol of conquest. The decisive moment came when Gladstone announced his conversion to the policy of disestablishment of the Church of Ireland. Backed by the Nonconformists, Gladstone achieved his aim, with effect from 1 January 1871.

In 1880 J.C. Ryle spoke of "the senseless bitter crusade of liberationists against the Establishment, which if successful, would only paganise the rural districts".[778] Towards the end of the century, the Nonconformist voluntary system did not generate the funds to meet its ministry needs in the country, and Church leaders did not want to be in the same predicament .[779] A few years later, Ryle referred to the lecturers that the Liberation Society paid "to go throughout the country, making violent attacks on the union of Church and state". It also produced "large quantities of tracts, containing statements about the Church of England of a very erroneous character, which will not bear investigation".[780] It was the Nonconformists who were "with some noble exceptions…the chief agitators for disestablishment".[781]

In the late 1880s, a serious campaign for the disestablishment of the Anglican Church in Wales began. It was driven by a potent cocktail of its relative weakness (although evangelicals had previously been vigorous there)[782] and by nationalism and Nonconformist antagonism to a church

[777] C.T. Bateman, "Missionary Efforts in the Metropolis", in *The Religious Life of London* (R. Mudie-Smith (ed.)) (1904) p.317.

[778] J.C. Ryle, *Churchmen and Dissenters* (1880) p.9.

[779] J.C. Ryle, *Principles for Churchmen* (1884) pp.323, 330 and 352-353.

[780] Ibid., p.313.

[781] Ibid., p.317.

[782] Since the 1850s, "the missionary fervour, practical holiness and preaching abilities of the evangelical clergy" had "spearheaded the parochial transformation" of that church but, in the 1880s, the "evangelicals were being eclipsed" by the Ritualists, see D.D. Morgan, *The Span of the Cross* (1999) pp.27-28. By then Welsh evangelicals seem to have become disorganised, see R.L. Brown, *The Welsh Evangelicals* (1986) pp.151-152.

that was abandoning its roots and turning Tractarian.[783] In 1895, the House of Commons carried the second reading of a bill to disestablish the Church in Wales, but the government fell before it went further. In England, motions to disestablish the Church of England were proposed from time to time, but without seriously going anywhere. Nevertheless, they spread alarm.

15.5 Other Church privileges go

In other areas, the privileges of the Church of England disappeared – or the disadvantages attaching to Dissent were removed. In 1868, the ability to enforce Church rates was abolished after a "prolonged and bitter conflict".[784] The Church moved to annual subscriptions and weekly collections. In 1880, it became possible for Nonconformist funerals to be held in parish churchyards. This might not seem much of a concession and many clergy thought it reasonable. Previously, either the local Anglican minister overlooked Nonconformist practice, or the Nonconformists accepted the Anglican funeral rite. However, the proposal was vigorously contested since some Anglicans saw the controversy as stirred up by liberal politicians to justify interference with the Church of England. Any surviving Nonconformist grievances were removed by the Burial Grounds Act 1900. Two years before that, the Marriage Act 1898 removed the need for a civil registrar at weddings in Nonconformist and Roman Catholic churches.

15.6 The Nonconformist Conscience

The growing political power of the Nonconformists flowered in the 1890s into the "Nonconformist Conscience". The role of Christians in politics was not new. Wilberforce had used Parliament as an instrument for furthering godliness in the nation. Edward Miall in his influential *The British Churches in Relation to the British People* (1849) had affirmed that Christianity "demands of all who believe in it, that it shall be the reigning influence in whatever they undertake". He asked rhetorically whether any man was at liberty to put aside any influence "whereby our fellow-man may be materially profited?"[785]

[783] Ibid., pp.157-161.

[784] *Nonconformity and Politics* (1909) p.92.

[785] E. Miall, *The British Churches in Relation to the British People* (1850) p.295.

The emphasis on politics helped change the meaning of Nonconformism or, perhaps more accurately, crystallised the division of Nonconformity into two types – political and religious. In 1877, Joseph Parker recalled a time when "the term 'Nonconformist' marked a high degree of religious ardour rather than a high degree of political vehemence".[786]

The soubriquet the 'Nonconformist Conscience' first appeared in the context of the fall from power, in 1890, of Charles Stewart Parnell, the leader of the Irish Nationalists, then in alliance with the Liberals. Parnell was found to be an adulterer. As the Liberals depended on the Nonconformists and they found his conduct unacceptable, events were set in motion that led to his departure from political leadership. The three features of the "Nonconformist Conscience" have been defined as: "a conviction that there is no strict boundary between religion and politics; an insistence that politicians should be men of the highest character; and a belief that the state should promote the moral welfare of its citizens".[787]

However, it was not until 1909 that the question was seriously raised as to whether Nonconformity was becoming too political. In that year, the anonymous author of *Nonconformity and Politics* argued that "Nonconformity, in making corporate political action bulk so largely upon its programmes, is forsaking its first ideals, substituting a smaller thing for a greater, and committing itself to a course of action which entails upon Nonconformity a heavy loss in all the things most essential to it if it is to be faithful to its original call."[788] In 1907, membership of all the main Nonconformist denominations fell. The secularising effect of an undue focus on politics by Nonconformism was noted.

15.7 An opportunity for secularism to expand

The differences between the denominations created a desire in many people for peace and a readiness to "sacrifice God's truth". A "spurious liberality" set in. Towards the end of the century, the squabbles of the sects made it "fashionable now to say that all sects should be equal – that all creeds should be regarded with equal favour and respect"; this also pointed to an equal treatment of other religions.[789] Furthermore, the

[786] J. Parker, "The Absorption of Dissenters", in *The Times*, 19 October 1877.

[787] D.W. Bebbington, *The Nonconformist Conscience* (1982) p.11.

[788] *Nonconformity and Politics* (1909) p.3.

[789] J.C. Ryle, *Principles for Churchmen* (1884) p.xxi.

fact that Ritualism repudiated the Protestant idea that God "deals with nations as they deal with him – that national prosperity and national decline are ordered by him"[790] and had adopted the idea of continued progress meant that, if such an idea became dominant, there was no loss in adopting a secularist agenda in government policy.

15.8 Conclusion

Underlying the attacks by the Nonconformists on the Established Church were two principles, and neither principle reflected a desire to secularise the state. First, it was argued that an established church was contrary to "religious equality". It was

> flagrantly unjust for the Government to increase the power of the ministers of a particular church by investing them with exceptional privileges and an artificial social position, and to use the national resources for the maintenance of forms of religious teaching and worship which are regarded with hostility by a large proportion of the people.

Why should, it was asked, the national wealth – of which irreligious men were part proprietors – be appropriated to the support of a Christian church?[791] Secondly, the Nonconformists had the conviction

> that the political organisation of a country is the worst machinery that can be employed to provide for the maintenance of religious worship and the propagation of religious truth, and that any organic relation between the Christian church and the secular government does more to secularise the church than to Christianise the state.[792]

Only by taking away the social dignity, political authority and national wealth conferred upon its ministers, would the Church of England see

[790] Ibid., pp.335-336.
[791] R.W. Dale, *The Politics of Nonconformity* (1871) p.10.
[792] Ibid., p.9.

the "perfect triumph of its spiritual power".[793] These arguments made headway.

The emphasis on politics by the Nonconformists and their attacks on the Established Church, combined with the doctrinal disputes within the denominations, enabled the enemies of doctrinal Christianity to emphasise the squabbling nature of the Protestant sects. In doing so, they had opportunity to advance the ideology of secularisation and to secularise the state, a development that Ritualism and likewise liberal theology, in different ways, encouraged. For the Nonconformists themselves, the emphasis on politics distracted many, and led them to wandering off into the highways and byways of life. For Church and chapel, the warning of St Paul to the Galatians was not heeded: "If you bite and devour each other, watch out or you will be destroyed by each other."[794] Ironically, this was at the very time when both had probably their greatest concentration of the converted within their ranks. However, as St Paul had found long ago, vigorous evangelistic campaigns bring a backlash among the unconverted.

[793] Ibid., p.32. Gladstone, staunch High Churchman as he was, thought that some concessions had to be made to "secure the Church" in the way that "the shipmaster throws cargo overboard to save the lives of passengers and crew", cited in G.I.T Machin, *Politics and the Churches 1869-1921* (1987) p.2.

[794] Galatians 5:15.

16

SUMMARY OF PART 2

16.1 Overview

The spiritual revival, around 1859, represents probably the highpoint of Christianity in the nation. However, its influence was not uncontested and it generated a virulent reaction; many outside the churches wanted rid of Christianity, or at least its doctrinal and supernatural elements, or to redefine them and to create what would effectively be a new religion, fashioned according to human taste. Furthermore, men had slipped into the churches during their huge numerical expansion in the first half of the nineteenth century who were unconverted, or whose doctrinal understanding was deficient, or whose views could be shaped by prevailing intellectual fashion. They too wanted to change what they found in the churches, but in the hope of drawing in the unreached – even if the result was a new religion, in an old building. Individuals from these two groups were natural allies and strengthened each other in their attacks on the orthodox. New religions seeping in from the East and elsewhere also caused a stir; and the differences between the Established Churches and Nonconformity made a united front to these challenges at a denominational level difficult. Indeed, the failure of the denominations to unite around the gospel and the lack of evangelical intellectual vigour in the universities perhaps explains the ultimate inability to repel the assaults on Christian doctrines in the last half of the nineteenth century. The underlying intellectual premises of the assaults were often not new, although at the time they were especially widely held in society and were both virulent and fair-seeming. Nevertheless, the organisations giving physical expression to the intellectual movements of the day were often "small and lacking in social significance".[795]

[795] S. Budd, *Varieties of Unbelief 1850-1960* (1977) p.2.

However, as the intellectual attacks on Christianity grew, evangelicals in Church and chapel did not give up on the evangelistic priority. Indeed, their endeavours in this direction grew also to new heights of zeal, sacrifice and creativity. There were certainly those, like the artist Holman Hunt, who dismissed the attacks of the "critics and theorists" as "the little carpings at words in the Bible". In his view, they overlooked "the cardinal facts that remain – that, to wit, from the little beginning of Abraham's leaving Padan-Aram, the whole of the active-minded people of the world have been blessed with an inspiring religion, which has endowed Shakespeare and the poor in hospital equally with noble and patient hope".[796]

[796] W.B. Scott, *Autobiographical Notes of the Life of William Bell Scott* (1892) (W. Minto (ed.)) vol.1, p.314.

Part 3

Responding to the new challenges (1859-1900)

17

MANY MORE SOULS TO WIN

17.1 Introduction

The emergency for the churches – created by rapid population growth during the first half of the nineteenth century – continued for the rest of the century. Between 1851 and 1901, the population of Great Britain grew from just over 20.8[1] million to 37 million souls. Furthermore, Great Britain was no longer a green and pleasant land. The percentage of the English and Welsh population living in urban areas grew from 50.2 per cent in 1851 to 77 per cent in 1901.[2] Agricultural workers poured into the cities, as the local need for their services fell away.[3] Britain was the most urban place on earth and London the world's largest metropolitan area.

To the churches, population growth, and its changing distribution, presented three major challenges. First, how to win so many souls for the Lord; and to do so on very different terrain to that on which souls had previously been won. A contemporary wrote, "The world is fast coming to consist of so many huge cities; and in them is to be fought the great battle between light and darkness".[4] In this fight for souls in the cities, the churches were not assisted by "The heavens declaring[ing] the glory of God, the skies proclaim[ing] the work of his hands"[5] – smog and, later, buildings obscured the heavens and the skies. The claim to souls would primarily rest on the summons of revelation.

Secondly, meaningful inroads into converting the working class remained to be made. In 1860, with the consequences of the 1859 Revival

[1] J. Black and D.M. MacRaild, *Nineteenth-century Britain* (2003) p.56. In 1851, the population of England and Wales was nearly 18 million.
[2] Ibid., p.80.
[3] M.R. Watts, *The Dissenters* (2015) vol.3, pp.123-124.
[4] J. Macpherson, *Revival and Revival Work* (N.D.) p.60.
[5] Psalm 19:1.

about to bite in London, Lord Shaftesbury – in a speech to the House of Lords – declared, with perhaps a little deliberate exaggeration, that not two per cent of the working men of London attended a place of worship. In his view, some parts of Lambeth were more unbelieving than Sierra Leone. Indeed, congregations of that distant land had contributed to a fund to build a church in Lambeth.[6]

Thirdly, facets of what was later called the "social problem" emerged. The social problem would grow to include, as Randall Davidson, a future Archbishop of Canterbury, remarked, "the problem of the unequal and inadequate distribution of what we call 'this world's goods,' the wrongs and rights of capital and labour, the education question, the fearful problems of intemperance, of impurity, of the overcrowded and ill fashioned dwellings of the poor".[7] Every Christian grouping sought to solve these problems, often using similar methodologies. The Church of England was especially troubled by the "social question" because, as the Established Church, it was most closely connected with the failings of the state.[8]

[6] Lord Shaftesbury, *Speech of the Right Hon. the Earl of Shaftesbury in the House of Lords, Feb 24, 1860 on the Holding of Special Religious Services in Theatres* (1860) pp.4-6.
[7] S. Dark, *Archbishop Davidson and the English Church* (1929) p.60.
[8] K.F. Inglis, *Churches and the Working Classes in Victorian England* (1964) pp.7-9.

18

EVANGELISTIC STRATEGIES TO WIN THE MASSES FOR CHRIST

18.1 Introduction

During the last half of the nineteenth century, the tools to reach the burgeoning populace with the gospel were a mixture of new and old. Those of the past included preaching inside and outside of church, the witness of the liturgy, teaching in families, homes, workplaces and schools, personal conversation and the passing on of tracts and Christian books. There were also the new visitation societies, additional clergy to visit parishioners at home, and more colporteurs.[9] Furthermore, the last half of the nineteenth century saw the usage of these evangelistic tools systemised, expanded and intensified. New ideas and organisations were also explored, established and developed. However, before we consider them, it is worth remembering that ultimately conversion is the work of God. Some, like Priscilla Stewart, later the wife of the important missionary leader C.T. Studd, were converted through a dream and a separate vision that demanded repentance.[10]

Today, the preachers of the era are still remembered. Many a mother prayed that her son would be a preacher and those prayers were answered.[11] An unusual number became household names, especially among the Nonconformists. Pre-eminent among them was the Baptist Charles Haddon Spurgeon. He drew vast crowds, as he preached for

[9] For a weekly timetable of an evangelical minister in the 1880s, see J.B. Lancelot, *Francis James Chavasse* (1929) pp.79-82.

[10] J. and B. Benge, *C.T. Studd* (2005) pp.66-67. The full account is found in Worldwide Evangelisation Crusade, *Priscilla Livingstone Studd* (N.D.) pp.8-9.

[11] See, for example, J. Wood, *The Story of the Evangelization Society* (N.D.) p.108. Spurgeon always attributed his success as a preacher to the prayers of his mother.

upwards of an hour of his over two-hour service at the Metropolitan Tabernacle at Elephant and Castle.[12] A visit to the metropolis from within the Empire, or the English-speaking world, was not complete without a visit to hear Spurgeon in full flow. Spurgeon's publications sold in vast quantities, including his sermons. The average Spurgeon sermon sold 25,000 copies each week, at 1d each. His sermons were a favourite of the colporteurs.[13] A controversial Spurgeon sermon, like that on baptismal regeneration, sold 350,000 copies. Around 1870, the monthly circulation of *The Sword and the Trowel*, the Metropolitan Tabernacle's magazine, was 15,000.[14] Visitors to the Metropolitan Tabernacle noted that the "striking feature" of the congregation was that men "greatly preponderated".[15]

Other Nonconformists also drew vast congregations, achieving national and, indeed, international renown. Many had preached and taught in Sunday school since their teenage years.[16] Foremost among these, and perhaps best remembered today, are William Booth (the founder of the Salvation Army) and the transatlantic American evangelist D.L. Moody. They both had a hunger to win souls for Christ. We will look

[12] C.M. Davies, *Unorthodox London* (1876) pp.40-42.

[13] J. Rennie, *Seed-Time and Harvest* (N.D.) p.30.

[14] M. Hopkins, *Nonconformity's Romantic Generation* (2004) p.158.

[15] "The Down-grade of Dissent", in *The Record*, 4 November, 1887, p.1071.

[16] For example, R.W. Dale was 15 when he preached first – to those assembled in a cottage, see A.W.W. Dale, *The Life of R.W. Dale* (1898) pp.17-18. Spurgeon first taught at a Sunday school – aged around 16 – and first preached to farm labourers, in a thatched cottage, not much later, see A. A. Dallimore, *C.H. Spurgeon* (1984) pp.27 and 32-33. J. Clifford was 15 when he first preached at a secret service held with his friends. He was soon speaking at the young people's prayer meeting and, within a year or two, his name was added to the Nottingham Local Preachers' Association, see J. Clifford, "My First Sermon", in 8 *The Young Man* (1894) pp.306-309. Silvester Horne had charge of a class of small boys, at 14 or 15, and preached his first sermon – in a farm kitchen – to a handful of village folk when he was not much more than 16, see *The Life of Charles Silvester Horne* (1920) (W.B. Selbie (ed.)) p.6. Hugh Price Hughes preached his first sermon, lasting 20 minutes, in a small cottage when he was 14. Six or seven attended – and he distributed tracts to local houses before preaching. At the same age, his name was entered on the Swansea Methodist circuit as a lay preacher, see H.P. Hughes, "My First Sermon", in 8 *The Young Man* (1894) pp.336-338. Joseph Parker was 18 when he felt compelled to take a New Testament and first preach – after a lay preacher had finished his sermon – to around 100 village rustics who had assembled in front of the village saw-pit, see J. Parker, "My First Sermon", in 8 *The Young Man* (1894) pp.13-14. He had already been "in the habit of addressing boy's meetings".

at their work in more detail shortly, together with that of the Methodist, Hugh Price Hughes.

In the 1840s, the Congregationalists had been concerned at their lack of eminent preachers, attributing this to an undue emphasis on doctrine in their training.[17] In the last half of the nineteenth century, they rectified this deficiency by producing a large number of celebrated preachers, including R.W. Dale, Joseph Parker, Newman Hall, Robert Horton and Silvester Horne. The Baptist John Clifford was also highly regarded. Some of these men benefited from the newly-opened University of London[18] and some were among the first Nonconformists to enter Oxford University. Horton achieved the best first in his year at Oxford in classics, was president of the Oxford Union and was a college oarsman.[19] Eloquent, intelligent, passionate and generally well-educated, these men were able to engage with the culture and politics of the day, as well as its religion. But, as contemporaries noted, the emphasis on learning did not generally lead to evangelists "eloquent and mighty in the Scriptures."[20] M.R. Watts observes that many of the Dissenting preachers of the last half of the nineteenth century did not produce "the results, in terms of conversions, secured by their more ignorant and less well-trained predecessors half a century earlier".[21]

The Tractarian Henry Parry Liddon was the best-known Anglican preacher. The leading Anglican figures tended to preach their first sermon after leaving one of the older universities. For example, F.W. Farrar did not preach his first sermon until the day of his ordination – and then

[17] P. Rylands, *The Pulpit and the People* (1847) pp.72-81.

[18] Dale came first and took the gold medal in philosophy at the University of London master's degree examination in 1853, see A.W.W. Dale, *The Life of R.W. Dale* (1898) p.82. "John Clifford took four degrees at the University of London between 1858 and 1866, two of them firsts," see M.R. Watts, *The Dissenters* (2015) vol.3, p.200. Newman Hall also obtained more than one bachelor's degree from the University of London, including, like Clifford, one in law. Hughes, in 1868, was one of the first three who stayed on for an extra year at the Wesleyan Richmond College to obtain a University of London degree. In 1880, he received a master's degree in philosophy from the same institution, see C. Oldstone-Moore, *Hugh Price Hughes* (1999) pp.21, 25-26 and 80. Many Nonconformist ministers also received honorary degrees, often from major Scottish or American universities, see M.R. Watts, *The Dissenters* (2015) vol.3, p.211.

[19] E. Kaye, *Mansfield College, Oxford* (1996) p.48.

[20] I.H. Murray, "A Hundred Years Ago (II.) The Death of John Angell James", in 15 *Banner of Truth*, April 1959, p.8.

[21] M.R. Watts, *The Dissenters* (2015) vol.3, p.213.

at a workhouse service on Christmas Day.[22] William Sinclair preached his first sermon in church the year after his ordination, although he had delivered school addresses.[23]

Danger lurked for the preacher. The leading Church evangelical, Daniel Wilson, observed that "There is a spiritual rivalry which is very apt to creep in and spoil our work". He added that in preaching it was easy to prepare "what will be most attractive and applauded", but not what tended to "edification – direct appeals to the heart and conscience; the bold exposure of sin; the pressing home of personal religion on our people. The simple, plain, honest statement of the whole truth as it is in Jesus".[24] At Bath William Haslam found plenty of "evangelical" preachers with large and attentive congregations, but they seemed satisfied with them. His lament was that "there were no conversions: plenty of the *word* of the Spirit, without any of the *work* of the Spirit!"[25] Others pointed to the need to pray in the evangelistic meeting for the "manifested presence and power of the Holy Spirit".[26]

William Haslam did not find that "the way of exposition and teaching" alone led to conversions; that was the way of the "Scribes".[27] Preachers "must work in the line of the operation of the Holy Spirit, whose primary work is to convince of sin: we must aim at bringing the sinner to see

[22] Archdeacon Farrar, "My First Sermon", in 8 *The Young Man* (1894) pp.56-58.

[23] Venerable Archdeacon Sinclair, "My First Sermon", in 8 *The Young Man* (1894) pp.132-133.

[24] D. Wilson, "Parochial Ministrations and the Spirit in Which to Conduct Them", in 61 *The Christian Observer for the Year 1861* (1861) pp.174-181.

[25] Author's italics. W. Haslam, *"Yet Not I"* (N.D.) pp.38-39 and 322.

[26] W.E. Smith, *Address to Evangelists* (N.D.) p.26.

[27] W. Haslam, *"Yet Not I"* (N.D.) p.76. A similar view was expressed by Captain Smith of the Evangelization Society, see W.E. Smith, *Address to Evangelists* (N.D.) p.27. Haslam suggested that the parties found in the Jewish Church at the time of Christ could all be found in the church of his day. The Sadducees of Jesus' time, who took away from the Scriptures and did not believe in "resurrection, or angels or spirits", were the nineteenth century theological liberals who are "broad and free in their views". The Pharisees, who added the traditions of men not in the Bible, were represented by those who follow the Roman Catholic tradition: and the Scribes, who held the Bible in the letter, but "woefully lacked that experimental knowledge of truth which constitutes spiritual vitality" were those who "go by the Scripture in the letter" but who did not know the power of God. There were also the disciples, each of whom knew the Lord, see W. Haslam, *Notes of an Address on Faith at St Paul's Cathedral, February 1874* (N.D.) pp.iv-viii.

that he is dead in trespasses and sins, that he is lost *now*".[28] It was also necessary that a preacher "should be a *witness*, as well as a *minister* of the truth". Preachers who wanted conversions should say not only "that Christ died, but '*He died for me*'; not only to preach salvation, but to add, '*I am saved*'".[29] Such preaching led to a reaction from the congregation. In 1872, when Haslam moved to the Curzon Chapel Mayfair, some members of the congregation thought his preaching identified him as mad – and left. Others were drawn to it.[30]

A further problem with reaching the nation through preaching was that gospel preachers were mainly limited to the towns; outside of them, energy and doctrinal clarity was often lacking. The Nonconformists referred to one rural area with a radius of eight miles containing 54 parishes and 60 clergymen, but only one known to preach the gospel.[31]

But reaching the nation was not just about the preachers. In the previous century, John Wesley had said: "give me a hundred men who fear nothing but sin and love nothing but God, and I will revolutionise the world". However, by 1859 the population of Britain had more than tripled since Wesley's day. During our period, it nearly doubled again. Accordingly, the great evangelist of the day, D.L. Moody, emphasised, after "good men" – of which there were many – "good methods". A number of evangelistic methodologies emerged, often built on developments earlier in the century, particularly those deriving from America. We will call them "seeker-friendly evangelism", "aggressive evangelism", "transatlantic evangelism" and, towards the end of the century, "holistic evangelism" – which we look at in a later chapter. However, this does not mean that each of these evangelistic approaches was separate. For example, the work of the Salvation Army embodied a number of these methodologies,[32] but such categorisation assists clarity of analysis.

In some quarters, the expectation of likely evangelistic achievements was high. In 1869 Hugh Price Hughes expected to convert Dover,

[28] Author's italics. W. Haslam, *"Yet Not I"* (N.D.) p.242.

[29] Author's italics. Ibid., p.80.

[30] Ibid., pp.315-325.

[31] J. Waddington, *Congregational History, 1850-1880* (1880) vol.5, p.433.

[32] Furthermore, General Booth held that "there are two distinct fields of religious activity – the field of aggressive evangelism and the pastoral field", see H. Begbie, *Life of William Booth* (1920) vol.1, p.157.

when he arrived there as his first charge.[33] Others wanted to soften the message – allegedly in order to increase its effectiveness among the masses – while on the conservative side, "holiness" teaching appeared. *The Family Treasury of Sunday Reading* suggested that "The surest way for a church to gain a larger congregation, *is to be faithful to the one it has*, however small."[34] The basis for this view was that Scripture taught that the "servant who is faithful over a few things, will be made ruler over many things". It recalled the advice that one young minister received, who complained of the smallness of his congregation: "It is as large a one as you will want to give account for in the Day of Judgment."[35]

18.2 Seeker-friendly evangelism

Throughout the Victorian era, getting the poor to church remained difficult. The working classes possessed a "general indifference... to our religious institutions".[36] A government report, just before our period began, noted, "the mute invitation...offered by the open door of a religious edifice" did not lead the "multitudes...to join in what to them would be a mystic worship, and give ear to truths which...are...on their first announcement, utterly distasteful".[37] Seeker-friendly evangelism sought to make changes to church services in order to encourage the masses to attend them.

18.2.1 *More services*

One solution was to run more services, so that the timing of the services did not hinder attendance. For example, Edward Bickersteth, at Christ Church, Hampstead, ran a service every day and, as the Bishop of Exeter, he recommended this practice to his clergy, so that their churches were in daily use. Among the Brethren and other evangelistic-minded churches, evening services to preach the gospel became more common, facilitated by the new gas lighting in urban areas.[38]

[33] C. Oldstone-Moore, *Hugh Price Hughes* (1999) pp.28-29.
[34] Author's italics. "How to Increase a Congregation", in *The Family Treasury of Sunday Reading* (1859) p.27.
[35] Ibid., p.26.
[36] E. Miall, "Preface to the First Edition", in *The British Churches in Relation to the British People* (1850) p.v.
[37] H. Mann, *Religious Worship in England and Wales* (1854) pp.96-97.
[38] T. Grass, *Gathering to His Name* (2012) p.134.

18.2.2 *Shorter services*

The "higher, more spiritual, and more intelligent" regular Church services did not appeal to the working classes.[39] At the risk of breaking the law, a new lighter form of service was pioneered in connection with the opening of the London theatres for services. There was a hymn, a chapter of the Bible was read, then an extempore prayer, then another hymn and a sermon. It was thought that even among "the higher classes there are not a few who would feel the refreshment of an occasional service of this kind".[40] In February 1860 London Diocese launched special missionary services in selected churches across the diocese to which "the working people in their working dress" were "specially invited to attend".[41] Already, special shorter evening services ran at St Paul's Cathedral and Westminster Abbey for the upper and middle classes in need of conversion.[42]

18.2.3 *New types of venue for services*

Some thought that the working classes did not attend church or chapel because of their unfamiliar architecture. One solution was to hold services elsewhere and, in 1859, services for the working classes resumed at Exeter Hall. In December of that year, the Nonconformists broadened the experiment by holding a service at the Britannia Theatre, Hoxton. William Brock, of the Bloomsbury Baptists, preached. Those attending numbered 3,500. A further 2,000 were turned away.[43] The following Sunday, the Congregationalist Baldwin Brown preached at another crowded service. This, though, was not an entirely evangelical venture. *The Revival* noted that Baldwin Brown had "doctrinal sympathy" with Mr Maurice and it "regretted that men of such principles should be pushed forward in connection with these special services".[44]

Nevertheless, at the beginning of 1860, a non-denominational move to throw open some of the capital's leading theatres for Sunday services

[39] "Religious Services in Theatres, and Ultra-Parochialism", in 60 *The Christian Observer for the Year 1860* (1860) p.280.
[40] Ibid., p.281.
[41] "London Diocesan Home Mission", in *The Record*, 17 February 1860, p.1.
[42] E. Hodder, *The Life and Work of the Seventh Earl of Shaftesbury, K.G.* (1887) p.563.
[43] "Sunday Evening Services in a Theatre", in *The Revival*, 31 December 1859, p.179.
[44] Ibid.

commenced. On 1 January 1860 the Congregationalist luminary Newman Hall preached at 3 pm to an "overwhelming audience". In the evening, George Mansfield, the Rector of All Hallows Thames Street, preached to an "equally large and attentive congregation". At Saddlers Wells, J.B. Owen, incumbent at St Jude's Chelsea, preached "to an immense congregation". At the Britannia Theatre, Hoxton, the Wesleyan minister, Richard Roberts, spoke.[45] The theatres were filled with

> costermongers [itinerant traders], street cadgers and labourers; women in fluttering rags, many with babies in their arms; boys in their shirt-sleeves and corduroys; young men and maidens in their gaudy 'Sunday best'; and here and there a few persons in attire denoting that they belonged to the 'better' classes.[46]

In June 1860, as the series of sermons at the Victoria Theatre closed, everyone in the "vast assembly", bar 200, stayed behind for a short time of prayer.[47]

Lord Shaftesbury "stood at the helm", directing the progress of the theatre services movement.[48] He often assisted at the Victoria Theatre's services, reading the lesson in a way that "caused the people to understand".[49] He calculated that on one Sunday alone, 18,630 people who would otherwise not have attended a worship service attended a theatre service.[50] Edwin Hodder, Shaftesbury's biographer, records the moving attempts of the poor as they were exposed to, and tried, hymn singing for the first time. In the House of Lords, Shaftesbury defended holding divine service in the theatres. Some of their Lordships were astonished, if not outraged, by this development. In April 1862, the theatres were still "filled with attentive, and often riveted listeners, week after week and month after month".[51]

[45] "The Theatres", in *The Record*, 2 January 1860, p.2.
[46] E. Hodder, *The Life and Work of the Seventh Earl of Shaftesbury, K.G.* (1887) p.564.
[47] "Preaching in the Theatres", in *The Record*, 4 June 1860, p.2.
[48] E. Hodder, *The Life and Work of the Seventh Earl of Shaftesbury, K.G.* (1887) p.564.
[49] Ibid., p.565.
[50] Lord Shaftesbury, *Speech of the Right Hon. the Earl of Shaftesbury in the House of Lords, Feb 24, 1860 on the Holding of Special Religious Services in Theatres* (1860) p.9. See also "Religious Services in Theatres, and Ultra-Parochialism", in 60 *The Christian Observer for the Year 1860* (1860) pp.276-284.
[51] "The Revival in London", in *The Revival*, 12 April 1862, p.115.

Others were equally adventurous in selecting their preaching venues. Tents were widely used for missions, by organisations like the Evangelization Society. Their range of tents accommodated from 200 to 500 people, although larger tents could be provided.[52] William Booth's mission – that grew into the Salvation Army – began in a tent in the Mile End Road, on the site of a former Quaker burial ground. Moody often preached in a circus or a moveable metal shed. Robert Horton used an iron church for the beginnings of his work in Hampstead.[53] However, it was the Wesleyans who most thoroughly investigated the best building for evangelistic work and, for this purpose, settled on a large central hall.[54] Halls became what the open air had been for eighteenth-century evangelism – "places of a *noncommittal* character to which a man may go...without committing himself in any way to agreement with that which is being spoken".[55] The Methodists built them in number and they were led by "powerful personalities".[56] Central halls were large: some, such as those at Nottingham and Birmingham, were vast. As well as providing large auditoriums, there was space for social enterprises; and the services were bright and might include an orchestral band and two well-sung solos. Manchester's Central Hall was built on the site of what had once been a Wesleyan chapel, but which had closed when its well-to-do members moved to the suburbs. The Manchester Central Hall revived Manchester's Methodism.[57] At these halls the rule that Methodist leaders should only be in place for three years was relaxed.[58] Some people accused the new halls of succeeding through sensationalism. The Methodist class system, going back to Wesley's day, which gave zeal to its members through their acceptance of regular spiritual oversight,

[52] J. Wood, *The Story of the Evangelization Society* (N.D.) pp.236-237.
[53] R. Horton, *An Autobiography* (1917) pp.50 and 55.
[54] J.E. McCulloch, *The Open Church for the Unchurched or How to Reach the Masses* (1905) p.176. See also K.F. Inglis, *Churches and the Working Classes in Victorian England* (1964) pp.92-95.
[55] Author's italics. Cited in J.E. McCulloch, *The Open Church for the Unchurched or How to Reach the Masses* (1905) pp.176-177.
[56] "The Future of our Church", in *The Methodist Recorder and General Christian Chronicle*, 3 May 1906 p.16.
[57] "The Manchester Central Mission", in *The Wesleyan Methodist Church Record*, April 1902 pp.116-117.
[58] M.R. Watts, *The Dissenters* (2015) vol.3, pp.135-136.

was in general decline.[59]

Many denominations established small mission halls in the back streets, worked by a missionary who spent every day in the homes of his people. The secret to their success was the "good preaching of the good old gospel".[60] Once a person was converted, the aim was to move them on to church or chapel. Until converted, the preaching in the churches was thought to be beyond the comprehension of the "poor and ignorant and even of the most educated classes who neither know their Bibles nor understand the most ordinary theological expressions".[61] In mission hall work, a denominational emphasis was found to be unhelpful, although attachment to a church providing regular support in workers and money was important.[62] Some commentators argued that it was only mission halls rooted in the back streets that reached the poorest.[63]

A cottage meeting or lecture was a way to reach out to the more distant parts of a country parish, although they need not take place in a cottage – a village schoolroom, the parsonage kitchen or the farmer's outhouse could be more convenient. Equally, they could be employed in the towns and cities. An Irish bishop, lecturing at St Paul's Cathedral, suggested having "four cottage lectures in four different parts of the parish, spread over the four successive weeks of the month". He found

[59] K.F. Inglis, *Churches and the Working Classes in Victorian England* (1964) pp.98-99 and M.R. Watts, *The Dissenters* (2015) vol.3, pp.145-146.

[60] W. Cuff, "Letter", in *The British Weekly*, 27 January 1888, p.242 and H.E. Stone, "Letter", in *The British Weekly*, 9 March 1888, p.363.

[61] W.M. Smith, "The London-Mission Hall Census", in *The British Weekly*, 10 February 1888, p.279.

[62] Ibid.

[63] A.G. Brown, "Letter", in *The British Weekly*, 27 January 1888, p.242 and H.E. Stone, "Letter", in *The British Weekly*, 9 March 1888, p.363. The view was challenged that the large mission halls did not reach the poorest. The honorary secretary of the Evangelization Society suggested that the "poorest and shabbiest" felt as welcome as the "richest" in even the "showiest mission-hall" – in a way that he did not in the churches, see W.M. Smith, "The London-Mission Hall Census", in *The British Weekly*, 10 February 1888, p.279 and see also G. Kirkham, "The London Mission Hall Census", in *The British Weekly*, 9 March 1888, p.362. See also "The London Mission-Hall Census", in *The British Weekly*, 24 February 1888, p.315 and A.G. Brown, "The London Mission-Hall Census", in *The British Weekly*, 17 February 1888, p.310. There was an ongoing concern that mission hall work led to attenders who did not grow-up spiritually, see H.W. Webb-Peploe, "Letter", in *The British Weekly*, 27 January 1888, p.242 and Mrs H. Grattan Guinness, "Letter", in *The British Weekly*, 20 January 1888, p.230.

the week-day cottage lecture to be "one of the best and surest methods of securing large and regular attendances at the parish church" and of ensuring that the attenders were in a position to profit from the Sunday services.[64] It was important for the clergy not to substitute the cottage lecture for house-to-house visitation. Experience showed that if you did, the flock substituted the lecture for the Sunday services.[65] Apart from the lecture, a cottage meeting might include singing, prayer – both liturgical and extempore – and some liturgy. Some cottage meetings developed into separate parish churches, such was the origin of the Anglo-Catholic parish of St Mary Magdalene, Bradford.[66]

A "room church"[67] or mission room was another venue to reach the masses. A lay visitor would visit local households and, where they were received, they invited the father and everyone else back to a short and simple service in a room. The service often consisted of a reading, a sermon and a prayer and was over in 20 minutes, although the clergyman would stay on to speak to those who wished to talk to him.[68] Numerous room churches were started. In 1887 Liverpool Diocese had 50 licensed mission rooms[69] and more were required.[70] For this purpose, buildings holding 400-500 people were wanted.[71] The London Bible and Domestic Female Mission especially made use of mission rooms. In them the 'ragged' listened to the Bible being read – and were told of the love of Christ straight from the loving lips of women.[72]

The running of a room mission service could test the need to build a church or chapel.[73] For example, Kidderminster's Old Meeting House, in looking to reach out to neighbouring towns and villages, started

[64] W.P. Walsh, "Cottage Lectures", in *Homiletical and Pastoral Lectures* (1879) p.361.
[65] Ibid., p.371.
[66] S. Baring-Gould, *The Church Revival* (1914) pp.294-295.
[67] "The Church Congress", in *The Times*, 10 October 1879.
[68] See also W. Cadman, "Pastoral Visitation", in *Homiletical and Pastoral Lectures* (1879) pp.318-319.
[69] J.C. Ryle, *A Charge Delivered to the Clergy of the Diocese of Liverpool at his Third Triennial Visitation* (1887) p.17.
[70] Ibid., p.22.
[71] Ibid.
[72] "How Wears the Missing Link?", in *God's Message in Low London* (N.D.) pp.13-14 and 22-23 and E. Platt, *The Story of the Ranyard Mission 1857-1937* (1937) pp.75-76.
[73] J.C. Ryle, *A Charge Delivered to the Clergy of the Diocese of Liverpool at his Third Triennial Visitation* (1887) p.22.

mission services at Crossway Green and, in 1862, at the nearby towns of Stourport and Bewdley. As a result, first a chapel at Crossway Green was built and then, "In 1870, the very beautiful mission chapel and school, at Stourport, were opened".[74] The Old Meeting House also ran room services for the aged and infirm. In some places, a coffee house, with some form of religious instruction or worship attached, was used to reach the masses.[75]

In the countryside, in the middle years of the nineteenth century, the appetite for evangelistic preaching was such that barns might be used for services every night for a number of weeks, being larger and holding more than small country churches.[76] Sometimes 1,000 gathered in the snow.[77] Around the parish of Buckenham, in Norfolk, remarkable scenes of revival unfolded.[78]

18.2.4 *The Pleasant Sunday Afternoon ("PSA") movement begins*

In 1875 the PSA movement commenced work, pioneering a new Nonconformist 'seeker-friendly form' of service. It sought to win the lads who, at the age of 15, drifted from the Sunday schools and the working man.[79] A service lasted 45 minutes and was "bright and brotherly, evangelistic and practical, plenty of singing, palpitating with life from beginning to end". The sermon might be ten minutes.[80] John Blackham, the movement's founder, from the Ebenezer Congregational Church at West Bromwich, began it with 120 young men whom he reached, by invitation, on the local streets.[81] Within ten years of its beginning and within eight miles of its place of origin at West Bromwich, 35,000 men

[74] G. Hunsworth, *Baxter's Nonconformist Descendants* (1874) pp.67 and 69.
[75] See E.R. Cotton, *More About our Coffee-Room* (1878).
[76] W. Haslam, *"Yet Not I"* (N.D.) pp.196, 210-216, 244, 258 and 298.
[77] G. Guinness, *"She Spake of Him"* (1872) pp.34-38.
[78] W. Haslam, *"Yet Not I"* (N.D.) pp.300-301.
[79] Some doubted the concept. The title suggested that only something pleasant would attract the working man – and gave "the half-hint that the other services of the churches were not pleasant", W.Y. Fullerton, *F.B. Meyer* (N.D.) p.108.
[80] "The Father of the P.S.A", in *The Christian World*, 8 February 1906 p.11. For an overview of the PSA, see K.F. Inglis, *Churches and the Working Classes in Victorian England* (1964) pp.79-85 and 92 and M.R. Watts, *The Dissenters* (2015) vol.3, pp.176-179. At the opposite end of the social scale some members of the nobility also desired short sermons, see W. Haslam, *"Yet Not I"* (N.D.) p.319.
[81] J.W. Tuffley, *Grain from Galilee* (1935) pp.9-10.

met regularly on a Sunday afternoon for a service.[82] The organisation then spread across the country. Some of the groups making up the PSA movement were very large. The group attached to the Congregational Tabernacle at Hanley in Staffordshire began with 1,200 after Blackham's launch campaign. "Throughout the Potteries, streamers twenty-five feet long were posted on hoardings, and 100,000 handbills were delivered by willing agents, house-to-house, in the streets, at the gates of the 'pot-banks'".[83] This group's membership peaked at 1,680.[84] John Blackham claimed that the movement's growth exceeded that of the Salvation Army.[85] "During the first great flush of success", it started many auxiliary services, including help with learning, sick provident funds and a penny savings bank.[86] Some became concerned that PSA movement meetings might degenerate into entertainment. In 1894, the movement entered Scotland – Pleasant Monday Evenings, for women, having already started.[87]

18.2.5 *Ending pew rents*

Pew rents discouraged members of the working classes from attending church. A few free pews did not help, as their occupants were looked down on in a way that the Bible proscribed. In London, where the regime was most entrenched, between 1870 and 1876, the number of Anglican churches without pew rents advanced from 10 to 30 per cent.[88] By 1890, pew rents existed only in 2,042 churches, but most of these were the new parish churches in the cities and larger towns.[89] The Congregationalists followed the Anglicans in seeking to end pew rents.[90]

[82] D. Killingray, "The Pleasant Sunday Afternoon Movement: Revival in the West Midlands, 1875-90?", in *Revival and Resurgence in Christian History* (2008) (K. Cooper and J. Gregory (eds)) pp.262-274.
[83] J.W. Tuffley, *Grain from Galilee* (1935) p.19.
[84] M.R. Watts, *The Dissenters* (2015) vol.3, p.177.
[85] D. Killingray, "The Pleasant Sunday Afternoon Movement: Revival in the West Midlands, 1875-90?", in *Revival and Resurgence in Christian History* (2008) (K. Cooper and J. Gregory (eds)) p.264.
[86] J.W. Tuffley, *Grain from Galilee* (1935) p.20.
[87] Ibid., pp.21-22 and 36-37.
[88] K.F. Inglis, *Churches and the Working Classes in Victorian England* (1964) p.52.
[89] Ibid., p.54.
[90] Ibid., pp.106-108.

Wesleyan Methodists more tenaciously kept them, in many areas.[91]

18.2.6 *An enhanced role for music and singing*

The churches, to draw a crowd, sought to tap into the fact that their contemporaries found in music "a pleasure and recreation that surpassed all others".[92] *The Times*, on 16 July 1875, explained that "Some people, in view of what they call the stagnation of religious life, have recommended greater variety in services and more singing, and in many of our churches there have been produced high-class music and a gorgeous ceremonial."[93] The aim was to offer an attractive and happy worship experience. In Ritualist churches, robed choirs became common and others followed. Sir Arthur Blackwood thought that evangelical churches, by developing the musical quality of their services to compete with the Ritualists, "trained people to receive the very doctrines which were feared".[94] Even the hitherto more puritanical Congregationalists took to hymns and choirs. Organs also became more numerous, although the leading King's Weigh House Church still had no organ when its pastor, Thomas Binney, died in 1874.

Singing was important to the street evangelists, in order to draw a crowd. For example, the evangelist John Hambleton, at the beginning of his work, prayed "for a fellow labourer who could sing so that in the open air we might attract people". Shortly thereafter, he met Edward Usher who was "a good singing man". Hambleton refers to them as being "yoked together" for a time[95] and that "From that hour souls were brought to God."[96] Groups of marching singers might also draw a crowd to a mission hall.[97] In 1860, advertisements for Richard Weaver's presence at Cumberland Market, near Regent's Park, referred to the fact that he would both sing and preach.[98]

[91] Ibid., pp.95-96 and M.R. Watts, *The Dissenters* (2015) vol.3, p.166.
[92] J. Walvin, *Leisure and Society, 1830-1950* (1978) p.97.
[93] The same points were also made in the next decade, see J.M. Lang, "The Decline in Church Attendance", in *The Christian Monthly and Family Treasury* (1882) p.13.
[94] *Some Records of the Life of Stevenson Arthur Blackwood* K.C.B. (1898) (H.S. Blackwood (ed.)) p.353.
[95] G. Green, *John Hambleton* (2009) p.16.
[96] J. Hambleton, *Buds, Blossoms, and Fruits of the Revival* (N.D.) pp.13-14.
[97] G. Green, *John Hambleton of Liverpool* (2009) pp.10-11.
[98] J. Paterson, *Richard Weaver's Life Story* (2012) p.118.

Moody's helper, Ira Sankey, developed congregational singing for an evangelistic purpose. Sankey was a soloist, lead singer of the choir and capable on the accordion. His music and singing drew people in and reinforced Moody's message. Some thought he was more of an attraction than Moody. *The Times* reviewer of the opening night of their 1875 London mission enthused of a Sankey solo that "to say that this solo was rendered with the utmost impressiveness is but the barest justice". Sankey overruled Moody in public when he thought Moody chose the wrong hymn.[99] *The Times* reviewer did not have much to say about Moody. In 1875, it is said that more people heard Sankey sing than listened to all Bach's works during the entire nineteenth century.[100]

William Booth, the period's other great revivalist, took music in a slightly different direction. In 1878 brass bands[101] were formed to blow down the opposition. Youths in Salisbury were drowning the hymn singing of the Salvation Army – the latter retaliated with a brass band.[102] In 1881 the tambourine appeared and music-hall tunes were adopted for Salvation Army songs. Within a year of a musical department being established, there were 400 Salvation Army bands "crashing into a repertoire" of 88 hit tunes.[103] Music was the key to open many doors. Thomas Champness was the first Methodist evangelist to use a harmonium in the open air. It "opened the way for the gospel to many a heart".[104] "Under the influence of music", Hugh Price Hughes declared, "men would do and dare and suffer that of which they would not otherwise dream".[105] Unusually for a Methodist, he was in favour

[99] "The American Revivalists", in *The Times*, 10 March 1875.

[100] Cited in J. Pollock, *Moody Without Sankey* (1983) p.124.

[101] The use by the Salvation Army of the brass band illustrates the insight of Booth into contemporary culture – and his ability to use it for his purposes. Advances in technology made brass instruments relatively cheap – and brass bands sprang up in every conceivable institution. "Brass band music could be guaranteed to raise interest and support wherever it struck up", see J. Walvin, *Leisure and Society, 1830-1950* (1978) p.104. Its use represented the implementation of one of the seven principles upon which the Salvation Army rested: "Willingness to try new methods of adaption and attack", see E. Douglas and M. Duff, "Introduction" to *Commissioner Railton* (1921) p.xvi.

[102] O. Chadwick, *The Victorian Church* (1987) pt.2, pp.291-292.

[103] R. Collier, *The General Next to God* (1965) p.70.

[104] E.M. Champness, *The Life Story of Thomas Champness* (1907) p.194.

[105] Cited in C. Oldstone-Moore, *Hugh Price Hughes* (1999) p.83.

of sung liturgical services.[106]

However, music was a two-edged sword. If it was the attraction, then the music had to fit the taste of the target audience. This was understood by the successful Methodist West London Mission. By 1905 it had a different musical element at each of its three Sunday services. There was "a large choir" and emphasis on congregational singing in the morning,[107] a "first-class brass band" at the afternoon service[108] and, in the evening, a full 80-instrument orchestra.[109] If musical fashion changed, so must a church's music – if it was to keep its audience.

All this meant that churches could tie themselves up in knots about the right type of music and hymns. Spurgeon, although supportive of Moody and Sankey, commented in 1875 – the year of their great mission to London – that "We are too apt to get into fine harness and tie ourselves up with rules and methods...Why, dear me, if we are to have a special service, one brother must have it conducted on the Moody method, and another can only have Sankey hymns. Who, then, are we that we must follow others? Do not talk to us about innovations, and all that; away with your rubbish!"[110]

Reliance on music to melt the hearts of a congregation might move an individual's confidence from the power of the gospel and shift it to the efficacy of the singing and music. Again, Spurgeon saw the issue clearly. He commented, "Dear friends, we know that souls are not to be won by music". Otherwise "it would be time for preachers to give way to opera singers".[111] Furthermore, the words of hymns became less effective in communicating theological truths, as hymn writers followed changes in theology. In 1880, R.W. Dale complained that hymns were now about man and not God.[112]

The emphasis on music did not advance everywhere. An Anglican visitor to Spurgeon's Metropolitan Tabernacle found that hymns, unaccompanied by musical instrument, could be sung with "striking

[106] Ibid., pp.81-83.
[107] J.E. McCulloch, *The Open Church for the Unchurched or how to reach the Masses* (1905) p.62.
[108] Ibid.
[109] Ibid., p.66.
[110] Cited in I.H. Murray, *The Forgotten Spurgeon* (1973) p.226.
[111] Ibid.
[112] R.W. Dale, *The Evangelical Revival* (1880) p.162.

effect" and form one of the "brightest features" of morning service.[113] Neither were the more puritan of the evangelical Anglicans driven by music. In 1875 Henry Allon wrote that "their services are as bald, and their singing as uncouth, as the Book of Common Prayer will permit them to be".[114] Some Brethren gospel halls did without music in their gospel services, because the unconverted should not be asked to sing about what was untrue in their own experience.[115] Lord Radstock, preaching at a gospel service, told his congregation not to sing the hymn "Just as I am, without one plea, But that thy blood was shed for me", unless they could truly sing it, "for it was better not to sing than sing a lie". A listener, Sir Henry Norman, who could not truly sing the hymn, decided henceforth only to go to Church services. However, at the first of these he attended the service was closed by "Just as I am." "That night Sir Henry Norman responded to the Saviour's request, and was able to sing with the heart "Just as I am, Thou wilt receive, Wilt welcome, pardon, cleanse, relieve."[116]

18.2.7 *The use of leisure and amusements for evangelistic purposes*

Some suggested reaching the masses through the provision, by Church and chapel, of amusements and leisure activities. In the 1870s, the working classes began to have more free time, albeit still limited. Those supportive of the approach argued that the question was whether such time would be spent under Christian or un-Christian influence.[117] In response, a plethora of church, chapel and mission hall clubs and associations mushroomed across the country, including those for concerts, lectures (those on science were seen as particularly helpful, given the way that unbelief used science),[118] debates, gym and other sporting activities. For instance, in Liverpool in 1885, of the 112 football teams in the town, 25 had church associations.[119] Such clubs and assemblies, it was asserted,

[113] "The Down-grade of Dissent", in *The Record*, 4 November 1887, p.1071.
[114] *Sermons Preached in the King's Weigh House Chapel, London. 1829-1869. By T. Binney* (1875) (H. Allon (ed.)) p.xxxix.
[115] T. Grass, *Gathering to His Name* (2012) p.135.
[116] "A Titled Man's Striking Conversion", in *Young Life*, March 1931 p.9.
[117] T.M. Macdonald, "How to Reach Working Men", in *Homiletical and Pastoral Lectures* (1879) p.411.
[118] Ibid., pp.413-414.
[119] J. Walvin, *Leisure and Society, 1830-1950* (1978) p.87. Everton F.C., grew out

were "stepping-stones by which men will be induced to pass into higher scenes of intercourse with the clergyman and his helpers" – occasions to make an "*earnest invitation* to the direct means of grace".[120]

Leading Christian sportsmen used their kudos to promote the public standing of Christianity. This was important, as the working classes tended to think that Christianity was "unmanly" and a premium was placed on showing the opposite to be the truth. There was no better example of this than C.T. Studd. Moody convicted him of "worldliness" at Cambridge in 1882. C.T. Studd was Cambridge University's cricket captain and the best all-round cricketer of his day. Later that year, he was at the crease – undefeated – when England lost the match to Australia that established the Ashes cricket series. In the 1880s, he visited many universities, promoting Christianity and missionary endeavour. His departure for the Chinese mission field created a further stir.[121]

However, using leisure for evangelistic purposes had its perils. It was easy for the Bible and its message to be lost in the need to amuse and entertain. As a result, the work of the church could take on a secular tone.[122] A Wesleyan protesting about a chapel's Pleasant Sunday evening musical observed that "the world has much more power in secularising the church, than the church has in evangelising the world".[123] The influential Baptist pastor Archibald Brown argued that the church had ceased to speak out against the frivolities of the day and had instead adopted them. He made the point that Scripture did not call the church to provide amusement for the people, but to preach the gospel. He noted that the prophets were persecuted not because they amused the people, but because they refused to.[124] He found that the emphasis on amusements

of the football team of the mainly middle-class St Domingo's Methodist church. St Domingo's, an amalgamation of three Methodist churches, was founded in 1870. The football club came out of the church's cricket team – at the end of the 1870s. In the early years, there was a great deal of overlap between church and football club; a club chairman was later both choirmaster and trustee of the church. St Domingo's no longer exists. In 1971, it amalgamated with another church and its land was sold, see the important work J. Corbett, *Everton: The School of Science* (2003) pp.2-3.

120 Author's italics. T.M. Macdonald, "How to Reach Working Men", in *Homiletical and Pastoral Lectures* (1879) p.415.

121 "Missions to China", in *The Times*, 5 February 1885.

122 T.M. Macdonald, "How to Reach Working Men", in *Homiletical and Pastoral Lectures* (1879) p.412.

123 M.R. Watts, *The Dissenters* (2015) vol.3, p.180.

124 A.G. Brown, *The Devil's Mission of Amusement* (N.D.) pp.6-8.

worked havoc among young converts and that "under the shadow of the name of Christ young people are being introduced to the 'world'".[125] As a protest against the use of amusement as an evangelistic weapon, he produced a tract entitled *The Devil's Mission of Amusement* (1889); it was designed to be freely given away. The copy in the British Library is marked "145th thousand".

18.2.8 *The 'institutional' church is established*

An 'institutional' church sought to comprehensively provide for the recreational, social and intellectual well-being of its members. It was a Christian response to the attractions of secular entertainment and culture. Michael Watts suggests that John Clifford's Westbourne Park Chapel, with its attached institute, became in 1878 the first such church in England, and its example was "followed by scores of others".[126] Earlier, Clifford had started a Mutual Improvement Society.[127] At its peak, in 1892, the Westbourne Park Institute had 1,500 members. It provided scientific and literary lectures, geological excursions, archaeological visits, concerts, and classes in languages, mathematics, elocution, shorthand, building construction, dress-making and geometry. There was also a reading room, library, and a literary and debating society. Later, a gymnasium and laboratory were added. At the Barry Road Chapel in Dulwich, Hugh Price Hughes also set about creating an institutional church, and two new buildings were built – one to accommodate 600 children and a library, together with a "large reception room designated for social gatherings". There was also a separate lecture hall able to seat 1,000. Together, these buildings enabled "the church to become a social as well as religious centre of the community". While Hughes was at the chapel, between 1878 and 1881, its membership more than doubled. At an eight-day mission, "65 men, 130 women [and] 200 children went into the vestries as penitents". Hughes also attributed his success to the adoption of the Anglican morning service – which enabled local people

[125] A.G. Brown, "The London Mission-Hall Census", in *The British Weekly*, 17 February 1888, p.310. See also M.R. Watts, *The Dissenters* (2015) vol.3, pp.179-180.
[126] Ibid., pp.168-169.
[127] Ibid., p.175. Mutual Improvement Societies still flourished and later became known as Literary Societies, see C. Oldstone-Moore, *Hugh Price Hughes* (1999) pp.55-56 and 83.

to escape "from the Ritualistic churches".[128] He was willing to advance towards Anglicanism to do so, adopting a sung morning service and establishing a choral society.

Even where a chapel did not have the ambition to be an institutional church, many sought to offer enough facilities to make them the centre of their respective communities.[129] The institutional churches by meeting local educational, social and cultural needs rebutted, whether consciously or not, the thesis of Matthew Arnold's *Culture and Anarchy* that the Nonconformists were Puritans who lived apart from, and did not understand, contemporary culture.[130] However, in doing so, such chapels risked shifting their focus.

18.2.9 *A new translation of the Bible is produced*

Between 1881 and 1885, a new translation of the Bible, the Revised Version, was published, reflecting contemporary scholarship. It became the first translation since the King James Bible to gain popular acceptance, but it was not without its critics.[131]

18.2.10 *New technology is adopted*

Technology was used creatively to draw the masses. Lord Shaftesbury was fond of recalling his experience of holding a magic lantern show in Whitechapel. His audience numbered 400 ragged and illiterate people; another 400-500 were turned away. The slides told the crucifixion story – the last slide being of Jesus standing at the door and knocking. Lord Shaftesbury said, "What you see there, is going on at the door of every house in Whitechapel" – and he invited the audience to throw open the doors of their hearts to him. They were moved to tears.[132]

At the West London Mission, Professor Fleming, Fellow of St John's College, Cambridge was "Director of Lantern Entertainments". He found "picture teaching" the means to stimulate the imagination and arouse inquiry, so that the foundations for adult education and the demand for better things could be laid. Biographies were popular; a series of

[128] Ibid., pp.82-84.
[129] M.R. Watts, *The Dissenters* (2015) vol.3, p.170.
[130] Ibid., pp.181-190.
[131] A.J. Brown, *The Word of God Among all the Nations* (1981) pp.117-118.
[132] E. Hodder, *The Life and Work of the Seventh Earl of Shaftesbury, K.G.* (1887) p.748.

lectures might embrace world-builders such as St Paul, Savonarola, Tyndale, Luther and Bunyan.[133] Lantern technology rendered outdated the colourful illustrations of the Working Men's Educational Union.[134]

18.3 Aggressive evangelism

A further solution to the problem of getting the masses to church was to systematically invade the "dingy territories" of the poor, "by *aggressive* Christian agency".[135]

Aggressive evangelism went back to the ideas that Thomas Chalmers initiated towards the end of the second decade of the nineteenth century and later published in *The Christian and Civic Economy of Large Towns*. Chalmers focused on house-to-house visitation – to reach those left without the gospel by the normal round of church services. In our period, the scope of aggressive evangelism widened to embrace revivals, mission weeks and longer campaigns – supported by "house-to-house visitation, street preaching, tract distribution [and] district prayer meetings".[136] Crowds were drawn through extensive advertising, including the use of newspaper advertising, music, posters and flyers.[137] The Salvation Army added marching and bands to these methodologies to draw the lost. The Methodist minister Thomas Champness "developed amazing ingenuity in attracting crowds. He rang a hand-bell, carried sandwich-boards, displayed a horrible array of heathen relics – anything to lure sinners" to hear the gospel message.[138]

[133] J.A. Fleming, "Free Popular Lantern Lectures", in *Advance!* November 1890 p.21.
[134] S.G. Green, *The Story of the Religious Tract Society* (1899) p.118.
[135] Author's italics. H. Mann, *Religious Worship in England and Wales* (1854) p.97.
[136] E. McHardie, *James Turner; or, How to Reach the Masses* (1875) p.viii.
[137] J.M. Lang, "The Decline in Church Attendance", in *The Christian Monthly and Family Treasury* (1882) p.12. See also G. Thorne, *The Great Acceptance* (N.D.) pp.50-51. Aggressive evangelism could create its own difficulties. Lang thought that the church had learnt too much "the art of puffing". Further, the invitation to leave one church to crowd another, weakened the regular church-going habit. Others criticised the posters and other material used by the Salvation Army, as likely to "offend the refined taste or religious prejudices of better taught and cultured people". The Salvation Army responded to critics by asserting that announcements were issued in the form they took because they wanted: (1) them read. Most religious ones were not; (2) to appeal to a particular class, namely "drunkards, gamblers, harlots, blasphemers, thieves, and neglecters of God and Salvation generally;" and (3) that class to come, see W. Booth, *All About the Salvation Army* (1885) p.12.
[138] J.I. Brice, *The Crowd for Christ* (1934) p.23.

The message of aggressive evangelism was clear. It was the "full-orbed exhibition of gospel truth, illumined by the glory of the cross. Christ must be set forth in all his offices. Sin must be denounced in all its enormity, its hideousness and malignity. The conscience must be probed; that of the sinner alarmed and awakened; that of the believer instructed and quickened. Salvation, full, free, and present, must be offered, and not only offered, but urged and pressed upon the heart; not merely as a privilege, but as a duty instant and imperative, demanded by the inflexible authority of God, and enforced by impending death and a coming eternity."[139]

Open-air work provided a further opportunity to reach those "people who could not be reached by other means".[140] In London, at the end of June 1862, open-air services were held in Hyde Park, St James's Park, Regent's Park, Primrose Hill, Victoria Park, Highbury and Kennington. The services at Hyde Park started at 3.30 pm and finished past 9 pm.[141] Those fit to preach on such occasions were few – either because of want of courage or because of lack of confidence in their natural gifts to do so.[142] Men were also wanted to go into the courtyards and alleyways, where people lived, to preach.[143] Easier to deliver was a church evening evangelistic service.[144] Some churches used open-air preaching immediately before a gospel service, in order to draw listeners to the latter.[145]

Practitioners of aggressive evangelism expected success. Hugh Price Hughes drew a distinction between those who held a week of special services to reach the lost and those who held "Revival Missions". It was the latter that he thought produced conversions. He thought eight days

[139] W. Cooke, *The Revival of Religion* (N.D.) p.6.

[140] W. Haslam, *"Yet Not I"* (N.D.) p.167. See also G. Guinness, *"She Spake of Him"* (1872) p.146.

[141] "The Parks and Open-Air Preaching", in *The Revival,* 3 July 1862, p.253 and "Thanksgiving and Prayer", in *The Revival*, 3 July 1862, p.249.

[142] Even a strong evangelical like Pennefather thought that he lacked the physical strength for it, or the calling, see R. Braithwaite, *The Life and Letters of Rev. William Pennefather* (N.D.) p.363.

[143] W.D. Maclagan, "The Church and the People", in *The Church and the Age* (1870) (A. Weir and W.D. Maclagan (eds)) pp.451-452.

[144] J.T. Davidson, "The Non-Church Going: How Can Our Churches Reach Them?", in *The Christian Monthly and Family Treasury* (1882) p.143.

[145] T. Grass, *Gathering to His Name* (2012) p.137.

the right length for such missions; starting on a Sunday. Each day was to begin with a prayer meeting, with a short Bible reading at noon and an evangelistic service in the evening. These might be supplemented by "afternoon services for women, late evening services for young men or for young women engaged in shops, and short services in factories for working men".[146] After the evening service, some thought there must be a prayer meeting – to "offer up special supplication on behalf of sinners and seekers of salvation".[147] In the week before the mission, special prayer meetings were held to invoke the blessing of God.[148] Others thought Revival Missions needed to be preceded by preparatory meetings of the church – "for solemn humiliation before God" – at which the minister, the deacons and the whole church confessed their sins.[149] The need for a special speaker was discouraged, lest people lost confidence in the regular minister – although it was accepted that some were better able to secure conversions than others.[150]

It was not the events of the Revival Mission week itself that were key to its success, but the prior deployment of the methods of aggressive evangelism – and the follow-up afterwards. Without them, it was a "mistake to excite expectation in the church".[151] The Methodist William Cooke stated that new converts needed to be publicly admitted into fellowship and given a copy of the Methodist rules, so that they were placed "under the most solemn obligations to a pure morality".[152] They were not to be encouraged to aspire for high office, "but to do all they can for the conversion of others". He added, "Thousands have relapsed through sheer inertness, or the want of something to do...let labour be found for them, in tract distribution, in Sunday-school teaching, in cottage prayer meetings, in collecting for missions, or some other

[146] H.P. Hughes, "Revival Missions", in 5 *The Christian Miscellany and Family Visitor* (1881) (3rd series) p.125.
[147] W. Cooke, *The Revival of Religion* (N.D.) p.10.
[148] H.P. Hughes, "Revival Missions", in 5 *The Christian Miscellany and Family Visitor* (1881) 3rd series) p.59 and W. Cooke, *The Revival of Religion* (N.D.) pp.8-11.
[149] Ibid., p.3.
[150] Ibid., p.7.
[151] H.P. Hughes, "Revival Missions", 5 *The Christian Miscellany and Family Visitor* (1881) (3rd series) p.59.
[152] W. Cooke, *The Revival of Religion* (N.D.) p.14.

suitable means of usefulness".[153] The parable Jesus told – of the master who told his servants in the country to "Go out to the roads and country lanes and make them come in, so that my house will be full" – guided the thinking and activities of many.[154]

18.3.1 *A work for all*

Youth did not exempt a Christian from aggressive evangelism. As we have seen, many of the best-known preachers of the era gained their evangelistic spurs while young. Hugh Price Hughes distributed tracts and preached soon after his conversion at the age of 14.[155] Hay Aitken, later the Church of England's best-known evangelist, as an undergraduate at Oxford in 1862, was part of a scheme to take tracts to nearby villages. For three years he did so, accompanied by others.[156] In the mid-1870s, Robert Horton, later a leading Congregational minister, was part of an undergraduate scheme to visit and take tracts to the slums of Oxford.[157]

Many of the noble, rich and learned were also committed to aggressive evangelism. As has been observed, "Many evangelists of a new and remarkable type appeared in the early [1860s], men of entire devotion and singleness of eye, gifted with social position, education and charm, giving up the scanty leisure of their official lives to make known the good news of divine love".[158] As the Evangelization Society discovered, when their members crossed the land holding missions, the working man would come to hear in a hall a "'Captain' or a 'Lord'" or one of their own class, when they would not attend a religious service in church.[159] The Evangelization Society also discovered that listeners were more convinced of the message when it was delivered by those giving up their leisure to deliver it. Tracts like George William MacCree's *Unexpected Conversions* (1863) encouraged Christians to action.

[153] Ibid., p.15.
[154] Luke 14:23b. W. Cadman, "Pastoral Visitation", in *Homiletical and Pastoral Lectures* (1879) p.312 and J.C. Ryle, *Expository Thoughts on the Gospels: Luke* (1983) pt.2, pp.162-163.
[155] C. Oldstone-Moore, *Hugh Price Hughes* (1999) p.15.
[156] C.E. Woods, *Memoirs and Letters of Canon Hay Aitken* (1928) p.91.
[157] R. Horton, *An Autobiography* (1917) p.35.
[158] E. Trotter, *Lord Radstock* (N.D.) p.143. For further members of the peerage involved in earnest Christian work, see G.E. Morgan, *R.C. Morgan: His Life and Times* (1909) pp.136-141.
[159] Evangelization Society, *Preaching the Gospel; or, Evangelists and Evangelization* (N.D.) pp.4 and 39-40.

Among the best known of these upper-class evangelists was Lord Radstock. He enjoyed a world-wide ministry – which was especially effective in Russia – but he also had his own mission hall in London[160] and was well-known to organisations such as the Evangelization Society. Sir Arthur Blackwood, the first Secretary to the Post Office, was another mission preacher, with an establishment background well-known to the Evangelization Society. In January 1868, notwithstanding a successful career in government service, he regularly preached three times a week and, in one week, just when he wanted rest, five times![161] In April 1875, he gave three or four addresses at the Opera House for D.L. Moody.[162] In May, preaching at the Brighton Corn Exchange, 1,500 crammed in. A "most interesting inquiry meeting" resulted.[163] However, such work, even for men like Lord Radstock, was not without opposition – especially from those clergy who rejected instantaneous conversion.[164]

The expected evangelistic commitment of the affluent went beyond a caste of distinguished lay evangelists. When Hugh Price Hughes arrived as the Methodist superintendent at Oxford in 1881, he explained "that every office-holder was expected to engage in the task of visiting every house in Oxford". Furthermore, even the richest went.[165] Applying the techniques of aggressive evangelism and nurturing the intellect, his efforts brought in "large numbers of converts".[166] On one occasion, he "announced from the pulpit that the congregation was to march through the streets in the manner of the Salvation Army and led by himself". The congregation duly processed through the city to fields where an open-air service was held. Thousands were drawn.[167]

Furthermore, the work of the evangelist was also no longer being left to the locally born. A survey drawn from the pages of two local newspapers in the Chatham area reveals that between 1859 and 1935, ten black evangelicals, plus a "good number of Salvationists", preached or

[160] D. Fountain, *Lord Radstock of Mayfield* (1984) pp.62-63.
[161] *Some Records of the Life of Stevenson Arthur Blackwood K.C.B.* (1898) (H.S. Blackwood (ed.)), p.255.
[162] Ibid., p.307.
[163] Ibid., p.309.
[164] E. Trotter, *Lord Radstock* (N.D.) pp.144 and 159-160.
[165] C. Oldstone-Moore, *Hugh Price Hughes* (1999) p.94.
[166] Ibid., pp.92-96.
[167] Ibid., p.99.

conducted missions in the lower Medway area.[168] At Manchester, in the autumn of 1876, Thomas Johnson, a former slave who gained his freedom when Richmond fell to the United States army, undertook mission work with the YMCA.[169] Shortly afterwards, he attended Spurgeon's Pastors' College – but he was not the first of an ethnic minority to attend.

Aggressive evangelism was not the exclusive preserve of evangelical individuals and enterprises. For example, a Broad Churchman, like Archbishop Tait, preached in the open air with the Open-Air Mission at Covent Garden.[170] At St Paul's Cathedral, the clergy were informed that "*If you want to get to a man's heart, you must go to his house.*"[171] Another Archbishop of Canterbury, E.W. Benson (on the High Church side), supported the formation of the Church Army (1882), once attempts to woo the Salvation Army into the Church of England fold failed. The Church Army's original calling was as "a working men's mission to working men". By 1900 it possessed a "troop of 65 vans manned by travelling evangelists, and more than 600 evangelists and nurses helping the parochial clergy".[172]

The Ritualists also adopted aggressive evangelism. One observer thought they had got, what he called, "gush" just as much as the Evangelical party.[173] At an 1864 parish mission in Liverpool, they handed out leaflets asking, "Are you ready to die? Do you wish to go to heaven when you die? Will you begin now to prepare yourself?"[174] They also sent off individual clergy to labour in the slums – to create

[168] D. Killingray, "Black Evangelicals in Darkest Britain 1770s-1930s", in *British Evangelical Identities Past and Present* (2008) vol.1, p.131.

[169] T.L. Johnson, *Africa for Christ. Twenty-eight Years a Slave* (1882) p.29.

[170] A.J. Greenbank, *'This is the Lord's Doing': The Open-Air Mission 1853-2003* (2003) p.8. However, the Broad Church and Pre-Raphaelite painter Ford Madox Brown, in his painting *Work*, in his representation of a tract distributor made it clear that he thought tract distribution was a "comic" exercise, while the same painting represented F.D. Maurice and Thomas Carlyle as serious figures, see T. Barringer, *Men at Work* (2005) pp.50-51, 63-66 and 74.

[171] Author's italics. T.M. Macdonald, "How to Reach Working Men", in *Homiletical and Pastoral Lectures* (1879) p.402. See also W. Cadman, "Pastoral Visitation", in *Homiletical and Pastoral Lectures* (1879) pp.311-331.

[172] K.F. Inglis, *Churches and the Working Classes in Victorian England* (1964) p.45.

[173] C.M. Davies, *Orthodox London* (1876) p.404.

[174] I.D. Farley, *J.C. Ryle: First Bishop of Liverpool* (2000) p.218. See also O. Chadwick, *The Victorian Church* (1987) pt.2, p.287.

mission churches – and created their own lay evangelistic organisations, such as the Church of England's Working Men's Society (1876).[175] An active Anglo-Catholic church, such as St Jude's Bradford, like many an evangelical church, had Sunday and ragged schools, organisations for distributing literature, a number of organisations for distributing different types of aid and a vision for planting mission churches.[176] One commentator summarised the position in 1879 as follows: "The whole land is now full of religious movement – every county, every town, of whatever class, every section of society. Church and Dissent, High Church and Low Church, vie with each other in revival services and in homely mission work."[177]

However, a key issue was that many Church of England clergy did not want aggressive evangelism in their parish without their permission. For instance, in the 1860s the evangelist and clergyman William Haslam was often in trouble with local clergy, his bishop, or the Archbishop of Canterbury, for accepting many invitations to preach in halls and barns outside his parish. Only in later years, as the benefits of increased congregations were recognised, did the animosity to him melt away.[178]

18.3.2 *A relentless and growing work*

As one well-known evangelist completed his campaign in a city, the next might arrive to open his – and to sweep up remaining doubters.[179] A new voice could often work wonders.[180] Once an individual was converted, he was expected to join in aggressive evangelism. For example, Archibald Brown, the week after his conversion, was taken by Sir Arthur Blackwood to a group of railway navvies and they were told that he "would come every morning during their breakfast time and read the word of God to them".[181] Archibald Brown later became a very effective Baptist minister, baptising over "5,000 who have been

[175] For a brief overview of the work of this society, see K.F. Inglis, *Churches and the Working Classes in Victorian England* (1964) p.46.

[176] S. Baring-Gould, *The Church Revival* (1914) pp.291-295.

[177] J.H. Rigg, *The Present Position of Christianity and the Christian Faith in this Country* (1878) p.9.

[178] W. Haslam, *"Yet Not I"* (N.D.) pp.282-289.

[179] N. Scotland, *Apostles of the Spirit and Fire* (2009) p.222.

[180] J. Wood, *The Story of the Evangelization Society* (N.D.) p.104.

[181] *Some Records of the Life of Stevenson Arthur Blackwood* K.C.B. (1898) (H.S. Blackwood (ed.)) pp.222-224.

converted by the same gospel that won me".

The larger men's home mission agencies continued to grow until towards the end of the nineteenth century. By 1860, the London City Mission and the Anglican Scripture Readers' Association together employed 494 men as full-time evangelists.[182] By 1884, the London City Mission alone had, in the words of Lord Shaftesbury at a dinner in his honour at the Mansion House, "450 men going out every day to carry counsel and consolation to the very depths of human misery".[183] "Between 1869 and 1884 the London City Mission claimed to have persuaded 115,412 people to attend worship".[184] In the year 1881-1882 alone, it distributed nearly four million religious tracts and just over 18,000 Bibles, New Testaments and other portions of the Scriptures.[185] That year, it saw over 3,000 drunks reclaimed, sent just over that number of children to school, induced 189 couples to marry and closed 147 shops on the Lord's day.[186] The Open-Air Mission also grew dramatically so that, by 1878, it possessed 398 accredited preachers. That year, they delivered 700,000 tracts. Auxiliary organisations had been established early in its life in many towns and places. By 1890, it had over 1,000 accredited preachers.

New home mission organisations were also established, such as the non-denominational Evangelization Society (1864). It grew out of the endeavours of laymen to reach the lost in the 1859 Revival. This had been led by itinerant laymen preaching across the land. As a result, "some gentlemen devised a 'Registry of Evangelists,'" which could be consulted by those looking for preachers for local missions.[187] In 1867

[182] D.M. Lewis, *Lighten their Darkness* (1986) p.120. Different dioceses would establish their own Scripture Readers' Society. For example, by 1887, the new Diocese of Liverpool had 45 readers, see J.C. Ryle, *A Charge Delivered to the Clergy of the Diocese of Liverpool at his Third Triennial Visitation* (1887) p.15.

[183] "Lord Shaftesbury at the Mansion-House", *The Times*, 6 March 1884.

[184] M.R. Watts, *The Dissenters* (2015) vol.3, p.133.

[185] Tract distributors were often accused of extravagance in their distribution of literature – it was recognised that many were thrown away. However, they observed that "in the parable of the sower only one of four kinds of soil yields any increase", see F. Cockrem, *Gawin Kirkham* (N.D.) p.103.

[186] "The London City Mission", in *The Times*, 6 May 1882. In 1875, one preacher thought no less than 30,000 shops were open on the Lord's day, see G.W. M'Cree, *Nineveh and London: A Sermon* 11 May 1875.

[187] Evangelization Society, *Preaching the Gospel; or, Evangelists and Evangelization* (N.D.) p.11.

it was remodelled and renamed the Evangelization Society, being an association of men to preach the gospel only – and to add "new life and vigour to all".[188] It also gave advice to those seeking to run missions, drew up mission schedules for its evangelists and provided their travelling expenses and salary.[189] It also provided an array of tents for the mission meetings themselves. Attacking theological error was to be avoided.[190] It enjoyed significant backers drawn from the nobility and professional classes, including Robert Baxter, whose prominent law firm evolved into Norton Rose Fulbright.[191] The Evangelization Society later took over the work of the Scottish Evangelistic Association and did a considerable work north of the Borders. Other Christians worked with particular groups, such as London's costermongers.[192] The Scottish Faith Mission was established in 1886.

Denominations also had their own vigorous home missions, while dioceses, districts and individual churches established evangelistic arms and open-air teams. Some were distinct organisations, such as the Metropolitan Tabernacle's Evangelists' Society. In some working-class districts, a public school or university college might take full, or partial, responsibility for arranging missions there. In 1887 schools or colleges took full or partial responsibility for at least 16 Church of England missions in London.[193] Cheltenham Ladies' College had a mission in the Bethnal Green area which influenced Maud Royden, one of the pioneers of women's ordination in the next century. Great numbers of people could also be deployed for individual evangelistic events. In Birmingham, May 1893 saw the Nonconformists organise 4,000 people for house-to-house visitation.[194]

[188] W.E. Smith, *Address to Evangelists* (N.D.) p.1. For the recommended form of a gospel address by a member of the Evangelization Society – and what to exclude – see ibid., pp.15-20 and 30-48.

[189] No charges were made, although a discreet thank offering was taken, J. Wood, *The Story of the Evangelization Society* (N.D.) pp.236-237.

[190] Ibid., p.5.

[191] Ibid., p.161 and A. St. George, *A History of Norton Rose* (1995) pp.28-40. For other significant society figures who backed the Evangelization Society, see pp.6-7 and 46-47.

[192] "The Friend of the Poor in Golden Lane", in *The Sword and the Trowel* (1875) pp.520-528.

[193] K.F. Inglis, *Churches and the Working Classes in Victorian England* (1964) p.29.

[194] E.K.H. Jordan, *Free Church Unity* (1956) p.37.

Members of mission organisations worked relentlessly. A missionary with the London City Mission worked 36 hours a week on door-to-door visitation. Running the mission congregations that emerged out of this work was extra. Unsurprisingly, in the summer of 1860, between 50 and 60 of the London City Mission's missionaries were under medical care, working reduced hours.[195] In the early 1870s, Ellen Ranyard, looking back, commented that "There never was such a score of years of missionary effort as these have been, nor one in which such effort has been quickened by every appliance of modern invention and social progress."[196] The division of London into postal districts, and the new Cassell set of nine cheap maps, enabled every court and blind alley to be identified for missionary endeavour. By the end of the century, those endeavours led Charles Booth, the great social commentator, to observe that London is "dotted with buildings devoted to this [mission] work. In the poorer parts especially, in almost every street, there is a mission; they are more numerous than schools or churches, and only less numerous than public-houses".[197]

In the country, a Nonconformist county evangelist acted as "a kind of pastor, village confidant, and itinerant gospeller". One such Baptist evangelist, near Dorchester, covered land 50 miles in circumference, extending to 17 parishes and with 5 chapels or preaching stations.[198] One such station was a former cart shed, where 150 could sit for a mid-week service. When the evangelist first arrived in one village, he asked to read and pray in 50 houses, but was permitted to do so only in seven. Ten years later, he was cordially welcomed in all the village's houses.[199] The affluent could be won.[200] Some country preachers led a less nomadic life. Philip Gosse of the Brethren, in the years between 1860 to 1881, saw his meeting at St Marychurch near Torquay grow from 30 to 40 attending to about 120 members, "mostly poor and working people in the midst of much worldliness and popery".[201] On a Sunday morning he "broke

[195] See D.M. Lewis, *Lighten their Darkness* (1986) p.247.

[196] "How Wears the Missing Link?", in *God's Message in Low London* (N.D.) p.20.

[197] Cited in D.M. Lewis, *Lighten their Darkness* (1986) p.275.

[198] G.H. Pike, "Out with a County Evangelist", in *The Sword and the Trowel* (1875) p.103.

[199] Ibid., p.106. On house visitation in the country, see ibid., pp.173-174.

[200] Ibid., pp.109-110.

[201] E. Gosse, *The Life of Philip Henry Gosse* (1890) pp.330-331, 354 and 367.

bread" with his flock; on an evening he preached a gospel sermon.[202] He engaged his own Biblewoman to help with visiting.[203]

18.3.3 *A bold work*

Aggressive evangelism required boldness. At Kidderminster, men were buttonholed in the street for a Nonconformist three-day mission, 40 being converted.[204] In response to the question of how to get men saved, General Booth wrote: "By talking to them, publicly in the open air and indoors, about their own sin, ingratitude, and death; about judgment, hell, and heaven; the love of God, and the voluntary suffering and death Jesus Christ endured on their behalf".[205] Those seeking conversion were encouraged to kneel in penitent form.[206] The methods were successful, but not all liked them. Booth admitted that "many of our methods are very different to the religious usages and social tastes of respectable and refined people, which may make those measures appear vulgar, that is, in bad taste to them; but this does not make them wrong in the sight of God. On the contrary, we think this adaption of measures to the state of the masses is abundantly justified by the extraordinary things which God has set his prophets to do, in order to arrest the attention of the people and also by the innovations connected with the work of Jesus Christ and his apostles. And if it can be proved from the results that these methods lay hold of the ignorant and godless multitudes, compelling them to think about eternity, and attend to their soul's salvation, we think they are thereby proved to be both lawful and expedient."[207]

At the race track and many other places aggressive evangelism was unwelcome.[208] Nevertheless, at Epsom, the evangelist Henry Moorhouse

[202] Ibid., p.356.
[203] Ibid., p.363.
[204] R. Horton, *An Autobiography* (1917) p.75.
[205] W. Booth, *The Doctrines and Discipline of the Salvation Army* (1881) section 28(3).
[206] Hugh Price Hughes preferred the congregation to kneel in silent prayer at the end of a service. He then invited all who wanted to be true Christians to stand up and kneel down again. He then liked them to come to an inquiry room to make their peace with God, rather than stay in the chapel where singing and praying continued, see H.P. Hughes, "Revival Missions", in 5 *The Christian Miscellany and Family Visitor* (1881) (3rd series) p.124.
[207] W. Booth, *All About the Salvation Army* (1885) p.10.
[208] Physical assaults on evangelists, were relatively rare, save at the race track, see J. Wood, *The Story of the Evangelization Society* (N.D.) pp.88-89.

and colleagues "boldly raised the standard of the cross amidst the wild excitement of the race. Nothing daunted by the rude jostling of the angry crowds, the raillery, the blasphemy, and the ferocious use of the horse whip and all sorts of missiles, they preached Jesus and left the issue with their Master".[209] The racecourse work yielded some outstanding prizes, even though some Christians thought it "inconsistent and out of place".[210] One such crown resulted from the conversion of Hanmer William Webb-Peploe, who became – for the first 20 years of the twentieth century – probably the leading Evangelical Anglican clergyman. A key element in his conversion was when a young man asked him to read a piece of paper. It read "Reader, if you died tonight, would your soul be in HELL?" Webb-Peploe fled from the race track. Shortly thereafter he was converted. Another for whom the race track was the beginning of the road to conversion was the later evangelist, E.H. Kerwin. He received a tract on the train while playing cards on the way to Doncaster races. However, it was a verse of Scripture on a banner at the race track that he could not get out of his mind. The Lord used other circumstances to follow up that impression and, two months later, he was converted.[211]

18.3.4 *Open-air preaching*

The years of the 1860s were the golden age of street evangelists. In London, the Open-Air Mission calculated in its Tenth Annual Report that "in the middle of summer there are nearly 500 Open-Air services held every Sunday in London and its suburbs by clergymen, ministers, missionaries, and other preachers".[212] It found that as "the opposition decreases, the interest and encouragement increase more and more".[213] Its concern was that many who took up open-air preaching had more "zeal than knowledge". The Evangelization Society found that "crowds would flock to town-halls, barns or other undenominational buildings" to hear lay evangelists, in a way that was unknown later.[214] In Wales,

[209] J. Macpherson, *Henry Moorhouse* (N.D.) p.39 and "Epsom Races", in *The Revival*, 2 June 1864, pp.343-344.
[210] Ibid.
[211] G.H. Pike, *Beneath the Blue Sky* (1888) pp.145-147.
[212] *The Open-Air Mission Tenth Annual Report* (1863) p.8.
[213] Ibid., p.10.
[214] J. Wood, *The Story of the Evangelization Society* (N.D.) p.22.

people could listen to half a dozen sermons in a day.[215] Great preaching festivals were held in the open air to which all those living in an area streamed on a holiday.[216] Lord Shaftesbury addressed the annual meeting of the Open-Air Mission in March 1884, at the Mansion House, with the Lord Mayor presiding. He was "old enough to recollect when open-air preaching was looked upon as the vilest thing imaginable", as offensive to the magistrate as the mob. Now, his Lordship observed, they were "met in the palace seat of justice of the chief justice of this great city", with him "giving us...the greatest encouragement to continue this good work". His Lordship added that, within a stone's throw from the hall where they were assembled, "on the steps of the Royal Exchange, the worthy Archbishop Tait also preached the word of God in the open air".[217] Lord Shaftesbury saw the work as tending "to fill the churches and chapels".[218] He was thankful that the nation had such an institution which promoted self-control, as it was by this principle in the hearts of men – and not, in the main, by the police or the army – that order was maintained.

There were many outstanding practitioners and organisations committed to open-air preaching. In the Church of England, bishops advocated it in charges to their clergy.[219] In 1888 Holden Pike, that great observer and recorder of the acts of the late nineteenth century evangelicals, published his *Beneath the Blue Sky: Preaching in the Open-Air*, to stimulate and inform the preachers themselves and to set before the public some facts about the work.[220] In 1890, Gawin Kirkham published *The Open-Air Preacher's Handbook.* It was based upon his contribution to Holden Pike's work, but added guidance on preparing for preaching outside, together with material on various other connected matters, such as sermon outlines. Its first edition of 3,000 copies sold out in less than two months – so a second edition was prepared.

[215] G.H. Pike, *Beneath the Blue Sky* (1888) p.164.

[216] Ibid., pp.164-169. For example, at Haverfordwest one Whitsuntide, to listeners numbered in their thousands, a free 'dinner' was provided after two morning sermons, and tea was served between the two afternoon and two evening sermons, see ibid., p.167.

[217] Ibid., pp.286-287.

[218] Ibid., p.289.

[219] Ibid., p.143.

[220] G.H. Pike, "Preface" to *Beneath the Blue Sky* (1888) p.iii.

Nevertheless, some denominations, at the three-quarter mark in the century, were losing their enthusiasm for open-air preaching. From his pulpit G.W. MacCree thought it necessary to urge the Primitive Methodists – who now had "scholars, orators and divines" and were looking to build fine chapels in London – to "never renounce open-air preaching, processing and camp meetings. If you do you deserve to be buried". He wanted powerful, not fine or learned, preaching. The latter, he commented, did not produce conversions.[221] In 1860, their last female itinerant had retired.[222]

18.3.5 *Publications*

Huge amounts of written material were published for evangelistic purposes. Spurgeon urged his congregation to give them away by the million.[223] In 1874, the Religious Tract Society distributed 22 million tracts – well over double what it had achieved in 1849.[224] Some people, not without effect, sent them anonymously to others.[225] Some, especially younger believers, came together to form 'Tract Distribution Bands'. They handed out tracts on a Saturday afternoon and carried out open-air work in the cities. During the summer they might conduct a tract distribution campaign in a particular county.[226] In the early 1880s, the Methodist Thomas Champness started the *Joyful News* – "an evangelistic weekly for the common people" – aimed at converting the lost and spreading evangelistic fervour. The third issue saw one man converted after reading it as he sat drinking in a public house.[227] The *Joyful News* was influenced by the earlier *War Cry* of the Salvation Army and it, in turn, influenced *The Church Army Gazette*; "all three had the same mission – the salvation of souls".[228] In 1888 the Scripture Gift Mission was established. This made available portions of the Bible, with illustrative pictures of places "made famous by the sacred story",

[221] G.W. M'Cree, *Nineveh and London: A Sermon,* 11 May 1875 pp.8-9.
[222] H. McLeod, *Religion and the Working Class in Nineteenth-Century Britain* (1984) p.30.
[223] C.H. Spurgeon, "Fields White for Harvest", in *Metropolitan Tabernacle Pulpit* (1867) vol.12, p.462.
[224] S.G. Green, *The Story of the Religious Tract Society* (1899) p.81.
[225] Ibid., pp.83-84.
[226] T. Grass, *Gathering to His Name* (2012) pp.137-138.
[227] J.I. Brice, *The Crowd for Christ* (1934) p.31.
[228] Ibid., p.34.

to be given away free, "with soul-saving results".[229] Some books of general religious purpose led to conversions. For example, a copy of F.W. Farrar's published sermons on the Lord's Prayer was passed on and converted someone who later established a Brethren gospel hall.[230]

18.3.6 *Colporteurs*

During the second half of the nineteenth century, many colportage societies were at work in the kingdom, enjoying particular success in Scotland. Spurgeon noted that, since the Reformation, "the sale of religious books has always been a main help to the cause of truth. You may be quite sure that this would naturally be so, because the sale of irreligious books is a mainstay to the cause of evil."[231] But the colporteurs' literature brought enlightenment, counteracting the "impure and seductive literature" in circulation.[232] One colporteur, asked if he had any works by Tom Paine, after suffering initial rejection by his questioner, had the joy of seeing him converted.[233] Another colporteur persuaded a man to buy Sir Arthur Blackwood's *The Shadow and the Substance* (1866). It converted him, so he bought 25 copies "to give to his special friends. Of these, 13 had told him that they owed their salvation to the book".[234]

The colporteur's work was not limited to selling literature, but had great similarities to that of many other Christians reaching out to the working classes; it was "testimony to the power and value of the aggressive principle".[235] It was observed that a colporteur

[229] "Jubilee of the Scripture Gift Mission", in *The Christian Herald and Signs of our Times*, 9 June 1938, p.526.
[230] R. Farrar, *The Life of Frederic William Farrar* (1905) pp.310-311.
[231] G.H. Pike, "*The Life and Work of Charles Haddon Spurgeon*", vol.4, p.212, in G.H. Pike, *The Life and Work of Charles Haddon Spurgeon* (The Banner of Truth Trust (1991)) vol.2.
[232] G.H. Pike, "*The Life and Work of Charles Haddon Spurgeon*", vol.3, p.167, in G.H. Pike, *The Life and Work of Charles Haddon Spurgeon* (The Banner of Truth Trust (1991)) vol.1.
[233] F.H. Wrintmore, *Two Feet for God* (1974) pp.17-18.
[234] *Some Records of the Life of Stevenson Arthur Blackwood* K.C.B. (1898) (H.S. Blackwood (ed.)) pp.332-333.
[235] G.H. Pike, "*The Life and Work of Charles Haddon Spurgeon*", vol.3, p.163, in G.H. Pike, *The Life and Work of Charles Haddon Spurgeon* (The Banner of Truth Trust (1991)) vol.1.

> converses with the inmates about their souls, prays with the sick, and leaves a tract at each cottage. He is frequently able to hold prayer meetings, open-air services and Bible-readings. He gets a room [a meeting place] if possible, and preaches; founds Bands of Hope, and makes himself generally useful in the cause of religion and temperance. He is, in fact, first of all a missionary, then a preacher, and by-and-by in the truest sense, a pastor.[236]

Many colporteurs went on to careers as full-time evangelists.[237] Colporteurs became "the most likely agency for the evangelisation of the poor in the rural districts,"[238] being an efficient form of home missionary service.[239] Colporteurs from different societies and denominations had a natural bond with each other.[240] However, they were not always welcome. Publicans could sneer when offered religious books[241] – and a colporteur preaching in a market place near London was pelted with rotten oranges; but such a response became infrequent.[242]

Some colporteur organisations grew very quickly. For example, the Christian Colportage Association was founded in 1874. Its origins go back to Arthur Smith, a converted costermonger. After his conversion, while praying, he was shown that he should use his barrow to hawk Bibles, rather than lumber. Robert Paton, a wealthy Christian, saw him in action and was impressed; he called a meeting at the home of his friend, Quintin Hogg. At that meeting the Christian Colportage Association

[236] Cited in A.A. Dallimore, *C.H. Spurgeon* (1984) p.117. For the qualities of a colporteur see J. Rennie, *Seed-Time and Harvest* (N.D.) p.45.

[237] *A Marvel of Grace, the Late William Taylor* (1895) p.51.

[238] G.H. Pike, "On the Road with a Colporteur", in *The Sword and the Trowel* (1875) p.424 and J. Rennie, *Seed-Time and Harvest* (N.D.) pp.54-56.

[239] G.H. Pike, "*The Life and Work of Charles Haddon Spurgeon*", vol.4, p.299 and vol.5, p.40, in G.H. Pike, *The Life and Work of Charles Haddon Spurgeon* (The Banner of Truth Trust (1991)) vol.2.

[240] For the main institutions, see J. Rennie, *Seed-Time and Harvest* (N.D.) pp.46-47. See also G.H. Pike, "*The Life and Work of Charles Haddon Spurgeon*", vol.3, p.163, in G.H. Pike, *The Life and Work of Charles Haddon Spurgeon* (The Banner of Truth Trust (1991)) vol.1.

[241] *A Marvel of Grace, the Late William Taylor* (1895) p.38.

[242] "The Eighth Annual Report of the Metropolitan Tabernacle Colportage Association", in *The Sword and the Trowel* (1875) p.337 and G.H. Pike, "On the Road with a Colporteur", in *The Sword and the Trowel* (1875) p.427.

was born. Lord Kinnaird was its first treasurer.[243] By 1889, it had 110 colporteurs. By 1893, this number had risen to 140.[244]

The growth of Spurgeon's Metropolitan Tabernacle Colportage Association, established in 1866, was more fitful. Its fourth annual report recorded that, although in some areas it was expanding, it had vacated a number of areas – including Shrewsbury, because of "the poverty of the people, and consequent smallness of the sales, although a most promising mission field".[245] That report noted that, in the previous year, it had an average of nine colporteurs. However, by 1878, with the work still growing, it had 94 colporteurs. That year, its colporteurs made, in aggregate, "the remarkable number of 926,290 visits".[246] The colporteur at Wellow, Isle of Wight, in six years revived the long-standing local Baptist church, previously a picture of sadness.[247] Spurgeon regarded his Colportage Association as "second to none of his institutions in value and utility".[248]

At the end of the nineteenth century, the three largest colporteur societies employed 371 colporteurs in Britain – and there were around another 30 smaller agencies, although some of these worked in Ireland. Scotland had the highest number of colporteurs per head of population.[249] Systematically, they visited more than 20,000 villages every month in the United Kingdom, together with the farm-houses and scattered cottages lying in-between. To many of these villages, colporteurs were the only visitors – and the only ones "come to tell them the way of salvation" – although the clergy could be helpful, encouraging their people to buy.[250] The colporteurs also visited the sick.[251]

James Rennie was a colporteur, sent by the Religious Tract and Book Society of Scotland to the villages of Bedford and Hertfordshire,

[243] F.H. Wrintmore, *Two Feet for God* (1974) pp.15-16.
[244] Christian Colportage Association, *Diamond Jubilee 1934* (1934) p.2.
[245] *The Fourth Annual Report of the Metropolitan Tabernacle Colportage Association* (1871) pp.4-5.
[246] A.A. Dallimore, *C.H. Spurgeon* (1984) p.119.
[247] A. Mother, "Colportage: its Benefits", in *The Sword and the Trowel* (1878) p.352.
[248] G.H. Pike, "*The Life and Work of Charles Haddon Spurgeon*", vol.3, p.166, in G.H. Pike, *The Life and Work of Charles Haddon Spurgeon* (The Banner of Truth Trust (1991)) vol.1.
[249] J. Rennie, *Seed-Time and Harvest* (N.D.) p.60.
[250] Ibid., pp.17-21.
[251] Ibid., pp.21-22.

where there was "often great spiritual darkness and ignorance of the gospel".[252] At the beginning, people said "'It is of no use...for I know I won't buy, and it will only be troubling yourself for nothing'".[253] Rennie persevered; the literature was well presented and inexpensive. He sold, in 30 years, 341,166 volumes, 752,257 magazines and small books, and 3,000,000 tracts, together with 30,000 Bibles.[254] Rennie wrote that "The quiet house-to-house visitation by earnest Christian men, the circulation of gospel books and magazines, and the straight personal dealing with individuals at their own homes, have proved to be a most effective agency."[255] As visits to the seaside by the public grew, the colporteurs followed, setting up their horse-drawn 'Bible carriages';[256] they also appeared at fairs and markets. However, Rennie noted that towards the end of the century people wanted moral tales, not Richard Baxter's *The Saints' Everlasting Rest* (1650) or the *A Call to the Unconverted* (1657), which 20 years before sold well.[257] Nevertheless, the moral stories were a much better alternative to the "trashy, sentimental tales" that were so widely circulated. The latter, in his view, filled "a man's head with foolish notions", pandered "to his worst passions" and consumed "a large amount of time".[258] Where the colporteurs were active, the bookshops testified to improved reading tastes.[259]

18.3.7 *In the country*

In the country, lay evangelists spread out. They were

> men who devoted the very best of their years to the Master's service, thinking little of payment...passing along from place to place, year after year, reviving sleepy churches and starting new societies in farm houses and cottages, which afterwards blossomed into active centres of religious work.[260]

[252] Ibid., p.17.
[253] Ibid., p.16.
[254] Ibid., p.15.
[255] Ibid., p.18.
[256] Ibid., p.29. See also T. Grass, *Gathering to His Name* (2012) pp.138-139.
[257] J. Rennie, *Seed-Time and Harvest* (N.D.) p.17.
[258] Ibid., p.33.
[259] Ibid., pp.41-45.
[260] I.C. Watson, *The Life Story of Thomas Langton of Malton* (1896) p.11. See also G.E. Morgan, *R.C. Morgan: His Life and Times* (1909) pp.164-167.

An example of such a man was Thomas Langton, instrumental in the conversion of thousands. As he travelled the dales and wolds of Yorkshire, new chapels sprang from his work.[261] The work of men such as Langton was fortified by the work of the colporteurs and the other evangelistic organisations. Indeed, a travelling evangelist, like Richard Weaver, was earlier a colporteur.[262] The denominations, though, were less enthused by the benefits of the travelling evangelist, much preferring to affirm the role of pastors and teachers.[263]

18.3.8 *Later, aggressive evangelism softens*

Yet, as the century wore on, there was a tendency for the message of aggressive evangelism to soften. In 1882 *The Christian Monthly and Family Treasury* ran a piece headed "Evangelistic Preaching: Why is it not more Successful?" Its conclusion was that preachers too much emphasised the "all-embracing love and mercy of God and the willingness of Christ to save" their hearers. "The average careless Protestant", it suggested, already believed this. Their problem was that since they believed salvation might be had at any time, there was no need to "be in a hurry to procure it nor at pains to purchase it either by strictness of life or regularity of attendance on ordinances". They needed to be told to pick up their cross daily. In 1884 Francis Chavassè, at his church of St Peter-le-Bailey Oxford, although noting many positive signs, observed that "Scarcely a middle-aged layman is to be found amongst us who will undertake direct spiritual work."[264] However, the message that God was love, it was thought, helped Roman Catholics – who looked to good works for salvation, but who failed to recognise that their sins were forgiven at the cross.[265]

18.4 William and Catherine Booth and the Salvation Army

William and Catherine Booth were remarkably effective evangelists in the revival of 1859. However, after the establishment in 1865 of the

[261] Ibid., pp.35-37 and 39-46. For some experiences of a Primitive Methodist travelling evangelist, see J. Flanagan, *The Romance of Evangelism* (1902).
[262] Dr and Mrs Palmer, *Four Years in the Old World* (1866) p.425.
[263] Ibid., pp.428-430.
[264] J.B. Lancelot, *Francis James Chavasse* (1929) p.91.
[265] "Evangelistic Preaching: Why is it not more Successful?", in *The Christian Monthly and Family Treasury* (1881) pp.143-145.

forerunner of the Salvation Army, they recognised that new approaches and techniques were needed. They made two discoveries. First, that members of the masses were the most effective way to reach the masses – and extraordinary success crowned this discovery.[266] By January 1879, the Salvation Army had 127 full-time evangelists – 100 of them converted at its meetings – with 1,900 voluntary speakers, holding 75,000 services a year. That year, a clergyman – explaining why the Church had been so ineffective in reaching the working classes – observed that often their only experience of Christianity was through their so-called Christian employers which led "into contempt and hatred of their religion".[267] Some Salvation Army officers from the lower classes were among the most gifted evangelists of the day and, in Rodney 'Gipsy' Smith, the Salvation Army had (for a time) the most gifted of the next generation as well.[268] Booth wrote that the Salvation Army "has made greater progress during the time it has been in existence than any religious movement of the last hundred years, some say greater than any since the apostles' days. Tens of thousands who were the most godless in the community are now apostles of salvation, living and preaching the gospel in every land."[269]

The second discovery was that "the poor would listen in great numbers provided that they were not asked to enter a church".[270] The alternative was open-air meetings and new techniques to gather a crowd. It was said that William Booth would "play any honourable trick, perform any antic, to win attention".[271] Furthermore, Booth systemised and amplified the techniques necessary to draw a crowd. In 1885, he attributed the Army's success to the following practices:

1. By holding meetings out of doors, and marching singing through the streets, in harmony with law and order.
2. By visiting public-houses, gin palaces, prisons, private houses, and speaking to and praying with all who can be got at.

[266] Others like Thomas Champness made a similar discovery, see J.I. Brice, *The Crowd for Christ* (1934) pp.43-44.
[267] T.M. Macdonald, "How to Reach Working Men", in *Homiletical and Pastoral Lectures* (1879) p.390.
[268] H. Murray, *Sixty Years an Evangelist* (N.D.) p.15.
[269] W. Booth, *All About the Salvation Army* (1885) p.7.
[270] O. Chadwick, *The Victorian Church* (1987) pt.2, p.286. A discovery Lord Shaftesbury made also, see E. Hodder, *The Life and Work of the Seventh Earl of Shaftesbury, K.G.* (1887) pp.747-748.
[271] O. Chadwick, *The Victorian Church* (1987) pt.2, p.288.

3. By holding meetings in theatres, music halls, saloons, and the other common resorts of those who prefer pleasure to God, and by turning factories and other strange buildings into meeting rooms, so securing hearers who would not enter ordinary places of worship.
4. By using the most popular song tunes and the language of every-day life to convey God's thoughts to everyone in novel and striking forms.
5. By making every convert a daily witness for Christ, both in public and private.[272]

Although it was easy for some to adopt a superior attitude towards the Salvation Army, it did a significant work – one that others were not doing. As Professor Chadwick observed, the Salvation Army "saved the drunks by conversion, not by relief nor by medicine".[273] Although the American revivalists like Caughey, Finney and the Palmers had reached all classes bar the lowest, the Salvation Army reached "human beings so low in the scale that no other church could get down to them", although usually the converts were from the lower middle class.[274] Indeed, Booth liked to go for the worst individuals, as their conversion drew the most attention.[275] The Salvation Army did so notwithstanding physical attacks. Being a Salvationist was not easy in the late nineteenth century. The Skeleton Army was set up to destroy it, by those opposed to the Salvation Army's stand against alcohol. In 1882, 669 Salvation Army soldiers were knocked down, kicked or brutally assaulted, of whom 251 were women, and 56 buildings were wrecked by a mob.[276] There were martyrs. The first was one of Booth's early Mile End converts, Mrs Susannah Beaty. She was kicked to death.[277] The police often looked on and did nothing, or they imprisoned or fined the Salvationist.[278] At Wolverhampton, the Salvation Army could not find a place for its services because the police

[272] W. Booth, *All About the Salvation Army* (1885) pp.5-6.
[273] O. Chadwick, *The Victorian Church* (1987) pt.2, p.296.
[274] Ibid., p.293. See also M.R. Watts, *The Dissenters* (2015) vol.3, pp.129-132.
[275] The later evangelist, Samuel Chadwick, had as one of his four principles of evangelism "That the way to fill empty churches is to raise the dead, i.e., get dramatic conversions", see J.I. Brice, *The Crowd for Christ* (1934) p.98.
[276] H. Begbie, *Life of William Booth* (1920) vol.2, p.4.
[277] R. Collier, *The General Next to God* (1965) p.108.
[278] Ibid., pp.108-109.

feared the disturbances that would result.[279] Other evangelicals could be hostile. A celebrated evangelical leader is reputed to have replied, when asked what he thought of the Salvation Army that "He did not like it at all but he believed that God Almighty did."[280]

Perhaps the extraordinary success of the Salvation Army was the divine hand's answer to evangelicalism's search for respectability in the mid-nineteenth century. It is interesting to note that there lies in the British Library a pamphlet stamped "1 Ĩ Ma[rch/y?] 1859"[281], by William Arthur, entitled *May We Hope for a Great Revival?* It sold well – the copy in the British Library is marked "Fiftieth thousand". Arthur was hoping that a revival similar to the one then occurring in the United States would break out here and speculated on its form. He noted that people thought revival might begin with prayer gatherings, as it had in the United States – but Arthur asked the question, "What, if once more the Lord should humble all existing instrumentalities by raising up some new and unwelcome one to do the work?" He had already commented: "What, if our national pride in greater propriety and order should be rebuked by the permission of extravagances which have not occurred elsewhere?"[282]

In reviewing the course of the revivals of previous centuries, Arthur noted a declining level of violence. The Reformation had the stake; the Puritan epoch witnessed the "conflicts of the sword"; and eighteenth-century evangelists were beaten up – even the well-known ones might see a companion stoned to death.[283] The Salvation Army, as perhaps the most vigorous element to have its roots in the 1859 Revival, engendered the most savage response. In 1863, at the height of the revival, *The Revival* noted that "intolerance and even persecution are but evils of the human heart" and would come if "divine and providential restraints" were removed.[284] Certainly, the brewery heir Frederick Charrington, when handing out tracts entitled "*This Way to the Pit*" to visitors to a local

[279] "Latest Intelligence", in *The War Cry*, 27 December 1879 p.4.
[280] W. Booth, *In Darkest England and the Way Out* (1890) p.280. For a summary of the strengths and weaknesses of the Salvation Army from an evangelical perspective, see H.C.G. Moule, *The Evangelical School in the Church of England* (1901) pp.65-67.
[281] The original does not specify the month in further detail.
[282] W. Arthur, *May We Hope for a Great Revival?* (1859) p.5.
[283] Ibid., p.8.
[284] "Signs of the Times", in *The Revival*, 5 February 1863, p.62.

music hall, was assaulted by a number of roughs sent by its proprietor. In the tumult that followed, he was arrested and spent a night in the cells of Bethnal Green Police Station.[285]

18.5 The Mission Movement in the Church of England

Some suggest that, in the 1850s, J.C. Ryle, in conjunction with Hugh McNeile and J.C. Miller, launched the first parish mission at St Martin's Church, Birmingham.[286] In 1864 a leading High Church preacher, like H.P. Liddon, drew 2,000 people on more than one occasion to a Lent Mission at Newbury parish church.[287] However, the beginning of "missions properly so-called"[288] within the Church of England is generally attributed to the Anglo-Catholics and, in particular, to November 1869 when they launched the Twelve Days' Mission to London. The evangelical William Haslam attributed the replacement of the word "mission", for special preaching services, to those "who love to copy Rome and Romish phrases".[289]

The official handbills of the Twelve Days' Mission described it as "12 days of prayer and preaching for the conversion of sinners".[290] It was to be "an assault on Sin and Satan".[291] *The Times* called it, to a "great extent, a novelty in the Church of England". It "roused considerable interest... among all classes".[292] After all, missions were seen as the province of the Nonconformists and their evangelical allies. *The Times* attributed the mission to the clergy of All Saints Margaret Street and St Alban's Holborn.[293] They were inspired by the work of the Society of St. John

[285] F.N. Charrington, *An Oasis in the Desert* (N.D.) pp.20-27.

[286] J.C. Ryle, *A Charge Delivered to the Clergy of the Diocese of Liverpool at his Third Triennial Visitation* (1887) pp.34-35. For some illustrative Nonconformist missions, see R. Horton, *An Autobiography* (1917) pp.69-76.

[287] J.O. Johnston, *Life and Letters of Henry Parry Liddon* (1904) p.68.

[288] See H.C.G. Moule, *The Evangelical School in the Church of England* (1901) pp.58 and 60 and C.E. Woods, *Memoirs and Letters of Canon Hay Aitken* (1928) p.100.

[289] W. Haslam, *From Death into Life* (1897) p.161. So also H.C.G. Moule, *The Evangelical School in the Church of England* (1901) p.60.

[290] "The Mission Services", in *The Times*, 25 November 1869.

[291] W.D. Maclagan, "The Church and the People", in *The Church and the Age* (1870) (A. Weir and W.D. Maclagan (eds)) p.444.

[292] "The Mission Services", in *The Times*, 23 November 1869.

[293] Ibid. Churches "where a 'high' ritual is practised, or 'high' doctrines are taught, those of St Margaret, Munster Square and St Andrew's, Wells Street...held aloof", see "The Mission Services", in *The Times*, 25 November 1869.

the Evangelist – known as the Cowley Fathers – who, since 1866, had run religious "revivals" in various country towns. William Bennett, a preacher at the Twelve Days' Mission, asserted that it was to them that "the Church owes, under God, the revival of parochial missions".[294] It would later be noted that High Church evangelism hinged more on "specific missions, by brotherhoods and sisterhoods, than [that of] the Evangelical section of the Church".[295]

To William Bennett, the appeal of the mission was that it arrested attention by offering novelty.[296] Furthermore, a missioner could be more direct with his listeners than the parish priest. The sermon was the principal work of the mission – the aim being that listeners made their confession to a priest.[297] Each day, at the mission's principal centres, a huge number of services were conducted – often up to four eucharistic and other forms of services.[298] The availability of confession was openly advertised.[299] In most of the churches involved, the mission concluded with a service whereby parishioners were recalled to their baptismal vows. The clergy, after the service, retired to hear confessions – to a late hour.[300] *The Times* observed that confession was "part and parcel of the religious 'revival', differing only in a very slight degree from the practice of the Roman Catholic Church".[301] The reintroduction of confession to, and spiritual direction by, a priest pointed to renewed clericalism in the Church.[302]

[294] W.J.E. Bennett, "Dedication Preface" to *Mission Sermons Preached at S. Paul's, Knightsbridge, at the London Mission of November, 1869* (1870) p.v. See also J. Kent, *Holding the Fort* (1978) pp.241-242 for other claimants as to the title of being the prime movers of the Twelve Days' Mission.

[295] J.H. Rigg, *The Present Position of Christianity and the Christian Faith in this Country* (1878) pp.8-9.

[296] W.J.E. Bennett, "Dedication Preface" to *Mission Sermons Preached at S. Paul's, Knightsbridge, at the London Mission of November, 1869* (1870) pp.xi-xii.

[297] Ibid., p.xii.

[298] J. Kent, *Holding the Fort* (1978) pp.259-260.

[299] "St Paul's, Knightsbridge", in *The Times*, 15 November 1869.

[300] "The Mission Services", in *The Times*, 25 November 1869. The creation of the service for the renewal of baptismal vows – being outside the Prayer Book – and the focus on confession, led to episcopally imposed limits on such activities in future missions, see "Meeting of the London Clergy at Sion College", in *The Times*, 11 October 1870. For the mission, its background and aftermath, see J. Kent, *Holding the Fort* (1978) pp.236-294.

[301] "The Mission Services", *The Times*, 23 November 1869.

[302] See J. Kent, *Holding the Fort* (1978) pp.283-284.

The Twelve Days' Mission involved up to 120 parishes.[303] Some who took part rejected its prevailing theology – but hoped that "this closer fellowship in the work of our common Lord and Master may do much to break down the prejudices and to remove the suspicions which too often exist between men of different ways of thinking who are yet moved by a true love for the same Saviour, and by an earnest desire to win souls for him".[304] One who was involved was the curate William Hay Macdowall Hunter Aitken. Prior to attending university, he had been assistant missioner at Thurso to his uncle, Hay Macdowall Grant, when the 1859 Revival struck Scotland. Aitken was much more sympathetic to Ritualism than his vicar, the evangelical William Pennefather. Perhaps, Aitken's involvement with the Twelve Days' Mission provided the contacts for him to later become, as he did, the "pre-eminent" English "missioner".[305]

Substantial numbers attended the Twelve Days' Mission and huge energy went into drawing them. For example, Father Stanton went into the "by-ways and alleyways, followed by a band of enthusiastic Churchmen, using extempore prayers and singing extempore litanies", to draw people under the hearing of the gospel.[306] *The Times* commented on the directness and fervency of the preaching[307] but, in retrospect, the mission was noted not so much for "its own immediate results as in the effect it had alike upon the Church and on the nation".[308] It was seen as a model for reaching the nation in future.[309]

In 1874 the Anglo-Catholic spiritual assault on London was renewed with another major mission. It was led by the Bishops of London, Winchester and Rochester – the expectation being that the area covered was as broad as the Church.[310] Remarkably, William Haslam, the revivalist, was one of those invited to address the missioners at St Paul's

[303] Ibid., pp.236 and 259.

[304] W.D. Maclagan, "The Twelve Days' Mission", in *The Times*, 16 November 1869.

[305] H.C.G. Moule, *The Evangelical School in the Church of England* (1901) p.60.

[306] "The Mission Services", in *The Times*, 25 November 1869.

[307] "The Mission Services", in *The Times*, 23 November 1869.

[308] C.E. Woods, *Memoirs and Letters of Canon Hay Aitken* (1928) p.101.

[309] See W.D. Maclagan, "The Church and the People", in *The Church and the Age* (1870) (A. Weir and W.D. Maclagan (eds)) pp.442-453. For Anglo-Catholic approaches to missions, see J.W. Horsley and N. Dawes, *Practical Hints for Parochial Missions* (1878).

[310] "The London Mission and the Confessional", in *The Times*, 7 February 1874 and C.M. Davies, *Orthodox London* (1876) pp.372-407.

Cathedral[311] before the mission's launch. The evangelical Sir Arthur Blackwood, who took part later, had the joy of receiving a letter from a former servant who had been converted during a prayer meeting for the mission.[312] Anglo-Catholic clergy expressed their dissatisfaction with the means recommended by evangelicals – which they thought had "a natural tendency to excite and break down the nervous system" – and evangelicals were concerned with the use of confession as part of the mission.[313] The London Mission was followed by missions in a number of northern cities.[314]

A further mission to London was launched in the autumn and winter of 1884-1885. Moody's return and success, to which we will come shortly, stirred the Church of England to launch it – as the solution to London's half-empty churches in the poorer districts. The mission was on a scale greater than ever before attempted, with more parishes than ever involved.[315] The city, because of its size, was divided into two; an East London Mission in November 1884[316] and a mission to the west, in February 1885. The East London Mission also included help with regard to housing, temperance and "penitential" women.[317] Again, concerns were expressed that the mission would be used to introduce the confessional.[318] Unfortunately, the Bishop of London, the instigator of the mission, died between its two parts – leading to fears that the second half of the mission would break up into a series of parochial missions.[319] Certainly, as *The Times* noted, there were different ways

[311] W. Haslam, *"Yet Not I"* (N.D.) pp.330-333. For the address, see W. Haslam, *Notes of an Address on Faith at St Paul's Cathedral, February 1874* (N.D.).

[312] *Some Records of the Life of Stevenson Arthur Blackwood* K.C.B. (1898) (H.S. Blackwood (ed.)) p.302.

[313] "'The London Mission of 1874'", in *The Times*, 10 December 1873 and "The London 'Mission'", in *The Times*, 14 February 1874.

[314] J. Kent, *Holding the Fort* (1978) p.282.

[315] "The East London Mission", in *The Times*, 15 November 1884.

[316] For the details, see ibid., "The East London Mission", in *The Times*, 17 November 1884 and "Throughout This Week There Are Other Matters", in *The Times*, 18 November 1884.

[317] Ibid.

[318] Ibid.

[319] "The London Mission", in *The Times*, 7 February 1885. Temple, of *Essays and Reviews* fame, as the nominee to the bishopric, opened the mission by addressing the clergy at Westminster Abbey. *The Times* summary of his address suggests that he thought that the power of mission lay in its "novelty" to stir the masses, "The London Mission", in *The Times*, 9 February 1885.

of drawing attention to the services. At St Giles-in-the-Fields, at 8 pm, half a dozen gentlemen stood outside the church and "affectionately" invited passers-by into the service, while at St Thomas Regent Street "the choir and clergy in full vestments, with cross and banners, and lanterns swinging from tall poles, issue into the crowded streets chanting penitential litanies or singing popular hymns to simple tunes".[320] "Public demonstrations" had become very much part of High Church witness.[321]

The Twelve Days' Mission ignited a movement of Anglican missions across the cities, towns and villages of the nation, with evangelicals taking a leading, but certainly not the only, part.[322] Hay Aitken was the pre-eminent missioner of this movement, with wide appeal across party lines, as he blended theologies which others found incompatible. He was given the soubriquet of the "High-Church Methodist" like his father, Robert, before him. He taught fervently the need for conversion but, under Tractarian influence, united to it the need for Sacramental Grace.[323] He worked effectively with the Ritualists, like George Wilkinson, at the great Leeds mission of 1875. Aitken took his father's old church there, with great success – while Wilkinson and others preached and emphasised the importance of confession elsewhere.[324] The work of such missioners was arduous. Hay Aitken would not take a mission of less than 18 days; he found the best work was done on the second and third Saturday nights. Often, missions were extended beyond the allotted time,[325] although bishops were wary about them. A proposed extension of Hay Aitken's first independent mission at Stroud was vetoed by the Bishop of Gloucester, on the ground that it would cause undue excitement.[326]

[320] "The London Mission", in *The Times*, 13 February 1885.

[321] J.H. Rigg, *The Present Position of Christianity and the Christian Faith in this Country* (1878) p.9.

[322] For an account of some of these missions, see C.E. Woods, *Memoirs and Letters of Canon Hay Aitken* (1928) pp.135-169. Relationships between the evangelist and local pastor was key to the success of a mission – and guidance was provided, see Dr Fish, "Evangelists and Revivals", in *The Sword and the Trowel* (1875) pp.115-121.

[323] C.E. Woods, *Memoirs and Letters of Canon Hay Aitken* (1928) pp.124-126. Hay Aitken was persuaded to become a full-time evangelist by Moody, who offered to guarantee his stipend, during Moody's mission to London of 1875, see ibid., pp.145-146.

[324] Ibid., p.136 and J. Kent, *Holding the Fort* (1978) pp.282-283.

[325] C.E. Woods, *Memoirs and Letters of Canon Hay Aitken* (1928) p.107.

[326] Ibid., p.101.

A mission sermon could be long. In 1874 a duke, listening to Hay Aitken at the Curzon Chapel Mayfair, urged: "Hang the fellow! He preached seventy minutes!"[327] A mission sermon might be published for evangelistic purposes. For example, the 20 sermons of Hay Aitken's "Ten Days' Mission" at Brighton in January 1875 reached a third edition in 1876[328] – and at a reduced price, so as to extend circulation. In January 1876, he returned to Brighton for a further mission. A volume of his sermons preached at All Souls Church Brighton and the Royal Pavilion and a volume of his sermons preached at St Margaret's Church Brighton and again at the Royal Pavilion were also published.[329] Individual sermons were published separately and testimonies of the power of written sermons to convert appeared.[330] Many churches produced their own hymn books for mission services – whether for services in schoolrooms, homes, temporary churches,[331] factories, warehouses or workshops.[332]

By the mid-1880s, Kent suggests Ritualist revivalism was in decline, but it had "helped to make the Church of England safe for Anglo-Catholicism".[333] George Body – after Aitken, the most popular parochial church missioner, and a definite Ritualist – thought the clergy used parish missions "as a means of raising the church life of their people, rather than of gathering in the ungodly".[334] Body's missions, though, certainly seem to have increased attendances in the churches where he preached.[335] In the 1890s, Charles Gore founded the Community of the Resurrection at Mirfield; it became "a school of missioners largely engaged in parochial missions".[336] As ritual was introduced to the eucharistic service, it became harder to identify occasions when a

[327] W. Haslam, *"Yet Not I"* (N.D.) p.335.

[328] H.M.H. Aitken, *"Ten Days' Mission"* (1876) (Third ed.) p.vi.

[329] H.M.H. Aitken, *"The Brighton Mission"* (1876) (Second Series) and *"The Brighton Mission"* (1876) (Third Series).

[330] C.E. Woods, *Memoirs and Letters of Canon Hay Aitken* (1928) pp.285-286.

[331] Christ Church, Hampstead, *The Church Mission Hymn Book* (1873).

[332] T.M. Macdonald, "How to Reach Working Men", in *Homiletical and Pastoral Lectures* (1879) p.403.

[333] J. Kent, *Holding the Fort* (1978) p.294.

[334] See K.F. Inglis, *Churches and the Working Classes in Victorian England* (1964) p.30.

[335] S. Baring-Gould, *The Church Revival* (1914) pp.292-293.

[336] J.L. Rees, *Timothy Rees of Mirfield and Landaff* (1945) p.63.

communion service led to the conversion of a major evangelist – such as Howell Harris and Charles Simeon.

Even before the mid-1880s, not every mission had been a triumph. Hay Aitken often struggled in London. His missions in Manchester (1877) and Liverpool (1878) were also difficult.[337] In 1881 he founded the Church Parochial Mission Society and, during his lifetime, it supplied missioners to clergy.[338] The Earl of Cairns was its first chairman – a distinguished Lord Chancellor – and a number of leading evangelicals were involved, such as H.W. Webb-Peploe and Lord Arthur Kinnaird, as well as those of broader views. The work of the Church Parochial Society became more complicated when, in 1883, Hay Aitken concluded that he no longer believed in the torment of the wicked, but in conditional immortality. Invitations to conduct missions were withdrawn. The Church Parochial Mission Society passed a resolution dissociating itself from the idea, but it did not condemn those who held that view.[339] Aitken's mission work continued, but he observed that, increasingly, the church did not have "the ear of the locality" and churches were half-full.[340] There might still be spiritual triumphs – such as his 1888 mission to Belfast, or where he was well-known. His 1888 mission to St Helens Parish Church led to the establishment of a Men's Bible Fellowship that quickly reached 650[341] – but he was now regularly troubled by the ineffectiveness of mission work and the governing board of the Church Parochial Mission Society was split. By 1895, even a visit to Belfast produced "a day of small things". Everywhere, there was an "ever-increasing indifference of the masses to the 'mission' form of appeal".[342] He then turned to mission work in North America – from where his reputation as "one of the very greatest preachers of the two Continents" drew a steady stream of invitations to speak.[343]

[337] C.E. Woods, *Memoirs and Letters of Canon Hay Aitken* (1928) pp.153-154. For other discouragements (and encouragements), see ibid., pp.163 and 166-169.
[338] Ibid., pp.149 and 160-161. For the missions of another Anglican clergymen, see F. Pigou, *The Acts of the Holy Ghost* (1908).
[339] See generally, ibid., pp.170-182.
[340] Ibid., p.197.
[341] "St Helens Parish Church Men's Bible Class", in *Church and People*, April 1939 p.24.
[342] C.E. Woods, *Memoirs and Letters of Canon Hay Aitken* (1928) p.205.
[343] Ibid., p.213. He preached over 22,000 sermons, a record beaten, in one view, only by John Wesley, ibid., pp.272 and 277-278.

18.6 Transatlantic evangelism and the Moody missions

The Americans Moody and Sankey embodied the new evangelism – whether in 'seeker-friendly' or 'aggressive' form. In their hands, between 1873 and 1875, evangelistic campaigns reached their apogee for the century.[344] Finney had worked mainly with the Congregationalists, Caughey and the Palmers working with the Methodists, but Moody also drew in evangelical Churchmen. He was not on good terms with that other great revivalist, General Booth.

Moody and Sankey's arrival in England was providential. Moody felt God wanted him to be an evangelist, but he was running a set of magnificent religious institutions in Chicago. These included the largest YMCA building in North America, a Sunday school of over a thousand (the fame of which saw President Lincoln visit it on the way to his inauguration) and Moody's own flourishing church. They were all burnt down in the great Chicago fire of 1871. Moody took the hint and came to England to run evangelistic services. When he arrived, he found those who had invited him were either dead or had forgotten him. There was one invitation left – an invitation to speak in York, from a chemist, the secretary of the local YMCA. Moody had not bothered to commit to this invitation. Therefore, to the surprise of the YMCA secretary, Moody arrived unannounced. Nevertheless, a mission was launched. It was a triumph. Moving to Newcastle and Sunderland, similar missionary success followed. Subsequent meetings in Edinburgh and Glasgow saw visitors attend them from all parts of Scotland; "deputations were sent from these centres over the country".[345] By 1875, Moody was preaching to huge crowds and his fame spanned the North Atlantic. In York, Moody had met the young F.B. Meyer, who greatly helped him, and their ongoing relationship linked Moody's legacy with that of the next generation.

Moody sought decisions for Christ from his hearers. Those moved by his preaching were counselled in inquiry rooms and made certain for Christ. One contemporary attributed the ability of Moody to three things. First, the service was limited to an hour. Second, half the hour was devoted to the singing of hymns. Third, his preaching style was

[344] English preachers went the other way.

[345] G.A. Smith, *The Life of Henry Drummond* (1899) p.60.

different from his contemporaries.[346] It was colloquial, made greater use of anecdotes and illustrations drawn from personal experience and was less doctrinal in content. Moody appealed to all classes. In 1875, he preached at 7.30 pm to the working classes of the East End at Bow Common, and at 9.00 pm to the aristocratic and upper middle classes at the Opera House, Haymarket.[347] There were no attacks on Catholic doctrines, so Roman Catholics attended. Indeed, all variety of Christians were welcome to the supporters' platform. On one occasion, the High Church Gladstone exclaimed to that arch-liberal Matthew Arnold, standing beside him on Moody's supporters' platform, "'I thank God I have lived to see the day when he should bless his church on earth by the gift of a man able to preach the gospel of Christ as we have just heard it preached!' At which Matthew Arnold retorted, 'Mr Gladstone, I would give all I have if only I could believe it.'"[348]

Moody's preaching style was ideally suited to a society impregnated with scriptural knowledge and values. He also knew how to target unbelieving men with believing wives. He preached that "you may have a praying wife now that weeps over you, pleads with you to come to Christ; but there will be no wife there to weep with you and pray for you – you will be separate then".[349] He forced people to think through how they responded to their knowledge and the beliefs of their family members. It was not enough to be respectable. Indeed, he thought that "the Church is dying of respectability".[350] He reaped a rich harvest. How many were converted will never be known this side of heaven but, in

[346] "The Father of the P.S.A.", in *The Christian World*, 8 February 1906 p.11.
[347] J. Pollock, *Moody without Sankey* (1983) p.142 and C.E. Woods, *Memoirs and Letters of Canon Hay Aitken* (1928) p.140. His son said he went to the opera house first, see W.R. Moody, *D.L Moody* (1930) p.225. There are suggestions that Moody was less successful at drawing the working classes, see K.F. Inglis, *Churches and the Working Classes in Victorian England* (1964) p.65. However, it is suggested that "especially men, were convinced of sin, and professed faith in Jesus Christ as their Saviour", see G.A. Smith, *The Life of Henry Drummond* (1899) pp.54 and 56.
[348] J. Pollock, *Moody without Sankey* (1983) p.140.
[349] D.L. Moody, *The London Discourses of D.L. Moody* (1875) p.111.
[350] See ibid., p.134. In the last half of the nineteenth century, up to the final decade, Nonconformity was increasingly middle class – and losing its appeal to the unskilled worker, see M.R. Watts, *The Dissenters* (2015) vol.3, pp.104-109.

1875, over 1.5 million people heard Moody in London.[351] In Birmingham, R.W. Dale's Carrs Lane church alone received 120 converts as new members from Moody's 1875 campaign in that city.[352] In eight months in 1883-1884 his hearers numbered 2.2 million people. His preaching converted a new generation of preachers, including Tommy Bewes, the father of a dynasty of Church of England ministers and evangelicals – enduring into the 21st century. Moody returned to England in 1892. It was not quite the triumph of the past, but Moody still had a power over hearts that was leaving others. Hay Aitken was troubled and humbled that "many of us who can preach as well as Moody, and with many more natural advantages, should yet fail with our hundreds, where he succeeds in bringing in his thousands".[353]

However, one should not assume that England in the 1870s was a hotbed of Christian zeal. Contemporaries thought that "the scepticism of the present age was one of the greatest difficulties to be overcome".[354] Congregationalists and others could be hostile to Moody.[355] *The Times*, in covering the opening night of the Moody and Sankey London campaign, wrote of them having "inaugurated their campaign against the religious indifferentism of London".[356] Its coverage of the early weeks of the mission was mocking.[357] The following gives a flavour of its view of Moody: "one is reminded of what Dr Johnson said with reference to Wesley – that he wrote and spoke more than he read – a remark which applies with much greater force here".[358] *The Times* suggested that Moody's success rested on meetings where the:

[351] J. Pollock, *Moody without Sankey* (1983) p.150. Some put the figures higher, at 2.5 million, W.R. Moody, *D.L Moody* (1930) p.225. Some suggest that Moody's second mission was less effective, R. Horton, *An Autobiography* (1917) p.69. Moody's sermons from his London campaign are set out in D.L. Moody, *The London Discourses of Mr D.L. Moody* (1875).

[352] A.W.W. Dale, *The Life of R.W. Dale* (1898) pp.319-320. See also C.E. Woods, *Memoirs and Letters of Canon Hay Aitken* (1928) pp.139-140 and M.R. Watts, *The Dissenters* (2015) vol.3, pp.126-127.

[353] C.E. Woods, *Memoirs and Letters of Canon Hay Aitken* (1928) p.206.

[354] "The International Christian Convention", in *The Times*, 7 May 1875.

[355] A.W.W. Dale, *The Life of R.W. Dale* (1898) pp.317 and 320 and G.A. Smith, *The Life of Henry Drummond* (1899) p.56.

[356] "The American Revivalists", in *The Times*, 10 March 1875.

[357] Especially "The American Revivalists", in *The Times*, 19 March 1875 and "Week More of Revivalism", in *The Times*, 26 March 1875.

[358] Ibid.

> Puritan clergy of the Establishment have fraternised with their Nonconformist sympathisers to promote the success of the movement, which has been powerfully aided, not only by the religious press, but also by zealous house-to-house visitation[359]...in the course of which the visitors have left circulars announcing the meetings and urging all who can do so to attend.[360]

Indeed, the house visitation was on a massive scale. In London 800 superintendents were required and 16,000 visitors.[361] Moody, in his opening talk, said that "To move London there must be not only fervent prayer but the united efforts of ministers, Sunday-school teachers and fathers and mothers."[362] Successful mission work in the 1870s required much prayer, unity, boldness and sheer hard work. The churches had learnt the lesson missed in the 1859 revival.

18.7 Workplace missions

Reaching people in their workplace was a key part of late nineteenth century evangelism. In 1880 the Railway Mission was founded to share the gospel with railway workers. Branches were set up and mission halls established in the great rail centres and in the more remote ones. Sunday schools were started and individuals were converted. For those in the military a number of agencies came into being including the Soldiers' Christian Association (1887). There was also the evangelistic and philanthropic work of a formidable group of evangelical ladies all of whose work was shaped by the 1859 revival. Their work included the soldiers' homes of Mrs Daniell and her daughter and those of Miss Elsie Sandes across the Empire. For the Royal Navy Agnes Weston established her Royal Sailors' Rests.[363] For seamen Reginald Radcliffe's Strangers' Rests were established. For household servants, a master might call them after breakfast every morning to read to them the Bible, make a few remarks and to pray.[364]

359 Catherine Booth was another great believer in house-to-house visitation. Towards the end of her life she said: "I esteem this work of house-to-house visitation next in importance to the preaching of the gospel itself", see C. Bramwell-Booth, *Catherine Booth* (1973) p.153.
360 "The American Revivalists", in *The Times*, 10 March 1875.
361 J. Radcliffe, *Recollections of Reginald Radcliffe* (1896) p.221.
362 "The American Revivalists", in *The Times*, 10 March 1875.
363 "A Mission with a Message", in *The Christian Herald and Signs of our Times*, 17 March 1938, p.257.
364 E. Gosse, *The Life of Philip Henry Gosse* (1890) p.358.

18.8 'Faith' missions

The last half of the nineteenth century was the great period of 'faith' missions, although travelling evangelists, especially Brethren evangelists, had developed the idea of "Living by faith", earlier in the century.[365] In their work they looked "to God alone for support" and did not ask for money.[366] Perhaps the best-known men who lived by faith were the Brethren members Hudson Taylor, with the China Inland Mission, and George Müller, with his orphanages and schools; but there were also others, such as the Joyful News Ministry, established by the Methodist minister Thomas Champness.[367] This sent young lay evangelists to village greens, chapels and into farmers' homes.[368] They did not come with the need for the expensive education of the ministerial class.

Marvellous stories circulated about God's provision for the work of these faith ministries. On one occasion, Müller had no money for bread at breakfast time but, when grace was over, a baker was at the door with loaves for the orphanage – sent by some unknown and unprompted benefactor. Charles Dickens, who lacked enthusiasm for Müller's theological principles, was impressed by his work.[369] Müller brought up just over 10,000 orphans. His schools educated over 120,000 children.[370]

Others took a very different view as to the means of funding their ventures. William Booth and Thomas Barnardo directly asked the public for money. Dickens thought that Müller, by telling of his prayers, worked to bring them about. Moody also viewed faith missions with a "certain degree of misgiving". In his view, all missions depended upon prayer and voluntary gifts – and "To stress the point that there was no

[365] See T. Grass, *Gathering to His Name* (2012) pp.13, 33-34, 41 and 46-47.

[366] J. Hambleton, *Buds, Blossoms, and Fruits of the Revival* (N.D.) p.9.

[367] John Hambleton and Richard Weaver are other examples of non-Brethren members adopting the living by faith approach to sustain their evangelistic endeavours, see *Buds, Blossoms, and Fruits of the Revival* (N.D.) p.9 and J. Paterson, *Richard Weaver's Life Story* (2012) pp.62-63 and 74. There were also organisations led by women such as Ranyard's London Bible and Domestic Female Mission, see "How Wears the Missing Link?", in *God's Message in Low London* (N.D.) p.6.

[368] J.I. Brice, *The Crowd for Christ* (1934) pp.34-39 and 73-75. For other individuals working on the faith principle, see I.C. Watson, *The Life Story of Thomas Langton of Malton* (1896) pp.33-34 and 51-53.

[369] C. Dickens, "Brother Müller and his Orphanage-work", in *Household Words*, 7 November 1857, pp.433-438.

[370] Müller also ran a chapel, numbering 2,000, at the time of his death.

appeal was but an astute method of soliciting."[371] In 1871 the Children's Special Service Mission ("CSSM") adopted a "qualified faith" position. Collections for ordinary work would not be publicised but, where a new effort was required, approaching friends was permissible. It found that the qualified faith approach did not work. In 1876 CSSM's means of funding moved to traditional lines.

18.9 The continuing rise of Christian women's work

Evangelicals in the first half of the nineteenth century were encouraged by the results of the work of women. In the last half of the century, their involvement in running a great range of activities – including evangelistic campaigns, social work and educating the young – was expanded and institutionalised. They also funded the building of mission halls, raised money for home missionaries, gave money to meet the needy[372] and edited church newspapers.[373] There were good practical reasons for this development – women outnumbered men in the churches, especially in the working-class districts. There were also more women than men to reach because, in the general population, women exceeded men in number by between five to seven percent.[374]

The recently established London Bible and Domestic Female Mission gave a platform to less-educated women to hold out the gospel as Biblewomen. Between November 1859 and November 1860 its number of full-time Biblewomen jumped from 35 to 137.[375] By the early 1870s it had more than 250 agents.[376] Its Biblewomen could be fearless in the gospel cause. One went to a factory to speak to women workers at a lunch-time. The factory manager thought his workforce "devils" and was against the attempt. The Biblewoman persevered and, although initially scorned and mocked, a weekly dinner-hour meeting was established at which she preached.[377] A Biblewoman could also look back on her day and find that she had been "welfare worker, instructor in cookery and hygiene, minor-ailment centre nurse and above all, her best friend to

[371] W.R. Moody, *D.L. Moody* (1930) p.381.
[372] I. Howat and J. Nicholls, *Streets Paved with Gold* (2003) pp.228-229.
[373] J.I. Brice, *The Crowd for Christ* (1934) p.33.
[374] J. Black and D.M. MacRaild, *Nineteenth-century Britain* (2003) p.56.
[375] See D.M. Lewis, *Lighten their Darkness* (1986) p.221.
[376] "How Wears the Missing Link?", in *God's Message in Low London* (N.D.) p.6.
[377] E. Platt, *The Story of the Ranyard Mission 1857-1937* (1937) pp.83-86.

many a weary woman".[378] Dioceses also started to employ Biblewomen "to hold mothers' meetings and do work which can be better done by women". In 1887 Liverpool Diocese had 31 Biblewomen.[379]

Ladies of the 'better' classes supervised the London Bible and Domestic Female Mission's Biblewomen. No lady need offer her services on a basis that it was "merely honorary or intermitting: she must be depended upon for the vigilant performance of her own particular duties".[380] It is telling that the Pre-Raphaelite painter Ford Madox Brown, in his well-known painting *Work*, in which he seeks to encapsulate all aspects of mid-Victorian life, includes only two women – both are middle class and one is distributing tracts.[381] Moody saw the visitation of the poor by ladies as the key to his missions.[382] A vicar of All Saints South Lambeth predicted that if lady visitors and the other organisations were taken away for three months "the church would be almost empty".[383] By the mid-1860s, the High Church deployed its ladies in primarily educational, but sometimes more wide-ranging, social activities.[384] The numbers in their sisterhoods, generally devoted to charitable works, were also growing. By the end of the century more than 10,000 had tried that way of life.[385]

The first institution to give formal status to women's work was that of Mildmay which, in 1860, made its women workers undenominational deaconesses. Two hundred Mildmay deaconesses were soon working

[378] Ibid., p.78.

[379] J.C. Ryle, *A Charge Delivered to the Clergy of the Diocese of Liverpool at his Third Triennial Visitation* (1887) p.16.

[380] L.N.R., *The Missing Link* (1861) p.299. For the development of Christian work by ladies see also G.E. Morgan, *R.C. Morgan: His Life and Times* (1909) pp.148-153 and 294-302.

[381] The other woman "avoids work altogether", see T. Barringer, *Men at Work* (2005) pp.50-51 and 63-66.

[382] "He said he should certainly advocate the agency of women helpers, and the higher the class of women the better. He believed it was the bounden duty of women, and of ladies especially, to go out as district visitors, and where they had time on their hands to engage in a house-to-house visitation. If they could only get the women to go round and search out the sick, the afflicted, and the oppressed, and bring all the agencies that had been suggested into full working order, they would very soon work such a glorious reform in the world as had never been seen before", see "The International Christian Convention", in *The Times*, 7 May 1875.

[383] J. Cox, *The English Churches in a Secular Society* (1982) p.65.

[384] P. Davie, *Raising up a Faithful People* (1997) pp.55-60.

[385] S. Mumm, *All Saints Sisters of the Poor* (2001) p.xii.

at any one time.[386] In 1862 Dr Tait, the Bishop of London, appointed the first Anglican deaconess. However, there was an ongoing lack of clarity about what such a role involved. She was a "woman set apart by a Bishop...for service in the church";[387] but what form of service? In 1882 Bishop J.B. Lightfoot of Durham noted the difficulty, rooted in the Bible's teaching, of defining the precise limit of a woman as a religious teacher; but he assured his clergy that "in the philanthropic and charitable work of the Church, which is her proper sphere, her capabilities are inexhaustible".[388] One view was that "When the heart of a woman has been won to the love of Christ, it is her happiness, her delight, to be employed in works of mercy. The truth of this is attested by the large number of voluntary workers among us."[389] In 1888 the Ladies' Home Mission Union was formed – to pray and raise funds for the work of the CPAS.[390] In 1891, a training college for ladies was founded at Blackheath and the first woman worker was appointed in the parish of Spitalfields.[391] A few years later another was founded at Bristol. Formal recognition of the deaconess role was given by the Lambeth Conference of 1897, but the functions of a deaconess, and how to become one, were not set out in the canons of the Church of England until 1920.

Elsewhere, deaconesses spread across the other denominations "for house-to-house visitation, mothers' meetings and tract distribution".[392] In 1887, formal denominational-based training was first provided when Katherine Hughes, the wife of Hugh Price Hughes, established the "Sisters of the People". In 1889, when the massive Wesleyan West London Mission launched *Advance!* (its monthly magazine), the leading

[386] K. Heasman, *Evangelicals in Action* (1962) p.39.

[387] M.J. Roxburgh, *Women's Work in the Church of England* (1958) pp.2-3. Popularisers of the role saw it as "the training of women for works of charity, whether as recognised members of the staff of the Church or not", J.M. Ludlow, *Women's Work in the Church*, (1865) p.217. At the apostles' time, deaconess had been "strictly excluded from the priestly functions of public teaching and worship", ibid., p.214.

[388] "The Bishop of Durham's Charge", in *The Manchester Guardian*, 15 December 1882.

[389] Cited in I. Howat and J. Nicholls, *Streets Paved with Gold* (2003) p.231. The London City Mission did not employ female mission workers to avoid the work being seen as that for women and leading to the supply of male recruits drying up.

[390] Lady Dynevor, "*Our Ladies' Home Mission Union*", in *Church and People, April* 1889 p.14.

[391] "Milestones", in *Church and People,* October 1938 p.55.

[392] M.R. Watts, *The Dissenters* (2015) vol.3, p.171.

article was devoted to them. They were described as

> educated, cultivated women, and are as much at home in the mansions of the rich as the homes of the poor. Their work is very varied; they hold mothers' meetings, Bible classes for working-girls, and have their reception-day at the house for all classes of people.[393]

A picture of a "Sister of the People" adorned the cover of the second issue (and those of future issues) of *Advance!* The Sisters also talked politics to men – and the sisterhood proved to be "an innovative institution for the development of women leaders".[394] In 1890 the Baptist Deaconesses' Home and Mission was founded, under the direction of F.B. Meyer. In 1895 the Wesleyan Methodists debated admitting women to Conference (their governing body), but the proposal was narrowly defeated.[395]

Meanwhile, the YWCA expanded its work with young women by merging in 1877 with Lady Kinnaird's home for young women. Before the merger, the YWCA had 150 branches and 12,000 members.[396] The agent of this merger was another leading female evangelical, Mrs Catherine Pennefather. Her husband had been the Rector of St Jude's Mildmay Park and had established the Mildmay deaconesses.[397] The merged organisation had substantial backers. The principal donor to its first headquarters office in Regent Street, London, was the very wealthy Samuel Morley. It also grew quickly. By 1885, it had 8,517 members in London, an addition of 1,538 members on the previous year.[398] In the student world, by 1894, women worked in the women's colleges to promote Christian work.[399]

From the second half of the nineteenth century, women started to go as single missionaries to Africa and Asia – where they made a "unique

[393] M. Bottome, "An Interview with Sister Lily", in *Advance!*, October 1889, p.6.

[394] C. Oldstone-Moore, *Hugh Price Hughes* (1999) pp.168-169.

[395] Ibid., pp.291-293.

[396] Young Women's Christian Association, *Our Eighty Years* (1935) p.11.

[397] C. Binfield, *George Williams and the Y.M.C.A.* (1973) pp.328-329. See also *A Study of the World's Y.W.C.A* (1924) pp.6-7.

[398] "Young Women's Christian Association", in *The Times*, 18 April 1885.

[399] T. Tatlow, *The Story of the Student Christian Movement of Great Britain and Ireland* (1933) p.56. Victorian women also established the Ladies' National Association for the Repeal of the Contagious Diseases Acts, the first British political organisation conducted entirely by women. Its secretary and most effective speaker was Josephine Butler.

contribution".[400] Amanda Berry Smith was a slave freed in America who in 1878 came from there to Britain. She was a Methodist and part of the 'Holiness' movement. The leaders of the Keswick Convention welcomed her – and she spoke there that year. A great number of evangelistic opportunities followed, until she left for India in the autumn of 1879.[401] She returned for evangelistic work in November 1889, leaving the following September.

British-born women were also teaching and preaching back at home.[402] Ellen Ranyard's Biblewomen taught women in "Mother's classes". Some classes led to "Father's classes". One lady enjoyed remarkable success,[403] and another lady ran two sessions a week for men between 7.30 and 10 pm, with 100 men attending. "The first hour and a half was devoted to instruction in reading, writing and arithmetic…The last hour was given up to Bible instruction and singing".[404] In 1893 the little and elderly Mrs Maynard took a Nonconformist mission in Putney High Street. The congregation did not think that the time was ripe for a mission – and having a woman speaker was unorthodox. Attendances were small, but Hudson Pope, the future great child evangelist (aged 14) and his friend were the converts.[405]

Some women were led into preaching when the success of their Sunday school, or other teaching opportunities, led to the creation of a church. It was difficult to stand back and hand it over to another.[406] Others, like Fanny Guinness, became preachers because their husbands

[400] Some mission agencies sent out only women missionaries to work with women, such as the Church of England's Zenana Mission Society. It was started in 1880, to evangelise women in India through education and medical help – and came out of the Interdenominational Indian Female Normal School Society, founded in 1852. A missionary observed that female missionaries: "demonstrated that there was another career open to women besides marriage. They raised the age of marriage. And they introduced the teaching and nursing professions as channels through which young Asian and African women would serve their own people," see M. Warren, *The Church Militant Abroad: Victorian Missionaries in the Victorian Crisis of Faith* (1970) p.69.

[401] N. Scotland, *Apostles of the Spirit and Fire* (2009) pp.192-195.

[402] See generally J. Murray, "Gender Attitudes and the Contribution of Women to Evangelism and Ministry in the Nineteenth Century", in *Evangelical Faith and Public Zeal* (1995) (J. Wolff (ed.)) pp.105-111.

[403] "How Wears the Missing Link?", in *God's Message in Low London* (N.D.) pp.44-48.

[404] E. Platt, *The Story of the Ranyard Mission 1857-1937* (1937) pp.81-82.

[405] P.M. St. John, *R. Hudson Pope* (1967) pp.20-21.

[406] L. Wilson, *Constrained by Zeal* (2000) pp.204-205.

were well-known evangelists and someone was needed to address women's meetings. Success at these led to speaking at mixed meetings,[407] especially if the husband failed to turn up and someone had to speak. If the talk produced conversions, then a wife, like Mrs Frances Haslam, might move into regular speaking engagements.[408] William Haslam also had another female helper in his work – Geraldine Hooper, a descendant of the Marian martyr, John Hooper, Bishop of Gloucester. She worked at first with Haslam at Bath, supporting his work with singing, running a prayer meeting, establishing a gospel meeting and other forms of help. This led to speaking engagements. Such was her success that she began her own missions. At Dunstable in May 1866 the building put up for her addresses sat 3,000 and was full nightly. On the Sunday evening, the numbers reached 4,000. Returning in July 1866, it was calculated that 7,000 packed the pavilion.[409] In 1867, she spoke with Hay Macdowall Grant and proved the more popular of the two.[410] In 1872 she and her new husband replaced the Booths in Whitechapel when the latter were ill.[411] However, the preaching took its toll; she died early, aged 31.[412] In her ten years of speaking she became "the most celebrated of the female preachers of the 1860s"[413] – preaching 4,000, perhaps 5,000, times "and rarely without winning souls".[414] She was identified as the female Spurgeon.[415]

The right of women to preach was a theological issue. The preaching

[407] C.W. Mackintosh, *Dr Harry Guinness* (1916) p.11.

[408] W. Haslam, *"Yet Not I"* (N.D.) pp.187-188, 207 and 209-210.

[409] G. Guinness, *"She Spake of Him"* (1872) pp.49, 58 and 60.

[410] Grant initially was against women's ministry but was won over by "the results of her labours", ibid., pp.91-92. For a male evangelist to share an evangelistic campaign with a female speaker was not unknown, see Thomas Langton and Miss Wilson at Pelton Fell, I.C. Watson, *The Life Story of Thomas Langton of Malton* (1896) p.170.

[411] G. Guinness, *"She Spake of Him"* (1872) p.165.

[412] The mourners at her funeral numbered between 10,000 and 15,000, see ibid., p.218.

[413] N. Dickson, Hooper [*married name* Dening], (Emma) Geraldine Henrietta Hamilton *Oxford Dictionary of National Biography* (2004). See also W. Haslam, *"Yet Not I"* (N.D.) pp.161-174 and 206-207 and 209-215. Another popular evangelistic preacher of the late 1860s was Miss Octavia Jary. A mission in the spring of 1867 saw two or three thousand assemble to hear her on a number of occasions at Ashbourne, Derbyshire. "Many were brought to Christ, noticeably of the better class", see J. Wood, *The Story of the Evangelization Society* (N.D.) pp.18-20.

[414] G. Guinness, *"She Spake of Him"* (1872) pp.10 and 41.

[415] Ibid., p.76.

of Geraldine Hooper was justified by reference to the words of the prophet Joel – that, in the latter days, God would "pour out his Spirit upon sons and *daughters*, upon servants and *handmaids*" and upon the conversions resulting from her speaking.[416] The issue was particularly acute among members of the Holiness movement. William and Catherine Booth first argued, when they were engaged, over a woman's right to preach. Although he was against it, all he could say was, "I would not stay *you*, if I had power to do so. Altho' *I should not like it*".[417] Five years later in 1860, Catherine Booth first preached in church – after writing a tract on the subject, prompted by the preaching of the American Phoebe Palmer.[418] Catherine Booth spoke for an hour on the Prodigal Son and was soon speaking for an hour and a quarter.[419] In *Female Ministry; Or Women's Right to Preach the Gospel* (1859), she drew a distinction between preaching the gospel to a man – which was acceptable – and "teaching as is domineering, and as involves usurpation of authority over a man".[420] Catherine Booth was clear that the married man was head of the household. She wrote to William, prior to marriage, to exhort him to be prepared to exercise his duty as head of the household and not to consider the job of bringing up the children that of the mother alone.[421] Perhaps that is why Booth found it easy to encourage her preaching; she acknowledged his authority.

In the Salvation Army, the role of women advanced step by step. First, women were evangelists and some were very effective and courageous ones;[422] then they led a corps jointly with another woman; next they had

[416] Author's italics. See ibid., p.xi. Hooper's biographer, Mrs Guinness, puts well the arguments in favour of female evangelistic preaching in ibid., pp.243-253.

[417] Author's italics. See A.M. Eason, *Women in God's Army* (2003) p.40.

[418] For the circumstances and steps that led to Catherine Booth preaching, see P.J. Walker, *Pulling the Devil's Kingdom Down* (2001) pp.17-34 and C. Bramwell-Booth, *Catherine Booth* (1973) pp.147-168. It has been observed that "one could argue that the holiness churches pioneered the ministry of women and that the history of feminism in the United States will not be complete, nor even fully understood, until this fact is taken into account", "Preface" to *Holiness Tracts Defending the Ministry of Women* (1985) p.vii.

[419] P.J. Walker, *Pulling the Devil's Kingdom Down* (2001) p.33.

[420] C. Booth, *Female Ministry*, p.13 reproduced in *Holiness Tracts Defending the Ministry of Women* (1985).

[421] C. Bramwell Booth, *Bramwell Booth* (1933) p.3.

[422] See, for example, the work of Marianne Pawson during the Chester revival of 1882, G. Green, *Revivals and other Great Events* (2014) pp.34-41.

charge of important undertakings, such as the Women's Training Home; and then finally became leaders of larger units, such as a division.[423] From 1878, women officers enjoyed equal rights with the men. William Booth would say, "The best men in my Army are the women."[424] All the same, apart from the pulpit, it is said that "men assumed commanding and decision-making responsibilities at the corps and administrative levels", unless blood or relational ties to the General were involved.[425] However, by allowing female Booth family members into positions of authority, "the Salvation Army was the first organisation to prove that working women possessed the talent to lead".[426] It also trained up many able preachers who had a wider ministry elsewhere. For example, in 1882 Mary Jane Featherstone, a Salvation Army Officer and an able preacher, married Smith Wigglesworth and resigned her commission.[427] They became an effective mission team. She preached while he did the counselling and made sure of the new converts, until she trained him up to preach. Smith Wigglesworth went on to become one of the founders of the modern Pentecostal movement of the next century.

18.10 The adult school movement

The adult school movement aimed to win working men and women to Christ through teaching.

> The education provided by the adult schools was firmly rooted in the scriptural and Christian tradition of the nineteenth-century Sunday school, but with this had been blended a curriculum which might include an element of almost any literary, philosophical or scientific theme, depending on the knowledge and interests of the teachers and their pupils.[428]

[423] For a summary of the growth of the role of women in the Salvation Army, see B. Booth, *Echoes and Memories* (1925) pp.161-172.
[424] R. Collier, *The General Next to God* (1965) p.110.
[425] A.M. Eason, *Women in God's Army* (2003) p.155.
[426] R. Hattersley, *Blood & Fire* (1999) p.440. See pp.199-200 for the influence of George Railton in allowing women to lead in the Salvation Army.
[427] S.H. Frodsham, *Smith Wigglesworth* (1974) pp.17-21.
[428] C. Charlton, "Introduction" to J.W. Rowntree and H.B. Binns, *A History of the Adult School Movement* (1985) p.iii.

Adult schools tended to meet on Sunday mornings. Social and recreational activities were often added to their educational meetings. By 1871, the adult school movement had about 8,000 members.[429] In 1874, the Quakers established an extra-denominational church in Birmingham for members of their schools. It soon had 1,000 members.[430]

Having been "cradled" by the Quakers,[431] in the 1870s the adult school movement gained wider traction, especially amongst the Congregationalists. A mission run by the Bunhill Adult School, in conjunction with the Evangelization Society, led to the names of 64 men and 50 women being followed up after the mission.[432] R.W. Dale looked "upon the movement with the largest hope, in relation to the future of religious life in this country", saying: "I believe that the movement is only in the earliest stage of a great and glorious history".[433] Nearby, the adult school movement spawned the PSA movement after John Blackham, running a morning adult school at West Bromwich, launched one in the afternoon.[434] The adult school movement also developed a social side in the form of savings funds, coffee carts in place of alcohol and clubs of various sorts for members and their children. By the turn of the century, its numbers exceeded 50,000.[435]

18.11 Christian student movements

In 1858 the Cambridge University Church Missionary Society began. In 1862 the Cambridge Daily Prayer Meeting started and there were evangelistic visits to venues in Cambridge from well-known evangelists, such as Sir Arthur Blackwood.[436] In 1877 CICCU was formed and, in 1879, a similar student Christian group at Oxford.[437] In the mid-

[429] J.W. Rowntree and H.B. Binns, *A History of the Adult School Movement* (1985) p.25.

[430] Ibid., pp.22-23.

[431] *Directory of Adult Schools 1911* (1911) p.5.

[432] J. Wood, *The Story of the Evangelization Society* (N.D.) p.65.

[433] E. Smith, *Mending Men* (N.D.) p.149.

[434] J.W. Rowntree and H.B. Binns, *A History of the Adult School Movement* (1985) p.26.

[435] Ibid., p.19.

[436] *Some Records of the Life of Stevenson Arthur Blackwood* K.C.B. (1898) (H.S. Blackwood (ed.)) pp.323-325.

[437] For an overview of the origins of late nineteenth-century student religious societies in the universities, see T. Tatlow, *The Story of the Student Christian Movement of Great*

1870s, Robert Horton described the Evangelical party at Oxford as maintaining "a genuine but feeble life", although this is a little harsh.[438] In Scotland, the religious revivals of the 1860s led to the formation of various Christian student groups and, in 1874, the Medical Prayer Union commenced in London's medical schools.

Moody's second evangelistic campaign of 1881-1884 increased the numbers of these student organisations. At Cambridge, over 200 men stood on the last night of his campaign to indicate that they had received blessing. Looking back, Handley Moule, Principal of Ridley Hall theological college, observed that "among the scores of true, deep, lasting conversions were not a few of men well-known and of powerful influence".[439]

Moody's time at Cambridge, partly through contact with its cricket captain, C.T. Studd, was also important because it set the stone rolling which set off an avalanche of student and missionary work across the globe. By doing so, it shifted the focus of evangelistic endeavours. Studd was perhaps England's best-known sportsman at the time. The previous summer he and his two brothers had been part of the Cambridge University side that soundly defeated the touring Australians. Studd scored 118 runs in the first innings and 15 not-out in the second. He took eight wickets. He was also, as we have seen, the last English wicket standing in the original Ashes series. Under Moody's influence – and with six others from Cambridge, including Stanley Smith, the stroke of the Cambridge boat – Studd went as a missionary to China. The Cambridge Seven, as Studd and his fellow missionaries were known, raised the profile of mission and Christian work within the universities. They went off to China after a packed Exeter Hall meeting in 1885, which had George Williams of the YMCA in the chair.[440]

The following year, Moody organised a student conference at Mount Hermon, Massachusetts, in conjunction with the YMCA. Out of this

Britain and Ireland (1933) pp.6-16.

[438] R. Horton, *An Autobiography* (1917) p.34. For a more positive view, see W.F. Scott, "Evangelical Churchmanship at Oxford", in *The Record*, 3 March 1933, p.114; J.D. Mullins, "Evangelicalism in Oxford in the Late Seventies", in *The Record*, 24 March 1933, p.165; and P.E. Wilson, "Evangelicalism in Oxford", in *The Record*, 31 March 1933, p.177.

[439] J.B. Harford and F.C. Macdonald, *Handley Carr Glyn Moule* (1922) p.95.

[440] "Missions to China", in *The Times*, 5 February 1885.

conference came the Student Volunteer Movement for Foreign Missions in the United States. Its watchword was "The evangelisation of the world in this generation". Soon, similar organisations were established in other countries including, in 1892, the Student Volunteer Missionary Union of Great Britain and Ireland.

Today, it is difficult to fully appreciate the enthusiasm and energy that, in the last decades of the nineteenth century, went into overseas missions. By the time of the first Quadrennial Student Missionary Conference in Liverpool in 1896, there were 1,038 volunteers, of whom 212 had already sailed.[441] By 1933, 3,600 members of the Student Volunteer Missionary Union of Great Britain and Ireland had gone abroad with British missionary societies. This emphasis on missions meant that many of the most committed and best minds went overseas. In the years ahead, there were insufficient men of the right quality contending for the gospel in the nation's theological colleges. Indeed, whereas the 1859 Revival primarily stimulated home evangelistic organisations, much of the spiritual energy that flowed out of the second Moody mission flowed overseas. One author wrote of "the burning activity of missions during those ten years, 1890-1900, after the opening up of Africa by Stanley and others, not in Africa only, but in China, India, Japan, and among the aborigines of North and South America". He added: "Most of the pioneer undertakings of the eighties had by that time overcome the initial stage, and were witnessing year by year the formation of Christian communities among the darkest heathen at a rate which fills the chronicler with amazement...Doors which might soon be closed were opening in all directions. The leaders in every enterprise were shouting to the rank and file to enter the breaches they had made and seize the strongholds, before the enemy had time to rally his forces."[442]

Reference to future missionary work is to get ahead of ourselves. To recruit missionaries from any specific university required a pre-existing student organisation. Accordingly, in 1893 the Inter-University Christian Union was established.[443] Even in the 1890s, establishing a student Christian Union was not easy. At Bristol, the Secretary of the

[441] R. Rouse, *The World's Student Christian Federation* (1948) p.56.
[442] C.W. Mackintosh, *Dr Harry Guinness* (1916) p.49.
[443] T. Tatlow, *The Story of the Student Christian Movement of Great Britain and Ireland* (1933) pp.49-51.

new organisation stood in a corridor of the Arts Faculty asking men if they knew of a Christian man. The answer he received was that there was not one. Colleges also refused permission to hold meetings, or even to put up notices.[444] The first experience of any new Christian Union "was usually great apathy and a very small meeting".[445] In 1895, the Inter-University Christian Union dropped the words Inter-University, as too elitist. It became the British College Christian Union and was later further renamed as the Student Christian Movement of Great Britain and Ireland.[446] It adopted as a doctrinal basis that its work and purpose was "in full harmony with a belief in Jesus Christ as God the Son and only Saviour of the world".[447]

18.12 Children's education

The role of the churches in education – and especially that of the Anglican National Society for Promoting the Education of the Poor – grew; by 1867, a million and a half children were in Church day-schools. However, there were 1,693 parishes[448] with no day-school and Parliament – under the influence of those who wished to secularise education and the Dissenters (who did not like the influence of the National Society for Promoting the Education of the Poor) – decided to act. The Education Act 1870 established a system of school boards of locally elected members, drawing their funding from the local rates, to provide a board school for places lacking adequate school facilities. A board school left no space for a ragged school. Lord Shaftesbury saw the implications. He wrote,

> The godless, non-Bible system is at hand; and the ragged schools, with all their divine polity, with all their burning and fruitful love for the poor, with all their prayers and harvests for the temporal and eternal welfare of forsaken, heathenish, destitute, sorrowful, and yet innocent children, must perish under the all-conquering march of intellectual power.[449]

[444] Ibid., pp.52-53.
[445] Ibid., p.54.
[446] In 1895, the co-ordinating body of the various national associations emerged, the World Student Christian Federation.
[447] Ibid., p.66.
[448] H.J. Burgess and P.A. Welsby, *A Short History of The National Society* (1961) p.34.
[449] Cited in J.L. Hammond and B. Hammond, *Lord Shaftesbury* (1936) p.258. But

Some ragged schools became board schools; others concentrated on their welfare side, including biblical activities.[450] Out of one, Quintin Hogg laid the foundations of today's Westminster University.[451]

More generally, the Education Act 1870 set in motion forces that reduced the involvement of Church and chapel in national education and reduced its religious purpose and content. Where a board school was established, it could not teach denominational distinctives. The religious teaching that resulted was "cold, stiff, starched."[452] It might also give up on doctrine altogether. William Forster, the Minister of Education responsible for the Education Act, declared, in accordance with the spirit of the age, his confidence that children will be taught "the great truths of Christian life and conduct", while their "poor little minds" will be spared "theological dogmas".[453] Benjamin Disraeli made the point that "a religion without formularies is a new religion".[454] By the 1920s, Disraeli was proved right. Ironically, the religion that resulted was "from its very indefiniteness, incapable of influencing character or conduct".[455] Furthermore, Lord Shaftesbury shrewdly noted that if religion in the new schools was not examined, it was unlikely that the teachers would pay attention to it.[456]

A further challenge to the hold of Christianity on the nation's thinking arising from the Education Act was the risk that, through state involvement, the link between secular and religious knowledge would be severed, so that the former ceased to recognise its divine origin. Spurgeon alluded to the dangers of this on a number of occasions. In 1872, he observed that unless religious education accompanied secular

Shaftesbury recognised something needed to be done for all the nation's children, see T.N. Kelynack, *The Progress of Child Welfare During the Last Half Century* (1922) pp.9-10.

[450] The Ragged School Union became the Shaftesbury Society and, in 2008, Livability. See also ibid., pp.15-16.

[451] C. Booth, *Life and Labour of the People in London* (1903), Third Series: Religious Influences vol.7, pp.390-393.

[452] T.N. Kelynack, *The Progress of Child Welfare During the Last Half Century* (1922) p.12.

[453] Ibid., p.10.

[454] Cited in S. Dark, *Archbishop Davidson and the English Church* (1929) p.181.

[455] Ibid.

[456] T.N. Kelynack, *The Progress of Child Welfare During the Last Half Century* (1922) p.12.

education you would "only do what has been done in Hindustan – convert men from idolatry into atheism, and bring people from the stupidity of a dormant intellect into the vicious activity of an intellect that seeks for anything but God".[457] Later he commented: "Secular knowledge *per se* may be very good, but it is easily turned into evil unless it be combined with and salted with the pure and better knowledge of the word of God."[458] Surprisingly in Victorian England, Spurgeon spoke of the Bible being "persecuted" in the schools by a minority; he termed them "half a dozen infidels".[459] A further problem was that, with the emergence of the teaching profession through the Education Act, the link between clergy and school weakened.

Nevertheless, in the short-term, the Education Act stimulated the schools work of the British and Foreign School Society and its Anglican counterpart, the National Society for Promoting the Education of the Poor. By 1874, the Church of England expended nearly as much on education of the poor as on clergy salaries[460] and, to the relief of the CPAS, the Bible was being taught in board schools.[461] Towards the end of the century, one of the tasks of Bishop Ryle in his new Liverpool Diocese was to establish new Church schools.[462] Individuals also sought to rectify some of the problems arising from the new approach to religious teaching. Francis Peek encouraged the London School Board to introduce voluntary examinations in Scripture, with presentation Bibles and Testaments for those who did best in them. By 1896, over 300,000 students had sat the exams; similar ideas being pioneered elsewhere.[463]

[457] G.H. Pike, "*The Life and Work of Charles Haddon Spurgeon*", vol.5, p.40, in G.H. Pike, *The Life and Work of Charles Haddon Spurgeon* (The Banner of Truth Trust (1991)) vol.2.

[458] "Mr Spurgeon on Denominational Schools", in *The Observer*, 1 November 1875. Lord Shaftesbury was of a similar view. He wrote in his diary: "I dread, sadly dread these schemes of national education." They were "a death-warrant to the teaching of evangelical religion. *It had better be called 'a water-rate to extinguish religious fire among young people'*". Author's italics. Cited in J.L. Hammond and B. Hammond, *Lord Shaftesbury* (1936) p.236. Later he would write of the "zealots of secular knowledge. Everything for the flesh, and nothing for the soul; everything for time and nothing for eternity", cited in ibid., p.237.

[459] "Mr Spurgeon on Denominational Schools", in *The Observer*, 1 November 1875.

[460] *Christianity in Great Britain* (1874) pp.11-13.

[461] E.J. Speck, *Church Pastoral-Aid Society* (1881) p.156.

[462] See I.D. Farley, *Ryle, First Bishop of Liverpool* (2000) pp.136-143.

[463] S.G. Green, *The Story of the Religious Tract Society* (1899) pp.129-131.

However, after 1870 some denominations felt less need to provide education. For instance, after 1843 the Wesleyan Methodist Conference built around 850 schools[464] but towards the end of the century, it gradually started to reduce their number.

With the creation of a national education system, the importance of Sunday schools to education, other than religious teaching, decreased. Philip Snowden, the first Labour Chancellor of the Exchequer, recalled that, in the early 1870s, the practice of devoting half the Sunday school lesson to spelling, stopped.[465] However, the numbers of Sunday scholars rose. By 1900, they approached 6.8 million[466] although, as a percentage of the population under 15, they peaked at 57 per cent around 1880. The working classes expected their children to attend, whereas the attendance level by children of the better-off was always lower. The demand for teachers created a voluntary religious army, especially since Sunday schools were often the centre for agencies working for the moral reformation, and social improvement, of the poor.[467] By the beginning of the twentieth century, a minister looking back over the previous 25 years wrote that the greatest proportion of the additions to Free Church membership had come through the Sunday schools, as "the old-time method of 'conversion' has sensibly diminished".[468] All the same, there was much wastage between Sunday school and church.[469] The link between child and church once the child left Sunday school was quickly broken. Many in the working classes found Christianity "unmanly".[470]

To be effective spiritually, Sunday schools needed someone aiming at soul-winning. An exemplary model of such a person was the Metropolitan Tabernacle's Lavinia Bartlett. A member since February 1856, in the summer of 1859 she started a senior class of three girls. By March 1861 she had 50 girls. For the last 12 years during which she

[464] R.E. Davies, *Methodism* (1976) p.153.

[465] P.V. Snowden, *An Autobiography* (1934) vol.1, p.25.

[466] P. Brierley, *UK Church Statistics 2005-2015* (2011) section 14.4, p.7.

[467] R.W. Dale, *The Evangelical Revival* (1880) pp.35-37.

[468] H. Mann, "Facts and Forces not Enumerated", in *The Religious Life of London* (R. Mudie-Smith (ed.)) (1904) p.274.

[469] See R. Gill, *The 'Empty' Church Revisited* (2003) p.131 and R. Currie, A. Gilbert and L. Horsley, *Churches and Churchgoers* (1977) pp.86-88.

[470] T.M. Macdonald, "How to Reach Working Men", in *Homiletical and Pastoral Lectures* (1879) p.389.

conducted the class, the numbers averaged between 600 and 700. By the time of her death in 1875, somewhere between 900 to 1,000 members of her class had joined the membership of the Metropolitan Tabernacle.[471]

The last four decades of the nineteenth century saw a distinct attempt by evangelicals to build up their presence in private education. Their general aim was to foster education – with a perception, at times, that the Oxford Movement and the Anglo-Catholic Woodward schools were the enemy. In 1866 Trent College was founded. Monkton Combe followed in 1868; the college that became St Lawrence's College in 1879; and Dean Close in 1886. In 1902, Weymouth College was added to the holdings of The Evangelical College and School Company.[472] In 1900, at a speech day for Trent College, Webb-Peploe declared that they were proud that the "boys were going to be taught to be loyal, honest and upright Churchmen."[473] However, near the end of the century, a layman observed that the benefits these schools offered were not widely known, lamenting that parents were less concerned about securing a "heavenly inheritance" for their children, than securing for them "a better position in life".[474] In 1875 the Wesleyan Methodists established the Leys School Cambridge, the 'Eton of Methodism,' for the children of Methodist laymen.

18.13 Missions to children

Spurgeon said, "I have more confidence in the spiritual life of the children I have received into this church, than I have in the adults".[475] Nevertheless, scepticism existed in some quarters concerning child conversion.[476] Many involved in teaching children Christianity rested "satisfied with the mere communication of knowledge, leaving to the distant and uncertain years of maturity the great question of conversion".[477]

However, some evangelists rejected this view. They realised that its root might "be traced to the same rationalistic spirit that revolts against

[471] E.H. Bartlett, *Mrs Bartlett and her Class* (1877) p.53.

[472] M. Wellings, *Evangelicals Embattled* (2003) pp.89-91. See also K. Harris, *Evangelicals and Education* (2004) p.329.

[473] "The Midlands", in *The Record*, 13 July 1900, p.665.

[474] "Middle Class Schools", in *The Record*, 30 July 1897, p.769.

[475] Cited in R. Carswell, *And Some Evangelists* (2005) p.121.

[476] "Notices of Books", in *The Sword and the Trowel* (1875) p.40.

[477] J. Macpherson, *Revival and Revival Work* (N.D.) p.276.

sudden conversion, because the suddenness does not admit of that lengthened play of human reason and human effort without which proud man is unwilling to be saved...It is salvation by the works of the law."[478] Often a mission included meetings for the local youth. For instance, Catherine Booth's eldest son Bramwell was converted at a meeting she addressed for children as part of an eight-week mission in Walsall.[479] Methodist churches on Child Sunday might run a series of evangelistic services. At such a service, on 2 November 1875, the future evangelist Thomas Cook was converted.[480] In 1879, Thomas Champness – having run children's services on a Sunday during a near three weeks mission in the town of Blyth – recorded 50 children "wishful to serve God".[481] Hugh Price Hughes thought that a preliminary to a "Revival Mission" was to invite all the older children to be involved and to run a special service of song for children on the Sunday afternoon of the first week of the mission.[482] Those who attended were to be exhorted to make a decision for Christ and to bring their family and friends to the evening service.

18.13.1 *Dedicated children's mission organisations*

Evangelistic work with children also benefited from the establishment of new organisations dedicated to their needs.

The Children's Special Service Mission

The Reverend Edward Payson Hammond was an effective American evangelist who adapted his gift to become "the first evangelist to children". He "did not stint emotion".[483] He was in New York at the time of its 1859 Revival. In 1860-1861, Hammond came to Edinburgh to complete his studies and got caught up in the revival there as an itinerant evangelist.[484] His big idea was simple: informal, special services for children and their Sunday school teachers, with no pulling of punches

[478] Ibid., p.277.

[479] C. Bramwell Booth, *Bramwell Booth* (1933) p.3.

[480] H.T. Smart, *The Life of Thomas Cook* (1913) p.18.

[481] E.M. Champness, *The Life Story of Thomas Champness* (1907) p.195.

[482] H.P. Hughes, Revival Missions, 5 *The Christian Miscellany and Family Visitor* (1881) (3rd series) p.61.

[483] J.C. Pollock, *The Good Seed* (1959) pp.16-17. On Hammond generally, see N. Scotland, *Apostles of the Spirit and Fire* (2009) pp.165-186.

[484] R. Carwardine, *Transatlantic Revivalism* (2006) pp.185-186.

on the atonement. This was followed by the children's enquiry meeting at which any child could stay behind for questioning and spiritual help. Children as young as four would respond to the call of Christ.[485] Hammond also made great use of music, encouraging singing before the service began and encouraged children pledging to follow Jesus to put it in writing.[486] Hammond came to London to speak at Baptist Noel's John Street Chapel in Holborn. Among Hammond's hearers, one night in the early summer of 1867, was a Sunday school teacher called Josiah Spiers. Listening to Hammond, Spiers was convinced of the methodology.[487]

Spiers went home and launched a service for 15 children in a friend's Islington drawing room. It was a great success; 30 years later, of the 14 still living, 9 were active in Christian work. Across the capital, others discovered that the cheerful hymns and simple gospel truths warmed the hearts of many children. It was said that the "'missing link' between regular, rather unrewarding, teaching at Sunday school and the child's discovery of personal faith", had been found.[488] CSSM was born, later to become Scripture Union. In 1868 Spiers merged his work with the similar work of William Pennefather at St Jude's, Mildmay Park, also inspired by Hammond.

In 1868, Spiers went on "holiday to Llandudno in North Wales and held a spontaneous children's meeting on the beach. He drew the text 'God is Love' in the sand, invited children to decorate it, and then told them a Bible story. The beach mission was born".[489] The work of the CSSM focused, but not exclusively, on the children of the wealthy. The latter were neglected by the ragged and Sunday schools and other institutions working with children. Their parents had the money to go to the beach. In 1880, a long-standing tradition – whereby CICCU supplied undergraduates for beach missions – began. In 1892 the CSSM held its first camp for boys, near Littlehampton. Meanwhile, in 1879, under the auspices of CSSM, the name 'Scripture Union' first appeared or, to be exact, 'The Children's Scripture Union'. Its original work was to provide a Bible reading programme for children. In 1887 Bible reading notes were added. By then, 328,000 were members of the Union.

[485] N. Scotland, *Apostles of the Spirit and Fire* (2009) pp.180 and 183.
[486] Ibid., pp.181-183.
[487] See E.P. Hammond, *The Conversion of Children* (N.D.) pp.39-43.
[488] J.C. Pollock, *The Good Seed* (1959) p.18.
[489] Ibid., p.14.

Spiers went on to become the first CSSM evangelist to children. He held meetings in town halls and mechanics institutes – preferably, any public building, bar a church. Meetings were non-denominational and – for members of boarding schools and families who did not allow their children out at night – started at 11 am. For everyone, there was an evening meeting at 7 pm. Spiers believed his task was to convert. Many, in a gospel-soaked culture, had been almost persuaded to become Christians. What the young needed was a special opportunity to give their hearts to God. The message was "the love of the Saviour for little children...Brimstone, and fire, and torments, and all the religious persuasive threats of past juvenile teaching were happily conspicuous by their absence".[490] The numbers were huge. A week-long mission in Bristol drew 10,000. Spiers liked long missions. As he said, "I never care to go anywhere for less than five days, and much prefer eight or ten days, as we always see much more blessing when the mission can be extended beyond the week".[491] With each mission went strong marketing efforts. Posters appeared on gas-lamp posts and were handed out at church doors and at street corners. Children attending were given free picture leaflets – on the condition that a portfolio be made to preserve them[492] (unless a child was too poor to buy cardboard).

Boys' and Girls' Brigades

In 1883, in Glasgow, the Boys' Brigade was founded by William Smith for boys aged 12 and above.[493] Brigades were attached to churches and a Bible class was part of its activities. The Boys' Brigade rested on the twin pillars of "Discipline and Religion". Discipline came first, on the basis of chronological priority.[494] The Boys' Brigade wanted to promote "true Christian manliness" and gave significant service to various mission agencies, especially the Church Missionary Society. It targeted those who had progressed beyond Sunday school, but who were not yet of age to join the YMCA. It gave a militaristic twist to Sunday-school work with children, just as the Salvation Army did with adults. Others recognised its

490 Ibid., p.35.

491 Ibid., p.26.

492 For more detail on the evangelistic work of Josiah Spiers, see ibid., pp.24-32.

493 R.S. Peacock, *Pioneer of Boyhood* (1954) p.133.

494 Ibid., p.26.

success and emulated it. In 1891 the Church Lads' Brigade was started. In 1893 the Girls' Brigade was established, beginning in Ireland. Before that, the Anglican Girls' Friendly Society had been founded. In 1899 a Free Church competitor, the Boys' Life Brigade, was established.

Christian Endeavour

Christian Endeavour was another interdenominational organisation dedicated to working with children. Its origins lay in the United States but, in 1887, the first permanent British Christian Endeavour Society was founded in Crewe. It seemed to offer a new way of drawing in the young to church – when Sunday schools failed to pass so many members on. By 1896, when the first annual meeting of the British Christian Endeavour Union was held, membership of Christian Endeavour Societies exceeded one and a half million. By 1900, 6,000 societies were registered with it, most being attached to Baptist, Congregational and Primitive Methodist Churches. The Wesleyans started their own equivalent, the Wesley Guild, with a greater literary and social function.[495] Active members of Christian Endeavour pledged to "strive to do whatever [God] would like to have me do"[496] and to attend and participate in a monthly consecration meeting, except in special circumstances. An analysis of Christian Endeavour members in Reading and district suggests that the organisation was much better than Sunday schools at leading its members into church membership.[497]

Caravan Mission to Village Children

In 1892 S.J. Hewlett and George Goodman set out with a horse and open carriage – their Bible carriage – on a tour of the villages and hamlets of Berkshire, Hertfordshire and Surrey, to reach children. The tour was successful and soon the work, which had been limited to the summer months, became all the year round and also embraced parents.[498]

495 M.R. Watts, *The Dissenters* (2015) vol.3, p.175.
496 F.E. Clark, "Beginnings", in *Sixty-Five Years of Christian Endeavour* (1946) (W.K. Chaplin and M.J. Street (eds)) p.16.
497 M.R. Watts, *The Dissenters* (2015) vol.3, p.176.
498 See "A Mission with a Message", in *The Christian Herald and Signs of our Times*, 3 February 1938, p.111.

18.14 New buildings

New churches were built, often faster than the growing population and its changing distribution required.[499] When John Sinclair, the Vicar of Kensington and Archdeacon of Middlesex, died, he left 23 new parishes and upwards of 30 new churches.[500] He had an immense iron church built in his vicarage's garden which sat 1,200. Iron churches were seen as temporary structures, to meet the challenge of sudden population growth before a permanent structure could be built.[501] The Methodists built great central halls and the Congregationalists built splendid churches, to vie with the Establishment in dignity and form. The yearbooks of the Congregational Union of the early 1860s are sprinkled with drawings of them. The London Baptist Association pledged to build at least one new chapel a year.

At the other end of church architecture, mission halls proliferated. They housed up to one sixth of those attending services. In 1888, a survey identified 873 mission halls in London. The parish of Holy Trinity, St Marylebone, provides an illuminating example of how, after 1859 – when William Cadman took up its incumbency – a parish church and its mission halls and rooms interacted to keep the church building at the centre of parish religious life, while reaching out to all parts of the parish. Cadman divided his parish of 14,000 souls into a number of districts, with five mission halls to work them, each with curate and staff. Every district held Sunday services at its mission hall, and a service at the parish church on a different night of the week. In temporary rooms across every district, the clergy held, weekly, two or three short services of 20 or 30 minutes or so. Ten or twelve attended each service. In this way, Holy Trinity drew a quarter of its parish each week to church, an accepted standard of the time. There were 28 services a week in the parish.[502]

As new buildings were erected, overall attendances rose.[503] However, numbers did not keep up with the growth in new buildings, so the

[499] M.R. Watts, *The Dissenters* (2015) vol.3, pp.111-117.
[500] Archdeacon Sinclair, "My First Sermon", in 8 *The Young Man* (1894) pp.132-133.
[501] W.J. Hopkins, *The Advantages to be Derived by the Adoption of Moveable Wooden Churches for Temporary Purposes Instead of Iron Ones* (1888) p.3.
[502] L.E. Shelford, *A Memorial of the Rev. William Cadman* (1899) pp.55-61.
[503] R. Gill, *The 'Empty' Church Revisited* (2003) pp.100-101.

average attendance declined.[504] For instance, in London of the 1880s, in the morning churches were 43.7 per cent full,[505] while mission halls were less than 13 per cent full, although in the evening the latter were half-full.[506] By this time, some thought there were too many – and too feeble – churches.[507] Many Nonconformist ones were built on debt, in the expectation of future growth. If that growth did not appear, that debt became a burden – absorbing the energy of the congregation to pay it off.[508]

18.15 Friendship evangelism

Evangelism in the late nineteenth century was not all missions, open-air preaching, house-to-house visitation and tract distribution. Even those who supported these activities, such as George Williams, the founder of the YMCA, thought the key to reaching young men was friendship. As he put it: "Get to know the names of young men. Take one at a time. Write a letter to him, give him a shake of the hand, ask him to have a friendly cup of tea; talk kindly naturally with him; take him for a walk; show him a little kindness, and you will get hold of him."[509] Frederick Charrington, the heir to the great Charrington brewery in the Mile End Road, was converted when a friend asked him whether he was saved; Charrington refused to discuss the matter – finding the topic unpleasant – but agreed to read John 3 when he was next alone. The next night, he did so. He later wrote that "I came to the words, 'He that believeth on the Son hath everlasting life'. I realised that I, too, possessed 'eternal life.'"[510] As a result, he gave up his brewing career and began mission work with children in the Mile End Road. This led him into a range of activities, not dissimilar to the Salvation Army, and the founding of

[504] Ibid., p.98.
[505] Ibid., p.105.
[506] "Census of the Mission Halls of London", in *Supplement to The British Weekly*, 13 January 1888, pp.217 and 230.
[507] "Opinions from Other Quarters", in *The Christian Monthly and Family Treasury* (1882) p.204 and "Too Many and Too Feeble Churches", in *The Christian Monthly and Family Treasury* (1882) p.205.
[508] G. Milburn, *Primitive Methodism* (2002) p.73.
[509] C. Binfield, *George Williams in Context* (1994) p.17.
[510] G. Thorne, *The Great Acceptance* (N.D.) pp.19-20.

the Tower Hamlets Mission.[511] When he, as the heir of the Charrington Brewery estate, presided over the annual meeting of the Band of Hope at Exeter Hall in February 1873, the Strand was blocked for hours – such was the sensation.[512]

18.16 Revivalism is established

In early 1859, William Arthur, when reviewing contemporary religious developments, wondered if the "extraordinary quickening"[513] of the churches in America would be paralleled in England. He hoped for a great revival – by which "we mean such a manifestation of the converting power of God, as shall mark a new epoch in the moral and religious history of mankind".[514] He instanced, as examples of such revivals, those of the previous three centuries – the Reformation, the great Puritan revival, and that of Whitefield and Wesley. The religious stirrings in America led him to hope for "not the conversion of a few scores in this town, or a few hundreds in that city...but a pervasive, national quickening, reaching into every parish, going into the centre of society, striking its highest and its lowest extremes, and carrying forward the cause of vital religion as far in advance of its position at this day as the revival of last century and its results have, up to this time, carried it beyond the position it then occupied".[515] At a time of revival, it was not that men were "more holy, more devoted, more prayerful, or more richly possessed of the knowledge of God's word than others, or than the same men at other times." No, a revival was pre-eminently an expression of God's sovereign grace and power – and one for which men might pray.[516]

[511] F.N. Charrington, *An Oasis in the Desert* (N.D.).

[512] G. Thorne, *The Great Acceptance* (N.D.) p.25.

[513] W. Arthur, *May We Hope for a Great Revival?* (1859) p.2.

[514] Ibid., p.4.

[515] Ibid. See also M. Bruen, *History of the Revivals of Religion in the British Isles* (1836) p.3, H.C. Fish, *Handbook of Revivals* (N.D.) pp.11-23 and D.M. Lloyd-Jones, *Revival* (1992) p.7.

[516] *Reminiscences of the Revival of '59 and the Sixties* (1910) p.15. It's worth noting that, even in 1859, a revival could mean "something of excitement, a movement exhibiting great emotion, a stir in the town, prayer meetings, preachings extraordinary, tract distributing" – or a revival of love in the believer, see "What is Revival?", in *The Revival*, 20 August 1859, p.25. For a helpful discussion of the differences between the terms revival, mission, reformation, renewal and church growth, see B.H. Edwards, *Can We Pray for Revival?* (2001) pp.9-30.

Yet, by the end of the third quarter of the nineteenth century, a revival was understood as a work of man. A revival was a special service or meeting, at which non-believers were told about the person and work of Jesus.[517] The origin of this change is attributed to the American evangelist Charles Finney, preaching and writing in the second quarter of the nineteenth century. In his view, conversions were encouraged by careful planning and "excitements". However, it is worth noting that the idea that people could co-operate in bringing about revival took root as conversions increased in the early 1800s – alongside the appearance and growth of new evangelical organisations. So, in 1832, the editor of *The Revivalist* thought that people could "attempt a revival of religion" when he asked, rhetorically, has God "not promised to pour out his Spirit in answer to prayer? Did he ever refuse success to sincere, well directed, and persevering efforts?"[518] By 1853, the former Puseyite turned evangelical, William Haslam, suggested that "revivals – that is, the refreshing of believers and the awakening of sinners – ought to take place wherever the gospel is preached in faith and power".[519] However, revival could be prevented by division within the churches and want of holiness.[520]

The 1859 Revival coinciding, as it did, with widespread evangelistic endeavours, hastened the change in meaning of the word revival – from a sovereign work of God of widespread influence, to man's evangelistic endeavours. Men like William Arthur, who urged that prayer be made for revival, were aware of the dangers of replacing an act of God with that of man. He cautioned that "everything like an effort to get up a revival" must be shunned. He added "Let those…known as revivalists take care that they do not thrust themselves into view".[521] Nevertheless, at a time when many summoned the nation to "repent and believe", whether in

[517] "The confusion of a mission with a revival is far worse than bad etymology; it is bad theology. It is not only that the root idea of the word 'mission' is that of 'being sent', and the root idea of the word 'revival' that of living afresh; there is as great a difference between the things themselves. A mission represents the ordinary work of the Christian Church; a revival is an extraordinary work of God", see D.G. Fountain, *E.J Poole-Connor, "Contender for the Faith"* (1966) p.98.

[518] "Address", in *The Revivalist* (1832) p.3 and "Nature of a Religious Revival", in *The Revivalist* (1832) pp.172-174.

[519] W. Haslam, *From Death into Life* (1897) p.174.

[520] "What Prevents a Revival of Religion", in *The Revivalist* (1861) pp.130-131 and 145-147.

[521] W. Arthur, *May We Hope for a Great Revival?* (1859) p.14.

church or on street corner, it was easy to confuse the 1859 Revival with meetings held by those like William Booth and the Open-Air Mission, which were part of it. Given the ongoing work of Booth and others, and its spiritual fruitfulness, once the 1859 Revival died away, it was understandable that a "revival" should be popularly seen as something instigated by human activity. The life of Humphrey Jones who, with his revival meetings, lit the spark of the 1859 Revival in Wales, illustrated the danger of the new approach. He believed in the methods of Finney, but became mentally unstable when, later, a host of converts were not produced each time he preached.[522]

The 1873-1875 campaign of Moody completed the process whereby a revival was understood as an evangelistic campaign. However, Moody himself knew that, to convert his listeners, the Holy Spirit had to be at work. On the opening night of his 1875 mission to London, Moody preached:

> You have got great preachers here – I do not believe London ever knew a day when it had so many great and good preachers as at the present time. It is not that; it is not human power that London wants, it is divine power; it is not eloquence of man, it is the eloquence of heaven, the power of the Holy Ghost breaking men's hearts. That is what London wants.[523]

Moody knew that power. As Handley Moule wrote, there was "a power abroad not of man but of God, rather preceding than following the track of the evangelists, preparing the ground for the sower".[524] However, as Moody's great campaign was run in the full glare of the national press, popular attention focused on the campaign itself, rather than the power behind it. Moody's campaign completed the shift, that David Bebbington discerns in the Victorian era, away from interest in community-based revivals, to ones "concentrated on large-scale efforts in industrial and mercantile centres, holding meetings in vast halls, and targeting not particular congregations but whole cities".[525]

[522] See E. Evans, *Two Welsh Revivalists* (1985) pp.7-28.

[523] D.L. Moody, *The London Discourses of D.L. Moody* (1875) p.5.

[524] H.C.G. Moule, *The Evangelical School in the Church of England* (1901) p.61. See also *Reminiscences of the Revival of '59 and the Sixties* (1910) pp.10-11.

[525] D. Bebbington, *Victorian Religious Revivals* (2012) pp.3, 13 and 274.

The confidence of many in "Revival Missions", as some called them, was complete. Hugh Price Hughes declared in 1881 that he had never known them to fail "where there has been adequate preparation".[526] The acceptance that revivals were the same as an evangelistic campaign, albeit with the presence of the Holy Spirit prayed for, especially among the poor, became accepted in many quarters. For example, Professor Chadwick, in his opus magnum on the Victorian Church, devotes over 13 pages to revivals, but only half a paragraph to that of 1859. The great weight of his work on revivals is devoted to the emergence of the Salvation Army (and its imitator, the Church Army), its work with the poor and the "antics" of William Booth to gain a hearing for the gospel. Otherwise, Chadwick associates revival with a new focus on open-air preaching and more frequent parochial missions. The Moody missions also only get a sentence (albeit long) in the 13-plus pages on revival.

The new use of the word "revival" had important consequences. It removed from parts of the church the expectation that God – as distinct from men and women, through an evangelistic campaign – can do great things. It also led to the word falling into disrepute, as signifying something "savouring of excitement, something abnormal in religious experience, something evanescent and lacking in practical effect".[527] The year 1859 saw the last great national revival, although regional revivals (in the old sense of the word) still occurred.[528]

18.17 The settlement movement

It was recognised that "The congregation of the wage-earning classes in districts of their own is a product of modern civilisation".[529] Previously, rich and poor lived side-by-side. It was suggested that their separation made the working classes impervious to civilisation and the gospel.[530]

[526] H.P. Hughes, "Revival Missions", in 5 *The Christian Miscellany and Family Visitor* (1881) (3rd series) p.123.

[527] *Reminiscences of the Revival of '59 and the Sixties* (1910) p.24.

[528] Some suggest that the first half of the 1880s were a special time of divine favour, see C.W. Mackintosh, *Dr Harry Guinness* (1916) pp.15-16 and 116. Note also Handley Moule's comment on Moody's campaigns of the mid-1870s and early 1880s, H.C.G. Moule, *The Evangelical School in the Church of England* (1901) pp.61-62.

[529] J. Gorst, "'Settlements', in England and America", in *The Universities and the Social Problem* (1895) (J.M. Knapp (ed.)) p.3.

[530] For an excellent account of the Settlement Movement, see K.F. Inglis, *Churches and the Working Classes in Victorian England* (1964) pp.143-174.

The idea behind the settlement movement was for graduates to go and live together in a poor neighbourhood and to reach out to the local community, under the leadership of resident clergy. Out of term-time, undergraduates would come down to reinforce the work. Unlike a college mission church which, if successful, became an independent parish church, a settlement provided the opportunity for continuous work.

The theological underpinning of the various settlements was as varied as the theology of the day. The first settlement was Toynbee Hall in Whitechapel, founded by the Reverend Samuel and Henrietta Barnett in 1885. The Barnetts were theologically broad and the driving force behind their work was the desire to bring the culture of the educated to, rather than to convert, the poor. The same year, the High Church founded Oxford House, also in the East End, to inject a little more religion and mission into things. Others, such as Browning Hall, stood for "the Labour movement in religion"[531] and, at St Pancras, the Passmore Edwards Settlement was for those whose Christianity "has become a system of practical conduct, based on faith in God and on the inspiring memory of a great teacher, rather than a system of dogma based on a unique revelation".[532] By 1898, Barnett noted 13 university settlements in London,[533] with others in Glasgow, Bristol, Manchester and Edinburgh. At that time, Barnett thought Toynbee Hall's success was to mitigate class suspicion and to inspire local government with a higher spirit.[534] They were, though, losing momentum. The suspicion was that people joined them as 'do gooders' to further their career in government, parliament or the civil service.[535] Watts suggests that, of the various initiatives to convert the urban poor, "Least successful... were the settlements".[536] However, their social work was influential. For instance, the PSA movement traced the origins of the measure to

[531] *University and Social Settlements* (1898) (W. Reason (ed.)) p.181.

[532] Ibid., p.182. Its founder was Mrs H. Ward, the author of *Robert Elsmere*, see W.S. Peterson, *Victorian Heretic* (1976) p.183.

[533] There were other settlements not always having a university basis. For a full list, see *University and Social Settlements* (1898) (W. Reason (ed.)) pp.179-190.

[534] S.A. Barnett, "University Settlements", in *University and Social Settlements* (1898) (W. Reason (ed.)) p.11.

[535] K.F. Inglis, *Churches and the Working Classes in Victorian England* (1964) pp.172-174.

[536] M.R. Watts, *The Dissenters* (2015) vol.3, p.140.

introduce old-age pensions to one of its meetings at Browning Hall.[537]

18.18 Catechetical teaching declines

At the beginning of our period, John Angell James, the Congregationalist minister at Carrs Lane, Birmingham, encouraged the churches to return to the "catechetical method of instructing children" and to teach less geography and natural history.[538] He also felt the chronology and the narratives of revelation, admittedly important, were being given a weight that only the "person and work of the Redeemer and the doctrines that cluster around the cross deserve". The advantages of teaching the catechism to all were seen in the life of one young Scotsman from an unbelieving family who had learnt the Shorter Catechism as a child. Invited to a mission service, but not convicted by the talk, he was afterwards asked by the minister "Will you decide for Christ?" Then the whole plan of salvation through "Christ's substitutionary offering of himself on the cross" rushed across his mind – and he was converted. He was soon leading his friends to Christ – and became an evangelist with the Evangelization Society. The society found it did not need to train him in the "Five Points" of redemption.[539] Later, John Macpherson, a keen observer of the evangelical scene, reminded parents: "no means of instructing the young can effectually supersede the catechetical method". In his view, "systematic theology is essential to breadth of religious intelligence, depth of religious conviction".[540] He foretold that if it were abandoned, the result might perhaps be "more religion, but with certainly less backbone in it".[541]

Yet catechisms, as a means of teaching religious truth, fell out of favour until the end of our period. Writing in 1880, R.W. Dale, the successor of John Angell James at Carrs Lane, thought religious instruction to children consisted in teaching them the names of the

[537] J.W. Tuffley, *Grain from Galilee* (1935) pp.72-76. See also W. Ward, "P.S.A. Brotherhood Page", in *The Christian Herald and Signs of our Times*, 6 January 1910, p.18. On the role of Nonconformists in introducing old age pensions in the early twentieth century, see M.R. Watts, *The Dissenters* (2015) vol.3, pp.316-320.

[538] J.A. James, "What is the Spiritual State of the Churches?", in *The Works of John Angell James* (1861) vol.9, p.429.

[539] J. Wood, *The Story of the Evangelization Society* (N.D.) pp.99-103.

[540] J. Macpherson, *Revival and Revival Work* (N.D.) p.281.

[541] Ibid.

kings of Israel and Judah, or working on a map of Palestine, or reading descriptions of biblical countries, or of the Temple.[542]

A number of reasons for the decline in the use of catechisms have been suggested. Some point to the growing scepticism and the inability to identify a catechism that secured general assent,[543] or to a change in teaching methodology which rejected memorising a text. High Churchmen attributed the decline to the substitution of a sermon on Sunday afternoons, for catechising after the second lesson at evensong.[544] For evangelical Anglicans, teaching the Church Catechism presented a conundrum. On the one hand, catechists said, "in my baptism; wherein I was made a member of Christ, the true child of God, and an inheritor of the kingdom of heaven". This, they did not believe. On the other hand, teaching the Church Catechism made more likely the fulfilment of the baptismal vows taken on behalf of a child. It presented to the child the idea that every child has duties towards God. A leading evangelical thought that public catechising, linked with the baptism of infants, removed "scepticism as to the propriety of binding babies by promises which they could not understand".[545]

Towards the end of our period, the use of catechisms revived. In the 1890s, High Churchmen reinvigorated catechetical teaching through the method of St Sulpice.[546] This was a system of catechising, not a catechism. It involved carefully planned mass instruction of the young and was an attempt to give more definite content to the increasingly vague pietism of the Sunday schools. In 1894 Spencer John Jones, Rector of Batsford with Moreton-in-Marsh, popularised the method with his *The Clergy and the Catechism*. Within three years, it reached its sixth edition.[547] To counter the accusation that the catechism was

[542] R.W. Dale, *The Evangelical Revival* (1880) p.264. But some Congregational churches seemed to have a different approach, see G. Hunsworth, *Baxter's Nonconformist Descendants* (1874) p.69.

[543] Dale thought catechetical teaching was no longer possible, nor indeed the "elaborate doctrinal sermons" (R.W. Dale, *The Evangelical Revival* (1880) p.267) when "the authority of the theological tradition is lost", ibid., p.266.

[544] W.H.B. Proby, *Annals of the "Low-Church" Party in England* (1888) vol.1, p.355.

[545] E.A. Knox, *Pastors and Teachers* (1902) pp.104-105.

[546] See P. Davie, *Raising up a Faithful People* (1997) pp.77-83.

[547] Evangelicals rejected the work, as "St Sulpice is subordinated to Mr Jones" and for "its certain very pronounced views", "The Method of St Sulpice", in *The Record*, 14 September 1900, p.873.

but the words of men, Spencer Jones made it clear that the Bible must be used to expand, explain and illustrate the relevant topics. It was not rote learning. In 1898 the Catholics first published the so called "Penny Catechism". It was a great success. As late as 1999, long after it had gone out of use, one writer to *The Times* suggested that if its use were restored, "I am sure our understanding of God's nature would be much clearer and more concise".[548] In 1899, the Free Church Catechism was launched, to plaudits, as a means of expressing the unity between the Free Churches making up the National Free Church Council.[549]

18.19 Family religion

The late 1850s and early 1860s witnessed a burst of activity in the launch of magazines and periodicals dedicated to ensuring that the Sabbath was used for religious purposes.[550] For example, *The Family Treasury of Sunday Reading* (1859) included practical and devotional papers, articles on apologetical and exegetical matters, sermons, biographical and historical pieces[551] and what it called "an entirely new feature in this periodical – a series of 'Home Lessons for the Lord's Day'". This was to help parents systematically teach divine truth, which was a duty "*sadly neglected by many*". An "hour *punctually* and *constantly*" was to be spent in teaching the Bible, with the Gospel of Matthew being the proposed starting point. Andrew Cameron, *The Family Treasury's* editor, observed that "Neglected children are almost certain to be lost."[552] Spurgeon suggested that "the Sabbath literature of our families might be as vivacious and attractive as the best of amusing serials, and yet as deeply earnest and profitable as the soundest of divines would desire".[553] William Cooke, a Methodist, reminded the parents of unconverted children that "However amiable their manners and superior their accomplishments, they are enemies to God, under the curse of the violated law, and every moment exposed to everlasting perdition." He

[548] T. Wynn, "The Spirit and Image of God", in *The Times*, 16 January 1999.
[549] C. Oldstone-Moore, *Hugh Price Hughes* (1999) pp.280-282.
[550] J.L. Altholz, *The Religious Press in Britain 1760-1900* (1989) p.48.
[551] J.C. Ryle's oft reprinted and substantial work *Christian Leaders of the 18th Century* first appeared as a series of articles in its 1866 and 1867 issues.
[552] Author's italics. "Home Lessons for the Lord's Day (no.1)", in *The Family Treasury of Sunday Reading* (1859) pp.vii and 11.
[553] C.H. Spurgeon, "Preface" to *The Sword and the Trowel* (1875) p.iii.

urged: "Besides the ordinary routine of domestic worship, take your children alone, one by one, for close appeals to the conscience and importunate pleading with God...rest not until the great work is done."[554]

In the mid-1870s, a commentator listed the means of instruction and conversion for children in the following order: the family; the school or class; the evangelistic service, or sermon; and the inquiry-room,[555] or conversation. In the home, the tools for this work were as follows: "The example of parents; prayer, social and secret; the word of God; the catechism, or systematic training in the knowledge of the great principles; and sacred song, or psalms, hymns and spiritual songs."[556] The singing of songs was a recent innovation of "incalculable value"; in which mothers took the lead to sing the gospel. The future theologically liberal Bishop Hensley Henson wrote of his childhood in the 1860s and 1870s: "It was my father's good custom to have family prayers, morning and evening. At this function, I was required to read aloud the psalms for the day." Henson's fondness for the psalms he thought might not "be unconnected with this experience".[557] Hudson Pope, the great child evangelist of the twentieth century, born in 1879, attributed his "amazing knowledge" of the Bible to his mother's teaching as a child and the weekly Bible classes prepared for him, as a nine-year-old, by his 19-year old sister.[558]

Such approaches were not true of all "godly" parents and families. In 1865 *The Revival* lamented that the children of many were slipping into "fearful laxity and indulgence", the young being allowed to act and dress as they please. Such training was thought unlikely to enable its subjects to withstand the "coming flood of wickedness".[559] In 1876, to remedy the situation, the Mothers' Union was started by the redoubtable Mrs Mary

[554] W. Cooke, *The Revival of Religion* (N.D.) p.12.

[555] Not every evangelistic organisation was committed to inquiry rooms. The Evangelization Society's policy was to refrain from their use, although an individual evangelist was permitted to use them and, through attending such a room before his conversion, one of its leading evangelists, William Taylor, was moved close to becoming a Christian, see *A Marvel of Grace, the Late William Taylor* (1895) pp.22-25.

[556] J. Macpherson, *Revival and Revival Work* (N.D.) p.280.

[557] H.H. Henson, *Retrospect of an Unimportant Life: 1863-1920* (1942) vol.1, p.3

[558] P.M. St. John, *R. Hudson Pope* (1967) p.17.

[559] "Personal Devotedness to the Lord Jesus", in *The Revival*, 13 July 1865, p.1. J.M. Lang, "The Non-Church Going: How Can Our Churches Reach Them?", in *The Christian Monthly and Family Treasury* (1882) p.75.

Sumner, in the Winchester diocese.[560] Its principles were "that in family life character is formed – that religion should be taught in the homes, both by word and example – that upon mothers, in the main, rests the responsibility of training the young people, and that this training is a profession, and must be learnt like any other profession".[561] In 1879 the Religious Tract Society published *The Boy's Own Paper*, as "Juvenile crime was being largely stimulated by the pernicious literature circulated among our lads." Lord Shaftesbury often spoke in public against this literature. He was "struck by the beauty of its composition, and by the artful way in which the most wicked and foul ideas were conveyed."[562] The Secularists were blamed for it. *The Boy's Own Paper* provided a better example to its readers. The first article was entitled "My First Football Match"[563] and the paper was an immediate success. It was followed by *The Girl's Own Paper* (1880).[564]

However, the trend remained towards "the increasing laxity of parental rule" – it was becoming "Parents, obey your children."[565] In 1890, Mrs Sumner placed the blame on the educationalists and philanthropists for taking away from working-class parents the God-given responsibility for training children. Rich parents, she believed, acted in the same way – handing their children over to governesses, tutors and schools – while they were caught up in "their interests, their amusements and the exigencies of society".[566] A few years later, Bishop Westcott thought, "In our schemes of reform the family has too often been forgotten; though we need, I think above all things, to labour for the restoration or development of simple family life. Legislative changes have tended to weaken the sense of home responsibility...If it be said that such

[560] Mary Sumner was the daughter-in-law of that evangelical bishop, Charles Sumner – and niece of the first evangelical Archbishop of Canterbury, John Sumner. A short history of the Mothers' Union is found in *The Mothers' Union 1876-2001* (2001).
[561] M. Sumner, *Women's Work Among Women* (1890) p.5.
[562] E. Hodder, *The Life and Work of the Seventh Earl of Shaftesbury, K.G.* (1887) p.747.
[563] "My First Football Match", in *The Boy's Own Paper*, 18 January 1879.
[564] S.G. Green, *The Story of the Religious Tract Society* (1899) pp.127-128.
[565] J.M. Lang, "The Non-Church Going: How Can Our Churches Reach Them?", in *The Christian Monthly and Family Treasury* (1882) p.75. See also T.M. Macdonald, "How to Reach Working Men", in *Homiletical and Pastoral Lectures* (1879) pp.395-396.
[566] M. Sumner, *Women's Work Among Women* (1890) p.3.

fellowship is impossible...our state is condemned."[567] Another bishop, Handley Moule, noted that "the calming, deepening power of the well-kept Lord's day is a waning thing in too many evangelical families".[568] Nevertheless, in some places, old practices lingered. For example, in 1889 the Provost of King's College, Cambridge, assumed that most of the undergraduates of that college were from homes where family prayers were the custom.[569]

18.20 More bishops and better episcopal organisation

In the mid-1850s, evangelicals had been encouraged by the growing willingness to see bishoprics not as a "dignity or a prize", but as a place for labour.[570] Later, there was increasing agitation for the bishops, with their cathedral staffs, to lead the evangelistic charge to reach the masses. The ordinary parochial clergy had enough to do already. As a result, the new dioceses of Truro and St Albans (both 1877), Liverpool (1880), Newcastle (1882), Southwell (1884) and Wakefield (1888) came into being. An Act was also passed to facilitate further suffragan bishops. Walsham How, the Bishop of Bedford, who led the East End mission of 1884, was one of these. However, notwithstanding these developments, there remained issues relating to the running of the Church. For example, in a paper published in 1884, Bishop Ryle referred to "Our large undivided dioceses, our too often useless cathedrals". He also pointed to our "ill-constituted Convocation".[571]

From the mid-1860s, the movement towards establishing diocesan conferences – at which the issues facing the Church could be addressed – facilitated evangelistic initiatives, such as the founding of organisations of lay evangelists.[572] However, in the paper referred to in the paragraph above, Bishop Ryle still noted the Church's "helpless inability to arrange systematic co-operation of clergy and laity".[573]

[567] B.F. Westcott, *The Incarnation A Revelation of Human Duties* (1892) p.29. See also H.C.G. Moule, *The Evangelical School in the Church of England* (1901) p.114.
[568] Ibid.
[569] See G.M. Trevelyan, *English Social History* (1978) p.503.
[570] "The New Year", in 57 *The Christian Observer for the Year 1857* (1857) p.4.
[571] J.C. Ryle, *Principles for Churchmen* (1884) p.350.
[572] K.F. Inglis, *Churches and the Working Classes in Victorian England* (1964) pp.31-33.
[573] J.C. Ryle, *Principles for Churchmen* (1884) p.350.

18.21 Conclusion

In terms of evangelistic strategies, the late nineteenth century emphasised spreading the word of God with boldness, creativity, innovation and hard work – unmatched, as the phrase of the times was, "since the apostles". The results were often very impressive and churches and chapels grew. Such growth was not without its physical challenges. As in apostolic times, there were threats to the life, limb and pocket of those involved. Even the cultivated Edward Studd was threatened with financial loss if he ran an evangelistic meeting with the Evangelization Society, near his Hampshire mansion.[574] Isaac Levinsohn, a Jew born in Russia, upon becoming a Christian in 1872, received death threats from his fellow Jews.[575] He survived to become a prominent evangelist.

Furthermore, aspects of the "new methods" attracted concern as the nineteenth century advanced. Archibald Brown noted that, at the beginning of his ministry, "The preaching used to be the sole attraction... now it is one of the least. Choirs, solos, cornets, stringed bands, organ recitals...are the baits held out. The Bible is being shelved...The great aim seems to be to make a service 'bright' and 'pleasant' rather than soul searching...Pleasing the people has taken the place of warning them."[576] In 1875, an article appeared in Spurgeon's *The Sword and the Trowel* entitled "How to Preach so as to Convert Nobody". The key, it was observed, was to drop sin, the particular sins of the audience, the atonement and hell from the discourse – while developing its literary qualities and making it short.[577] In London, attendance at a place of worship began to be taken as a sign of "a profession of religion".[578]

Spurgeon, towards the end of his ministry, thought that the excess of innovation had led to "a hardening process" to the gospel "among the masses". It was now much harder "to win attention to the word of God". People no longer flocked to hear those preaching the gospel of Christ as they had in the middle decades of the nineteenth century. Spurgeon

[574] J. Wood, *The Story of the Evangelization Society* (N.D.) p.79.

[575] I. Levinsohn, *The Story of Isaac Levinsohn* (1891) pp.79-82.

[576] A.G. Brown, "The London Mission-Hall Census", in *The British Weekly*, 17 February 1888, p.310.

[577] "How to Preach so as to Convert Nobody", in *The Sword and the Trowel* (1875) pp.443-445. See also Evangelization Society, *Preaching the Gospel; or, Evangelists and Evangelization* (N.D.) pp.93-95.

[578] C.H. Spurgeon, *An All-Round Ministry* (1960) p.296.

thought that the explanation for the "distaste for the ordinary services of the sanctuary…in some measure, lies in the direction little suspected. There has been a growing pandering to sensationalism...I feel deeply grieved at some of the inventions of modern mission work."[579] Some clergy thought they had to become showmen, varying the attractions, otherwise people would not come. Some Ritualist services were simply "theatre".[580] Furthermore, if people came to church, they did not expect the contents to unduly delay them. In 1882, John Pentland Mahaffy, in his little book entitled *The Decay of Modern Preaching*, noted that people were no longer willing to go to church at 12 noon and leave at 2.15 pm. Any preacher, apart from one with the "highest powers", was regarded by his hearers "as a sort of social criminal" if he went "beyond half an hour".[581] Consistent teaching of biblical doctrines through catechisms, to ingrain them in the heart, fell off – as did the daily routine of family worship and teaching.

Finally, behind all the human endeavours to reach the unbelieving, the work of divine providence must never be lost from view. For example, Cornelius, the father of the future evangelist Gipsy Smith, was converted in the late 1860s when he and his two brothers felt a great spiritual hunger. Speaking of it to the landlady of a beer shop, under similar conviction, she gave them a copy of *Pilgrim's Progress*. When it was read to them they "felt the smart of sin, and wept like little children".[582] Shortly thereafter, Cornelius spoke to a road repairer he passed by and confessed his spiritual disquiet. The road repairer took him to a chapel that night and Cornelius was converted; followed shortly thereafter by his brothers, parents and a great uncle. Soon the brothers were engaged in Christian work and attracting the encouragement of William Booth.[583]

[579] Ibid., pp.296-297.
[580] "Attendance at Public Worship in Large Towns", in *The Manchester Guardian*, 7 November 1881.
[581] J.P. Mahaffy, *The Decay of Modern Preaching* (1882) pp.3-4.
[582] R. Smith, *Gipsy Smith his Life and Work* (N.D.) pp.46-47.
[583] Ibid., pp.49-61.

19

MATERIAL HELP

19.1 The social problem

Accompanying the challenge of reaching the urban masses was how to solve the social problem, especially the dreadful home and work conditions of the masses. These conditions were inconsistent with the dignity of people created in the image of God, hardened them to the gospel, left converts open to the temptation of sin and demanded action from a good Samaritan. As a response, an evangelical parish might provide books for the sick, soup in time of cholera, schools and school books for children, a penny bank, a lending library and a maternity fund. For the especially needy there was also cooked rice, relief tickets and local collections, together with charity sermons for all to help pay for them, along with a host of evangelistic initiatives.[584] Some saw social work as an example of the glory, compassion and reality of the living God. For instance, Spurgeon founded and ran a very substantial orphanage at Stockwell. When challenged by an agnostic about his beliefs, he pointed – after his usual arguments failed to dent his questioner's position – to the failure of unbelievers to provide help to the needy, in contrast to the works that sprang from Christianity. Spurgeon ended the conversation with the triumphant cry, "The God who answers by orphanages, let him be God!".[585] Tellingly, the marketing blurb for Holden Pike's biography of Charles Haddon Spurgeon described him as "preacher, author, and philanthropist".[586]

19.1.1 *The range and quality of Christian social work*

Lord Shaftesbury had no time for those who spoke against improving public health on the basis that "more thought should be given to the

[584] "The English Evangelical Clergy", in 3 *Macmillan's Magazine* (1860) p.120.
[585] Author's italics. A.A. Dallimore, *C.H. Spurgeon* (1984) p.130.
[586] "The Best Life of Mr Spurgeon", in *The British Weekly*, 17 February 1888, p.311.

soul and less to the body".[587] While others fled London during cholera epidemics, agents of the London City Mission risked their lives to bring aid, as did Spurgeon in his first year of ministry there.[588] As he pithily put it: "the laws of cleanliness and health are as binding upon us as those of morality".[589]

The 1859 Revival coincided with the establishment of many philanthropic organisations[590] and Moody's work further stimulated philanthropy.[591] Evangelical house visitation programmes meant that they understood working-class needs and they established both general organisations to help the poor and specialised agencies to meet every contingency.[592] More widely, Heasman – the pioneer in charting Christian social activity – lists the following areas where Christian organisations worked: "There were infant nurseries for babies, homes for older children, evening institutes for teenagers, reformatories for children convicted in the courts, organisations to try to reduce drunkenness, crime and prostitution, asylums for the insane, care for the families of servicemen and for those whose jobs took them away from home, and canteens for workers in some of the outdoor occupations."[593] Some organisations for social help, like the National Society for the Prevention of Cruelty to Children, drew leaders from a wide religious spectrum, although its first President was Lord Shaftesbury and its first Secretary was the Congregational minister Benjamin Waugh.[594]

Much Christian social work was pioneering. In 1860, Pennefather's Mildmay Institution[595] introduced well-conceived, properly-executed and sustained training for social work. Its experience influenced the social science courses begun in some universities in the twentieth

[587] G.B.A.M. Finlayson, *The Seventh Earl of Shaftesbury 1801-1885* (1981) p.410.

[588] I. Howat and J. Nicholls, *Streets Paved with Gold* (2003) pp.13-19.

[589] C.H. Spurgeon, "The Voice of the Cholera", in *Metropolitan Tabernacle Pulpit* (1867) vol.12, p.448.

[590] K. Heasman, *Evangelicals in Action* (1962) pp.8 and 14.

[591] G.A. Smith, *The Life of Henry Drummond* (1899) pp.61-62. See also "Glasgow United Evangelistic Association", in *The Christian*, 13 September 1968 p.17.

[592] K. Heasman, *Evangelicals in Action* (1962) pp.9-10. For another excellent account of Victorian evangelical philanthropy, see also I. Bradley, *The Call to Seriousness* (1976) pp.119-134. House visitation for religious and social purposes was not an exclusive evangelical domain, see J. Covert, *A Victorian Marriage* (2000) p.191.

[593] K. Heasman, *Evangelicals in Action* (1962) pp.9-10.

[594] W.G. Robinson, *Benjamin Waugh* (1961) p.9.

[595] K. Heasman, *Evangelicals in Action* (1962) p.38.

century. Mildmay also became the first organisation to pay its less-well-off workers for their work helping the poor, thus creating the forerunners of modern paid social workers. Mildmay paved the way for the professionalisation of social services and by doing so provided the guidelines for subsequent state intervention.

In 1866 Mildmay developed its own nursing arm when two of its deaconesses, at a time of an outbreak of cholera, volunteered to go into some of London's worst slums, where even the police feared to enter, to care for the sick and their dependants. The *Younghusband Report* (1959) into social and health workers acknowledged that with regard to the services within its ambit "without exception each owes its origin to voluntary effort, often religious in its inspiration".[596]

An initiative of the Salvation Army provided an early model of the benefit of health and safety at work and of concern for the environment. Matches, in the late nineteenth century, were made with yellow phosphorus, the fumes of which rot the jaw and ultimately kill those exposed to it. Alternatives to yellow phosphorus existed, but the match-makers said they were too expensive and would destroy their market. General Booth campaigned for the use of a new type of red phosphorus match – albeit more expensive. He set up a factory to make them. The leading match manufacturers, after a struggle, followed suit.

Often, Christian social work was more parochial and arose from the needs of the hour. For example in 1881, with the snow lying thick around Kenilworth, the local minister organised the clearing of the snow on the roads so that the traffic could proceed.[597]

19.1.2 *The Temperance movement*

The Temperance movement deserves separate treatment from other Christian social concerns because of the importance that Church and chapel attached to the abuse of alcohol. William Haslam, no theological liberal, working with the poor of Bath in the early 1860s, thought that "it was impossible to labour with any hope of permanent success till some plan could be devised for checking this cursed and cursing

[596] *Report of the Working Party on Social Workers in the Local Health and Welfare Services* (1959) para.192. See also K. Heasman, *Evangelicals in Action* (1962) pp.9-10.
[597] C. Pennefather, *"Fervent in Spirit"* (N.D.) pp.13-14.

influence".[598] The biographer of James Flanagan, that most effective Primitive Methodist evangelist, traced the process of his conversion to his wife engaging a temperance enthusiast to challenge him to sign the pledge.[599] D.L. Moody in the summer of 1882 held a meeting in Glasgow for reformed alcoholics. "Over 800 sat down to tea, of all ages and ranks."[600]

The damage alcohol did was manifest. In Liverpool in 1899, a survey found that of 600 children born to inebriate mothers in prison, 335 were stillborn or died within two years of birth. It also led to stunted growth, other health issues, family breakdown and neglect of education.[601] Frederick Charrington, the brewing heir, led a vigorous campaign against London's music halls in the early 1880s because intoxication on their premises made them a centre for prostitution and caused the destruction of young girls and the breakdown of marriages.[602]

The Temperance movement involved huge numbers of people. By 1897, the Band of Hope, fighting alcohol drinking by children, had 3.28 million members.[603] In Liverpool, at the end of J.C. Ryle's episcopate, 191 out of 205 churches held a Temperance Sunday. This is not to say that every Christian did not drink. John Ruskin, in his Christian period, visited Spurgeon with a couple of bottles of his father's finest red wine; his father was a wealthy vintner. All the same, Spurgeon preached at temperance events and saw his children inducted into the Band of Hope. Such endeavours, though, had little impact on government policy during our period. One view was that "so enormous a part of our revenue is derived from the drinking habits of the working classes" that it had put the consciences of the legislators to sleep.[604]

[598] W. Haslam, *"Yet Not I"* (N.D.) p.64.
[599] R.W. Russell, *The Life of James Flanagan* (1920) pp.16-17.
[600] G.A. Smith, *The Life of Henry Drummond* (1899) p.135.
[601] "History of Hope UK" (May 2008) p.2, www.hopeuk.org/wp-content/uploads/History.pdf, accessed 21 October 2016.
[602] F. N. Charrington, *The Battle of the Music Halls* (N.D.).
[603] "History of Hope UK" (May 2008) p.2, www.hopeuk.org/wp-content/uploads/History.pdf, accessed 21 October 2016.
[604] W. Cadman, "Pastoral Visitation", in *Homiletical and Pastoral Lectures* (1879) p.406.

19.1.3 *Setting up trades unions*

For many Nonconformists, involvement with, and leadership of, the newly established trades unions was a natural extension of their faith. George Edwards, after conversion to Primitive Methodism, read theology and realised that "social conditions were not as God meant them to be". Methodism, especially Primitive Methodism, in the coalfields and in agriculture, was the most effective religious movement in seeing its members reach leadership positions in the new unions. Many of these leaders were lay preachers. They started meetings with prayer and used chapel buildings for union meetings.[605] They learnt their skills in speaking, leadership and the organisation of men in the Primitive Methodist chapels.[606]

19.1.4 *The relationship between social help and evangelism*

As our period started, evangelism and social help were perceived as separate Christian duties – separate, but mutually reinforcing. For example, in the early 1860s, the rules of the London Bible and Domestic Female Mission provided that Biblewomen were to sell Scriptures cheaply to the poor for five hours every day. For this, they were paid two shillings a day. During other hours, they were to pursue benevolent activities, including needlework, cooking and cleanliness – for which they were unpaid.[607] The aim was to teach the poor to look after themselves, rather than to look to others.[608] The work was recognised by contemporaries as radical – a "new chapter in the history, not only of Christianity, but of civilisation".[609] The underlying philosophy was that "The woman is appointed for the physical civilisation of communities. She is to 'guide the house'...and this part of the education of the women of the working classes has been little cared for".[610] Often, the poor shut the door in the face of a Biblewoman and said: "We want bread instead of Bibles", but some listened to the Bible being read to them.[611] It was the

[605] M.R. Watts, *The Dissenters* (2015) vol.3, pp.271-277.
[606] G. Milburn, *Primitive Methodism* (2002) p.55.
[607] L.N.R., *The Missing Link* (1861) p.298.
[608] Ibid., p.297.
[609] Under "New Books" at end of ibid.
[610] Ibid., p.279.
[611] Ibid., p.63.

Bible first, but on the second visit concern for the body as well as the soul was manifested.[612] As a result of this need, in 1868, The London Bible and Domestic Female Mission added a new role of "nurse" to its work[613] but, nevertheless, its Biblewomen continued to feel the pressure to alleviate physical suffering. Accordingly, in 1873 The London Bible and Domestic Female Mission created the role of a "Pioneer" for lady superintendents of Biblewomen. Their role was to ensure that Bible canvassing remained the first priority of Biblewomen and that they did not "degenerate into a mere agency for giving relief".[614] By 1889, The London Bible and Domestic Female Mission in London possessed 140 Biblewomen and 70 nurses under the guidance of 160 lady superintendents.[615] However, outside London – and under the superintendence of Ellen Ranyard – where Biblewomen were established, too often Bible work ceased to be the primary element.[616] As William Haslam noted of "temporal relief" and "spiritual advice", as he reached the poor of Bath: "It is very difficult to combine these two good works; and more difficult not to do so."[617]

For those who did not like evangelism, but who were committed to good works, the possibility of directing evangelicals away from preaching by affirming social help appealed. An early example – a comment that appeared in a local Exeter paper – was aimed at Geraldine Hooper's preaching there. The author suggested that, instead of "spending precious time in praying and talking", she would have been better employed in "zealously...alleviating the pangs of hunger experienced by the poor in our midst".[618] Perhaps, because Hooper was a woman, the challenge at the time was more plausible; but the charge would be repeatedly made against evangelicals and, in a growing chorus, towards the end of the century when holistic evangelism would emerge.

[612] Ibid., p.285.

[613] See "Link after Link; or, Bible Women Nurses", in *God's Message in Low London* (N.D.) pp.3-64. Similar works were started in other cities, see "District Nursing in Bristol City", in 6 Biblewomen and Nurses (1889) pp.64-66.

[614] E. Platt, *The Story of the Ranyard Mission 1857-1937* (1937) pp.50-51.

[615] "Biblewomen and Nurses", in 6 *Biblewomen and Nurses* (1889) p.3.

[616] "How Wears the Missing Link?", in *God's Message in Low London* (N.D.) pp.26-27.

[617] W. Haslam, *"Yet Not I"* (N.D.) p.27.

[618] G. Guinness, *"She Spake of Him"* (1872) pp.73-74.

19.1.5 *An embryonic Christian welfare state*

Most late nineteenth century Christians did not believe that state intervention was the means to solve every social problem. They affirmed voluntarism – the view that, without state aid, "vital needs could be met by direct appeals to believing hearts and consecrated purses". Spurgeon, for instance, believed that voluntarism "was the best instrument of Christian charity".[619] He saw the hand of God in the establishment of his orphanage work. In the summer of 1866, at the church prayer gathering, he prayed for a new work and the means to implement it. A few days later, a letter arrived from someone he did not know offering £20,000 to establish a work for the education and training of orphan boys. The work was later extended to girls.[620] In Spurgeon's eyes, and in the eyes of thousands of Nonconformists, the foundation of the Stockwell Orphanage illustrated the power of voluntarism. Similar views were espoused by others, such as Charles Baring Young. He gave up being an MP to establish, in 1886, Kingham Hill School in Oxfordshire, to train working-class boys in "the Christian faith and way of life".[621] He educated 200 boys a year at his own expense and then left his fortune to support the ongoing work. The school continues to this day. He believed that "The tendency of Government Departments is to become wasteful, fussy and autocratic".[622] However, by 1890 Hugh Price Hughes – illustrating the changing thinking of many evangelicals – thought "that private charity is quite unable to cope with the gigantic and growing pauperism of London".[623] He added that "private benevolence and voluntary societies have broken down altogether". This may reflect the fact that private giving fell, along with Christian earnestness, at the end of the nineteenth century. His conclusion was that "it is both legitimate and necessary for the state to use all the resources of civilisation to abolish pauperism".

[619] T. Curnow, E. Hulse, D. Kingdom and G. Thomas, *A Marvellous Ministry* (1993) p.97.

[620] A.A. Dallimore, *C.H. Spurgeon* (1984) pp.126-129.

[621] A.F. Jarvis, *Charles Baring Young of Daylesford* (1950) p.35.

[622] Ibid., p.28.

[623] H.P. Hughes, "The Problem of London Pauperism", in *Advance!*, November 1890, p.23.

19.2 Funding it all

Philanthropic work was expensive. However, as *The Revival* commented, "There are not a few Christian manufacturers...who are devoting either the whole or a large part of their profits to the cause of missions. They... sustain the heralds of salvation."[624] They also "pioneered measures to improve the living and working conditions of their employees" – in the form of medical assistance, cheap meals and housing, educational help, paid holidays, and involvement in profit sharing schemes.[625] Their numbers included the Nottingham Liberal MP and textile manufacturer Samuel Morley, "rumoured to be the richest commoner in England".[626] He was behind Moody and Sankey, was a great supporter of the YMCA, the Salvation Army and Frederick Charrington's work in the East End, funded and built many chapels and was at his most generous in educational matters.[627] He also supported the establishment of – and helped fund – the National Labourers' Agricultural Union, by the Primitive Methodist Joseph Arch.[628] But there were many others, and not limited to the ranks of Christian manufacturers – the Barclays, the W.H. Smiths, the Colmans and the Peeks, just to name a few – who gave lavishly and spawned business empires, the names of which are recognisable today. However, if Morley had a rival in terms of the amount given, it was the Baroness Burdett-Coutts, whose wealth came from Coutts Bank. Her generosity tended towards assisting the Church.[629] Above them all was Lord Shaftesbury. He did not have Morley's wealth, but he organised philanthropy.[630]

But it was not just the very rich who were generous. Spurgeon's work with his orphanage was almost a national icon. People and churches gave to it on a lavish scale. In November 1875, he records that the town of

[624] "Self-Supporting Missions", in *The Revival*, 2 June 1864, p.337.

[625] M.R. Watts, *The Dissenters* (2015) vol.3, pp.278-282.

[626] C. Binfield, *George Williams and the Y.M.C.A.* (1973) p.230. See also K.F. Inglis, *Churches and the Working Classes in Victorian England* (1964) p.101.

[627] It was also said of Morley that "No appeal for a sick girl needing a holiday, no small tea for a group in a crowded district, no expense for a Saturday half-holiday outing, nothing was too small for his attention", see E. Kinnaird, *Reminiscences* (1925) p.70.

[628] M.R. Watts, *The Dissenters* (2015) vol.3, p.277.

[629] D. Owen, *English Philanthropy 1660-1960* (1965) pp.413-420.

[630] See generally on Victorian philanthropists C. Binfield, *George Williams and the Y.M.C.A.* (1973) pp.230-255. On Morley generally, see D. Owen, *English Philanthropy 1660-1960* (1965) pp.401-408.

Reading organised a bazaar for it and raised £1,158 – truly, he declared, "royal munificence".[631] Colonel Gordon, later to be famous as General Gordon of Khartoum, adopted "a singular austerity of living" in order to fund "a variety of charitable expenses".[632] When Booth wanted to help the needy, the Salvation Army launched its own self-denial week in which members gave up something for a week. The first such week raised £4,820, mainly in pennies and half-pennies. Many evangelical leaders of the nineteenth century raised funds to increase stipends of clergy, in poorer or newer areas of work.

19.3 Conclusion

By the end of our period, Christians had marked out the areas where social care was needed and heavily invested in providing it. They had, in widening the working opportunities for women, identified the group of people who were to sustain social care and introduced training for them. They had also been involved with establishing trades unions which, in some ways, were voluntary self-help organisations. In finding new ways to look after their employees, many of the leading Christian employers were at the cutting edge of developments. In some quarters, there were no limits on the expectations of what the churches could achieve in the field of social reform. General Booth, as we will see in the context of holistic evangelism, thought that, with national support, the Salvation Army could provide a solution to poverty and destitution, but not all supported him. Others believed that the challenge of the poor was too big for the churches and appealed for government aid. In doing so, they paved the way for state intervention. Indeed, some issues of social reform, like limits on the working hours in industry championed by Lord Shaftesbury, could only be achieved by government intervention. The same was generally true of the temperance issue – always the matter which generated the most enthusiasm from the churches, but one on which governments were cool.

The emphasis on eradicating social evils may have led some people, under the influence of F.D. Maurice, to rewrite their doctrine of sin. This approach received an apparent impetus from science. By the late 1870s,

[631] C.H. Spurgeon, *The Metropolitan Tabernacle: its History and Work* (1876) p.109.
[632] L. Strachey, *Eminent Victorians* (1971) p.198.

there were those who held that evolution meant that right and wrong no longer represented eternal realities. Morality no longer existed. One view was that "All things are on the bosom of an irresistible out-flowing stream, and we are what we are in virtue of an unavoidable necessity." Sin needed to be redefined – and conduct which government was popularly being asked to prohibit was one possible definition of it.[633] By the end of the nineteenth century, Dominic Erdozain suggested that sin was no longer perceived by many as a permanent desire to rid the soul of God, but some "failure" or "weakness" that could be corrected by human effort. If sin was no more than some unfortunate habit, then salvation was no more than the expression of the virtues, and this could be achieved without divine help.[634] However, at the end of the century, evangelicals holding to orthodoxy, such as J.C. Ryle and General Booth, continued to appreciate the difference between sin, which led to hell, and human failure, which could be remedied by human effort.

However, some leading evangelicals, like John Clifford, president of the Baptist Union – and whose epoch lasted well into the twentieth century – used language which potentially confused salvation from God's judgment on sin with social salvation. He suggested that the purpose of preaching the gospel was because in its wake came social improvement. For example, in a Fabian Tract, he wrote that the emphasis on social action should mean no "slacking" in preaching of the gospel – the "primary work". He went on "History and present experience alike declare that no other name than that of Christ is given whereby we can have social salvation."[635] On this view, the purpose of preaching the gospel was to bring about social change. A social gospel was arising, which gospel preachers found made the gospel ineffective.[636] Interestingly, the Brethren, who did not dwell on social work, but the Second Coming, continued to prosper numerically throughout

[633] "New Light on Sin", in *The Family Treasury of Sunday Reading* (1879) p.6.

[634] D. Erdozain, "The Secularisation of Sin in the Nineteenth Century", in 62 *The Journal of Ecclesiastical History* (2011) p.61.

[635] J. Clifford, "Socialism and the Churches", in *Fabian Tract No. 139* (1908) p.13. Compare Acts 4:12.

[636] M.J. Lockhart, *W.P Lockhart* (1895) pp.240-242. Lockhart directly challenged Clifford after the latter's exposition of "The Christian Conception of Society" at the 1891 autumn meeting of the Baptist Union, see ibid.

our period.[637] However, they did use 'Gospel Tea Meetings' to reach the lower classes. These free 'meat teas' were followed by a gospel address.[638] They were also attentive to the needs of the poor and sick of their own members.[639]

[637] T. Grass, *Gathering to His Name* (2012) pp.87 and 116-117.
[638] Ibid., p.136.
[639] E. Gosse, *The Life of Philip Henry Gosse* (1890) pp.358 and 363-364.

20

HOLISTIC EVANGELISM

20.1 Introduction

At the mid-point of the nineteenth century, the Congregationalist Edward Miall – in a searching critique as to why the churches had failed to reach the nation – stated:

> A little more systematic benevolence, a little more practical regard to the earthly welfare of man...a little more kindly philanthropy such as that exhibited so conspicuously by their divine Master, would have constituted a very pleasing and harmonious background to... revelation.[640]

He had no particular projects for the churches to undertake. In some places, the church might supply water; in others, drainage, or improved dwellings or baths, washhouses or education and books.[641] In overseas missions, he noted that the church took the lead in instructing in the common arts and conveniences of life. He asked, therefore, why should the church not take the lead originating and conducting works of philanthropy at home?[642]

20.2 The civic gospel

In Birmingham, "Towards the end of the sixties a few...men made the discovery that perhaps a strong and able town council might do almost as much to improve the conditions of life in the town as Parliament itself".[643] Their "prophet" was George Dawson who inclined towards Unitarianism.

[640] E. Miall, *The British Churches in Relation to the British People* (1850) p.290.
[641] Ibid., p.293.
[642] Ibid., pp.294-295.
[643] A.W.W. Dale, *The Life of R.W. Dale* (1898) p.401.

He argued that "the odours of corporeal nastiness interfere even with the propagation of the gospel".[644] He also believed that "A great town exists to discharge towards the people of that town, the duties that a great nation exists to discharge towards the people of that nation."[645] Joseph Chamberlain, who taught in the Sunday and night schools attached to Dawson's church, made Dawson's ideas concrete.[646] In Birmingham, water and gas supplies were municipalised, slum housing cleared and "the art gallery and libraries were enlarged, and baths, parks, and open spaces were added to the city's amenities. It was a record of municipal progress which cannot easily be paralleled in any city in the world."[647] The death rate in the most populous districts of Birmingham fell dramatically. Chamberlain, as a Unitarian, was interested in education; he wanted schools controlled by local authorities and the education to be undenominational.[648] He also believed that it was the environment that shaped character. He believed it was no more "the fault of these people that they are vicious and intemperate than it is their fault that they are stunted, deformed, debilitated and diseased".[649] In a talk to a Quaker adult school, he observed that it was absurd "to preach morality to people who are herded together in conditions in which common decency is impossible".[650]

Assisting the endeavours of Dawson and Chamberlain in articulating and applying the civic gospel, was Dawson's long-time admirer, R.W. Dale. Dale sustained the civic gospel on the basis that "the living Christ was a reigning Christ, the Prince as well as Saviour of men, whose will is to be done on earth as it is done in heaven". His will was to be asserted in art, literature, commerce and politics.[651] A man of huge energy and ability, "He would never admit that religious devotion can excuse any neglect of private or public duty."[652]

[644] Cited in W. Wilson, *The Life of George Dawson* (1905) p.149.
[645] Ibid., p.151.
[646] Chamberlain turned from Unitarianism and religion on the death of his second wife, J.E. Powell, *Joseph Chamberlain* (1977) pp.30-32.
[647] C. Petrie, *Joseph Chamberlain* (1940) pp.13 and 17-19.
[648] Ibid., p.14.
[649] Ibid., p.18.
[650] Cited in M.R. Watts, *The Dissenters* (2015) vol.3, p.289.
[651] A.W.W. Dale, *The Life of R.W. Dale* (1898) p.398.
[652] Ibid., p.400.

20.3 A seminal book

As the century progressed, the idea that to reach the working class it was first necessary to meet their material needs took root in the soil of hitherto evangelical denominations like the Congregationalists and Methodists. The growth of this idea coincided with many Congregational leaders adopting a critical attitude to the Bible – and the recognition by men like R.W. Dale that they saw few converts from outside the church.[653] In 1883, the idea took institutional shape with the publication of the tract *The Bitter Cry of Outcast London*, probably by Andrew Mearns, a Congregational minister.[654] This received considerable publicity from the leading society journal *The Pall Mall Gazette*, under the editorship of W.T. Stead – a product of the 1859 Revival. *The Bitter Cry* struck a chord, as many "were preparing to move away from a strict emphasis upon salvation and the after-life to a genuine awareness of the importance of physical environment and social justice".[655]

The Bitter Cry appealed to the conscience of the churches. At a time of great wealth, it drew a link between slum housing and religious apathy; and between overcrowding and sexual immorality including, most controversially, incest. It pointed to areas of the East End where 39 out of 4,235 people attended church, some of these only once or twice a year.[656] It urged an evangelistic response and stated that the "Congregational Union have determined to open in several of the lowest and most needy districts of the metropolis, suitable mission halls as a base of operations for evangelistic work".[657] Congregationalism was beginning to repudiate its earlier view that its special mission was to the middle classes.

However, *The Bitter Cry* was no self-serving endeavour to broaden the appeal of Congregationalism in its outreach, only the love of Christ in its "simplest form" was to be presented. Help from any quarter was welcomed.[658] The state's involvement was implored, as the work was so large. *The Bitter Cry* stated that social amelioration must be completed

[653] M.R. Watts, *The Dissenters* (2015) vol.3, p.95.

[654] See A.S. Wohl, "Introduction" to *The Bitter Cry of Outcast London* (1970) (A.S. Wohl (ed.)) pp.14-15 for a discussion as to its author.

[655] Ibid., p.25.

[656] A. Mearns, "The Bitter Cry of Outcast London", in *The Bitter Cry of Outcast London* (1970) (A.S. Wohl (ed.)) p.57.

[657] Ibid., p.56.

[658] Ibid., p.71.

before "the Christian missionary can have much chance".[659] *The Bitter Cry* completed the shift in the thinking of the Baptist John Clifford, "from an individualistic to an environmental explanation of sin and poverty".[660] The state, under pressure from Lord Salisbury, responded.[661] *The Bitter Cry* also engendered a somewhat unusual sense of corporate sin – in that it was argued that every member of society was involved in the existence of slum accommodation.[662]

20.4 An influential Methodist, the Forward Movement and open-churches

In the early 1880s, the Methodists were generally in a better spiritual condition than the Congregationalists. For them, it was a time of revival. In 1884, Hugh Price Hughes witnessed 2,500 conversions.[663] All the same, despite his and other evangelistic successes, the entire nation was not converted. *The Bitter Cry*, by linking together drunkenness and sexual immorality as causes of sin of which the masses could neither let go nor repent, provided the explanation as to why the nation was so unconverted. For him and others, solving the housing and social condition of the masses was the key to enable the nation to be finally and fully reached.[664] Further, *The Bitter Cry* seemed to explain why the older a person was, the less likely they were to come to Christ – through the influence of drink and sexual immorality, they hardened themselves against the divine influence.[665]

London's Wesleyan Methodists responded to *The Bitter Cry* by raising a new mission effort to London and one operating upon new principles. Numerically weak in London, what members they had were solidly middle and lower middle class, as discipleship had lifted early converts up the social scale. Now they returned to reaching the working classes.[666] The new movement was known as the Forward Movement. As well as

[659] Ibid., p.69.
[660] M.R. Watts, *The Dissenters* (2015) vol.3, p.290.
[661] A.S. Wohl, "Introduction" to *The Bitter Cry of Outcast London* (1970) (A.S. Wohl (ed.)) pp.32-37.
[662] Ibid., p.26.
[663] C. Oldstone-Moore, *Hugh Price Hughes* (1999) p.103.
[664] Ibid., pp.107-134. See also P.S. Bagwell, *Outcast London: A Christian Response* (1987) p.143.
[665] Ibid., pp.104-105.
[666] J.E. McCulloch, *The Open Church for the Unchurched or How to Reach the Masses* (1905) pp.34-35.

reviving the Wesleyan Methodist presence in London, it also offered them the opportunity of breaking away from their chapel culture to the status of national church.[667]

The Forward Movement consisted of what was called "open-churches" – each

> organised for the purpose of aggressive evangelism in its immediate community, where as a rule, wholesome social and religious influences are deficient; the working principle of the organisation being to supplement the ordinary methods of the gospel, such as preaching, Sunday school and prayer meeting, by a system of practical kindness and service, ministering to the physical, social and intellectual, as well as to the spiritual needs, and reaching, as far as possible, all the people all the time, with the ultimate aim of saving the whole life through vital faith in Jesus Christ.[668]

Such churches looked similar to institutional churches, but that description was dismissed by some as implying that the work was placid.

The danger for the new movement was that undertaking social work might become a pre-condition to evangelism. If so, evangelism might cease in many parts. Others thought the gospel still worked – and that many, but not all, of the social problems were self-inflicted.[669]

The flagship of the Forward Movement was Hugh Price Hughes's West London Mission. This "from the beginning operated entirely outside the walls of churches and chapels". At St James's Music Hall, its inaugural meeting was on 21 October 1887 and the sermon was preached by C.H. Spurgeon.[670] Thereafter, on a Saturday night, a concert was held at St James's Hall before being moved to Exeter Hall, as a means of providing innocent amusement to the young. The Sunday services were at St James's Hall. The morning service was run

[667] For this thesis, see C. Oldstone-Moore, *Hugh Price Hughes* (1999) pp.137-138.

[668] J.E. McCulloch, *The Open Church for the Unchurched or How to Reach the Masses* (1905) p.51.

[669] See M.R. Watts, *The Dissenters* (2015) vol.3, pp.291-292 and F. Crozier, "Methodism and '*The Bitter Cry of Outcast London*' (1885)", in *The Bitter Cry of Outcast London* (1970).

[670] J.E. McCulloch, *The Open Church for the Unchurched or How to Reach the Masses* (1905) p.60. For a history of the West London Mission, see P.S. Bagwell, *Outcast London: A Christian Response* (1987).

for all and, in the evening, Hughes preached an evangelistic sermon for the unconverted. He was convinced that "Every Methodist minister must be a soul winner. Methodism cannot live without revivals and conversions."[671] These services were "remarkably fruitful".[672] In the afternoon, he held what "he called a 'conference', though it was actually a new type of sermon...'an attempt to deal separately, systematically, and permanently with the social aspects of the ethical teachings of Christ'".[673] He accepted Ruskin's dictum that "If our religion is good for anything, it is good for everything".[674] It was these sermons, plus a few other evangelistic ones, that Hughes published under the titles of *Social Christianity* (March 1889) and *The Philanthropy of God* (December 1889). They "constituted the first coherent expression of Hughes's Forward Movement theology".[675] Hughes put forward Christ as "the greatest of social reformers". He also developed the themes that "Christ came to save the nation as well as the individual"; that "it is an essential feature of his mission to reconstruct human society on the basis of justice and love"; and that "Christ intended human law to conform itself to his moral example".[676] Under Christian socialism, drinking and gambling were to be controlled – and the brothels closed. On occasion, the West London Mission's outdoor processions were mistaken as those of the socialists. This caused no disquiet, as when people listened to what they had to say, they found that "we are socialists in very deed – that we preach the universal brotherhood of man, and the universal love of God to all his creatures".[677]

In 1890, Hughes wrote that if we can triumph in the West End,

> we can triumph anywhere; if we fail there, no victory anywhere else can retrieve the fortunes of the day. The fact is that West London

[671] J.I. Brice, *The Crowd for Christ* (1934) pp.25-30. See also R. Currie, A. Gilbert and L. Horsley, *Churches and Churchgoers* (1977) p.40.

[672] J.E. McCulloch, *The Open Church for the Unchurched or How to Reach the Masses* (1905) pp.67 and 69. For an explanation of his success as an evangelist, see C. Oldstone-Moore, *Hugh Price Hughes* (1999) pp.103-106.

[673] Ibid., p.166.

[674] J.E. McCulloch, *The Open Church for the Unchurched or How to Reach the Masses* (1905) p.62.

[675] C. Oldstone-Moore, *Hugh Price Hughes* (1999) p.171.

[676] Hughes's thought in *Social Christianity* and *The Philanthropy of God* is helpfully summarised in ibid., pp.173-181.

[677] "The Services in Hyde Park", in *Advance!*, August 1890, p.170.

> is the microcosm of the great macrocosm which we call the British Empire. There you have representatives of every section of human society, and every aspect of life. It is the headquarters of business, of pleasure and of politics, and the only Christian organisations that will endure in the 20th century are those that can cope with the gigantic spiritual difficulties of West London, and exhibit the triumphs of the gospel within a mile of Piccadilly Circus.[678]

By the beginning of the twentieth century, the West London Mission drew "members of both Houses of Parliament, ladies of title, journalists, actresses, representatives of the learned professions, and visitors from almost every part of the world, as well as those usually reached by such religious efforts".[679] Furthermore, it was calculated that in the first 18 years of the mission, attendances at its main Sunday evening service numbered two million people, without reference to the network of overflow halls and other halls connected to the West London Mission holding services at the same time.[680] It seemed that Hughes had established the theology and institutions of a new and successful Methodism for the cities. He had also given it the hope, enthusiasm and confidence that characterised every period of spiritual revival.[681]

Yet, in the three years to 1893, growth in the Methodist churches was disappointingly small[682] – given the vastness of the available resources and the unprecedented opportunities, although "glorious revivals and extensive harvests" did occur. Hughes thought the problem was that the labourers were too few – and that Methodists did not work for Christ as they did for money and political parties. The Salvation Army's energy and commitment to the winning of souls was a rebuke to them, but suggested what could be achieved.[683] To remedy the situation,

[678] H.P. Hughes, "In the Heart of the Forward Movement", in *Advance!*, November 1890, p.18.

[679] J.E. McCulloch, *The Open Church for the Unchurched or How to Reach the Masses* (1905) p.67.

[680] Attendances at the main morning and evening services averaged 3,500, without use of overflow or other mission buildings, see ibid., p.68.

[681] "Easter Hope", in *The Methodist Times*, 6 April 1893, p.211.

[682] "Why not More Conversions?", in *The Methodist Times*, 6 July 1893, p.427.

[683] "Easter Hope", in *The Methodist Times*, 6 April 1893, p.211 and "Why is Missionary Progress so Slow?", in *The Methodist Times*, 4 May 1893, p.275.

Hughes constantly urged Methodists to preach the "plain, old-fashioned Scriptural gospel of 'Jesus and the resurrection'".[684] He also organised a mass march to Hyde Park, culminating in open-air preaching, and floated the idea of a simultaneous national mission, which reached fruition in the early years of the next century.[685]

If the labourers were few, the demands on Methodists – and especially the members of the Forward Movement – grew, so that they were pulled in many directions besides evangelism. Christopher Oldstone-Moore, in his biography of Hughes, observed that "Forward-Movement Methodism demanded a deeper and more strenuous spirituality than in the past". To support this view, he refers to Hughes's comment that Methodism's duty as a church is "many-sided and national. We have to take our legitimate share in the promotion of civic righteousness both local and imperial." He went on: "We have necessarily and greatly multiplied our devotional and philanthropic agencies over a wide area. To fill this immense channel of public and private usefulness we need a vaster supply from those springs in the mountains of God from whence cometh our help."[686] The new Methodism was taking its place in the world. However, it was still livelier than other parts of the Methodist church which *The Methodist Times* characterised as, in some places, "so respectable, so tame, so dumb".[687] By the turn of the century, developments seemed to vindicate the Forward Movement. In London, churches adopting its principles increased attendance by 22 per cent and membership by 105 per cent. These figures were the net increase after allowance for people moving to the suburbs. Attendances at chapels ignoring the principles of the Forward Movement dropped 44 per cent.[688] To what extent these numbers reflected movement within Methodist chapels is uncertain. Whether that increased membership would linger if the new Methodism was unable to sustain – for whatever reason – its social work, remained to be seen.

Elsewhere, "The principles, practices and even the name of the Forward Movement were" adopted by others. In the 1890s, the

[684] Ibid.

[685] C. Oldstone-Moore, *Hugh Price Hughes* (1999) p.253.

[686] Ibid., p.302.

[687] "Easter Hope", in *The Methodist Times*, 6 April 1893, p.211.

[688] J.E. McCulloch, *The Open Church for the Unchurched or How to Reach the Masses* (1905) p.51.

Congregationalists launched their own Forward Movement. Robert Horton's Lyndhurst Road chapel developed its existing work in Kentish Town – leading to a major mission with large buildings and the provision from Lyndhurst's congregation of 200 workers.[689] Hugh Price Hughes was a "featured speaker" at its opening.[690] Other Congregationalists launched their own mission halls. One of the most successful was the Wheatsheaf Hall built by the MP W.S. Caine which, between 1884 and 1894, grew to 250 members.[691] Horton was invited to go to Westminster Chapel, the denomination's largest chapel, to lead a Forward Movement of its London churches, but it was not to be.[692] However, the boast from the chairman of the Congregational Union was that no one could now say that "when wealth recedes from a neighbourhood, Congregationalism can no longer live here".[693] By the end of the nineteenth century Church and chapel in Lambeth ran at least 58 thrift, friendly and other societies aimed at self-help; 36 temperance societies; and sponsored 16 nurses and 10 gymnasiums (five by the Church of England and five by Nonconformists).[694]

20.5 The Salvation Army offers to run an organisation comparable to the welfare state

Yet the needs of the poor remained great. Before the solution of the welfare state was tried, General Booth suggested the idea of a Christian organisation running something akin to the welfare state.

Booth published, in 1890, *In Darkest England and the Way Out*. For him, parts of England were as dark as those of Central Africa explored by Henry Stanley. Booth numbered prostitutes in Great Britain at 100,000, the number matching that of the homeless. Half a million people were drunkards and, in one year, 160,000 people were convicted of drunkenness. In London alone, 933,000 people were destitute, of whom 300,000 were "starving". As Booth put it, England had "A population

[689] A. Peel and J.A.R. Marriott, *Robert Forman Horton* (1937) pp.150-151 and 156.
[690] C. Oldstone-Moore, *Hugh Price Hughes* (1999) p.221.
[691] J. Cox, *The English Churches in a Secular Society* (1982) p.44.
[692] *The Life of Charles Silvester Horne* (1920) (W.B. Selbie (ed.)) pp.151-152.
[693] Cited in M.D. Johnson, *The Dissolution of Dissent, 1850-1918* (1987) p.254.
[694] For a full account of the staggering range of activities run by the churches and chapels of Lambeth, see J. Cox, *The English Churches in a Secular Society* (1982) pp.58 and 299-301.

sodden with drink, steeped in vice, eaten up by every social and physical malady".[695] Within *In Darkest England*, he proposed a range of schemes that the Salvation Army would run to help the poor. These schemes included food and shelter depots, labour yards where people could work to pay for their food,[696] a model farm, a poor man's lawyer and a poor person's bank. There was also to be a matrimonial bureau where unmarrieds could register to meet members of the opposite sex.

Booth did not propose to depart from his focus on saving souls. However, he was appalled at what he saw in the "midst of the unparalleled wealth, and civilisation, and philanthropy of this professedly most Christian land".[697] He added, "My only hope for the permanent deliverance of mankind from misery, either in this world or the next, is the regeneration or remaking of the individual by the power of the Holy Ghost through Jesus Christ". He went on, "But in providing for the relief of temporal misery I reckon that I'm only making it easy where it is now difficult, and possible where it is now all but impossible, for men and women to find their way to the cross of our Lord Jesus Christ".[698] It may be that in the mid-1880s, as the expansion of the Salvation Army slowed, Booth looked for the cause of this slow-down and came to a conclusion about the need for social amelioration.[699]

Many in the churches supported Booth's scheme and thought it full of promise. Hugh Price Hughes thought it "the greatest social scheme which had ever been conceived in the interests of the poor".[700] Leading evangelicals, like Webb-Peploe and Joseph Parker, urged their people to support it. In Westminster Abbey, F.W. Farrar preached, using the Good Samaritan[701] as his example, that "mere isolated individual effort was helpless; the evil could only be met by the brave effort of the whole nation, the courageous self-denial of the whole church, and the hearty co-operation of all true Christians". He continued:

[695] W. Booth, *In Darkest England and the Way Out* (1890) pp.14-15.

[696] Churches also provided secular work to the unemployed to keep them from hunger, see J. Harries, *G. Campbell Morgan* (1930) p.53.

[697] C. Booth, "Preface" to *In Darkest England and the Way Out* (1890).

[698] Ibid.

[699] K.F. Inglis, *Churches and the Working Classes in Victorian England* (1964) pp.194-199.

[700] See "General Booth's New Book", in *Advance!*, November 1890, p.27.

[701] Luke 10:25-37.

> In legislation, the nation was doing nothing to meet the case. The church was doing a good work, but to plunge into the very depths of the existing misery and to dig down to the roots of vice and destitution she needed a more burning enthusiasm and a more powerful and unencumbered organisation...Benevolent societies and organisations were doing good work, but their efforts were too sporadic and too limited, and something more thorough, systematic, and fundamental was necessary.[702]

Farrar's support came notwithstanding his doubts about the theology and methods of the Salvation Army.

However, not everyone would support an organisation led by General Booth. In December 1890 and January 1891, Thomas Huxley wrote no fewer than 12 letters to *The Times* criticising *In Darkest England.*[703] Huxley later published them in a book. He saw Booth's scheme as a tendentious way of making people Christian. As he put it,

> Men are to be made sober and industrious, mainly, that, as washed, shorn, and docile sheep, they may be driven into the narrow theological fold which Mr Booth patronises. If they refuse to enter, for all their moral cleanliness, they will have to take their place among the goats as sinners, only less dirty than the rest.[704]

In his view, "harlotry and intemperance are sore evils, and starvation is hard to bear or even to know of; but the prostitution of the mind, the soddening of the conscience, the dwarfing of manhood are worse calamities".[705] Huxley also accused Booth of the vices that any leader of a sect is accused of today and more: "religious emotionalism"; inculcating "blind obedience" to the chief; "religious fanaticism"; "blackmail"; "extraction of money by intimidation"; "despotic social and religious regimentation"; "fanatical intolerance and personal ambition"

[702] "'In Darkest England'", in *The Times*, 10 November 1890. Farrar followed up his support of the Darkest England initiative with a powerful piece in his opening chapter of *Social and Present-Day Questions* (1892).

[703] For other responses to *In Darkest England*, see K.F. Inglis, *Churches and the Working Classes in Victorian England* (1964) pp.204-208.

[704] T.H. Huxley, *Social Diseases and Worse Remedies* (1891) pp.64-65.

[705] Ibid., p.58.

and (perhaps worst of all) "Boothism" – defined as "the utilisation of the workers for the furtherance of Mr Booth's peculiar projects".[706] Admirers of Huxley have seen this onslaught as an error of judgment.[707] Booth's invariable response to each letter, as it was discussed with his staff, was "Don't answer criticisms. Let's have a good meeting."[708] However, the Salvation Army did not raise the funds required to fulfil the plans set out in *In Darkest England*. From 1893-1894, Booth left the cause of social reform to others and returned to his first cause – "the great gospel of the changed heart".[709] But the direction of the Salvation Army's work had changed and it became part of the British way of life. A conversation between Booth and the young Winston Churchill shows Booth penetrating the Establishment, but as concerned with human salvation as ever. To a question from Churchill of whether Booth thought Churchill was converted, Booth responded, "No...you are not converted, but I think you are convicted."[710]

20.6 The state is deified

The Bitter Cry called for the state to intervene – to meet social need and to pave the way for evangelism. From this, it was not hard for certain Dissenters "to endow the state with religious attributes". For example, "Dale regarded 'Civil authority' as 'a divine institution'. Clifford went further, claiming...that 'the state is more sacred than any church...for the state stands for the whole people in their manifold collective life'".[711] Such perspectives invited the state to take over the role of the churches in good works. This it duly did in the twentieth century. By doing so, it weakened the role of the churches in society and the ties that bound their members together in mutual support. The invocation of the state to meet social need was also consistent with the view of many Dissenters that the Established Church must be removed from education.

[706] Ibid., p.75.
[707] O. Lodge, "Introduction" to T. Huxley, *Lay Sermons* (1910) p.xi.
[708] H. Begbie, *Life of William Booth* (1920) vol.2, p.168.
[709] Ibid., pp.179 and 199-200. It is said that Booth's social work was an expression of his religious conscience, but his view remained that "religious work is the greatest of all *social* works". Author's italics. See ibid., p.200.
[710] Ibid., p.445.
[711] M.R. Watts, *The Dissenters* (2015) vol.3, p.293.

21

WORKING TOGETHER TO WIN THE NATION FOR CHRIST

21.1 Background

William Haslam thought that, in evangelistic terms, "the chief characteristic of our age, as distinguished from every preceding one...is the spirit of unity that binds workers together".[712] Revival meetings might bring ministers and people from five or six denominations together to plead for the "liberation of captives".[713] "Social feuds" between rich and poor were forgotten before the "common object of bringing souls to the feet of Jesus".[714] Evangelism led to touching acts of kindness between members of different denominations. For example, a wealthy farmer who attended the Church of England provided a mare and a dog-cart, together with a weekly salary, to a Nonconformist county evangelist so that he no longer had to walk to his far-flung preaching stations.[715] Ecumenicalism was also evident in the many organisations committed to meeting human need and in the great pan-evangelical societies, such as the Bible Society and the London City Mission.[716] Behind this unity, Haslam discerned the hand of God further manifested by declaration of a "'Week of Prayer' – a time set apart for united prayer, all over the Christian world, for the outpouring of the Holy Spirit".[717] Furthermore, evangelistic ecumenicalism enjoyed practical expression in the work of the YMCA and YWCA – hugely successful interdenominational organisations, operating across nations. D.L. Moody was committed to their work. He started his full-time Christian work in Chicago where

[712] W. Haslam, *"Yet Not I"* (N.D.) p.34.
[713] P. Palmer, "Mrs Palmer's Labours", in *The Revivalist* (1859) p.186.
[714] "Letter from a Lady", in *The Revivalist* (1859) p.174.
[715] G.H. Pike, "Out with a County Evangelist", in *The Sword and the Trowel* (1875) pp.103 and 107.
[716] R.H. Martin, *Evangelicals United* (1983) pp.9-10.
[717] W. Haslam, *"Yet Not I"* (N.D.) pp.33-34

he was responsible for the first purpose-built YMCA building in the United States, a palatial affair. In his missions, he adopted the YMCA and YWCA pattern of Christians of all denominations working together – through united prayer and witness – to advance the work. Some criticised him for this; others attributed his success to it.

For some denominations, reasons of a linked history and outlook made reunion a possibility. For example, in 1868 the York Convocation addressed reunion between the Church of England and the Wesleyan Methodists – as the Wesleyans sought respectability and considered themselves akin to the Establishment. At around the same time, Matthew Arnold called for the Nonconformists to re-establish links with the Established Church – as part of his programme, set out in *Culture and Anarchy*, to rid themselves of their dogmatism. In 1888, the Anglicans drafted the Lambeth Quadrilateral – whereby they articulated the basis upon which reunion might be made with the Roman Catholic and the Orthodox Churches. The following year, notwithstanding, or perhaps because of, the increasing attacks of the Dissenters on the Church for its privileges, the Archbishop of Canterbury indicated the willingness of the Church of England to confer, on the basis of the Lambeth Quadrilateral, with other churches, to see "what steps can be taken, either towards corporate reunion, or towards such relations as may prepare the way for fuller organic unity hereafter".[718]

As the numbers attending the churches began to decline in the last years of the nineteenth century, organisational reunion between denominations became seen as the means of recovering spiritual vitality.[719] Hugh Price Hughes argued in 1891 that the reason why "'the overwhelming majority of the human race are heathen'...was because the churches were divided". Advocates of reunion pointed to the prayer of Jesus in John 17:20-23, to sustain their cause: may they "be brought to complete unity. Then the world will know that you sent me". That there were five major Methodist groups in the United Kingdom suggested that these words were insufficiently heeded.[720] Furthermore, there was a need for more

[718] Cited in E.A. Payne, *The Baptist Union* (1982) p.145. See also C. Oldstone-Moore, *Hugh Price Hughes* (1999) pp.230-239 and 260-266.

[719] M.R. Watts, *The Dissenters* (2015) vol.3, pp.214-215.

[720] Watts tells us that "The argument was repeated time and again over the next century in defiance of the evidence that the Nonconformist churches had grown at their fastest

money as meeting social needs grew in importance. A Methodist New Connection minister noted: "the power of propagation has relatively declined, or has come to be more and more dependent on large material resources...The social forces are against small denominations, and their struggles will be greater."[721]

However, the Baptists were unenthusiastic to Church overtures, but they desired reunion among themselves. In 1891, the General and Particular Baptists came together. The General Baptists (Arminian in tendency) were the smaller denomination. John Clifford, with Spurgeon having come out of the Baptist Union (it had been the main Particular Baptist organisation since 1813), united the Baptist Union with the General Baptists.

Nonconformists drew together through the National Free Church Council. This emerged in the early 1890s to resist the Romanism spreading from the Established Church,[722] to "take common action on great religious and social problems, to strive together to deepen their own spiritual life, and to win England for Jesus Christ".[723] It also reflected their coming together through the various denominational Forward Movements. It drew its members from local councils made-up of Nonconformist evangelicals, without reference to their denomination; there were no official representatives of the individual Nonconformist churches. By 1899, there were 500 councils and federations.[724]

This left the Anglican and Roman Catholic Churches free to discuss the possibility of reunion, which they did between 1894 and 1896. The Archbishop of Canterbury regarded the conversations without enthusiasm – in his view, they were an academic affair that had to be

rate in the years between 1790 and 1840, the period in which they were also the most divided", see ibid., p.213. It was also the period when most of the major Methodist groups came into being. Perhaps the truth referred to in John 17:20-23 was fulfilled when true believers came together to work together – and not by denominational merger.

[721] Cited in R. Currie, *Methodism Divided* (1968) p.88.

[722] The Church's infection "with semi-Romanism...and semi-unbelief" had long been seen by leading Church evangelicals as the reason why the Nonconformists would not embark on the Church's ship, see J.C. Ryle, *Principles for Churchmen* (1884) pp.308-309.

[723] E.K.H. Jordan, *Free Church Unity* (1956) p.30.

[724] Ibid., p.55. See generally M.R. Watts, *The Dissenters* (2015) vol.3, pp.216-217 and C. Oldstone-Moore, *Hugh Price Hughes* (1999) pp.238-240 and 272-280.

undertaken.[725] The Holy See responded by indicating that it did not recognise Anglican ordination.

In Scotland, 1896 saw the union of the Congregational and Evangelical Unions; they had been discussing merger for a decade.[726] James Morison, the latter's founder, died the previous year.

[725] See S. Dark, *Archbishop Davidson and the English Church* (1929) pp.90-96.
[726] Proposed Union Between the Congregational Union and Evangelical Union (1895).

22

THE NEED FOR HOLINESS TO WIN THE NATION FOR CHRIST

22.1 The benefits of holiness

Many Christians recognised that evangelism, practical help, brotherly unity and new theological organisations would only be used by God to change lives, and the nation, if those engaged were holy, that is set apart from the world and living lives of goodness and moral purity. It was said that it was not so much "the *means* employed as the spirit in which the work is done. Let there be more personal consecration, and more self-denial. Let the church be on fire, and the world will soon be in a blaze."[727] The great Methodist evangelist Thomas Cook thought that the "secret" of his effectiveness was that he had learnt "'the lesson that if we would convert sinners, we must revive saints. This is not only needful, because the converts in a period of revival are almost certain to conform to the type of the average professor, but because the harbouring of unkind feelings, the want of charity and forbearance, ill-will, the indulgence of prejudices or animosities, prevent the outpouring of God's Spirit, without which all our efforts are in vain'...Wherefore, in every mission he held great holiness meetings, and often preached on the subject to a thousand people every noon or afternoon for a week."[728]

Many agreed with the need for proper standards of conduct, from all theological parties. Bishop Ryle thought "the standard of living had become painfully low in many quarters".[729] But his standards were high. Bishop Samuel Wilberforce thought that "a resolution to attend theatres or operas disqualified a man for the parochial ministry".[730] Spurgeon,

[727] Author's italics. E. McHardie, *James Turner; or, How to Reach the Masses* (1875) p.viii and T.M. Macdonald, "How to Reach Working Men", in *Homiletical and Pastoral Lectures* (1879) pp.400-402.

[728] J.I. Brice, *The Crowd for Christ* (1934) p.58.

[729] J.C. Ryle, *Holiness* (1979) p.xvii.

[730] O. Chadwick, *The Victorian Church* (1987) pt.1, p.445.

at the end of his life, thought it disqualified a clergyman from being an evangelical. Frederick Temple, as the Bishop of London in the last quarter of the nineteenth century, continued his predecessor's refusal of a licence to Stewart Headlam, as the latter encouraged "young men and young women to be frequent spectators of ballet dancing".[731] But these men were becoming the exception. The great Congregationalist R.W. Dale, in 1880, saw that the taste that avoided the theatre, the ballroom and cards was vanishing; he did not entirely disapprove.[732] Each person had to decide "the true method of Christian living" and, in doing so, recognise no "human authority" but "the supremacy which belongs only to Christ".[733] These were fine sentiments, but fewer people seemed to know how the supremacy of Christ was expressed. As the importance of doctrine seeped out of the churches and the content of the faith became vague, religious ardour dissipated.[734]

22.2 How to achieve holiness

Some remained determined to seek holiness and competing views emerged on how to achieve it.[735] J.C. Ryle set out in his book *Holiness* (1877), the view that triumphed in the late twentieth century. Ryle offered holiness through struggle, self-exertion and the recognition of spiritual warfare. The American Robert Pearsall Smith and his wife, Hannah, opposed this view. For Pearsall Smith, holiness was something that could be obtained instantly through faith, without struggle, almost as a second conversion or baptism – leading to what was called "sinless

[731] K. Leech, "Stewart Headlam, 1847-1924 and the Guild of St Matthew", in *For Christ and the People* (1968) pp.75-76.

[732] R.W. Dale, *The Evangelical Revival* (1880) p.271.

[733] Ibid., pp.271-272.

[734] Ibid., pp.24-25, 161-163 and 169.

[735] These doctrinal differences caused difficulties. A good man could get things wrong. A bastion of evangelicalism, and early Keswick speaker, the Rev. Preb. H. Webb-Peploe, recalled that he had been accused of "Heresy! Heresy!! Damnable Heresy" by "the very centre of evangelical churchmanship", for being party to the first convention – although Webb-Peploe's standing in evangelical circles recovered. H. Webb-Peploe, "Early Keswick Conventions", in *The Keswick Convention* (1907) (C.F. Harford (ed.)) p.39. For a history of the early theological development of Keswick, see I. Randall, "The Keswick Convention and Anglican Evangelical Tensions in the Early Twentieth Century", in *Evangelicalism and the Church of England in the Twentieth Century* (2014) (A. Atherstone and J. Maiden (eds)) pp.89-94. On the background to the growth of the Holiness movement, see J. Kent, *Holding the Fort* (1978) pp.295-355.

perfectionism". Some thought Moody greatly encouraged this view, as "the effect of his teaching is to push the Christian virtues to the background that all the attention may be directed to his central fact that 'faith in Christ can be had this moment'".[736] Pearsall Smith disappeared from the public view after allegations of sexual impropriety.[737] Between the views of Ryle and Pearsall Smith was the so-called "Higher Life" view. This believed that holiness was not to be achieved through an ongoing struggle with the flesh, but through the ongoing walk of faith. Through faith, sin was "perpetually counteracted", but the idea found in Wesleyan convictions (a fourth view) that entire sanctification was possible through faith was rejected. In the nineteenth century it was the Higher Life view that prevailed at Keswick.

22.3 The importance of the Keswick Convention

The bastion of the "Higher Life" view was the annual Keswick Convention, founded in 1875. It was the forerunner of the many conventions that exist today – for taking Christians away from the bustle of everyday life to study the Bible and deepen and refresh spiritual life. By 1907, 10,000 attended Keswick for some part, including day-visitors. The emphasis on holiness and getting away from the daily grind with other Christians energised many of the activities outlined in this Part. It inspired a resting, buoyant trust that was the springboard for the active, manly Christian life that was perceived by many to be the ultimate aspiration for the Christian.[738] Keswick also enabled people to plan together. It also had from its beginning separate ladies' meetings at a time when "few…dared to accept the risen Lord's earliest commission to Mary in the way of giving his message so openly".[739]

After 1888, the Keswick Convention reinforced the importance of overseas missionary endeavours. From that year, its authorised history records that the missionary factor gained a "firm and in some years

[736] "The American Revivalists", in *The Times*, 16 July 1875.

[737] His daughter, Alys, was Betrand Russell's first wife. For an excellent account of the perplexing life and work of the Pearsall Smiths, see N. Scotland, *Apostles of the Spirit and Fire* (2009) pp.199-216.

[738] C. Binfield, *George Williams and the Y.M.C.A* (1973) p.221.

[739] Nugent, "Women at Keswick", in *The Keswick Convention* (1907) (C.F. Harford (ed.)) p.195.

a dominant place in Conventions".[740] For missionary recruiters, the Keswick Convention offered the best avenue to Christian students in Britain.[741] The Convention of 1891 was the means whereby the work of the Student Volunteer Movement for Foreign Missions was publicised in Great Britain. Future Conventions saw many other milestones passed in the development of Christian student work.[742]

Further, as many other organisations turned from orthodoxy in the late nineteenth century, Keswick had another part to play. This time, it was not winning the nation for Christ – it was preserving the faithful remnant. Its focus on holiness enabled it to do that. It believed in something – the traditional Christian doctrines including, as George Reginald Balleine (the historian of the Evangelical party in the Church of England) wrote, "that half-forgotten article of the creed, 'I believe in the Holy Ghost, the Lord and giver of life'".[743] Keswick drew the Anglicans, especially educated Anglicans, because they could afford the time. They would be the dominant evangelical grouping in the twentieth century. The Congregationalists, of whom Spurgeon despaired, rarely attended; nor did the Methodists, having a different view of holiness. In the twentieth century, it was the Congregationalists and Methodists who suffered the sharpest decline in numbers. Keswick preserved orthodoxy only by the judicious appointment of speakers and the orthodoxy of its leadership.[744] It also created its own other-worldly sub-culture, which was not always healthy for the church,[745] especially as its emphasis on one brand of holiness created a division within evangelicalism. However, although Keswick was not perfect, by bringing together Christians and giving them a view of a greater whole – while maintaining a biblical basis – it contributed to keeping orthodoxy alive in the difficult times to come.

[740] J.C. Pollock, *The Keswick Story* (1964) p.85.
[741] Ibid., p.112.
[742] Ibid., p.115.
[743] G.R. Balleine, *A History of the Evangelical Party* (1911) p.200.
[744] J.C. Pollock, *The Keswick Story* (1964) pp.96 and 103.
[745] Lloyd-Jones criticised Keswick for having contributed to a reduction of interest in biblical theology: I.H. Murray, *D. Martyn Lloyd-Jones: The Fight of Faith 1939-1981* (1990) pp.73-74.

23

NEW OPPORTUNITIES: INCREASING NATIONAL WEALTH AND LEISURE

23.1 Introduction

From the time of Wesley until 1859, the nation's wealth grew substantially. A Wesleyan minister observed that

> Men who were poor and humble at the time of their conversion have found themselves in good society, have been encouraged and aided by good practical suggestions and, stimulated by example, they have been taught industry, economy and enterprise, by the Holy Bible and a correct conscience; and, under all these influences, they have found themselves rising rapidly in wealth and consideration.[746]

The same observer reckoned that accumulating wealth was a trial that could arrest the march to heaven,[747] although there were biblical checks to prevent the nation plunging into hedonism, such as Sabbath observance. Robert Maguire, preaching at St Andrew's Holborn in 1859, asked "What is it that makes England what she is but because she honours the Sabbath?"[748] Contemporaries referred to the European "Continental Sabbath" as the explanation for why Britain had been lifted above her near neighbours. Writing in the late 1850s, George Eliot observed: "Evangelicalism...brought into existence...the idea of duty, the recognition of something to be lived for beyond the mere satisfaction of self...There was a divine work to be done in life, a rule of goodness

[746] "The Church in the Furnace", in *The Revivalist* (1858) p.125.
[747] Ibid., p.126.
[748] R. Maguire, *The Sabbath and its Perpetual Obligation* (1859) p.15.

higher than the opinion of their neighbours."[749] The following year, John Stuart Mill raised the spectre that the stricter Calvinists and Methodists might "put down all public and nearly all private amusements; especially music, dancing and public games".[750]

National wealth continued to grow between 1859 and 1900. Some saw the nation's wealth as a sign of God's favour, to be used for his purposes. During the 1860s and the following decades charitable giving flourished and with it an array of evangelical organisations. Others saw the new wealth as flowing from the nation's inherent talent and greatness – to be spent on self, or family. In 1869, Matthew Arnold complained: "Never did people believe anything more firmly, than nine Englishmen out of ten at the present day believe that our greatness and welfare are proved by our being so very rich".[751]

Changing theological attitudes influenced changing attitudes to wealth. *The Revival* warned that a new theology was appearing – "Religion made easy". "In these days of 'modern progress'", it explained, "the once straight and narrow way is become a 'royal road', a smooth and easy path".[752] Farrar, in his 1870 Hulsean lectures, noted that increased wealth might explain the infidelity of the times, as men, without a proper theological framework, became absorbed with its delights. In his view, "At the zenith of their civilisation nations have often been at the nadir of their faith" and "material advance may be moral retrogression".[753] Spurgeon – not one to be diverted from the Lord's work – perhaps gave a nod in the direction of contemporary culture when he opened the preface to the 1875 volume of *The Sword and the Trowel* with the words: "we have endeavoured, month by month, to provide for your entertainment and edification". The need for leisure and entertainment coloured all aspects of life across most classes and regions. This was particularly manifested in the ever-widening readership that the novelists drew – and in sport.[754]

[749] G. Eliot, *Scenes of Clerical Life* (1988) (T. Noble (ed.)) p.228.
[750] J.S. Mill, "On Liberty", in *J.S. Mill On Liberty in Focus* (1991) (J. Gray and G.W. Smith (eds)) p.101.
[751] M. Arnold, *Culture and Anarchy* (2009) p.39.
[752] "Christian Self-Denial", in *The Revival*, 6 July 1865, p.1.
[753] F.W. Farrar, *The Witness of History to Christ* (1892) pp.12-14.
[754] H. McLeod, *Religion and Society in England, 1850-1914* (1996) pp.197-200. See also M.R. Watts, *The Dissenters* (2015) vol.3, pp.163-167.

By the last decade of the nineteenth century, if not a little before, the ascent of leisure and entertainment in the national consciousness became unchallenged. In 1890, Mrs Sumner noted that it was fashionable to "cry up two panaceas for all the ills of life – secular culture and recreation".[755] Towards the end of the century, philanthropy declined. F.W. Farrar thought that as wealth had "increased, the proportion given to the service of God, and our neighbour, has become less and less".[756] In wealthy Liverpool, Bishop Ryle's appeals on behalf of hospitals, lifeboats and a seaman's orphan institution did not raise the expected funds.[757] He was also disappointed by the funds raised for the diocese's cathedral. The historian G.M. Trevelyan explained that "When religion had been transformed, from the 'public and documented system of beliefs, practices and aspirations' that it had been when the Queen came to the throne, into a 'provision for personal needs,' it could no longer influence the conduct of those who felt no need for themselves".[758] Entertainment became the replacement.

This is not to say that in the 1890s the nation entirely abandoned itself to hedonism. For example, the settlement movement – whereby graduates in the late nineteenth century went to live among the poor – was a new expression of "the obligations which the classes who possess culture and leisure have towards those who are less richly endowed".[759] However, as orthodoxy weakened, the numbers attracted by such movements dwindled and the motives for joining such movements became more mixed.

23.2 Limits on leisure activities

For leisure to expand its ambit, belief in the benefits of Sabbath observance – and the legal limits on Sabbath leisure activities – had to be eroded. Early changes were soon made. In 1860, the Crystal Palace was open on a Sunday. A further notable change arose in 1866, when Thomas

[755] Mrs Sumner, *Women's Work Among Women* (1890) p.2.
[756] F.W. Farrar, *Social and Present-Day Questions* (1892) p.101.
[757] See Farley, *J.C. Ryle, First Bishop of Liverpool* (2000) pp.194-204. Funds in Reading also seem tighter at the end of the century, see S. Yeo, *Religion and Voluntary Organisations in Crisis* (1976) p.149 and see generally S. Flew, *Philanthropy and the Funding of the Church of England 1856-1914* (2015).
[758] G.M. Trevelyan, *English Social History* (1978) p.506.
[759] J. Gorst, "'Settlements' in England and America", in *The Universities and the Social Problem* (1895) (J.M. Knapp (ed.)) p.3.

Huxley launched his "Sunday evenings for the people lectures". These lectures were on social subjects for the well-being of mankind. In 1868, the Court of Common Pleas (Baxter v. Langley) ruled that these lectures did not violate the eighteenth-century statute prohibiting entertainments or debates on a Sunday.[760] The statute was neatly circumvented by mixing up the lectures with sacred music – and calling the governing association the "Recreative Religionists". It was explained to the court that "the meaning of the phrase was not recreation in the ordinary sense, but that what was intended was a new form of religion by which it was hoped to interest the people at large in religious services".[761] In any event, the court refused to intervene. A few years later, in Liverpool, sacred music was again the weapon to open up the Sabbath. There, J.C. Ryle fought proposals to open a hall for sacred music – and an exhibition of pictures – on a Sunday. Although he lost these battles, they illustrate the issues over which battles were fought and the continuing limit on Sabbath leisure.[762] In 1896, the British Museum opened on the Sabbath.[763] But, in 1899, the storm of protest was sufficiently strong to stop certain newspapers publishing on a Sunday.[764]

By the end of the century, many clergy were against strict observance of the Sabbath. Some were against it because it suggested one day for God and six for man,[765] while the Ritualists with their intense focus on the eucharist, were less concerned about the rest of the day. Others, like Davidson, the Bishop of Rochester and a future Archbishop of Canterbury, agitated for the opening of libraries, museums and art galleries on a Sunday – so as to broaden the education of the working

[760] "The Court of Common Pleas, Westminster, Nov.19", in *The Times*, 20 November 1868.

[761] Ibid. For a summary of a lecture and justification for it, see C.M. Davies, *Unorthodox London* (1876) pp.29-34.

[762] I.D. Farley, *J.C. Ryle, First Bishop of Liverpool* (2000) pp.152-158. Most of the interested public supported him. The constant pressure of a few council members in the opposite interest was in the end decisive.

[763] Shaftesbury had killed off an earlier proposal, in 1856, see J.L. Hammond and B. Hammond, *Lord Shaftesbury* (1936) p.220.

[764] See J. Harries, *G. Campbell Morgan* (1930) p.60. In the 1870s the CPAS referred to the Sunday newspaper as the "destroyer" of religious principles in children and the "demoralising periodical", see E.J. Speck, *Church Pastoral-Aid Society* (1881) p.180.

[765] W.H.B. Proby, *Annals of the "Low-Church" Party in England* (1888) vol.1, p.379.

classes (he was a trustee of the British Museum). Using the Sabbath to educate artisans and the lower middle classes was increasingly tantalising to many church leaders.[766] The Trades Union Congress allied itself with the Sabbatarians – against Sunday opening. Serious evangelicals regarded it as "robbing the working classes of their rightful privilege of rest on the Lord's day".[767]

23.3 The impact of growing wealth on the working class

For members of the working class, increasing national wealth did not immediately lead to a substantial increase in free-time for church-going or leisure activities. In the early 1870s, the average working hours for manual workers was reduced – but only to 57 hours per week. As late as 1896, Thomas Mann wrote that some men, even in full-time work, earned so little that the mother must rise at five in the morning, leave her child with the nurse and start work at six with the men – until returning at night to commence house duties. Otherwise, the family starved.[768] Nevertheless, by the late 1870s churches were concerned to influence such leisure time as working men[769] had through the institutional churches and other means, while sport became a particular allure to the working man.

23.4 The impact of growing wealth on the wealthy

Leisure, as an alternative to religion, had the strongest allure for the upper and middle-classes. They had the time and money needed to engage in leisure. By the 1860s, the Bible Society noted the difficulty in getting out the middle-classes to collect subscriptions for Bibles, although they would collect and give money to fund others to do so.[770] Such developments meant that the gap in understanding between the working and middle-classes grew, to national disadvantage. On 1 April 1875 D.L. Moody warned a congregation – made up mainly of the middle classes and those who contemporaries considered as 'better' – that "Many

[766] See S. Dark, *Archbishop Davidson and the English Church* (1929) pp.66-70.
[767] E. Trotter, *Lord Radstock* (N.D.) p.163.
[768] T. Mann, *A Socialist's View of Religion and the Churches* (1896) p.15.
[769] T.M. Macdonald, "How to Reach Working Men", in *Homiletical and Pastoral Lectures* (1879) p.411.
[770] L. Howsam, *Cheap Bibles* (1991) pp.197-200.

Christians have so many things that their hearts are set upon here, and live so much like the world, that the world does not have any confidence in the Christianity of the nineteenth century."[771] As we have seen, Mrs Sumner, the founder of the Mothers' Union, thought that excess entertainment made the rich too busy to teach their children the faith.

This latter development may also explain Sarah Flew's finding in *Philanthropy and the Funding of the Church of England 1856–1914* (2015) that from the 1880s voluntary giving to the home mission organisations by the upper and middle classes that she examined fell away, as a generation of philanthropists died and were not replaced. Flew suggests that the reason for this reduction in giving by the wealthy may have been caused by a failure to teach the younger generation the concept of Christian stewardship. She also attributes the reduction in giving to the growth of the charity bazaar as a means of fundraising; this reflected the need of the giver to receive something for their gift and to be entertained in the process. William Wilberforce would also have probably explained the development by the increasing unwillingness of the Church to teach that everyone would "stand before God's judgment seat".

In the last quarter of the nineteenth century, C.H. Spurgeon's annual visits to the French Riviera, and especially his beloved Menton, popularised overseas holidays for Christians. Attending him, or visiting him there, was often a substantial group of people – and his holiday experiences were written-up and found their way into *The Sword and the Trowel*, where they were found to be "far more interesting than ordinary guide-books".[772] At Menton Spurgeon found rest from his intensive work and believed that "If anything can make me young and strong again, this will."[773]

[771] D.L. Moody, *The London Discourses of D.L. Moody* (1875) p.126.
[772] C.H. Spurgeon, *Autobiography* (1973) vol.2, pp.376-377.
[773] Ibid., p.368.

24

MORALITY

24.1 Overview

Christie Davies – in her insightful work *The Strange Death of Moral Britain* (2004) – writes that the last half of the nineteenth century witnessed the birth of what she calls "respectable Britain", a land where a great mass of the population adopted a spontaneous moral order that led to "a remarkable fall in the incidence both of crimes of violence and of crimes of dishonesty in England and Wales". Contemporaries noted that "Before the opening of the theatres for preaching the gospel, it was not safe for a decent person to walk on Sunday morning" through certain London districts. By 1864, with "tract distribution, street preaching, prayer, and other meetings" common – and with many conversions – it was possible to "walk quietly and tolerably securely from Bishopsgate to Bethnal Green".[774] Richard Carwardine comments that "At the height of the [1859] revival in Sunderland and North Shields there were no criminal cases to bring before the assize courts, and theatres and taverns were apparently closed".[775] In 1869, an evangelist working in the Golden Lane area "among the scum of London" remarked that "What all the paraphernalia of the law could not effect, namely, the prevention of crime, and the regeneration of the degraded inhabitants of Golden Lane, the gospel is accomplishing."[776] Christie Davies notes, more generally, that "Larcenies recorded by the police dropped from about 500 for every 100,000 of the population in 1857 and 1858 to fewer than

[774] "East of London", in *The Revival*, 19 May 1864, p.313.
[775] R. Carwardine, *Transatlantic Revivalism* (2006) p.196.
[776] "The Poor of Golden-Lane", in *The Revival*, 30 December 1869, p.5. In any event, morality through Royal Proclamation was on the decline. The last proclamation against vice was in June 1860, as parliamentary sovereignty eroded the role of royal proclamations, see A. Hunt, *Governing Morals* (1999) p.227.

300 in the 1890s".[777] At the same time, the efficiency of the police in detecting crime increased. In 1876, a barrister commented: "there never was in any nation of which we have a history, a time in which life and property were so secure as they are at present in England".[778] Marx and the sociologists had predicted that the working class, in their misery, would express their rage by resorting to crime. However, by 1900 the people "were more honest, more respectable, more moral"[779] than they had been in 1800 – despite the greater opportunities for envy that the nation's increased wealth brought.

Such moral change in the nation did not surprise evangelicals like J.C. Ryle – even if it did Marx. Ryle thought that it was not a nation's possessions, science, manufacturers or its democracy that kept a nation great. After all, since the beginning of the world, many great nations had fallen – including Egypt, Athens, Rome and, most recently, Spain. Rather, he affirmed, "The sinews of a nation's strength are truthfulness, honesty, sobriety, purity, temperance, economy, diligence, brotherly kindness, charity among its inhabitants". Ryle asked rhetorically, is there any "surer way of producing these characteristics in a people than by encouraging, and fostering, and spreading, and teaching pure Scriptural Christianity?".[780] As Gertrude Himmelfarb observed, "what sustained the Victorian ethic was essentially what had first sustained it – an unsectarian, latitudinarian evangelicalism".[781]

24.2 Sexual morality

A key aspect of respectable Britain was its growing sexual purity, although Secularists like Charles Bradlaugh were unconvinced of the merits of this.[782] Queen Victoria and the "purity of her court"[783] set the

[777] C. Davies, *The Strange Death of Moral Britain* (2004) p.3. See also G. Himmelfarb, *The De-moralization of Society* (1995) p.39.

[778] Cited in C. Davies, *The Strange Death of Moral Britain* (2004) p.7.

[779] Ibid., p.9. They were, though, far from perfect. Falsehoods told for gain were considered "trivial failings", see "Evangelistic Preaching: Why is it not more Successful?", in *The Christian Monthly and Family Treasury* (1882) p.145.

[780] J.C. Ryle, *Principles for Churchmen* (1884) p.336.

[781] G. Himmelfarb, *Victorian Minds* (1975) p.291.

[782] Bradlaugh's willingness to support sexual immorality helped turn some Secularist leaders to Christianity as providing the only basis for morality, see T. Larsen, *Crisis of Doubt* (2006) pp.123-124 and 160-161.

[783] E.H. Bickersteth, *Charge* (1886) p.29.

example. In the 1870s and 1880s, many of those who shaped – or were the products of – the 1859 Revival combined to provide the impetus for greater legislative intervention in sexual morality. The campaigns for sexual purity were rooted in the belief that social stability was dependent on public and private morality. Furthermore, in the 1880s the first signs of challenges to Britain's worldwide economic dominance were appearing – in the form of the United States and Germany. Spurgeon had taught that although, for individuals, "their punishment or reward is reserved for the next state", as "nations will not exist in the next world; there is no such thing as a judgment of nations" on "the last great day". Instead "The trial and punishment of nations takes place in this state."[784] The view was articulated that Rome fell to the barbarians; other nations were falling; and the United Kingdom would go the same way, if it did not change.[785] Later, Edward Bickersteth thought that the extent to which the "untold blessings to England and to that vast colonial empire entrusted to England" was due to the "wise and even government of our Queen", would be known on the last "day when the secrets of Divine Providence are disclosed".[786]

The Salvation Army was often at the forefront of sexual purity campaigns. In the 1880s, an extensive, white, sex slave-trade existed in London and throughout Europe. In 1885, a campaign against it began with a series of articles by the journalist W.T. Stead in the *Pall Mall Gazette* – aided by Bramwell Booth of the Salvation Army and Josephine Butler. It has been said that W.T. Stead "exposed the hell of child-harlotry with a force and energy never before known in journalism".[787] Then, in a sting operation organised by the Salvation Army, a child called Eliza Armstrong was purchased for five pounds from her mother. Her virginity confirmed by an independent third party, the plot was sprung. It caused a further massive furore in the press. The *Pall Mall*'s editor, Stead, was an actor in the plot.[788] This highly publicised operation,

[784] C.H. Spurgeon, "The Voice of the Cholera", in *Metropolitan Tabernacle Pulpit* (1867) vol.12, p.446.

[785] J. Weeks, *Sex, Politics and Society* (1989) p.87.

[786] E.H. Bickersteth, *Charge* (1886) pp.29-30.

[787] H. Begbie, *Life of William Booth* (1920) vol.2, p.42.

[788] Stead, is a curious figure in Christian history. Some thought him obsessed by sex, see M.R. Watts, *The Dissenters* (2015) vol.3, pp.298-300 and 303-304. He lost his life when *The Titanic* went down in 1912.

which marks the beginning of modern campaign journalism, contributed to the age of consent being raised from 13 to 16 by the Criminal Law Amendment Act 1885. It had only been raised to 13 in 1875. The Criminal Law Amendment Act also introduced new prohibitions against homosexual behaviour.[789] The same year saw the establishment of the National Vigilance Association, as the successor to the Society for the Suppression of Vice.[790] Its Council included Bramwell Booth, John Clifford, Hugh Price Hughes and W.T. Stead. It quickly spawned local committees, thereby creating a regional level of organisation for areas such as Sunderland and the North East and Birmingham and the Midland counties.[791] *The British Weekly* wrote of the national concern for chastity as a great uprising "which any statesman will treat with contempt at his peril".[792] It observed that the shops around the Strand, where indecent books and pictures were sold, were under "rigorous supervision".[793] In 1899, the London Council for the Promotion of Public Morality was established. The evangelist Samuel Chadwick had as one of his four principles of evangelism: "That it is an important part of the evangelist's sacred calling to hunt the wolf, i.e., to make war upon organised evil."[794]

However, it is possible to over-emphasise compliance with "Victorian respectability" in the sexual arena – certainly outside the committed Christian community.[795] In the 1860s, the Contagious Diseases Acts were quietly and quickly slipped through Parliament; they affirmed state-sanctioned prostitution where the prostitutes lived near military installations or in garrison towns. The justification for the Acts was said to be one of necessity. If this was true, it was suggested, God was

[789] See J. Weeks, *Sex, Politics and Society* (1989) pp.86-89.

[790] See "National Vigilance Association", in J. Green, *Encyclopedia of Censorship* (1990) pp.377-378 and C. Oldstone-Moore, *Hugh Price Hughes* (1999) pp.146-148.

[791] M. Huggins, *Vice and Victorians* (2016) pp.154-155. Huggins provides a good overview of the organisations that multiplied to bring about "respectable Britain" in the Victorian period, but is more circumspect as to their successes, see ibid., pp.147-171.

[792] "The Creed and Hope of Progress", in *The British Weekly*, 5 November 1886, p.1.

[793] "Tempted London", *The British Weekly*, 16 March 1888, p.366.

[794] J.I. Brice, *The Crowd for Christ* (1934) p.98.

[795] Even within that community voices were raised in the early 1880s to suggest that the possibility of a "persecution of Christians as Christians" was because they were not forceful enough in upholding sexual purity, see J. Butler, *Modern Heathenism Caused by Christian Faithlessness* (N.D.).

unjust in punishing those who satisfied their lusts with prostitutes.[796] Hugh Price Hughes argued that "the Contagious Diseases Acts are the flag – the visible sign of the triumph of lust. As long as that foul banner floats defiantly over the Palace of Westminster, the whole world can see that the allied forces of atheism, materialistic science, and debauchery have triumphed over Christian morals and humanity."[797] It was not until 1886 that the campaign by Josephine Butler and others to have repealed the Contagious Diseases Acts was successful. Furthermore, sexual fidelity was often lacking at the most illustrious levels. For example, when Winston Churchill was born on 30 November 1874, his parents had been married but seven months.[798] His father was a Cabinet minister and younger son of the Duke of Marlborough. Churchill's father died of what was thought to be syphilis. Nevertheless, illegitimacy fell steadily from its mid-century peak of around seven per cent, to four per cent by the century's end[799] – and first pregnancies before marriage fell from around 40 per cent of first pregnancies in the early nineteenth century to under 20 per cent in the early twentieth century.[800] However, at the end of the nineteenth century, even with a growing emphasis on the traditional family in evangelistic enterprises, Charles Booth commented: "With the lowest classes premarital relations are very common, perhaps even usual",[801] but matters were much better than they had been.

Further, just as aggressive evangelism gave rise to an aggressive intellectual attack on Christianity, so – as Jeffrey Weeks observes – "the moralistic campaigns around sexuality encouraged, as a response, a more radical position on sexuality".[802] The last decades of the nineteenth

[796] C. Oldstone-Moore, *Hugh Price Hughes* (1999) pp.35 and 37.

[797] Ibid., p.67.

[798] B. Johnson, *The Churchill Factor* (2014) p.40. Lord Curzon in the 1890s cbserved "the convention... that physical relationships must be restricted to married friends or girls from other backgrounds", D. Gilmour, *Curzon* (1994) pp.104-105.

[799] The level of illegitimacy in 1870 might be higher by between 10 and 30 per cent than the statistics suggest, see C. Davies, *The Strange Death of Moral Britain* (2004) p.15. Illegitimacy tended to be more of a problem in the rural districts, see P. Laslett, *Bastardy and its Comparative History* (1980) p.63.

[800] J. Weeks, *Sex, Politics and Society* (1989) p.73 See also P. Laslett, *Bastardy and its Comparative History* (1980) pp.54-55 who suggests a higher figure for first conceptions before marriage.

[801] See J. Weeks, *Sex, Politics and Society* (1989) p.60.

[802] Ibid., p.91.

century witnessed the emergence of "groups of people with a much more clearly defined sense of a homosexual identity".[803] Perhaps the growth in boarding schools encouraged the "simple substitutional homosexuality" that H.G. Wells observed amongst boarders at his school in the 1870s.[804] Further, the Catholic and Anglo-Catholic revivals were providing "a safe, queer space for the non-heterosexually inclined".[805] In Samuel Butler's *The Way of all Flesh*, Pryer, the High Church curate, with Ritualist friends, is said to declare, in the late 1850s, that "the priest must be absolutely sexless".[806] Some were already raising questions about Cardinal Newman's sexual attitudes – and Archbishop Benson's wife was sharing a bed with Lucy Tait, the daughter of the previous Archbishop of Canterbury.[807]

The general commitment to Christian morality was accompanied with a commitment by Christians to those who fell short. In 1860 C.H. Spurgeon preached to the Bloomsbury Baptists a sermon on behalf of the Society for the Rescue of Young Women and Children. He began by making it clear that adultery involved two parties. In contemporary society "he could not see why the sin of the man should be slurred over, and that of the woman brought forth". Society punished the women and thrust them out of every home and association. The Society for the Rescue of Young Women and Children was doing a good work, but its funds were exhausted. He added, "if there was anyone who could refuse to contribute on that morning to such a benevolent object, he did not envy him. He trusted there would be few such."[808] The *Younghusband Report* of 1959 picked out Josephine Butler and Dr Barnardo as among the few "courageous and far-sighted people" whose work with unmarried women and their children had helped to change social attitudes.[809]

[803] Ibid., p.111.

[804] H.G. Wells, *Experiment in Autobiography* (1969) vol.1, p.81.

[805] T.W. Jones, *Sexual Politics in the Church of England, 1857-1957* (2013) p.162.

[806] S. Butler, *The Way of all Flesh* (1966 (Penguin)) pp.260 and see also 257.

[807] T.W. Jones, *Sexual Politics in the Church of England, 1857-1957* (2013) pp.162-171.

[808] "Mr Spurgeon on the Social Evil", in *The Observer*, 15 April 1860. Under the "spirit of revival" many 'fallen women' were reclaimed. Their refuge previously called a 'penitentiary' and "very like a prison – gave place to the new… so that no harsh voice sounded, but rather the silver note of compassion – 'Go in peace and sin no more'," see G.E. Morgan, *R.C. Morgan: His Life and Times* (1909) pp.145-146.

[809] *Report of the Working Party on Social Workers in the Local Health and Welfare Services* (1959) para.192.

24.3 Changes in moral outlook towards the end of the century
Notwithstanding the difficulties of compliance with sexual morals, Davies argues that sustaining respectable Britain was a world view "that assumed that individuals were autonomous moral agents responsible for their own behaviour, that the innocent ought to be protected, the virtuous rewarded, and the guilty punished".[810] This is what she poignantly calls "moral Britain" – and it was sustained by the continuing impact of evangelical theology. Davies discerns the origins of the death of moral Britain as being in the last years of the nineteenth century. In those years also, many in the governing, educated and wealthy elites turned from the view that individuals were responsible actors to the view that they were the victims of circumstance or evolutionary forces beyond their control. The welfare of the masses was to be administered "in such a way as to minimise harm regardless of merit or guilt of the individuals concerned".[811] Furthermore, by the 1890s "to enthuse about suicide… was standard form among aesthetes and would-be bohemians".[812]

Such developments coincide with the increasing influence of Liberal Catholic theology; and William Wilberforce's view – that there was a divine judge to whom all would give account – ceasing to be widely taught in the churches. At the time, Holman Hunt, that most Protestant of the Pre-Raphaelite Brotherhood, observed in a letter to a sceptical friend that "we have a theory that there is no personal God, no Father watching over us and judging us, which in 100 years is steadily disintegrating society and producing fatal consequences, of which we as yet see not the end, which, as I believe, will be very terrible before long".[813] It was ironic that, as the incarnation and the idea of God dwelling with man replaced the atonement as the central issue of theology, many of the nation's leaders assumed that life was a game of blind chance. But then,

[810] C. Davies, *The Strange Death of Moral Britain* (2004) p.xi.
[811] Ibid., p.11. J.C. Pringle, attributed "the destruction of the idea of man as a responsible moral and spiritual being" in social work to 1885-1886 onwards, see J.C. Pringle, *Social Work of the London Churches* (1937) pp.210, 221 and 224.
[812] O. Anderson, *Suicide in Victorian and Edwardian England* (1987) p.242. To the extent that the figures are accurate, the number of suicides in England and Wales per million people slowly rose in the last half of the nineteenth century, see ibid., 80-81, although the rates varied by sex, age and locality, see generally ibid. From the 1870s, voluntary euthanasia "had articulate advocates", see ibid., p.243.
[813] W.B. Scott, *Autobiographical Notes of the Life of William Bell Scott* (1892) (W. Minto (ed.)) vol.1, p.314.

perhaps the incarnation was being used only to bless the practices of the Establishment?

By 1880, one leading Congregational teacher observed: "In morals we think of our own conscience – not of God's law; of our self-respect – not of God's approval; and we are distressed by self-reproach – not by God's displeasure and God's anger".[814] Perhaps such a change in morality did not surprise many. In 1861, as *The Christian Observer* noted, if the view of the authors of *Essays and Reviews* prevailed, then nothing of Christianity was likely to remain "excepting an inherently feeble system of morals, shorn of the help of all the motives which the gospel brings into action, and independent of divine grace".[815] By the end of the nineteenth century, the views of the authors of *Essays and Reviews* were prevailing in many quarters.

[814] R.W. Dale, *The Evangelical Revival* (1880) p.169.

[815] "The School of the Essayists, and the Church of England", in 61 *The Christian Observer for the Year 1861* (1861) p.30.

25

NUMBERS

25.1 Overview

Even after the great revival of 1859-1860, the number of people not entering a place of worship remained in many places stubbornly high. In London in 1866, Spurgeon thought that "the habitual forsakers of public worship are probably in a large majority".[816] *The Times*, a few years later, thought that the numbers not attending church were slightly lower – at a third of Londoners.[817] All the same, as far as overall attendances were concerned, in comparison with earlier ages, the third quarter of the nineteenth century was a good time for the churches. Local surveys produced by the regional press showed that, at least until the 1880s, the growth in Church and chapel attendance matched – if not at times exceeded – the rising population. Spurgeon knew of places "in England where there is scarcely a soul to be found at home at the hour of public worship".[818] At the Old Meeting House, Kidderminster, John Marsden, in an eleven and a half-year ministry, received into his church upwards of 300 people. In 1874, his successor wrote: "our position, numerically and financially, can scarcely ever have been better".[819] The Anglicans also rode the rising tide. For example, Edward Bickersteth, in his charge to

[816] C.H. Spurgeon, "The Voice of the Cholera", in *Metropolitan Tabernacle Pulpit* (1867) vol.12, p.448. In 1860, to give a sense of the magnitude of the work before it, the Scripture Readers' Association cited figures presented before the House of Lords that, in Southwark, 68 per cent of the population attended no place of worship; in Lambeth, 60.5 per cent; in Tower Hamlets, 53.5 per cent; in Finsbury, 53 per cent; and in Westminster, 50 per cent, see "The Sixteenth Report of the Church of England Scripture Readers' Association", in 2 *The Scripture Readers' Journal* (1856-60) p.416.

[817] "The Mission Services", in *The Times*, 23 November 1869.

[818] C.H. Spurgeon, "The Voice of the Cholera", in *Metropolitan Tabernacle Pulpit* (1867) vol.12, p.448.

[819] G. Hunsworth, *Baxter's Nonconformist Descendants* (1874) pp.69-70.

his diocese of Exeter, rejoiced in having confirmed 6,786 persons in the year to 7 May 1886. He thought that in only four per cent of his parishes were there "careless pastors", neither caring or growing the flock. He believed that the Church of England was "immeasurably more firmly rooted in the affections of her people than it was fifty years ago".[820]

It was only in the 1880s – Professor Chadwick suggests 1887[821] – that Church and chapel attendance, although not declining, ceased to match population growth. In that year Holden Pike, in his memoir of Queen Victoria's jubilee, includes in the list of the achievements of her reign "the growth of religious denominations… never before was there such an era of church and chapel building, of extension of mission abroad, and of philanthropic enterprise at home".[822] Meanwhile, the results of the various local surveys were pored over[823] – not because of what they suggested about the national standing of Christianity, although that was important – but because of what they indicated about the relative strengths of the Church of England and the Nonconformists. As the number of Nonconformists waxed, the case for the former to enjoy the privileges of being the Established Church waned.

25.2 1859-1880s: keeping up with the Nonconformists

In 1882, Andrew Mearns, the Secretary of the London Congregational Union, drew together the results from various newspaper surveys and published them, in table-form, under the heading *Census of Attendance at Public Worship.*[824] In the 78 towns covered in England and Wales, with a combined population of 3.629 million people, it suggested that

[820] E.H. Bickersteth, *Charge* (1886) pp.7, 15-16 and 30.

[821] O. Chadwick, *The Victorian Church* (1987) pt.2, p.232 and M.R. Watts, *The Dissenters* (2015) vol.3, pp.85-91. See also E.R. Wickham, *Church and People in an Industrial City* (1969) p.171; R. Gill, *The 'Empty' Church Revisited* (2003) pp.110-134; D.W. Bebbington, *The Nonconformist Conscience* (1982) p.2; and D.A. Reid, "Playing and Praying", in *Cambridge Urban History of Britain* (1840-1950) (2000) (M. Daunton (ed.)) vol.3, p.800. Some contemporaries thought a decline in church attendance might already have set in – see, for example, J.M. Lang, "The Decline in Church Attendance", in *The Christian Monthly and Family Treasury* (1882) pp.11-12.

[822] G.H. Pike, *Victoria Queen and Empress* (1887) p.95.

[823] "Church and Chapel Attendance", in *The Times*, 26 December 1881. There was no national census into religion similar to that of 1851, until 1979.

[824] It had a separate table for attendances at certain Scottish towns and cities. At Edinburgh, attendances numbered 101,606, out of a population of 228,190.

Church and chapel attendance on any Sunday was around 41.37 per cent of the population. However, this calculation made no allowance for those attending more than once. Making the assumption that Horace Mann had made in his report of 1851, for those going more than once, then around 25.5 per cent of the population attended church on a given Sunday. Another commentator, C.S. Miall, thought that the numbers attending more than one service had changed since 1851. He produced figures published in numerous newspapers, including *The Times* and *The Manchester Guardian*, for total attendances – on the basis that one quarter of the worshippers at the two services combined attended only one service.[825] On this basis, Miall calculated that 36.16 per cent of the population in the towns surveyed went to church. Some observers thought one third was a more fitting deduction, but he preferred to be cautious on numbers. In nearly every town evening services were larger than the morning by around 20 per cent. Today, the differences between the 1851 and 1881 surveys, in the aggregate numbers attending church, are explained on a number of grounds. These include differences in the weather on the day of the surveys; difficulties in counting those who went to church more than once; simple inaccuracies in the compilation of the various censuses; and by the fact that the Mearns Census was not national.[826] Considerable disparities existed in the level of church-going between towns. For example, in Liverpool, only 19.9 per cent of the population went to church; while in Barnsley, the figure was 16.8 per cent. However, in historic towns, such as Gloucester and Hastings, 50.7 per cent and 52.7 per cent of their respective populations attended church.[827] This gave credibility to Anglican arguments that the censuses of the early 1880s, by excluding the rural parishes, failed to reveal their

[825] "The Statistics of Church and Chapel Attendance", in *The Manchester Guardian*, 27 December 1881 and "Church and Chapel Attendance", in *The Times*, 26 December 1881. Mann had assumed, in 1851, that half of those attending in the afternoon had not been present in the morning – and one-third of those present in the evening had not been at either service.

[826] O. Chadwick, *The Victorian Church* (1987) pt.2, pp.218-238. Anecdotal evidence suggests that, at the end of the 1870s, the Anglicans were unaware of any decline in church going, see T.M. Macdonald, "How to Reach Working Men", in *Homiletical and Pastoral Lectures* (1879) p.388.

[827] "The Statistics of Church and Chapel Attendance", in *The Manchester Guardian*, 27 December 1881.

true national numerical strength.

The issue for the Church of England was keeping up with the Nonconformists. C.S. Miall provocatively published a table of six major towns that showed that, in connection with the "burning question"[828] of the day (the relative strengths of the denominations), the Church of England and the Nonconformists had, respectively, 36.9 per cent and 55.6 per cent of attendances at public worship.[829] However, the Bishop of Winchester argued that the surveys did not accurately reflect the rural strength of the Church of England.[830] Bishop Lightfoot, at Durham, also questioned the accuracy of such surveys, asserting that "they are instituted by particular persons with special ends in view". He believed that the surveys omitted the "early communions, mission-room services, children's schoolroom services and the like". He believed that there had been a "recent quickening of Church life", which swelled aggregate attendances.[831] In any event, the Church of England remained by far the largest denomination.

The Salvation Army added significantly to Nonconformist numbers. In 1881, a survey of 14 major towns suggested that its worshippers constituted 5.35 per cent of the total population.[832] At Hull, it made up 11,394 of the 63,138 people who attended a service, according to the Mearns 1882 Census. Its presence was the difference between there being a slight rise in the percentage of the population being worshippers and a slight fall.[833] But not all Nonconformist denominations grew sufficiently to exceed population growth. The numerical growth in the number of Primitive Methodist worshippers was slightly behind population growth and more so the United Methodist Free Churches. The Congregationalists just about kept up.[834]

In 1886, the newly established *The British Weekly* surveyed London's

[828] Ibid.

[829] Ibid.

[830] "The Bishop of Winchester on Mr Miall's Statistics", in *The Manchester Guardian*, 30 December 1881. The claim to have captured the country parishes was disputed: see "Church and Chapel Attendance", in *The Manchester Guardian*, 4 January 1882.

[831] "The Bishop of Durham's Charge", in *The Manchester Guardian*, 15 December 1882.

[832] O. Chadwick, *The Victorian Church* (1987) pt.2, p.229.

[833] Ibid.

[834] Ibid., p.227 and R. Gill, *The 'Empty' Church Revisited* (2003) p.98.

population, which had numbered 3,816,483 at the previous census in 1881. It found that 460,000 went to church or chapel in the morning and 410,000 in the evening.[835] It found these results "not disheartening, however much they leave to be desired".[836] The numbers excluded afternoon services, services for children and mission services. In November 1887, a census of mission hall attendance showed an additional attendance of 203,504 people.[837] The matter that drew the most comment in the religious press was the numerical weakness of the Salvation Army, especially in the East End.[838] Many eagerly grasped the opportunity to label it a failure. The numbers of Salvationists at morning, afternoon and evening services added up to 53,591.[839] The Salvationists responded by saying that their endeavours stirred up many who immediately, or later, moved on.[840] When the results of a tidying-up exercise into the census results were published the following year, their numbers fell to 45,172.[841] The same tidying-up exercise increased the total of worshippers at the services covered, including mission halls, to 1,167,312.[842] As a result, it was found that, in London, the proportion of the population attending Nonconformist chapels and missions had risen from less than 9 per cent in 1851, to 10.6 per cent in 1886-1887.[843] The 1886-1887 surveys also reassured the Church of England. Although the percentage of the population attending its services fell from 15 per

[835] The 1851 census found that attendances for morning, afternoon and evening services in London were respectively 460,168, 100,855 and 313,316 – being 874,339 in total. This census found London's population to be 2,362,236, see *Census of Great Britain 1851. Religious Worship* (1853) p.clxxxiv.

[836] "Our Religious Census of London", in *The British Weekly*, 5 November 1886, p.2.

[837] *The Religious Census of London* (1888) p.53.

[838] "Notes and Queries on the Mission Hall Census", in *The British Weekly*, 13 January 1888, p.201; "Mrs H. Grattan Guinness, Letter", in *The British Weekly*, 20 January 1888, p.230; "Notes of the Week", in *The British Weekly*, 27 January 1888, p.244; and "The "Methodist Times" and the Salvation Army", in *The British Weekly*, 3 February 1888, p.265. It was perhaps the weakness of the Salvation Army in the East End, where poverty was most acute, that led General Booth a few years later to combine evangelistic and social action, see "General Booth's New Book", in *Advance!*, November 1890, p.27.

[839] "Census of the Mission Halls of London", in *Supplement to The British Weekly*, 6 January 1888, p.197.

[840] "The London Mission-Hall Census", in *The British Weekly*, 17 February 1888, p.310.

[841] *The Religious Census of London* (1888) p.53.

[842] J.T. Stoddart, "The *Daily News* Census (1902-3) compared with the *British Weekly* Census (1886)", in *The Religious Life of London* (R. Mudie-Smith (ed.)) (1904) p.281.

[843] M.R. Watts, *The Dissenters* (2015) vol.3, p.89.

cent in 1851 to 11.8 per cent in 1886-1887, over half of all attendances were at its services.[844] The Roman Catholics were growing and, in some important areas, were very strong. In Westminster, the religious survey of 1886 showed that over 28 per cent of church attendances were Roman Catholic.[845]

In Wales, that citadel of Nonconformity, the growth in membership of its four main denominations (Baptists, Calvinistic Methodists, Congregationalists and Wesleyan Methodists) was startling. Numbering nearly 22 per cent of the adult population at the time of the religious census of 1851, the 1859 Revival increased that proportion to nearly 32 per cent. By 1881, nearly 35 per cent of the population aged 15 and over were members of one of these four denominations.[846] The vast majority of these spoke Welsh. Five-sixths of the Welsh speakers were outside the Church in Wales.[847]

But attending church did not necessarily mean that a person understood Christianity. Ryle thought that only one in 20 Anglicans knew why he was a churchgoer and, because of popular ignorance, he encouraged evangelical Churchmen to teach the Thirty-nine Articles.[848] Some churchgoers mocked the beliefs of others. For example, Philip Snowden wrote of his childhood in the 1870s, attending his local Wesleyan Methodist chapel in the West Riding of Yorkshire, that the local preacher's sermons had "the hell fire touch". He recalled that among the "humble weavers" there was an "earnest faith". However, his parents believed none of it. This, he described, "was the advantage of having parents who were too liberal in their religious views to approve such a theology".[849] This was the case even though his father, who "had a remarkable knowledge of the Bible",[850] was the Superintendent of the Sunday school and his father had a brother who was a "very strict

[844] Ibid., p.90. The raw statistics suggest that combined Church and chapel attendances fell in London from 26 per cent of the population in 1851 to 24 per cent in 1886-1887 – but it is thought that the explanation may lie in the accuracy of the underlying data, see ibid., pp.90-91.

[845] *The Religious Census of London* (1888) p.49.

[846] M.R. Watts, *The Dissenters* (2015) vol.3, p.86.

[847] See H.T. Edwards, *The Past and Present Position of the Church in Wales* (1879) p.5.

[848] J.C. Ryle, *Church Principles and Church Comprehensiveness* (1879) pp.42-43.

[849] P.V. Snowden, *An Autobiography* (1934) vol.1, p.28.

[850] Ibid., p.22.

Baptist". Of course, there had always been unbelief. When Snowden's maternal grandfather was on his death bed, in the early 1870s, the members of the local chapel came to sing and pray with him. The precedent of the thief who repented on the cross did not move his grandfather.[851]

25.3 The evangelical view of the times

Some continually sought to undermine the Evangelical party within the Church of England – by suggesting that it was well past its zenith and in decay.[852] Nevertheless, at least until 1880, if not later, its members were optimistic. Although in 1865 Lord Shaftesbury had observed that "The evangelical body, once so powerful, is in fact disappearing",[853] such concern proved to be transient. Dean Close, who had watched the progress of the Church of England Evangelical party since 1813, wrote to *The Times* in 1879 that it "was never so numerous or so influential [than] as at the present moment".[854] J.C. Ryle agreed. He thought that distinctively evangelical doctrines were preached in five times as many pulpits than 50 years previously and that there were at least ten times as many pulpits occupied in the large towns by evangelicals than 50 years before. He added: "those religious societies which are mainly supported by evangelical Churchmen are the largest, wealthiest and most powerful of the day".[855] The editor of *The Times* responded by indicating that he thought that, though the evangelicals had influenced other church parties,[856] evangelicals no longer put their "special doctrines…in the

[851] Ibid., p.23.

[852] E. Garbett, "The Evangelical School", in 1 *The Churchman* (1879-1880) pp.2-19 and J.C. Ryle, "Where are we?", in 1 *The Churchman* (1879-1880) pp.30-38.

[853] G. Battiscombe, *Shaftesbury* (1974) p.264.

[854] "The Decay of Evangelicalism", in *The Times*, 6 February 1879.

[855] William Haslam agreed with Dean Close and Ryle. He observed that, "There never was a time in the history of the Church when there were more believers, more true gospel preaching, more praise and testimony for God, than the present", see W. Haslam, *"Yet Not I"* (N.D.) pp.34 and 182.

[856] In doing so *The Times*'s editor echoed what others had already observed. For example, W.D. Maclagan, in 1870, writing in a collection of essays of middle-ground clergy, noted the need for more preaching which aimed at "conversion, and not only the edification of souls", see W.D. Maclagan, "The Church and the People", in *The Church and the Age* (1870) (A. Weir and W.D. Maclagan (eds)) p.458. Maclagan added that "nothing is more remarkable or more hopeful...than the very great increase of such preaching, even among certain extreme parties where it could have least been expected", ibid., p.459.

front". They had softened, and were different from their forebears.[857]

In 1879, J.C. Ryle, in an article published in *The Churchman*, thought that the evangelicals "possess the confidence of the majority of lay Churchmen – that is, of the middle classes and intelligent lower orders".[858] When he became the first Bishop of Liverpool, *The Manchester Guardian* published substantial extracts from this article as an expression of interest in evangelical views.[859] Ryle calculated that, in the late 1870s, evangelical congregations in the Church of England numbered 4,000 or 5,000.[860] At the beginning of 1887, *The Record*, although seeing many issues, observed that, in comparison with 50 years before, "the Church of England is more filled with zeal for the Lord and more established in the hearts of the people".[861]

The Nonconformists agreed about the strength of evangelicals in the Church of England. In 1880, one noted that the Nonconformists found it more difficult to make progress than 50 years before because then there were large towns of 100,000 with only one evangelical Church of England preacher, and some towns with between 10,000 and 20,000 inhabitants with none. In such circumstances, people drifted

857 "Dean Close and Canon Ryle Plead", in *The Times*, 6 February 1879. See also D. Wilson, "Introductory Address", in *Be Thou a Faithful Dispenser of the Word of God* (1878) p.5.

858 J.C. Ryle, "Where are we?", in 1 *The Churchman* (1879-1880) p.34.

859 "The First Bishop of Liverpool", in *The Manchester Guardian,* 16 April 1880.

860 J.C. Ryle, "Where are we?", in 1 *The Churchman* (1879-1880) p.35. R.W. Dale said, in a sermon of 1879, that seven or eight years earlier Ryle put evangelical clergy numbers at "not more than one-fifth, or at most one-fourth, of the clergy", R.W. Dale, *The Evangelical Revival* (1880) p.5. In 1868, Ryle had suggested there were 2,000 evangelical clergymen, although of all shades of opinion, see J.C. Ryle, *We Must Unite!* (1868) p.29. However, this was no more than the number of clerical subscribers to the CPAS and it thought that their number "could be considerably increased", see E.J. Speck, *Church Pastoral-Aid Society* (1881) p.154. In 1862, Dale put evangelical clergy at 8,000 to 10,000, but soon changed this to 7,000 to 10,000. However, his test for an evangelical clergyman was one who rejected baptismal regeneration, see A.W.W. Dale, *The Life of R.W. Dale* (1898) pp.171 and 176. To put these figures into some sort of context, in 1861 there were 19,195 clergy and 14,731 churches. Ten years later there were 20,674 clergy and 15,522 churches. By the latter date there were around 14,700 parishes or districts in England and Wales, see E.J. Speck, *Church Pastoral-Aid Society* (1881) pp.150 and 173.

861 "New Year's Thoughts", in *The Record*, 7 January 1887, p.13. See also J.C. Ryle, *A Charge Delivered to the Clergy of the Diocese of Liverpool at his Third Triennial Visitation* (1887) pp.28-36 and 64.

to the Nonconformists; now they had competition.[862] However, some Nonconformists had no worries about the competition. In 1878, Spurgeon celebrated 25 years at the Metropolitan Tabernacle and recalled how the work had begun with "A few poor, godly people" who had become "the nucleus of the present great host". He attributed developments to the doings of the most High in response to unceasing prayer and the aggressive evangelistic work of the flock. Year after year, the prayers had been answered. He was alert to the prospect that the seven good years might be followed by seven lean ones – and called for the reader to pray that "such a wretched supposition may not be realised".[863]

Methodism enjoyed a revival in the early 1880s, especially in the North of England, after a period of "indescribable gloom". There, Samuel Chadwick started his ministry;[864] Thomas Cook was a "youthful evangelist"; and Thomas Champness and others were all in full vigour. Hugh Price Hughes, in February 1883, wrote that Methodism was "stronger than ever, and more successful than ever".[865] Further, one commentator thought that the battle with science and philosophy was in a "more satisfactory" place than ten years past.[866] Many devout believers were scientists, including Sir John Herschel, Professors Phillips, Sedgwick, Stokes, Pritchard and Clerk Maxwell. The antagonistic Professor Tyndall was noted as a former assistant to the "great Faraday", who – whatever his other ability – had not learnt from his "sagacious master" that the "fear of the Lord is the beginning of wisdom".[867] Further, in 1878, the press was said to be characterised by "a sense of moral

[862] J. Waddington, *Congregational History, 1850-1880* (1880) vol.5, pp.441-442.

[863] C.H. Spurgeon, "Preface" to *The Sword and the Trowel* (1878) pp.iii-iv.

[864] J.I. Brice, *The Crowd for Christ* (1934) pp.97-98 and see also C. Oldstone-Moore, *Hugh Price Hughes* (1999) p.102.

[865] Ibid. Thomas Waugh in the early 1880s was a Connexional evangelist with Thomas Cook. He considered his special mission evangelistic appeals as being made in "virgin soil". Looking back 23 years later on those times he observed that hearers were not then adept at refusing "the offers of life". A 12-day mission resulted in 800 or 900, sometimes even 1,000 inquirers, see T. Waugh, *Twenty-Three Years a Missioner* (N.D.) p.67.

[866] J.H. Rigg, *The Present Position of Christianity and the Christian Faith in this Country* (1878) p.1. See also G, Deane, *The Relations of Church and Science: A Sermon*, August 1875.

[867] J.H. Rigg, *The Present Position of Christianity and the Christian Faith in this Country* (1878) p.19. Faraday was a Sandemanian, see G. Cantor, *Michael Faraday* (1993). Tyndall was his biographer.

responsibility...by a reverence of tone in regard to religious subjects, which can only be properly described as Christian".[868] This was very different from the position at the beginning of the nineteenth century.

However, the achievements of the 1870s and early 1880s only came about because of the vigour of contemporary Christians, in the face of challenges on many fronts. In the Preface to *The Christian Observer for the Year 1877*, its editor noted that the Church of England, for the past 12 months, had been subject to attack:

> The spirit of aggression – not of innovation merely – upon her entire position, doctrinal, constitutional, devotional, pastoral, an aggression supported by her own members, and characterised by high authority as nothing less than a conspiracy, has been as energetic and uncompromising as ever.[869]

That volume was the last volume of *The Christian Observer*, although a substitute, *The Churchman*, appeared in 1879 – the circulation of which soon exceeded that of the *Christian Observer*, even in the years when the latter was a "power in the Church".[870] Nevertheless, it became harder for an evangelical to become a bishop. In the mid-years of the century, the Prime Minister, Lord Palmerston, appointed many "Palmerston evangelicals" as bishops. However, Gladstone, it was said, had a "No Evangelical Need Apply" policy when it came to the appointment of bishops.[871] Between 1865 and 1900, only six outright evangelical bishops were appointed. Further, it was noted, if the leading figures in a parish were unsympathetic, even the most successful of preachers might witness fewer conversions – as the "poorer people did not listen with as much interest as they might have done".[872]

[868] Ibid., p.13.
[869] "Preface" to 77 *The Christian Observer for the Year 1877* (1877) p.iii.
[870] "Preface" to 1 *The Churchman* (1879-1880) p.iii and J.L. Altholz, *The Religious Press in Britain 1760-1900* (1989) p.17.
[871] P. Anglicanus, *How the Church of England May be Preserved* (N.D.) p.4.
[872] W. Haslam, *"Yet Not I"* (N.D.) p.311.

25.4 After the 1880s, church attendances fall away as a proportion of the population

Empty churches, in a particular area, were not a phenomenon that first arose in the late Victorian period. In 1860, many of the magnificent Anglican churches in the City of London attracted only 40 or 50 on a Sunday, as so few people then lived there.[873] Sometimes churches that became empty by virtue of population movement were taken over by others. In 1882, Bishop Lightfoot refers to acquiring four chapels from the Nonconformists in Sunderland, which they had abandoned because the congregations had migrated to a better neighbourhood.[874]

However, around 1887, if not slightly before, the increase in Church and chapel numbers across the nation seems to have ceased to keep pace with population growth.[875] Throughout 1882, *The Christian Monthly and Family Treasury* ran a series of articles, and organised a symposium, on the apparent decline in church-going, in both "crescent and terrace".[876] Many reasons for the decline were given. One commentator thought that an excess of advertising, a lack of spontaneity and long services, a preference for high-class music instead of presenting the truth,

[873] Lord Shaftesbury, *Speech of the Right Hon. the Earl of Shaftesbury in the House of Lords, Feb 24,1860 on the Holding of Special Religious Services in Theatres* (1860) p.7.

[874] "The Bishop of Durham's Charge", in *The Manchester Guardian*, 15 December 1882. A problem for the Nonconformists was that as their chapels were funded by the congregation; as wealthier members left for better parts, those remaining might be unable to support it, K.F. Inglis, *Churches and the Working Classes in Victorian England* (1964) pp.63-64.

[875] Population movement in the late nineteenth century means that although church attendances declined in particular areas, overall, the decline may not have been severe. For example, in 1887 – the year of the Down-grade Controversy – Spurgeon lamented: "Attendance at places of worship is declining, and reverence for holy things is vanishing", I.H. Murray, *The Forgotten Spurgeon* (1973) p.142. However, it may be that Spurgeon's view was informed – based as he was at the Elephant and Castle – by the sight of churches emptying in Inner London, as people moved to the newly built suburbs and used the railways to get to work. A leading evangelical at Holy Trinity, St Marylebone, was also struggling to keep open its network of mission halls and temporary rooms – as the wealthy of the Regent's Park area moved out and the character of its neighbourhood changed, see L.E. Shelford, *A Memorial of the Rev. William Cadman* (1899) pp.57, 68 and 91.

[876] J.M. Lang, "The Non-Church Going: How Can Our Churches Reach Them?", in *The Christian Monthly and Family Treasury* (1882) p.72. See also "Attendance at Public Worship in Large Towns", in *The Manchester Guardian*, 7 November 1881.

disagreements between the churches, the now frequent requests for money and, above all, the uncertainty about doctrine – as part of a wider attack on authority structures in all parts of life – was producing "irregular worshipping, a coming and going, merely as the individual likes". It was the prelude to a long decline in church going.[877] The same author, later in the year, added – as reasons for not attending church – the growing failure of parents to teach and train the young; and pew rents. There might be free seats, but their occupants were stared at. The existence of cheap-looking mission halls did not prove that the church cared for the poor. At Oxford, in 1884, Francis Chavasse complained that the "social air...is repressive and suppressive".[878] He observed that "The missionary spirit is dormant. The week-day congregations are stationary."[879]

The theological liberal Edward White suggested that the way to reach the masses was to dedicate the evening service, once a month, to an outreach service – at which a discourse, historical and interesting, was given. White's other proposed topics for discourse included natural theology, the confirmation of the Bible by modern discovery, and church history.[880] A few years later, the experience of the Secretary of the Open-Air Mission was that "the disposition to attend public worship is steadily decreasing". He attributed this to education and increased intellectualism, but also to the willingness of Christians to take a lax view of the Sabbath – and their dedication to entertainment – and a decline in open-air evangelism. However, where there was still the energy and confidence to engage in open-air work, there could be a startling response. The Presbyterian minister of Ossulston Street, Somers Town, London, Z.B. Woffendale, recruited 500 of his 830 members through open-air preaching – primarily through preaching by the bandstand at Regent's Park and on the Euston Road.[881] Campbell Morgan reopened Holloway Congregational Church just before the turn of the century. "Gathering about him a few earnest men and women", he "went out 'to

[877] J.M. Lang, "The Decline in Church Attendance", in *The Christian Monthly and Family Treasury* (1882) pp.12-14.
[878] J.B. Lancelot, *Francis James Chavasse* (1929) p.92.
[879] Ibid., p.91.
[880] E. White, "The Non-Church Going: How Can Our Churches Reach Them?", in *The Christian Monthly and Family Treasury* (1882) p.76.
[881] G. Kirkham, "The London Mission Hall Census", in *The British Weekly*, 9 March 1888, p.362.

compel' the people of the surrounding neighbourhood to 'come in'" – and they did.[882]

The problem of declining numbers was particularly acute in urban areas.[883] In London, between 1886 and 1902-1903, the total number of worshippers dropped by 150,000, even though the population rose by 500,000.[884] Almost all the decline was among Church of England parishes. In London, worshippers were well under a fifth of the population.[885] "The healthiest parishes were those with highly motivated clergymen, normally activists, either High or evangelical, who supplied a broad range of opportunities for philanthropic and religious service."[886] In London, people were "more eclectic than parochial".[887] Chadwick notes that "ministers who preached vehement sermons about hell often got larger congregations than the ministers who never mentioned the subject".[888]

The conversion of the working class was not achieved. Despite all the efforts, in 1879 the numbers to be converted were so great and the resources in comparison so few, that it seemed that "the work of evangelising the masses has almost to be begun".[889] However, those with a long memory believed that the "working classes were never so favourably disposed towards Christianity as they are now"[890] – but they remained unwilling to attend church. By 1890, it was acknowledged that "the Church of England and almost every other religious body had practically lost all effectual hold on the mass of the working classes".[891] In Bethnal Green, only 13.3 per cent went to any place of worship.[892] When,

[882] J. Harries, *G. Campbell Morgan* (1930) pp.59-60.

[883] See generally R. Gill, *The 'Empty' Church Revisited* (2003).

[884] J.T. Stoddart, "The *Daily News* Census (1902-3) compared with the *British Weekly* Census (1886)", in *The Religious Life of London* (R. Mudie-Smith (ed.)) (1904) pp.280-281.

[885] M.R. Watts, *The Dissenters* (2015) vol.3, p.371.

[886] J. Cox, *The English Churches in a Secular Society* (1982) p.178. The Evangelization Society assumed that a third of a town might never attend a religious service, see W.E. Smith, *Address to Evangelists* (N.D.) p.21.

[887] W. Haslam, *"Yet Not I"* (N.D.) p.337.

[888] O. Chadwick, *The Secularization of the European Mind* (1975) p.106.

[889] "The Church Congress", *The Times*, 10 October 1879.

[890] J.T. Davidson, "The Non-Church Going: How Can Our Churches Reach Them?", in *The Christian Monthly and Family Treasury* (1882) p.141.

[891] "'In Darkest England'", in *The Times*, 10 November, 1890.

[892] D.W. Bebbington, *The Nonconformist Conscience* (1982) p.5.

in 1892, F.B. Meyer went to Christ Church, Westminster Bridge Road, London, many had "gloomy prognostications" of his ability to draw them from the neighbouring slums. "It can't be done", was the view.[893] Those who went to church received "the 'ragging' of the workshop or the sneers of neighbours".[894] One new convert, in the summer of 1893, who told his workmates of his conversion, found that they had put rats in his jacket and tar in its pockets. His cap was nailed to the floor. However, he persevered in his witness and, within a week, two of his workmates at the farrier's shop where he worked were converted and others followed.[895]

The Nonconformists remained generally in good heart. Outside London, which commentators focused on, they kept their contact with, and drew recruits from, the working classes.[896] Their ministers, even those with very different theologies, might regularly meet together in congenial "Fraternals".[897] Their active members outnumbered those of the Church of England. Their numbers would not peak until around 1906-1907 – even though, as a proportion of the population, their numbers declined. They were confident and believed that the future rested with them.[898] Their decline in ministerial numbers was still to come.[899] In 1888, the Wesleyan Methodists had the luxury of being able to turn down 105 of their 150 ministerial candidates, including G. Campbell Morgan, one of the great preachers of the next century.[900] A few years earlier, they had turned down Thomas Cook from the ministry, even though his trial sermon witnessed five conversions.[901] The Baptists grew in number, especially those claiming spiritual descent from Spurgeon.[902] Effective

[893] W.Y. Fullerton, *F.B. Meyer* (N.D.) p.107.

[894] C. Booth, *Life and Labour of the People in London* (1903), Third Series: Religious Influences vol.7, p.429.

[895] J. Bryant, *Happy Jim* (1937) pp.34-35.

[896] M.R. Watts, *The Dissenters* (2015) vol.3, pp.120-124.

[897] R. Horton, *An Autobiography* (1917) pp.100-103 and *The Life of Charles Silvester Horne* (1920) (W.B. Selbie (ed.)) p.72.

[898] D.W. Bebbington, *The Nonconformist Conscience* (1982) pp.1-2.

[899] See H. McLeod, *Religion and Society in England, 1850-1914* (1996) pp.193-196.

[900] J. Harries, *G. Campbell Morgan* (1930) p.35.

[901] H.T. Smart, *The Life of Thomas Cook* (1913) pp.44-45.

[902] See J. Cox, *The English Churches in a Secular Society* (1982) pp.45-46; J. Munson, *The Nonconformists* (1991) pp.11-12; and J.T. Stoddart, "The *Daily News* Census (1902-3) compared with the *British Weekly* Census (1886)", in *The Religious Life of*

evangelists remained at work. Gipsy Smith records that the enquirers at his last mission of the nineteenth century, at Luton, numbered 1,080 – rather more than one in forty of the population.[903] Even in London John McNeill, the Scottish Free Church Presbyterian evangelist, drew half-a-million people to his "great London campaign" in the first six months of 1898. The last 12 nights were at the Royal Albert Hall.[904]

Churches with evangelistic zeal and biblical commitment grew, but their expansion, as the Brethren found, gently slowed,[905] as the unconverted became less willing to attend the gospel hall and less responsive to the preaching.[906] The Brethren, however, founded new evangelistic organisations – like Counties. This, a month after its founding, launched a tent campaign at Watford in May 1899 with a 500-seat marquee.[907] However, the funding of the leading mission agencies fell-off in the last decade of the nineteenth century, as did the number of the agents they employed.[908] This was not good, because their directness, especially with the working class, paid dividends. It was a City missionary who converted the farrier mentioned above. That farrier became known as 'Happy Jim' – and he enjoyed a long life as an evangelist, having previously been a notorious drunk.[909]

In Congregational churches "a certain dullness and stagnation in the religious life" was felt. There, the younger men, like Silvester Horne, thought that "The times demand not only a new construction of thought, but a new construction of method".[910]

Roman Catholic numbers grew. By 1900, there were over two million British Roman Catholic members.[911] Most were Irish, or of Irish stock, together with a growing number of celebrity converts, but

London (R. Mudie-Smith (ed.)) (1904) pp.288-290.

903 R. Smith, *Gipsy Smith his Life and Work* (N.D.) p.296.

904 A. Gammie, *Rev. John McNeill his Life and Work* (N.D.) p.126.

905 *The Christian Brethren as the Nineties Began* (1993) p.86, but see also T. Grass, *Gathering to His Name* (2012) pp.116-117.

906 Ibid., p.136.

907 "History", www.countiesuk.org/about-us/history, accessed 25 September 2017. For the background to the formation of Counties, see T. Grass, *Gathering to His Name* (2012) pp.144-146.

908 D.M. Lewis, *Lighten their Darkness* (1986) pp.278-279.

909 J. Bryant, *Happy Jim* (1937) pp.23-28.

910 *The Life of Charles Silvester Horne* (1920) (W.B. Selbie (ed.)) pp.72-73.

911 R. Currie, A. Gilbert and L. Horsley, *Churches and Churchgoers* (1977) p.25.

the middle classes remained resolutely resistant to Roman Catholicism. To encourage further converts – and as a sign of the acceptability of converting to Rome – in September and October 1878, four successive editions of *The Whitehall Review* carried lists of secessions to Rome since the Tractarian movement began. Later, in 1878, these lists were collected into a book, *Rome's Recruits*, listing converts to Rome in the nineteenth century. By 1884, this book was into its fifth edition and listed over 3,000 conversions.[912] More than a thousand names had been added since the last edition. Gladstone suggested the arrangement of the names of converts. It started with the names of the "Nobility and gentry" – 13 pages for the men alone – and then there followed the names of converts under the headings of the "Army", "the Navy", "the Medical and Legal professions", "Literature", "Architects", "War office", "Publishers", "Clergy and relatives of clergy", and then, under the relevant universities and their respective constituent colleges. The lady converts followed, listed under parallel headings – although some were included under previous sections, such as "Literature". There were 21 pages for lady converts under the heading "The Nobility and Gentry (Ladies)", including no less than seven duchesses. However, most Englishmen still condemned anything that carried "its votaries into the Roman precinct".[913] In 1879, to show that those going to Rome were far fewer than "those who embrace the truth",[914] *Protestant Recruits* was published – being a record of modern priests, monks, nuns and theological students leaving the Church of Rome. There was also a steady leakage of working-class members from Catholicism, but this seemed to slow towards the end of the century, as the number of priests and supporting organisations grew.[915] A "thinker" might change his theological position a number of times. For example, the Reverend Richard Waldo Sibthorpe was, in 1828, an associate of Baptist Noel at St John's, Bedford Row and "known as one of the most eloquent preachers of the Evangelical school". In 1841, he went over to Rome but returned to the Church of England in 1848, before returning to Rome for the last 14 years of his life. However, his obituary said he had no sympathy with

[912] W. Gordon-Gorman, *Converts to Rome* (1884).

[913] W.E. Gladstone, *Gleanings of Past Years* (1879) vol.7, p.233.

[914] M.R. Butler, *Protestant Recruits* (1879) p.3.

[915] K.F. Inglis, *Churches and the Working Classes in Victorian England* (1964) pp.119-142.

later developments in that church.[916]

In sum, for the quarter of a century after 1859, the forces hostile to Christianity, and a resurgent Christianity – albeit weakened through self-inflicted wounds because of political disputes between Church and chapel – competed, to an honourable draw. The numbers in the churches grew at least in line with the population. After around 1886, the new doctrinal developments spread beyond the vanguard of their early supporters and started to influence many across the nation. Furthermore, the Forward Movement of the Wesleyan Methodists and other churches began to take evangelism in a new direction, so that confidence in its success rested as much on social work as on the power of the message. Recruitment slowed, as the focus on and energy for evangelism was diluted and the changes to the gospel message, intended by human wisdom to make it more attractive to the masses, were found to render it powerless. Christians became unsure of the gospel, and if they were unsure of the message what did they have to go out and talk about? Those who believed in hell had the most powerful reason to talk to their children, neighbours, friends and passers-by. Dale refers to the moral nature of the times becoming "flaccid and sluggish".[917] Watts writes that "There is much evidence to suggest that liberal Nonconformists, in trying to adapt their religious beliefs to meet the challenges posed by evolution, higher criticism and the reaction against eternal punishment, blunted the edge of the gospel they preached and undermined their ability to win converts".[918] In July 1893, *The Methodist Times*'s leading article was headed "Why not More Conversions?"[919]

Interest in, and reliance upon, the nation's Christian heritage declined. Gifts to, and purchases of, the resources supplied by the Religious Tract Society plummeted between 1884 and1889. By 1899, the proceeds of sales were just under 60 per cent of what they had been in 1884 and subscriptions and donations began to dip.[920] The collapse in sales related to books, magazines and cards, but the sales of tracts were maintained.[921]

[916] "Obituary", in *The Times*, 12 April 1879.
[917] R.W. Dale, *The Evangelical Revival* (1880) p.161.
[918] M.R. Watts, *The Dissenters* (2015) vol.3, p.94.
[919] "Why not More Conversions?", in *The Methodist Times*, 6 July 1893, p.427.
[920] S.G. Green, *The Story of the Religious Tract Society* (1899) p.116.
[921] Ibid., p.122.

The new doctrines perhaps spurred the zealous on to greater urgency, but a great bulk of churchgoers became lukewarm in their faith. For many, orthodoxy was replaced by religious sentiment. This could be found without God. It could be got by a beautiful service and just as freely by the sea-shore and mountain side.[922] R.W. Dale suggested: "In our sorrow we expect to find consolation, not in the divine compassion, but in the soothing influence of religious meditation; and strength, not in the inspiration of God, but in the vigour and depth of religious emotion which may be stirred by noble thoughts concerning life and duty, or by the bold and heroic temper of a sacred song."[923]

Doubts began to be expressed in Nonconformist circles on the need for the new birth.[924] Like the Unitarians before them, education replaced the role of conversion in the thinking of such people and it "proved an important stimulus to the secularisation of Dissent".[925] Further, if there was no need for the new birth, then church discipline of a standard higher than that of the world was unnecessary and, it was argued, deterred individuals from joining a church.[926] Nevertheless, the ability of the liberal Nonconformist churches to draw teenagers and men and women in their twenties, declined. As they gave up on the need for conversion, a drift from them to the Church of England began.[927] In Scotland, within Presbyterian churches, a similar drift towards the Established Church appeared.[928] Professor Seeley noted, in *Ecce Homo*, that "Where the power of reclaiming the lost dies out of the church, it ceases to be the church. It may remain a useful institution, though it is most likely to become an immoral and mischievous one." Hugh Price Hughes, in citing Seeley in *The Methodist Times*, added that when the power to convert is lost, "the Christian Church is an organised hypocrisy and a living lie – the most deadly of all corrupt organisations".[929]

Nevertheless, those who held out the gospel prospered; in 1887, one writer to *The British Weekly* noted the "enormous growth of the

[922] R.W. Dale, *The Evangelical Revival* (1880) p.163.
[923] Ibid., p.169.
[924] M.R. Watts, *The Dissenters* (2015) vol.3, pp.96-100.
[925] Ibid., p.205.
[926] Ibid., pp.142-152.
[927] Ibid., pp.98 and 204.
[928] C.G. Brown, *Religion and Society in Scotland since 1707* (1997) p.47.
[929] "Why not More Conversions?", in *The Methodist Times*, 6 July 1893, p.427.

Brethren...the success of the Salvation Army...the daily increasing of the evangelicals of the Church of England" in comparison with "the evil of unbelief in many pulpits".[930] Thomas Cook, who started work as a lay evangelist with the Wesleyans, in 1880 saw 3,000 profess conversion in his first year of work with the Halifax and Bradford District Home Missionary Committee. The following year, there were more than 3,000 adults.[931] In 1882, on becoming the first Methodist Connexional evangelist, he saw "nearly six thousand people seeking salvation".[932] Cook never repudiated "the endless suffering of the lost" and was rarely short of a convert after a sermon – and he preached well into the twentieth century.[933] "He often told his students that they must not eliminate the element of fear from their preaching." One author thought he "reaped a richer harvest of souls than any minister since Wesley".[934] In the 1890s, Samuel Chadwick enjoyed notable evangelistic success from settled pastorates in Leeds.[935] If he was to preach for longer than an hour, he announced it the previous week. Even then the crowds came.[936] But elsewhere, it got more difficult – as the mass of churches articulated a different view as to the urgency of the message.

As the last decade of the nineteenth century dawned, the churches also lacked "pre-eminent personalities"[937] – as their greatest figures grew old or passed away. Lord Shaftesbury died in 1885; Spurgeon in 1892, aged 58. Furthermore, for many of his later years he was very ill. J.C. Ryle continued as Bishop of Liverpool until the end of the century, but he was already 74 in 1890 and possibly lingered in his role too long. Moody's last major mission in Britain ended in 1884, although he returned for less demanding ventures. Gawin Kirkham and John MacGregor, two great drivers of open-air work, both died in the early 1890s. Reginald Radcliffe, Richard Weaver and W.P. Lockhart, evangelists who came to the fore in the 1859 Revival, all died in the first six years of the 1890s.

930 W.J.C. Ward, "Are Nonconformists Departing from the Faith?", in *The British Weekly*, 11 November 1887, p.30.
931 H.T. Smart, *The Life of Thomas Cook* (1913) p.55.
932 J.I. Brice, *The Crowd for Christ* (1934) pp.50-53.
933 H.T. Smart, *The Life of Thomas Cook* (1913) pp.259 and 262.
934 J.I. Brice, *The Crowd for Christ* (1934) pp.54-55.
935 Ibid., pp.100-101.
936 Ibid., p.104.
937 H.C.G. Moule, *The Evangelical School in the Church of England* (1901) p.87.

Booth turned to social work in the late 1880s. He returned to evangelism after a few years and led the way in motor car evangelism in the next century, but he was 61 in 1890; Catherine Booth was already dead. On her passing it was preached, and not by a Salvationist, that "she had brought more souls to the feet of the Saviour than any other woman or man in this age or any other age".[938] The Booths were Arminian in doctrine, and Moody's doctrine fuzzy, but they loved souls and had energy, creativity and abundant organisational and leadership skills. It remained to be seen what would happen when lesser men followed their doctrine. Further, would "sound institutions" – as one theologian asked at the beginning of the twentieth century – "when worked not by genius but by fidelity and common wisdom", be able to deliver converts in an increasingly hostile world?[939] All the same, on the eve of the new century, the Religious Tract Society, the society that armed the other evangelical societies, celebrated its centenary with a meeting at the London Mansion House, with the Lord Mayor of London attending and the Queen consenting to becoming a patron.

[938] "The Late Mrs Catherine Booth", in *Advance!*, November 1890, p.26.
[939] H.C.G. Moule, *The Evangelical School in the Church of England* (1901) p.87.

26

SUMMARY OF PART 3

26.1 Overview

At the beginning of our period, although facing external and internal challenges, those promoting a gospel agenda were as strong, if not stronger, than ever before. The task confronting them was to use their position to reach the masses, while dealing with the internal divisions that related mainly to church organisation and structure. Strong economic factors were at work to provide the funds to sustain and expand the machinery that the previous two generations had put in place to reach the nation. Furthermore, with the happy fact of Lord Shaftesbury becoming the son-in-law to the Prime Minister, evangelicals had a voice into government – with an influence unmatched since Wilberforce.

To this already strong position, the 1859 Revival unleashed massive spiritual energy which reduced many to fear and trembling for their salvation. A wave of new evangelistic and social organisations resulted and the converts of that period put backbone into evangelical organisations for the remainder of the century. The revival also breathed new life into the moral reforms that Wilberforce, Hannah More and others initiated earlier in the century. The time coincided with the British Empire reaching its zenith.

In the quarter of the century that followed – in terms of creativity, self-sacrifice, zeal and the desire to win souls and to make the nation pleasing to God – it is hard to think of another half century quite like it. Great preachers abounded and drew congregations in the thousands. Transatlantic evangelism probably reached its peak. Yet, if anything, the danger was of making "an idol of parochial machinery"[940] and losing sight of the pulpit. Huge sums were raised to fund new building programmes

[940] J.C. Ryle, *Christian Leaders of the 18th Century* (1997) p.270.

and to establish new and expand existing Christian organisations. As J.C. Ryle commented: "It is hard to have many irons in the fire at once, and to keep them all hot".[941] The numbers of clergy and laity involved in Christian work, especially in education, were enormous. Politicians as powerful as Gladstone were only too aware of the danger of mishandling issues considered of importance to the denominations. Many thought that the nation's prosperity depended on its obedience to God.

But there was another side to it all. As the claims of Christ were held out and accepted by many, others were repelled. Scepticism grew where the tenets of biblical Christianity were preached vigorously. Many leading figures in science, politics, philosophy, literature, social and economic life found common cause with critics of the historicity of the Bible. As Gladstone put it, "the sceptical movement set in with a wide and subtle power".[942] In the early 1880s, Josephine Butler, speaking at a Christian Women's Union Conference, observed that "Open profession of scepticism is decidedly fashionable". She added that it required "some moral courage…at a London party to own to a belief in revelation".[943] Lord Shaftesbury, at a dinner to mark the grant to him of the freedom of the City of London in 1884, commented that

> the future is very dark...There never was, at any time...such a cool and systematic unbelief, and so largely acceptable; never such a succession of wild and pernicious opinions, which, though they pass away as rapidly as they come, distract and pervert the public mind. These agents, whatever be their name, atheists or agnostics are concentrated, organised, disciplined, aggressive. Children even are trained to be missionaries of evil.[944]

For those who did not like what they found in Christianity, other religions provided an alternative – especially as the British Empire made their tenets accessible.

The social standing of the Church, and sometimes parental

[941] Ibid. For an overview of this machinery in a lively evangelical church, at the beginning of our period, see R. Maguire, *Pastoral Letter Addressed to the Congregation of St James's, Clerkenwell* (1859).
[942] W.E. Gladstone, *The Impregnable Rock of Holy Scripture* (1890) p.258.
[943] J. Butler, *Modern Heathenism Caused by Christian Faithlessness* (N.D.) p.1.
[944] "Lord Shaftesbury at the Mansion-House", in *The Times*, 6 March 1884.

encouragement, often led men into ministry, rather than the love of God. Such men were not the fox-hunting parson of old, but they were yet to have Christ fully formed in them. They listened to what the world was saying, and gently, or aggressively, as the case might be, adopted its perspective. They were often clever and unafraid to express old heresies in new dress, with energy. They proclaimed a Bible without authority and promoted a religion stripped of the miraculous and the atonement, devoid of heaven, hell and final judgment, and one in which sin was irrelevant. Their most dangerous and damaging argument was that, in order for Christianity to reach the masses, certain biblical doctrines needed to be abandoned. Such an argument had appeal because Christians of the times wanted to reach everyone. However, the reality was that to move from orthodoxy was to leave God's path and with that came spiritual decay and an increasing weakness in numbers.

Furthermore, scepticism grew as Ritualism emerged out of the combined High Church/Tractarian parties. Beginning as an attempt to combat incipient theological liberalism and the fact that Protestantism had not converted the entire nation, Ritualism ironically increased those who were resistant to the gospel because it seemed a throw-back to a long-forgotten past, or worse. It attracted those who liked its aesthetic appeal but, for the mass of the population, it discredited the Church of England both through its teaching and through the conflict it created within the Church. It also undermined the importance of preaching – a principal means of getting the message out – as the emphasis on spectacle grew. As a positive observer of the Catholic Revival noted, "Instead of 'preaching houses', the churches became truly 'places of worship'".[945] Tait, the Archbishop of Canterbury, thought Ritualism a greater danger than free thought,[946] as perhaps did Ryle.[947] Shaftesbury, with greater foresight, when asked who was the greater danger, the Ritualists or the Neologians (those of the *Essays and Reviews* ilk) replied that "the first were a greater danger to the Church of England as an established institution, but the second were a greater danger to the Church of England as the Church of Christ".[948] The growing strength of the new theologies

[945] F. Bennett, *The Story of W.J.E. Bennett* (1909) p.187.
[946] S. Dark, *Archbishop Davidson and the English Church* (1929) p.8.
[947] J.C. Ryle, *Knots Untied* (1964) (G.E. Duffield (ed.)) pp.18-19.
[948] J.L. Hammond and B. Hammond, *Lord Shaftesbury* (1936) p.225.

was revealed when the publication of *Lux Mundi* revealed that the younger Anglo-Catholics at Oxford had absorbed liberalism – to the horror of their elders.[949] In the 1890s, Anglo-Catholicism and theological liberalism came together and Christian socialism reappeared in strength. Around this time, a fundamental shift in the prospects of biblical Christianity occurred. Robert Horton, the Congregational minister whose writings contributed so much to this shift, especially amongst members of his denomination, wrote, "The way of regarding the Bible, which in 1888 seemed to ignorance revolutionary and heretical, in 1891 was recognised as the result of a cautious and reverent admission of facts which could not be disputed".[950] Horton was troubled that, though many came to hear him, his preaching witnessed few conversions.[951]

The defence of the faith from intellectual attack was weakened: first, by the strong presence of scepticism within Oxford University; and then by the ancient universities losing their Christian allegiance. Previously, the Church of England's control of them gave it readily available thinkers and organisation to combat error. Now, when error appeared, it was more likely to taint the lingering Christian elements of the universities than to be repelled by them. Further, the attitude to knowledge – and what was truly knowledge – had changed. In the past, Anglican influence had meant that knowledge was connected with virtue and was to be understood as rooted in understanding God and his purposes. After 1870, the ancient universities no longer operated on these assumptions and they might well be hostile to Christianity. Anglican influence over science, which had been such a feature of earlier centuries, dissipated – and science was now pitted against Christianity. In 1884, Francis Chavasse, an evangelical minister in Oxford, attributed, in part, the difficulties of parish ministry to the advancing "secularisation of the University". He now needed to prop up college students under attack. It was pastoral visitation of the parish that languished and the unstable drifted from their moorings as Chavasse became "too little of the friend and too much of

[949] J.O. Johnston, *Life and Letters of Henry Parry Liddon* (1904) pp.360-376 and 383-384.

[950] R. Horton, *An Autobiography* (1917) p.94.

[951] A. Peel and J.A.R. Marriott, *Robert Forman Horton* (1937) pp.132, 152-153 and 157-159.

the preacher, and the work suffer[ed]".[952]

The timing of the loss of the universities to Church control was particularly unfortunate. The educated, of whom, with the new schools, there were now more than ever, were influenced by theories and systems – and these now multiplied in number and complexity not hitherto seen.[953] Furthermore, universities could act as breeding grounds for ideas contrary to Christianity, rather than, at best, the provider of an antidote to erroneous ideas.

The establishment of the new theological colleges did not compensate for the loss of influence over the universities. Indeed, as liberal ideas gripped the universities, the theological colleges tended to be more swayed by the ideas of their professional peer group in the universities than by their confessional basis. A further problem for the intellectual defence of Protestant Christianity was that the evangelical movement was, as R.W. Dale noted, "more eager to seek and to save the lost than to investigate the foundations of Christian doctrine".[954] It produced great preachers and organisers, but no original theologian of the first or second rank, or great historian committed to ensuring that church and state saw the doctrines of the Reformation as key to their respective successes.[955] Perhaps, with regard to the former, the loss of control of the ancient universities discouraged such activity, while Anglo-Catholicism in the history departments prevented the latter. Particularly damaging was the loss of so many graduates to the mission field. Their number grew substantially in volume in the 1880s.

The defence of Christianity against scepticism was also weakened by the divisions and rivalries between Church and chapel. Their disagreements over education, burial grounds and other matters gave their opponents a stick to beat them with. It also opened the way to greater involvement by the state in secular education and made securing the best possible provision for religious teaching in schools impossible. These disagreements did not prevent evangelicals across denominations

[952] J.B. Lancelot, *Francis James Chavasse* (1929) pp.91-92.

[953] W. Haslam, *"Yet Not I"* (N.D.) pp.128-129.

[954] R.W. Dale, *The Evangelical Revival* (1880) p.24.

[955] James Kirby sees J.C. Ryle and his popular work, *What Do We Owe to the Reformation?* (1877) as the leading evangelical exponent of this view, see J. Kirby, *Historians and the Church of England: Religion and Historical Scholarship, 1870-1920* (2016) p.183.

working together, but it must have added a degree of stress unhelpful to the successful prosecution of the work. For an evangelical like J.C. Ryle, knowing that a natural ally, like C.H. Spurgeon, was committed to disestablishment, must have added another burden to life, even though they were personally on friendly terms.

In the 1880s, the impact of scepticism became clearly visible. Ryle, as Bishop of Liverpool, was horrified by the figures for church-going in Liverpool – at a shade under 20 per cent.[956] It is difficult to know exactly when the tipping point came – when the numerical growth of Christianity no longer matched population growth – but it was at some point during the 1880s, or even late 1870s, whatever the energy of individual Christians, congregations and organisations.

In the late 1880s, the transition from the theology of the atonement to that of the incarnation, as the dominant theological model, was completed. In 1890, R.W. Dale began a book considering how Christianity was to be verified – given developments in modern thought – with the words that "There are large numbers of people...who cannot understand how it is possible, in these days, for intelligent, open-minded, educated men to believe in the Lord Jesus Christ."[957] Huxley thought all that was left with regard to Christianity was to rail around the ruins, to preserve them from desecration.[958]

As national wealth grew in the 1890s, instead of it flowing into gospel work and giving, as doctrinal convictions ebbed, it flowed into leisure and entertainments. Indeed, for a variety of reasons, the income of the Church of England was squeezed between 1837 and 1897 resulting in the average income of incumbents halving.[959] Mrs Sumner, speaking at the 1890 Church Congress at Hull, noted that "the rivers of immorality, intemperance, irreligion and infidelity are streaming over our cities and villages". Yet, she added, "there never was a time when such religious enthusiasm prevailed, such zealous fighting for God and right...and still the tide of sin rolls on".[960] Her solution to halting the tide of sin was

[956] "The Statistics of Church and Chapel Attendance", in *The Manchester Guardian*, 27 December 1881.
[957] R.W. Dale, *The Living Christ and the Four Gospels* (1890) p.1.
[958] W.E. Gladstone, *The Impregnable Rock of Holy Scripture* (1890) p.256.
[959] J. Kirby, *Historians and the Church of England: Religion and Historical Scholarship, 1870-1920* (2016) pp.218-219.
[960] Mrs Sumner, *Women's Work Among Women* (1890) p.2.

the Mothers' Union. Contemporaries saw that there was a battle going on between light and darkness – and which way it would turn out was unknown. The High Church William Proby, writing in 1888, thought that "the average amount of piety in the reformed Church of England is probably greater now than it has been at any other period since the country had become Christian".[961] With the benefit of hindsight, it can be seen that the years either side of 1859 represented the zenith of orthodoxy in Great Britain. There were troubles, but then Jesus had foretold that, in this world, this is what his followers would experience.[962]

[961] W.H.B. Proby, *Annals of the "Low-Church" Party in England* (1888) vol.1, p.4.
[962] John 14:1.

Glossary

Anglo-Catholicism: The movement within the Church of England that affirms many Roman Catholic beliefs and practices, within the framework of a national church. It grew out of the Tractarian and Ritualist movements.
Antinomianism: The belief that conformity with the moral law is unnecessary for those with faith.
Arianism: The chief feature of Arianism was its claim that Jesus was not a divine person. It has a long history, stretching back to Arius – who lived during the last half of the third and first half of the fourth century A.D..
Arminianism: Ideas popularised by the Dutch scholar Jacobus Arminius, who died in 1609. The following year, in response to Calvinism – the dominant Protestant theological outlook of the time – The Five Articles of Remonstrance were drawn up, to clarify the ideas of Arminians on key doctrines. Article I held that God elects to salvation those he knows beforehand will have faith in him. Article II affirmed unlimited atonement; the concept that Christ died for all. Article III affirmed the total depravity of man. Article IV repudiated the Calvinistic concept of irresistible grace, asserting that mankind has the free will to resist God's grace. Article V, rather than rejecting the notion of the perseverance of the saints, provided that it may be conditional upon the believer remaining in Christ.
Atonement: In the nineteenth century, the atonement, especially for evangelicals, meant the theory of the atonement known as penal substitution – whereby Christ died on the cross as a sacrifice for human sin, to satisfy the justice of God. Other explanations of the atonement can co-exist with penal substitution – such as the belief that Jesus died in the place of men, to free them from the power of sin, the devil and his allies, who held humanity captive.
Brethren: The origins of the Brethren go back to the 1820s and the work of a number of effective evangelists, the best known of whom is John

Nelson Darby. The appellation 'Brethren' indicated that being a Christian was more important than any doctrinal slant. Creeds were eschewed as divisive. They regarded as Christians all those who held the basic tenets of salvation. They also affirmed the role of the Holy Spirit as the "all sufficient guide" to God's people. Gifts from the Spirit, especially those of teachers and evangelists, were emphasised – and those possessing these gifts were freed to exercise them outside the Brethren Assembly. They had no ordained clergymen.

Broad Churchmen: A term used increasingly in the nineteenth century and traced back to W.J. Conybeare,[1] to refer to those who were not members of the Evangelical party, or the Tractarians and their successors, the Ritualists. They were less committed to biblical orthodoxy and often started with their own thinking to establish doctrine, or redefined traditional theological terms in a new way. Later in the century, members became known as Liberals – as the rejection of biblical ideas became more extreme.

Calvinism: The Five Points of Calvinism formulated by the Synod of Dort, ending in 1619. They are: total depravity (not that everything a man does is in itself wrong, but that man lives his life in rebellion to God and cannot save himself); unconditional election; limited atonement (Christ's atoning work was intended only for the elect – and not for the rest of the world); irresistible (or irrevocable) grace; and the perseverance of the saints. The most controversial of these doctrines are limited atonement and the perseverance of the saints. Many otherwise strong Calvinists have been hesitant over limited atonement. Such persons, in this book, are known as "moderate Calvinists".

Christian Socialism: The beginnings of Christian socialism are attributed to F.D. Maurice, around 1850. Maurice emphasised the Fatherhood of God, the brotherhood of man and that God is love – together with the need for co-operation, rather than competition, between men. He looked to baptism to bring about spiritual change, rather than affirming the need to "repent and believe". In the last quarter of the nineteenth century, Christian socialism took on a new vigour. Members of all parties were attracted to it, so that in different places it might take

[1] For a recent analysis of the origin, relevance and application of the Broad Church concept see, H. Schlossberg, *Conflict and Crisis in the Religious Life of Late Victorian England* (2009) pp.7-12.

on a ritualistic, broad, or evangelical colouring, according to the relevant individual's taste.

Church: The Church of England, as established since the Reformation.

Church of Scotland: The established Church of Scotland, as established since the Reformation and being Presbyterian in its form of government.

CICCU: The Cambridge Inter-Collegiate Christian Union.

Colporteur: An individual whose primary purpose was to travel the country selling religious literature. Many added to their primary role that of missionary, preacher and provider of social help.

Congregationalists: see Independents. Later in the nineteenth century, Congregationalism started to develop central organisations to help bind its churches together.

CPAS: The Church Pastoral Aid Society.

CSSM: The Children's Special Service Mission, later called Scripture Union.

CSU: The Christian Social Union.

Deism: Deists believed that God created the universe, but did not intervene in it. They therefore rejected the divinity of Jesus Christ.

Dissent: The Dissenters were those who could not accept an established church, or various of its doctrines and offices. The main Dissenting groups were the Congregationalists/Independents, Baptists, Methodists and Presbyterians, although there were smaller groups like the Quakers and Unitarians.

Evangelicalism: A notoriously difficult word to define, but it has its origins in the Greek word euaggelion, meaning gospel, or good news. It has been regularly used, historically, to distinguish those Christians who wanted a more energetic or zealous Christianity – both in word and deed – than most of their contemporaries. At its heart is a commitment to: the authority of the Bible; penal substitution as the means of reconciling man with God; and a recognition of the need for conversion "by the operation of the Spirit of God, before the soundest and most orthodox sentiments can have their proper influence".[2] Flowing from the work of conversion was the expectation of a life of good works.

[2] *The Works of the Rev. John Newton* (1827) p.174.

Evangelical Party: Evangelicals[3] within the Church of England.
High Churchmen: High Churchmen emphasised the importance of the sacraments and ceremonies in conveying grace – and attached great significance to the role of the national Church in the life of the nation.
Independents: Independents believed that a church should be governed by and made up of members of the local Christian community of the elect. They rejected bishops and other central institutions. From the late seventeenth century they were also increasingly known as Congregationalists, although the term Independent continued to be used into the nineteenth century, especially if their Calvinistic vigour in preaching was being affirmed.
Liberals: Late in the nineteenth century, Broad Churchmen began to be known as Liberals – as their differences with orthodoxy grew. Samuel Taylor Coleridge had earlier suggested that the portions of the Bible with authority were those that chimed with the spirit of the reader. Later in the century – as antagonism to the Bible's teaching hardened – it was found that fewer portions of the Bible chimed with the spirit of Liberal readers. The chasm between orthodoxy and liberalism was also widened as "two distinct conceptions – revelation by the Eternal Word, and actuation of the Holy Spirit"[4] – which the Bible held together, were separated by Liberals.
Liberal Evangelicals: Liberal Evangelicals were those individuals who regarded themselves as evangelicals – and who accepted as their heritage churches that had traditionally been in practice evangelical, like the Congregationalists – but who wanted to recast traditional evangelical doctrines. They emerged in number around the last quarter of the nineteenth century – and their desire to recast doctrine later spread to evangelicals across the denominations.
Limited Atonement: See Calvinism.
Methodists: John Wesley was the main founder of Methodism in the 1730s, as a group within the Church of England committed to sharing the gospel with zeal. After his death in 1791, Methodists separated from the Church of England, but thereafter they fragmented into a number of groupings. The largest group was always the Wesleyan Methodists, but

[3] For the use of the appellation "evangelical" in England from the time of the Reformation, see J.A. Thomas, *The Nation's Gospel: Reformation to Revolution* (2017) vol.1, pp.51-53.
[4] S.T. Coleridge, *Confessions of an Inquiring Spirit* (1886) p.73.

from its ranks emerged a number of other groups. The Methodist New Connection and the Reformers broke away over the authority and the role of the laity within the Methodist Conference, its governing body. The Primitive Methodists left as they thought that the Wesleyans lacked the zeal of their founder and desired respectability. The Bible Christians were not so much a breakaway; they grew out of the work of a Methodist minister with zeal. The Wesleyan Methodist Association left when the Wesleyans established their own training college for ministers.
Moderate Party: The dominant theological grouping in the Church of Scotland in the eighteenth century. They did not deny orthodox statements of faith, but "were very shy as to preaching its truths, spoke of it as containing antiquated notions...They flattered human nature as to its ability to obey the moral law".[5]
National Society for Promoting the Education of the Poor: The National Society for Promoting the Education of the Poor in the Principles of the Established Church throughout England and Wales.
Nonconformists: See Dissent.
Oxford Movement: See Tractarianism.
Penal Substitution: See Atonement.
Presbyterianism: Presbyterianism came out of the Reformation and refers to churches governed by representative assemblies of elders at a number of different levels. Presbyterian churches do not have bishops.
PSA Movement: The Pleasant Sunday Afternoon movement ran short afternoon services for working men. It also provided social help to them.
Quakers: Quakers emerged in the 1640s from the teachings and experience of George Fox. Quakers claimed that every man was enlightened by the 'divine light of Christ'. For Quakers the relationship between personal enlightenment and the Scriptures could vary. For some, their personal 'divine light' could take priority over, and contradict, the Scriptures. This made it difficult for orthodox Christian groups to work with them, but in the nineteenth century many evangelicals were able to work closely with many Quakers as their personal 'divine light' and the Scriptures pointed in the same direction. Quaker influence "far exceeded their numerical strength".[6]

[5] Cited in A.L. Drummond and J. Bulloch, *The Scottish Church 1688-1843* (1973) p.57. "They were under suspicion on the subject of the doctrines of the Fall and of original sin, of grace, salvation, and the atonement"; ibid., p.104.
[6] J. Munson, *The Nonconformists* (1991) p.3.

Real Presence: The doctrine that, in the service of the mass, or communion, when the words of consecration are pronounced by the priest, the bread and wine miraculously change into the very body and blood of the Lord Jesus Christ.

Ritualism: Ritualism grew out of the Tractarian movement in the 1850s – as the latter emphasised greater ritual in services, including the use of vestments, incense and candles. It led to the introduction of a range of Catholic liturgical practices into Anglicanism – and the emphasis on water baptism as the cause of spiritual regeneration.

Socinian: In the early sixteenth century, Laelius Socinus and his nephew Faustus Socinus breathed new life into Arian doctrines. They were most active in Poland, but Socinians appeared in England. Perhaps their most famous leader – although it is claimed he came to the same conclusions independently – was, in the seventeenth century, John Biddle. He denied original sin and hell.

Tractarianism: The movement among High Churchmen that appeared in 1833 – in opposition to governmental proposals to abolish various Irish bishoprics. The movement emphasised the apostolic succession of the Church – to resist political interference and to challenge Protestantism. It is also known as the Oxford Movement, by virtue of its place of origin. Members might also be called Puseyites, after one of their leaders.

Unitarians: Unitarians, unlike deists, believed in revealed religion; like deists, they did not assign divinity to Jesus Christ. Like the Quakers, their influence far exceeded their numerical strength.[7]

YMCA: The Young Men's Christian Association.

YWCA: The Young Women's Christian Association.

[7] Ibid.

A Timeline of Some Principal Events

References below to a book are to its date of first publication; and references to a society are to the year it was established/opened. Events in bold have been added on the right to provide the wider historical context. The matters on the left-hand side of the timeline refer to matters that have impeded, or might be considered to be part of a wider movement to impede, the spread of the gospel. Those matters on the right in ordinary type refer to matters that have advanced, or might be considered to be part of a wider movement to advance, the spread of the gospel. Some matters both impede and advance the gospel; in those cases, the relevant matter has been put where, on balance, its emphasis has probably led. Some matters might have been put on either side. For the sake of brevity, names of books, societies, denominations etc have been abbreviated.

Part 1

John Wesley dies	**1791**	**Louis XVI seeks to flee from the French Revolution**
		Spiritual revival in Wales
	1793	Scottish Colportage Society
Paine's *Age of Reason*	1794	J. Milner's *History of the Church* vol.1
E. Darwin's *Zoonomia*		
	1795	More's first *Cheap Repository Tract*
	1796	Watson's *Apology for the Bible*
		Charles Simeon rides into Scotland
	1797	Wilberforce's *Practical View of Christianity*
		Society for Propagating the Gospel at Home
		Baptist Home Mission
Malthus's *Principle of Population*	1798	
Schleiermacher's *On Religion*	1799	Religious Tract Society
		More's *Modern System of Female Education*
	1802	Society for the Suppression of Vice
		Christian Observer
		Paley's *Natural Theology*

	1803	Sunday School Union
Unitarian Evangelical Society	1804	Bible Society
	1806	Angell James ordained to minister at Carrs Lane
	1808	Society for Promoting Christianity among Jews
		British and Foreign School Society
	1811	Calvinistic Methodist Church
		Primitive Methodists
		National Society for Educating the Poor
	1815	**Battle of Waterloo ends French threat**
		Henry Ryder Bishop of Gloucester
Lord Macaulay champions novels	1816	
Owen publicly rejects Christianity	1817	
	1818	Parliament gives £1 million for new churches
		Church Building Society
	1819	Origins of Chalmer's
		Christian and Civic Economy
E. Irving minister in London	1822	
	1826	Shaftesbury enters Parliament
		Glasgow City Mission
T. Arnold Headmaster at Rugby	1828	*The Record*
Lyell's *Principles of Geology*	**1830**	**First public steam railway**
	1831	First Brethren chapel in England
		Lord's Day Observance Society
		Exeter Hall built
Maitland attacks Milner's *History*	**1832**	**First reform of the franchise**
Wilberforce dies	1833	
Tractarian controversy begins		
Carlyle moves to Chelsea	**1834**	**New Poor Law in England and Wales**
Strauss's *Life of Jesus*	1835	Baptist Noel's *State of the Metropolis Considered*
Communitarian Rational Society		London City Mission
Simeon dies	1836	CPAS
Mormon missions arrive in Britain	1837	Society for Additional Curates
	1839	Kilsyth revival in Scotland
	1840	Coleridge's *Confessions of an Inquiring Spirit*
The Nonconformist	1841	Caughey arrives from USA
	1843	Free Church of Scotland

TIMELINE

British Anti-State Church Assoc.	1844	Church of England Scripture Readers' Association
		Ragged School Union
		YMCA
White's *Life in Christ*	1846	Evangelical Alliance
A. Brontë's *Tenant of Wildfell Hall*		
Dawson proclaims Civic Gospel	1847	Band of Hope
	1848	**Revolutions across Europe**
		John Sumner Archbishop of Canterbury
	1849	Ruskin's *Seven Lamps*
		Finney arrives from USA
Maurice's *Christian Socialist Tracts*	1850	Gorham baptismal regeneration case
Expression "Secularism" coined	1851	First national religious census
Spiritualism the rage in London	**1853**	**Crimean War (ends 1856)**
Maurice's *Theological Essays*		Spurgeon starts preaching in London
		Open-Air Mission
		Ragged Church and Chapel Union
R.W. Dale at Carrs Lane	1854	
	1856	James McQuilkin of Ballymena converted
Buckle's *History of Civilisation*	1857	London Bible and Domestic Female Mission
Ruskin rejects Calvinism	1858	

Parts 2 and 3

C. Darwin's *Origin of Species*	1859	Revival and over one million converts in UK
J.S. Mill's *On Liberty*		London theatre services begin
Liberal Party formed		Lord Palmerston becomes Prime Minister
Secularism revives		Caughey, Finney and Palmers tour UK
Marx's *Political Economy*		
Macmillian's Magazine		
Cornhill Magazine		
Eliot's *Adam Bede*		
Brown's *Divine Life in Men*		
Incense used in church		

Essays and Reviews	**1860**	**HMS Warrior the iron-hulled battleship launched**
Spencer asserts new philosophy		Mildmay deaconesses
Crystal Palace Sunday opening		Catherine Booth preaches in church
Colenso's *Pentateuch*	1862	First Anglican deaconess
Gilchrist's *Life of Blake*	1863	
Renan's *Life of Jesus*		
	1864	Evangelization Society
	1865	Origins of the Salvation Army
Seeley's *Ecce Homo*	1866	
Marx's *Capital*	1867	CSSM
Arnold's *Culture and Anarchy*		
	1869	Anglican Twelve Days' Mission in London
	1870	**Education Act**
University religious tests removed	1871	
	1873	Moody's first missionary visit
Draper's *Conflict Religion/Science*	1874	Anglican London Mission
		Christian Colportage Association
	1875	Keswick Convention
		PSA Movement
Stephen's *English Thought*	1876	Mother's Union
Malthusian League	1877	CICCU
Guild of St Matthew		YWCA created through merger
Farrar's *Eternal Hope*	1878	First Institutional church at Westbourne Park
	1879	OICCU
	1880	Liverpool Diocese
	1881	Moody's second missionary visit
		Church Parochial Mission Society
	1882	669 Salvationists attacked
Drummond's *Natural Law*	1883	Boys' Brigade
		The Bitter Cry
	1884	Anglican East London Mission
Socialist League manifesto	1885	Anglican West London Mission
Shaftesbury dies		*Pall Mall Gazette* anti-sex trade campaign
		Lightfoot's *Apostolic Fathers*
		Toynbee Hall and settlement movement

TIMELINE

Mansfield College, Oxford	1886	
	1887	Spurgeon withdraws from Baptist Union
		West London Mission and Forward Movement
		Christian Endeavour
Ward's *Robert Elsmere*	1888	
Lux Mundi	1889	
Christian Social Union		
Nonconformist Conscience	1890	Booth's *In Darkest England*
Clarion Press	1891	
Spurgeon dies	1892	National Free Church Council
		Caravan Mission to Village Children
	1893	Inter-University Christian Union
		Girls' Brigade
Allen's *The Women Who Did*	1895	
White's *Warfare Science/Theology*	1896	
	1900	Adult school numbers exceed 50,000

Author's Profile

Jeremy A. Thomas read law at Queen Mary College, University of London and gained his Master's degree at Dalhousie Law School, Canada. He was called to the Bar in England by Gray's Inn, undertaking pupillage at shipping and commercial chambers, before joining Ashurst, the international law firm. At Ashurst he specialised in company and commercial law where he was the partner responsible for the firm's know-how.

Jeremy has made numerous contributions to legal periodicals, books and festschrifts relating to public international law (in particular international law in Asia), human rights and general commercial law. He was a founder member of the editorial board of the *Journal of the History of International Law.*

He attends All Souls Church Langham Place, where he serves as a Deputy Churchwarden. He is also a member of the Bishop's Council of the Diocese of London and the Two Cities Area Council. He is married with three children.

Index[1]

[1] This index covers the General Introduction to the series of which this volume is part, the Introduction to volume 2 and the main text of this book.